Labour at War

LABOUR AT WAR

France and Britain
1914–1918

JOHN N. HORNE

CLARENDON PRESS · OXFORD
1991

Oxford University Press, Walton Street, Oxford OX2 6DP
Oxford New York Toronto
Delhi Bombay Calcutta Madras Karachi
Petaling Jaya Singapore Hong Kong Tokyo
Nairobi Dar es Salaam Cape Town
Melbourne Auckland
and associated companies in
Beirut Berlin Ibadan Nicosia

Oxford is a trade mark of Oxford University Press

Published in the United States
by Oxford University Press, New York

British Library Cataloguing in Publication Data
Horne, John N.
Labour at war: France and Britain 1914–1918.
1. Great Britain. Labour movements, history   2. France.
Labour movements, history
I. Title
331.80941
ISBN 0–19–820180–X

Library of Congress Cataloging in Publication Data
Horne, John N.
Labour at war: France and Britain, 1914–1918 / John N. Horne.
p.   cm.
Includes bibliographical references and index.
1. Trade-unions—France—Political activity.   2. Trade-unions—
Great Britain—Political activity.   3. World War, 1914–1918—Social
aspects—France.   4. World War, 1914–1918—Social aspects—Great
Britain.   I. Title.
HD6687.H67   1990
322′.2′094109044—dc20
90–37796
ISBN 0–19–820180–X

Typeset by Latimer Trend & Company Ltd, Plymouth

Printed in Great Britain by
Courier International Ltd,
Tiptree, Essex

*To my father
and to the memory
of my mother*

All of us have now had the opportunity to realise and to convince ourselves of the truth of what was long since preached by the Communists and the Socialists, namely, that neither the production of all that is necessary for a nation nor the distribution of what is produced can be abandoned to the hazards of competition or to the lust for enrichment of private individuals . . .

Three years ago such a programme was described as a dangerous Utopia. Even the more advanced Socialist workers found it impossible to apply it at the time being; they left to the generations to come the task of such a reorganisation of society.

But now a widely spread feeling is arising which considers that an immediate solution of those first portions of the social problem is imperative. The difficulties lived through by the nations during the war have opened the eyes of a great number.

Consequently an immense work of social reconstruction has become unavoidable. It can no more be brushed away as a Utopia. People feel the need of reconstruction, and everyone can already distinguish its main lines.

And it is high time for the workers to hesitate no more; to take this work in hand without waiting for the State or upper classes to do it for them. Life itself has indicated the main lines of the reconstruction.

Prince Peter Kropotkin, 'An Open Letter to the Western Workingmen'. Published in the *Railway Review* (NUR), 29 June 1917, and in *La Bataille* (CGT), 2 July 1917.

Preface

THE subject of this study, organized labour during the First World War, stands at the intersection of two much larger and quite distinct historical problems. The first is the question of how and why reformism became the predominant orientation of labour and socialist movements in the industrial societies of central and western Europe during the twentieth century. The second is the question of how and why those same societies achieved the degree of cohesion which they manifested during the mobilization of 'total' war efforts between 1914 and 1918. That the relationship between the dynamics of societies at war and the evolution of labour movements is not arbitrary is attested to by the number of studies looking at the connection between labour radicalism and the First World War. Nothing like the same attention has been paid, however, to those substantial elements of organized labour (the majorities in the major belligerent societies, excepting Austria, Italy, and Russia) which supported the war effort until the end, to the terms on which they did so, and to the significance of this both for their own future development and for the war experience of the societies concerned.

Such a subject is doubly comparative. It assumes that, despite the deeply individualistic features imparted to labour movements by the national contexts in which they evolve, the essentially transnational processes which create them result in certain similarities. It also assumes that 'total' wars as they have affected twentieth-century industrial societies have exhibited similar features in different national settings. Both of these seem to me reasonable propositions. But they are only adopted for the purposes of the argument and are not taken as proved at the outset.

'Similar' is not 'the same'. The value of comparative history ought in part to reside in the measurement of difference. In addition to examining historical processes across national boundaries, comparison should also establish a perspective, a sense of relativity, on the distinctiveness of particular national cases. Perhaps comparative history needs no manifestos. But very little of it has been undertaken either in labour history or in the social history of the World Wars, especially at the level of research rather than of secondary synthesis. The jeopardy is double, and the need for clarity on the aims of the exercise doubly important.

This study originated in an observation and a question. The observation was that both the Confédération Générale du Travail (CGT)—the French trade union movement—and the Labour Party in Britain, emerged from the First World War with distinctive programmes of reforms, which responded to the war experience while also defining the future orientation of the two organizations. Both programmes planned the reconstruction of society in the light of a critical assessment of the social impact of the war, yet each also contained more general statements of principle. The reverberations of the two programmes (the *Programme Minimum* of the CGT and *Labour and the New Social Order*) continued for many years.

The question stemmed from reading the work of Arthur Marwick and others: how did labour participation in the war affect both organized labour and the national efforts? The answer seemed linked to the emergence of the reform programmes, and led to the hypothesis of this study. Labour movements participating in the war effort, in France and Britain, came to define their continued participation in terms of the reforms which they felt should, and hoped would, emerge during and above all after the war. These reform plans influenced the subsequent development of the labour movements and also constituted a significant feature of the process of wartime mobilization in the two societies. In other words, it is suggested that there was a specific labour reformism characteristic of France and Britain (for all the distinctiveness conferred by separate national settings) during the First World War. If correct, this would suggest that the process of societal mobilization in France and Britain was similar in at least one respect, and it would explain specifically why the war experience was important for the more general development of labour reformism. Testing the hypothesis clearly required establishing the nature of labour participation in the war effort, and investigating the role and significance of reform thinking, as well as of associated developments in the behaviour and function of organized labour, during the war. This accounts for the shape of the study.

Although conceived comparatively and rooted on both sides in archival research, the study depends on the French case for the substance of the demonstration, partly because it has suffered greater neglect by historians, partly because my own primary interest lies in French history. In particular, the discussion of the CGT required consultation of the Ministry of the Interior police intelligence files in the Archives Nationales (F_7 series), and of various collections in the Institut Français d'Histoire Sociale, as well as of the obvious printed sources, in order to reconstruct the politics of the movement. The papers of Albert Thomas, effectively in charge of the munitions effort from late 1914 to September 1917, were also indispensable for establishing the economic and social circumstances which CGT leaders confronted and the nature of their institutional participation in the economic mobilization (Archives Nationales, 94 AP). The British example has been used as a comparative check, in order to take the argument beyond the level of one national case, and also to establish a perspective on French labour participation in the war. Here the path was made easier by the pioneering studies of Royden Harrison, on the War Emergency: Workers' National Committee, and by J. M. Winter on the conversion of much of British labour to a moderate socialism during the war. But vital elements of the British case remained obscure, necessitating research on the principal labour organizations in the archives of the Labour Party and the Trades Union Congress (TUC), as well as through printed sources. Hopefully, the deployment of the British material is adequate to its task without making the book longer than it need be.

Three brief qualifications seem in order. First, while there is nothing arbitrary about a comparison between the French and British labour movements during the war, neither is there anything uniquely relevant about it. A comparison between either and the German, Italian, Austrian, Russian, or American cases would be as valid and might easily be as interesting. The same is true for comparisons between the two World Wars. Hopefully, others will push the comparative grid much further.

Secondly, this study is based on national labour leaderships. It seemed to me important to consider the hypothesis at this level first, not least because labour leaders were naturally in the forefront of formal labour participation in the war effort and of defining national labour reform programmes. I have sought to place these leaderships in the context of their 'movements', their relationships with business and the state, and the rapidly changing economic and social circumstances of the war and the *après-guerre*. But I am aware that much remains to be established about wartime labour at the regional and local levels.

Thirdly, wars, like other periods of concentrated upheaval, present peculiar problems of analysis. They are both a product of what has gone before and an original combination of factors, a point of new departures. Investigation of a hypothesis about a particular wartime labour reformism must restore to the war its specificity as a process, or accelerator of often conflicting processes, without drawing into war's vortex causes and explanations which properly apply to longer-term, pre- and post-war developments. An attempt is made to distinguish between these two fundamental dimensions, especially in Chapters 1, 7, and 9. But the balance between them is not always easy to establish and must, in any discussion of war and social change, lie near the heart of the debate.

Inevitably, in a work which began as a doctoral thesis and has been rewritten as a book, debts, intellectual and other, have accumulated. It is a pleasure to acknowledge them even if they cannot be repaid. Roderick Kedward, of the University of Sussex, gradually converted himself from the most tactful and supportive of supervisors into the most stimulating and encouraging of colleagues and friends. In particular, he vigorously counteracted occasional fluctuations in morale, when the 'big push' of a comparative study seemed bogged down and hints of a single country defeatism appeared; to him, special thanks are due. Patrick Fridenson, of the École des Hautes Études en Sciences Sociales, has been exceptionally generous with his time in commenting on both the thesis and the book. My thanks are also due to Jean-Louis Robert, of the Université de Paris I, and Jay Winter, of Pembroke College, Cambridge, for their critical encouragement. I of course remain responsible for the arguments of the book and for any errors of fact or interpretation which it may contain.

Among the many librarians and archivists who have helped me, I should particularly like to thank Mlle Colette Chambelland and Mlle Françoise Blum, of the Musée Social, Mme Denise Fauvel-Rouif and Mme Hélène Strub, of the Institut Français d'Histoire Sociale, M. Laurent Gervereau, of the Musée d'Histoire Contemporaine, for his help in finding the cover illustration, and M. Bruno van Dooren, for introducing me to the full riches of the Bibliothèque de Documentation Internationale Contemporaine, all in Paris; and in London, the librarians of the Labour Party and the Trades Union Congress. I should also like to thank the staff of the Library of Trinity College, Dublin, for their unfailing courtesy and help. I am grateful to the former Social Science Research Council for the postgraduate award which enabled me to undertake the thesis, and to the Grace Lawless Lee Fund and the Arts, Economic, and Social Sciences Research Fund, both of Trinity College, Dublin, which helped finance the additional research in France and Britain required to recast the thesis as a book.

Last, but far from least, I should like to acknowledge the support and encouragement of many friends, including Joe Azizollahoff in London and Bernard Frévaque, Jean Gordon, and Marie-Pierre Gueutier in Paris. Above all, I wish to thank my wife, Michèle Clarke, who has helped me in more ways than I can number.

J.H.

Dublin
July 1989

Contents

List of Figures

List of Tables

List of Abbreviations

AFL	American Federation of Labor
AN	Archives Nationales
ANEE	Association Nationale pour l'Expansion Économique
APP	Archives de la Préfecture de Police (Paris)
ASE	Amalgamated Society of Engineers
BDIC	Bibliothèque de Documentation Internationale Contemporaine
BSP	British Socialist Party
CAP	Commission Administrative Permanente (PS)
CDS	Comité de Défense Syndicaliste
CGL	Confederazione Generale del Lavoro
CGT	Confédération Générale du Travail
CRRI	Comité pour la Reprise des Relations Internationales
FBI	Federation of British Industries
FNCC	Fédération Nationale des Coopératives de Consommation
GFTU	General Federation of Trade Unions
IFHS	Institut Français d'Histoire Sociale
IFTU	International Federation of Trade Unions
ILO	International Labour Organization
ILP	Independent Labour Party
ISB	International Socialist Bureau
ISNTUC	International Secretariat of National Trade Union Centres
LPNEC	Labour Party National Executive Committee
LSI	Labour and Socialist International
MCGFTU	Management Committee of the General Federation of Trade Unions
MFGB	Miners' Federation of Great Britain
min.	minutes
NAC	National Administrative Committee (ILP)
NAEE	National Alliance of Employers and Employees
NUR	National Union of Railwaymen
PCTUC	Parliamentary Committee of the Trades Union Congress
PLP	Parliamentary Labour Party

PRO	Public Record Office
PS	Parti Socialiste
rep.	report
RILU	Red International of Labour Unions
SFIO	Section Française de l'Internationale Ouvrière (PS)
SHAT	Service Historique de l'Armée de Terre
SPD	Sozialdemokratische Partei Deutschlands
TUC	Trades Union Congress
UDC	Union of Democratic Control
UGT	Unión General de Trabajo
UIMM	Union des Industries Métallurgiques et Minières
USTICA	Union Syndicale des Techniciens de l'Industrie, du Commerce et de l'Agriculture
WEWNC	War Emergency: Workers' National Committee

Note on Terms

French *syndicalisme* and English 'trade unionism' are really different species of the same genus. But since the terms also denote the genus in each language, 'syndicalism' and 'trade unionism' are used interchangeably. In the same way, *patronat*, 'industrialists', and 'businessmen', though connoting slightly different realities in the two languages, are used synonymously. The term 'Syndicalism' (with capital) is reserved for the British variant of militant direct-action trade-unionism, influenced by French revolutionary syndicalism, which was especially prominent before the First World War. The term 'labour' (without capital) refers to the organized labour movement, or to its definitions and perceptions of working-class interests, in both countries. 'Labour' (with capital) is applied only to the political wing of organized labour in Britain. For the difference between *mouvement ouvrier* and 'labour movement', see p. 21 below.

1 The Context

To contemporaries, the first 'total' war was a bewildering yet strangely dynamic phenomenon. It rapidly generated its own dimensions of space and time. Its requirements seemed to penetrate every corner of the combatant societies. Its chronology soon included a heroic past—the autumn of 1914—and a future which expanded inexorably with the failure of each 'final' offensive. The war was no longer a feared or anticipated event, external and one-dimensional, with various possible consequences. It was the present, swallowing up large portions of the forseeable future, and breeding its own particular sense of normality. Whole societies, to borrow the French expression, 'installed themselves' in the war.

For labour movements this process was doubly complex. Disarmed by the failure of the Second International to present any serious opposition to the diplomatic crisis before the mobilizations occurred, socialists and trade unionists were especially vulnerable and disoriented once the cataclysm arrived. Subsequently, in varying degrees with or against the national tide, they sought to define their own reactions to the war, and hence their own interpretations of the social and political realities and chronological perspectives which it created. This is a study of two sets of responses, one in France, one in Britain, by those labour leaders who continued to support the national effort until the end. Whether or not the responses were similar in the two cases, and therefore more than a peculiarity of one national war experience, will be a central question.

In some respects, however, the contemporary sense of the war's uniqueness is misleading. Precisely because, in the words of the official French *Bulletin des usines de guerre*, 'it is the whole of society which feels involved', the war was a conflict between the fundamental resources—demographic, economic, social, and political—of each camp.[1] Although its exceptional nature and its ability to fuse national energies generated responses which were equally exceptional, the war also drew on larger patterns of social evolution. In the case of wartime labour movements, mutations within early-twentieth-century working classes, changes in industrial technologies, powerful impulses of attraction and repulsion between labour movements and the state, and many other developments were more than the backdrop to reactions to the war. They were the deep currents which, together with the shifting cross-winds of wartime events, helped shape labour responses—though labour and socialist leaders trying to impose some ideological coherence on the aberrant 'normality' of the war were rarely fully aware of this.[2] Some of these longer-term developments, especially as expressed in the French and British labour movements themselves, must therefore be outlined before the specific impact of the war on labour in the two countries can be investigated and compared.

(i) Labour Movements and Working Classes

The nature of the economic forces and social constituencies to which organized labour responded evolved rapidly from 1900 to 1930. After a twenty-year depression, the rate of economic growth increased sharply from the mid-1890s. Implementation of new technologies created new leading industries (steel, chemicals, electricity, motor cars). Larger, more concentrated forms of business organization, 'rationalized' processes of industrial production, widening demand in domestic economies, and intense trade competition all contributed to this formidable 'second wind' of industrialization.[3] There were noticeable fluctuations in economic activity, including a slump following the war, in 1920–1,

---

[1] *Bulletin des usines de guerre*, 1 May 1916, p. 1.

[2] G. Haupt, 'Why the History of the Working Class Movement?' *New German Critique* (New York), 14 (1978), pp. 3–24.

[3] D. Landes, *The Unbound Prometheus: Technological Change and Industrial Development in Western Europe from 1750 to the Present* (CUP, Cambridge, 1969), 231–358; F. Braudel and E. Labrousse (eds.), *Histoire économique et sociale de la France* (Presses Universitaires de France), iv, pt. 1, *1880–1914* (1979); pt. 2, *1914–1950* (1980); S. Pollard, *The Development of the British Economy, 1914–1967* (Edward Arnold, 1969).

and expansion brought its own problems of obsolescence and decay. But broadly speaking, the First World War occurred in the midst of, and reinforced, a longer-term reformulation and acceleration of European industrial growth which only subsided in the second 'great depression' of the 1930s.

The consequences of this for organized labour were considerable. To a certain extent, a remodelling of working classes occurred.[4] Skilled workers, the historic creators of organized labour, retained an important place in production and a vital role in the labour movements themselves, often transmitting traditions of organization and political commitment, and hence a class consciousness, to other sections of the working class. Yet their own economic position came under considerable pressure. This was particularly obvious in, but by no means confined to, the engineering and metallurgical industries, which were at the core of the new industrial growth, and which experienced a massive, temporary expansion through wartime munitions production. Well before the war in both France and Britain, intensified mechanization and new methods of workshop organization threatened the skilled status of the engineering worker and his control over the rhythm of production. 'Scientific management' as propounded by F. W. Taylor and his European disciples extended the vista of tightened management control over the workplace.[5]

The extent and consequences of this reorganization of the social relations of production are open questions. But already a sharp difference between the two countries seems clear. The well-established skilled industrial labour force of late Victorian and Edwardian Britain, with its entrenched defences (through work 'customs' and labour organization), was far better placed to moderate the pace and even resist the redefinition of the

[4] For a review of the literature on this theme, see J. Cronin, 'Rethinking the Legacy of Labor, 1890–1925', in J. Cronin and C. Sirianni, *Work, Community and Power: The Experience of Labor in Europe and America, 1900–1925* (Temple Univ. Press, Philadelphia, Penn., 1983), 3–19. See also P. N. Stearns, *Lives of Labour: Work in a Maturing Industrial Society* (Croom Helm, 1975); D. Geary, *European Labour Protest, 1848–1939* (Croom Helm, 1981); M. Perrot, 'La Classe ouvrière française au temps de Jaurès', in M. Rebérioux (ed.), *Jaurès et la classe ouvrière*, (Éditions ouvrières, 1981), 67–81; and G. Noiriel, *Les Ouvriers dans la société française, XIXᵉ–XXᵉ siècles* (Seuil, 1986), 120–94.

[5] On Taylorism, see M. de Montmollin and O. Pastré (eds.), *Le Taylorisme* (Maspero, 1984), and Bibliography, Secondary Works, part 1.

production process than skilled workers in France, facing a tardy but intensive industrialization without any comparable heritage of organization. Thus the influential skilled British union, the Amalgamated Society of Engineers (ASE), suffered a sharp defeat by employers over issues of control in 1897–8. But in reality, the local power of the engineering unions made employers slow to disturb the status quo right up to the war.[6] In France, the much newer and far weaker metal workers' organization was confronted before the war both by its failure to organize the new, semi-skilled proletariat which dominated the rapidly expanding iron industry of French Lorraine and by its impotence to control experimentation with 'Taylorism' in the nascent car industry.[7] In consequence, skill was defended by rather different strategies in the two engineering industries. But in both cases, the 'dilution' of skill in the armaments industries and the accelerated creation of a semi-skilled engineering workforce provided some of the most volatile fuel for labour militancy and unrest during and immediately after the war.

The development of new industrial sectors and the reinforcement of some traditional ones (mining, docks, and transport) were accompanied by changes not just in production processes but also in the size and nature of the workplace. This is especially clear in the case of less-industrialized France. The different, less dynamic trajectory of its nineteenth-century economic evolution resulted in a smaller scale of industrial organization than in Britain. Yet the First World War itself

[6] G. D. H. Cole, *Trade Unionism and Munitions* (Clarendon Press, Oxford, 1923), 45–51; J. B. Jefferys, *The Story of the Engineers, 1800–1945* (Amalgamated Engineering Union, Lawrence and Wishart, 1946), 150–73; J. Zeitlin, 'Engineers and Compositors: A Comparison', in R. Harrison and J. Zeitlin (eds.), *Divisions of Labour: Skilled Workers and Technological Change in Nineteenth Century England* (Harvester Press, Brighton, 1985), 185–250. For opposed views on the extent of the reconstruction of the social relations of production from 1880 to 1920, see R. Price, 'The New Unionism and the Labour Process', and J. Zeitlin, 'Industrial Structure, Employer Strategy and the Diffusion of Job Control in Britain, 1880–1920', both in W. J. Mommsen and H. G. Husung (eds.), *The Development of Trade Unionism in Great Britain and Germany, 1880–1914* (German Historical Institute/Methuen, 1985), 133–49 and 325–37 respectively.

[7] C. Gras, 'La Fédération des métaux en 1913–1914 et l'évolution du syndicalisme révolutionnaire français', *Le Mouvement social*, 77 (Oct.–Dec. 1971), pp. 85–111; G. Hatry, *Louis Renault: patron absolu* (Éditions Lafourcade, 1982), 68–86; N. Papayanis, *Alphonse Merrheim: The Emergence of Reformism in Revolutionary Syndicalism, 1871–1925* (Martinus Nijhoff, The Hague, 1985), 67–70.

testified to France's arrival in the rank of major industrial nations. Although the invasion of the autumn of 1914 devastated a leading industrial region with 16.3 per cent of French industrial concerns and 41 per cent of total steam power, a war economy was organized which furnished a large part of French munitions needs.[8] In the decade before the war, craft-based production in small workshops was still extremely important. In 1906, only 41 per cent of the industrial labour force worked in enterprises employing more than one hundred people, and 32 per cent were still in workshops with under ten workers. By 1921, with the figures respectively 57 per cent and 22 per cent, the triumph of the factory was secure.[9]

The recruitment and formation of the working class itself underwent significant changes. In addition to shifting relations between unskilled workers and the skilled élite, the growth industries recruited workers either from other industries or from outside the working class.[10] In France in particular, with a much smaller pre-war working class and a more sluggish population growth-rate, the first thirty years of the twentieth century witnessed an industrial enrolment from the still predominantly rural population.[11] The structural resistance of the French peasantry to any overwhelming transformation limited this process, and by the 1920s, French industry drew to a degree unparalleled in Europe on immigrant labour.[12] The percentage

[8] A. Fontaine, *L'Industrie française pendant la guerre* (Presses Universitaires de France, 1925), 45–7. For different assessments of the paths and benefits of industrialization (the second reducing the relative backwardness of France), see C. P. Kindleberger, *Economic Growth in France and Britain, 1851–1950* (Harvard Univ. Press, Cambridge, Mass., 1964); P. O'Brien and C. Keyder, *Economic Growth in Britain and France, 1780–1914* (Allen & Unwin, 1978); and M. Lévy-Leboyer and F. Bourguignon, *L'Économie française au XIXᵉ siècle* (Économica, 1985).

[9] C. Gide and W. Oualid, *Le Bilan de la guerre pour la France* (Presses Universitaires de France, 1931), 328.

[10] Stearns, *Lives of Labour*, 19–44.

[11] Noiriel, *Les Ouvriers dans la société française*, 132.

[12] G. Mauco, *Les Étrangers en France* (Colin, 1932); J. Vidalenc, 'La Main-d'œuvre étrangère en France et la première guerre mondiale (1901–1926)', *Francia*, 2 (1974), pp. 524–50; G. Cross, *Immigrant Workers in Industrial France: The Making of a New Laboring Class* (Temple Univ. Press, Philadelphia, Penn., 1983); J. Horne, 'Immigrant Workers in France during World War I', *French Historical Studies*, 14/1 (1985), pp. 57–88; 'Étrangers, immigrés, français', *Vingtième siècle* (special no.), July–Sept. 1985; G. Noiriel, *Le Creuset français: histoire de l'immigration XIXᵉ–XXᵉ siècles* (Seuil, 1988).

of women workers in industry declined in both countries over the long term. But the large, temporary increase in the female labour force during the war encouraged the shift of women workers to the newer industrial sectors.[13] In many respects, therefore, the early twentieth century was a crucial period for the formation of a working class based decreasingly on skill and attuned to the demands of mass industrial production.

The physical configurations of this class formation were especially important. Its internal relations, types of consciousness, and patterns of organization were structured not only by the workplace but also by the growth of densely settled industrial neighbourhoods, often close to the workplace or linked to it by proliferating urban transport systems, but also frequently isolated in social space from other groups.[14] Proletarian districts were reinforced during the war as old centres swelled with an influx of munitions workers and entirely new complexes mushroomed in hitherto non-industrial areas. These solidly working-class communities (the Clyde, the steel suburbs of Sheffield, the industrial *banlieue* of Paris, the thickening network of coal and manufacturing towns around St-Étienne, etc.) were the physical setting of, and a major contributing factor to, the growth of distinctive forms of working-class sociability and culture, laying special emphasis on values of community and solidarity.

Labour organization and collective action evolved rapidly under the influence of these economic and social changes. But a long-term increase in prices—itself generated by the economic expansion—constituted a direct spur to the two working classes to defend their purchasing power. Figure 1 indicates the sharp increase in the cost of living (after a long decline) which from 1896 in Britain, ten years later in France, brought *la vie chère* to

[13] See Append. IV.

[14] J. Cronin, 'Labor Insurgency and Class Formation: Comparative Perspectives on the Crisis of 1917–20 in Europe', in Cronin and Sirianni (eds.), *Work, Community and Power*, 20–48; S. Meacham, *A Life Apart: The English Working Class, 1890–1914* (Thames and Hudson, 1977), 194–220; J.-P. Brunet, *Saint-Denis, la ville rouge: socialisme et communisme dans la banlieue ouvrière, 1890–1930* (Hachette, 1980); M. Perrot (ed.), 'L'Espace de l'usine', special no. of *Le Mouvement social*, 125 (Oct.–Dec. 1983); M. Agulhon, *et al.*, *Histoire de la France urbaine*, iv, *La Ville de l'âge industriel* (Seuil, 1983), 39–59.

the front of labour preoccupations.[15] One response was a strengthening of the co-operative movement (historically much stronger in Britain). In both countries, the connections between the co-operatives and the labour and socialist movements were debated in the decade before the war, leading in the French case to the unification in 1912 of the socialist and 'neutral' currents

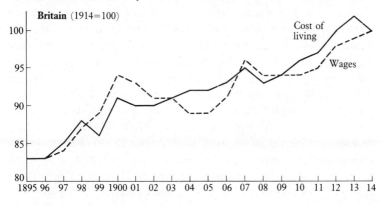

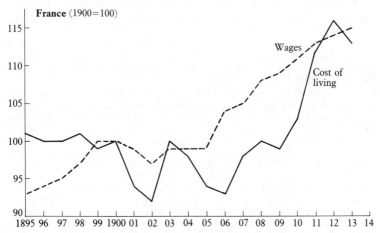

Fig. 1. Increase in the Cost of Living in Britain and France, 1895–1914

[15] A. L. Bowley, *Wages and Income in the United Kingdom since 1860* (CUP, Cambridge, 1937); H. Pelling, *Popular Politics and Society in Late Victorian Britain* (Macmillan, 1968), chap. 9; J. Lhomme, 'Le Pouvoir d'achat de l'ouvrier français au cours d'un siècle: 1840–1940', *Le Mouvement social*, 63 (Apr.–June 1968), pp. 41–69. P. N. Stearns backdates the decline in real wages to 1900–10 in *Revolutionary Syndicalism and French Labor: A Cause without Rebels* (Rutgers Univ. Press, New Brunswick, 1971), append. A.

of co-operation.[16] Alarming before the war to a generation unused to the phenomenon, inflation became vertiginous during and after the conflict (see Appendix I), heightening organized labour's concern to protect the working-class consumer.

Even more importantly, rising prices contributed to a major, long-term upsurge in strikes, from 1895 to the mid-1920s (see Figure 2).[17] The decade 1910 to 1920 and especially the years 1917–20, whose relative militancy was particularly marked in France, formed the most dynamic phase of this pattern (see Appendix II). Inflation forced trade unions to use their industrial power to maintain real wages and to restore disrupted wage differentials. But other factors also counted. The extremely tight labour market during and after the war, until the slump of 1920–1 (which especially in France broke the accumulating waves of industrial unrest), placed labour in an unusually favourable position. Demands for reduced work-time (fuelled by lengthened hours during the war) and recognition of the workers' right to leisure, plus issues of control over the production process, also motivated the 1917–20 movement.[18] Perhaps more fundamentally still, the strikes often centred, explicitly or

[16] J. Gaumont, *Histoire générale de la coopération en France* (FNCC, 1924), ii. 403–44; S. Pollard, 'The Foundation of the Co-operative Party', in A. Briggs and J. Saville (eds.), *Essays in Labour History 1886–1923* (Macmillan, 1971), 185–210.

[17] E. Shorter and C. Tilly, *Strikes in France, 1830–1968* (CUP, Cambridge, 1974); *British Labour Statistics. Historical Abstract 1886–1968* (HMSO, 1971), 396; J. Cronin, *Industrial Conflict in Modern Britain* (Croom Helm, 1979); id., 'Strikes and Power in Britain 1870–1920', *International Review of Social History*, 32/2 (1987), pp. 144–67; J.-L. Robert, 'Ouvriers et mouvement ouvrier parisiens pendant la grande guerre et l'immédiat après-guerre' (Thèse d'état, Paris I, 1989), 49. In the five-yearly average for 1915–19, the figures for the Seine established by J.-L. Robert have been used to correct the official figures for 1917, 1918, and 1919, which seriously under-represent the number of strikes and strikers. The Loire strike of May 1918 was ignored, and a conservative estimate of 30,000 has been added to the 1918 figure for this. In the current state of research, however, the overall figures for 1917 and 1918 (and hence the entire wartime average) remain a very rough approximation which almost certainly underplays the real scale of industrial unrest.

[18] Stearns, *Lives of Labor*, 300–31; G. Cross, 'Redefining Workers' Control: Rationalization, Labor Time and Union Politics in France, 1900–1928', in Cronin and Sirianni (eds.), *Work, Community and Power*, 143–72; id., 'Les Trois Huits: Labor Movements, International Reform, and the Origins of the Eight Hour Day, 1919–1924', *French Historical Studies*, 14/2 (1985), pp. 240–68; id., *A Quest for Time: The Reduction of Work in Britain and France, 1840–1940* (Univ. of California Press, Berkeley, Calif., 1989); C. Sirianni, 'Workers' Control in Europe: A Comparative Sociological Analysis', in Cronin and Sirianni, op. cit., 254–310.

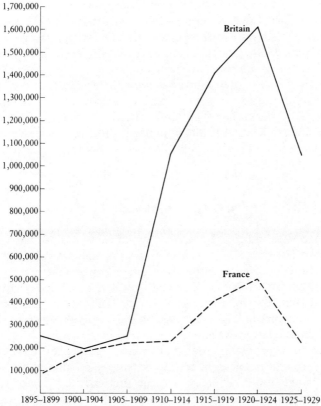

Fig. 2. Strikers in Britain and France (five-yearly averages), 1895–1929

implicitly, on the recognition by employers and the state of the right of trade unions to organize the workforce.[19] The war and its aftermath, together with the immediate pre-war years in Britain, thus formed a period of unprecedented industrial unrest and self-organization within both working classes.

The implications of this economic militancy were profoundly ambiguous for contemporary labour movements, and this has been paralleled by the ambivalence of subsequent historical interpretation. The mass strike movements can be seen either as

[19] Both 'unofficial' shop stewards' movements and 'official' labour were concerned to legitimate union control and representation in the eyes of state and employer. On the British case, see C. Goodrich, *The Frontier of Control: A Study of British Workshop Politics* (Bell, 1920), 4–19.

statements of protest and even revolt or as an 'apprenticeship'
in manipulating the economic levers available to a working class
concerned to deploy its influence essentially within the prevailing system.[20] The two views are not mutually exclusive in what
was, after all, a complex, multiple phenomenon. Both reflect an
undoubted reality of organized labour during the decade of the
war—the thrust to carve out an enlarged sphere of trade union
power. And the different, often conflicting views of industrial
action and trade unionism to which this gave rise became major
preoccupations of contemporary labour leaderships themselves.

(ii) The Industrial Organization of Labour

By 1914, the industrial organization of labour in Britain and
France differed markedly, reflecting not just distinctive trajector-
ies of industrialization but also a longer continuous history of
trade unionism in Britain. The CGT, at its first unified congress
in 1902, had a membership of 122,000. This rose to 390,000 in
1910–12, before falling to 256,000 by the outbreak of war.[21] The
TUC grouped over two and a half million members in 1914, for a
similar-sized population to that of France (see Appendix III). At
a very rough estimate, it might be suggested that the CGT
represented under 6 per cent of the unionizable workforce in
1914, compared to between 17 and 21 per cent for the TUC.[22]
   This was the difference between a trade unionism of 'active
minorities' and one which had embarked on mass enrolment.[23]

---

[20] Stearns, *Lives of Labor*, 300–31; Geary, *European Labour Protest*, 115–26;
Cronin, 'Rethinking the Legacy of Labor, 1890–1925', 3–19.
[21] E. Dolléans, *Histoire du mouvement ouvrier*, ii, *1871–1936* (Colin, 1946), 54;
J.-L. Robert, *La Scission syndicale de 1921: essai de reconnaissance de formes*
(Publications de la Sorbonne, 1980), 159–160.
[22] The higher British figure is calculated from the numbers for 1914 in W. A.
Orton, *Labour in Transition: A Survey of British Industrial History since 1914*
(Philip Allan, 1921), 272. The lower figure, for 1910, is that of H. A. Clegg, A. Fox,
and A. F. Thompson, *A History of British Trade Unions since 1889*, i, *1889–1910*
(OUP, Oxford, 1964), 466. The French figure is based on P. Sorlin's estimate of
approximately four and a half million as the size of the industrial work-force, in *La
Société française*, i, *1840–1914* (Arthaud, 1968), 163.
[23] For the French and British trade union movements, see Bibliography, Secondary Works, part 1.

If the skilled worker continued to play a crucial role in British trade unionism, the big battalions of miners and general railway workers (the Miners' Federation of Great Britain (MFGB) and the National Union of Railwaymen (NUR)) were a powerful force by the eve of the war. More generally, from the late 1880s, the 'new unionism' had made significant inroads into semi-skilled workers and into the mass of the unskilled 'general' workers.[24]

The CGT, by contrast, had a diminutive miners' federation (only fully united on the eve of the war), even allowing for France's small coal industry. The railway unions were also small, only partly as a result of repression following the abortive national rail strike in 1910, and not united until 1917. Above all, the importance of the textile workers, still constituting over 40 per cent of the industrial workforce before the war, barely registered with the CGT, where the textile workers' federation had under twenty-five thousand members in 1913. The metal-workers' federation gained in importance in the pre-war years, reflecting the qualitative and quantitative shift in French industrialization, but, as we have noted, it had trouble organizing beyond the ranks of the skilled.[25]

The CGT, therefore, represented not just a minority but also an élite of French workers, recruiting disproportionately among male skilled workers in the more traditional, less mechanized trades.[26] The largest federation in 1913 (17 per cent of total membership) was that of the building workers, while a congeries of small trades (match-making, jewellers, brush- and hat-making, printing, leather, furniture, and tobacco) provided a further 18 per cent. Geographically, the CGT was under-

[24] P. S. Bagwell, *The Railwaymen: The History of the National Union of Railwaymen* (Allen & Unwin), i (1963); R. Page Arnot, *The Miners* (Allen & Unwin), i, *A History of the Miners' Federation of Great Britain from 1910 Onwards* (1953); and E. J. Hobsbawm, 'The "New Unionism" Reconsidered', in Mommsen and Husung (eds.), *The Development of Trade Unionism in Great Britain and Germany*, 15–31.

[25] French labour history lacks the institutional trade union histories available in Britain. But see C. Bartuel and H. Rullière, *La Mine et les mineurs* (Librairie Octave Doin, 1923); G. Ribeill, *Le Personnel des compagnies de chemins de fer*, i, *Des origines à 1914* (Développement et Aménagement, 1980), 313–565, and ii, *Les Cheminots en guerre 1914–1920* (CERTES-ENPC, 1988), 93–207; for the metalworkers, Papayanis, *Alphonse Merrheim*.

[26] M. Guilbert, *Les Femmes et l'organisation syndicale avant 1914* (Éditions du CNRS, 1966), 29.

represented in the industrial departments of the north, east, and centre and drew disproportionately on the Midi and the towns of the centre, west, and south-west. Paris, still essentially a centre of artisan production, even as the industrial 'red suburbs' began to encircle it, had 30 per cent of the CGT's membership.[27]

These basic characteristics help explain the distinctive differences in structure between the two movements. They also provide part of the explanation for the revolutionary syndicalism which animated the rapid growth of the CGT between 1904 and 1908 and which, formally at least, continued to define its orientation until the war. The principal divisions within British trade unionism marked off skilled from semi-skilled and general workers, but the dominance of national organizations over local cross-trade groupings was well-established. Although the trades councils experienced something of a resurgence from 1900 to 1926, as one expression of strengthening local networks of communal organization, they remained a subordinate element in the vertical trade union structure.[28] This reflected the high density of industrialization and thus of labour organization in Britain.

In France, a more scattered industrialization and the numerical weakness of syndicalism favoured local bodies which maximized the cross-trade solidarity of small syndicats in individual towns and cities. Thus the local *bourse du travail* (the nearest French equivalent to the trades council) emerged in the 1890s as the foundation of French syndicalism.[29] The autonomous Fédération des Bourses du Travail only combined with the CGT, until then composed solely of syndicats and fédérations by trade and industry, in 1902. The unified confederation embodied this dual heritage, with each member enrolled twice, through the local *bourse*, and hence the national Fédération des

---

[27] M. Labi, *La Grande Division des travailleurs: première scission de la CGT, 1914–1921* (Éditions ouvrières, 1964), 249–53; Shorter and Tilly, *Strikes in France 1830–1968*, 155–6.

[28] A. Clinton, *The Trade Union Rank and File: Trades Councils in Britain, 1900–1940* (Manchester Univ. Press, Manchester, 1977), 4–7.

[29] J. Julliard, *Fernand Pelloutier et les origines du syndicalisme d'action directe* (Seuil, 1971); P. Schöttler, *Naissance des bourses du travail: un appareil idéologique d'état à la fin du XIXᵉ siècle* (1982; French trans., Presses Universitaires de France, 1985).

Bourses, as well as through the local syndicat and the national Fédération des Industries.[30]

Paradoxically, the relative weakness of French syndicalism made it easier to promote the idea of industrial federations at the expense of craft sectionalism, leading to the creation of the builders' and metalworkers' federations in 1907 and 1908 respectively. Although significant skill distinctions remained within such bodies, they provided a potent example to Syndicalist trade union leaders in Britain (notably the dockers' leader, Tom Mann) who advocated the restructuring of British labour into radical and demarcation-free industrial unions.[31] Both before and especially following the war, a major amalgamation movement occurred within British trade unionism. But instead of conforming to the rational schemes of the industrial unionists, it confirmed the old contours between skilled and unskilled, with many of the latter swelling the cross-trade 'general' unions.[32]

In both countries, however, tensions between the centralization of power in national structures and its devolution to local or rank-and-file level became palpable in the decade of the war. Shifting definitions of skill and of the 'frontier' of control in the workplace forced trade unions into counterveiling bids to exercise their power at both levels, in ways which were as likely to be competitive as complementary with each other. In France, geographic localism as much as skill particularism was the fault-line of this tension. In 1912–13, the CGT leadership declared that the local *bourse du travail* must be subordinated to groupings at the level of each département, the Unions des Syndicats, which alone could represent them nationally through the Fédération des Bourses.[33] Against this attempted

---

[30] L. Levine, *The Labor Movement in France* (Columbia Univ. Press, 1912), 155–8.

[31] T. Mann, *Tom Mann's Memoirs* (The Labour Publishing Co., 1923), 251–5; S. Price, 'A "French Revolution" in Britain before the First World War?' *Modern and Contemporary France*, 22 (July 1985), pp. 3–13.

[32] E. J. Hobsbawm, 'Artisan or Labour Aristocrat?' *Economic History Review*, 38/3 (1985), pp. 355–72; H. A. Clegg, *A History of British Trade Unions since 1889*, ii, *1911–1933*, (OUP, Oxford, 1985), 105–11 and 307–8.

[33] CGT, *18ᵉ Congrès national corporatif . . . tenu au Havre du 16 au 23 septembre 1912. Compte rendu des travaux* (Imprimerie de l'Union, Le Havre, 1912), 65–8; CGT, *Compte rendu de la conférence ordinaire des fédérations nationales et des bourses du travail . . . tenu les 13, 14 et 15 juillet 1913 . . . Paris* (Maison des Fédérations, 1914), 15. See also Chap. 5, below.

centralization (only fully implemented in 1918–19), the tradition of local autonomy for the *bourses* and syndicats provided the major framework for the dissident, minority syndicalism which emerged in many of the key munitions and engineering centres in 1917–19, and along the railway system in 1919–20. Informal networks of dissident shop stewards (*délégués d'atelier*) in some regions reinforced the oppositional syndicalism in engineering in 1917–19. But dissidence departed less from the formal structures of the trade union movement, at least until 1920–1, than in Britain. There, by contrast, a national unofficial shop stewards' movement (though with strong roots in certain regions) cut horizontally across the established trade union structures, in order to mount a more militant local defence of skilled engineering workers during the war.[34]

Organizational structures were a crucial issue during and immediately after the war. In the first place, both trade union movements, swollen by the waves of industrial unrest, reached an unprecedented size. The TUC by 1920 grouped six and a half million workers, while the CGT increased fourfold over its pre-war peak to well over one and a half million members in 1919. These heights could not be defended in the slump of 1920–1, and the CGT in particular fell back to seven hundred thousand by the eve of the 1921 schism (still twice its pre-war record).[35] But trade union leaders were, for much of the period concerning this study, attempting to organize and direct what, even in the case of the CGT, came close to a mass industrial organization.

Secondly, the contrasting systems of industrial relations within which the trade unions sought to deploy their strength were substantially modified—at least temporarily—by the shock of war. In Britain, district and even industry-wide collective bargaining between employers and unions had become significant in a number of industries by 1914. The state was not absent from this process; in the case of coal and the railways, it intervened directly, and trade unions were making increased use of the voluntary conciliation procedures operated by the Labour Department of the Board of Trade, though they rejected compulsion. But the essence of the system remained bilateral.

[34] J. Hinton, *The First Shop Stewards' Movement* (Allen & Unwin, 1973); Geary, *European Labour Protest, 1848–1939*, 142. See also Chaps. 5 and 6, below.

[35] Orton, *Labour in Transition*, 272; Robert, *La Scission syndicale de 1921*, 159–60.

Although in France local and district collective bargaining were not unknown, employer hostility to trade unionism was much more pronounced. The state showed periodic signs of wishing to take a distinctly interventionist line in industrial relations. Millerand, as the relevant minister in 1900, expanded a limited Napoleonic system of tripartite trade representation (employers, workers, and the state) and contemplated compulsory arbitration of industrial disputes. But CGT leaders not only rejected arbitration, but remained in varying degrees deeply distrustful of state intervention in industrial relations, especially when Clemenceau substituted intervention of a different kind by bloodily repressing CGT-led strikes in 1907–8 and attacking the confederation itself. Locally, however, prefects and magistrates did exercise a mediating function in disputes, and the lure of state action to buttress and institutionalize relatively weak labour organizations against recalcitrant employers continued to attract certain strands of syndicalism. Though the legislative record of the Office du Travail (a full Ministry of Labour from 1906) was fairly meagre before the war, sympathetic civil servants lent some promise to such hopes.[36]

In both countries, the war obliged the state to intervene actively in what became trilateral systems of industrial relations, under the imperative of organizing the munitions effort. The war, in fact, was a key moment in the development of a 'societal corporatism'—i.e. of a propensity for institutional bargaining between organized interests and the state to become a crucial adjunct to, if not a substitute for, more traditional representative politics. The war moved the frontier between state and society and brought the two interest groups which crucially mattered in the economic effort, business and labour, into a new relationship. The role of labour in this corporatist

---

[36] E. H. Phelps-Brown, *The Growth of British Industrial Relations: A Study from the Standpoint of 1900–14* (Macmillan, 1959); C. J. Wrigley (ed.), *A History of British Industrial Relations*, i, *1875–1914* (Harvester Press, Brighton, 1982), and ii, *1914–1939* (1987); Clegg, *A History of British Trade Unions since 1889*, ii. 97–105; J. Julliard, *Clemenceau, briseur de grèves* (Éditions Julliard, 1965); P. N. Stearns, 'Against the Strike Threat: Employer Policy towards Labor Agitation in France, 1900–1914', *Journal of Modern History*, 40/4 (1968), pp. 474–500; J.-A. Tournerie, *Le Ministère du travail: origines et premiers développements* (Cujas, 1971), 251–66; M. Perrot, 'Le Regard de l'autre: les patrons français vus par les ouvriers (1880–1914)', in M. Lévy-Leboyer, *Le Patronat de la seconde industrialisation*, (Éditions ouvrières, 1979), 293–306.

development and its longer-term significance will form a central theme of this study.

The value placed on local solidarity by relatively isolated syndicalist militants and the particular artisanal culture of late nineteenth-century French skilled labour, were important factors in the flowering of pre-war revolutionary syndicalism—what one historian has described as the culmination of a tradition of 'trade socialism', rooted in the world of the workshop and building site, and in the pride and autonomy of the *ouvrier professionnel*.[37] Although the war confirmed its disintegration as the prevailing orientation of the CGT, revolutionary syndicalism profoundly marked the entire period of this study and, indeed, much of the subsequent history of French trade unionism.

Most distinctive among its features was a faith in the self-sufficiency of labour's industrial action and organization, both in winning immediate gains and in ultimately transforming society. With the associated belief in class conflict, this expressed the all-too-real predicament of scattered syndicalist forces which depended on militant action and on solidarity in their primary struggle against a *patronat* hostile to any modification of its industrial authority. A large majority of the CGT subscribed to the primacy of 'direct action'—that is, of the strike and associated action—and to industry rather than politics as the essential field of endeavour for organized labour.

Revolutionary syndicalism was also a moral affirmation of the dignity and independence of skilled labour in an economy where the workshop and small factory still seemed credible symbols of the ideal of a decentralized, self-governing organization of industry. The resolution passed by the 1906 Amiens congress, and subsequently considered the doctrinal 'charter' of the CGT, declared that 'the syndicat, today a grouping of resistance, will be in the future a grouping of production and sharing out, a basis of social reorganization'.[38]

Logically, in such an orientation, the general strike was the lever for the 'emancipation of labour'. Although it had lost its earlier chiliastic attraction as the single act of revolutionary

---

[37] B. H. Moss, *The Origins of the French Labor Movement, 1830–1914* (Univ. of California Press, Berkeley, Calif., 1976), 136–55; M. Collinet, *Esprit du syndicalisme* (Éditions ouvrières, 1951), 11–19.

[38] H. Dubief, *Le Syndicalisme révolutionnaire* (Colin, 1969), 95–7.

expropriation, revolutionary syndicalist leaders and intellectuals retained it as the symbol of their approach down to the war by interpreting it more metaphorically, as the accumulating industrial strength of labour through the continuous practice of the strike, which might eventually transform economic and social relations. The emphasis thus switched to the educative role of industrial action in the creation of an organized working class.[39]

At the national level of the CGT, revolutionary syndicalism amounted to a powerful, though never precise or monolithic, ideology. The 'charter' of Amiens gave less than a full definition. In the interests of unity, it stressed the political neutrality of the CGT, accepting that syndicalists could also be members of 'parties and sects' independently pursuing the 'transformation of society'. Revolutionary syndicalists, however, were generally less apolitical than anti-political, expressing their hostility to the state through a strong antimilitarism and even anti-patriotism. They tended to reject both parliamentary socialism (with its belief in the efficacy of the existing state) and the Marxism of the Guesdist wing of the Parti Socialiste (PS), with its doctrinaire subordination of syndicalism to the revolutionary party.

The strength of this ideology owed a great deal to anarchism. Many revolutionary syndicalist leaders, though certainly not all, came from an anarchist background. This is true not just of obvious founding figures (Pelloutier, creator of the Fédération des Bourses du Travail in the 1890s, Yvetot, his successor at the head of the Fédération des Bourses in the unified CGT, or Pouget, founder of the celebrated anarchist paper, *Le Père Peinard*, in the 1890s, and a secretary of the CGT from 1902 to 1908), but also of the second generation, including Léon Jouhaux, general secretary of the CGT during the period covered by this study.[40] Although 'pure' anarchists disputed the

[39] V. Griffuelhes and L. Niel, *L'Objectif de nos luttes de classes* (La Publication sociale, 1910), 27; R. Brécy, *La Grève générale en France* (Études et Documentation Internationale, 1969); J. Julliard, 'Théorie syndicaliste révolutionnaire et pratique gréviste', in id., *Autonomie ouvrière: études sur le syndicalisme d'action directe* (Gallimard/Le Seuil, 1988), 43–68; id., 'Jaurès et le syndicalisme révolutionnaire', in Rebérioux (ed.), *Jaurès et la classe ouvrière*, 111–18.

[40] J. Maitron, *Le mouvement anarchiste en France*, vol. 1, *Des origines à 1914* (1951; Maspero, 1975), 265–330; id., *Paul Delesalle: un anarchiste de la belle époque* (Fayard, 1985), 115–57; B. Georges and D. Tintant, *Léon Jouhaux*, i, *Des origines à 1921* (Presses Universitaires de France, 1962), 31–2.

lure of syndicalism, revolutionary syndicalism remained deeply
marked by anarchism, and the syndicalist press before the war
was highly permeable to anarchist ideas and writers (Pierre
Monatte, creator of the most influential new syndicalist
periodical, *La Vie ouvrière*, from 1909 to 1914, was strongly
influenced by anarchism).[41]

Even nationally, however, there were important qualifications to the hegemony of revolutionary syndicalism. First, the
minority of Guesdists in the CGT, who were concentrated in
the federation of textile workers, had an entirely different
concept of trade unionism. Rooted in the more densely industrialized north, where conditions were closer to those experienced by the German Social Democratic Party or the Parti
Ouvrier Belge, the Guesdists had built a powerful local presence encompassing unions, co-operatives, local government
and parliamentary deputies, under the overall identity of the
PS.[42] It was to repudiate the demand of Renard, Guesdist
secretary of the textile workers, that the CGT should integrate
itself into this type of working-class organization, that the
majority formed behind the Amiens 'charter' in 1906.[43] The
Guesdists returned to the attack at the 1912 congress, provoking a further reassertion of syndicalist autonomy.[44]

Secondly, there was a moderate, reformist belief in the value of
the PS and parliamentary action, which was especially marked
among those syndicalists (notably railway workers and miners) in
whose industries state regulation and legislation played some
part (both the railway and mining companies operated renewable
concessions from the state).[45] Thirdly, and most important, a
'reformist' current existed within the large majority subscribing
to the basic ideals of syndicalist autonomy, direct action, and an

---

[41] C. Chambelland (ed.), *Pierre Monatte: la lutte syndicale* (Maspero, 1976), 53–127.
[42] C. Willard, *Les Guesdistes: le mouvement socialiste en France (1893–1905)*
(Éditions sociales, 1965), 234–42.
[43] CGT, *15ᵉ Congrès national corporatif ... tenu à Amiens du 8 au 16 octobre 1906.
Compte rendu des travaux* (Imprimerie de la Somme, Amiens, 1906), 157, 170–1.
[44] CGT, *18ᵉ Congrès national corporatif ... tenu au Havre du 16 au 23 septembre
1912. Compte rendu des travaux,* (Imprimerie de l'Union, Le Havre, 1912), 106–58.
[45] R. Trempé, 'Le Réformisme des mineurs français à la fin du XIXᵉ siècle', *Le
Mouvement social*, 65 (Oct.–Dec. 1968), pp. 93–107; J. Julliard, 'Jeune et vieux
syndicat chez les mineurs du Pas-de-Calais', in id., *Autonomie ouvrière*, 69–93;
Ribeill, *Le Personnel des compagnies de chemins de fer*, i. 556–65.

eventual decentralization of the economy. Typically, this reformism laid greater emphasis on a permanent bargaining framework, co-operated more readily with employers in state-initiated bipartite or tripartite institutions, and tried to organize welfare benefits along the lines of British and German unions. It was less liable to anti-patriotism, preferring to emphasize the political neutrality of the Amiens resolution.[46]

There was no simple division by craft or industry between the revolutionaries and reformists supporting the Amiens position. Even predominantly reformist groups (miners, railwaymen, printers) contained revolutionary minorities, and the reverse is true for revolutionary federations such as the metal and building workers. At least some contemporaries felt that if the CGT's voting system had reflected the numerical strength of the constituent organizations, the reformists would have prevailed.[47]

At the local level, even outside the Guesdist north, it is doubtful whether revolutionary syndicalism managed generally to establish itself as a predominant political culture within labour circles. An anti- or apolitical stance nationally by CGT militants not infrequently coexisted with local co-operation with socialists.[48] Often, indeed, personnel and organizations overlapped. Additionally, many strikes, even during the revolutionary syndicalist heyday of 1904–8, probably owed little at least to the *direct* influence of the latter.[49]

---

[46] F. Challaye, *Syndicalisme révolutionnaire et syndicalisme réformiste*, (Alcan, 1909), 119; J.-B. Séverac, *Le Mouvement syndical* (Quillet, 1913); 73–7; Levine, *The Labor Movement in France*, 193; M. Rebérioux (ed.), *Les Ouvriers du livre et leur fédération: un centenaire, 1881–1981* (Temps Actuels, 1981), 93–128.

[47] F. Challaye (*Syndicalisme révolutionnaire et syndicalisme réformiste*) considered that a proportional voting system would have produced a reformist majority. L. Levine (*The Labor Movement in France*, 193) considered this unlikely.

[48] J. Julliard, 'I Rapporti sindacati-partiti: la pluralità dei modelli storici e il caso francese', in M. Antonioni, I. Barbadori, *et al.*, *Sindacato e classe operaia nell'età della seconda internazionale* (Sansoni editori, Florence, 1983), 358–81; id., 'Indépendance réciproque et concurrence: le syndicalisme français et la politique d'action directe', in id., *Autonomie ouvrière*, 199–227. This reality was clearly driven home to Victor Griffuelhes, former general secretary of the CGT and one of the most influential revolutionary syndicalist leaders, in his visit to local labour organizations—almost none of which measured up to his ideals (Griffuelhes, *Voyage révolutionnaire: impressions d'un propagandiste* (Rivière, 1910)).

[49] Stearns, *Revolutionary Syndicalism*, 100–1.

Yet the revolutionary syndicalist approach to strikes was consonant with the conditions of industrial protest in much of France. Weak organizations struggling to establish their existence and recognition by employers, as well as a basic hold on wages and work conditions, relied on the *élan* of militancy and local cross-trade solidarity in the absence of funds, mass support, or a sympathetic state.[50] In this context, it should be stressed that the *bias* of revolutionary syndicalist support to the less mechanized, more artisanal sectors was just that. Revolutionary syndicalism also struck root among industrial factory workers.[51] The success of revolutionary syndicalism arguably lay in its pragmatic capacity to codify and reinforce the 'direct action' which characterized the strikes and union organization unfurling across much of France for the first time between 1904 and 1908. When stiff government and employer resistance reduced the strike success-rate, revolutionary syndicalist militants and intellectuals, and hence the CGT, slid into a long period of doubt and disorientation which was still unresolved on the outbreak of war.[52]

(iii) Labour and Politics

In both countries, the period 1900–14 confirmed and expanded the political and electoral strength of the labour and socialist movements, already apparent in the 1890s.[53] The changing comportment of the state towards workers, with intensified repression of industrial unrest (especially in France) but also an enlarged government role in industrial relations and social

---

[50] Julliard, 'Théorie syndicaliste révolutionnaire'.

[51] Y. Lequin, *Les Ouvriers de la région lyonnaise (1848–1914)*, ii, *Les Intérêts de classe et la république* (Presses Universitaires de Lyon, Lyons, 1977), 304–37.

[52] Maxime Leroy, one of the most astute contemporary observers of French syndicalism, firmly dates the crisis in the CGT from the clash with the Clemenceau government in 1908 (*La Coutume ouvrière* (Giard et Brière, 1913), i. 22–3).

[53] French socialists first established a significant parliamentary presence in 1893, with 50 deputies. The newly united PS gained 52 seats in 1906 and 103 in 1914. In Britain, the ILP had little national, though much local, electoral success in the 1890s. The new Labour Party won 30 seats in 1906 and 42 in Dec. 1910.

welfare, in turn affected the political attitudes of labour. The war, by simultaneously demonstrating the interventionist capacity of the state while crystallizing, through the Bolshevik revolution, a new model of revolutionary politics, proved as crucial a period for the political as for the industrial orientation of organized labour. But if this suggests a certain similarity in the broad chronology of labour's political experience in Britain and France, the nature of the two states as well as the political traditions of the two movements resulted in quite different labour attitudes to politics.[54]

The crux of these differences is suggested by a problem of translation. 'Labour movement' does not denote the same reality as *mouvement ouvrier*. The former encompasses the political organization of labour in an organic relationship with trade unionism (at least in the British 'model', less so in North America), whereas the latter distinguishes the industrial organization of labour from a separate socialist movement. The relationship between the industrial and political organization of labour and the degree to which the latter was characterized by socialism, differed markedly in the French and British cases.[55]

A number of reasons can be suggested for this. The state, as an administrative and coercive system, was historically more highly differentiated from society in France than in Britain. The nature and legitimacy of this strongly centralized, relatively autonomous structure were issues subtending much of French politics, to which the socialism emerging in the 1880s and 1890s was in part a response. Attitudes to the state constituted one of the main determinants of the various currents, with anarcho-syndicalists repudiating any state, Guesdists hostile to the 'class state', and

---

[54] See Bibliography, Secondary Works, part 1.

[55] There has been little comparative reflection on such differences of structure and tradition, with the exception of the studies by G. Haupt (see, *inter alia*, 'Socialisme et syndicalisme: les rapports entre partis et syndicats au plan international: une mutation?', in Rebérioux (ed.), *Jaurès et la classe ouvrière*, 29–66) and by J. Julliard (*Autonomie ouvrière*, pt. 2). Three international conferences have resulted in juxtapositions rather than comparisons: 'Avec ou sans l'état? Le mouvement ouvrier français et anglais au tournant du siècle', *Le Mouvement social*, 65 (Oct.–Dec. 1968); Antonioni, Barbadori, *et al.*, *Sindacato e classe operaia nell'età della seconda internazionale* (1983); and Mommsen and Husung (eds.), *The Development of Trade Unionism in Great Britain and Germany* (1985).

reformists encountering fierce resistance from fellow socialists in attempting to use the existing state—as the *cas Millerand* resonantly demonstrated.[56]

In Britain, the state was less ambitious in its pretentions to define the relations between economic and social groups. British law was less abstract and sweeping than the 1884 French law on syndicalism, which laid down the powers and functions of worker (and employer) organizations.[57] Nor was the state perceived generally by labour as an unwarranted concentration of arbitrary authority, to be contested as such. Paradoxically, the social and industrial reforms introduced by government in Britain in the decade before the war were much more extensive than in France. This was connected with the predominant social weight of the working class in Britain, on which the Liberals (unlike the French Radicals) increasingly politically depended. It is true that this state intervention plus repressive measures in response to the pre-war industrial unrest (including use of the army) did generate a socialist critique of the state, in the form both of the upsurge of Syndicalism and of the Guild Socialists' theoretical attack on the 'servile state'.[58] But the indifference of many trade unionists to socialism before the war, plus the tendency of most socialists to rely unquestioningly on the parliamentary process to oppose what was seen as the fundamentally *economic* power of capital, suggests that the state

[56] M. Perrot, 'Les Socialistes français et les problèmes du pouvoir (1871–1914)' in A. Kriegel and M. Perrot, *Le Socialisme français et le pouvoir*, (Études et Documentation Internationale, 1966), 9–92; B. Badie and P. Birnbaum, *Sociologie de l'état* (Grasset, 1979); N. Jennawi-Le Yaouanc, 'La Conception de l'état chez les idéologues du socialisme anglais et français avant 1914' (DEA diss., Université de Paris II, 1980); P. Birnbaum, 'États, idéologies et action collective en Europe occidentale', in A. Kazancigil, *L'État au pluriel: perspectives de sociologie historique* (UNESCO, 1985), 229–45.

[57] Case-law played a vital part in British trade unionism. But there was no attempt to provide global definitions of trade unions as occurred with the 1884 law (which notably confined trade unions to 'professional' questions).

[58] B. Holton, *British Syndicalism, 1900–1914: Myths and Realities* (Pluto Press, 1976); A. W. Wright, *G. D. H. Cole and Socialist Democracy* (Clarendon Press, Oxford, 1979), 72–101; D. Powell, 'The New Liberalism and the Rise of Labour, 1886–1906', *Historical Journal*, 29/2 (1986), pp. 369–93; J. Stone, *The Search for Social Peace: Reform Legislation in France, 1890–1914* (State Univ. of New York Press, Albany, NY, 1985).

did not provide the same stimulus as in France to the formulation of socialism.[59]

The contrast in the relative importance of socialism by 1914 was reinforced by the divergence in the political traditions of the two movements. In both cases, the matrix of a broader, democratic political culture was vital in the emergence of labour ideologies. But the language and associations of the latter were entirely different. In France, they reached back to the legitimating myths of 1789–94 and to the succession of nineteenth-century revolutions. Hostility to industrial capitalism and criticism, even rejection, of the existing state, were frequently combined with a commitment to the Republican tradition and, therefore, to a certain patriotism—that of France as the *patrie* of revolution and popular liberties. Republicanism and socialism, even revolutionary socialism, were for many socialists not only compatible but indissociable. Even the Guesdists proved more hostile to state than nation.[60]

In Britain, the continuity of the parliamentary system and the use of legislation as a relatively sensitive mechanism of adjustment to pressure for change, helped forge the link between an already strong trade union movement in the late nineteenth and early twentieth centuries and political Liberalism.[61] The revival of socialism in the 1880s substantially influenced the leadership of the 'new unionism' over the subsequent twenty-five years.[62] But the bulk of trade unionists remained uncommitted, even

---

[59] This is as true for Hyndman, the convert to Marxism, as for the Fabians or for the bulk of the Independent Labour Party. See n. 115 below; C. Tsuzuki, *H. M. Hyndman and British Socialism* (OUP, Oxford, 1961); A. M. McBriar, *Fabian Socialism and English Politics, 1884–1918* (CUP, Cambridge, 1962); R. E. Dowse, *Left in the Centre: The Independent Labour Party, 1893–1940* (Longman, 1966), 1–19.

[60] Willard, *Les Guesdistes*, 181–212; T. Judt, *Marxism and the French Left: Studies in Labour and Politics in France, 1830–1981* (Clarendon Press, Oxford, 1986), 24–114.

[61] For useful recent summaries of the literature, see K. D. Brown, *The English Labour Movement* (Gill and Macmillan, Dublin, 1982); J. Hinton, *Labour and Socialism: A History of the British Labour Movement, 1867–1974* (Wheatsheaf Books, Brighton, 1983); K. Burgess, *The Challenge of Labour: Shaping British Society, 1850–1930* (Croom Helm, 1980); and K. Laybourn, *The Rise of Labour: The British Labour Party, 1890–1979* (Edward Arnold, 1988).

[62] H. Pelling, *The Origins of the Labour Party 1880–1900* (2nd edn., OUP, Oxford, 1965), 192–215; E. J. Hobsbawm, 'Considérations sur le "nouveau syndicalisme", 1886–1926', in 'Avec ou sans l'état?' *Le Mouvement social*, 65 (Oct–Dec. 1968), pp. 71–9; id., 'The "New Unionism" Reconsidered'.

formally, to socialism until the new Labour Party constitution of 1918.[63] And the language of British socialism in its major variant after 1893, the Independent Labour Party (ILP), was reformist and eclectic. *Revolutionary* socialism and doctrinaire polemics remained doubly peripheral within the pre-war British labour movement.

The strength of French socialism and the relatively tardy emergence of French trade unionism, as well as its nature, help explain the contrast with Britain in the relationships between the political and industrial organization of labour. The well-organized British trade union movement only felt the need to establish a political wing in the 1890s and early 1900s when faced with employer counter-organization against the surge of unionization. The growing influence of the ILP also contributed to the establishment of the Labour Representation Committee in 1900.[64] But the new body was dominated by the block membership of the trade unions, the separately affiliated socialist groups (notably the ILP and British Socialist Party (BSP)) remaining a small minority (33,000 out of a total membership of 1,600,000 in 1914).[65] The Labour Party, as it became in 1906, was thus first and foremost the pragmatic expression of trade unionism as a political interest group. After the 1906 election it lobbied and supported the Liberal government. But its exact role, its relationship with the Liberals, the extent to which it should take the political initiative on matters beyond trade union defence, or even commit itself to socialism, were open questions in the pre-war period.

In France, socialist organizations had a political logic independent of trade unionism as the advance guard of Republicanism or, in the case of the Guesdists, as a revolutionary marxist party. Moreover, in a society where the working class was a minority, socialism necessarily, and with some success, appealed to sections of the peasantry and *classes moyennes*.[66] It

---

[63] See Chap. 6, below.

[64] Clegg, Fox, and Thompson, *A History of British Trade Unions since 1889*, i. 269–86; Pelling, *The Origins of the Labour Party, passim*.

[65] H. Pelling, *A Short History of the Labour Party* (Macmillan, 1961, and subsequent edns.), 156.

[66] Willard, *Les Guesdistes*, 316–25; T. Judt, *Socialism in Provence 1871–1914* (CUP, Cambridge, 1979).

was more than an expression of working-class politics, fundamental though these were. By comparison with Britain, therefore, the relationship between industrial and political organization was problematic as well as crucial. The different socialist groups in the 1890s had various 'models' for their connection with syndicalism. The Guesdists advocated the subordination of syndicalism to the party in the manner we have noted. Jaurès urged a unified but pluralist party with syndicats as one of the constituent elements, somewhat along the lines of the Parti Ouvrier Belge.[67] Neither approach survived the emergence of the autonomous CGT and the collapse of socialist unity plans in the wake of the Dreyfus Affair.

When socialist unity was finally achieved, in 1905, the Section Française de l'Internationale Ouvrière (SFIO) not only encompassed a variety of understandings of socialism but also consecrated the separate political and industrial organization of French labour. Within the new party, a range of views persisted on relations with the CGT—from anti-parliamentary socialists at one extreme, who shared close affinities with the revolutionary syndicalists, to the Guesdists at the other.[68] The broad centre was occupied by those—Jaurès himself, Allemanists, Blanquists, and 'reformists' such as Albert Thomas—who all in different ways urged close and sympathetic co-operation with the CGT while accepting organizational separation.[69] A number of nationally important socialists also held positions within the CGT. Such personal co-operation was strengthened in the period immediately before 1914 through the joint socialist-syndicalist campaign against the threat of war and the three-year military-service law. None the less, the institutional and ideological separation of the CGT from the PS remained a crucial feature of organized labour in France, not only during

[67] Willard, *Les Guesdistes*, 352–60; M. Rebérioux, 'La Conception du parti chez Jaurès', in Rebérioux (ed.), *Jaurès et la classe ouvrière*, 83–100.

[68] M. Rebérioux, 'Les Tendances hostiles à l'état dans la SFIO (1905–1914)', *Le Mouvement social*, 65 (Oct.–Dec. 1968), pp. 21–36.

[69] Rebérioux, 'La Conception du parti chez Jaurès'; M. Dommanget, *Edouard Vaillant: un grand socialiste, 1840–1915* (La Table Ronde, 1956), 456–86; J. Howorth, *Edouard Vaillant: la création de l'unité socialiste en France (Éditions et Documentation Internationale/Syros, 1982), 195–217;* B. W. Schaper, *Albert Thomas: trente ans de réformisme social* (Assen, Van Gorcum, 1959), 72–3.

the war but also during the post-war schisms which gave birth
to French communism.

(iv) International Labour

Internationalism was important in both labour movements not
just because the war occasioned, if only in part causing, the
collapse of the Second International and precipitated schisms in
the international socialist and trade union organizations in
1919–20 (ahead of most domestic schisms), but also because
labour and socialist internationalism cast a sharp light on its
own natural corollary, the nationalism and national identities of
the various labour movements and working classes.[70] Too little
is known, unfortunately, about the relative strengths of national
and internationalist feeling among workers beyond labour organizations and leaderships, especially before 1914. Even the
views of ordinary trade unionists and socialists have not been
substantially investigated.[71] This makes it difficult to know how
far the undoubted anti-war feelings and internationalist sentiment which existed in the French, British, and other labour
movements expressed a more general phenomenon or, on the
contrary, worked against the grain in a period when both
nationalism and the means of its dissemination (universal
primary education, the mass press) were strengthening. What is
increasingly evident is that even within the language, actions
and formal declarations of the labour movements, especially in

---

[70] For these two dimensions to the history of international labour, see Bibliography, Secondary Works, part 2.

[71] G. Haupt, 'Guerre ou révolution? L'Internationale et l'union sacrée en août
1914', in Haupt, *L'Historien et le mouvement social*, (Maspero, 1980) 199–235; '1914:
la guerre et la classe ouvrière européenne', special no. of *Le Mouvement social*, 49
(Oct–Dec. 1964); A. Kriegel, 'Août 1914; nationalisme et internationalisme ouvriers',
Le Pain et les roses (Presses Universitaires de France, 1968), 207–43; J. Howorth,
'French Workers and German Workers: The Impossibility of Internationalism,
1900–1914', *European History Quarterly*, 15/1 (1985), pp. 71–97; M. Van der Linden,
'The National Integration of European Working Classes (1871–1914)', *International
Review of Social History*, 33/3 (1988), pp. 285–311; R. Gallissot, R. Paris, and
C. Weil, 'La Désunion des prolétaires', special no. of *Le Mouvement social*, 147.
(Apr–June 1989) (esp. R. Gallissot, 'La Patrie des prolétaires', pp. 13–25).

their opposition to war, national allegiances seriously, perhaps fatally, qualified an internationalist faith.

The CGT combined most forcefully the themes of antimilitarism and antipatriotism. The refusal to respond to a national mobilization in the event of war on the grounds that international working-class solidarity pre-empted all else, and that war only expressed the interests of capital and reaction, remained its position until 1914. The special CGT congress called in November 1912 at the height of the the first Balkan war, affirmed that the organization 'does not recognize the right of the bourgeois state to dispose of the working class'.[72] Such a position derived logically both from the CGT's insistence on autonomy from the state and 'politics' and especially from the anarchism which animated revolutionary syndicalism as an ideology.

But the internal divisions in the CGT marked its international as much as its domestic policy, especially since international policy became really important only after 1911, at a time of growing doubt and disorientation for the organization. In particular, many syndicalists distinguished antimilitarism, fuelled by the domestic use of the army in industrial disputes, from antipatriotism. At the 1908 Marseilles congress, support for the former was virtually unanimous whereas the latter was opposed by a large minority.[73] Revolutionary syndicalist leaders themselves grew increasingly cautious in their anti-war policy. At the conference of the Fédération des Bourses in 1911, all the delegates except one declared that their own members' frame of mind lent small encouragement to the hope that there would be mass support for a strike in opposition to a military mobilization.[74] From 1912, although CGT leaders sustained their anti-war and even antipatriotic rhetoric, they quietly abandoned the notion of a revolutionary general strike in the event of war,

---

[72] A. Kriegel and J.-J. Becker, *1914: la guerre et le mouvement ouvrier français* (Colin, 1964), 24–5; Georges and Tintant; *Léon Jouhaux*, i. 120–1.

[73] CGT, *16ᵉ Congrès national corporatif . . . tenu à Marseille du 5 au 12 octobre 1908. Compte rendu sténographique des travaux* (Imprimerie Nouvelle, Marseilles, 1909), 212–16; Levine, *The Labor Movement in France*, 178–9.

[74] J. Julliard, 'La CGT devant la guerre 1900–14', in id., *Autonomie ouvrière*, 94–111; S. Milner, 'The French Confédération Générale du Travail and the International Secretariat of National Trade Union Centres (1900–1914); French Syndicalist Attitudes towards Internationalism and the International Labour Movement' (Ph.D., Aston, 1987), 358–433.

concentrating instead on co-operating with the PS in mobilizing labour opinion to prevent war.[75]

It was, indeed, the socialists, and especially Jaurès, who
expressed a more complex relationship than vintage revolutionary syndicalism allowed between a class and a national identity
within French labour. The antimilitarism defined by Jaurès in
L'Armée nouvelle (November 1910) and deployed by the PS in
1912–14 in its campaign against the three-year military-service
law, pivoted on the association, rather than dissociation, of
Republican patriotism and socialist internationalism.[76] Jaurès
demanded the integration of the working class into the national
community. He asserted the workers' right to participate in
legitimate national defence, but also their duty to employ all
measures, including an international preventive general strike,
against bellicist pressures in France. It was this approach to
internationalism which prevailed during the immediate pre-war
years in the campaigns of organized labour.

Ironically, the sense of national distinctiveness was heightened by the differences and misunderstandings which occurred within the international labour and socialist organizations themselves. The deliberate ambiguities of the Second
International's anti-war policy, in order to accommodate profound national differences, are well known. So, too, is Jaurès's
defence of Republican and parliamentary democracy against
the SPD.[77] But the International Socialist Bureau was riven by
dissensions between different national delegates, which were

---

[75] Julliard, 'La CGT devant la guerre 1900–14'; Kriegel and Becker, *1914: la
guerre et le mouvement ouvrier français*, 40; J.-J. Becker, *1914: comment les français
sont entrés dans la guerre* (Presses de la FNSP, 1977), 89–98; Papayanis, *Alphonse
Merrheim*, 71–81; Milner, 'The French Confédération Générale du Travail', 438–9.
In particular, CGT leaders carefully distinguished their position from the ultra-left
antipatriotism of Gustave Hervé and his followers within the PS (see the manifesto
issued to this effect in 1912 by Jouhaux, Griffuelhes, Voirin, Savoie, and Bled,
reproduced in *La Revue socialiste, syndicaliste et coopérative*, 2 (1912), pp. 281–2).

[76] J. Jaurès, *L'Armée nouvelle* (1910; Éditions de l'Humanité, 1915), 361–2; H.
Goldberg, *The Life of Jean Jaurès* (Univ. of Wisconsin Press, Madison, Wis., 1962),
417–57; Kriegel, 'Août 1914: nationalisme et internationalisme ouvriers'; and ead.,
'Jaurès en juillet 1914', *Le Pain et les roses*, 171–205.

[77] J. Braunthal, *History of the International*, i, *1864–1914* (1961; English trans.,
Nelson, 1966), 281–2 and 320–56; G. Haupt, *Socialism and the Great War: The
Collapse of the Second International* (Clarendon Press, Oxford, 1972); I. Muller, *De la
guerre: le discours de la deuxième internationale, 1889–1914* (Droz, Geneva, 1980), 243–80.

usually hidden in order to preserve the appearance of mono-lithic internationalism.[78]

Even more significantly, the CGT engaged in a fluctuating contest with the German trade union movement's leadership, and notably with its secretary, Karl Legien, within the International Secretariat of National Trade Union Centres (ISN-TUC) from 1901. This first attempt at a distinct trade union international (nominally it became the International Federation of Trade Unions (IFTU) in 1913) was dominated up to the war by the irreconcilability of the French and German conceptions of trade unionism. For the Germans, the Second (socialist) International—from which the autonomous CGT was excluded—was the proper forum for political issues, and they consistently blocked the CGT's attempts to introduce the question of anti-militarism into ISNTUC conferences.[79] Equally aggravating for revolutionary syndicalists like Griffuelhes, Yvetot, and Jouhaux was the apparent superiority complex of the Germans, with their financially prosperous mass unionism, towards the diminutive CGT—a superiority driven home by the fact that the Germans largely financed the ISNTUC, with Legien acting as its secretary. This accumulation of mistrust undermined the CGT's confidence in international trade union action during the crisis of July 1914, and resurfaced as a major international preoccupation of the CGT leadership during and after the war.[80]

British Labour's internationalism drew as much on an older but still highly influential tradition of liberal internationalism as on socialism. Wars were seen as inherently reactionary and unnecessary and the possibility that a democratic Britain might become entangled in the conflicts of continental militarism were

[78] J. Howorth, 'The Left in France and Germany, Internationalism, and War: A Dialogue of the Deaf, 1900–1914', in E. Cahm and V. Fiscera, (eds.), *Socialism and Nationalism in Contemporary Europe, 1848–1945*, 3 vols. (Spokesman Books, Nottingham, 1978–80), i. 7–19; and id., 'French Workers and German Workers'.

[79] J. Sassenbach, *Twenty-Five Years of International Trade Unionism* (IFTU, Amsterdam, 1926); L. Lorwin, *Labor and Internationalism* (Macmillan, 1929); Milner, 'The French Confédération Générale du Travail'; ead., 'The International Secretariat of National Trade Union Centres 1901–1913', *International Review of Social History*, 33/1 (1988), pp. 1–24.

[80] For the pre-war tension, and especially an abortive meeting between Jouhaux and Legien in Brussels late in July 1914, see Milner 'The French Confédération Générale du Travail', 417–23.

especially reproved. The language of international class solidarity was superimposed on this foundation, with the ILP (the driving force behind Labour internationalism) collaborating with radical Liberal 'pacifists' before and especially during the war.[81] Since the preservation of Britain and its democratic liberties from external (and, to a lesser extent, domestic) militarism, as well as the pursuit of a moderate, parliamentary socialism, lay at the core of ILP policy, the nation was not repudiated— only nationalism. But ILP international policy never entirely won over the Labour Party before the war. Many trade unionists remained suspicious of ILP internationalism or at best indifferent to international questions. Although the January 1912 Labour Party conference voted to 'investigate' the feasibility of a general strike against war (in the advocacy of which to the International itself, the ILP had played a key role), the response of the unions remained inconclusive.[82] The British labour movement as a whole barely spoke with a united, let alone enthusiastic, voice on international affairs.

Pre-war socialist internationalism, though relying first and foremost on the distinctive strengths of the trade union and socialist movements to prevent war (parliamentary pressure, mass demonstrations, the general strike) also drew on the concepts of 'bourgeois internationalism'—national self-determination, disarmament, compulsory arbitration, and the abolition of secret diplomacy—in short, a kind of international democracy, permanently to outlaw war. Such ideas, popularized through the Hague Peace Conferences of 1899 and 1907, were the essence of the radical Liberal stance in Britain and also marked Radical foreign policy in France.[83] They strongly influenced the ILP and, in a minor key, emerged in the SFIO. Both Jaurès in *L'Armée nouvelle* and Vaillant at the 1913 PS

---

[81] See, for example, the declaration against war by the British section of the International, on 1 Aug. 1914, quoted in R. Miliband, *Parliamentary Socialism* (Merlin Press, 1961), 42. See also Dowse, *Left in the Centre*, 24–8; C. Cline, *Recruits to Labour: The British Labour Party, 1914–1931* (Syracuse Univ. Press, Syracuse, NY, 1963).

[82] D. J. Newton, *British Labour, European Socialism and the Struggle for Peace, 1889–1914* (OUP, Oxford, 1985).

[83] F. S. L. Lyons, *Internationalism in Europe, 1815–1914* (Sythoff, Leiden, 1963), 338–54; A. J. P. Taylor, *The Trouble-Makers: Dissent over Foreign Policy* (Hamish Hamilton, 1957), 87–119; Z. Steiner, *Britain and the Origins of the First World War* (Macmillan, 1977), 128–70; L. Bourgeois, *Pour la société des nations* (Georges Crès, 1914).

congress considered them one of the means available to international socialism to prevent war.[84] They were also adopted by the Copenhagen congress of the Second International in 1910.[85] The labour and socialist enthusiasm for 'Wilsonism' and a new international order which developed during the war thus had autonomous pre-war roots.[86] More generally, the shifting relationship between class and national identities which international questions highlighted and the terms in which various currents associated or dissociated them, constituted one of the essential frames on which the experience of the war and its aftermath was woven in both labour movements.

(v) On the Eve of the War

Chronic since 1908 and the clash with the Clemenceau government, the disorientation of the CGT was becoming acute on the eve of the war. Formally, the 'charter' of Amiens and its associated beliefs continued to define the outlook of the confederation. In December 1911, Léon Jouhaux expounded the principles of French syndicalism to an audience at the Brussels Maison du Peuple.[87] Still in his thirties, the former matchworker from Aubervilliers, in the semi-rural northern suburbs of Paris, had emerged in the wake of the 1908 crisis as the *protégé* of Griffuelhes and the revolutionary syndicalist candidate to the general secretaryship of the CGT, a post he held from 1909 to 1947.[88] It is not surprising that for his Belgian audience, Jouhaux defined the tenets of classic revolutionary syndicalism, repudiating the class state and any possibility of an *entente* between

---

[84] *L'Armée nouvelle*, 329–37; *Parti socialiste, 10ᵉ congrès national tenu à Brest les 23, 24 et 25 mars 1913. Compte rendu sténographique* (n.d.), 246–7.

[85] A. Van Der Slice, *International Labor, Diplomacy and Peace, 1914–1919* (OUP, Oxford, 1941), 23–4.

[86] A. J. Mayer, *Political Origins of the New Diplomacy, 1917–1918* (Yale Univ. Press, New Haven, Conn., 1959). See also Chaps. 2 and 8, below.

[87] The speech was published twice, in France as *Notre syndicalisme* (La Publication sociale, 1912), and in Belgium as *Les Tendances syndicales: le syndicalisme français par L. Jouhaux: le syndicalisme allemand par Johann Sassenbach* (Des Presses de L. Urdal et Co., Brussels, 1912).

[88] Georges and Tintant, *Léon Jouhaux*, i. For the early years, see M.-A. Renauld, 'Documents: mémoires de Léon Jouhaux', *Le Mouvement social*, 47 (Apr.–June 1964), pp. 81–109.

workers and the *patronat*. We have already noted that less than a year later, at the 1912 Le Havre congress of the CGT, the revolutionary syndicalist leaders rebuffed the attempt by the Guesdist textile leadership to reopen the question of socialist-syndicalist relations with a reaffirmation of the 1906 'charter'.

But despite this, symptoms of the organization's malaise proliferated. Stagnating membership and the declining success-rate of strikes prompted internal acrimony over the nature of syndicalist organization and the merits of 'militant minorities'. A sharp cleavage opened up within revolutionary syndicalist ranks between those, like Jouhaux and Merrheim, the influential secretary of the Fédération des Métaux, who favoured more centralized discipline, higher subscriptions, and a mass membership, and those who defended a more traditional revolutionary militancy.[89] This was the principal issue at the July 1913 conference of the Fédération des Bourses du Travail, at which the CGT leadership presented its organizational reforms subordinating local *bourses* to the departmental Unions. Both Merrheim and Jouhaux urged this as the key to a new union strategy in which carefully prepared, specific campaigns for more modest but realistic goals would define the path of syndicalist growth—a strategy which both men emphasized until the outbreak of the war.[90]

This new realism was endorsed almost unanimously at the 1913 conference, but caused major internal divisions within the

[89] E. Chaille, 'L'Évolution de la C.G.T.', in *La Revue socialiste, syndicaliste et coopérative*, 2 (1912), pp. 140–4; H. Lagardelle, 'Les Difficultés du syndicalisme', *Le Mouvement socialiste*, 244 (Sept.–Oct. 1912), pp. 161–4; P. Monatte, 'La CGT a-t-elle rectifié son tir?' *La Vie ouvrière*, 93 (Aug. 1913), pp. 129–39. All three, from different angles, identify the emergence of a new realism between the twin dangers of 'political' socialism and anarcho-syndicalist or 'hervéiste' insurrectionalism.

[90] CGT, *Compte rendu de la conférence ordinaire des fédérations nationales des bourses du travail ... tenu les 13, 14 et 15 juillet 1913 ... Paris* (Maison des Fédérations, 1914), esp. the speeches by Jouhaux (pp. 46–7) and Merrheim (pp. 55–6). Jouhaux's article, 'L'Action directe' (*La Bataille syndicaliste*, 9 Jan. 1913), significantly reframed the traditional revolutionary syndicalist idea by divesting it of its violent and insurrectionary nuances. A 'Déclaration à propos de l'action confédérale' was issued after the 1913 conference to summarize the new policy, and was signed by Jouhaux, Dumoulin, Lapierre, Lenoir, Merrheim, Labbe, Blanchard, Lefevre, Voirin, Bled, Minot, Vignaud, Savoie, Puyjalon, Sarda, Monatte, Gauthier, Monnier, Moulinier, Ranty, Delzant, Charbonnier—most of whom (Monatte being the clear exception) eventually supported the wartime or post-war *majoritaire* position (*Le Mouvement socialiste* (July–Aug. 1913), pp. 126–29).

two main revolutionary syndicalist organizations, the Fédération des Métaux and the Fédération du Bâtiment. The leadership of the *métaux*, at a tense congress in September 1913, applied the new confederal approach despite bitter resistance by a 'revolutionary' minority, which later expelled Merrheim from his own local union (in which it held a majority), the latter itself being subsequently excluded from the federation.[91]

In the Fédération du Bâtiment, the crisis in recruitment, numerically stagnant but with a high turnover, and the failure of a major Paris building strike in 1911—together with the shift in confederal orientation—also triggered internal conflict. Nicolet, a Paris plumber who had been the federation's first secretary in 1907 and was re-elected in 1912, attacked the anarcho-syndicalists who dominated the Paris organizations for the revolutionary *élan* with which they embarked on unsuccessful strikes, demanding a leadership more representative of the provinces and more cautious in its approach to industrial action. The Paris revolutionaries and their leading personality, Raymond Péricat, condemned what they saw as a move towards reformism and syndicalist bureaucracy, prompting Nicolet's resignation in 1913. A bitterly divided 1914 congress had to arbitrate between the two tendencies.[92] The Paris revolutionary syndicalists chose the non-re-eligibility of sydicalist functionaries as the symbolic issue (at the price of refusing to allow their leading figures to stand again for national leadership). They

[91] *Fédération des ouvriers des métaux, Compte rendu des 1ᵉʳ et 2ᵉ congrès nationaux tenus à Paris . . . août 1911 et . . . septembre 1913* (Maison des Fédérations, n.d.), especially Merrheim's and Jouhaux's speeches, pp. 96–9; APP B/a 1605, police report on the 1913 congress; Gras, 'La Fédération des métaux en 1913–1914', 102; Papayanis, *Alphonse Merrheim*, 52–5.

[92] *Fédération nationale . . . du bâtiment, rapport du comité. Questions à l'ordre du jour du congrès national, Bordeaux . . . 7. . . 11 avril 1912* (La Cotypographie, Courbevoie, 1912), esp. 13–14 (membership) and 90–112 (strikes); *Compte rendu des travaux du 4ᵉ congrès national, tenu à Bordeaux, les 7, 8, 9, 10 et 11 avril 1912* (Imprimerie du 'Travailleur du Bâtiment', 1912); J. Nicolet, 'La Crise syndicaliste', *Le Travailleur du Bâtiment* (Sept. 1913); *Fédération nationale du bâtiment, 5ᵉ congrès national . . . du lundi 13 au vendredi 17 avril 1914. Rapports sur les questions à l'ordre du jour* (Maison des Fédérations, n.d., but 1914); esp. pp. 14–29 on strikes and 45–9, on falling membership; *Fédération nationale du bâtiment, 5ᵉ congrès national, Paris . . . 13 au 17 avril 1914; Compte rendu des séances* (L'Union Typographique, Villeneuve-Saint-Georges, 1914), esp. pp. 27–112, for the clash of Nicolet and Péricat.

were overwhelmingly defeated, opening the way to a moderate group (notably Chanvin, a relatively unknown sculptor-decorator from Paris, and Picart, an architectural draftsman), who ran the building workers' federation throughout the war.[93] Jouhaux made an unplanned but important intervention at the congress in which he drew the parallel between Merrheim's position in the metalworkers and that of Nicolet. He denied that the shift in orientation was reformist, but declared that 'revolutionaryism does not exclude foresight and intelligence' and a more pragmatic industrial policy.[94]

The syndicalist malaise surfaced in other ways too. CGT leaders began to revise their views on industrial capitalism in a phase of intensive growth and consolidation. This produced the firm conviction in Merrheim that organized labour had seriously to study the economic evolution of industry in order to contest it, a conviction shared by Pierre Monatte in *La Vie ouvrière* and also by Jouhaux.[95] Merrheim, who from his background in the Nord had emerged by 1908 as the dominant force in the new Fédération des Métaux, produced three monographs on the metallurgical industry between 1908 and 1913.[96]

There were signs of an even more radical revision among the central knot of CGT leaders. As early as 1910–11, Griffuelhes contrasted the backwardness of French business and the acute tension of its industrial relations with the dynamism of industry in countries such as America, arguing that a productive capitalism would create a more prosperous working class and powerful

---

[93] Moulinier, a plumber, and Chanvin, were elected joint secretaries in 1914, but the former died in 1915. Péricat retained his seat on the Comité Confédéral, where he was the only advocate of resistance to the mobilization on 1 Aug. 1914, and where he remained true to his pre-war anarchist and pacifist views throughout the conflict (R. Brécy, *Le Mouvement syndical en France, 1871–1921: essai bibliographique* (Mouton, 1963), 85).

[94] *Fédération nationale ... du bâtiment, 5e congrès national ... 1914*, 106.

[95] Gras, 'Merrheim et le capitalisme'; Papayanis, *Alphonse Merrheim*, 59–70; C. Chambelland (ed.), *Pierre Monatte: la lutte syndicale* (Maspero, 1976), 61–127; Georges and Tintant, *Léon Jouhaux*, i. 99. Jouhaux and Griffuelhes published a short-lived *Encyclopédie du mouvement syndicaliste* from Dec. 1911 to May 1912, with somewhat the same aim as *La Vie ouvrière*.

[96] Most notably, with Francis Delaisi, the economist, *La Métallurgie: son origine et son développement* (Éditions de la Fédération des Métaux, 1913), a comprehensive and impressive study.

labour movement.[97] Jouhaux picked up the theme in 1913, apropos a dispute in the Breton fishing industry.[98] Merrheim tackled a crucial variant of the idea immediately before the war—the introduction of 'scientific management' techniques (dramatizing the issue of a mass, unskilled workforce) in the car industry. Initially, after major non-union strikes against *chronométrage* at Berliet (Lyons) in 1912 and Renault in early 1913, Merrheim condemned (along with most other labour commentators) what he saw as an attempt to reduce wages and erode the ethos of the skilled worker, confirming the 'moral degradation' of the proletariat. By March 1914, however, he had begun to modify his analysis. He suggested that Taylorism had at least shown a revolution in industrial methods to be inevitable, and argued that an informed and powerful labour movement should adapt the development to its own benefit while eliminating its abuse.[99]

These hesitant and ambiguous modifications in the attitudes of leading syndicalists to industry were underlined by the nearly unanimous vote of the 1910 CGT congress in favour of voluntary collective contracts with the *patronat*.[100] The impossibility of conducting a successful trade unionism without some institutionalized relationship with business seemed accepted by many revolutionary syndicalists as well as reformists. A parallel ambiguity emerged after 1912 in relation to the state. Despite continued allegiance to the ideal of syndicalist autonomy and apoliticism, the logic both of co-operating with the PS in mounting an anti-war campaign and of pressing for reforms on specific labour issues from 1912 (reduction of working hours

[97] V. Griffuelhes, 'L'Infériorité des capitalistes français', *Le Mouvement socialiste* (Dec. 1910), pp. 329–33, and 'Stagnation capitaliste', ibid. (Jan. 1911), pp. 34–7.

[98] 'La Crise sardinière: le point de vue syndical', *La Bataille syndicaliste*, 11 Jan. 1913.

[99] The shift is marked by the difference between two sets of articles, the first, 'La Méthode Taylor', in *La Vie ouvrière*, 20 Feb. 1913, pp. 210–26 and 5 Mar. 1913, pp. 298–309, and the second, retaining the same title, in *La Vie ouvrière*, 20 Mar. 1914, 345–62 and 5 Apr. 1914, pp. 385–98. For the anti-time-and-motion strike at Renault, see P. Fridenson, *Histoire des usines Renault*, i, *Naissance de la grande entreprise (1898–1939)* (Seuil, 1972), 70–9; id., 'Les Ouvriers français de l'automobile jusqu'en 1914', *Sociologie du travail* (July–Sept. 1979), pp. 297–321.

[100] CGT, *17ᵉ Congrès national corporatif ... tenu à Toulouse du 3 au 10 octobre 1910. Compte rendu des travaux* (Imprimerie Ouvrière, Toulouse, 1911), 334–6.

and introduction of the *semaine anglaise,* or half day on Satur-
day, and opposition to *la vie chère*) implied the need to
influence the state and politicians as well as the *patronat*.[101]

These divergences within revolutionary syndicalist ranks
remained unresolved and partly covert up to the outbreak of
war. According to a police report of July 1913, 'the anarchists of
the confederation wage a bitter struggle against the moderates,
to whom Jouhaux has rallied', and Jouhaux and Merrheim in
turn resented the attempt to portray them as 'traitors to the
working class'.[102] The two leaders constantly reiterated the
compatibility of the new realism with basic revolutionary
syndicalist values and goals, and there was no discernible
attempt to realign the syndicalist currents behind a new overall
programme or philosophy.[103] A referendum conducted among
the industrial federations and departmental unions in the early
summer of 1914 on the issues to be discussed at the forthcoming
confederal congress, showed that much of the CGT membership shared both the new realism and the ambivalence over its
implications for the movement's orientation. Shorter working
hours and the *semaine anglaise* headed the list of issues to be
discussed with seventy-one votes, followed by fifty-seven for
the CGT's attitude to the 'mouvement social' and for its
principles of general action.[104] Scheduled for the autumn and
widely expected to clarify the CGT's orientation, the congress
of Grenoble was never held.[105] The war intervened.

Although the PS suffered less obviously than the CGT from
a crisis of identity in the final years of peace—its membership

---

[101] For the domestic reform campaign, see the decision of the 1912 congress,
CGT, *18ᵉ Congrès national corporatif ... tenu au Havre du 16 au 23 septembre
1912 ...,* 193–6, and the Comité Confédéral's report to the congress scheduled for
Sept. 1914, *Rapports des comités et des commissions pour l'exercice 1912–1914
présentés au 19ᵉ congrès corporatif ... tenu à Grenoble du 14 au 19 septembre 1914*
(Maison des Syndicats, 1914), 57–8.

[102] APP B/a 1605, rep. 29 July 1913.

[103] Georges and Tintant, *Léon Jouhaux,* i. 100. The police reports of 1913 and
1914 stressed both the disorientation of the CGT and the subterranean nature of
the struggle between tendencies, beneath a superficial ideological accord (APP B/a
1605 and AN F₇ 13574, and, in particular, in the latter series, 'Notes rétrospectives
sur les divisions intérieures du Comité Confédéral de la CGT', 10 Sept. 1915).

[104] AN F₇ 13581, reps. 18 June and 10 July 1914. Anti-militarism and opposition
to the three-year military service law gained only 35 votes.

[105] AN F₇ 13574, rep. Apr. 1914.

and electoral strength expanded steadily—there was a sharp tension between its constituent currents. As usual during the entire period from 1900, this was especially acute over the question of reforms and participation in government. The issue emerged anew from 1911 (at the Saint-Quentin congress) with a reformulation of reformism on the right of the party which laid special emphasis on municipalization and nationalization as economic strategies for progressively achieving socialism. The principal spokesmen of this tendency were the academic economist and socialist activist from the Deux-Savoies, Edgar Milhaud, and Albert Thomas, the baker's son from Champigny-sur-Marne and former scholarship boy at the École Normale Supérieure, who edited the reformist *Revue Socialiste, syndicaliste et coopérative* and, still in his early thirties, entered parliament in 1910.[106]

Interest in nationalization and municipalization was nothing new among French socialists. But this initiative was significant first, because it defined a new, decentralized form of public ownership, associating consumers and producers in running the concern and thus avoiding charges of *étatisation*, or fostering the bureaucratic state, and secondly, because it embryonically sketched out a new, piecemeal strategy of socialist advance. 'Only the transformation of capitalist property into social property', stated Thomas in a 'Déclaration Socialiste' to the Chamber in 1910, 'will free the workers ... It is in the interest of the nation as of the proletarians that the most crushing capitalist monopolies should be urgently transformed into democratically run social services'.[107]

---

[106] Founder of the influential periodical, *Les Annales de la régie directe*, Milhaud was above all a theorist of non-state forms of nationalization and an academic economist at the University of Geneva (P. Dogliani, 'Edgar Milhaud e la rivista internazionale "Annales de la régie directe" (1908–1924)', *Annali della fondazione Luigi Einaudi*, 19 (1985), pp. 195–249). For Thomas's importance as the leading figure on the right of the PS immediately before and during the war, as well as an influential figure in syndicalist circles and in the co-operative movement, see Schaper, *Albert Thomas: trente ans de réformisme social*, 51–200; M. Rebérioux and P. Fridenson, 'Albert Thomas, pivot du réformisme français', *Le Mouvement social*, 87 (Apr.–June 1974), pp. 85–97; and M. Fine, 'Towards Corporatism: The Movement for Capital-Labor Collaboration in France, 1914–1936' (Ph.D. thesis, Univ. of Wisconsin, Mad., Wis., 1971).

[107] Repr. in *La Revue socialiste, syndicaliste et coopérative*, 2 (1910), pp. 5–7.

This reformist initiative received a good deal of support among elements of the PS, including the Fédération de la Seine, with its strong Blanquist and Allemanist roots, which developed its own municipal programme. It was also endorsed by the CGT federations most open to parliamentary action, the *cheminots* (railway workers) of the state network and the miners.[108] But it was vehemently opposed by the Guesdists at the 1911 and 1912 party congresses, since it flagrantly contradicted their understanding of the class state which had to be *politically* conquered by socialism. Nationalization failed to gain majority support or a place on the socialist electoral programme in 1914.[109]

In reality, the overt adoption of specific reformist strategies would have unbalanced the delicate equilibrium of currents composing the PS. For this reason Jaurès shunned the suggestion in 1914 that *de facto* co-operation with the Radicals against the three-year military-service law should be converted into a formal electoral alliance—a renewal of the centre-left bloc which had helped shatter socialist unity plans in the wake of the Dreyfus affair.[110] The effect of the 1913–14 campaign, which confirmed the pre-eminence of Jaurès's leadership, was one of negative integration, uniting the party in opposition to the menace of war and what was perceived as a resurgence of militarism and domestic reaction. After the outbreak of war, it was the threat to the nation, rather than a change of views on the state, which drew leading socialists (including Guesde) into governmental participation.

Like the PS, the British labour movement found that reform strategies became an increasingly insistent question in the immediate pre-war years. Many, though not all, historians

[108] J.-C. Dufour, 'Les Nationalisations dans l'histoire du mouvement ouvrier français (jusqu'à la deuxième guerre mondiale)' (DES diss., Université de Paris, 1969), 75–7; J. Horne, 'L'Idée de nationalisation dans les mouvements ouvriers européens jusqu'à la deuxième guerre mondiale', *Le Mouvement social*, 134 (Jan.–Mar. 1986), pp. 11–14.

[109] *Parti socialiste. 8ᵉ congrès national tenu à Saint-Quentin ... avril 1911. Compte rendu sténographique* (n.d.), 250–90; *Parti socialiste. 9ᵉ congrès national tenu à Lyon ... février 1912* (1912), 238–53. The latter involved a particularly revealing clash between Thomas and Guesde on the very principle of nationalization. For the 1914 socialist programme, see *Le Mouvement socialiste*, 261–2 (1914), pp. 215–37.

[110] A. Thomas, *La Politique socialiste* (Rivière, 1913), 48–59; *Parti socialiste. 11ᵉ congrès national tenu à Amiens ... janvier 1914. Compte rendu sténographique* (1914), 234–5 and 373–4 (for Jaurès).

agree that Labour was making steady inroads into the working class, substituting the politics of class for the social harmony variously preached by old and New Liberalism. But the precise nature of those politics—whether cautiously defensive of a narrowly defined Labour interest tied tightly to the industrial concerns of trade unions, or entailing a broader, latently socialist redefinition of the collective good, remains an open debate, and one underpinned by differing evaluations of pre-war working-class culture.[111]

The Labour Party's parliamentary record between 1906 and 1914 furnishes some evidence for both views. On various issues such as unemployment, minimum wages, and old age pensions, Labour MPs condemned the inadequacy of the Liberal government's measures and proposed more sweeping alternatives. Yet the failure of both the Labour parliamentary leadership and the trade union MPs to support the Minority Poor Law Commission Report, drafted by the Webbs, against the less radical 1911 National Insurance Act, which favoured the unions in its administration, suggests that trade union self-interest could act as a brake on the acceptance of coherent, more abstract principles of social reform.[112]

Rather than an integrated programme, the Labour Party had a series of demands linked by loose commitment to broad social change and 'collectivism'. But the party remained ideologically cautious, and the issue of reform emerged pre-eminently through matters of organization and tactics. For Labour's very success, however incomplete, in eroding working-class Liberalism, faced it inexorably with the inner contradiction of its own electoral and parliamentary co-operation with the senior party. The essential, and unresolved, choice was whether to continue

---

[111] Pelling, *Popular Politics and Society in Late Victorian Britain*, chap. 1, and id., 'La Classe ouvrière anglaise et les origines de la législation sociale', *Le Mouvement social*, 65 (Oct–Dec. 1968), p. 48; R. I. McKibbin, *The Evolution of the Labour Party 1910–1924* (OUP, Oxford, 1974), 70–1; J. M. Winter, 'Trade Unions and the Labour Party in Britain', in Mommsen and Husung (eds.), *The Development of Trade Unionism in Great Britain and Germany, 1880–1914*, 359–70; and K. D. Brown (ed.), *The First Labour Party, 1906–1914* (Croom Helm, 1985).

[112] E. Halévy, *The Rule of Democracy (1905–1914)* (1932; English trans., Ernest Benn, 1934); McBriar, *Fabian Socialism and English Politics*, 329–36; K. D. Brown, *Labour and Unemployment, 1900–1914* (David and Charles, Newton Abbot, 1971), 164–74; D. Martin, 'Ideology and Composition', in Brown (ed.), *The First Labour Party*, 17–37; Winter, 'Trade Unions and the Labour Party in Britain'.

supporting the Liberals in the dwindling hope of further social reform or, in the unfavourable conditions of the restricted franchise (which left over four million working-class males without the vote), and an electoral system benefiting the two established parties, to opt for complete independence.[113] On to this basic question of strategy, the socialist minority tried to graft the broader issues of socialist commitment and ultimate goals. Yet the moderate socialist project was a long-term one. Philip Snowden, as a leading figure in the ILP, was not being unduly pessimistic when he wrote in 1911:

it is doubtful whether we shall have in this country within the next generation an avowed Socialist Party, built up by the elimination or destruction of other political parties, which will be sufficiently strong to take the reins of government.[114]

The pre-war industrial unrest put pressure on Labour's political options. Although the Syndicalist critics of parliamentary politics remained numerically marginal, the danger that they might give a doctrinal edge to industrial dissidence forced the leading spokesmen of 'collectivism' and moderate socialism to mount counter-attacks on revolutionary trade unionism, and to sharpen their own political self-definition in the process.[115] And in a more restrained and pragmatic manner, the Triple Alliance of miners, railwaymen, and dock and transport workers, formed in 1914 partly to channel rank-and-file pressure, seemed to promise the concentrated strength and focused leadership in the industrial sphere which were so markedly absent in the political and parliamentary domain.[116]

---

[113] McKibbin, *The Evolution of the Labour Party*, 70–1; R. Douglas, 'Labour in Decline 1910–24', in K. D. Brown (ed.), *Essays in Anti-Labour History* (Macmillan, 1974), 105–25; M. Pugh, *Electoral Reform in War and Peace, 1906–1918* (Routledge & Kegan Paul, 1978); Horne, 'L'Idée de nationalisation dans les mouvements ouvriers européens', 14–16.

[114] *Labour Leader*, 16 May 1911, quoted in Douglas, 'Labour in Decline', 124–5.

[115] Notably J. Ramsay MacDonald, *Syndicalism: A Critical Examination* (Constable, 1912); P. Snowden, *Socialism and Syndicalism* (Collins, 1913); B. and S. Webb, *What Syndicalism Means* (Garden City Press, Letchworth, 1912).

[116] P. S. Bagwell, 'The Triple Industrial Alliance, 1913–22', in Briggs and Saville, (eds.), *Essays in Labour History*, 96–151; G. A. Phillips, 'The Triple Industrial Alliance in 1914', *Economic History Review*, 24/1 (1971), pp. 55–67; Clegg, *A History of British Trade Unions since 1889*, ii. 114–17.

Major differences between French and British labour were inherent in the opposed structures of the two movements and in quite different labour and socialist traditions—not to mention the overarching contrast in labour relations with the state and *patronat* in the two countries. But such differences notwithstanding—and they form the parameters to a study of the war years— reforms and reformism as issues emerged with new sharpness in both the French and British labour movements in the years preceding the war. In neither case was there a doctrinal debate remotely equivalent to that which occurred at the turn of the century when Bernstein and others sought to 'revise' the formal Marxist canons of German Social Democracy. But the growing political influence of the working class, the diverse potential of its industrial organization, ebbing after rapid, often volatile growth in France, swelling and traversed by mass unrest in Britain, and the tension between class and national identities dramatized by international labour organization and the threat of war, all combined in different ways to produce an acute sense (inside and outside its own ranks) of organized labour's potential as an agent of social change. The debates within both movements over the scale and mode of such change intensified—before the war apparently cancelled them, substituting its own novel agenda.

2 The 'Choice of 1914': Labour Participation in the National Efforts during the War

THE switch by most French and British labour and socialist leaders in under a week from repudiating to accepting a European war was dramatic. In retrospect, the ambiguities of pre-war labour and socialist internationalism make the turn-about less surprising. But the sheer speed with which the crisis swept Europe into war and the bulk of labour and working-class opinion into support of their national efforts, profoundly disorientated labour and socialist leaders. Policies carefully elaborated to avoid conflict between national and international allegiances were swamped overnight. Peacetime preoccupations, let alone the role of socialism and trade unionism as agents of economic and social change, seemed suspended for the duration. Inevitably, there was a strong feeling of disruption on the part of labour leaders, of mental disjuncture with the immediate past.

Yet the discontinuity was not total. In the crisis atmosphere of the late summer and autumn 1914, labour leaders drew selectively on the attitudes of the pre-war past and sought to fit them to the changed reality of the war. The resulting adjust-ment of perspectives and language added up to what might be called the 'choice of 1914', a choice which underlay labour participation in the war efforts down to November 1918.

(i) The 'Choice of 1914'

At its deepest level, the decision to support the war effort carried with it the statement, overt or implied, that the preservation of organized labour itself and of its goals and functions was identified with the protection of existing society and its institutions against outside threat. Nation and labour, nation and working class, were perceived in the light of the international crisis to be intimately connected.

This was not necessarily a reasoned position. Labour leaders were rallying in an emergency to what they accepted as the national cause. The existence of the nation in the French case, its fundamental interests in the British, clearly seemed threatened. But the nation was also seen in more abstract and ideological terms as incarnating the defence of democratic principles against the aggression of 'militarist', 'imperialist', and 'autocratic' regimes (the terms being interchangeable).

In this sense, the 'choice of 1914' reaffirmed the liberal democratic traditions which were interwoven into the political cultures of organized labour in both countries, into many of the currents of socialist thought, and into the circumstances of trade union organization since the 1870s and 1880s.[1] It also confirmed the steady extension of mass participation in politics during the fifty years preceding the war. The crisis demonstrated that the nation could be claimed by labour movements as a source or their own identity. By the same token, it posed in acute form the question of labour and working-class responsibilities to the nation as a whole.

The PS strongly reaffirmed the revolutionary democratic tradition of French republicanism. Not only the followers of Jaurès but also the old revolutionaries, Guesde and Vaillant, cast themselves as tribunes of the nation in arms. The language and precedents of *l'An II* and of 1870–1—historically powerful moments of revolutionary patriotism and popular identification with the nation—floated over the French socialists' experience of autumn 1914 and the battle of the Marne.[2] The Groupe socialiste in parliament proclaimed constantly the association of socialist, republican, and national identities.[3]

---

[1] See Chap. I, sect. iii, above.

[2] See, for example, Vaillant's editorials in *L'Humanité* in Sept. and Oct. 1914, reaffirming both the revolutionary traditions of Paris and the patriotic credentials of the revolutionary socialist tradition in France.

[3] *Le Parti socialiste, la guerre et la paix: toutes les résolutions et tous les documents du parti socialiste de juillet 1914 à fin 1917* (Librairie de l'Humanité, 1918), 73–8 and 110–12.

British labour leaders were a little slower openly to embrace the national cause and to define it as the defence of democracy. They were not exposed to the threat of invasion and they shared the more general disorientation entailed in accepting that Britain had finally terminated a century of imperial aloofness to become an active partner in one of the two blocs struggling over the European balance of power. Initially Labour leaders blamed the war on the diplomatic system as such, prolonging the radical Liberal analysis of pre-war years, in which official Labour and ILP policy had shared. On 7 August, W. C. Anderson, chairman of the Parliamentary Committee of the Trades Union Congress (PCTUC—the nearest the TUC came to having an executive), and Arthur Henderson as the new secretary of the Labour Party, published a letter reluctantly accepting the war but considering it to have been caused by 'Foreign Ministers pursuing diplomatic policies for the purpose of maintaining a balance of power (in which) our own national policy of understandings with France and Russia only was bound to . . . endanger good relations with Germany.'[4]

Ramsay MacDonald, who had just resigned as secretary of the party, and much of the ILP with him, maintained the view that the war was the product of an élitist and unacceptable system for managing the European balance of power, which Britain should have shunned, thus endowing Britain at the outset with an anti-war movement unparalleled in other countries.[5] But within a month, and with the help of popular outrage at the German invasion of Belgium and France, the bulk of the leaders of the national Labour committees fully endorsed the national effort in what was held to be a conflict between opposed political systems and values. In mid-October, in order to 'clear away once and for all misconceptions which have been circulated as to the attitude of the British Labour movement', most Labour MPs and members of the national committees issued a manifesto.

The British Labour movement has always stood for peace . . . [But the] refusal of Germany to the proposal made by England that a conference of the European powers should deal with the dispute between Austria

---

[4] G. D. H. Cole, *Labour in Wartime* (Bell, 1915), 29.
[5] Dowse, *Left in the Centre*, 20–34; D. Marquand, *Ramsay MacDonald* (Cape, 1977), 167–74.

and Servia, the peremptory domineering ultimatum to Russia, and the rapid preparations to invade France, all indicate that the German military caste were determined on war if the rest of Europe could not be cowed into submission by other means ... [The Labour Party] realised that ... the victory of Germany would mean the death of democracy in Europe.[6]

The break with pre-war positions was greatest in the case of the CGT. Jouhaux embraced republican and Jacobin patriotism with particular enthusiasm. On 4 August, in a spontaneous and emotional funeral oration for Jaurès, he declared: 'Emperors of Germany and Austria-Hungary, Prussian squires and Austrian lords who, through hatred of democracy, desired war, we undertake to sound the death-knell of your reign.'[7] Revolutionary syndicalist colleagues may have felt more reserved, and some, such as Merrheim and the leadership of the Fédération des Métaux, were soon strongly opposed to Jouhaux's patriotism. But there is no evidence that his funeral oration was criticized in the Comité Confédéral, and the bulk of the committee shared his basic premiss.[8] Early in 1915, the committee declared that:

However urgent may be our desire to re-establish peace between the peoples who are today belligerent, we cannot forget that Belgian territory is still almost entirely occupied and that our northern and eastern *départements* are in the same situation, and that in addition the essential conditions for social progress are the inviolability and the independence of peoples.[9]

In both countries, labour leaders made quite explicit the connection between the self-preservation of democracy and the nation and the conditions for the continued growth of the

[6] Cole, *Labour in Wartime*, 55–6; C. Howard, 'MacDonald, Henderson and the Outbreak of War, 1914', *Historical Journal*, 20 (1977), pp. 871–91.

[7] L. Jouhaux, *A Jean Jaurès: Discours prononcé aux obsèques de Jean Jaurès par Léon Jouhaux, secrétaire de la Confédération Générale du Travail* (La Publication Sociale, P.-M. Delesalle, 1915), 11.

[8] Speeches of Merrheim and Jouhaux to the 1919 CGT congress, CGT, *20e Congrès national corporatif ... (Lyon, 15–21 septembre 1919). Compte rendu des travaux* (L'Union Typographique, Villeneuve-Saint-Georges, 1920), 169–90 and 227–52; 'Alphonse Merrheim et sa "correspondance confidentielle"', in V. Daline, *Hommes et idées* (Éditions du Progrès, Moscow, 1983), 292; Georges and Tintant, *Léon Jouhaux*, i, 141–3.

[9] *La Bataille syndicaliste*, 2 Feb. 1915.

labour and socialist movements. As Jouhaux stated in his valediction to Jaurès:

We do not want the few liberties which we have prised with such difficulty from the forces of evil to sink without trace. Our desire was always to enlarge the people's rights, to expand the field of liberties. It is in harmony with this desire that we reply 'present' to the mobilization order. We shall never wage a war of conquest.[10]

The October 1914 Labour manifesto held in almost identical terms that if Germany triumphed 'working class aspirations for greater political and economic power would be checked, thwarted, and crushed, as they have been in the German Empire'.

It is important to stress the fact that most labour leaders in 1914–15 endorsed the national effort in these terms, and saw the war as a conflict between opposed political systems and values. The subsequent criticisms by different currents of pacifism, the post-war condemnation of 'social-chauvinism' by the Bolsheviks and by nascent communist movements, and the growing inter-war consensus that the war had been avoidable and had lasted four and a half years only because the masses in each country had been misled by their own national propaganda, all contributed to the view that the First World War was not essentially a struggle between opposed systems and ideologies.[11] This view has continued to shape the history of labour in 1914–18 though a revolution has occurred in the historiography of the causes of the war. Research in the last twenty-five years has underlined the extent to which the impetus for the war came from the highly unstable political system of Wilhelmine Germany and the expansionist aims of its ruling élites, while work in France has pointed to the strength of popular feeling in 1914 that an essentially pacific France had been the victim of

---

[10] Jouhaux, *A Jean Jaurès*, 11.

[11] A classic and influential example of the 'betrayal' thesis is A. Rosmer, *Le Mouvement ouvrier pendant la première guerre mondiale*, i, *De l'union sacrée à Zimmerwald* (Librairie du Travail, 1936), ii, *De Zimmerwald à la révolution russe* (Mouton, 1959). For communist condemnation of socialist participation, see A. S. Lindemann, *The 'Red Years': European Socialism versus Bolshevism, 1919–1921* (Stanford Univ. Press, Stanford, 1974), 17–20. For influential inter-war views on the crucial role of propaganda, see H. D. Lasswell, *Propaganda Technique in the World War* (1927; new edn., MIT Press, Boston, Mass., 1971), 10–12, and G. Demartial, *La Mobilisation des consciences* (Éditions Rieder, 1927), 115–18.

German aggression.[12] Without entering the debate on the origins of the war, these new conclusions should help us to understand how labour leaders in France and Britain could, without being propaganda victims, identify with the national cause in essentially ideological terms.

They should also help us understand the resilience of the 'choice of 1914'. By 1917–18, 'pro-war' labour leaders were critical of the allied governments (the Americans excepted) for their failure to commit themselves to 'democratic' war aims— that is, to a non-expansionist peace settlement based on the right to national self-determination and on new international institutions (notably the 'Society of Nations'). The war to defend national democracies had become a war to build an international democracy. Though symbolized by Woodrow Wilson from the end of 1916, such ideas had been espoused by the pro-war majorities of the PS and CGT from February 1915, as we shall see in greater detail (Chapter 8). The British trade union movement, more indifferent to international questions before the war and readier simply to endorse government war aims in the first half of the war, only came to such ideas in 1917—though they flourished in the ILP from the outset. In both cases, these criticisms during the last two years of the war of the inadequacy of official war aims were accompanied by the suspicion that if the basis for a negotiated peace should prove to exist, both the French and British governments would have to be pushed into recognizing and pursuing it.

But criticism of official war aims did not imply a rejection of the war. The central debate of 1917, for example, over allied labour and socialist participation in an international socialist conference in Stockholm to discuss the basis for a negotiated peace was interpreted by many labour leaders as a step which would strengthen, not weaken, the allied effort. Where the French and British governments prevented labour delegations attending for fear that this might be interpreted as a sign of

[12] See, in particular, the controversy surrounding the publication of F. Fischer's two works, *Germany's Aims in the First World War* (1961; English trans., Chatto & Windus, 1967) and *The War of Illusions* (1969; English trans., Chatto & Windus, 1975), and J. Joll's synthesis, *The Origins of the First World War* (Longman, 1984). On French responses in 1914, see Becker, *1914: comment les français sont entrés dans la guerre.*

defeatism, both Jouhaux and Henderson argued that Stockholm would help detach the progressive forces of the Central
Powers from their own national efforts and win them to the
'democratic' aims of the Entente. From the autumn of 1917, the
Labour Party took the lead in developing an allied labour and
socialist peace strategy (which rallied the French socialist and
CGT majorities) aimed at gaining the support of the German
and Austrian labour movements for a 'democratic' peace settlement and simultaneously at persuading the French and British
governments to commit themselves to the same goal.[13]

This labour diplomacy undeniably represented an important
shift, seeking as it did to capture and channel increasing
war-weariness and dissatisfaction with worsening economic
conditions (overtly pacifist movements drew on the same dis-
contents). But the crucial point is that it was an extension, not a
rejection, of the 'choice of 1914'. It represented a divergence
from official views of what the war was about but not a
repudiation of the national effort. We now know that notwithstanding the vote of the SPD deputies and a majority in the
Reichstag for non-annexationist peace aims in July 1917, civilian support for expansion and the power of the High Command
in Germany were such that efforts to negotiate peace were
probably doomed to failure.[14] If the allies wished to avoid a *paix
allemande*, they had no alternative—short of a revolutionary
collapse of the Central Powers—to seeking military victory, and
the Armistice in the end was brought about by a combination of
the two. But there was, for French and British labour leaders,
no incompatibility between continued support for the military
effort and the demand that 'Wilsonism' should become the
official allied *credo*, or the belief that a compromise, negotiated
peace along those lines *might* be possible. The CGT and British
labour majorities continued to back the military effort (most
vocally during the crisis caused by the German spring offensive
in 1918) while pursuing their labour diplomacy.[15]

It might be objected that what has been described as the
'choice of 1914' was in reality no choice at all. The apparently

[13] See Chap. 8 n. 21, below.
[14] Fischer, *Germany's Aims in the First World War*, 391–404; G. Pedroncini, *Les
Négociations secrètes pendant la grande guerre* (Flammarion, 1969), 106–7.
[15] See Sect. ii, below and Chap. 5, sect. iv, below.

open and ideological acceptance of the national war effort by so many labour and socialist leaders may simply have camouflaged a forced acquiescence in a role which could not be avoided, for fear of repression or of desertion by working-class opinion at large. Fear of repression may have had some initial influence on French labour leaders, despite the assurances of Malvy, minister of the Interior, that the known antimilitarist and revolutionary militants listed in the notorious *Carnet B* would not be rounded up. But a comparison suggests that there were other 'choices' open to labour leaders in 1914. A passive neutrality might have been declared, like that of the Italian Socialist Party after May 1915 ('neither support nor sabotage').[16] Alternatively, acknowledgement of the necessity for the national defence might have been distinguished from any endorsement of the special justice of the allied cause, through the even-handed condemnation of *all* governments—or of capitalism—for the war, and through the insistence *above all else* on a negotiated peace. This, with various nuances, was the position taken up by the moderate pacifism associated with Jean Longuet in the PS, by Alphonse Merrheim and the less extreme *minoritaires* in the CGT, and by much of the ILP in Britain. The fact, therefore, that the *majoritaires* of the CGT, a good portion of the French socialist leaders, and a clear majority of the Labour Party and TUC chose to interpret the war, even in 1917–18, as being at its irreducible minimum about the defence of political democracy shows that the 'choice of 1914' was one of conviction, not contingency.

(ii) The Politics of Labour Participation in the National Efforts

In accepting and identifying with a *national* war effort, labour leaders were by definition proposing to do something more—to participate in it. From the start the conflict showed a propensity to become a 'total' war by involving civil society to an unprecedented—and unanticipated—degree. The process of societal mobilization involved more than the military effort, colossal though that turned out to be, or even the munitions effort,

---

[16] G. Arfé, *Storia del socialismo italiano, 1892–1926* (Einaudi, 1965), 212–23.

which began to take shape in France from late September 1914 and in Britain from the winter and early spring of 1915. It also entailed the *political* activation and co-ordination of different organizations, groups, and social classes behind the military and economic mobilizations. As the war dragged on, it equally meant maintaining their support for the war and preserving a basic consensus on the meaning and necessity of the national effort.

The state played a central role in this political mobilization of society through its emergency wartime enabling powers, through the terms on which it organized the industrial effort, and through propaganda and censorship. But the political mobilization was not purely governmental or government-induced. Organizations and social groups participated of their own accord. In many respects, the war stimulated the self-mobilization of different elements in society behind a multi-faceted war effort. The terms and intensity of participation by different organizations varied within and between belligerent societies and also fluctuated with the phases of the war. But they were central to the resilience of the different powers and to their varying abilities to sustain a long war effort.[17]

From the outset, there were basic differences in the military mobilization in France and Britain which in turn affected the nature and rhythm of organized labour's participation in the broader political mobilization. In France, compulsory mass mobilization swept three and a half million men into the army in 1914 and gave the military authorities an important role in civil society. In Britain, by contrast, the initial war effort was

[17] There are no really adequate studies of the process of societal mobilization in France, or of the role of the state within it. See, however, P. Dogliani, 'Stato, imprenditori e manodopera industriale in Francia durante la prima guerra mondiale', *Rivista di storia contemporanea*, 4 (1982), pp. 523–59; J. Horne, 'A Parliamentary State at War: France 1914–1918', in A. Cosgrove and J. I. McGuire (eds.), *Parliament and Community* (Appletree Press, Belfast, 1983), 211–35; and F. Bock, 'L'Exubérance de l'état en France de 1914 à 1918', *Vingtième siècle*, 3 (1984), pp. 41–51. For Britain, see A. Marwick, *The Deluge: British Society and the First World War* (Macmillan, 1965), and K. Burk (ed.), *War and the State: The Transformation of British Government, 1914–1919* (Allen & Unwin, 1982). More general discussions are S. Andrzejewski, *Military Organisation and Society* (Routledge & Kegan Paul, 1954), and A. Marwick, *War and Social Change in the Twentieth Century* (Macmillan, 1974). A much broader, more conceptual study, but with considerable relevance to wartime mobilization, is P. Nettl, *Political Mobilization* (Faber, 1967).

resolutely civilian and voluntary. Just over a million men had volunteered by December 1914, avoiding any immediate need for conscription, and the army had no role in domestic administration.[18]

These differences affected the kind of unwritten compacts on which labour's political self-mobilization was based. The fact that British labour was participating in a voluntary military mobilization for the first eighteen months of the war profoundly influenced its view of the conflict. The Labour Party and TUC leaderships threw themselves into recruiting campaigns not just to express their support for the war but to fend off the alternative of military conscription. Behind this lay a deep identification with the popular tradition of democratic freedoms held to distinguish England from continental states, a tradition which, in a more patrician variant, many Liberals shared, including Asquith himself as prime minister. A joint meeting of the Labour Party National Executive Committee (LPNEC) and the Parliamentary Labour Party (PLP) on 26 April 1915 endorsed Labour's recruiting activities by 15 votes to 10, against a largely ILP opposition.[19] When in September 1915, Asquith and Kitchener (minister for War) painted a bleak picture of manpower shortages to a meeting of the LPNEC, PCTUC, and PLP, they established a subcommittee to step up the recruiting drive and save the voluntary system.[20]

Yet the menace of conscription grew inexorably as military needs outstripped the flow of volunteers. Labour leaders, in the logic of their position, found themselves simultaneously endorsing the war with enthusiasm and repudiating compulsion. At the September 1915 Trades Union Congress, the determination to overcome German 'militarism' was overwhelmingly proclaimed, but a PCTUC resolution opposing conscription was carried unamimously.[21] The Labour Party

---

[18] P. Sorlin, *La Société française*, ii, *1914–1968* (Arthaud, 1971), 21; P. E. Dewey, 'Military Recruitment and the British Labour Force during the First World War', *Historical Journal*, 27/1 (1984), p. 200.

[19] LPNEC, min. 1915, 34.

[20] *Report of the Labour Party Conference, Bristol, Jan. 1916* (LPNEC report); LPNEC, min. 1915, 74, 84–8; PCTUC, *Quarterly Report* (Dec. 1915), 4; *Labour Year Book* (1916), 70–1; M. Sanders and P. Taylor, *British Propaganda during the First World War* (Macmillan, 1982), 102–6.

[21] *Report of the Trades Union Congress, Bristol, September 1915 (1915)*, 79–91.

conference at Bristol on 26–8 January 1916 approved by a very large majority the electoral truce and recruiting campaign, 'being convinced that the issues in the present European War are of transcendent importance to the democracies of this and all other countries.' But an equally large majority condemned conscription as being 'against the spirit of British Democracy and full of danger to the liberties of the people'.[22]

The details of the conscription crisis in the first half of 1916 do not concern us here. The essential point is that faced with the inadequacy of volunteer manpower for the army, and confronted by the irresistible confluence of the Conservative campaign for compulsion with the Liberal conscription lobby around Lloyd George, Labour swallowed conscription, however reluctantly. The Labour leaders closest to government (and centrally Henderson as a minister) were persuaded by the government's arguments. When assured by Asquith that military conscription was not a prelude to Labour's nightmare, industrial conscription (that is, the suspension of civilian status for all male industrial workers), the PLP and the LPNEC withdrew their threat to end Labour participation in the all-party coalition-government.[23] The Labour Party conference of late January 1916 which rejected the first conscription act also clearly repudiated any idea of active resistance to it, and endorsed the Labour presence in government. In April, when confronted with the second conscription bill extending compulsion to married men, the PCTUC and LPNEC hesitantly, but in the end decisively, approved it.[24]

[22] Report of the Labour Party Conference, Bristol, January 1916 (1916), 105 and 116.

[23] C. Wrigley, David Lloyd George and the British Labour Movement (Harvester Press, Brighton, 1976), 164–74; R. J. Q. Adams and P. Poirier, The Conscription Controversy in Great Britain 1900–1918 (Macmillan, 1987), 139–40, 162–8.

[24] Kitchener, Asquith and Lloyd George addressed a joint meeting of the LPNEC, PCTUC, Management Committee of the General Federation of Trade Unions, and the major trade unions, on 26 Apr. 1916. They explained the gravity of the continuing manpower shortage and argued that there was no alternative to extending conscription to married men. On 27 Apr., in a succession of votes, the PCTUC endorsed the government's intentions, though the LPNEC hesitated a while longer (PCTUC, min. 27 Apr. 1916; LPNEC, min. 1916, 68–77). At the TUC in Sept. 1916, a composite resolution, passed virtually unanimously, opposed the principle of conscription but contented itself with calling for its abolition at the end of the war (Report of the Trades Union Congress, Birmingham, September 1916 (1916), 266–9).

Labour leaders and the national labour organizations largely accepted conscription because they could see no alternative or because they subordinated their opposition to a deeper, continuing approval of Labour support for the war. But the conscription crisis implicitly redefined the terms of that support. By 1916, the war effort was fomenting disquiet among Labour leaders in a number of other areas. The inadequacy of government provisioning arrangements in the face of shortages and rapidly mounting prices forced the national Labour committees into organized protest on behalf of working-class consumers and, in particular, into demanding greater state intervention in the economy. At the same time, the various industrial concessions agreed by trade union leaders appeared to have found little reciprocating echo among employers. In the war industries, profits were rising visibly, barely checked by very light 'excess' profits taxation. All this produced demands in the Labour Party for a more energetic, egalitarian organization of the war effort.[25]

This more critical view of the war effort resulted in conflicting pressures on the Labour Party's participation since May 1915 in the Asquith coalition. Increased involvement or total withdrawal were both possible means of pressuring government for the stronger action which Labour now demanded. The conscription crisis itself had resulted in the Labour Party and TUC being consulted as political partners at the highest level of national politics.[26] With the continuing manpower difficulties and broadening clash of approach to the whole economic mobilization in 1916, Lloyd George emerged as the leading champion of a strongly interventionist, and apparently more egalitarian, approach to the domestic economy. In the course of the political crisis of early December 1916, in which he ousted Asquith and restructured the government, he promised the national Labour committees much of what they had demanded in vain from Asquith—including state control of mines and shipping and firm action on food supplies.

---

[25] See Chap. 6, below.

[26] Notably in the meetings of national Labour leaders with Asquith and Kitchener on 27 Sept. 1915, with Asquith on 12 Jan. 1916, and with Asquith, Kitchener, and Lloyd George on 26 Apr. 1916.

The celebrated 'doping seance' worked: the Labour leaders endorsed Lloyd George, and received a considerably enhanced presence in the new coalition.[27] Arthur Henderson was one of only five members of the inner, war cabinet—a supreme symbol of Labour participation in the political mobilization. Labour MPs were also appointed to two new ministries, Pensions (George Barnes) and Labour (John Hodges). The creation of the latter was a long-standing Labour demand and equally symbolized the weight of Labour participation in the national effort. Yet the endorsement of Lloyd George had only been voted after considerable debate and by a small majority on the LPNEC (18 to 12), while at the Labour Party conference in Manchester a month and a half later (23–5 January 1917), a vociferous minority urged complete Labour withdrawal from government.[28]

As it turned out, the Lloyd George government did not produce satisfactory solutions (from a Labour point of view) to the domestic problems caused by the war, despite its firmer grip on the military effort. Moreover, pressures on labour leaders and government alike intensified in 1917–18. Industrial unrest increased sharply and the influential Shop Stewards' and Workers' Committee Movement challenged the national trade union leadership in the engineering industry.[29] As we have noted, the Labour Party and TUC also drafted their own 'democratic' international programme towards the end of the year under the impulse of Wilsonian peace aims, the February revolution in Russia, and the international labour diplomacy surrounding the ill-fated Stockholm conference.

These combined pressures helped provoke Labour's disengagement from the official political mobilization of the war

[27] D. Lloyd George, *War Memoirs of David Lloyd George* (rev. edn., Odhams Press, 1938), i. 624–5; T. Jones, *Lloyd George* (OUP, Oxford, 1951), 92–3. For the 'doping seance', or Lloyd George's long speech to labour leaders on 7 Dec. 1916 (the day after he ousted Asquith), see Lloyd George, op. cit., i. 624–32; the LPNEC report to the Labour Party conference in Jan. 1917, and also Henderson's account to the same, *Report of the Labour Party Conference, Manchester, January 1917* (1917), 3–4, 43, 87–8; J. H. Thomas, *My Story* (Hutchinson, 1937), 43–6; and M. I. Cole (ed.), *Beatrice Webb's Diaries, 1912–24* (Longman, 1952), 72–4.

[28] Cole, *Beatrice Webb's Diaries, 1912–24*, 73.

[29] R. Lowe, *Adjusting to Democracy: The Role of the Ministry of Labour in British Politics, 1916–1939* (Clarendon Press, Oxford, 1986), 87–105.

effort. There was no formal dissociation from the government, the resignation of Henderson over the refusal of passports for Stockholm being carefully presented on both sides as a personal affair.[30] But from mid-1917, the Labour ministers were more and more isolated within their own party, and their demands for unquestioning loyalty to the government (including the suppression of all discussion of a negotiated peace) fell on deaf ears at conferences where the party was busy defining its own domestic and international policies.[31] At the same time, the support of the large majority of the Labour Party for the military effort was never in doubt, and after the rebuff of the German offensive in 1918, the LPNEC recorded its

deep sense of gratitude for ... the heroic resistance offered by our Armies in the field ... Such magnificent courage and resolution—so consistent with the best British traditions—imposes an imperative obligation upon all sections of the country to assist in the final overthrow of militarism and [to] secure for the world a lasting and democratic peace.[32]

The participation of the labour movement nationally in the political mobilization of British society for the war thus operated on several levels and evolved in relation to the war effort. Participation in government was important but by no means defined the phenomenon. It underlined the initial convergence of government and Labour views on a voluntary military effort and on rather vague affirmations of the 'democratic' nature of the allied cause. Successive shifts in Labour leaders' perceptions of the war effort and war aims, in response to the conscription crisis, dissatisfaction with the Lloyd George government's domestic record, and international events in 1917, drove a wedge between Labour and official views without diminishing Labour support for the national effort. What from the start had been a self-mobilization by Labour leaders of their movement occurred on increasingly differentiated terms.

The circumstances which shaped the French political mobilization were rather different. The mass military mobilization,

[30] Lloyd George, *War Memoirs*, ii. 1116–40; Wrigley, *David Lloyd George and the British Labour Movement*, 216–17.
[31] G. N. Barnes, *From Workshop to War Cabinet* (Herbert Jenkins, 1923), 189–207.
[32] LPNEC, min. 1918, 128.

and the powers bestowed on the army and the Ministry of War by the 'state of siege' legislation, abruptly subjected France to military authority in a manner unknown in Britain, where the enlarged executive powers conferred on the government by the Defence of the Realm Act remained firmly in civilian hands.[33] Additionally, the Ministry of the Interior held the *Carnet B* in readiness. A number of CGT leaders were on the list, among them several subsequent pillars of the majority, including Jouhaux.[34] All this amounted potentially to an alternative, essentially authoritarian administrative model which might be applied for the duration of the emergency, completely over-turning normal definitions of legitimate social and political activity.

The pressure to implement such arrangements should not be underestimated. Leading officials concerned with internal security, as well as Clemenceau, urged L.-J. Malvy, the Radical minister of the Interior, to arrest the *Carnet B* militants. After consultations, however, Malvy declared himself opposed to a measure which the absence of any sign of working-class resistance rendered superfluous as well as potentially divisive. The premier, Viviani, agreed and the entire council of ministers voted to suspend the arrests on the eve of the mobilization.[35]

The non-application of the *Carnet B* was the founding act of what came on both sides to be seen as a 'policy of confidence' by government in organized labour. It was endorsed by successive administrations, at least until Clemenceau's arrival in power in November 1917. In part this reflected the result of the April–May 1914 elections, which had produced a centre-left majority in the Chamber and brought figures like Viviani and Briand

---

[33] P. Renouvin, *Les Formes du gouvernement de guerre* (Presses Universitaires de France, 1925), 28–32.

[34] J.-J. Becker, *Le Carnet B: les pouvoirs publics et l'antimilitarisme avant la guerre de 1914* (Klincksieck, 1973), 167–73. Sixty of the 142 names on the Parisian list were those of revolutionary syndicalist leaders, including such future wartime *majoritaires* as Savoie, Bled, Marie, and Marck, in addition to Jouhaux.

[35] L.-J. Malvy, *Mon crime* (Flammarion, 1921), 37–8; General Messimy, *Mes souvenirs* (Plon, 1937), 146–8; Becker, *1914: comment les français sont entrés dans la guerre*, 379–400.

(both fairly sympathetic to labour by their past and orientation) to the premiership for the first two thirds of the war.[36] As the munitions effort highlighted the industrial implications of labour support, Albert Thomas, its principal architect, also played an important role in defining and applying the 'policy of confidence'.[37] But the core of the policy remained confidence in organized labour's *political* self-mobilization, and the key figure here, by virtue of the formidable concentration of administrative and police powers in the Ministry of the Interior, continued to be Malvy. It was he, down to his forced resignation in August 1917, who was responsible for defining the legal status of trade unions under the emergency wartime legislation as well as for the general state of civilian morale and internal security.

Malvy claimed that his approach was to give 'to democratic France the maximum liberty compatible with national defence', and from the start he defended the right of trade unions to function as normally as possible.[38] Until September 1915, the military authorities held a central responsibility for domestic order, thereafter being subordinated to the civilian powers outside the 'army zones'. Malvy (and the government more generally) intervened to protect trade union activity from constraint and repression by the army. Jouhaux admitted in December 1915 that meetings had only been possible because 'the government leant with all its force on the military authorities'.[39] At the end of 1915, Malvy made his 'policy of confidence' quite explicit in his instructions to the prefects: 'I invite you generally to avoid all procedures which might provoke irritation in the working class, which, since the beginning of the war, has manifested the most loyal patriotism.'[40]

[36] Viviani had started out as a socialist and Briand as a revolutionary syndicalist sympathizer. More recently, as a pre-war centre-left Republican, Briand had attempted to develop a conciliatory approach to labour (M. G. Dézès, 'Participation et démocratie sociale: l'expérience Briand de 1909', *Le Mouvement social*, 87 (Apr.–June 1974), pp. 109–36.)

[37] See pp. 66–77, below.
[38] Malvy, *Mon crime*, 107.
[39] AN F, 13574, rep. 18 Dec. 1915.
[40] Malvy, *Mon crime*, 91.

Technically, the unions were supposed to restrict their discussions and activity to questions of 'corporate' interest, in accordance with the 1884 law. With the growth of minority syndicalist criticism of both the war and the majority's participation in the national effort, the law served as the basis for a distinction between normal trade union questions, considered a legitimate part of that effort (wages, conditions, and so on), and 'political' pacifism. Yet even when reinforcing the distinction, during the strikes of May–June 1917, Malvy urged a conciliatory approach, instructing the prefects to let syndicalists know 'that the government in no way intends to hinder their syndicalist liberty, that it intends to respect the free discussion of their professional interests'.[41] As we shall see, Malvy and the CGT leadership co-operated closely to resolve the strikes.

Malvy clearly believed that the bulk of the industrial workforce and of the syndicalist movement continued to support the war effort. Even when faced with the strikes of May–June 1917 (which in the case of the munitions workers were illegal), he refused to accept that they were *politically* motivated, let alone linked to the mutinies on the western front.[42] It was this view which he was forced to defend in July 1917 against his enemies to the right who accused him of complicity in, or at least negligence towards, a vast pacifist plot orchestrated from Germany. 'A democracy', he argued in self-defence to the Chamber,

has other duties than to launch itself into battle against labour organizations and to restrain syndicalist liberties at the moment when all social classes find themselves in the trenches, mingled in the same love of the *patrie*.[43]

Naturally, the counterpart to conciliation and 'confidence' was constant surveillance and, where needed, repression. The whole syndicalist movement was observed very closely indeed

---

[41] Circular of 26 June 1917, SHAT, 6N 148 (Fonds Clemenceau).
[42] On this, Malvy was undoubtedly correct; see Chap. 5, below.
[43] *Journal officiel, chambre des députés, débats parlementaires* (1917), 1710.

(through the widespread use of *mouchards*, or police spies).[44] But by and large, the breaking up of meetings, arrest of militants, and suspension of newspapers or seizure of tracts were reserved for those threatening the *political* mobilization by preaching resistance to the war, and care was taken not to lump together all strikes and other manifestations of labour discontent into this category.

The 'policy of confidence' underwrote the political mobilization of French labour leaders on behalf of the war effort. It was tangible proof of the CGT majority's thesis that in defending *patrie* and republic, they were also preserving organized labour—a point constantly made to the minority. It is difficult, too, to imagine the PS supporting the national effort in the same terms without such a policy (the Groupe socialiste had lobbied Malvy at the end of July 1914 to warn against the application of the *Carnet B*).[45]

It might be argued that the accession to power of Clemenceau, *bête noire* of pre-war organized labour and apparently bent on suppressing all dissident views in pursuit of military victory, demonstrates the opposite—for the CGT leadership maintained its support for the national effort to the end. Clemenceau's premiership provoked bitter socialist and syndicalist criticisms. But Malvy out of office, and especially during his trial in mid-1918, became the public symbol for the CGT majority leadership of an alternative 'policy of confidence' in organized labour by comparison with which Clemenceau, but not the war effort itself, was condemned.[46] Moreover, Clemenceau and Louis Loucheur, Albert Thomas's successor as minister of Armaments, in fact continued some of the central features of the 'policy of confidence'. If the repression of 'pacifism' and 'defeatism' intensified (especially after the strikes of May 1918), a certain tolerance of 'economic' strikes and even contact with

[44] This yielded the rich stock of police reports which make possible a detailed internal political history of the major labour and socialist organizations. Comparable, though much less comprehensive, surveillance of the British labour movement seems to have been a product of the war itself, starting only in 1917.

[45] H. Rouger, *L'Action socialiste au parlement (1914–1919)* (Librairie du Parti Socialiste et de l'Humanité, 1919), 3–4.

[46] See Chap. 5, below.

labour leaders were maintained.[47] Clemenceau's premiership placed considerable strain on state–labour relations. It served further to differentiate the self-mobilization of the CGT majority leadership behind the national effort, but did not negate it.

The CGT *majoritaires* expressed their political support for the national cause in several ways—by acknowledging the primary importance of the military effort, by observing an informal industrial truce, and by co-operating in the industrial mobilization.[48] Yet the tradition of syndicalist autonomy and the institutional separation of the CGT and PS deflected the principal onus for mobilizing and maintaining *formal* political support for the national effort on to the socialists. Unlike the British trade unions, with their organizational preponderance within the Labour Party, the CGT never faced making or associating itself with the supreme gestures of supporting a parliamentary *Union sacrée* or entering government. The closest it came to such acts (and with which the 'pacifist' *minoritaires*, from 1915, reproached the *majoritaires*) were Jouhaux's role as *délégué à la nation* in 1914 and the CGT's participation in an emergency welfare body, the Comité au Secours National, set up to cope with the social disruption occasioned by the mobilization, and in which ecclesiastics and right-wing politicians also joined.

Jouhaux undoubtedly ceded to his own enthusiasm for the revolutionary precedent of 1792 and a popular national mobilization when, in accompanying the government to Bordeaux during the battle of the Marne, he agreed to become a 'delegate to the nation'—though he by no means saw this as class collaboration. It was in any event, a personal and short-lived

---

[47] D. R. Watson, *Georges Clemenceau: A Political Biography* (Methuen, 1974), 285–6; J.-B. Duroselle, *Clemenceau* (Fayard, 1988), 831–44.

[48] There was no resolution comparable to the formal industrial truce of the British labour movement in 1914. But the self-denying ordinance on strikes to mark 1 May during the war, and the Comité Confédéral's refusal to countenance *minoritaire* suggestions of industrial action to protest against conditions in munitions production, made the *majoritaire* position quite clear (AN F₇ 12891, 'Le Mouvement syndicaliste, année 1916', 8, 28–9).

initiative.[49] Participation in the Secours National, agreed by the Comité Confédéral of the CGT, dovetailed with the labour movement's effort of social solidarity within its own ranks in 1914.[50] None of this was equivalent to the parliamentary and governmental participation of the PS in the war effort, with Jules Guesde and Marcel Sembat becoming ministers in the coalition formed on 26 August 1914 under the impact of the German invasion, followed by Albert Thomas as under-secretary (later minister) of armaments at the Ministry of War from May 1915.

The PS, drawing, as we have noted, on its traditions of revolutionary republicanism and on the justification of legitimate national defence elaborated by Jaurès in *L'Armée Nouvelle*, endorsed the official war effort more or less unquestioningly throughout the first year of the war. Thereafter, tensions quickly developed within the party along two distinct lines.

The first of these fissures concerned the organization of the war effort. Socialist deputies took a leading part in the three-cornered battle between parliament, government, and the High Command in 1915–16 to re-establish civilian control over the

---

[49] According to three retrospective texts by Jouhaux and one by the Comité Confédéral (but almost certainly Jouhaux's formulation), the *délégués à la nation* were originally conceived by Guesde in late Aug. 1914, at the moment of the invasion crisis and formation of the national coalition, purely as a means of associating labour leaders with the national defence. It was in this expectation that Jouhaux withdrew to Bordeaux with the government in early Sept. This conception of the *délégués* was rejected by political circles at Bordeaux. A more official propaganda function was suggested, touring cities with non-labour figures to promote the *Union sacrée*, which Jouhaux repudiated. A third variant was then agreed between Jouhaux and Sembat, socialist minister of Public Works, whereby the former would visit industrial centres re-establishing contact with the syndicalist base and conducting an enquiry into the unemployment crisis triggered by the war. This was vetoed by the interim Comité Confédéral, which had remained in Paris under Merrheim's leadership. Not without bitterness—and even a crisis of self-confidence in his own position—Jouhaux returned to Paris to face criticism and misunderstanding. AN F₇ 13583, rep. of Dec. 1916 CGT conference speech by Jouhaux; *Rapports des comités et des commissions pour l'exercice 1914–1918 présentés au 19ᵉ congrès corporatif ... juillet 1918* (Imprimerie nouvelle, 1918), 7–8; CGT, *19ᵉ Congrès national corporatif ... (Paris, 15–18 juillet 1918). Compte rendu des travaux* (Imprimerie Nouvelle, 1919), 225; CGT, *20ᵉ Congrès national corporatif ... (Lyon, 15–21 septembre 1919). Compte rendu des travaux*, 229–30. See also Daline, 'Alphonse Merrheim et sa "correspondance confidentielle"', 296–9, and Georges and Tintant, *Léon Jouhaux*, i. 149–53.

[50] See Chap. 3, below.

military direction of the war.[51] They also intervened on a variety of wartime economic issues to urge (like the Labour Party from 1916) a more energetic and egalitarian approach.[52] In both cases, the Groupe socialiste was inspired by the revolutionary mobilization of 1792–4 (including the economic interventionism of the Jacobins), and indeed stood for a kind of updated, wartime version of Jacobinism, ideally directed by the socialists themselves, as their model of the political mobilization. This made them increasingly critical of both the Vivani and Briand governments' handling of the war effort. It also alienated a small minority of right-wing socialists who advocated the continued subordination of criticism to the larger effort and who established a succession of propaganda bodies to this end.[53]

The demand for a mobilization more in keeping with a socialist understanding of the republican tradition was also treated coolly by the much larger 'minority' which began from 1915 to open the second fissure by pressing the case for a negotiated peace.[54] The intensifying pressure from the moderate *minoritaires* associated with Jean Longuet helped push the pre-war majority in 1917 into accepting the possibility of a negotiated peace and the need for a formal allied declaration of 'democratic' and non-interventionist war aims. This further distinguished the socialist *majoritaires* from official views of the war effort, especially after Clemenceau arrived in power.[55] Yet

---

[51] *Le Parti socialiste, la guerre et la paix*, 95–7, 118; J. C. King, *Generals and Politicians: Conflict between France's High Command, Parliament and Government, 1915–18*, (Univ. of California Press, Berkeley, Calif., 1951), 113–39.

[52] See Chap. 3, below.

[53] Notably the Comité de propagande socialiste pour la défense nationale, founded in May 1916 to 'place at the service of the national defence everything which was still healthy and good in socialism' (H. Bourgin, *Le Parti contre la patrie: histoire d'une sécession politique* (Plon, 1924), 98), and from July 1918, the daily paper *La France libre*, which had the support of forty socialist deputies (*La France libre*, 5 July 1918).

[54] Characteristic is the difference between the Renaudel and Longuet motions presented to the congress of the Fédération de la Seine in Dec. 1916, immediately before the national congress of the PS. Longuet's resolution demanded the re-establishment of the Second International and urged the government to explore the possibility of a negotiated peace. Renaudel's motion declared that 'the nation and the working class, being menaced, have the imperative duty to safeguard their independence', and demanded an intensified war effort (repr., AN F₇ 13073).

[55] *Le Parti socialiste, la guerre et la paix*, 189–99.

like the Labour Party, the socialist *majoritaires* continued to give their primary allegiance to the military effort and to see the war as irreducibly one between legitimate democratic self-defence and German militarism. Although the *majoritaires* (identified with Renaudel) lost their preponderance to the moderate *minoritaires* at the October 1918 party congress, their position is important because it demonstrates the compatibility of a sustained socialist political mobilization behind the national military effort with growing criticism of government organization of that effort, and of the war aims to which it was directed.

No more than in the case of British Labour was there a simple identification of syndicalist and socialist leaders with the official mobilization of political support for the war by the state. 'Pro-war' labour leaders became increasingly critical of government on war aims and on a range of domestic issues. The *Union sacrée* of 1914 was the suspension of politics in favour of the military mobilization. It could not survive the reintroduction of complexity, and therefore politics, by the war itself into the process of societal mobilization.[56] Options and alternatives opened up. This did not undermine the deeper 'choice of 1914' by pro-war labour and socialist leaders but it did force them to emphasize the distinctiveness of the terms on which they participated in the national defence.

(iii) Trade Unions and the Industrial Mobilization

If the political importance of labour support for the war was obvious from the outset, economically trade union leaders found themselves marginalized by the initial suspension of normal activity in the expectation of a purely military outcome to events. Only as the reality of industrialized warfare dawned did they move from being spectators on the sidelines to spokesmen for a group—the industrial, and especially skilled, workers—which had become vital for national success.

In essence, the industrial relations of both countries during the war were a three-way relationship of inherently unequal

---

[56] For a similar argument, see J.-J. Becker, 'Union sacrée et idéologie bourgeoise', *Revue historique*, 538 (July–Sept. 1980), pp. 65–74.

strength. The state relied on the collaboration of business-men—Lloyd George's 'men of push and shove'—to improvise a munitions effort. Despite limited experimentation with state-run factories, private industry supplied the bulk of munitions and other military needs. As Albert Thomas observed:

> The method employed consisted of . . . calling on the good will of all, and letting them set to freely. We encouraged the industrialists. We showed them that they would not be ruined by working for the war, and that their initiative would find its reward. We supplied them with raw material, granted loans to expand factories or to build new ones . . . and found them the necessary manpower.[57]

Organized labour was the disadvantaged third corner of the triangle. Translating the 'choice of 1914' into industrial terms meant, first and foremost, avoiding disruption of vital war production. We have noted that CGT leaders voluntarily and informally operated a strike ban during the war. A conference of Labour Party and trade union leaders in late August 1914 urged that, for the duration of the war, 'a serious attempt should be made by all concerned to reach an amicable settle-ment before resorting to strike or lock-out.'[58]

But if trade union leaders were participants in the collabora-tive venture of the industrial mobilization, they were also concerned to defend their members' interests against the most damaging aspects of that mobilization. They were forced on to the defensive not only by the potentially increased power of industrialists, invited to 'set to freely' against a legally shackled work-force, but also by the state itself, which demanded a transformation of the labour market (notably by controlling and directing the labour supply and 'diluting' skilled labour in engineering) in the interests of maximizing defence production. Resolving the tension between participation in the munitions effort and the defence of trade union interests was the underly-ing preoccupation of the 'pro-war' industrial labour leaderships in both countries throughout the war. And having sacrificed the

---

[57] AN 94 AP 141. For the industrial mobilization in both countries, see Bibliography, Secondary Works, parts 3 and 4.

[58] Cole, *Labour in Wartime*, 44–5; *Labour Year Book* (1916), 22; Orton, *Labour in Transition*, 18.

strike weapon, foundation of normal industrial relations, whatever the degree of collective bargaining, they had to find other ways of defending their own views, especially to the interventionist wartime state. Consultation, delegations, lobbying, and moral persuasion became the substitute for industrial relations based on the ultimate sanction of the official strike.[59]

Differences both in the trade unionism of the two countries and in the forms taken by the military and industrial mobilizations shaped the way in which trade union leaders coped with these conflicting pressures. Not only was the CGT smaller and weaker than the British trade union movement, but its Fédération des Métaux had less clear territory to defend than its British counterpart, the ASE, because French metallurgical workers had not established the same wealth of special 'customs' by which British engineering workers institutionalized their skill and defended it on the labour market.[60] These 'customs' lay directly across the path of dilution. The disparity in the relative strengths of the two trade union movements was multiplied by differences in the degree of disruption caused by the military mobilization and by the initial improvisation of the munitions effort. With no early mass military mobilization in Britain and no compulsion until 1916, trade union membership actually rose during the first two years of the war. In France it plummeted. Until 1916–17, when the rhythm of war production and mounting labour grievances began to push syndicalist numbers up past pre-war levels, CGT leaders were strongly aware that they presided over a disrupted and diminished organization, in which basic communication had either broken down or was skeletal (Appendix III).[61]

Furthermore, the initial recruitment of labour to French munitions was haphazard in the extreme. From late September 1914, mobilized workers were hastily pulled back from the front and deployed in the interior, often far from their original homes, thus adding to the disruption of French industrial geography provoked by the invasion of the industrial northeast. The workers concerned included unskilled as well as skilled, and many who were neither—the notorious *embusqués*

[59] See Bibliography, Secondary Works, part I.
[60] See Chap. I, above.
[61] See Chap. 4, below.

(shirkers) seeking refuge in safe industrial jobs.[62] Mobilized workers were allowed to join unions and, as Albert Thomas later clarified, they were to earn normal civilian wages. But they remained subject to military direction and discipline and were forbidden to strike.[63] In Britain, by contrast, a free labour force, firmly implanted in its pre-war industrial and geographic frameworks, had to be wooed by the government in 1915 into waiving its craft customs and its legitimate disruptive potential for the duration of the war.[64]

These factors help explain why the British government (in the shape of Lloyd George, as minister of Munitions) engaged in formal bargaining with union leaders over the introduction of dilution and the banning of strikes in the war industries. Even the compulsion involved in the July 1915 Munitions of War Act was underwritten by prior labour agreement. In France, no such formal responsibility for the industrial mobilization was asked of, or given by, syndicalist leaders. Their relationship with government was fundamentally a consultative one, through which they sought to influence the form of the industrial mobilization to take account of their members' needs.

It might be asked why the French government engaged in such consultation when the power conferred on it by a mass military mobilization and by a gravely weakened syndicalist movement delivered it of the constraints hampering its British counterpart.[65] But to have ignored the CGT would have been to deny the 'policy of confidence'. It would also have been short-

[62] R. Pinot, 'Les Industries métallurgiques et la guerre', Le Parlement et l'opinion (Oct. 1916), pp. 990–1015; Fontaine, L'Industrie française pendant la guerre, chap. 3.

[63] 'Statut du "mobilisé industriel"', Bulletin des usines de guerre, 15 (7 Aug. 1916), pp. 119–20; P. Baudry, Guide de l'ouvrier militaire affecté dans une usine travaillant pour la défense nationale (n.d.); W. Oualid, 'The Effects of the War upon Labour in France' in C. Gide (ed.), Effects of the War Upon French Economic Life (Clarendon Press, Oxford, 1923), 139–91; W. Oualid and C. Picquenard, Salaires et tarifs: conventions collectives et grèves. (La politique du ministère de l'armement et du ministère du travail) (Presses Universitaires de France, 1928), 139–60.

[64] A British commission of enquiry into French munitions' production late in 1915 reported that '(the use of) non-qualified labour, male and female, has not presented the same difficulties in France as in England. The conditions imposed by the trade unions over wages and work, have been virtually suspended' (Labour Gazette, Jan. 1916, pp. 8–9).

[65] Thomas's advantage in this regard was a theme of Lloyd George's speeches in 1915 (D. Lloyd George, Through Terror to Triumph (Hodder and Stoughton, 1915), 107 and 135).

sighted since the *potential* power of the CGT and the metal-workers' federation, as skilled labour became a critical factor in the national effort, was considerable. Above all, it would have run quite counter to the inclinations of Albert Thomas as the effective director of the munitions effort from October 1914 and its official organizer from May 1915 to September 1917.[66]

Thomas's pre-war career, with his belief both in the need for a moderate, mass trade unionism in France on the British or German patterns and in the legislative path to economic and social reform, predisposed him to establish a working relationship with the CGT.[67] If he accepted the motor role of private enterprise and profit in the munitions drive, he was also ready to experiment in shaping the wartime state's relationship with labour. In particular, he solicited syndicalist leaders as the official spokesmen for the working class, recognizing that organized labour had legitimate interests to defend. In coming to office, he reversed Millerand's policy early in 1915, as minister of War, of considering labour legislation to be suspended for the war, and he declared in the face of often savage wage-cuts that pre-war pay norms must be maintained in the war factories.[68] Although Thomas never ceased calling for patriotic sacrifices from labour, he in fact understood that in a long and complex industrial effort, some protection of working conditions and living standards, and recognition of the CGT's right to speak on behalf of war workers, were preconditions of success.[69]

[66] Thomas was put in charge of railway co-ordination by the socialist minister of Public Works, Marcel Sembat, in Oct. 1914. He rapidly became the key person organizing the withdrawal of mobilized workers from the front, in close association with industrialists. He was appointed to the newly created Under-Secretaryship of Artillery and Munitions at the Ministry of War in May 1915. Although this did not become a full Ministry of Armaments until Dec. 1916, the reasons were political, to preserve the authority of the Ministry of War and its privileged relationship with the army. But from its inception, the Under-Secretaryship was every bit as much the organizational motor of the munitions drive as was the Ministry of Munitions in Britain (A. Ferry, *Les Carnets secrets d'Abel Ferry 1914–1918* (Grasset, 1957), 91, 98; Schaper, *Albert Thomas*, 98–121).

[67] See Chap. 1 n. 106, above.

[68] AN F, 13366, reps. 12 Feb. and 6 Apr. 1915; Oualid and Piquenard, *Salaires et tarifs*, 31; Schaper, *Albert Thomas*, 115.

[69] See, for example, two speeches delivered at Le Creusot, the first in Aug. 1915 (*Le Temps*, 25 Aug. 1915), the second in Apr. 1916 (*Bulletin des usines de guerre*, 1 May 1916, p. 2).

Nor was he alone in this. Sembat, as minister of Public Works until October 1915, and successive ministers of Labour adopted a similar stance.[70] All three ministries subscribed to the construction of a collaborative framework within which labour leaders might participate in the industrial mobilization.[71] This operated at three levels—personal access by labour leaders to ministers and civil servants, to raise specific grievances concerning individuals or groups of workers; 'mixed' commissions, together with business and state representatives, in which broader policy was discussed or enacted; and the regulation of industrial conflicts.

Throughout the war, and especially down to Clemenceau's accession to power, CGT leaders acted incessantly as interlocutors for their membership with ministers on a range of questions. These stretched from grievances over wages and conditions to endless conflicts with local and military authorities over the right to engage in union activity. In 1917–18, the protection of persecuted militants (often *minoritaires*) and demands for government intervention to end strikes on favourable terms were added to the list.[72] In order to allow syndicalism to function as this safety-valve, Thomas from the start sheltered key national CGT leaders by suspending their call-up for the forces—and the CGT leaders in turn used these exemptions to buttress their position (thus Merrheim had three of his secretaries in the metalworkers' federation exempted from service).[73] Much criticized by right and left as proof of the self-interest and political favouritism linking union leaders and government, the exemptions were in fact evidence of the importance attached by the state to the participation of organized labour—and especially unionized engineering workers—in a successful industrial mobilization.[74] As Albert Thomas revealed, after

[70] See pp. 89–90, 98–112, 114, 178–9, 278, below.

[71] Oualid and Picquenard, *Salaires et tarifs*, 33–4. By a decree of 18 Oct. 1917, after Thomas's departure, the Ministry of Labour, virtually eclipsed by the powers of Thomas's administration, recovered some of its authority both in industrial relations and in overall questions of the labour supply.

[72] The reports on the war factories and on the CGT in the F_7 series of the Archives Nationales bear ample witness to this function.

[73] AN F_7 13366, n. of 29 Feb. 1916.

[74] The preservation of syndicalist cadres was only one aspect of the exemptions, which were overwhelmingly economic in their motivation—with half a million *mobilisés* in war factories by 1917.

leaving office, his first act on being appointed head of the munitions effort had been to ask the CGT leadership for the 'list of trade union activists in the engineering industry so that they could be given exemption status in the factories'.[75]

Thomas and his ministerial colleagues went much further by seeking to draw the CGT leadership into a more sustained, organizational collaboration covering different aspects of the economic effort, through various types of 'commissions mixtes'. These were concentrated in two areas—the munitions effort and the labour supply.[76]

As early as October 1914, Thomas had solicited the Fédération des Métaux's agreement to notify him of all complaints regarding the munitions effort. The day after formally taking charge of munitions, he told Merrheim that 'he wanted his passage at the Under Secretaryship to be marked by results on the workers' side'.[77] But the close collaboration desired by Thomas was never fully realized.

The metalworkers' leadership did indeed bombard Thomas with grievances until autumn 1915—and never entirely stopped. But they became convinced that faced with industrialists bent on forcing down wages and undermining conditions, neither Thomas nor his staff of military 'labour controllers', charged with supervising the flow and utilization of manpower in private armaments factories, had sufficient counterveiling power to impose guarantees for labour. On these grounds, in mid-1915, Merrheim refused to provide the list of the metalworkers' membership requested by Thomas so that he could grant exemptions to ensure the supply of skilled engineers.[78]

[75] AN F₇ 13595, rep. 25 Dec. 1917.

[76] CGT, *Rapports des comités ... pour l'exercice 1914–1918*, 5–37; R. Picard, *Le Mouvement syndical durant la guerre* (Presses Universitaires de France, 1927), 55–77; Georges and Tintant, *Léon Jouhaux*, i. 178–83. The CGT also participated in a range of welfare bodies, including not only the Comité au Secours National but also organizations for military allocations (to soldiers' wives) and war orphans. Additionally, the CGT took part in departmental 'commissions mixtes' to revive economic activity (see Chap. 3, below), while Jouhaux participated in a Conseil National des Économies established to consider economic priorities (AN F₇ 12891, 'Le Mouvement syndicaliste, année 1916', 10–11).

[77] *L'Union des métaux*, 62 (May–Dec. 1915), pp. 3–4; IFHS, 14 AS 219, Commission Exécutive, Fédération des Métaux, min. 29 May 1915.

[78] IFHS, 14 AS 219, Commission Exécutive, Fédération des Métaux, min. 19 June and 1 July 1915.

Similarly, when the Dalbiez law was enacted in August 1915, with the goal of examining the entire munitions work-force to remove the *embusqués* and establish each mobilized worker's entitlement to war work by seniority and professional qualification, the Métaux leadership refused to take part in the regional 'commissions mixtes' set up to enforce the act. For although they had supported the act and fought for the inclusion of the commissions, they held that the latter had no guaranteed independence.[79] In a kind of summit meeting between Merrheim and Thomas in August 1915, at which the membership list and the Dalbiez commissions were discussed, Merrheim made it clear that he did not doubt Thomas's goodwill, but that the Federation could not 'take on the heavy responsibilities stemming from [Thomas's] functions . . . [when] it is the Comité des Forges [the iron masters' professional body] which is the master and imposes its will.'[80]

Jouhaux, who disliked Merrheim's 'negative' attitude at the summit, and the majority of the Comité Confédéral, differed somewhat from the metalworkers' view. Critical of the Dalbiez commissions in reality, they continued to endorse the principle even as the commissions faded into disuse within six months of the act (both Thomas and the industrialists were desperate to expand the munitions work-force, and were not willing to let the commissions evict the *embusqués* from the factories).[81] Jouhaux remained convinced of the need for some kind of delegates responsible for the workers' well-being in the war plants.[82]

More immediately, however, he and the Comité Confédéral approved syndicalist participation in two Commissions mixtes established by Thomas to advise on the wages and welfare of munitions workers. The first, set up in April 1916, was the Comité du Travail Féminin, with the task of considering

[79] J. Horne, 'L'Impôt du Sang: Republican Rhetoric and Industrial Warfare in France, 1914–18', *Social History*, 14/2 (May 1989), pp. 201–23.

[80] IFHS, 14 AS 219, Commission Exécutive, Fédération des Métaux, min. 14 Aug. 1915.

[81] AN F₇ 13366, reps. of 30 Nov. and 6 Dec. 1915 for CGT criticisms. At the beginning of 1916, the syndicalist members of the commission in the Seine resigned.

[82] *La Bataille*, 17 Dec. 1916. Jouhaux was impressed by the shop steward system in the British engineering industry.

'improvements [to be introduced] in the material and moral situation of women working in the [armaments] industry'. Jouhaux was initially the only CGT delegate, but after his threatened resignation, Thomas persuaded him to remain and to co-opt two other syndicalists. The CGT stayed on the committee until the end of the war, contributing to its deliberations on maternity care, crèches, wage-levels, and the suitability of women to different forms of factory work, and thus to Albert Thomas's considerable social provisions for women munitions workers.[83]

The second body, the Commission Consultative du Travail, was far more ambitious, representing the pinnacle of Thomas's attempt administratively to incorporate the unions into the munitions effort. The commission was composed of senior civil servants, technical and medical officers, and Jouhaux plus five other trade unionists, representing workers in the state arsenals. Thomas envisaged that it would consider the tangle of social and economic problems confronting the munitions labour force, notably:

[the] situation of the [temporary] labour force (mobilized men ... women, foreign and native workers); regulation of work so as to avoid fatigue which would harm production; the hygiene and safety of workers, plus safety measures; wages, pensions and health insurance; measures to be taken for lodging, cheap food and transport.[84]

This was a formidable agenda. In its majority, the Comité Confédéral supported participation, to reconcile (as one member put it) the interests of the workers with war production. Merrheim was opposed not on principle but because the invitation was a personal one, from Thomas to Jouhaux, and because he remained sceptical about Thomas's real powers.[85]

[83] A detailed published report of the work of the Comité du Travail Féminin is *Protection et utilisation de la main-d'oeuvre féminine pendant la guerre* (Ministère de la Reconstitution Industrielle, 1919). Reports and minutes of the committee are in AN 94 AP 135 (Fonds Thomas). For Jouhaux's initial reaction, see AN F₇ 13572, CGT, Comité Confédéral, 25 July 1916 (rep. 27 July).

[84] AN 94 AP 122 (Fonds Thomas), n. of 6 Apr. 1916. The report of the Comité Confédéral to the 1918 CGT congress passed swiftly over the Commission Consultative du Travail, observing that it met only a few times. Fairly full documentation exists, however, in AN 94 AP 122. See also Oualid and Picquenard, *Salaires et tarifs*, 416–19.

[85] AN F₇ 13821, CGT, Comité Confédéral, rep. of meeting, 13 May 1916.

The whole venture was indeed doomed by the omission of the *métaux* and by the initial restriction of the commission to *state* establishments, when so much of the improvised munitions effort was occurring in the private sector. At the outset Jouhaux warned Thomas that the real battle lay in forcing employers to raise wages at least in line with wartime inflation and to implement basic welfare measures. 'If collaboration does not produce results, it is natural that the labour movement would not capitulate before the ever-increasing and arrogant demands of the employers without a fight.'[86]

The syndicalists dominated the short existence of the commission, from June to the end of 1916, with their criticisms.[87] But the reports and recommendations which resulted were clearly insufficient, for by the end of the year the CGT delegates had departed.

The labour supply—dwindling in 1916, suffering a famine in 1917, and perhaps the most serious constraint on the domestic war effort—was a second natural area in which ministers sought to consult the CGT. Although dilution was not subject to formal negotiation, the government was keen to win broad syndicalist endorsement for its desperate attempts to recruit women and especially foreign and colonial labour to the munitions effort—a potentially explosive issue on the shop floor. Both Thomas and Métin, minister of Labour, kept CGT leaders personally informed of measures to import foreign labour in 1915–16, and reassured them that equal wages and conditions would be enforced to safeguard the position of French workers.[88] In June 1916, Métin established a consultative joint commission on labour placement, the Commission Nationale du Placement, consisting of equal numbers of business and labour representatives as well as politicians and civil servants, to thrash out general principles of labour supply both

[86] AN 94 AP 122, letter to Thomas, 30 June 1916.

[87] See, for example, Jouhaux's criticisms in the meeting of 5–6 June 1916 and late Nov. (rep. 28 Nov.) in AN 94 AP 122. Thomas agreed to broaden the recommendations of the committee to take in private enterprise (AN F$_7$ 12891, 'Le Mouvement syndicaliste, année 1916', 8).

[88] e.g. AN 94 AP 135 (Fonds Thomas), n. from Métin, minister of Labour, to Thomas, 2 Oct. 1916.

during and after the war.[89] Together with an inter-ministerial manpower commission, with executive powers, the Commission Nationale du Placement tried to become the central agency recruiting and distributing all manpower resources in 1917.[90] The goal was illusory as different services and ministries competed fiercely for scarce labour resources, but the CGT delegates sought to use the two commissions to ensure that the mass recruitment of women and foreigners did not further undermine unionized male workers.[91]

There were other national joint commissions—notably a consultative commission established in November 1917 to consider the most effective utilization of mines for the war effort, and a Commission des Traités Internationaux du Travail, set up by the Ministry of Labour from 1917 to 1919.[92] But 1915–16, the period in which the industrial mobilization was organized, marked the apogee of the phenomenon, and there was a sharp reduction in innovation subsequently. In 1917–18, with the upsurge in industrial unrest, official attempts to secure syndicalist co-operation rapidly focused on wages and strikes.

Initially, the control exercised by the authorities over a largely conscript munitions work-force (through the ban on strikes backed up by military sanctions) seemed adequate. But by 1917, little more than a third of the aviation and armaments workers were *mobilisés* (see Table 1). The quite legal involvement of civilians in strikes and the inflationary pressures which forced some mobilized workers into illegal industrial action, convinced Thomas that industrial relations must be placed on a new footing. This was an unconsciously ironic tribute to the argument of the CGT that he had failed even to maintain pre-war wage-rates, let alone raise them in line with inflation, in the

---

[89] CGT, *Rapports des comités ... pour l'exercice 1914–1918*, 24; *Journal officiel, chambre des députés, documents parlementaires*, 1916, 5518, for the decree establishing the Commission; and IFHS 14 AS 213a, no. 4 (Fonds Picart), for the minutes of its meetings. The Commission grew out of a body, the Office Central de Placement for the unemployed and refugees, set up in Oct. 1914 to deal with the dislocation of the labour market at the beginning of the war.

[90] AN 94 AP 135, letter of Métin to Thomas, 5 Jan. 1916, for the origins of the inter-ministerial commission. The minutes of the latter for much of 1916–17 are in AN F_{14} 11333–4.

[91] See Chap. 3, below.

[92] See Chap. 8, below.

TABLE 1. Composition of the Munitions Labour Force

	Ministère de l'Armement	Sous-Secrétariat de l'Aviation	Total	%
Mobilized labour	575,962	35,395	611,357	36
French and Belgian civilian males	470,864	39,328	510,192	30
Foreign labour	170,895[a]	3,541	174,436	10
Female labour	379,495	20,759	400,254	24
Total	1,597,216	99,023	1,696,239	100

[a] includes 29,194 prisoners of war

Source: AN F$_{14}$ 11334, Commission Inter-ministérielle de la main-d'œuvre, 1 July 1917.

face of employer resistance. But the new system was not necessarily to the CGT leadership's liking.

After a particularly serious strike in December 1916–January 1917 at the Paris engineering firm of Panhard-Levassor, whose work-force, significantly, was over half female, Thomas extended the relatively favourable wage-settlement by decree to all munitions workers in the Paris region. This was the beginning of a permament, state-backed system of negotiated wage-settlements which was eventually extended to all war industries. Its purpose was to raise, regularly revise, and enforce a single schedule of wage-rates for each region, preferably agreed by labour and business representatives (to this end there were regional joint commissions), but imposed by the state if necessary. By unifying wage-rates between factories and establishing clear criteria for differentials, it was hoped that wage rivalry and strikes might be avoided. To add force to this hope, a second decree imposed a system of compulsory conciliation and arbitration, thus banning strikes. Both decrees had full governmental approval.[93]

---

[93] R. Picard, La Conciliation, l'arbitrage et la prévention des conflits ouvriers: expériences du temps de guerre (Lang, 1918), 9–10; Oualid and Picquenard, Salaires et tarifs, 194–215; and AN 94 AP 139 (Fonds Thomas) for press cuttings on the introduction of the new system.

The response of syndicalist leaders was ambiguous. The majority within the Comité Confédéral and the Fédération des Métaux welcomed Thomas's recognition of the decline in real wage-rates—'a first step in the direction which we have constantly indicated' as Jouhaux termed it.[94] At the same time, compulsory arbitration was almost unanimously rejected in a tradition stretching back to the fierce resentment aroused by Millerand when he tried to introduce the idea in 1900.[95]

In reality, the results were complex and the unions gained a good deal in wage increases through the new system.[96] Moreover, as a *quid pro quo* for the unions' heightened sense of vulnerability, Thomas instituted (under syndicalist pressure) a system of factory-level worker delegates. This responded to the desire of Merrheim and Jouhaux, among others, for a more localized labour 'control' over factory conditions after the fiasco of the regional Dalbiez *commissions mixtes*. The attitude of the CGT leadership to Thomas's industrial relations reforms (which prevailed until the end of the war) will be discussed more fully in a subsequent chapter.[97] The point to stress here is that while syndicalist leaders participated *faute de mieux* in the new arrangements, they remained highly critical and took no formal or administrative responsibility for them.

---

[94] *La Bataille*, 18 Jan. 1917. A meeting of the Commission Exécutive of the Fédération des Métaux on 27 Jan. 1917 approved the general approach to wage increases while considering the minimum wage much too low (AN F₇ 13366, *Appel de la fédération des métaux: à ses organisations, à leurs militants.*)

[95] *La Bataille*, 18 Jan. 1917, for Jouhaux's hostility; AN F₇ 13366, *Appel de la fédération des métaux*, for a round condemnation by the *métaux* leadership. At an inter-union meeting of the metalworkers of the Seine, in Feb. 1917, Hyacinthe Dubreuil, secretary of the Mécaniciens, lamented: 'We thought that [Thomas's] socialist ideas were going to allow him to defend us, but we were wrong. The pre-war socialist has totally disregarded his ideals and delivered the working class bound hand and foot to the bosses' (AN F₇ 13366). The metalworkers maintained their condemnation to the end of the war ('Rapport fédéral', to the July 1918 metalworkers' congress, *L'Union des métaux*, 68 (July 1918), p. 14).

[96] In Apr. 1917, an inter-ministerial conference on wage-scales was established to extend the system to all war-work. (*Bulletin des usines de guerre*, 9 July 1917; Oualid and Picquenard, *Salaires et tarifs*, 202–5). For the actual working of the system see Chap. 5, below.

[97] See, pp. 176–96, below.

In all, there were distinct limits to the CGT's participation in the industrial mobilization. The *minoritaires* castigated Jouhaux and his colleagues as *embusqués* and accused them of betraying revolutionary syndicalist principles.[98] But even here there were important nuances. While a libertarian revolutionary syndicalist, like Péricat of the Paris building workers, opposed syndicalist participation in the Commission Consultative du Travail because he condemned the war, Merrheim, as we have seen, judged the issue on the grounds of efficacy.[99] Although the *métaux* leadership was less disposed to participate in the various joint commissions than the confederal majority, it continued to lobby ministers and parliament on behalf of its own policies.

Undoubtedly, the wartime role of the *majoritaires* marked a new departure. It brought them into contact with industrialists and, to an even greater extent, with ministers and civil servants. The very concept of *commissions mixtes* was rooted in the traditions of reformist syndicalism and appeared to principled revolutionaries to breach the canons of syndicalist autonomy. Participation in them implied at least the possibility of an entente with enlightened administrators and politicians on certain questions. The openness to labour and social reform which had been evident before 1914 among some centre-left politicians and the civil servants of some departments, notably the Ministry of Labour, was reinforced by the urgency of labour questions during the war and by the broad acceptance of an enlarged role for the state. Albert Thomas also assembled a team of administrators—many of whom were socialist academics or experts temporarily enrolled in the civil service—which included Arthur Fontaine (from the Ministry of Labour), François Simiand, the economist, Mario Roques, and

---

[98] This was the stock in trade of clashes between hardline *minoritaires* and the *majoritaire* leadership, both on the Comité Confédéral (see, for example, the bitter exchange on 7 Oct. 1916 as tension mounted in advance of the CGT conference (AN F₇ 13569), when Bourderon called Bled and Jouhaux *embusqués* and Antourville regretted 'that the CGT participates in all these mixed commissions in which it will get bogged down'), and in the wartime conferences of the CGT and the July 1918 congress.

[99] AN F₇ 13569, CGT, Comité Confédéral, min. 13 May 1916; AN F₇ 13821, rep. of same meeting, 16 May 1916.

Charles Dulot, also from the Ministry of Labour.[100] Labour leaders extended their contact with these civil servants and with politicians and businessmen by participating in several associations for the study of economic and social questions.[101]

Yet most of the syndicalist participation in the industrial mobilization was consultative. In effect, CGT leaders found themselves plunged into uncharted waters by the war. Skilled status did not, as in Britain, represent fairly clearly defined areas, the temporary shift in whose markers was up for negotiation. Rather, the tidal pull of the war accelerated the permanent displacement of skill and indeed the restructuring of the working class, both geographically and sectorally, as women and foreigners seeped or flooded into new reaches of the economy. The CGT *majoritaire* leaders tried to engage in a process of social bargaining over the terms on which this should occur. They used their contacts with the state to lobby for their own views. But they did not formally negotiate accords behind which they undertook to rally and discipline their members, and the level of criticism remained high.

From the point of view of those opposed to the war and to contact with the state, this might seem like betrayal. But, whatever view is taken of the *majoritaire* approach, Jouhaux was right when he asserted that it never amounted to an endorsement of the official industrial mobilization. He accepted that the CGT had 'collaborated'

if to undertake representations, present observations, formulate demands, is called collaboration. If, on the other hand, as I believe, the

---

[100] Arthur Fontaine, permanent director of the Ministry of Labour, collaborated closely with Albert Thomas both on war contracts and on the allocation of labour and working conditions (Schaper, *Albert Thomas*, 108, and B. Lavergne, *Les Idées politiques en France de 1900 à nos jours: souvenirs personnels* (Librairie Fischbacher, 1965), 132). Simiand, librarian at the Ministry of Labour, and professor at the École des Hautes Études, became (along with another academic, Mario Roques), the right-hand man of Albert Thomas at the headquarters of the munitions effort, in the Hôtel Claridge on the Champs-Elysées. Both Simiand and Roques, like Thomas, were alumni of the École Normale Supérieure (Oualid and Picquenard, *Salaires et tarifs*, 100; M. Lazard, *Francois Simiand, 1873–1935: l'homme, l'oeuvre* (Association pour le progrès social, 1935), 6–7; and Schaper, op. cit., 197–8). Charles Dulot was among Thomas's close collaborators both in the munitions effort and subsequently (Fine, 'Towards Corporatism' 35–40).

[101] See Chap. 7, below.

word collaboration denotes responsibility in the political direction of
the government, we never engaged in that collaboration.[102]

British trade unions, by contrast, shared a more formal
responsibility for the industrial mobilization. Although the
principal trade union leaders had unilaterally and voluntarily
agreed an industrial truce, this was insufficient for government.
The absence of control over the bulk of adult male workers
which the military mobilization initially conferred on the
French government, the continued numerical strength of the
unions, and the relatively high level of strike activity in 1915
(see Appendix II), necessitated more formal agreement. Even
when conscription was introduced in 1916, industrial workers
were not subordinated to military discipline *until* they had been
withdrawn from the work-force. Not only the renunciation of
strikes but also the mass of interlocking problems involved in
assembling a munitions workforce and maximizing production
were thus necessarily the subject of bargaining between government and labour leaders. The element of compulsion increased
steadily, but successive governments continued to seek the
accord of trade union leaders to ensure the success of the
various measures.[103]

The leaderships of the main skilled or single-industry unions
(the ASE, the miners, the railway unions) fought a long,
defensive battle to protect a dwindling sphere of union autonomy in the face of the state's twin imperatives of mobilizing a
massive industrial effort while channelling as many men as
possible into the military forces. At the same time, further
conflicts of interest set the skilled engineers against those
general unions which represented semi-skilled workers
encroaching on skilled terrain in 'diluted' munitions work.

---

[102] *19ᵉ Congrès national corporatif . . . (Paris, 15–18 juillet 1918). Compte rendu
des travaux*, 226–7.

[103] The British government achieved a result close to the French situation
through the Munitions of War Act and conscription. Indeed, Thomas's decrees of
Jan. 1917 finally gave him the power to ban strikes of *civilian* war workers secured
by Lloyd George eighteen months before in the July 1915 act. But the notion that
men were civilians *until* assigned to a military unit was preserved (Lloyd George,
War Memoirs, ii. 1566–7; Wrigley, *David Lloyd George and the British Labour
Movement*, 218–31).

These fairly well-known conflicts only concern us here for the light they cast on the nature of official trade union participation in the industrial mobilization. The voluntary 'Treasury Agreements' of March 1915 between government, industrialists, and trade union leaders placed a moratorium on strikes in favour of a binding arbitration system for the duration of the war and established procedures for 'diluting' skilled labour on munitions work.[104] But the difficulty of constraining union members in some localities to observe the accords impelled Lloyd George to introduce the Munitions of War Act in July 1915. This banned strikes in the war industries, formalized the arbitration system, provided for 'dilution' and substitution, and empowered the state to direct engineering workers into munitions work and to control their job mobility once there.[105]

Lloyd George called the act 'an honourable bargain and a patriotic bargain', and trade union leaders, after extensive negotiations, indeed agreed to its provisions.[106] Although the MFGB proved refractory, and won exemption (along with the cotton operatives), the miners' executive undertook to use the industry's well-established bargaining procedures and, failing that, arbitration, in order to avoid strikes. The NUR supported the legal prohibition of strikes until the end of the war, as did the leaders of the engineering unions. The 'choice of 1914' was a compelling argument. As Robert Young, secretary of the ASE, wrote in the union's journal following a strike on Clydeside in early 1916:

If arbitration has not worked out to the satisfaction of many members, that is no argument, under present national conditions, for stoppage of work ... We have given our pledge, not to the Government as a Government, but to the nation through the Government ... We are dealing with the nation's requirements while in a state of war.[107]

Union leaders gained few real concessions in return. They insisted on the inclusion in the bill of a limited provision for

---

[104] *Official History of the Ministry of Munitions* (HMSO, 1920–4), vol. i, pt. 2, 85–8; Cole, *Trade Unionism and Munitions*, 70–4; *Labour Year Book* (1916), 59–62.

[105] *Official History of the Ministry of Munitions*, vol i, pt. 4; *Labour Year Book* (1916), 76–7. An amendment of Jan. 1916 extended the act to shipbuilding, war-related construction, and to some public utilities.

[106] *Report of the Trades Union Congress, Bristol, September 1915*, 355.

[107] *Amalgamated Engineers' Monthly Journal and Report*, Apr. 1916, p. 40.

taxing 'excess' war profits, in recompense for labour's 'sacrifice'. They acquired representation on a new body, the Central
Munitions Labour Supply Committee, established to advise
the Ministry of Munitions on 'dilution'. They also won verbal
acknowledgement by ministers (including Balfour for the Conservatives) that 'dilution' was a purely wartime expedient and
that trade union 'customs' would be restored with the peace.[108]

But these were limited allowances in exchange for a formal
compact by which union leaders assumed moral responsibility
for the basic form of the munitions effort in a manner without
parallel in France. The promises on restoration were not
binding. No specific terms were set for the introduction of
'dilution' (affecting such crucial matters as wage differentials
between skilled and unskilled, women's pay, and changes in the
engineering production process). Nor did union leaders consider broadening the compact to take in the cost of living or
tighter state control on industry. The patriotic mood which
most union leaders shared in 1915 and their normal propensity
to confine themselves to narrowly industrial matters (broader
questions being the province of the Labour Party) biased the
1915 'bargain' firmly in favour of industrialists and the state.

Subsequently, both the state and trade union leaders sought
to modify the understanding in their own favour, with the state
forcing the pace. The struggle ranged over various issues—
'dilution', wage-rates and differentials, labour mobility, and the
'combing out' of male workers for the army. Skilled workers
were at odds with the semi-skilled or unskilled on many of these
questions. Semi-skilled engineering workers, for example,
resented the skilled engineers' attempt (successful for a good
part of the war) to secure an immunity against call-up while the
semi-skilled, often doing nearly identical work, had no choice
but to go.[109] Conversely, piece-rates eroded the skilled time-
rates in engineering, provoking the cabinet to try and restore

---

[108] Cole, *Trade Unionism and Munitions*, 241–4.

[109] *History of the Ministry of Munitions*, vol. vi, pt. 1; Orton, *Labour in Transition*,
76–87; Cole, *Trade Unionism and Munitions*, 129–41; R. Hyman, *The Workers'
Union*, (Clarendon Press, Oxford, 1971), 120; Wrigley, *David Lloyd George and the
British Labour Movement*, 186–7; G. R. Rubin, 'Explanations for Law Reform: the
Case of Wartime Labour Legislation in Britain, 1915–1916', *International Review of
Social History*, 32/3 (1987), pp. 250–70.

differentials in 1917–18.[110] Yet the general unions (with the exception of the Workers' Union) accepted the principle of the post-war reinstatement of skilled 'customs' and the TUC as a whole committed itself to the restoration of skilled status.[111] Both the strength of the skilled unions within the movement and a defensive reflex—seeking to preserve established union positions—made restoration the minimum price of trade union participation in the industrial mobilization, and the government's evasiveness over the issue (its eventual legal commitment extending only to specific munitions work and not to broader defence production, including shipbuilding and aircraft production) made this one of the bitterest sources of contention. Only after the Armistice was there an unequivocal official undertaking to restore the pre-war status quo.[112]

In fighting to secure the best conditions or greatest autonomy for their members, craft, 'industrial' and general unions took part to an unprecedented degree (and even more than in France) in state bodies. The PCTUC had long acted as the TUC's direct lobby of government. But wartime requirements produced the novel phenomenon of substantial participation by a variety of individual unions in government organizations and national negotiations.[113]

Thus, the ASE used the Central Munitions Labour Supply Committee to influence the process of dilution. It approved the Committee's circulars, especially those proposing equal wages for women dilutees plus clear differentials between skilled and unskilled labour, and prevailed on Lloyd George to empower their application. But the general unions with members in engineering were also involved in negotiating such issues.[114] Elsewhere, the MFGB negotiated (from February 1917) with the government-appointed Coal Controller, the cotton unions

---

[110] *History of the Ministry of Munitions*, vol. v, pt. 1, 167–93; G. R. Askwith, *Industrial Problems and Disputes* (John Murray, 1920), 426–45; Clegg, *A History of British Trade Unions since 1889*, ii. 182–3.

[111] Hyman, *The Workers' Union*, 122.

[112] Cole, *Trade Unionism and Munitions*, 193–4, 245–7.

[113] Clegg, *A History of British Trade Unions*, ii. 209–10; A. Reid, 'The Impact of the First World War on British Workers', in R. Wall and J. Winter (eds.), *The Upheaval of War: Family, Work and Welfare in Europe, 1914–1918* (CUP, Cambridge, 1988), 221–33.

[114] Orton, *Labour in Transition*, 62–75; Cole, *Trade Unionism and Munitions*, 115–28, 157–75; Hyman, *The Workers' Union*, 119–21.

participated in the Cotton Control Board, and so on.[115] Many of these bodies also had employer representation—amounting to the British equivalent of the *commissions mixtes*.

As in France, disparities in wage-rates between establishments and districts as well as eroded differentials between the skilled and semi-skilled, were a source of unrest. And like their cross-Channel colleagues, British trade union leaders found that whatever their misgivings over compulsory arbitration, they stood to benefit from an arrangement which both simplified the process of determining wages and swung the weight of government behind their regular increase. Following an agreement between the ASE, the Workers' Union (with a large number of semi-skilled munitions workers), and the Engineering Employers' Federation in February 1917, wage-rates were applied nationally in engineering and revised three times a year by the principal wartime arbitration body, the Committee on Production—established in 1915, but to which trade union representation was now added. Comparable arrangements were made for mining and the railways. Thus, under state sponsorship, the war reinforced the trend to national collective bargaining.[116]

Yet such collaboration did not turn the trade unions into simple administrative spokes in the wheels of the official mobilization. By and large, union leaders saw their contact with government as the means of defending their members in abnormal conditions. Significantly, the leading national figures of the MFGB and the NUR, Robert Smillie and J. H. Thomas, both refused Lloyd George's offer of ministerial office.[117] Union leaders frequently raised critical questions—indeed, in the case of the ASE, often the same as those posed by the radical shop stewards' movement. The ASE executive, for example, bitterly condemned attempts by the government to limit the mobility of skilled engineering workers through the infamous Leaving

[115] G. D. H. Cole, *Labour in the Coal-Mining Industry (1914–1921)* (Clarendon Press, Oxford, 1923); Page Arnot, *The Miners*, ii, 170–3; Clegg, *A History of British Trade Unions*, ii. 209.

[116] *History of the Ministry of Munitions*, vol. v, pt. 1, 77–85; Askwith, *Industrial Problems and Disputes*, 415–25; Hyman, *The Workers' Union*, 86–91; Clegg, *A History of British Trade Unions*, ii. 163, 177–8.

[117] R. Smillie, *My Life for Labour* (Mills and Boon, 1924), 174–82; J. H. Thomas, *My Story*, 43–5.

Certificates (employer permission to change jobs) and negotiated a slightly less restrictive arrangement in 1917. It also resisted government efforts to 'comb out' skilled engineers for the front and won the 'Trade Card' scheme from the new Lloyd George government by which the ASE itself granted exemptions to its own members—though the government, avid for military reserves, subsequently tried to withdraw the system amid much acrimony. These were issues which also galvanized the rank-and-file movement of skilled engineers and helped provoke the May 1917 strikes.[118] Thus the ASE leadership was scarcely a mouthpiece for government views. As with the CGT *majoritaires*, however, it was sharply distinguished from the movements of internal union opposition by its refusal to condone disruptive industrial action.

The 'choice of 1914' logically implied participation by 'pro-war' labour leaders in the national effort. At the same time, it imposed constraints on labour action. Anything undermining the military effort or hindering war production was incompatible with labour support. This rendered official labour leaderships vulnerable to those who rejected the 'choice of 1914' or who urged the full use of organized labour's power to protect its interests.

Yet the 'choice of 1914' equally meant that labour leaders supporting the war did so not at the behest of government or through simple absorption into a mood of patriotic resistance, powerful though the latter was in 1914–15. Rather, there occurred the 'self-mobilization' of organized labour, by which its own identity and concerns, as interpreted by the leaderships, were placed behind the national cause. As the war continued, however, it confronted labour with a range of difficult political and industrial questions. The tension between those questions and the prior 'choice of 1914' constituted the basic magnetic field within which the 'pro-war' leaderships in both countries had to chart their responses to the war.

---

[118] Cole, *Trade Unionism and Munitions*, 145–6; Jefferys, *The Story of the Engineers*, 182–7; Hinton, *The First Shop Stewards' Movement*, 196–212; Wrigley, *David Lloyd George and the British Labour Movement*, 184–204.

3 Responding to the War: The French Labour Movement and Wartime Problems

LABOUR leaders reacted first and foremost to the declaration of war in 1914 as a national emergency. But almost from the outset, the military mobilization generated a host of domestic social problems. The separation of couples and families, as men joined the forces, and the paralysis of much normal economic activity, quite literally brought the war home to the bulk of the population, and especially to the economically vulnerable. Pressing in Britain but potentially devastating in France, these side-effects of the military mobilization forced labour leaders to respond to the crisis at a second level, as a social emergency, in which they had rapidly to improvise new ways of carrying out traditional functions of working-class defence.

Although the war gradually assumed its own sense of normality, social problems—far from disappearing—multiplied as consumer prices began inexorably to rise and as the industrial mobilization in 1915 created a large munitions work-force. The social impact of the war on labour thus became a major preoccupation (at different rhythms in France and Britain) of the labour leaderships who abided by the 'choice of 1914'.

(i) Autumn 1914

In France, the labour response to the social emergency centred on a new organization founded to link socialists and syndicalists at the national level—the Comité d'Action. The committee stemmed from the obvious need for the CGT and the PS to economize their skeletal forces after the mobilization by collaborating in a closer and more institutionalized form than had ever been possible before the war. The initiative seems to have been a joint one. The Comité Confédéral on 3 September 1914 authorized the participation of the CGT, and a joint meeting on 6 September with various socialist organizations—the national Commission Administrative Permanente (CAP), the parliamentary Groupe Socialiste, and the Fédération de la Seine—resulted in the founding of the Comité d'Action. In the confused atmosphere of the German invasion, it was envisaged partly as a means of self-defence against the punitive attitudes which the government and the military might still adopt towards organized labour, especially if the Germans besieged Paris. This was the moment at which the bitter wrangle broke out over Jouhaux's departure with the government for Bordeaux, and the precedent of the Commune was palpably in the air. But the surveillance reports of the Préfecture of Police stress that the labour movement's main concern was economic rather than political self-protection, as the Comité d'Action's first communiqué itself made clear.

The Commission's [sic] function is to tighten the links between militants and organizations, and by that means to make them most effective in present circumstances, and in helping the public authorities in all the questions which concern the life of the working-class population (provisioning, unemployment, soup kitchens, separation allowances, etc.) and in the national defence.[1]

The composition of the Comité d'Action was subsequently enlarged to include members of the Fédération Nationale des Coopératives de Consommation (FNCC).[2] Its explicit aim was thus to establish a single labour voice in answer to the social disruption and sense of discontinuity provoked by the war. Day-to-day business was handled by the secretary, Louis

---

[1] *La Bataille syndicaliste* and *L'Humanité*, 10 Sept. 1914; *Rapport sur l'action générale du comité présenté le 20 novembre 1915* (1915) (hereafter *Rapport . . . 1915*), 1–2; APP B/a 1605, 'Note sur l'attitude de la C.G.T. et de l'Union des Syndicats de la Seine pendant la période de crise qui a précédé la mobilisation et depuis l'ouverture des hostilités', 31 Oct. 1914; H. Dubreuil, *Employeurs et salariés en France* (Félix Alcan, 1934), 79–81; J. Horne, 'Le Comité d'Action (CGT-PS) et l'origine du réformisme syndical du temps de guerre (1914–1916)', *Le Mouvement social*, 122 (Jan.–Mar. 1983), pp. 33–60.

[2] *L'Humanité*, 3 Oct. 1914.

Dubreuilh, who was also the general secretary of the PS.[3] But the full committee met frequently both in the autumn of 1914 and thereafter, and from the beginning of October, subcommittees covering a range of questions were set up.[4]

Much of the Comité d'Action's initial activity assumed that wartime circumstances were unique, and the solutions went no further than the emergency at hand. In its concern with material aid for soldiers and providing information for dislocated families on their missing relatives, the committee expressed a working-class variant of the more general mood of national solidarity in September 1914, as the battle of the Marne disrupted communications between civilians and the front. It was this mood which makes the CGT's participation in the Comité au Secours National, however it may have been interpreted subsequently, typical of the feelings in labour circles in Paris during the autumn.[5] The Comité d'Action not only approved participation but, in the person of Jules Bled,[6] became the principal organizer of the 'popular meals' of the Secours National, on the model of the *soupes communistes* of pre-war strikes. Over a million meals were provided in October for the Seine alone and fifty million subsidized meals were served down to late 1916.[7]

The committee was more critical of the national effort where it felt feasible measures were being ignored. Price controls and the

---

[3] From mid-1915, the burden of work, especially correspondence, led to the appointment of another socialist, H. Prêté, as permanent secretary of the committee (AN F$_7$ 13571, rep. 31 Aug. 1915).

[4] (1) military separation allowances and unemployment relief, (2) rents, (3) work, (4) information for the families of dead or wounded soldiers, (5) information for the families of prisoners, (6) clothing and other donations to soldiers, (7) ambulances and nursing homes, (8) provisioning measures (*L'Humanité*, 3 Oct. 1915; APP B/a 1605, 'Note sur l'attitude de la C.G.T', 31 Oct. 1914). For the changes in the subcommittees in 1916, see p. 131, below.

[5] See Chap. 2, above.

[6] (1879–1961) Parisian market gardener, founder member of the Parisian Syndicat des Jardiniers and secretary of the Fédération Nationale Horticole, 1904–14. From 1913 to 1918, Bled was secretary of the Union des Syndicats de la Seine. A pre-war revolutionary syndicalist, and also a socialist, he collaborated closely with Jouhaux during the war. The biographical notes provided on key French syndicalist and socialist figures are taken from J. Maitron and C. Pennetier (eds.), *Dictionnaire biographique du mouvement ouvrier français* (Éditions ouvrières, 1973–?), pt. 3, *1871–1914*; pt. 4, *1914–1939*, unless otherwise specified.

[7] *L'Humanité*, 21 Dec. 1914 and 5 Nov. 1916; CGT, *Rapports des comités ... pour l'exercice 1914–1918*, 6.

preservation of scarce stocks (notably sugar) as well as larger military separation allowances—the only support for many working-class women—and their extension to artisans, share-croppers, and common-law wives, were the subject of vigorous demands. But these measures all concerned exceptional circumstances which it was universally felt, in the autumn of 1914, would end like the war itself in a matter of months.[8]

By contrast, the acute unemployment triggered by the mobilization seemed to have larger implications. It certainly reached formidable proportions before the industrial mobilization began to absorb the surplus labour in early 1915. In October 1914, unemployment stood at a monthly average of 35 per cent, and it was still 20 per cent in January 1915. As Jouhaux later recalled, 'the fields, factories and offices were deserted *en masse*'.[9] With the limited nature of pre-war French social security measures and the scale and suddenness of the crisis, unemployment was the most tangible and threatening aspect of the more general disruption occasioned by the war and it dramatized the normal vulnerability of workers to lay-offs—especially because a comparable crisis was predicted to accompany demobilization. The impact of the unemployment was compounded by the attempt of many employers to profit from the economic conjuncture by lowering wages.[10]

Both the Comité d'Action and labour leaders more generally proposed solutions which, in the interests of national solidarity, claimed recognition of the particular needs of workers as well as an organizational role for the labour movement itself. This foreshadowed the dominant approach subsequently adopted by labour leaders as the industrial mobilization gathered pace.

In Paris, where the better-off districts had emptied at the German advance, the working class, as in 1870, faced both

[8] Horne, 'Le Comité d'Action (CGT-PS)', 35–6. For military separation allowances and also perceptions of the duration of the war, see J.-J. Becker, *The Great War and the French People* (1980; English trans., Berg, Leamington Spa, 1985), 17–21, 105–12. Representatives of the Comité d'Action sat on the Commission supérieure des Allocations Militaires (*Rapports des comités ... pour l'exercice 1914–1918*, 11).

[9] L. Jouhaux, *Réceptions de Gompers à la Confédération Générale du Travail, 24 et 26 septembre 1918* (1918), 13–14; A. Créhange, *Chômage et placement* (Presses Universitaires de France, 1927), 68; P. Izard, *Le Chômage et le placement en France pendant la guerre* (Sagot, 1920), 46–80; B. G. de Montgomery, *British and Continental Labour Policy* (Kegan Paul, Trench and Trubner, 1922), chap. 24.

[10] See Chap. 2, above.

economic disruption and a German siege. And as in 1870,
workers' organizations took the initiative in responding to both,
treating directly with the military administration. When Gallieni, the military governor, ordered a fortified entrenchment to
be built around the capital, the building workers' unions seized
on it as a vast public works project capable of providing relief
for a building-work-force in enforced idleness since early
August. Through Paul-Boncour, a socialist on Gallieni's staff,
it was agreed that the Syndicat des Terrassiers would supply
fifteen to twenty thousand men a day, at union rates of pay, to
the private contractors responsible for the job. The Comité
d'Action endorsed this solution with enthusiasm.[11]

The outcome was divisive. By early November, both the
Comité d'Action and the Terrassiers were accusing some contractors of sacking union men and undercutting the agreed rate.
Eventually, the military authorities themselves reduced the rate
and began to bypass the union movement in recruiting, while
the Terrassiers, for their part, tried to build on their earlier
advantage and extend unionization and impose winter-working
rules. Each side accused the other of cynically manipulating the
Union sacrée to its own end.[12] It is not surprising if the
Terrassiers tried to take advantage of the initial accord. With
their secretary, Hubert, they had been in the front rank of the
Paris revolutionary syndicalists within the Fédération du Bâtiment before the war, and were rapidly to become a key element
of the pacifist opposition to the war. But the 'pro-war' labour
leaders also felt that the employers' attitude betrayed the *Union
sacrée*, an experience amplified subsequently in the munitions
effort. The Comité d'Action protested formally:

[These abuses] prove that the immense sacrifices, moral and material,
currently accepted by the proletariat, as much at home as on the

---

[11] Gallieni, *Mémoires du général Gallieni: défense de Paris* (Payot, 1920), 118–20;
J. Paul-Boncour, *Entre deux guerres: souvenirs sur la IIIᵉ république*, i, *Les Luttes
républicaines, 1877–1918* (Plon, 1945), 244–6.
[12] APP B/a 1605, rep. 'Au sujet d'ouvriers occupés aux travaux du camp
retranché', 23 Sept. 1914 and 'Note sur l'attitude de la C.G.T.', 31 Oct. 1914;
Syndical Général des Ouvriers Terrassiers ... du département de la Seine, *A nos
adhérents: rapport moral et financier: du 1er août 1914 au 1er janvier 1918* (Société
Ouvrière d'Imprimerie, Courbevoie, 1918), 10–16; for the Comité d'Action's
protests, see *Rapport ... 1915*, 9–12 and *L'Humanité*, 2 Nov. 1914.

battlefields, neither touch nor move the great majority of the *patronat*.[13]

Another response to the crisis fared rather better. In November 1914, the CGT devised a national plan for reactivating the economy and thus dealing with unemployment. This almost certainly owed something to the contact which Jouhaux made with Sembat, in the latter's capacity as minister of Public Works, at Bordeaux. Approved by the Comité Confédéral on 22 November 1914, the plan was formally submitted to Sembat three days later with a letter from Jouhaux explaining its purpose.[14]

The CGT envisaged a series of local *commissions mixtes temporaires* for the duration of the war, on which representatives of trade unions and the *patronat*, under a government-appointed chairman, would look at ways of rekindling economic activity. They were also to ensure that union wage-rates and conditions were maintained, in opposition to the experience of the Paris entrenchment and the capital's clothing and engineering industries.

The CGT and the Comité d'Action developed a campaign around the document in favour of what was termed a *renaissance industrielle*. This soon came to mean not simply a reprise of economic activity but a qualitative change under the stimulus of war, with new techniques and a new role for labour.[15] The aspiration is clear, though the ideas remained inchoate. The political incorporation of the labour movement into the war effort was to be differentiated, so that labour organizations, while supporting the national cause, might exert some critical

[13] *Rapport ... 1915*, 12.

[14] An ephemeral Commission du Travail, consisting of Sembat, Vaillant, and Jouhaux, was set up to consider unemployment before the battle of the Marne, but it did not survive the removal of the government to Bordeaux (CGT, *Rapports des comités ... pour l'exercice 1914-1918*, 6-7). Jouhaux planned to use his role as a *délégué à la nation* to co-ordinate action against unemployment (see Chap. 2 n. 49, above). *La Bataille syndicaliste*, 25 Nov. 1914, for the plan; AN F₇ 13574, rep. 25 Jan. 1915, for the covering letter; AN F₇ 13574, rep. 24 Dec. 1914, for CGT approval.

[15] The theme was developed in numerous articles, especially by Jouhaux, in *La Bataille syndicaliste* during the winter and spring of 1914-15 (e.g. 'Soucis ouvriers, calculs patronaux', 11 Jan. 1915, and 'Pour un outillage plus perfectionné', 28 Jan. 1915).

control over their economic destinies. As Jouhaux explained to Sembat:

For the workers' side, we suggest that the national federations, the *syndicats*, the *bourses du travail*, the *unions départementales du travail*, could provide the delegates who, by virtue of their technical knowledge and their professional capacities, will be able to render a major service to the industrial renaissance, to the workers' cause.

In the event, it was not the well-intentioned projects of gravely weakened labour organizations which solved unemployment, but the industrial mobilization. Yet the CGT initiative was not fruitless. February 1915 saw the constitution of Commissions Mixtes Départementales pour la Reprise du Travail which were loosely derived from the CGT proposal. The prefects were invited to establish commissions (existent on a voluntary basis since the autumn in some *départements*) with equal worker and *patronal* representation to facilitate the return to 'a normal economic life'. The goal was distinctly more restrained than that of the original CGT proposition. But by late August 1915, 59 commissions had been set up and by October 1918 there were 64 in 63 *départements*.[16] Moreover, the Commission Mixte pour le Maintien du Travail of the Seine acquired a national significance largely because its labour delegates were leading figures in the CGT. Together with some progressive administrators and centre-left and socialist politicians, the CGT leaders formed a group, as we shall see, which took a critical and reforming approach to many of the problems raised by the war in the Paris region.

For all their limitations as purely advisory bodies with a less radical brief than that envisaged by Jouhaux and the CGT, the departmental *commissions mixtes* testify to the syndicalist leadership's desire to win some permanent benefit for labour from the economic disruption caused by the outbreak of war, a desire which, according to a police report of early 1915 'thus

---

[16] 'Commissions mixtes pour la reprise du travail', *Bulletin du ministère du travail*, July–Aug. 1915, pp. 202–15, and ibid., Aug–Oct. 1918, 353–60; Ministère du Travail, *Travaux des commissions mixtes départementales pour le maintien du travail national* (Imprimerie Nationale, 1918), 4 vols.; APP B/a 1605, 'Note sur l'attitude de la C.G.T. et des organisations syndicales du département de la Seine depuis le mois de janvier dernier', Apr. 1915, 3; *Rapports des comités ... pour l'exercice 1914–1918*, 9–11.

marked a new orientation in the tactic employed by the leaders of working-class opinion'.[17]

(ii) Protecting the Working-Class Consumer

On official figures, prices rose well ahead of wages throughout the war, roughly doubling to the end of 1917 and trebling to the end of 1919, with especially sharp increases in the first six months of hostilities, the spring of 1917, and the summer and autumn of 1918 (see Appendix I).[18] Labour calculations showed even higher inflation, and this was confirmed by Thomas's Commission du Travail for the big munitions centres, where intense competition for scarce accommodation and profiteering by shopkeepers sent prices soaring above national inflation rates. Yet although on official estimates, wage-rates lagged behind prices, calculating the movement of living standards remains problematic. Contemporary images of high wages in the war industries, though partly an optical illusion which failed to discount for inflation, had some substance. Certain workers, especially women, were able to shift to better-paid sectors, while unemployment virtually disappeared. Complex combinations of piece-rates, overtime, and cost-of-living bonuses make it hard to estimate total income as opposed to basic rates. What is clear, however, from *L'Humanité*, the Fédération des Métaux, and other sources, is that much of contemporary working-class and labour opinion *felt* that living standards had declined or only kept pace with inflation through considerable effort by workers themselves.[19]

[17] AN F₇ 13574, rep. 25 Jan. 1915.

[18] L. March, *Le Mouvement des prix et des salaires pendant la guerre* (Presses Universitaires de France, 1925); J.-L. Robert, 'Les Luttes ouvrières en France pendant la première guerre mondiale', *Cahiers d'histoire de l'institut Maurice Thorez*, 23, 1977, pp. 41–3.

[19] A. Luquet, reports in *L'Humanité* on living and working conditions in Paris (Oct. 1915) and the Loire and Lyons regions (June–July 1916); report of the Fédération des Métaux, *L'Union des métaux*, Dec. 1916; A. Roche (secretary of the Bourse du Travail of Roanne), 'Le Problème de la vie dans un ménage ouvrier', *La Clairière*, 15 Dec. 1918, pp. 1655–9; AN 94 AP 129, rep. July 1916, for the views of Albert Thomas's official labour controllers on exorbitant rents and food prices in the Loire and Lyons regions; *Bulletin des usines de guerre*, 13 Nov. 1916, pp. 230–1, for the summary of the Commission du Travail.

Inflation was compounded by shortages. The deterioration of an understaffed railway system, the decline in agricultural production, and the German U-boat campaign from 1916, added queues and empty shelves to the consumers' lot. By the autumn of 1915 there were signs of working-class unrest at the particularly steep price rises in Paris. In 1917 and especially 1918, protest at prices and shortages was an important aspect of strikes in some of the large munitions centres.[20]

Labour leaders responded with two distinctive but complementary reflexes. The first envisaged state intervention to control prices and regulate distribution. The second sought ways of increasing the provision of vital consumer necessities. Socialists, syndicalists, and *coopérateurs* collaborated closely, with the Comité d'Action playing a central role. In October 1915, the committee charged its cost of living subcommittee with drafting a series of reports on provisioning problems, notably meat, coal, sugar, dairy, and cereal products, whose ideas were taken up by the CGT, the FNCC, and the Groupe Socialiste.[21]

The first solution proposed by labour—that of state regulation of market forces—drew on a long popular memory. It assumed that although the imbalance between supply and demand contributed to inflation, the real cause was the rapacity of suppliers, middle-men and small shopkeepers. For a traditional enemy there was a traditional solution—*taxation* and *réquisition*, that is, the limitation by the state of the price of vital goods with its essential corollary, the right to requisition supplies from those who refused to sell within the designated limit. It was all the easier to demand this economic Jacobinism

[20] For Parisian discontent in 1915, see Becker, *The Great War and the French People*, 132–40, and Robert, 'Ouvriers et mouvement ouvrier parisiens', 18–150. For the consumer protests in 1918, see the specially commissioned reports from the postal censorship in SHAT 16N 1470, and the monthly reports to the Ministry of the Interior (Direction de la Sûreté Générale) from Oct. 1917 in SHAT 16N 1538.

[21] The principal sources for the Comité d'Action are the irregular accounts of its meetings in *L'Humanité* and *La Bataille syndicaliste*; reports in AN F₇ 13074 and 13571, and in APP B/a 1605; and the published reports of the committee, especially (for an outline) *Rapport . . . 1915* and *Rapport du comité d'action, 2ᵉ année, octobre 1915 à octobre 1916* (hereafter *Rapport . . . 1916*), all in IFHS, Fonds Picart, 14 AS 213 (5) 386. For the role of the Comité d'Action in the broader provisioning campaign, see the report of the meeting to discuss this held by the Union des Syndicats de la Seine, the Comité Confédéral of the CGT, and the Comité d'Action in Dec. 1915 (*La Bataille*, 13 Dec. 1915).

in the context of a political mobilization which constantly invoked the precedent of *l'An II*.[22] The Comité d'Action and the socialist deputies both pushed for their own version of such an approach and endorsed the tentative moves of government in the same direction, notably with a law of 16 October 1915 authorizing the requisitioning of wheat and flour for civilian use. They actively lobbied on behalf of Malvy's bill for sweeping powers of *taxation* and *réquisition* in relation to all basic consumer goods, and protested to the government when, in April 1916, the bill emerged emasculated from the Sénat, guardian throughout the war of a conservative, free-market approach to economic matters.[23]

The second labour approach—augmenting the provision of necessities—turned on the traditions of skilled workers and labour organizations themselves. The decline in supply was to be limited, if not reversed, by the return of qualified men from the front to key sectors and by the involvement of working-class organizations—the trade unions in increasing production and the co-operative movement in retailing. Thus, the Comité d'Action recommended that frozen meat (virtually unknown in pre-war France) should be imported on a massive scale and distributed through municipalities and co-operatives, with Daudé-Bancel, secretary general of the FNCC, charged with instructing working-class consumers how to prepare it. Both the Comité d'Action and the syndicalist paper *La Bataille syndicaliste*, now retitled *La Bataille*, undertook a veritable publicity campaign in favour of frozen meat.[24] The Comité d'Action, the CGT and the socialist deputies also urged the government to increase cereal production by making the cultivation of unfarmed land compulsory under the aegis of a

[22] *Journal officiel, chambre des députés, documents parlementaires*, 1915, no. 1366, pp. 1045–7 (socialist bill on *taxation* and *réquisition*), and *Journal officiel, chambre des députés, débats parlementaires*, 1915, p. 1844 (Mistral's speech).

[23] P. Pinot, *Le Contrôle du ravitaillement de la population* (Presses Universitaires de France, 1925), 6–8; C. Meilhac, *et al.*, *L'Effort du ravitaillement français pendant la guerre et pour la paix, 1914–1920* (Félix Alcan, n.d.), 22–4; Comité d'Action, *Rapport . . . 1916*, 8; AN F₇ 13571, rep. 20 Apr. 1916; min. of Comité Général of the Union des Syndicats of the Seine, 12 Apr. 1916, p. 13.

[24] Comité d'Action, *Rapport . . . 1916*, 4; *La Vie chère: rapport relatif aux mesures à prendre pour enrayer la hausse de la viande*, 15 Dec. 1915 (report of the Comité d'Action, signed by Henri Sellier and Gaston Lévy); L. Jouhaux, 'A l'aide des coopératives', *La Bataille*, 8 Dec. 1915.

commission mixte, in every commune, on which the agricultural workers' unions would be represented.[25]

Coal, one of the most vital, and vexed, provisioning problems, illustrates especially clearly this dual labour approach. Coal prices soared during the war, well above the general level of inflation in the earlier years. The German occupation of the richest mining districts and the mobilization of the miners reduced an already insufficient production. France depended on Britain for the balance, and the consequent shortage was already acute by the second winter of the war, with municipal rationing introduced in Paris in 1916. To make matters worse, domestic and imported coal were sold at different rates, with the cheaper home supplies being monopolized by the big industrial users, leaving the domestic consumer to pay the higher import rates.

At the end of 1915, the Commission des Mines in the Chambre des Députés proposed that a government-controlled, two-tier system of prices be established, with domestic consumers buying at the lower price.[26] The Comité d'Action fully endorsed this interventionism, and backed up its case with a substantial report by Alexandre Luquet.[27] The committee condemned the Sénat for characteristically amending all substance out of the original proposal. It also turned its hostility on to Sembat and his *chef de cabinet*, Léon Blum, who were responsible for government coal policy and opposed two-tier price controls (official policy was to press the British to reduce their export prices). When Sembat and Blum appeared before the Comité d'Action in August 1916, they found their audience hard to convince, and Jouhaux replied:

[25] Comité d'Action, *Rapport . . . 1916*, 7; *La Voix du peuple*, 1 May 1916, in which the Comité Confédéral supported the project; 'L'Organisation de la production agricole', in *La Bataille*, 27 Jan. 1917, for the resultant CGT policy on agriculture.

[26] *Journal officiel, chambre des députés, débats parlementaires*, 1916, pp. 3384–5, for the Durafour bill, emanating from the Commission des Mines; H. Bruggeman, M. Poëte, and H. Sellier, *Paris pendant la guerre* (Presses Universitaires de France, 1925), 31–2; G. Sardier, *Le Ravitaillement en charbon pendant la guerre* (Larose, 1920), 63–79.

[27] (1874–1930) born in Bourges but a Parisian from late adolescence, Luquet was a hairdresser and secretary of the Fédération des Coiffeurs from 1898 to 1919. Initially a revolutionary syndicalist, he was, during the war, a leading reformist. He was also, from 1896 until his death, an active socialist (originally in the Parti Ouvrier Français), and one of the key national figures linking the CGT and PS.

I know this is a rather difficult question to resolve, but I also know that the working-class population, which has made so many sacrifices, is beginning to murmur against this excessive increase in coal prices.[28]

But in parallel with the argument on pricing, the Comité d'Action, the CGT, and the mining deputies also called on the government to increase coal production by returning miners from the trenches and technically modernizing the mines in conjunction with the miners' own organizations. The Fédération du Sous-Sol itself developed these ideas. The difficulty of imposing such changes on reluctant coal companies made nationalization the natural term of the argument, and in 1916–17, the federation, the Comité Confédéral of the CGT, and the mining deputies demanded nationalization as the only sure way of expanding wartime coal production, with the deputies presenting an unsuccessful nationalization bill to parliament in November 1916.[29]

Arguably the most successful aspect of organized labour's response to the plight of the working-class consumer was the co-operative boom. Despite losing 40 per cent of its members and resources in the invasion, the FNCC saw its constituent societies increase from 1,200 to 1,500 during the war, and its turnover from 9 to 42 million francs.[30] The co-operatives

[28] AN F₇ 13571, rep. 12 Aug. 1916; Comité d'Action, *La Vie chère: rapport sur la question du charbon* (Dec. 1915), and *Rapport . . . 1916*, 5. For the Comité d'Action's support for the Durafour bill and subsequent condemnation of the Sénat, see AN F₇ 13571, rep. 23 Oct. 1915. For official policy, see Marcel Sembat, 'Les Cahiers noirs', in *Cahiers et revue de l'OURS*, 161 (May 1985), pp. 10–11.

[29] Bureau Fédéral of the Fédération du Sous-Sol, 'La Hausse des charbons', *La Bataille*, 2 July 1916; C. Bartuel, 'Pourquoi nous manquons de charbon', *La Clairière*, 1 Aug. 1917, p. 11; Bartuel and Rullière, *La Mine et les mineurs*, 88–9.

[30] Chap. 1 n. 16, above; *3ᵉ Congrès national et conférence coopérative interalliée tenu à Paris, les 22, 23, 24 et 25 septembre 1916. Compte rendu* (Bureau de la Fédération Nationale, 1917); *4ᵉ Congrès national tenu à Paris les 30 septembre, 1ᵉʳ et 2 octobre 1917. Compte rendu* (L'Émancipatrice, 1917); *5ᵉ Congrès national tenu à Paris les 22, 23 et 24 septembre 1918. Compte rendu* (Fédération Nationale des Coopératives de Consommation, 1918); *L'Action coopérative* (the review of the FNCC, fortnightly until Aug. 1914 and restarted as a monthly, Jan. 1916); *L'Émancipation*, the review of what had been the 'neutral' current before unification in 1912; reports in *La Bataille* and *L'Humanité*; and the wartime publications of the secretary general of the FNCC, A. Daudé-Bancel, *Le Mouvement ouvrier français pendant la guerre* (1915), *La Coopération pendant et après la guerre* (FNCC, 1916), *Le Protectionnisme et l'avenir économique de la France* (Giard et Brière, 1916), and *La Reconstruction des cités détruites* (La Presse Sociale, 1917). The figures are from Albert Thomas's speech to the 1918 congress, p. 10.

benefited directly from labour involvement in the Comité au
Secours National, being largely responsible for the Comité
d'Action's 'popular meals'. Even more important was the role
of Albert Thomas. Thomas was president of the FNCC and
took an active part in its wartime congresses. It is scarcely
surprising, therefore, that the FNCC presented a report to one of
the first meetings of the Commission du Travail in June 1916,
calling for the massive recourse to co-operatives to provide
lodgings, shops, and restaurants in the mushrooming munitions
centres, nor that it benefited from large-scale state patronage
thereafter. The FNCC established contracts with the Ministry
of Armaments to provide the bulk of canteens in munitions
factories, state and private, and received subsidies from
both government and employers. In February 1918, as part of
Clemenceau's onslaught on the subsistence crisis, a Conseil
Supérieur de la Coopération institutionalized the co-operative
movement's role in the state's provisioning arrangements.[31]

In other respects, there remained a gulf between labour
policies on prices and provisioning and official measures for
most of the war. Relatively little was done before 1918 to
control prices, and those in power most open to labour views
(such as Malvy) were hampered by the calculated inertia of the
senators as well as by the complexity of the problems. Equally,
the redeployment of skilled labour from the front to key sectors
of the economic effort, though it did occur, was on nothing like
the scale envisaged by labour leaders.

These felt, therefore, that they had good reason to be critical
of government, especially as the position of working-class
consumers deteriorated rapidly during the U-boat crisis of

---

[31] A. Thomas, *La Coopération et les usines de guerre* (Bibliothèque de l'École
Coopérative, 1919); AN 94 AP 122, for the FNCC report; *Bulletin des usines de
guerre*, 13 Nov. 1916, p. 232, for the official response. By mid-1918, 45 canteens,
restaurants, etc. were run by the state, 328 were controlled by employers, and 932
were organized by co-operatives (M. Frois, *La Santé et le travail des femmes pendant
la guerre* (Presses Universitaires de France, 1926), 36). The Ministry of Armaments
set up a *Fonds coopératif des ouvriers des usines de guerre* in 1916, to which employers
contributed, with Renault and the Société Commentry, Fourchambault, Decazeville making early grants of 10,000 francs each (AN 94 AP 122, and *Bulletin des
usines de guerre*, 13 Nov. 1916, p. 232). In May 1917, the government was
authorized by law to grant 2 million francs to consumer co-operatives (Ministère du
Travail, *Encouragement aux sociétés coopératives ouvrières* (1919)). For the Conseil
supérieur de la Coopération, see ibid.

spring 1917. In May 1917, for example, the Comité Confédéral of the CGT issued a *Déclaration* cogently summarizing the labour programme in defence of the consumer.[32] Faced with the decimation of grain imports by German submarines, it demanded sweeping *taxation* and *réquisition*—'not a single grain of wheat unused while the fate of the nation is at stake'. At the same time, it urged a massive productive effort—the equivalent for *ravitaillement* of the munitions drive—with the state intensifying coal and food production and reorganizing the merchant marine and the railways—'if no grain of wheat should remain unused ... no railway wagon should remain unoccupied'. But inescapable manpower shortages limited the potential for a production drive. And only in the last year of the war did Clemenceau bring in nationally anything resembling the state control of provisioning demanded by labour leaders (notably through price controls and rationing).

(iii) The Manpower Crisis: The Wartime Labour Market, Women and Foreign Workers

The competition between the military and industrial mobilizations for scarce manpower had become critical by 1916 and defied resolution as long as the war lasted. The combination of a labour famine and abnormal state intervention in the labour market—first by the military control over mobilized workers and, second, by large-scale official efforts to recruit women and foreigners for the war industries and agriculture—created an unprecedented situation for labour, and especially syndicalist, leaders. Solicited by the state for their help in easing the manpower crisis, the latter saw the opportunity to institutionalize a more 'rational' operation of the labour market, entrenching the power of the syndicats. Yet the mass utilization of women and foreigners intensified the restructuring of the labour force

---

[32] 'Déclaration', issued as a brochure and published in *La Bataille*, 21 May 1917.

already evident before the war. Deeply threatening, this development rendered all the more urgent the use of wartime circumstances to establish some syndicalist control over the recruitment
of women and foreigners to new areas of industrial work.

Initially, of course, the problem was an oversupply of labour
with the economic paralysis caused by the military mobilization
of autumn 1914 and the flood of northern and Belgian refugees
into the rest of France. Labour placement was one of the
questions which the Commissions Mixtes Départementales
pour la Reprise du Travail were invited to consider, and a
number of them set up placement offices. The government
reinforced this initiative by turning the temporary Office Central du Placement des Chômeurs et Réfugiés into an Office
National du Placement to co-ordinate the embryonic system.
Early in 1916, all municipal placement offices were required to
establish administrative *commissions paritaires* (with equal
employer and worker representation), and placement offices
were made compulsory in every *département* on the same basis.
The war therefore saw the implementation of a multi-tiered
labour placement system with official funding and the administrative participation of organized labour. This stood in sharp
contrast to the rudimentary national provisions for labour
placement in pre-war France and was a belated equivalent of
the labour exchanges in Britain and Germany.[33]

For the CGT, such a system offered the hope of the permanent
regulation of the post-war labour market through a public
system along lines long advocated by the syndicats in notoriously
casual trades such as baking, hairdressing, and cafés. Syndicalist
enthusiasm was especially evident in the Seine. The Commission
Mixte pour le Maintien du Travail of the Seine was, as we have
noted, virtually a laboratory for social experimentation. It created
as one of its priorities an Office Départemental de Placement et
de la Statistique du Travail of the Seine covering the volatile
Paris labour market, and run by a *commission paritaire*. There was
broad agreement from the employer delegates, but the initiative

---

[33] A. Luquet, 'L'Organisation du marché du travail', *La Clairière*, 15 Sept. 1917,
pp. 158–67, and 1 Oct. 1917, pp. 220–8; A. Savoie, 'La Répartition de la main-
d'oeuvre sera-t-elle assurée dans l'avenir?' *La Clairière*, 1 Nov. 1917, pp. 318–24;
Izard, *Le Chômage et le placement en France pendant la guerre*, 13, 40–50; Créhange,
Chômage et placement, 4–5, 45–61.

came from an alliance between the worker delegates, almost all well-known national leaders of the CGT, and Henri Sellier,[34] a strategically placed socialist militant who was also a councillor for the Seine and a civil servant with the Ministry of Labour. It was he who drafted the report on the placement office.[35] From early on, the placement office was perceived as significant both for the war itself and for the organization of the demobilization— a preoccupation mirrored in the Commissions Mixtes pour le Maintien du Travail of other *départements*.[36] A police report of mid-1915 confirmed that the Paris experiment had been warmly received in syndicalist circles, while Luquet, with long experience of casual labour in the hairdressing trade, wrote:

Thus, under the imperious necessity of the most obvious needs of the national effort, a rational institution of public placement is being elaborated which is already giving excellent results, and which after the war will give even more appreciable ones.[37]

The departmental placement system did indeed come into its own in 1919, with the demobilization. From 1915 to 1918, however, the problem was not placing labour but finding it. Thomas's munitions service, the Ministry of Labour, and the Ministry of Agriculture spawned a plethora of often competing agencies which sought to channel women and foreign workers into vital war production.[38] CGT leaders in particular tried to utilize their organizational participation in the economic mobilization—notably the Commission Mixte Départementale

---

[34] (1883–1943) a civil servant and eventually general secretary of the Syndicat des Fonctionnaires. He was a close supporter of Vaillant in the PS. A councillor for the suburban municipality of Puteaux, he was a member of the Conseil Général of the Seine during and after the war, and became a senator in 1935. He was Minister of Health in the 1936–7 Popular Front government.

[35] Izard, *Le Chômage et le placement en France pendant la guerre*, 76–81; H. Sellier and E. Deslandres, *La Constitution de l'office départemental du placement et de la statistique du travail de la Seine: son action et ses travaux, du 1er novembre 1915 au 30 octobre 1918* (Conseil Général de la Seine, 1918), esp. 54–87 for the functioning of the office; *Travaux des commissions mixtes départementales pour le maintien du travail national*, i, *Seine*.

[36] H. Sellier, *L'Humanité*, 8 May 1916.

[37] *Le Petit parisien*, 28 Nov. 1915. For the police report, see AN F₇ 13574, rep. July 1915.

[38] Oualid and Picquenard, *Salaires et tarifs*, 28; Créhange, *Chômage et placement*, 46; J. Godfrey, *Capitalism at War: Industrial Policy and Bureaucracy in France, 1914–1918* (Berg, Leamington Spa, 1987), 184–6.

pour le Maintien du Travail of the Seine and the advisory Commission Nationale de Placement—to define the ground-rules by which this remodelling of the wartime working class should occur.

Women and foreign workers, during the war, threatened a syndicalist movement largely composed of skilled males not so much by their overall numbers as by their invasion of new sectors and new geographical areas, and by their role in the changing labour process.[39] The proportion of women in the total industrial labour force only rose from just under 30 per cent before the war to 37.2 per cent in 1917, before declining to 32 per cent in the slump of autumn 1920. But 22.3 per cent of the engineering work-force was female in January 1918 compared to only 6.5 per cent of a much smaller work-force in 1914. Unpublished official figures for mid-1917 confirm this huge growth in absolute numbers, with 400,000 women working in armaments and aviation, or 24 per cent of the total (see Table 1 and Appendix IV). In the biggest munitions centre, the Paris region, 100,000 women constituted a third of the armaments work-force. Yet although women embarked on new types of work, with many entering factories for the first time, the numbers of women employed in the traditional sectors of textiles

[39] For official policy on using women and foreigners in the industrial mobilization, see *Bulletin des usines de guerre*, esp. 'L'Initiative industrielle', 3, 15 May 1916, p. 17; *Bulletin du ministère du travail*, various issues; the records of the Commission inter-ministérielle de la main-d'oeuvre in AN F$_{14}$ 11333-4; AN 94 AP 129 and 135 (Fonds Thomas); 'Labour Conditions in the Manufacture of Munitions in France', *Labour Gazette*, Jan. 1916, pp. 8-9; P. Hamp, *La France, pays ouvrier* (Éditions de la Nouvelle Revue Française, 1916); Oualid and Picquenard, *Salaires et tarifs*, 62-7; General Pédoya, *La Commission de l'armée pendant la grande guerre* (Flammarion, 1921), 259-325; Lt.-Col. Reboul, *Mobilisation industrielle*, i, *Des fabrications de guerre en France de 1914 à 1918* (Berger-Lavrault, Nancy, 1925), 170-2; M. C. Volovitch, 'Essai sur l'évolution et la composition de la main d'oeuvre industrielle pendant la guerre de 1914-1918', (Maîtrise diss., Université de Paris, 1968); J. Cavignac (ed.), 'La Classe ouvrière bordelaise face à la guerre (1914-1918). Recueil de textes', *Cahiers de l'Institut Aquitain d'Études Sociales* (Bordeaux), 4 (1976), pp. 49-86; J.-W. Déreymez, 'Les Usines de guerre (1914-1918) et le cas de la Saône-et-Loire', *Cahiers d'histoire (Lyon, Grenoble)*, 26/2 (1981), pp. 151-81; Dogliani, 'Stato, imprenditori e manodopera industriale in Francia durante la prima guerra mondiale'; P. Fridenson, 'The Impact of the First World War on French workers', in Wall and Winter (eds.), *The Upheaval of War*, 235-48; Robert, 'Ouvriers et mouvement ouvrier parisiens', 320-619.

and clothing, and thus exposed to notorious exploitation and abysmal wages, remained higher than those in engineering.[40]

The number of immigrants in the industrial and agricultural labour force remained below the pre-war total. But since there had been an exodus of immigrants in 1914, the reintroduction during the war of over half a million foreign workers (excluding prisoners of war) was highly visible. Moreover, the ethnic composition of the immigrants changed markedly. Before the war, Belgium and Italy had been the main suppliers. A substantial proportion of the influx of Belgian refugees went into war work, but Spain now became the biggest single supplier of immigrant workers (over a third of the total), while a further third came from China and the colonies, mainly North Africa and Indo-China (see Appendix IV). This mass introduction of 'exotic' labour, though it foreshadowed the inter-war pattern of immigration, was unprecedented for France, or indeed any western industrial society. Overall, about half the immigrant workers joined the armaments work-force, comprising 10 per cent of the total (see Table 1), with possibly a further 30 per cent of immigrants engaged on the land.[41]

---

[40] Frois, *La Santé et le travail des femmes pendant la guerre*; March, *Le Mouvement des prix et des salaires*, 287–95; A. Aftalion, *L'Industrie textile en France pendant la guerre* (Presses Universitaires de France, 1925), 15–18; M. Dubesset, F. Thébaud, and C. Vincent, 'Les Munitionnettes de la Seine', in P. Fridenson (ed.), *1914–1918: l'autre front* (Éditions ouvrières, 1977), 189–219; J. McMillan, *Housewife or Harlot: The Place of Women in French Society, 1870–1940* (Harvester Press, Brighton, 1981), 101–88; F. Thébaud, *La Femme au temps de la guerre de 1914* (Stock, 1986), 169–88; J.-L. Robert, 'Women and Work in France during the First World War', in Wall and Winter (eds.), *The Upheaval of War*, 251–66.

[41] Chap. 1 n. 12, above; 'Proposition Landry', in *Journal officiel, chambre des députés, documents parlementaires*, 28 Dec. 1915, no. 1632; *L'Œuvre économique*, 25 Apr. 1917 (special no. on foreign labour); J. Lugand, *L'Immigration des ouvriers étrangers en France et les enseignements de la guerre* (Martinet, 1919); L. Chassevent, *Appel à la main-d'oeuvre étrangère pour l'agriculture française* (Rousseau, 1919); Instituto de Reformas Sociales, *Información sobre emigración española a los paises de Europa durante la guerra* (Madrid, 1919); B. Nogaro and L. Weil, *La Main-d'oeuvre étrangère et coloniale pendant la guerre* (Presses Universitaires de France, 1926); H. Pirenne, *La Belgique et la guerre mondiale* (Presses Universitaires de France, 1928), 275–82; J. Van der Stegen, 'Les Chinois en France, 1915–1929' (Maîtrise diss., Université de Paris X, 1974); G. Cross, 'Towards Social Peace and Prosperity: The Politics of Immigration in France during the Era of World War I', *French Historical Studies*, 11/4 (Fall 1980), pp. 610–32; Horne, 'Immigrant Workers in France during World War I'.

The fears aroused among labour leaders by the use of women and foreigners on war work extended beyond the war itself. The decimation of adult French males on the Western Front, added to pre-war labour shortages, suggested that the recruitment of sufficient industrial labour would be a long-term problem. The possibility of a permanent rise in levels of female industrial employment conflicted with the strong natalist sentiment emerging in wartime France.[42] The likelihood of a continued increase in the use of foreign labour, an eventuality which had already alarmed the pre-war CGT, represented an even greater menace. The Fédération des Métaux had stood by helpless as a predominantly Italian and non-unionized labour force was employed in the rapidly expanding metallurgy complex in the Meurthe-et-Moselle (French Lorraine). The proliferation of foreigners in engineering and metallurgy during the war and the tensions created by the use of non-European labour compounded syndicalist fears.[43]

Elementary self-defence dictated that the CGT leadership try and organize women and immigrants, as well as lobbying the government to enforce equal wages and welfare protection (in accordance with Albert Thomas's declared policy). In the case of women, one of the earliest initiatives came from the clothing workers' federation. The clothing trade was over three-quarters female and its wages and conditions, for women working at home and in sweat shops, were notorious. They had been the subject of several pre-war enquiries, and with price inflation and wage-reductions in 1914–15 (85 per cent of Parisian clothing manufacturers reduced wages by between 25 per cent and 50 per cent), the situation of many women clothing workers became critical. Parliament rushed through a pre-war bill providing minimum wages for women domestic workers, in July 1915, while syndicalist attention focused unusually clearly

---

[42] R. Tomlinson, 'The Politics of Dénatalité during the French Third Republic, 1870–1940' (Ph.D., Cambridge, 1984), 114–32.

[43] For pre-war syndicalist attitudes to foreign labour, see A. Delevsky, *Antagonismes sociaux et antagonismes prolétariens* (Marcel Giard, 1924), 250–307; G. Pirou, 'La Main-d'oeuvre étrangère en France', *Revue socialiste, syndicaliste et coopérative*, May 1912, pp. 407–27; CGT, *Compte rendu de la conférence ordinaire des fédérations nationales des bourses du travail ... tenu les 13, 14 et 15 juillet 1913 ... Paris*, 38–9; AN F₇ 13581, reps of 18 June and 10 July 1914; and G. Noiriel, *Longwy: immigrés et prolétaires, 1880–1980* (Presses Universitaires de France, 1984), 198–212.

on the problem of subsistence industrial wages for women and on the vulnerability of families with a single, female income.[44]

In 1915, the male-led Fédération de l'Habillement, severely weakened by the war, tried to rebuild itself around a campaign for the protection of women workers. Its leaders, and notably the secretary, Pierre Dumas,[45] enthusiastically supported the two *commissions paritaires* set up to administer the minimum wages for female domestic workers in Paris, and on which the federation was represented.[46] They also launched a Comité Intersyndical d'Action contre l'Exploitation de la Femme in July 1915, together with the socialist feminist, Gabrielle Duchêne, in order to organize women workers and to campaign for improved pay and conditions.[47]

This committee quickly won wider support from other unions, and notably from the Fédération des Métaux, also beginning to react in the autumn of 1915 to a burgeoning female work-force.[48] A brochure issued by the committee in 1917, *Le Travail de la femme pendant la guerre*, summarized the approach defined at numerous Paris meetings during the previous eighteen months.[49]

[44] McMillan, *Housewife or Harlot*, 60–4; Thébaud, *La Femme au temps de la guerre de 1914*, 169–88.

[45] (1875–1960) a tailor, and general secretary of the Fédération de l'Habillement, 1909–20. Born in the Hérault, he worked in the east and south as a young man (including the Jura and Geneva), where he frequented anarchist circles. A revolutionary syndicalist in the CGT, he moved to a more moderate position just before the war. Exempt from military service due to a limp, he was a leading reformist during and just after the conflict. In the early 1920s, he gravitated to the corporatism and fascism of Georges Valois.

[46] AN F₇ 12891, 'Le Mouvement syndicaliste, année 1916', 71–2; AN F₇ 13575, rep. 29 Feb. 1916.

[47] AN F₇ 12891, 'Le Mouvement syndicaliste, année 1916', 19; APP B/a 1605, 'Attitude de la C.G.T. et des organisations syndicales du département de la Seine depuis le 15 Juillet 1915' (n.d.), according to which, the Comité Intersyndical d'Action was founded on 19 July 1915 by the Syndicat de la Chemiserie-Lingerie, with the support of 30 organizations; P. Dumas, 'Les Ouvrières de l'aiguille', *La Bataille syndicaliste*, 11 June 1915, and 'La Main-d'œuvre féminine devant la CGT', *La Bataille*, 1 Dec. 1915; Rosmer, *Le Mouvement ouvrier pendant la première guerre mondiale*, ii. 62; and Thébaud, *La Femme au temps de la guerre de 1914*, 186–7.

[48] IFHS, 14 AS 219, min. of the Commission Exécutive, Fédération des Métaux, 2 Oct. 1915 and 18 Mar. 1916; AN F₇ 12891, 'Le Mouvement syndicaliste, année 1916', 63–4, 117–21.

[49] A. Découzon, *Le Travail de la femme pendant la guerre* (L'Union Typographique, Seine-et-Oise, 1917; copies in IFHS 14 AS 213 (3) 275 and AN F₇ 13366). For meetings in 1916–17, see *L'Humanité*, 4 and 28 July 1916, and 11 Feb. 1917, and *Le Populaire*, 12–25 Feb. 1917, 8 ('Dans les syndicats').

It highlighted the problems of women supporting families on what were still treated by industrialists as supplementary wages, with few concessions in hours and conditions to their maternal functions, and focused in particular on 'l'industrialisation de la femme'—the massive penetration of unskilled female labour into machine work on exploitative piece-rates. An enquiry by the Fédération des Métaux in the autumn of 1915 had confirmed that women were being widely used in the war industries to increase the rhythm of work and undercut male wages.[50] *Le Travail de la femme* urged women to unionize in order to achieve equal pay with men, a duty, it suggested, which they owed the men at the front unable to defend their own civilian wage-rates.

The Comité Confédéral of the CGT pursued similar policies to the Comité Intersyndical towards women workers (as did the Union des Syndicats of the Seine).[51] In particular, Jouhaux made equal wages and protective welfare measures for women workers the twin themes of a report which he presented to the Commission Mixte Départementale pour le Maintien du Travail of the Seine in February 1916, and which he subsequently submitted as the view of both that Commission and of the CGT to Albert Thomas's Comité du Travail Féminin, shortly after its inception in April 1916[52] The work of this committee until the end of the war and the stream of official instructions in the *Bulletin des usines de guerre* suggest that the syndicalist case met with some official sympathy, converging with the views of Thomas himself and of the enlightened civil servants, politicians, technical experts, and more open employer representatives who composed the Comité du Travail Féminin.[53] There was broad agreement that the exploitation of women evident early in the war should be

[50] 'Salaire et travail des femmes', *L'Union des métaux*, May–Dec. 1915, pp. 9–13. See also P. Dumas, 'La Main-d'œuvre féminine devant la CGT', *La Bataille*, 1 Dec. 1915, and M. Capy, 'Salaires de guerre', *Le Midi socialiste*, 15 Mar. 1916, and 'État-patron', ibid., 3 Apr., 1916.

[51] AN F₇ 12891, 'Le Mouvement syndicaliste, année 1916', 18; min. of Commission Générale, Union des Syndicats of the Seine, 1916, 38.

[52] AN F₇ 12891, 'Le Mouvement syndicaliste, année 1916', 18–21; L. Jouhaux, 'Les Femmes travaillent, produisent', *La Bataille*, 28 Jan. 1916; *Travaux des commissions mixtes départementales pour le maintien du travail national*, i, *Seine*.

[53] Comité du Travail Féminin, *Protection et utilisation de la main-d'œuvre féminine dans les usines de guerre*, provides a summary of the committee's work. Albert Thomas's set of its minutes and reports is in AN 94 AP 135.

checked. In September 1916, the principle of equal remuneration was declared (nearly a year after Britain, where the Central Munitions Labour Supply Committee endorsed the same idea in late autumn 1915), and a variety of welfare measures along the lines of those envisaged by the CGT were introduced in an essentially paternalist spirit, including crèches, separate hygiene facilities, and women superintendents modelled on those of the Ministry of Munitions.[54]

The long-term prospect of increased levels of female factory work—especially in traditional skilled male preserves—brought out the full ambivalence of the CGT leadership towards women. Some permanent rise, in the light of wartime losses of adult males, was accepted as inevitable. This implied a continued campaign to unionize women workers. But the same preoccupation led syndicalists to echo more general natalist fears for the reproduction of the 'race', and this in turn reinforced a traditional family ethic within organized labour, by which the non-working mother was seen as the guarantor of a strong, 'moral' working-class and labour movement.[55] Such an ethos responded to real enough concerns, but also hid a continuing fear of female wage competition and a cultural unwillingness to accept women workers as equals. The net result was a frequently expressed hope that many *munitionnettes* would eventually yield their places to returning men.[56]

Thus, Jouhaux consistently warned in 1916 against the permanent use of women on the same scale as in wartime ('if, in France today, there is the problem of furnishing munitions, there

[54] Comité du Travail Féminin, op. cit.; *Bulletin des usines de guerre*, 16 July 1917, 90–5, for a summary of the protective measures introduced for women; Frois, *La Santé et le travail des femmes pendant la guerre*; and, for the origins of the *surintendantes*, A. Fourcaut, *Femmes à l'usine en France dans l'entre deux guerres* (Maspero, 1982), 11–19. The *Bulletin des usines de guerre* amply testifies to Thomas's interest in the British experiments, and Rowntree's scheme in the Ministry of Munitions was cited by Jouhaux as an example to follow in 'Les Femmes travaillent, produisent', *La Bataille*, 28 Jan. 1916.

[55] J.-L. Robert, 'La CGT et la famille ouvrière, 1914–1918: première approche', *Le Mouvement social*, 116 (July–Sept. 1981), pp. 47–66.

[56] J. Bouvier, *Mes mémoires* (Maspero, 1983), 135–9; Dubesset, Thébaud, and Vincent, 'Les Munitionnettes de la Seine', 202–9; McMillan, *Housewife or Harlot*, 159–62; Thébaud, *La Femme au temps de la guerre de 1914*, 185–8.

remains, for tomorrow, that of the birth-rate')[57] And not surprisingly, Merrheim and the Fédération des Métaux, without the ASE's promises on the restoration of trade union 'customs', were especially ambivalent about women workers, under a veil of paternalism and solicitude for the family. Merrheim, on his numerous speaking tours throughout France, frequently called for the unionization of women. But he equally often advocated strict limits on their employment. He told a meeting of the élite Union des Mécaniciens of the Seine that women were being used as the stalking-horse of Taylorism (like the ASE in Britain, the Union des Mécaniciens refused to admit semi-skilled women workers as members). And in July 1916, Merrheim informed some metallurgical workers at Albi, in the Tarn, that:

Women must be defended by being forbidden [access to] the workshop; as for widows and orphaned girls, if they work in factories, their exploitation must be avoided, and if they replace a man, they must get equal pay for equal work.[58]

This probably sums up the balance of the *métaux* official position, to judge by the resolutions passed at the national committee meeting in September 1917 and the congress of July 1918, which advocated unionizing women but also considered that 'the systematic introduction of women into the workshop is in absolute opposition to the creation and existence of the family *foyer*.'[59]

If there was doubt over the post-war role of women in industry, CGT leaders were quite certain that immigrants would be a permanent and major feature of the labour market—and thus an unambigous threat. As Luquet wrote in *L'Humanité* early in 1916:

After the war, when our own have laid down arms and can once again take up their tools, the women who occupied their posts in the hell of industry will relinquish their place to their [male] companions. Will

---

[57] L. Jouhaux, 'Les Femmes travaillent, produisent', *La Bataille*, 28 Jan. 1916, and 'Protection élémentaire et obligatoire de la femme', *La Bataille*, 8 Dec. 1916.

[58] AN F₇ 13366, rep. 3 Aug. 1916; rep. 27 Nov. 1916 for Merrheim's speech to the *mécaniciens*; Rosmer, *Le Mouvement ouvrier pendant la première guerre mondiale*, ii. 117.

[59] *L'Union des métaux*, July 1918, p. 13, and Sept. 1918, p. 7; Robert, 'Women and Work in France', 261.

it be the same if ... female labour is replaced by Asian or African labour ...?[60]

This anxiety appeared as early as autumn 1914. The Terrassiers and the Comité d'Action protested against the importation by some contractors of Italians for the *camp retranché* at less than union rates, and the Fédération des Métaux complained about Sembat's decision to admit Italians for the nascent munitions effort while high unemployment subsisted among refugees from Belgium and the north.[61] But it was the beginning of active official recruitment of foreign, and especially colonial, workers in 1915, plus the tide of peasants escaping across the Pyrenees from rural hardship in neutral Spain, which really convinced the bulk of the CGT that immigration was one of its gravest wartime problems.

The depth of rank-and-file anxiety became clear to CGT leaders in the winter of 1915–16, during their tours in the provinces trying to reinject life into the syndicalist movement.[62] As immigration intensified in early 1916, stories abounded. Jouhaux heard that 50,000 Chinese were to be recruited, though Métin, the minister of Labour, reassured him that the figure was really 5,000.[63] In May, Merrheim reported the wild rumour that a million Italians were to come, while in July he evoked to the engineering workers of St-Juéry (in the Tarn) the spectre of a million Spanish, Italians, and Russians flooding in after the war to undercut French wages.[64] Jouhaux summarized the broad syndicalist reaction:

It is, of all questions, the one which incontestably interests the labour movement the most and it requires a rapid solution ... On the one hand, we find ourselves faced with the pressing need for manpower for industry, the war, agriculture, a need which cannot be satisfied. On the other hand, we realize perfectly well that if we are unable to demand

---

[60] 'Pour la production de guerre', *L'Humanité*, 9 Feb. 1916.

[61] APP B/a 1605, rep. of 23 Sept. 1914; IFHS 14 AS 219, Commission Exécutive, Fédération des Métaux, 10 Jan. and 3 Apr. 1915 (correspondence between Merrheim and Sembat).

[62] AN F₇ 13569, CGT, Comité Confédéral, 31 Dec. 1915; F₇ 12891, 'Le Mouvement syndicaliste, année 1916', 13.

[63] AN F₇ 13569, CGT, Comité Confédéral, 8 Apr. 1916. An article on the subject in *La Bataille* by Jouhaux on 17 Mar. was censored.

[64] AN F₇ 13571, Comité d'Action, min. 13 May 1916; AN F₇ 13361, rep. 30 July 1916.

and win serious guarantees on the conditions for the importation of quantities of workers of a culture other than our own, the interests of French workers will be sacrificed and exploitation by big business will be made easier.[65]

Jouhaux's response was to produce a comprehensive plan which accepted the long-term need for immigration but sought to define 'serious guarantees'. This was approved by the Comité Confédéral in February 1916 and distributed throughout the movement.[66]

Just as CGT leaders used the unemployment crisis of late 1914 to suggest incipiently that the economic shock of war should be harnessed to the positive ends of a *renaissance industrielle* and an institutionalized role for organized labour in bringing about an economic revival, so the immigration issue allowed these ideas to be developed further. Jouhaux's report tied the CGT's acceptance of foreign labour to the creation of a dynamic industrial economy based on a prosperous, high-wage labour force, and therefore on domestic demand, rather than on a wage-cutting scramble for foreign markets.

It would be stupid if, on the pretext of conquering foreign markets, French industry neglected its own internal markets. And since the best consumer is the working class, the higher interest of the country and the real interest of national industry consist in having as client a working class with high wages, better working conditions, and an enlarged capacity for consumption.

Immigration, in consequence, was to be strictly regulated so as to reinforce, not threaten, this fundamental economic recipe. 'This appeal to foreign labour must be made in a methodic and rational way, avoiding economic and social disruption, and new levels of misery ...'.

Internationally, the report felt that such regulation should be achieved by inter-governmental labour treaties, setting the size and conditions of migratory flows, and by placing recruitment firmly in the hands of the labour movements of the countries of origin. Domestically, the reformed labour placement system was to ensure the rational distribution of immigrants, avoiding

---

[65] AN F₇ 13571, Comité d'Action, min. 5 June 1916.
[66] AN F₇ 13569, CGT, Comité Confédéral, min. 31 Dec. 1915 and 5 Feb. 1916; AN F₇ 12891, 'Le Mouvement syndicaliste, année 1916', 13–14. The report was published in a CGT brochure, *Questions ouvrières* (1916).

local unemployment, while equality in wages, conditions, and trade union rights with French workers were to avoid competition in the labour market. A national commission was also envisaged through which delegates of the ministries concerned, of the central and departmental placement offices, and of trade unions and employer organizations would monitor the local requests for foreign labour and enforce the whole system. In short, immigrant labour was to be used on a nationally agreed basis solely to remedy the demographic weakness of wartime and post-war France.

This report formed the basis of CGT policy on immigration until well after the war.[67] It was pursued internationally with foreign labour movements. Late in April 1916, the CGT sent a delegation to Rome to discuss labour controls over the migration of workers with its Italian equivalent, the Confederazione Generale del Lavoro (CGL).[68] A month later, a meeting of Italian, Belgian, British, and French trade unionists in Paris, for 1 May, endorsed the CGT report.[69] An accord was also signed in San Sebastian, in October 1916, between Jouhaux and Barrio, secretary of the Unión General de Trabajo (UGT), the Spanish socialist trade union body, which sought to ensure that the trade unionists among the Spanish immigrants were enrolled in the Union des Syndicats of their French destination.[70] From July 1916, the question of the international control of immigration by organized labour became one of the foundations of the attempt to revive the international trade union movement within the allied camp (see Chapter 8).

As with the use of women on munitions work, there was a certain convergence of syndicalist and official views on the issue of immigration. General Gallieni, as minister of War in late

[67] The report was debated extensively by a meeting of the Union des Syndicats of the Seine, 1 May 1916 (Commission Générale, Union des Syndicats de la Seine, min. 1916, 30–8), and was endorsed by all the major federations and many local organizations. See also L. Jouhaux, 'L'Immigration, notre point de vue', in *La Bataille*, 22 Sept. 1916.

[68] AN F, 12891, 'Le Mouvement syndicaliste, année 1916', 15; AN 94 AP 135, note from Barère, French ambassador in Rome, to Briand, 9 May 1916.

[69] AN F, 12891, 'Le Mouvement syndicaliste, année 1916', 15–17; AN F, 13569, CGT, Comité Confédéral, min. 1 May 1916.

[70] AN F, 12891, 'Le Mouvement syndicaliste, année 1916', 17; AN F, 13569, CGT, Comité Confédéral, min. 7 Nov. 1916; *Le Populaire*, 6–12 Nov. 1916; for the text of the accord, see *Rapports des comités ... pour l'exercice 1914–1918*, 22–3.

1915, observed that the question would have to be handled carefully to avoid 'the inconvenience which might arise from the brusque transplantation of yellow and black men'.[71] As we have seen, ministers were keen to keep the CGT informed about the recruitment of workers abroad, and they granted the confederation a place on the Commission Nationale de Place-ment and the inter-ministerial manpower commission as both of these bodies tried jointly to control the whole field of labour resources in 1916–18.[72]

Jouhaux's plan for regulating foreign labour—after first being endorsed (like the parallel guidelines on women workers) by the Commission Mixte pour le Maintien du Travail of the Seine—provoked the main debate on the issue in the Commission Nationale de Placement.[73] There were divergences. The Com-mission side-stepped the CGT's idea that formal inter-govern-mental accords on labour migration should be included in the peace treaty at the conclusion of the war. It also refused to accord immigrants the right to engage in all forms of trade union activity. But the central principles, that immigration should be regulated and that the national labour force should be protected through guarantees on equal wages and conditions, were accep-ted. It was also agreed that the public labour placement system was the natural mechanism for distributing immigrant labour, and that the Commission Nationale de Placement itself might act as the national regulatory body demanded by the CGT.[74]

Nor was the consensus confined to principles. Official fears of working-class hostility to immigration lay explicitly behind the Franco-Italian accord negotiated by Albert Thomas in mid-1916, which stipulated equal wages and conditions. The inter-ministerial manpower commission became the principal agency

[71] AN 94 AP 135, note from the minister of War, 17 Dec. 1915. Métin, minister of Labour, replied confirming that the protection of domestic French labour was of paramount concern and outlining plans to stagger the arrival of non-white workers to avoid racial tension (ibid., n. of 4 Mar. 1916).

[72] See pp. 71–2 above; AN F₇ 13569, CGT, Comité Confédéral, 8 Apr. 1916; AN 94 AP 135, n. of 25 July 1916 on meeting of CGT with Métin; AN F₇ 12891, 'Le Mouvement syndicaliste, année 1916', 14–15.

[73] J. Borderel, 'La Main-d'œuvre étrangère à la commission mixte du départe-ment de la Seine', *Le Parlement et l'opinion*, Nov. 1916, pp. 1108–17; IFHS, 14 AS 213a, no. 4 (Fonds Picart), min. of Commission Nationale de Placement.

[74] IFHS, 14 AS 213a, no. 4 (Fonds Picart), min. of Commission Nationale de Placement, 17 Nov. 1916.

for ensuring its implementation and drafting comparable contractual agreements with other immigrant groups.[75] The Commission des Traités Internationaux du Travail set up by the
Ministry of Labour in 1917 under Arthur Fontaine had the
explicit function of working out bilateral labour treaties covering immigration among other subjects. With the addition of
labour and business representatives, it played a crucial role in
preparing the immigration agreements negotiated in April and
September 1919 with Poland and Italy respectively, and which
broadly conformed to the CGT's policy.[76] It is clear, therefore,
that the CGT's views, underscored by the possibility of popular disaffection (and in 1917–18 there were several serious race
riots), influenced the manner in which foreign labour was
recruited by the state.

The acute labour shortage produced by the war, the fact that
only the state was in a position to organize the importation of
much of the foreign labour, and the state's direct intervention
in the labour market, made central government control over the
use of women and foreigners on war work acceptable to a broad
spectrum of opinion. The reality was fairly chaotic. But ministers, officials, and some employers could share the CGT's basic
contention that only such regulation ensured a minimum protection for skilled males as well as for women and foreigners,
while maximizing the recruitment to the war effort from these
vital sources. At the same time, CGT leaders relied on the state
to help implement their policy since they clearly felt ambivalent
about organizing the two categories—despite their formal pro-
testations. Notwithstanding the campaign of the Comité Intersyndical contre l'Exploitation de la Femme, craft barriers
impeded the unionization of women in engineering, and there is
no evidence of a concerted national drive to organize non-
European immigrants.

---

[75] AN 94 AP 135, n. of 25 July 1916. In reply to a letter from Jouhaux about
immigrants in Oct. 1916, Métin assured him that 'Nothing has been, nor will be,
done without the bodies on which we desired the participation of the representatives of labour organizations being kept informed' (94 AP 135, n. of 2 Oct. 1916).
For another view of the consensus, see Cross, 'Towards Social Peace and Prosperity', 617–19.

[76] *Bulletin du ministère du travail*, 1919, append., 'Commission des traités
internationaux de travail'; ibid. (Jan.–Feb. 1920), pp. 20–5; Cross, 'Towards Social
Peace and Prosperity', 622–3; id., *Immigrant Workers in Industrial France*, 46–55.

Yet the convergence of syndicalist and official views on women and foreign workers was far from total. There were, for example, important undercurrents of disagreement even within the apparent wartime consensus on the French economy's long-term dependence on foreign labour. Many *patrons* were converted from their pre-war preference for a free market in immigrant labour to state recruitment and regulation, but more in the interests of securing a ready labour supply than for the social reforms which interested the CGT. The umbrella business lobby organization founded in 1915, the Association Nationale d'Expansion Économique (ANEE), treated immigration as one of the major questions confronting it. But although accepting the need for equal wages to be specified in advance through fixed-term contracts in order to protect French workers, it envisaged no role for organized labour in the immigration process, ignored the question of trade union rights for foreign workers, and emphasized the danger that 'morally' (i.e. politically) undesirable immigrants might be allowed in.[77]

More importantly still, the real wages of women and foreigners were, despite Thomas's declared policy, often less than those of French males. Equal pay could be side-stepped by ascribing whole categories of work to women and foreigners within a reorganized labour process. Or it could be ignored. Adequate inspection and independent control of private employers, or even of state arsenals, was difficult in a vast and hastily assembled munitions effort, where maximum production for the national defence was the overriding priority. Women's wages remained below those of men (even on comparable work)—though the gap narrowed in 1917–18—while the colonial and Chinese workers in state arsenals (at least down to 1917) received much less than French workers, despite the equality of treatment stipulated in their contracts.[78]

The government undoubtedly alleviated some of the worst conditions in crowded munitions centres by building barracks for both women and foreigners, and by providing or subsidizing

[77] P. de Rousiers, 'Régime des travailleurs étrangers en France', *L'Expansion économique*, June 1917; H. D. Peiter, 'Men of Goodwill: French Businessmen and the First World War (Ph.D., Michigan, 1973), 190 ff.
[78] March, *Mouvement des prix et des salaires*, 287–95; Horne, 'Immigrant Workers in France', 76–7; Robert, 'Women and Work in France', 259.

various social facilities (crèches, canteens, etc.). But the poor living and working conditions of both groups remained evident until the end of the war, and were underlined in 1917–18 by racial tensions and by the involvement of women in strikes.

CGT leaders therefore continued to feel vulnerable to both groups, and especially to immigrants, as skilled workers were 'combed out' for the front in the last year of the war, under the loi Mourier of August 1917. In February 1918, for example, Loucheur had formally to reassure the Fédération des Métaux, who accused him of planning the mass importation of mobilized Italian workers, that only French nationals would replace engineering workers sent to the trenches.[79] For the post-war future, strict state regulation of the labour market, with active syndicalist participation, seemed merely the indispensable minimum in order to protect organized labour against changes in the labour force and the labour process of which syndicalist leaders remained deeply critical.

(iv) Defending the Skilled Worker: Technology, Taylorism, and the Labour Process

The thrust of CGT policy was to make the *capacités profession-nelles* of the skilled worker the key human factor in the economic war effort. For this reason, the Comité Confédéral and the Commission Exécutive of the Fédération des Métaux supported the Dalbiez law of August 1915, since it sought to ensure that only genuine skilled workers were returned from front to factory, while resisting as far as was decently possible the reverse 'combing out' of young skilled workers, which culminated in the Mourier Law of August 1917. As Jouhaux tersely summed it up in September 1917:

We must produce, and for that men are indispensable . . . The national defence will not be disorganized simply because several hundred thousand workers are withdrawn from combat units in order to make the land productive, to extract coal and minerals, to activate machines![80]

---

[79] *L'Union des métaux*, Jan. 1918, and SHAT 10 N 63, rep. of deputy Abel Ferry, for the metalworkers' accusations; *Bulletin des usines de guerre*, 18 Feb. 1918, p. 343, for Loucheur's circular.

[80] 'Production-richesses', *La Bataille*, 24 Sept. 1917.

The CGT leaders were supported in this view by Albert Thomas, who repudiated the idea that large numbers of war workers could be retrieved for combat without damaging munitions' production and the country's industrial future.[81]

What the CGT leaders meant by the full use of the skilled worker is illustrated by the question of dock labour. By the spring of 1915, French ports were badly congested as a workforce decimated by mobilization tried vainly to cope with an explosion of imports. Labour leaders argued that dock reorganization could play a key role in easing the coal shortage and the general rise in prices. As early as January 1915, Jouhaux called for the expansion and modernization of the ports, with the preservation of the dock labour force, plus the development of railways and canals, in order to endow France with a modern distributive system. The war seemed to provide a stimulus for the modernization of a key element of the French economy, provided this was not thwarted by business interests. Commenting on the congested ports, Jouhaux asked:

Are we going to experience a profound transformation of our methods of production? Is the *patronat* going to leave behind its routine practices? Will we live through a veritable industrial renaissance?[82]

Early in June 1915, Sembat advised Jouhaux that the employers in the Channel ports were introducing Chinese labour, threatening both the skilled labour grades and the unions. Jouhaux and Clément Vignaud,[83] secretary of the dockers' federation, went immediately to organize the docks at Rouen and Le Havre.[84] In Le Havre, the local union offered to co-operate with the Chamber of Commerce, which co-ordinated the port's activity, by organizing and training inexperienced workers to replace the 70 per cent loss of dockers to the army. It also proposed a general modernization, with additional cranes, and the protection of the established work-force by the return of the mobilized dockers plus an increase in wages. The

---

[81] Horne, 'L'Impôt du Sang: Republican Rhetoric and Industrial Warfare', 201–23.

[82] *La Bataille syndicaliste*, 4 Jan. 1915.

[83] (1866–1931) from the Charente-Inférieure, Vignaud worked in factories and as a docker, becoming secretary general of the Bourse du Travail of La Pallice, near La Rochelle, from 1907 to 1912, and national secretary of the Fédération des Ports et Docks from 1912 until at least 1925.

[84] AN F₇ 13574, rep. 14 June 1915.

suggestions were ignored.[85] On 11 August 1915, Jouhaux advanced a national version of this plan which included a joint office, attached to the Ministry of Public Works, through which employers and trade unionists would rationalize the ports, with the unions supplying the labour.[86]

The CGT plan was not accepted, and the organization of the docks remained contentious for the remainder of the war.[87] But Vignaud and Jouhaux's approach prefigured the CGT leadership's views more generally on the wartime role of the skilled worker. A number of union leaders demanded the 'rationalization' of their industries under the stimulus of war, by which they meant technical and administrative modernization based on higher wages and productivity plus shorter hours, in the planning of which organized labour would play a crucial role. Thus, as we have seen, the Fédération du Sous-Sol pinned its hopes of expanding coal production both on the return of mobilized miners and on the modernization of the mines.[88] Casimir Bartuel,[89] secretary of the miners, summarized this programme in March 1917 as:

Wages matching needs and the daily expenditure of effort; the rational utilization of time, tools, and equipment; ... the recognition of the workers' rights and a due measure of workers' control in the running of the mines.[90]

In a similar vein, as the transport crisis became acute in 1916, the moderate leaders of the railwaymen and their parliamentary

[85] C. Vignaud, 'La Main-d'œuvre dans les ports', *La Bataille syndicaliste*, 10 July 1915; C. Lepilliez, 'Les Ouvriers et le mouvement ouvrier du Havre de 1914 à 1927' (Maîtrise diss., Rouen, 1972), 63–82.

[86] *La Bataille syndicaliste*, 11 Aug. and 20 Sept. 1915.

[87] See various reports in AN F$_{14}$ 11333, minutes of the Commission interministérielle de la main-d'œuvre.

[88] Bureau Fédéral of the Fédération du Sous-Sol, 'La Hausse des charbons', *La Bataille*, 2 July 1916; 'La Crise du charbon', ibid., 24 Nov. 1916; and 'La Main-d'oeuvre dans les Mines', ibid., 22 Dec. 1916; *Fédération nationale des travailleurs du sous-sol, Compte rendu officiel des travaux du 3e congrès national extraordinaire, 23–6 mars 1917* (Imprimerie des Travailleurs Réunis, Carmaux, 1917), 21–7.

[89] (1869–1946) born in the Aveyron, Bartuel worked as a coal miner in the Loire, where he became secretary of the regional miners' federation. An 'independent reformist socialist', he became secretary of the national federation in 1911. He retained this position throughout the war and was a leading reformist within the CGT.

[90] C. Bartuel, 'Richesse des houilles', *La Bataille*, 25 Mar. 1917.

spokesmen (notably Marcel Cachin) demanded the return of skilled personnel from the army, higher wages, and reduced hours (there was evidence of train crews working a sixteen-hour stretch), and the upgrading of equipment and standardization of procedures across all the railway companies. They also demanded that the unions be consulted over these changes.[91] When the first congress of the unified Fédération Nationale des Cheminots was held in January 1917, its concluding resolution stated that:

the personnel is in no way responsible for the transport crisis; the collaboration of delegates of the personnel, designated by the Federation, with the power to carry out enquiries and to monitor changes . . . is the only way of making appreciable improvements in the deplorable situation of the transport system.[92]

Generally, CGT leaders termed these various changes the 'reorganization of work'. To the extent that the industrial mobilization held up a mirror to French economic backwardness, mechanization and more integrated production were advocated as the key to the munitions effort and to a dynamic postwar industrial economy based on high wages. Technological evolution and working-class prosperity were seen to be inseparable. The concept of the 'reorganization of work' was used both to condemn the 'routine practices' and cosy cartels ('economic Malthusianism') held to characterize pre-war French business, and to encapsulate the CGT's fundamental demand that the industrial war effort should be founded on the *capacités professionnelles* of the skilled worker and involvement of the labour movement. As such, it became a leitmotiv of Jouhaux and other labour leaders in 1915–16. As the Comité Confédéral of the CGT put it in a circular issued in the winter of 1915–16:

To prepare the intensification of production in all fields is to work for the growth of the general good, it is to favour [our] winning greater, deeper improvements . . . To show that the introduction of technical perfections is practicable, that through it, new resources will be

---

[91] M. Bidegaray, *Contre les compagnies: pour la nation* (1917), with preface by Marcel Cachin; AN F₇ 12891, 'Le Mouvement syndicaliste, année 1916', 77–81; E. Le Guéry, 'Emploi rationnel des forces ouvrières chez les cheminots', *La Bataille*, 22 Sept. 1916.

[92] *La Bataille*, 29 Jan. 1917.

unleashed without demanding excessive and depressing work from the human motor, that is to do a syndicalist's work.[93]

Munitions production and the engineering industry were the fundamental test for this approach. It was here that the pace of technological advance was fastest, and also that the greatest threat to skilled workers lay, from non-skilled operatives and from changes in the production process. During the war, the new 'American methods' which had already menaced skilled engineering workers before 1914 became widely publicized, and were applied (often incompletely) in certain sectors, especially vehicle production and the state arsenals. 'Dilution' of skilled work (that is, the intensification of the division of labour) was the most widespread development, but it was closely related to greater mechanization of production (more specialized lathes, pneumatic hammers, etc.), and to more integrated production processes, with mechanical lifting and transport and, in some cases, assembly lines. The 'scientific management' advocated by the French disciples of Taylor, such as le Chatelier, which promised to raise productivity by 'rationalizing' human movements, was particularly ventilated. Under the collective appellation of the 'rational organization of work', these new methods were discussed by engineers, industrialists, and officials.[94] Albert Thomas was one of their principal champions in government, advocating them tirelessly in the *Bulletin des usines de guerre*, and requesting his officials to investigate the applicability of Taylorism and other forms of 'scientific management' to the state arsenals.[95]

There was a considerable overlap in theme between the labour idea of the 'reorganization of work' and this debate on 'American methods', and the former must in part be seen as a response to

---

[93] *La Bataille syndicaliste*, 18 Oct. 1915.

[94] See Bibliography, Secondary Works, part 1.

[95] R. F. Kuisel, *Capitalism and the State in Modern France: Renovation and Economic Management in the Twentieth Century* (CUP, Cambridge, 1981), 34–7; Fridenson, 'The Impact of the First World War on French Workers', 237–8. For examples of Thomas's views, see 'L'Initiative industrielle', *Bulletin des usines de guerre*, 15 May 1916, p. 17, and his circular, 'Pour augmenter le rendement de la main-d'œuvre', *Bulletin des usines de guerre*, 8 May 1916, p. 11. Thomas asked Arthur Fontaine to look into Taylorism, etc. (min. permanent section of the Commission Consultative du Travail, 5th sess., 23 Aug. 1916, AN 94 AP 122).

the latter. But there was no simple productivist consensus in the engineering industry between industrialists, technocrats, and labour leaders. Merrheim, for example, confirmed his conversion just before the war to a critical acceptance of 'Taylorism'. In a special issue of *L'Œuvre économique* in June 1917 devoted to the subject, he considered that 'a rational, intelligent use of manpower is obligatory unless we want to see the failure of our industry'. But he condemned the manipulation of movement measurement and productivity bonuses to exploit workers, when workers should be the principal beneficiaries.[96]

This was the key distinction. For CGT leaders, the 'reorganization of work' was to lessen, not increase, exploitation as they understood it, by reducing hours and raising wages. But the munitions effort was not a model experiment in the new methods. As we have already seen, the agreement in principle between Albert Thomas and labour leaders that the social protection of workers should not be suspended but stepped up during the war, that wage levels should be protected against inflation, and that organized labour should be consulted over the industrial mobilization, produced a good deal of discord in practice. The CGT (Jouhaux as well as Merrheim) became increasingly sceptical of Thomas's ability, when driven by the imperative of maximizing engineering production, to impose the controls necessary to protect labour, and especially to protect the skilled male.[97]

The fields in which the skilled male was under threat were interconnected. The use of foreign and female labour in new areas, the erosion of apprenticeships (a major preoccupation of the CGT delegates on the Commission Mixte pour le Maintien du Travail of the Seine in 1915), the reduction of wage differentials between skilled time-rates and semi-skilled piece-rates, and the growth in 'arbitrary acts' (that is, in the reinforcement of authoritarian power in the work-place, notably with military sanctions), all helped undermine the skill and sense of

---

[96] A. Merrheim, 'Notes sur le système Taylor', *L'Œuvre économique*, 10 June 1917.

[97] See, in particular, the minutes of the Commission Exécutive of the Fédération des Métaux (IFHS 14 AS 219) and Jouhaux's interventions on the Commission Consultative du Travail (AN 94 AP 122).

status of the male syndicalist.[98] But at the core of this preoccupation lay the changes in the production processes themselves, especially (though not exclusively) in the engineering and metallurgical sector. Thus, in July 1915, both Merrheim and Dubreuil, secretary of the Union des Mécaniciens de la Seine, argued to the Commission de l'Armée of the Sénat that only the preservation of skilled wage differentials could ensure increased output. A police report of the same date noted that:

the introduction into France of numerous, perfected machines from America is not liked by the workers who are certain that the *patrons* are getting the war administration to pay them their new machinery which, after the war, will restrict the need for labour.[99]

In the spring of 1916, the Fédération des Métaux formulated these criticisms in a circular, *A la classe ouvrière organisée: à l'opinion publique*. It rolled the manipulation of the labour market, new manufacturing techniques, and profiteering on state contracts, into a comprehensive indictment. The circular denounced

the wages, generally insufficient, which are paid especially to mobilized workers who, being under military authority, cannot defend themselves by ordinary means, whereas the *patrons* are given all the credit they need to improve their plant, thus allowing them to gain a triple profit, from the exploitation of women and mobilized labour, from increased output from the [new] machinery, and from the scandalous prices paid for *matériel* and munitions.[100]

From early 1916, the Comité Conféderal of the CGT conducted its own campaign, parallel to that of the Fédération des Métaux, to publicize munitions workers' grievances.[101] We

---

[98] For apprenticeship, on which the CGT delegates presented a comprehensive report, see *Travaux des commissions mixtes départementales pour le maintien du travail national*, i, *Seine*, 28.

[99] AN F₇ 13366, rep. 24 July 1915.

[100] *L'Union des métaux*, 63, May 1916, p. 3.

[101] IFHS 14 AS 219, Commission Exécutive, Fédération des Métaux, min. 5 Feb. 1916, circular from the CGT, applying a decision of the Comité Confédéral of 31 Dec. 1915, to all syndicats in engineering asking them to be 'the intermediaries between (the Comité Confédéral) and the mobilized workers in the metallurgical factories and in all industries working for the national defence', over questions of wages, conditions, changes in the labour process, and so on. This angered Merrheim who felt it implied that the Fédération des Métaux had done nothing. See also AN F₇ 12891, 'Le Mouvement syndicaliste, année 1916', pp. 8–10, and Rosmer, *Le Mouvement ouvrier pendant la première guerre mondiale*, ii. 168.

have already noted that after a fleeting and rather stormy
presence, the syndicalist delegates finally quit Albert Thomas's
Commission Consultative du Travail.[102] By spring 1917, and
prompted by the first serious strikes, Jouhaux proclaimed that
the obvious crisis of the working-class consumer was now
matched by the acute dissatisfaction of the industrial worker,
especially in munitions. The discrepancy between the 'reorganization of work', seen as the ideal of a munitions effort founded
on the skilled worker, and the reality of the new manufacturing
arrangements, formed the core of Jouhaux's case, namely, that
the industrial mobilization should be the catalyst for the introduction of a new industrial order, combining high productivity
with increased working-class living-standards and with an
unprecedented role for syndicalism in organizing industrial
production and curbing the authority of the *patronat*.

Work is poorly organized everywhere and it must be reformed, and
not only in the domain of the state . . .
New methods, progress, will only penetrate to the extent that their
management is undertaken by a technical administration in which
workers' delegates collaborate.
To associate all the forces of production in equal discussion and
decision-making is to ensure the effective implementation [of the new
methods] and better output.
So long as the conditions of work, the allocation of the machinery,
the remuneration of the work-force, remain the prerogative of the
patronat's will alone, things will continue to go from bad to worse
until, suddenly they snap . . .
Let labour play a major role, let production be scientifically and
humanely organized, and there will be a better utilization of forces,
preventing progress appearing to be the worker's enemy.[103]

Precisely because the authority of the industrialist was the
principal enemy, the issue of 'worker control', meaning at its
minimum official syndicalist involvement in reorganizing the
production process, became acute. The Fédération des Métaux,
as we have seen, condemned the Dalbiez commissions,
designed to vet the munitions labour force for bogus skilled
workers, or *embusqués*, because the commissions lacked genuine
independence. Both the *métaux* and the CGT *majoritaires* by

---

[102] See pp. 70–1, above.
[103] L. Jouhaux, 'L'Intervention de l'état', *La Bataille*, 30 Mar. 1917.

1917 insisted on the need for a local level of syndicalist 'control' in workshop and factory which would provide the instrument for ensuring that unavoidable changes in industrial organization were not fundamentally detrimental to the skilled males who remained the core of the CGT's social constituency.

Almost from the outset, French labour leaders responded to the war not just as a national cause but as a succession of economic and social problems specifically affecting the working class. These included the severe but short-lived unemployment crisis of autumn 1914, the difficulties faced by working-class consumers, the changes wrought by the industrial mobilization in the labour market, and a substantially modified production process, especially in the engineering industry. These problems stimulated syndicalist and socialist leaders to propose solutions reflecting their view of labour's interests. They also prompted organizational experimentation with the advocacy of various *commissions mixtes* or *paritaires*, to institutionalize labour participation in the economic mobilization, and with the establishment of the Comité d'Action to bridge the historic cleavage between the PS and the CGT. All of this amounted to a highly pragmatic and essentially defensive response to the experience of war. But the very preoccupation with new defence strategies for the skilled worker and therefore with an alternative, critical view of the industrial mobilization, contained in embryo a broader reorientation of action and ideology.

4 Planning the Post-War World: The French Labour Movement and Reform, 1915–1916

A NUMBER of French labour leaders considered that, for all their immediacy, the social problems spawned by the war had not merely a broader but specifically a post-war relevance. Out of this view developed a tendency to consider the war's wider significance for the future of society. The experience by labour leaders of August 1914 as a moment of ideological dislocation reinforced this tendency. As the sense of overwhelming emergency occasioned by the outbreak of war gave way to the feeling that the war was a new normality, a semi-permanent state, labour leaders began to probe the future by its unfamiliar light, searching for threads of continuity. In so doing, they tried to relate the major features of the war from their perspective—the political self-mobilization of organized labour, the munitions effort, the possibilities for peace—to past doctrines and to the more permanent preoccupations of organized labour. The more the war became a protracted, complex process, the more insistently it seemed to pose the question of how, and how much, it would permanently alter the pre-war world. In differing degrees, labour leaders and the central institutions of the CGT, the PS and the co-operative movement sought answers to this question as a corollary to their participation in the national effort.

(i) The CGT and the 'Economic Reorganization' of Post-War France

One of the first ways in which the general question of the post-war future presented itself to labour leaders was over the physical reconstruction of the north-east, a problem already created by the devastation left in the wake of the German retreat from the Marne. It threatened to assume major proportions after the war, not least because so much of French industrial capacity was contained within the occupied and fighting zones. Much of the more general debate, which was lively in parliament and elsewhere, turned on whether the state was liable to pay indemnities for war damage and on whether individuals receiving these had a corresponding obligation to use them as part of a general reconstruction effort. Governments did little to go beyond this legal wrangle and prepare either the content or the administration of a reconstruction programme.[1]

Socialists, syndicalists, and *coopérateurs*, on the other hand, were interested from the start in doing just that. In June 1915, the Comité d'Action published a report on the *Reconstruction des Cités Détruites*, prepared by a specially established subcommittee, the moving force behind which was Achille Picart,[2] secretary of a small white-collar union in the Fédération du Bâtiment and prominent in the federation's moderate wartime leadership.[3] The report underpinned the labour campaign, whose originality lay in viewing the reconstruction of the northeast as a possible microcosm of the benefits which might be derived more generally from the social and economic changes wrought by the war. The Comité d'Action's report subordinated the question of indemnities to the state's social responsibility to the region as a whole. It urged the government to use the wartime destruction to eliminate for good the worst social problems of a heavily industrial region through reforms in housing, town planning, and public hygiene.

[1] W. MacDonald, *Reconstruction in France* (Macmillan, 1922), 34–58; *Journal officiel, chambre des députés, documents parlementaires*, 1916, no. 2345, pp. 1175–242 ('Rapport fait au nom de la commission des dommages de guerre').

[2] (1878–1962) a quantity surveyor, Picart became secretary of the Syndicat des Dessinateurs in 1907, and a member of the Commission Exécutive of the Fédération du Bâtiment in 1913. Revolutionary syndicalist before the war, and reformist during it, he played an important role in the inter-war labour movement.

[3] *Reconstruction des cités détruites et dommages de guerre; Rapport ... 1915*, 15; *Rapport ... 1916*, 13–14. The subcommittee had 10 members, 7 from the CGT (Jouhaux, Picart, Merrheim, Chanvin, Doumencq, secretary of the Dessinateurs et graveurs en bois, the railway workers' leader, Toulouse, and Michaud, of the Plombiers et couvreurs), 2 from the Socialists (Braemer and Sellier), and Daudé-Bancel from the FNCC.

The justification was only in part greater social equality. The reconstruction of the north-east was seen as one of the means of solving the problem of reconversion to a peacetime economy. It was also to be a working demonstration of the fundamental thesis of Jouhaux and the CGT that modernized production and the enlarged demand coming from a prosperous, high-wage working class, were in tandem the best guarantors of post-war industrial prosperity.

Advantage must be taken of the wholesale destruction of a large number of towns and villages in order to reconstruct these urban areas in accordance with new needs, modern standards of traffic regulation, hygiene and aesthetics. Our generation would never be forgiven if . . . it did not raise up healthier, more beautiful and more gay cities . . .

[This reconstruction] would rapidly draw the whole country in its wake, towards a new and intensive phase in the development of our national prosperity, towards new levels of economic, political, and social progress.[4]

The plan also envisaged an entire structure of regional and local organizations—*commissions mixtes* on the grand scale— through which the major economic forces would participate in planning the reconstruction. By this means, syndicalism was to entrench its control over the labour supply, working conditions, and wage-rates.

The Comité d'Action, socialist deputies, and the CGT lobbied government and parliament throughout the war on this programme.[5] But officialdom avoided any commitment to this kind of ambitious social planning, and, for labour leaders, the reconstruction of the north-east was perhaps most important as a symbol of the wider post-war world. This was especially the case among the *majoritaires* of the CGT. Two incidents in particular illustrate the extent to which they gave serious thought to the shape of post-war France as it might emerge from the trauma of war.

The first was the launching of *La Bataille* in November 1915. *La Bataille syndicaliste*, the daily paper of the CGT founded in

---

[4] *Reconstruction des cités*, 4–5.

[5] AN F₇ 13571, rep. Comité d'Action, 14 Mar. 1916; *Journal officiel, chambre des députés, documents parlementaires*, 1916, no. 2345, p. 1187 ('Rapport fait au nom de la commission des dommages de guerre'); see also Picart's articles in *La Bataille*, 4 and 6 Nov. 1916.

1911 with trade unions as its principal shareholders, was wound up in the autumn of 1915. With its print-run halved to just over 20,000 following the mobilization, restarting the paper with individuals as shareholders was a means of protecting reduced union funds from liability for the paper's debts.[6] But it was also a political manoeuvre. The new paper fell firmly under the control of Jouhaux and his allies, who confirmed the exclusion of *minoritaire* views which had already been apparent—and bitterly resented—in preceding months.[7] Hinting strongly that some of the funding for the new paper came from Malvy's secret funds, the executive of the Métaux refused all dealings with it.[8]

But *La Bataille* also marked an important moment in the developing concern of CGT leaders with the consequences of the war. A *Déclaration* appeared in the first number on 3 November, which argued that the role of the paper was to preserve open communications within the syndicalist movement so that it could anticipate and exploit to the full the malleable circumstances of the post-war world—'Let us hope

[6] AN F₇ 13574, rep. 25 Jan. 1915. For the relaunching of *La Bataille*, the main sources are AN F₇ 13574, reps. Sept.–Nov. 1915; AN F₇ 12891, 'Le Mouvement syndicaliste, année 1916', 129–34; IFHS 14 AS 219, Commission Exécutive, Fédération des Métaux, min. 2 Oct. 1915; R. Rolland, *Journal des années de guerre, 1914–1919* (Albin Michel, 1952), 525–8; and documents in Rosmer, *Le Mouvement ouvrier pendant la première guerre mondiale*, i. 67–9. See also Georges and Tintant, *Léon Jouhaux*, i. 420–9; and C. Gras, *Alfred Rosmer et le mouvement révolutionnaire international* (Maspero, 1971), 142–3.

[7] AN F₇ 13574, rep. 27 Sept. 1915. Some of the most vehement criticisms at the final shareholders' meeting on 26 Sept. 1915 came from Desbois, an anarchist and former editor of Hervé's *La Guerre sociale*, and his mistress, Marcelle Capy, both of whom claimed to have been censored by Marie and Grandidier, two of the editors. Capy circulated her denunciation as a brochure. For a graphic portrayal of the chaos and acrimony of the meeting, see Rosmer's letter to Monatte in C. Chambelland and J. Maitron (eds.), *Syndicalisme révolutionnaire et communisme: les archives de Pierre Monatte* (Maspero, 1968), 205–6.

[8] Merrheim claimed on several occasions that *La Bataille (syndicaliste)* received Malvy's subventions (AN F₇ 13574, reps of 27 May and 2 Dec. 1915). The police report, 'Le Mouvement syndicaliste, année 1916' (AN F₇ 12891), concluded its section on *La Bataille*: 'Like many papers born during the war, it is at the mercy of the "special aid" which will not be extended beyond certain limits and a certain period.' The 'special aid' in question was almost certainly the subvention of the Ministry of the Interior. On the suggestion of H. Dubreuil, the Métaux executive published a condemnation of the new paper (IFHS 14 AS 219, Commission Exécutive, Fédération des Métaux, 6 Nov. 1915). Merrheim's handwritten draft of the tract is in the same collection.

that tomorrow there will be an economic resurgence matched by a resurgence of labour, for which we must be ready.' The *Déclaration* was signed by seventy trade unionists, more than twenty of whom were members of the Comité Confédéral.[9]

The press remained an important expression of the syndicalist preoccupation with reform. Not only did *La Bataille* carry numerous articles on the subject, but in 1917, when its financial future again seemed threatened, the paper issued a brochure entitled *La Bataille dans la Bataille* which appealed for new subscribers by re-dedicating the paper to the cause of post-war reform.[10] A monthly journal, *La Clairière*, was founded at the same period (1 August 1917) in order to provide a more reflective approach to the same questions. One of its two administrators, Marcel Laurent,[11] was closely associated with Jouhaux, becoming assistant secretary of the CGT in 1918. The first issue described the journal's aim as 'dissipating the befogged atmosphere' of the pre-war CGT and building on the wartime strength of the syndicalist movement in order to prepare the country's 'economic renaissance'. The bulk of the articles in *La Clairière* concerned wartime problems and post-war reform, and were written principally by *majoritaires* from the Comité Confédéral, though professional journalists and writers also contributed, such as François Depré, Pierre Hamp,

[9] The 'Déclaration' was also circulated as a brochure. The signatories who were beyond doubt members of the Comité Confédéral were: Charbonnier and Chanvin (Bâtiment), Lefevre (Bijoux), Le Guéry (Diamantaires), Fénot (Employés), Michaud (Plombiers), Dumas (Habillement), Gauthier (Inscrits Maritimes), Puyjalon and Vignaud (Ports et Docks), Bled (Union Départementale de la Seine), Charlier (Sciage-façonnage), Guinchard, Jaccoud, and Quillent (Moyens de Transport), Toulouse and Thierry (Chemins de Fer), Picart (Bâtiment), Doumenq (Dessinateurs et graveurs en bois), Jouhaux, Calvayrac (assistant secretary of the CGT), and Guibert (Passementiers à la main).

[10] IFHS 14 AS 213 f (34). The leading *majoritaires* of the Comité Confédéral writing in *La Bataille* were Dumas, Le Guéry, Lefevre, Picart, Guinchard, and, less often, Bled and Chanvin (the last-mentioned used the building workers' paper, *Le Travailleur du bâtiment*, as a *majoritaire* organ). From 1916, Bartuel, of the miners, and Bidegaray, of the railwaymen, also contributed. Jouhaux, however, appeared most frequently.

[11] (1887–1966). From the Seine-et-Oise, Laurent was a grocery shopworker and active in Parisian syndicalism. Mobilized as a nurse, he was back in Paris by 1917, from which point he became a leading moderate in the CGT. From 1918 to 1923, he was assistant secretary of the CGT and in Dec. 1918 he succeeded Savoie as secretary of the Fédération de l'Alimentation.

Léon Harmel, and Maxime Leroy, as did some international figures, including Kropotkin.[12] In effect, *La Clairière* acted as the theoretical mouthpiece of the majority in the last sixteen months of the war and subsequently. In 1918, majority CGT leaders also wrote for *L'Information ouvrière et sociale*, the paper founded by Albert Thomas and Charles Dulot, an official at the Ministry of Labour, as a forum for official, business, and labour views on economic and social reform.[13] But this was simply an additional string to a doctrinal and journalistic preoccupation with post-war reform which had been sounding through the CGT majority's own press for three years.

The second incident illustrating this preoccupation was rather different. In early March 1916, Jouhaux accepted an invitation to address a banquet of one of the leading employers' organizations, the Fédération des Industriels et des Commerçants Français, in order to give 'a labour point of view on the economic reorganization of tomorrow'. The result, published as a brochure by the Comité Confédéral, became instantly notorious in *minoritaire* eyes as a candid confession of Jouhaux's betrayal of revolutionary syndicalist principles, and it has been accepted ever since as a touchstone of his personal evolution during the war.[14]

To the rather angry meeting of the Comité Confédéral following the speech, as well as in his introduction to the brochure, Jouhaux stressed that it was a purely personal statement. In reality it had a larger significance. On 4 March, the day of the banquet, a secret meeting of *majoritaires* discussed the threat from *minoritaire* pacifist propaganda, and notably from the periodic *Lettres aux abonnés de la vie ouvrière*.[15] Jouhaux announced that he had accepted the invitation to the banquet in order to 'dispel the legend which presents the CGT as a bunch of ranters', and he read out his speech to general

---

[12] The principal union leaders writing in *La Clairière* were Jouhaux, Bartuel, Dumas, Savoie, Luquet, Keufer, Lefevre, Bled, Cnudde (Textile), Dret (Cuirs-et-Peaux), Picart, Réaud (Inscrits Maritimes), Guinchard, Toulouse, Hodée (Horticulteurs), Laurent, and Rambaud (of the Coiffeurs)—in short, many of the most prominent *majoritaires*.

[13] Fine, 'Towards Corporatism', 35–40.

[14] For the instant condemnation of Jouhaux by the *minoritaires*, see AN F₇ 13569, CGT, Comité Confédéral, min. 11 Mar. 1916; AN F₇ 12891, 'Le Mouvement syndicaliste, année 1916', 26–8; and *L'Union des métaux*, no. 61, May 1916.

[15] AN F₇ 13575, rep. 6 Mar. 1916.

approval. He could not admit this subsequently without revealing the existence of the secret *majoritaire* meetings (which continued for most of the war). But the speech was not a personal whim. It was a concerted attempt to sharpen the doctrinal self-definition of the *majoritaires* at a point when pacifism was beginning to find an audience.

In his introduction to the brochure, *Une attitude, un programme*, Jouhaux marked the distance which he felt the CGT had travelled since August 1914.[16] The organized working class, he suggested, was no longer content simply to defend the positions won in peacetime against external aggression (the point of the funeral oration for Jaurès) nor even to claim specific reforms on unrelated issues arising from the war. It now required an entire programme of post-war development, related to the shock of the war, in which syndicalism itself would play a leading role.

The speech itself made three basic points. The first was Jouhaux's reply to a view widely held in business and government circles during the war, namely, that the military contest would be followed by a bitter economic conflict, in which Germany would intensify her pre-war incursions into French markets, at home and abroad. This apprehension slid easily into an economic nationalism which envisaged tariffs and a competitive scramble to modernize French industry as weapons of the trade war. The ANEE was founded as a broad business pressure group in 1915 precisely to prepare these weapons, and Clémentel, as the influential minister of Commerce from October 1915 until the end of the war, conceived his role in a similar light.[17] Even some journalists writing in *La Bataille syndicaliste* accepted these premises.

Jouhaux made it abundantly clear that he rejected them.[18] He repudiated an undue concentration on exports and especially rejected any notion that wages should be kept low and hours long in the cause of French industrial competitiveness in

---

[16] IFHS 14 AS 213 (2) 184.

[17] Peiter, *Men of Goodwill*, 71–3, 190–1; Godfrey, *Capitalism at War*.

[18] L. Jouhaux, 'Il faut préparer l'organisation', *La Bataille*, 4 Nov. 1915; cf. P. Brulat, 'Après la guerre', ibid., 19 Nov. 1915, and id., 'Le Salut est en nous', ibid., 1 Dec. 1915.

international markets. Developing the argument used in relation to foreign labour, he stressed that if industrial modernization was potentially the great legacy of the war, it should, first and foremost, benefit the working class. The benefits of higher productivity should be distributed directly to the national market in the form of higher wages and shorter hours. The industrial inadequacy starkly revealed by the munitions effort should provide the stimulus for a radical modernization at the centre of which would be the 'reorganization of work' as understood by labour leaders. And Jouhaux employed what in 1917–18 became the virtual slogan of the *majoritaires*; 'the minimum time at work for the maximum production'. If industrial reform were tackled seriously, Jouhaux felt, it would ensure international competitiveness as well as rising living standards. In any event, he argued, organized labour favoured international co-operation rather than competition between workers, as envisaged over the migration question.

Jouhaux's second point was the moral one that labour's participation in the national effort carried a reciprocal obligation by French society, notably the state and *patronat*, to concede major post-war reforms:

[The] end of hostilities must not mark a return to the [former] disavowal of the rights of the organized working class . . .

Labour must, if a real economic renewal is to occur, occupy the place in this country which is its due in the conduct of modern societies.[19]

His final point was the role he envisaged for organized labour. Again, the kernel of his perception came from the war effort. He argued that economic change was a collaborative process, in which the absolute power of capital would gradually concede a growing authority to labour in a development which Jouhaux termed 'industrial democracy'. This was really an extension of the feeling that the industrial mobilization ought to be founded on the skilled worker and his *capacités professionelles*.

The capitalist should be guided only by the concern to develop his industry in the general interest. He should see the worker as his

---

[19] *Une attitude, un programme*, 16.

collaborator, to whom he should give a great deal of liberty ... The man-machine is a poor worker ...[20]

Mindful of the ideological function of the speech, to map out some doctrinal self-definition for the CGT majority, Jouhaux also formulated this idea more broadly. He warned the industrialists that he by no means preached simple peace and an end to class conflict, nor renounced the complete transformation of society. But he suggested that class antagonism could be productively channelled and used to intensify industrial progress, since both the antagonists, capital and labour, had by their nature a common interest in modernization. Tentatively, Jouhaux was trying to recast the mobilizing myth of revolutionary syndicalism, the expropriation of capital through the general strike, as the gradual conquest by organized labour of recognition and power. This would create an 'industrial democracy' parallel to the political democracy established by the republic—and it was the economic equivalent of universal suffrage which Jouhaux hoped French labour might gain from the war. The endorsement which this hesitant redefinition received from the secret assembly of *majoritaires* and from the subsequent, acrimonious meeting of the Comité Confédéral (where publication was voted by 27 to 5, with 4 or 5 abstentions) was neither passive nor nominal, as is demonstrated by the way in which these ideas were developed during the remainder of 1916 into a full-scale programme.[21]

The Comité d'Action played a leading part in this development, reaching the pinnacle of its own importance in the process. According to its second annual report, post-war reform was 'the most important question of all those presented to us by the reality of the war.'[22] In January–February 1916, the committee discussed

the question of the organization of work on the morrow of the war and the means of intensifying the industrial production and the commercial development of the country which need, as of now, to be envisaged.[23]

[20] Ibid., 9.
[21] AN F$_7$ 13569, CGT, Comité Confédéral, 11 Mar. 1916; AN F$_7$ 12891, 'Le Mouvement syndicaliste, année 1916', 27–8.
[22] *Rapport ... 1916*, 15.
[23] *La Bataille*, 28 Jan. and 18 Feb. 1916; *L'Humanité*, 12 and 26 Feb. 1916.

But it proved so difficult to devise one plan encompassing the range of specific questions involved that in a reshuffle of the subcommittees, on 15 April 1916, a new subcommittee was established solely to consider what was termed the 'economic reorganization' of post-war France, and charged with providing a *vue d'ensemble* for the Comité d'Action's work.[24]

Almost immediately, however, the new subcommittee ran into difficulties. Since post-war reform, both practically and symbolically, explored the relationship between wartime abnormality and more permanent realities, it placed a huge weight on the wartime association between the CGT and PS, provoking nothing less than a crisis in relations between them.

Throughout 1915–16, the Comité d'Action grew in importance for CGT leaders, whereas the reopening of parliament offered the socialists a more familiar means of making their voices heard. The committee increasingly became the mouthpiece of syndicalists, *coopérateurs*, or of socialists with strong syndicalist connections. In 1916, the CGT provided half the active membership (see Table 2).[25] If attendance at one third (9) or more of 27 possible meetings indicates active participation, the CGT delegates outnumbered socialists by 10 to 8, with 2 delegates from the FNCC. Moreover, the CGT delegates were especially active in the attempt to prepare a reform programme. In the reshuffle of April 1916, they provided the secretaries of six out of ten subcommittees, as well as five out of seven members of the new 'economic reorganization' subcommittee (Jouhaux, Luquet, Bled, Merrheim, and Chanvin, the others being Lévy and Compère-Morel).[26]

[24] AN F, 13571, rep. 17 Apr. 1916; *L'Humanité*, 24 Apr. 1916.

[25] The membership list in the second annual report differs slightly from the attendance reported in *L'Humanité*. This may be because *L'Humanité* missed some meetings or because official delegates, busy elsewhere, sent substitutes. The annual report, however, does not provide attendance figures.

[26] The CGT secretaries of the reorganized subcommittees in April 1916 were Doumencq (separation allowances), Luquet (rents), Merrheim (war work), Dumas (co-operative workshops and military contracts), Jouhaux (work and wages), and Chanvin (reconstruction of the cities of the north-east). The others were Poisson, FNCC (parcels for soldiers), Lévy and Braemer (CAP of the PS), responsible for *la vie chère* and refugees respectively, and Dejeante, deputy, in charge of relations with the Groupe Socialiste. In addition to being more prominent, the syndicalist leaders were also younger, mainly in their forties (reflecting the *sursis d'appel*), whereas the socialists, in their fifties and sixties, represented an older generation (Camélinat had been Directeur de la Monnaie in the Commune).

TABLE 2. The Comité d'Action in 1916: Membership and Frequency of Attendance (out of a possible 27 Meetings)

Name	Affiliation	Attendance	Name	Affiliation	Attendance
Dubreuilh	PS	27	Longuet	PS	5
Camélinat	PS	25	Sellier	PS	5
Doumenq	CGT	25	Brétin	PS	4
Beuchard	PS	24	Daudé-Bancel	FNCC	4
Bled	CGT	24	Hubert-Rouger	PS	4
Braemer	PS	24	Marty	FNCC?	4
Chanvin	CGT	22	Roland	PS	4
Dumas	CGT	21	Bon	PS	2
Guiber	CGT	20	Chevallier	FNCC	2
Jouhaux	CGT	17	Deguise	PS	2
Merrheim	CGT	17	Ducos de la		
Luquet	CGT(PS)	16	Haille	PS	2
Chausse	PS	15	Breim	?	1
Toulouse	CGT	14	Dret	CGT	1
Brion	CGT	11	Grandvallet	PS	1
Comprère-Morel	PS	11	Guinchard	CGT	1
Dejeante	PS	11	Mauger	PS	1
Poisson	FNCC	10	Morin	PS	1
Berthaut	FNCC	9	Renaudel	PS	1
Ramadier	FNCC	7	Roldes	PS	1

Source: L'Humanité, 1916.

In addition to this growing syndicalist bias, the Comité d'Action also became critical of the socialist deputies. As early as October 1915, the rest of the committee denounced the delegates from the Groupe Socialiste for their indifference, a protest repeated in April–May 1916 as post-war reform became a major issue.[27] In mid-May, the anger of the committee (and the embarrassment of its more faithful socialist members) penetrated to the Groupe Socialiste.[28] The deputies and the committee decided to co-ordinate their approach to post-war reform, which the deputies had independently begun to consider. For a while relations improved. A new Commission Mixte d'Études Économiques was established on 20 May to draw up a joint reform programme. It consisted of the secretaries of the Comité d'Action's subcommittees and the Groupe Socialiste's own committee on post-war reform.[29]

Jouhaux clearly hoped that the Comité d'Action would be turned from a temporary wartime agency into the fulcrum of sustained co-operation between socialists, syndicalists and *coopérateurs*, stretching into the post-war world. He described this ideal to a special meeting of the Comité d'Action and of all socialist deputies early in June.

If we wish to end the unorganized state in which we currently find ourselves, and if we wish to succeed in constituting a veritable proletarian power, we will only be able to do so if we create serious links between the various organisms in which the workers are grouped. At every step we will encounter problems which have to be resolved in two ways: alongside the affirmation of socialism, envisaging a radical transformation of society, we must search for a formula applicable within the framework of existing society. Ideal solution, practical and immediate solution—that is the dual aim which should spur us on.[30]

It is easy to understand why this vision of collaboration appealed to syndicalists, to whom it promised a presence by

---

[27] AN F₇ 13571, rep. 23 Oct. 1915 and 17 Apr. 1916.

[28] Ibid., reps 16 and 22 May 1916 (on meetings held on 13 and 20 May); *L'Humanité*, 24 May and 2 June 1916, reports on the same two meetings. The Groupe Socialiste conceded the charge of negligence in attendance at the Comité d'Action, and strengthened its delegation for the second meeting, on 20 May, which mapped out the procedure for tackling post-war questions.

[29] Comité d'Action, *Rapport ... 1916*, 15–16; AN F₇ 13571, rep. 22 May 1916.

[30] AN F₇ 13571, rep. 5 June 1916.

proxy in parliament. It is equally easy to see why most socialist deputies, given the traditional divisions between the PS and the CGT, should have been less enthusiastic. A gravely depleted syndicalist movement had little to offer in return.

Although some leading deputies, such as Compère-Morel and Renaudel, were well-disposed to Jouhaux's idea, the real enthusiasts within the PS were those who were also active in, or especially sympathetic to, the CGT.[31] They constituted a distinct group on the Comité d'Action itself (see Table 2). Luquet and Gaston Lévy[32] were both prominent in the CGT and PS, and Lévy emerged as the key young protagonist of closer links between the bodies. Additionally, several of the older socialists active on the committee, Chausse, Dejeante, and Berthaut, came from a background of Allemanist or Blanquist Parisian socialism, making them particularly sympathetic to revolutionary syndicalism.[33] The significance of this link is confirmed by the role of the veteran Blanquist leader, Vaillant, on the Comité d'Action. At a funeral meeting held for him in late December 1915 by the socialist federation of the Seine, at

[31] Ibid.; J. Compère-Morel, 'Songeons à demain', *L'Humanité*, 14 Apr. 1916; P. Renaudel, 'Renaissance économique', ibid., 9 June 1916; Bourgin, *Le Parti contre la patrie*, 115.

[32] (1882–1944) born in Nancy, Lévy grew up in Paris where he became a bank clerk and founded the bankworkers' *syndicat*. He was a *majoritaire* and member of the CGT's Comité Confédéral in 1914–18. From 1905 active in the Fédération de la Seine of the PS, he became its secretary, member of the CAP, and responsible for propaganda in the party. Also an active *coopérateur*, he advocated closer links between the strands of the labour movement. At the Le Havre CGT congress in 1912, in the debate on socialist-syndicalist relations, he argued for 'maintaining the autonomy of the two forces'.

[33] Luquet, Berthaut, and Dejeante shared a common link in the socialist section of the twentieth arrondissement. Berthaut and Dejeante also shared a common turning-point in the past. Both were Allemanist municipal councillors who left the Parti Socialiste Ouvrier Révolutionnaire in 1896 in protest at the proportion of the conciliar salary which the party insisted they contribute to party funds. They formed an Alliance Communiste Révolutionnaire in close touch with the Blanquists, and in 1901 joined the Parti Socialiste de France of Guesde and Vaillant (Maitron (ed.), *Dictionnaire biographique du mouvement ouvrier français* pt. 3, *1871–1914*, xi. 334–5). For Blanquist sympathy for the CGT, see Dommanget, *Edouard Vaillant*, 178–9; Howorth, *Edouard Vaillant: la création de l'unité socialiste en France*, 195–203; Robert, 'Ouvriers et mouvement ouvrier parisiens', 1326–47. Luquet became deputy for Vaillant's old constituency in the twentieth arrondissement in 1928.

which many of the Comité d'Action were present, Jouhaux paid homage to Vaillant's influence on labour's wartime interest in 'economic democracy'.[34]

Despite these impulses of convergence, the programme of post-war reforms produced by the Commission Mixte d'Études Économiques in November 1916 was less the expression of real socialist-syndicalist collaboration than the voice at one remove of the Comité d'Action. It is difficult to establish the precise balance of influence within the Commission Mixte, but it seems certain that the Comité d'Action was the stronger partner. Although the Groupe Socialiste's own subcommittee on post-war reforms (under Bedouce and Bretin) had drawn up a list of questions before the Commission Mixte first met, it was the outline plan of the Comité d'Action's subcommittee which formed the basis of the joint discussions. Lévy later stated that the November programme followed the Comité d'Action's ideas closely, and, as we shall see, the parliamentary socialists interpreted post-war reform more restrictively.[35] Both the origins of the November programme and its content indicate that it reflected the views of the three components of the Comité d'Action—first, and most importantly, the core of CGT leaders (Jouhaux, Bled, Pierre Chanvin,[36] and probably Merrheim); secondly, figures equally active in the CGT and PS (Luquet and Lévy); and thirdly, *coopérateurs*, especially those from the 'socialist' tradition, who saw co-operation as a vehicle of social

---

[34] *L'Humanité*, 24 Dec. 1915. Vaillant had been a keen member of the Comité d'Action and actively fostered closer syndicalist links by his approach to the war effort (Dommanget, *Edouard Vaillant*, 251–7).

[35] For Lévy's opinion, see AN F$_7$ 13571, rep. 16 Jan. 1917. See also *La Bataille*, 8 June 1916, and *L'Humanité*, 9 June 1916, for reports of the meeting of the Commission Mixte on 3 June at which both Luquet and Lévy insisted that the Comité d'Action outline be used as the basis of the Commission's deliberations, rather than the questions listed by the socialist deputies. In Nov., the Commission Mixte rejected a series of amendments proposed by Bedouce (AN F$_7$ 13571, rep. 21 Nov. 1916).

[36] (1865–1938) a moderate, Chanvin's election as joint secretary of the Fédération du Bâtiment in 1914 indicated the crisis of orientation in this bastion of revolutionary syndicalism. The death of his colleague in April 1915 left Chanvin as sole secretary, which he remained down to the schism of 1921, when the *minoritaires*, under Péricat, were triumphant. Chanvin was a vocal supporter of Jouhaux on the Comité Confédéral, at meetings, and in the press, especially *Le Travailleur du Bâtiment*.

transformation in association with other types of labour organization. Ernest Poisson,[37] secretary general of the FNCC and
member of the socialist CAP, and Lévy were key figures here,
and indeed had jointly published an article in April 1916 which
anticipated some of the themes of the subsequent November
programme of the Commission Mixte.[38] The latter thus stands
as the culmination of the Comité d'Action's attempt to look at
the effect of the war on post-war French society.

The programme echoed Jouhaux's reformist distinction
between the ultimate ideal and the immediately practicable
reforms through which the ideal might be approached. The
ideal was the eventual collectivization of the economy.

The disorder caused by the permanent conflict of private interests . . .
will persist despite all efforts at organization, based solely on the profit
motive, by classes or nations, so long as the working class has not been
able to make social harmony prevail by the socialization of the means
of production and exchange, and the international understanding of
the workers.[39]

But the programme's main thrust consisted of a plan for the
immediate 'economic reorganization' of post-war France. This
expressed the feeling, acute among *majoritaire* labour leaders by
1916, that the war had signalled the demise of at least the
laissez-faire form of industrial capitalism. As the programme
declared: 'No economic method has been able to withstand the
torment [of the war].' Pre-war concern at economic concentration, monopolies, and international forms of business organization, plus intimations of transformed processes of production,
were intensified by the munitions effort and by fears of a

---

[37] (1882–1942) born the son of a civil servant in Normandy, Poisson studied law.
An Allemanist, he was among the founders of the socialist movement in conservative
Normandy at the turn of the century. He failed several times before the First World
War to become a deputy, but was appointed to the CAP of the PS in 1914. Active
from 1904 in the Norman co-operative movement, he played a leading role nationally
in co-operative unification and was, from 1912, the first general secretary of the
FNCC. Poisson published numerous articles and, following the war, several books,
including *La République coopérative* (1920; English trans., 1925).

[38] G. Lévy and E. Poisson, 'Le Prolétariat et la "renaissance" de la France',
L'Avenir, Apr. 1916, pp. 55–60.

[39] *Rapport de la commission mixte d'études économiques*, 1, in IFHS, 14 AS 213 (5)
386) (Fonds Picart), and AN 94 AP 406 (Fonds Thomas). The slightly different
typescript initially presented to the Commission Mixte is in IFHS 14 AS 213a, doss.
3. The full report was reproduced in *La Voix du peuple*, Dec. 1916.

ruthless trade war to come. At the same time, massive state intervention seemed to overturn most of the shibboleths of orthodox pre-war economic theory and practice, and hint at ways of channelling the transforming energies of war to the advantage of the working class. It was only a short step for labour leaders to suggest that if the state could mobilize industry for the war it could also mobilize industry for peace and social reform.

The actual changes proposed clustered around two central images. The first was a productivist vision of a modernized French economy based on intensified industrial output, with the latest techniques, higher productivity, and greatly enhanced working-class living standards—in short, on an idealized vision of the industrial mobilization.

The immediate economic reorganization should have as its basis the uninterrupted development of national or industrial equipment and machinery and the unlimited dissemination of general and technical education. It should have as its aim the employment of all talents, the utilization of all material resources, and the application of all inventions and discoveries; the stimulation of private initiatives by removing all excuses . . . for sterile and deadly routines; the prevention of all voluntary restrictions on production and all overworking of producers. . .

The working class must thus direct the national effort in this direction. . .[40]

This last sentence focuses the second image, that of a post-war economy typified not just by high growth but also by a shift in the economic balance of power towards the working class within capitalism. This, of course, had been at the heart of CGT leaders' views on the industrial mobilization and of Jouhaux's argument to the industrialists in March 1916. But here, the concern with *participation*, through *commissions mixtes*, workers' delegates, etc., was broadened into an outline model of a planned but decentralized economy, with a greatly enlarged public sector and real power in syndicalist hands.

Delegates of workers and consumers were to establish a framework of economic planning for industries 'where the dispersion of businesses still allows the operation of enterprise and free competition', which would set the size and nature

---

[40] *Rapport de la commission mixte d'études économiques*, 1.

of production, control technological innovation, share profits above normal interest and dividend rates, and build up the industry's financial reserves. The programme also envisaged that the state would increasingly collectivize sectors of the economy, notably where monopoly conditions prevailed and where the state had conceded areas of the public domain to private interests. Although not specified, this almost certainly referred to mines and railways. As with the framework of economic planning, however, the form taken by the collectivized industries, whether at national or local level, was to be decentralized, being administered by delegates of the producers and consumers concerned.

The economic reorganization will only be able to achieve its fullest effect if the Nation reasserts, maintains, or establishes its social right over the ownership of collective wealth and the means of producing and exchanging this, *and if it increasingly entrusts* the management of this collective wealth in an autonomous but responsible form to the départements, the communes, and co-operatives, *and above all to new collective organizations*, endowed with their own legal status, and administered by the qualified representatives of the producers and consumers.[41]

This is the central passage of the Commission Mixte's post-war programme. Here, the limited forms of institutional participation by workers in the economic mobilization, urged and partly achieved by labour leaders, were broadened into a reformist vision of an increasingly collectivized post-war economy, in which the potential power accruing to the state would be carefully checked by new, participatory forms of management. The ideas, as we shall see, drew on pre-war debates in reformist circles, syndicalist and socialist, over the possible forms which nationalization and municipalization might take. But for the first time, erstwhile revolutionary syndicalist leaders, with their hostility to the state and belief in worker power, considered how such principles might be translated into specific proposals for new forms of economic ownership and management.

The new economic role proposed for organized labour was accompanied by the ideal of the social protection of workers as one of the principal goals of the post-war 'economic reorganization'. In this, the programme demanded acknowledgement of the

---

[41] Ibid., 2.

fact that France had become an industrial society and claimed corresponding recognition and reforms on behalf of the working class. A series of measures was outlined, covering housing, unemployment, illness, old age, and also a self-protective control by the labour movement over the labour market in matters such as the employment of women and foreigners. This was simply an extension and co-ordination of the specific proposals made by labour organizations over the previous two years.

After publication of the report, CGT-PS co-operation declined. In late December 1916, the programme was presented to the national congress of the PS and the conference of the CGT. But whereas, in the CGT, it was actively used by the *majoritaire* leaders to imprint a firmer stamp on their wartime orientation, in the PS it barely made a mark.[42] Significantly, it was Gaston Lévy, thoroughly sympathetic to the syndicalist approach, who presented it to the socialist congress. But Albert Bedouce,[43] speaking for the socialist deputies on post-war change, confined his contribution to fiscal reform. The divergence between the CGT and the Groupe Socialiste surfaced at the Commission Mixte d'Études Économiques on 13 January 1917. Despite Lévy's protest that 'if we do not produce something from this first effort, they will say in the Bourses (du Travail) and in the sections of the Party that we have failed', it was agreed that the socialist deputies and the Comité d'Action should work along separate lines on post-war reform.[44]

The failure to co-ordinate reform plans resulted partly from different attitudes to the question. But it also reflected the disintegration of socialist-CGT co-operation more generally.

---

[42] *La Voix du peuple*, Dec. 1916; AN F$_7$ 13583, account of the CGT conference; Jouhaux's summary in *La Bataille*, 4 Jan. 1917; summaries of the socialist congress in *L'Humanité*, 28 Dec. 1916, and *Le Midi socialiste*, 29 Dec. 1916.

[43] (1869–1947) born in Toulouse, Bedouce became a leading figure in the city's socialism. He worked initially as a bank employee and commercial salesman. Member of the Guesdist Parti Ouvrier Français from 1893, he was also deeply influenced by Jaurès, and united Toulouse socialism in advance of the creation of the SFIO in 1905. First socialist mayor of the city, he founded *Le Midi socialiste*, a daily, in 1908, and was deputy for Toulouse from 1902 to 1919 and 1928 to 1940. A supporter of the pro-national defence majority in 1914–18, he played a leading role in trying to reconcile it with the Longuettist minority in 1916–17.

[44] AN F$_7$ 13571, rep. 16 Jan. 1917.

Socialist deputies continued to ignore CGT and Comité d'Action proposals.[45] Even more seriously, the old syndicalist critique of parliamentary politics resurfaced. The winter of 1916–17 was a turning-point in the war, with provisioning shortages and the emergence of mass industrial unrest. CGT leaders, who in war conditions were in closer touch with shifts in working-class mood than socialist deputies, required urgent action whereas the deputies were prisoners in economic matters of a conservative Sénat. At one especially bitter meeting of the Commission Mixte on 11 November 1916, Compère-Morel, as a stalwart Guesdist, observed that 'a little bit of dictatorship' might be needed to break the Sénat. Jouhaux condemned Compère-Morel for feeding syndicalist anti-parliamentarianism.

Truly, the picture which you paint of the capabilities and understanding shown by members of parliament would delight the heart of irreducible anti-parliamentarians. Notice, Compère-Morel, that for me there is no question of anti-parliamentary or anarchist theories, which I shall perhaps take up again after the war, but rather of knowing where to find the means, the organ, which will express against private and individual interests, the general interest.[46]

At a meeting in mid-January, Jouhaux (preoccupied with the major metalworkers' strike at Panhard-Levassor in Paris) added that 'he had had enough of theories and demolishing society in speeches'.[47] At a meeting of the Commission Mixte in mid-February, Jouhaux urged that if the 'public powers' (and thus the whole apparatus of parliamentary government and pressure group lobbying) did not produce immediate satisfaction, the labour movement should 'resume its complete liberty' and openly attack the authorities.

Tomorrow, the working masses, faced with a desperate situation, would not pardon us for not having told the truth and agitated in order to force the hand of the political leaders of the country.[48]

Despairing of finding in parliament the instrument of the 'general interest' which might deliver the desired solutions, the

---

[45] Ibid., rep. 11 Nov. 1916; *L'Humanité*, 29 Nov. 1916.
[46] AN F₇ 13571, rep. 11 Nov. 1916.
[47] Ibid., rep. 15 Jan. 1917.
[48] Ibid., rep. 10 Feb. 1917.

CGT *majoritaires* placed increasing reliance on direct propaganda campaigns, into which the strikes could themselves be incorporated, in order to press their criticisms of the economic mobilization and plans for post-war reforms. Neither the Comité d'Action nor the Commission Mixte d'Études Économiques was entirely abandoned. But the former, now almost totally identified with the CGT lost its *raison d'être* and dwindled in importance, while the latter led a much reduced and spasmodic existence until the end of the war.[49]

The institutional and ideological cleavages in the French labour movement had acted as a sharp brake on the collaborative impulse. Neither the Comité d'Action nor the Commission Mixte succeeded in becoming a crucible for joint labour post-war planning, and in consequence this planning flowed into an essentially syndicalist mould. Where the entire November 1916 programme left little trace in the PS, the CGT's well-known *Programme minimum* of post-war aims adopted in December 1918 was in large part a verbatim reproduction of the earlier document.[50] The reformism which emerged in 1916 as a coherent doctrinal response to the war was fashioned, and ultimately weakened, by this bifurcation of organization and tradition, becoming an essentially syndicalist rather than joint phenomenon. This was of major consequence for the French labour movement during the war and long after it.

(ii) The Parti Socialiste and Post-War Reform

It might be asked why, even if the CGT and the PS failed to pursue a common post-war programme, the emphasis on a specific war reformism should have been so much weaker and more diffuse among the socialists. As we have seen, socialists collaborated with syndicalists and *coopérateurs* in defending the

---

[49] The Commission Mixte continued to meet in the first half of 1917 and *L'Humanité* contains reports of occasional meetings in 1918. In mid-Feb. 1917, it was decided to reduce meetings of the Comité d'Action to one a month, on urgent matters only, with the large economic questions being referred directly to the Commission Mixte (ibid., rep. 19 Feb., 1917).

[50] J.-L. Robert, 'Les "Programmes minimum" de la CGT de 1918 et 1921', *Cahiers d'histoire de l'institut de recherches marxistes*, 16/2 (1984), pp. 58–78.

material conditions of workers. They shared a common 'economic jacobinism' when criticizing the industrial mobilization and official attitudes to the economic effects of the war. Although the CGT tended to predominate in questions of manufacturing and working conditions, the socialists intervened vigorously to combat *la vie chère* and to demand adequate provisioning arrangements. Thus, in late October 1916, the socialist deputy Bretin expounded to the Chamber the policy on *ravitaillement* of the Commission Mixte d'Études Économiques, demanding *taxation, réquisition,* and rationing on a wide range of basic goods as the only means of averting serious disturbances.[51] The socialists in particular took up the question of rents, and fought a protracted battle to maximize the moratorium granted on rents to mobilized men and their families and to those suffering from wartime inflation, and to minimize state compensation to landlords.[52]

Local collaboration between socialists, syndicalists, and *coopérateurs* paralleled that at the national level. The Commission Mixte pour le Maintien du Travail of the Seine indicates how CGT delegates could co-operate with municipal socialists like Henri Sellier on a range of pragmatic issues, including labour placement, women, and immigrant workers. This was by no means exceptional. Local Comités d'Action reproduced national collaboration between working-class organizations. Socialists were involved in administering numerous municipalities, and in general they combined with the local syndicalist and co-operative movements to participate in municipal campaigns and organizations for adequate *ravitaillement*, rent controls, aid to soldiers and refugees, and so on.[53] The increasingly dense threads of local labour organization evident in the pre-war years provided, in spite of the mass call-up, the warp and weft of working-class participation in the process of societal mobilization behind the national effort.

In some instances, socialist preoccupation with the economic effects of the war did generate a more substantial war

---

[51] Rouger, *L'Action socialiste au parlement*, 21–2.

[52] Ibid., 24–8; A. Luquet, *La Législation sur les loyers de la guerre: ce que tout le monde doit savoir* (Librairie de l'Humanité, 1919).

[53] *Rapport . . . 1916*, 3; AN F$_7$ 13571, reps. 15 Feb., 10 Apr., and 17 Apr. 1916; Cavignac (ed.), 'La Classe ouvrière bordelaise face à la guerre', 90–102; Dogliani, 'Stato, imprenditori e manodopera industriale', 531–9.

reformism, with post-war implications. In Paris, for example, the kind of reformist ideas advocated by the CGT *majoritaires* were also shared by a number of socialists, as we have noted in relation to the Comité d'Action. In December 1916, for example, when both the CGT and PS were scheduled to discuss the November programme of the Commission Mixte nationally, the same ideas were avidly debated in socialist circles in the capital. The ninth section of the Fédération de la Seine adopted a programme of reforms including the mobilization of capital, the requisitioning of war factories, solutions to the 'problems' of women and foreign workers, the 'socialization' of production, and co-operation with the CGT for the 'economic reorganization' of France.[54] The congress of the federation went on to pass a resolution signed by Sellier, Poisson, and Renaudel, and by Dubreuil and Prêté, secretaries of the Comité d'Action, which, if it was mainly a justification of socialist participation in the national defence, also demanded a range of health and welfare measures which would 'realize in peacetime the principles of social solidarity which have governed the action of the working class during the war'.[55]

Yet the impact of such ideas nationally on the PS remained limited. One explanation lies in the degree to which socialist *majoritaires* were circumscribed by their conception of socialism as the historical fulfilment of Jacobinism, and thus absorbed by the imperatives, and language, of national defence. This is illustrated by the socialist deputies, the bulk of whom remained firmly *majoritaire* throughout the war.[56] In their efforts to reassert parliamentary control over the war effort and to goad

[54] 'Les Problèmes économiques', *Le Populaire*, 18–24 Dec. 1916.

[55] AN F$_7$ 13073, copies of the three resolutions put to the congress. For the particularly important role of the Socialist section of the twentieth *arrondissement* in the national Comité d'Action, see Robert, 'Ouvriers et mouvement ouvrier parisiens', 1340–7.

[56] For the Groupe Socialiste, see *Le Parti socialiste, la guerre et la paix*; Bourgin, *Le Parti contre la patrie*; Rouger, *L'Action socialiste au parlement*; A. Zévaès, *Le Parti socialiste unifié et la guerre* (Éditions de l'Effort, 1919); reports in *L'Humanité* and *Le Midi socialiste*; and parliamentary debates and documents in the *Journal officiel*. The contributions of 14 prominent socialist deputies to parliamentary debates from 1915 to 1918 have been examined (13.5% of the total of 103 socialist deputies), drawn from across the political spectrum of the Groupe Socialiste: Auriol, Bedouce, Jean-Bon, Cachin, Compère-Morel, Dejeante, Groussier, Longuet, Mauger, Mistral, Pressemane, Renaudel, Théo-Bretin, and Valière.

government into a more vigorous and egalitarian economic effort, they necessarily advocated political innovations in support of their modern version of the popular mobilization of *l'An II*. Thus, in bitter frustration at the conservatism of the Sénat and the leisurely pace of parliamentary procedure (and possibly stung by the criticisms of the Comité d'Action), some socialist deputies at the end of 1916 suggested that the Chamber and Sénat should vote together as the Assemblée Nationale in order to ensure the swift passage of measures of *salut public*—'the little bit of dictatorship' with which Compère-Morel outraged Jouhaux.[57] But this and other reforms were seen principally, though not exclusively, as measures for winning the war rather than as the point of new and long-term departures.

This becomes especially clear in the vexed question of the principles governing the munitions effort, with mobilized workers suffering fundamental restrictions of liberty while industrialists benefited from their new relationship with the state, not least by abnormally high levels of profit. The Groupe Socialiste responded with two bills in 1915, both proposed by Paul Mistral.[58] The first, in May, attacked profiteering on war contracts. It proposed that all war contracts signed since the beginning of the war should be reviewed to ascertain real profit margins, and that profits above 10 per cent should be taxed heavily.[59] The second, in August, was more comprehensive. It envisaged the requisitioning of all mines and factories engaged

---

[57] G. Bonnefous, *Histoire politique de la troisième république*, ii, *La Grande Guerre, 1914–18* (Presses Universitaires de France, 1967), 211; P. Renaudel, 'Vers l'Assemblée nationale', *L'Humanité*, 15 Dec. 1916; and Bracke, 'Prendre le taureau par les cornes', ibid., 17 Dec. 1916. A specially established parliamentary commission rejected the socialist proposal on the grounds that it would constitute a revision of the 1875 constitution.

[58] (1872–1932) Mistral was born and died in Grenoble, whose socialism he dominated for many years. A white-collar worker from a poor background, who became a successful wine wholesaler, he joined the Parti Ouvrier Français in 1893. Editor of the socialist paper of the Isère, *Le Droit du Peuple*, 1903–1910, and deputy for Grenoble from 1910 until his death, Mistral supported the *Union sacrée* in 1914, but gravitated to the moderate pacifist current of Longuet. At the Tours congress in December 1920, he formulated the resolution repudiating the 'Twenty-One Conditions' for adherence to the Third International. In the 1920s, he was active as a reforming mayor of Grenoble.

[59] 'Proposition de loi tendant à limiter les profits des fournisseurs de la guerre...', *Journal officiel, chambre des députés, documents parlementaires*, 1915, no. 887, pp. 382–3.

on war work for the duration of the war, with due compensation, and with the existing owners and managers retained as state employees. Mistral argued that this would make war production more centralized and efficient, as well as more equitable between labour and capital. It was the application of 'economic Jacobinism' to a central problem of the industrial mobilization.[60]

These two proposals were the ideal by which the socialist deputies judged the munitions effort. Throughout the war they condemned the failure of successive budgets to go beyond the minimal, and widely flouted, excess profits legislation of 1915, and introduce progressive taxation on personal wealth and income, so drawing on the nation's capital resources to pay for the war. Bedouce, long a specialist on tax reform, and Vincent Auriol,[61] leading socialist member of the Commission des Finances in the Chamber, became the principal spokesmen along with Mistral on the issue.[62] Although essentially an emergency measure of wartime equity—'to bring within the common law of sacrifice war industry profits and the privilege of fortune'—tax reform evoked a wider resonance.[63] It resurrected one of the main themes of the Left's successful electoral campaign in April–May 1914. It also served notice that fiscal reform would become a central issue once more for the Left in a

---

[60] 'Proposition de loi tendant à organiser la production de guerre par la réquisition des mines et des établissements industriels . . .', ibid., 1915, no. 1187, pp. 850–1; A. Hennebicque, 'Albert Thomas et le régime des usines de guerre, 1915–1917', in Fridenson (ed.), *1914–1918: l'autre front*, 111–44.

[61] (1884–1966) born in the Haute-Garonne, Auriol studied at the Faculty of Toulouse, and joined the SFIO in 1905. Editor of *Le Midi socialiste*, he was a deputy from the Haute-Garonne, which he represented until 1947. Not mobilized during the First World War, due to the loss of an eye, he was, with Bedouce, the party's financial expert and one of the centrist conciliators in 1917–18. He signed the letter to the CAP of 29 July 1920 against the Third International, and remained with the PS at Tours. Minister of Finance in the 1936–7 Blum government, and active in the Resistance during the Second World War, he was President of the Fourth Republic from 1947 to 1954.

[62] Auriol reported to the Chamber in 1917 that war profits were extremely high, widespread, and disguised, and that only a little more than 10% of the excess profits tax due for the first eighteen months of the war had been paid (*Journal officiel, chambre des députés, documents parlementaires*, 1917, no. 3052, pp. 252–6, and no. 4053, pp. 1852–6; *Le Midi socialiste*, 8 and 9 Jan., 1918).

[63] *Journal officiel, chambre des députés, débats parlementaires*, 1916, pp. 622–623.

peacetime economy struggling to absorb the impact of the war. A declaration of the Groupe Socialiste, read to the Chamber in March 1916 by Auriol, warned that:

At the end of the war, in the first hours of the peace, we will not have any mechanism sufficiently resistant, sufficiently adapted to the needs of the moment, to avoid the enormous deficit of an increased budget, to service the interest on the [national] debt, to restore economic life, to repair war damages, to provide pensions, to undertake social reforms . . .'.[64]

The requisitioning of war industries was urged as a strictly wartime measure. But its egalitarian, jacobin rigour inevitably conflicted with the compromises made by Albert Thomas in his improvization of defence production. The government acknowledged the moral logic of Mistral's case but rejected it as impracticable. Instead, the government endorsed the bill proposed by the Commission de l'Armée in the Chamber, which propounded the idea of a close financial and technical control of private contractors, enabling the state to regulate production and limit profiteering, and which also proposed a new form of contract, the *régie intéressée*, whereby the state directly shared in profits in proportion to its loans to the contracting company. This philosophy of tight state control on an essentially private enterprise munitions effort (the state arsenals apart) while still allowing the indispensable incentive of high profits, was an idealized version of the approach actually adopted by Albert Thomas.[65] In a drawn-out debate, in June 1916 and February–April 1917, the socialist deputies repudiated Thomas's approach—and even more so, that of François de Wendel, the steel magnate and conservative deputy, who held that controls and profit-limitation would 'kill the hen with the golden eggs'.[66] In reply to Thomas's defence of state control and the *régie*

[64] Ibid.; *Le Midi socialiste*, 20 Mar. 1916.

[65] *Journal officiel, chambre des députés, documents parlementaires*, 1916, no. 1773, pp. 194–201.

[66] *Journal officiel, chambre des députés, débats parlementaires*, 9 June 1916, pp. 1311–12; J.-N. Jeanneney, *François de Wendel en république: l'argent et le pouvoir, 1914–1940* (Seuil, 1976), 47–8. Thomas made a brief comment on 9 June (ibid., 1315). But his major speech came on 27 Feb. 1917 (*Journal officiel, chambre des députés, débats parlementaires*, 1917, pp. 496–501).

intéressée as inaugurating a new relationship between state and industry, the socialist deputy, Jean Bon, remarked pointedly:

Monsieur le ministre de l'Armement, you have just shown us that you have done exactly what others would have done in your place. From you, and above all from one of our own, we expected something else.[67]

Only at the end, having lost their amendment reintroducing the requisitioning of war factories, did the Groupe Socialiste accept a compromise. They proposed a second amendment extending Thomas's wartime approach to the reconversion to a peace economy. State arsenals were to manufacture the vital goods for rebuilding the *régions dévastées* and the transport infrastructure of the whole country. Private factories engaged in war production were to be similarly used on the basis of the *régie intéressée*, and this form of association between state and private capital was to be permanently promoted through the government's budget. This plan, of April 1917, was the most comprehensive pronouncement on post-war reform by the socialist deputies during the war.[68]

Although ruled technically out of order as an amendment, the socialist plan was warmly received by Albert Thomas. The socialists succeeded in inducing the Chamber to establish a Commission sur la Réorganisation Économique, to which the plan was referred, and it became the key to their attitude to post-war reform in the last eighteen months of the war. Valière, a socialist deputy, took it as his yardstick in condemning the complete absence of government policy on post-war reconstruction, in contrast to Britain and Germany, during the first parliamentary debate on the subject in March 1918. He complained that the Sénat and Albert Thomas's successor, Loucheur, had both opposed the original socialist proposals, thus rendering the Commission sur la Réorganisation Économique impotent, while Clemenceau, in his obsession with *la guerre intégrale*, had stifled official discussion of reconstruction. This parliamentary deadlock lasted until the Armistice, with the

---

[67] Ibid., 505.
[68] Ibid., 4 Apr. 1917, pp. 1091–2; 'Proposition de loi tendant à la réorganisation économique', *Journal officiel, chambre des députés, documents parlementaires*, 1917, no. 3253, pp. 447–8.

socialist deputies adding little to their proposals for post-war reform.[69]

It is clear, therefore, that the socialist deputies attached less importance to post-war economic reform, and interpreted it more narrowly, than did the CGT or the Comité d'Action and Commission Mixte d'Études Économiques. It remained subordinate to their commitment to a more equitable and vigorous war effort, which they saw themselves as uniquely fitted to direct. Where it did emerge, its focus was limited. Tax reform and the maintenance of state involvement in industrial production were important points. But they were less comprehensive and radical than the Commission Mixte's programme of November 1916. Valière, commenting on the April 1917 socialist plan, accepted that:

The system which we propose to you does not in any way resemble a system of pure collectivism or of state collectivism; it is simply the current system based on the way society [now] functions. We are simply asking you to accord to a certain number of industrialists and merchants ... the subventions which they will need ... to put their intelligence and industry to work.[70]

The nature of the conflicts within both the CGT and the PS suggest a further reason for the weaker emphasis on post-war reform among socialists. In the CGT, the clash between *majoritaires* and *minoritaires* turned as much on the former's co-operation with the state as on the conflict between internationalist and national allegiances. For *minoritaires*, and especially for the more libertarian among them, the war marked a breach in the domestic as well as the international orientation

---

[69] *Journal officiel, chambre des députés, débats parlementaires*, 15 Mar. 1918, pp. 944–54. Valière also argued this in 'La Réorganisation économique', *Le Midi socialiste*, 20 Aug. 1917, and again on 8 Mar. 1918. For an almost identical view on the consistent failure of the government and parliament to heed socialist promptings and prepare immediate post-war economic plans, see Bedouce, 'Demain', *Le Midi socialiste*, 5 Apr. 1918. This failure pushed the socialist deputies into using the Commission Mixte d'Études Économiques as a means of looking at the possible post-war uses of the *usines de guerre* (Bedouce, 'Notre avenir industriel', *Le Midi socialiste*, 29 June 1918). Right at the end of the war, the Groupe Socialiste renewed its campaign for coal nationalization and the *régie intéressée* (Rouger, *L'Action socialiste au parlement*, 42–3; Dogliani, 'Stato, imprenditori e manodopera industriale', 558).

[70] *Journal officiel, chambre des députés, débats parlementaires*, 4 Apr. 1917, 1093.

of the CGT. The entire identity of pre-war revolutionary syndicalism seemed menaced. The *majoritaire* leadership, in response, explored the 'choice of 1914' in both dimensions, emphasizing domestic questions as much as, if not more than, international issues, at least in part to contain the growing *minoritaire* challenge.

In the PS, by contrast, the conflict was chiefly between the primacy of national defence on the one hand and the attempt to resurrect pre-war internationalism in a move to end the war on the other. International issues thus shaped the basic wartime topography of the PS, reducing other questions to subsidiary geographical features. The political traditions of French socialism probably favoured this distinction. Those who backed the war effort saw themselves above all as defending the revolutionary heritage of the nation rather than as betraying socialist first principles by participating in the 'bourgeois' state. The national crisis and the perceived treason of German Social Democracy in supporting German aggression justified what was seen as exceptional participation in a purely temporary wartime regime. Criticisms, and plans for reform, tended to remain circumscribed by this frame of reference.[71]

This was clearest of all with the Guesdists, who distinguished sharply between state and nation. Defence of the latter did not confer legitimacy on the former. As Lebas, former Guesdist mayor of Roubaix in the occupied north, put it in 1916:

Did the party which sent [socialist ministers] to their new and elevated posts thus abandon tactics based on class struggle? Not at all; their entry into ministries simply signified that French socialism was aware of the very critical situation in which the country found itself due to the invasion . . .[72]

The veteran Guesdist, Compère-Morel, argued in a significantly titled article in *L'Humanité* in May 1916, 'Tels nous étions, tels nous restons' ('As we were so we remain'), that the unity of worker and bourgeois against the ruling élites of Germany did not change the essence of socialism and that class conflict would resume after the war until 'socialism achieved'

---

[71] See Bibliography, Secondary Works, part 1.

[72] J. Lebas, *La Guerre et la politique du parti socialiste français* (L'Avenir, 1916), 9.

put an end to it.[73] Other currents were more open to the connection between participation in the national effort and post-war reform. But the divergence between the traditions within the party worked against the emergence of a national consensus among the *majoritaires* on the connection between the war and reform. And the fact that the moderate *minoritaires* accepted the logic of the national defence and even of involvement in its organization, reduced the onus on the *majoritaires* to justify participation in the war effort other than by their views of the international and military situations.

Thus, *L'Humanité*, the voice of Renaudel and the 'pro-war' majority until October 1918, did not mount a campaign in favour of war reformism to strengthen the majority (any more than Renaudel himself did at party congresses), despite running articles on different aspects of reform. Equally, when a number of leading socialists tried (and failed) at the October 1917 Bordeaux congress to hitch together Renaudel's majority and the moderate pacifists around Longuet, they did not attempt to create a consensus based on post-war social reconstruction— despite the involvement of Bedouce and Auriol. Rather, they emphasized the common ground on defence and diplomacy, including Renaudel's reluctant acceptance of an international socialist conference while the war was in progress. At most, Bedouce, Auriol, Valière, and others used *Le Midi socialiste* (the influential Toulouse paper of the would-be conciliators) to publicize the approach to post-war reform adopted in parliament.[74] Marcel Cachin admitted in the same paper in January 1918 that the 'programme of economic democracy' developed during the war was the work of the CGT. The principal organ of the moderate *minoritaires*, *Le Populaire*, remained dominated by international questions in 1916–18, with Paul Louis (journalist, member of the CAP, and labour historian) something of a lone voice in arguing that social reform was the issue on which the

[73] *L'Humanité*, 12 May 1916.
[74] Articles in *Le Midi socialiste* by V. Auriol (30 Aug. and 4 Sept. 1917), M. Sembat (14 Oct.), and J. Longuet (17 Oct.). See also Bourgin, *Le Parti contre la patrie*, 191–2; Rosmer, *Le Mouvement ouvrier pendant la première guerre mondiale*, i. 204, 210; and R. Wohl, *French Communism in the Making* (Stanford Univ. Press, Stanford, 1966), 80.

party might re-establish its pre-war unity.[75] Nor did the far
Right of the party make any greater use of domestic reform
plans. Neither the Comité de Propagande Socialiste pour la
Défense Nationale nor the new daily paper, *La France libre*,
established in July 1918 by a coalition of right-wing socialists,
including forty deputies, developed the idea of war as an agent of
social change. Support for the national cause trumped all else.[76]

The idea of a specifically wartime reformism remained fragmented and subordinated to other concerns within the PS.
There were individuals with a sustained interest, local socialist
organizations, in Paris and elsewhere, which generated a vision
of reforms developing from the war, and labour leaders active in
the PS and the CGT, like Luquet and Lévy, who hoped to
make the programme emanating from the Comité d'Action a
project uniting the entire labour movement.

But none of this was enough to produce a national redefinition of socialism in terms of reformism and of the economic and
social experience of the war. Socialist identification with the
tradition of republican patriotism restricted many socialists'
vision of the war to the national emergency created by the
German invasion. This vision often extended little further than
a jacobin critique of the official mobilization, and a demand for
openly 'democratic' French war aims. Traditional hostility to
the 'bourgeois' state, ironically, reinforced the reluctance of
some of the most committed protagonists of the national
defence to think in terms of post-war reform. And the *minoritaire* challenge came over the resurrection of international
socialism to promote a negotiated peace. Understandably, the
majoritaires of the PS responded on the same issue. Only release

[75] M. Cachin, 'Le Droit ouvrier nouveau', *Le Midi socialiste*, 15 Jan. 1918; P.
Louis, 'Problèmes économiques de l'après-guerre', *Le Populaire*, 28 May and 4 June
1916, and 'Un Programme d'action', ibid., 3 Nov. 1917.

[76] Bourgin, *Le Parti contre la patrie*, 98–106. When the Comité de Propagande
Socialiste pour la Défense Nationale failed, Bourgin established a successor organization, the Comité Socialiste pour la Paix du Droit, in 1918. As the name implied, it was
concerned principally with war aims and national defence until the Armistice, its
main piece of propaganda being entitled *Le Parti socialiste et les buts de guerre* (1918)
(Rosmer, *Le Mouvement ouvrier pendant la première guerre mondiale*, ii. 186–7).

from the invasion, in November 1918, began to unfreeze the terms of political conflict in the Parti Socialiste. It was the CGT, less formally implicated in the official war effort and more ideologically disoriented on the eve of the war, which developed a sharply critical view of the social and economic effects of the war on labour, and which, at the war's end, claimed to present labour's account to the nation.

(iii) Majoritaires *versus* minoritaires*: The Politics of Post-War Reform in the CGT*

The division of the CGT began in the autumn of 1914. Perhaps because of the importance attached to doctrinal and strategic questions by French syndicalists, the Comité Confédéral was the cockpit of this division and a centre of real decision-making (in a manner unparalleled, in the British case, by the PCTUC). From the row over Jouhaux's departure with the government for Bordeaux in September 1914, refusal of the 'choice of 1914' turned on hostility to syndicalist collaboration with the government as well as on resurgent internationalism. Pierre Monatte invoked both, in the first overt gesture of opposition, when he resigned from the Comité Confédéral in December 1914, protesting at its refusal to contemplate attending an international conference organized by Scandinavian socialists.[77] In 1915–16, several centres of syndicalist opposition to the war emerged and overlapped. The network of contacts created by Monatte's *La Vie ouvrière*—though the review itself ceased publication during the war—provided a centre of intellectual opposition—which included the émigré Trotsky.[78] Two pre-

---

[77] P. Monatte, 'Pourquoi je démissionne du comité confédéral', in AN F₇ 13372, 'La Propagande pacifiste', annexes, and Rosmer, *Le Mouvement ouvrier pendant la première guerre mondiale*, i. 177–80; AN F₇ 13372, 'La Propagande pacifiste', 'Dans les milieux ouvriers', 7; Maitron and Chambelland (eds.), *Syndicalisme révolutionnaire et communisme*, 45–85.

[78] L. Trotsky, *My Life* (Thornton Butterworth, 1930), 212.

war bastions of revolutionary syndicalism, the Fédération des Métaux and the anarchist-influenced syndicalism of the Paris building industry, were natural sources of pacifism. The anarchist movement itself, split in two by the war, gave influential support to both *minoritaires* and *majoritaires*. Militant primary school teachers active in the minority teachers' trade union, illegally affiliated to the CGT, were a further kernel of pacifism, and the Unions des Syndicats of certain *départements*, notably the Rhône (Lyons), showed anti-war stirrings from early on.[79]

The pivotal personality in the syndicalist opposition to the war was undoubtedly Merrheim. An intimate of Monatte, he enjoyed close contact not only with the established militants of the Fédération des Métaux but also with the pacifist potential of the restructured work-force in the munitions industry. From the start, he used his frequent tours of local metalworkers' *syndicats* to co-ordinate pacifism in the provinces. From October 1914, in the 'group' of *La Vie ouvrière*, and from early 1915 on the Comité Confédéral of the CGT, Merrheim campaigned against the *jusqu'au boutiste* language of the *Union Sacrée* and in favour of an early, negotiated end to the war.[80] In February 1915, he attended an inter-allied socialist conference in London in order to oppose the majority of the CGT delegation. In April 1915, he demanded that the CGT show its independence from the whole mobilization process by organizing a May Day demonstration. Though an isolated voice, he

---

[79] For the syndicalist opposition, see AN F$_7$ 13372, 'La Propagande pacifiste', 'Dans les milieux ouvriers'; APP B/a 1605, various reports; G. Dumoulin, *Carnets de route* (Éditions de l'Avenir, Lille, 1938), 65–97; Rosmer, *Le Mouvement ouvrier pendant la première guerre mondiale*, 2 vols.; Maitron and Chambelland (eds.), *Syndicalisme révolutionnaire et communisme*, 86–213; Chambelland (ed.), *Pierre Monatte: la lutte syndicale*, 128–50. For the Paris building workers' pacifism, see Syndicat Général des Ouvriers Terrassiers ... du département de la Seine, *A nos adhérents: rapport moral ... du 1er août 1914 au 1er janvier 1918* and Robert, 'Ouvriers et mouvement ouvrier parisiens', 622–35. For the Fédération des Métaux, see IFHS, 14 AS 219, min. of the Commission Exécutive of the Fédération des Métaux, and the ten wartime numbers of *L'Union des métaux*, 61 (Aug. 1914/May 1915) to 70 (Sept. 1918/Feb. 1919). For the teachers, see AN F$_7$ 13372, 'La Propagande pacifiste', 'La Propagande pacifiste des instituteurs syndiqués', and for anarchism, see ibid., 'Dans les milieux anarchistes'. See also Bibiliography, Secondary Works, part 1.

[80] See n. 114, below.

and Albert Bourderon[81] produced the first wartime issue of
L'Union des métaux for the traditional *fête* of organized labour
without submitting it to the censorship.[82]

This proved to be an influential statement, which also
marked the parameters of Merrheim's pacifism. With its ring-
ing assertion, 'this war is not our war', it resuscitated pre-war
internationalist ideals in a bold appeal for an end to the war,
foreshadowing the programme preached by Woodrow Wilson
eighteen months later (no annexations, national self-determination, disarmament, and compulsory arbitration). It also
strongly condemned the wartime 'collaboration' of the CGT
with the state. Yet it observed certain restraints. No appeal was
made to sabotage the war effort or boycott the national defence,
and no link was formulated between opposing the war and
promoting revolution.

Together with scattered strikes and daytime meetings on the
first of May, the appearance of *L'Union des métaux* openly
established a pole of opposition whose existence was confirmed
by the first wartime conference of the CGT in August 1915.[83]
Jouhaux had sought to avoid such a meeting as a harmful
admission of internal discord. But on 30 May, Bourderon
succeeded in getting the Comité Confédéral to approve a

[81] (1858–1930) born in the Loiret to a republican peasant family, Bourderon
became a barrel-maker and moved to Paris as a young man. Active in both Allemanist
socialist politics and syndicalism, he founded the Fédération du Tonneau in 1903.
Minoritaire for most of the war, he was a key link between socialist and syndicalist
oppositions. In 1918, however, he rallied to the CGT majority and in 1921 remained
in the CGT.

[82] *L'Union des métaux*, 61 (May 1915); IFHS 14 AS 219, Commission Exécutive,
Fédération des Métaux, min. 29 May 1915; Chambelland and Maitron (eds.),
Syndicalisme révolutionnaire et communisme, letters of Merrheim to Monatte, 23 Feb.
1915 (pp. 95–9), Rosmer to Monatte, 24 Feb. 1915 (pp. 112–16), 9 Apr. 1915
(pp. 121–2), 22 Apr. (pp. 123–4), 29 Apr. (pp. 125–8), and 8 May 1915 (pp. 128–30);
Daline, 'Alphonse Merrheim et sa "correspondance confidentielle"', 322–3 and
328–31; Rosmer, *Le Mouvement ouvrier pendant la première guerre mondiale*, i. 250–
70; A. Kriegel, *Aux origines du communisme français* (Mouton, 1964), i. 104–5; and
Gras, *Alfred Rosmer et le mouvement révolutionnaire international*, 129–33.

[83] APP B/a 1605, 'Note sur l'attitude de la CGT et des organisations syndicales du
département de la Seine depuis le 1er Avril 1915', 15 July 1915; AN F₇ 13272 ('Le 1er
mai 1915–1918'); Chambelland and Maitron (eds.), *Syndicalisme révolutionnaire et
communisme*, Rosmer to Monatte, 10 May 1915 (p. 130); Rosmer, *Le Mouvement
ouvrier pendant la première guerre mondiale*, i. 250–70; and Kriegel, *Aux origines du
communisme français*, i. 104–5.

conference by a large majority, suggesting that many of the majority also wished to clarify the CGT's wartime stand.[84] At the conference, Merrheim and Bourderon pushed home their initiative, declaring that they intended to 'try the leaders of the CGT'. They repeated the charge-sheet of the May Day issue of *L'Union des métaux*, and Jouhaux and Luquet, for the majority, were forced to defend the primary commitment to the 'choice of 1914' and their support for the military effort. Seventy-nine organizations supported the *majoritaire* resolution, but 10 abstained and 27 voted for the *minoritaires*.[85]

During the subsequent eighteen months, Merrheim's pacifism provided the minimum basic programme rallying opposition to the war within the CGT. He and Bourderon were the two French representatives at the international conference of socialists at Zimmerwald, in September 1915, where they resisted Lenin's persuasive case for turning war resistance into the preparation of revolution. They adhered to a majority resolution confirming the moderate pacifism which they had already defended in France. On their return, they were founding figures, on 21 November 1915, of the Comité d'Action Internationale, which aimed to direct a campaign for 'an immediate and unconditional peace' and against 'the loyalist members (of the CGT)

[84] AN F₇ 13574, CGT, Comité Confédéral, 30 May 1915; *L'Union des métaux*, 62 (Dec. 1915). Where the police report gives 22 for and 7 against, Merrheim gives 19 for, 10 against, and 6 abstentions. For Merrheim's surprise at Bourderon's initiative, to which he had not been alerted, see Chambelland and Maitron (eds.), *Syndicalisme révolutionnaire et communisme*, Merrheim to Monatte, 30 July 1915, p. 142. For the *minoritaire* policy of pressing for conferences and congresses, see Kriegel, *Aux origines du communisme français*, i. 105–7.

[85] *L'Union des métaux*, 62 (Dec. 1915); CGT, *Rapports des comités ... pour l'exercice, 1914–1918*, 15–19; AN F₇ 13583, various accounts, including a 32-page typed report, apparently the only summary of the speeches made which exists; APP B/a 1605, 'Attitude de la CGT et des organisations syndicales du département de la Seine depuis le 15 juillet 1915', n.d. (but early autumn 1915), 6–12; Rosmer, *Le Mouvement ouvrier pendant la première guerre mondiale*, i. 343–67. According to the official CGT circular after the conference, 118 organizations had been represented, with the vote on the *majoritaire* resolution 81 for, 27 against, and 10 abstaining. *L'Union des métaux* claimed that the vote was 79 for, 27 against, and 10 abstaining, since two organizations' delegates arrived late. The summaries of the speeches in F₇ 13583 show clearly that Jouhaux had to defend the very fact of 'collaboration' in the national effort against the attacks of Bourderon, Merrheim, and Péricat.

who had sold themselves to the government'. The committee changed its name to the Comité pour la Reprise des Relations Internationales (CRRI) in February 1916, with a socialist section under Bourderon and a syndicalist section under Merrheim, and became the umbrella organization of intensive pacifist activity. It was under the committee's aegis that the *Lettres aux abonnés de la vie ouvrière* were issued by Alfred Rosmer,[86] the former secretary of *La Vie ouvrière* who hoped to use the review's old network of committed readers in building a pacifist movement.[87]

Yet tensions grew within this *minoritaire* consensus. Anarchists and revolutionary syndicalists sought to give a more libertarian and intransigent tone to their rejection of the war and to their condemnation of the CGT's betrayal of revolutionary values. Strengthened by the second international socialist conference at Kienthal, in April 1916, which Merrheim and Bourderon were prevented by the government from attending and which reinforced the link between pacifism and revolution, and by Trotsky's presence in Paris, this tension led to sharper attacks on the *majoritaire* leadership of the CGT and hinted at a rift among the *minoritaires* themselves.[88] In August 1916, the syndicalist (and more radical) component of the CRRI established a distinct Comité de Défense Syndicaliste (CDS), whose

---

[86] (1887–1964) Born of French immigrants in the USA, Rosmer (real name Alfred Griot) was brought up in Paris where he became a clerical worker. An intellectual, theatre critic, and journalist, he moved from anarchism to revolutionary syndicalism through the influence of Dunois and Monatte, becoming chief international correspondent of *La Vie ouvrière*. Mobilized to non-combatant occupations, he was a pivotal figure in the syndicalist opposition to the war. With Monatte won to the Bolshevik Revolution, he joined the PCF, leaving it, with Monatte, in 1924 for the Trotskyist opposition.

[87] AN F₇ 13372, 'La Propagande pacifiste', 'Dans les milieux ouvriers', 11–13; ibid., 'Dans les milieux socialistes', 6–10; M. Fainsod, *International Socialism and the Great War* (Harvard Univ. Press, Cambridge, Mass., 1935), 61–74; Rosmer, *Le Mouvement ouvrier pendant la première guerre mondiale*, i. 368–419, and ii. 21–6; Kriegel, *Aux origines du communisme français*, i. 105, 122–9; Wohl, *French Communism in the Making*, 62–73; Chambelland and Maitron (eds.), *Syndicalisme révolutionnaire et communisme*, 181–213, 243; Gras, *Alfred Rosmer et le mouvement révolutionnaire international*, 136–72; Daline, 'Alphonse Merrheim et sa "correspondance confidentielle"', 339–42; Papayanis, *Alphonse Merrheim*, 93–5.

[88] AN F₇ 13372, 'La Propagande pacifiste', 'Dans les milieux socialistes', 12–13; Rosmer, *Le Mouvement ouvrier pendant la première guerre mondiale*, ii. 70–113.

aim was to 'struggle against the deviation of the labour move-ment effected by the confederal majority'. In response to an inter-allied trade union conference held at Leeds in July 1916, and the programme of CGT-inspired international reforms which it approved (and which the *majoritaires* issued as a pamphlet, *Questions ouvrières*), the CDS published *L'Action de la Majorité Confédérale et la Conférence de Leeds* as the first in a series of brochures condemning what it saw as a spurious internationalism, as well as the reformist evolution of the majority in general.[89] Increasingly, Raymond Péricat,[90] the anarcho-syndicalist leader of the Paris building workers and former secretary of the Fédération du Bâtiment, became the driving-force behind the new body, which adopted the lan-guage of pre-war revolutionary syndicalism to condemn the *majoritaires* while urging the link between pacifism and revolu-tion. Merrheim initially supported the CDS. But the contrast between his own pacifism, entirely in tune with Wilson's stated peace aims from the end of 1916, and the revolutionary pacifism of Péricat, hovering on the brink of outright defeatism, grew increasingly apparent. Also fearful of encouraging syndicalist

---

[89] Rosmer remains vague about the founding date of the CDS (*Le Mouvement ouvrier français pendant la première guerre mondiale*, ii. 195–7), and subsequent historians have differed widely. In fact, as the remarkable 'Le Mouvement syndica-liste, année 1916' (AN F₇ 12891), 43, and AN F₇ 13575, CGT, rep. 12 Sept. 1916, make clear, the CDS was founded at the end of Aug. 1916, though as A. Kriegel noted, its roots go back to the parallel socialist and syndicalist organization of the CRRI (*Aux origines du communisme français*, i. 126–7). A second pamphlet, *Aux organisations syndicales! à leurs militants!* in Nov.–Dec. 1916, condemned the *majoritaires* for betraying the principles of revolutionary syndicalism and explicitly publicized the CDS attack in advance of the Dec. 1916 CGT conference. Further CDS pamphlets in 1917 were R. Péricat, *Maîtres et valets* (on the expulsion of the CDS from the Paris Bourse du Travail by the Union des Syndicats de la Seine), and H. Dubreuil, *La Vraie Cassure*. These are all reproduced in A. Sowerwine and C. Sowerwine (eds.), *Le Mouvement ouvrier français contre la guerre, 1914–1918* (Éditions d'Histoire sociale 1985), vol. iii.

[90] (1873–1957) born in the Seine-et-Marne, Péricat was a building worker who became secretary of the Fédération du Bâtiment from 1908 to 1912, and led it in the confrontation with the Clemenceau government in 1908. Partisan of 'direct action' and anti-militarism, Péricat was the only member of the Comité Confédéral of the CGT to advocate resistance to the mobilization in Aug. 1914. Mobilized until June 1916, he was a founding member of the CRRI and CDS. He was imprisoned from May to Dec. 1918 for his role in a pacifist *minoritaire* congress held in May. Founder of the far-Left paper *L'Internationale* in February 1919, he co-operated with Monatte in animating a revolutionary syndicalist opposition in the CGT and played a key role in its schism.

disunity, Merrheim parted company with the CDS in June 1917.[91]

The development of the syndicalist opposition in 1914–16 presented a triple threat to the *majoritaires*, and especially to Jouhaux. It challenged their mobilization of organized labour behind the national effort. It reawakened the pre-war controversy over the relevance of revolutionary syndicalist values. And from late 1916, it threatened to establish a dangerous junction with the potentially explosive discontent of the hastily recruited working populations in the large munitions centres.

The *majoritaires* never stopped defending the original significance of the 'choice of 1914'—the right of self-defence against an aggressor in the interests both of the nation and the working class. As we have observed, they modified their position during the war to allow for the cautious pursuit of a negotiated peace, provided that the military effort was not thereby imperilled. But they never rejected its essence. The *majoritaire* leaders devoted much energy to converting this primary aspect of the 'choice of 1914' into a full international policy. One of their first policy statements of the war, on 2 February 1915, implicitly repudiated Monatte's protest of two months before. It reaffirmed the legitimacy of the military effort as the precondition for building the 'United States of the World'.[92] Shortly afterwards, a CGT delegation attended the inter-allied socialist conference in London, where Jouhaux and a group of British trade unionists sought to define a specifically inter-allied trade union policy, stressing the international dimension of economic and social reforms.[93] As the war continued, the CGT *majoritaires* developed an international reformism which was intimately linked to their national programme of post-war reforms (see Chapter 8).

Domestically, however, the *majoritaires* initially responded to the *minoritaire* challenge simply by reasserting the 'choice of 1914' and by invoking the spirit of working-class solidarity and mutual aid in the national emergency. This was the message on

[91] AN F₇ 13372, 'Dans les milieux ouvriers', 18–21; Rosmer, *Le Mouvement ouvrier pendant la première guerre mondiale*, ii. 195; Kriegel, *Aux origines du communisme français*, i. 226–7; Maitron (ed.), *Dictionnaire biographique du mouvement ouvrier français*, pt. 3, *1871–1914*, xiv. 72; Papayanis, *Alphonse Merrheim*, 96–7.

[92] *A l'internationale ouvrière: aux organisations centrales nationales*, in IFHS, 14 AS 213/18, and repr. in *La Bataille syndicaliste*, 2 Feb. 1915.

[93] See Chap. 8, below.

1 May 1915 of the first wartime issue of the official CGT bulletin, *La Voix du peuple* (issued six times during the war). Jouhaux, writing in *La Bataille syndicaliste*, hinted at the reformist theme—'Let us not cast our minds back to the past, let us not dwell too much on the horrors of the present, let us boldly scour the future to discover there the shape of a new life'.[94] And he sounded it more insistently as relations with Merrheim and Bourderon worsened in the approach to the August conference. On 10 May, Jouhaux told the Comité Confédéral that the 'revival of work and especially the reconstruction of factories in the invaded départements' should become a major concern of the CGT (in June the Comité d'Action published its report on the same subject).[95] At the Comité Confédéral on 26 June 1915, Merrheim read out a denunciation of Jouhaux's wartime record, signed by the entire Commission Exécutive of the Métaux. After Merrheim and Blanchard had stalked out (to shouts of 'jesuits, skunks' from Jouhaux's supporters), Jouhaux defended the 'choice of 1914' at length ('the manifesto of the metalworkers—mere thistle-down; only Jaurès's funeral will remain historic'), and he ended by arguing that the CGT should respond immediately to the social problems created by the war and also draft plans for a 'peace which will permit social and democratic evolution'.[96]

Jouhaux sought to turn the theme of reform into a counter-weight to the *minoritaires'* pacifism at the conference itself. Preliminary notice insisted that in addition to the *majoritaires'* record, the economic and social impact of the war would also be discussed, and three weeks before the conference, Jouhaux seemed optimistic that the tactic was working.

Twenty or so replies have come in from the provinces. Almost all call for a deep discussion on 'labour conditions during the war'. The other

---

[94] 'Espoir et courage', *La Bataille syndicaliste*, 1 May 1915; *La Voix du peuple*, 1 May 1915. The Comité d'Action made an appeal in the same terms (*L'Humanité*, 1 May 1915). For meetings held on 1 May in response to these appeals, see APP B/a 1605, 'Note sur l'attitude de la CGT et des organisations syndicales du département de la Seine depuis le 1er Avril 1915', 15 July 1915, and Cavignac (ed.), 'La Classe ouvrière bordelaise face à la guerre', 91–2.

[95] AN F₇ 13574, CGT, Comité Confédéral, min. 10 May 1915.

[96] Jouhaux resigned following further hostile remarks from Péricat, only to be reconfirmed in office by a vote of confidence (32 to 5, with 5 abstentions). AN F₇ 13574, CGT, Comité Confédéral, 26 June 1915, rep. 28 June; IFHS, 14 AS 219, Fédération des Métaux, Commission Exécutive, 1 July 1915.

question on the agenda, the 'Current situation of syndicalism', which hides the peace question, the real object of the congress [*sic*], does not for the moment seem to excite the provincial organizations.[97]

In fact, with the *majoritaires* forced onto the defensive by the *minoritaires*, reform was barely mentioned at the conference. But this proved a turning-point. Though the *majoritaire* leaders easily survived their first test within the movement, the *minoritaire* vote drove home to them the need to escape from a purely static defence of the 'choice of 1914'. Along with the importance of retaining control of reviving local organizations, this encouraged the *majoritaires* to develop the theme of wartime and post-war reform into a programme, and eventually a doctrine.

In mid-October 1915, the *majoritaires* sent out a circular which regretted that the conference had not found time to discuss the economic questions raised by the war and urged that their consideration should not be left until the end of hostilities. Listing issues which foreshadowed the November 1916 programme (reconstruction of the devastated regions, labour placement, immigrant workers, and an 'industrial renaissance' leading to a general reorganization of the economy), the circular placed the sights of the CGT firmly on the post-war future:

we have a duty to speak out in the name of the interests of the working class, and we must foresee, for a future unfortunately still far off, conditions which will favour the fulfilment of our proletarian hopes.[98]

'Propaganda tours' of the country followed in the winter of 1915–16 which allowed the *majoritaires* to tune in to local preoccupations as they formulated policies on issues such as foreign and female labour and *la vie chère*.[99] They were thus

---

[97] AN F₇ 13574, circular of 2 July 1915; ibid., CGT, Comité Confédéral, min. 23 July 1915.

[98] *La Bataille syndicaliste*, 18 Oct. 1915; CGT, *Rapports des comités ... pour l'exercice 1914–1918*, 17.

[99] Officially, the tours represented the entire Comité Confédéral. But the six delegates, besides Jouhaux, were all *majoritaires*—Lefevre, Chanvin, Guinchard, Gauthier (secretary of the Fédération des Inscrits Maritimes), Georget (treasurer of the Fédération du Sous-Sol, replacing Bartuel), and Venant, of the Union Départementale du Nord (AN F₇ 13574, CGT, Comité Confédéral, min. 10 Dec. 1915). See also ibid., CGT, Comité Confédéral, rep. 20 Dec. 1915 and AN F₇ 13569, CGT, Comité Confédéral, rep. 31 Dec. 1915; and for the meeting organized in Paris in association with the Comité d'Action and the Union des Syndicats de la Seine, *La Bataille*, 13 Dec. 1915 and AN F₇ 13574, rep. 13 Dec. 1915.

able to present themselves as the vigorous and pragmatic defenders of labour interests and the real voice of the labour movement.

Minoritaire activity after Zimmerwald made the *majoritaires* redouble their efforts. *La Bataille syndicaliste* was relaunched shortly before the founding of the Comité d'Action Internationale as a deliberate and successful bid to take over a central organ of the syndicalist media. Jouhaux's speech in March 1916 to the Fédération des Industriels et des Commerçants Français was not a personal gesture but, as we have seen, an attempt endorsed by the confederal majority to provide a more doctrinal definition of the *majoritaire* position in order to counteract the effect of Rosmer's *Lettres aux abonnés de la vie ouvrière*. On 1 May 1916, the *majoritaires* appealed to local organizations to hold regional conferences on wartime and post-war reform, in contrast with the rather lack-lustre effort a year earlier. The May Day issue of *La Voix du peuple* argued that these conferences would be a means by which 'our syndicalism will be truly and forcefully reborn, and we will then be able to work usefully for the reforms which are indispensable to us', and the journal went on to list all the reform issues being discussed nationally.[100]

Over the following months, the Unions des Syndicats of several *départements* held conferences which endorsed the *majoritaire* emphasis on reforms. The Union des Syndicats de la Seine organized its conference in four sessions from 30 April to 3 June.[101] Because of the overlap between its leading figures

[100] AN F₇ 12891, 'Le Mouvement syndicaliste, année 1916', 28–31; AN F₇ 13575, CGT, Comité Confédéral, rep. 29 Apr. 1916; *La Voix du peuple*, 1 May 1916 (esp. Jouhaux's editorial, 'Action et but').

[101] AN F₇ 12891, 'Le Mouvement syndicaliste, année 1916', 97–101; Union des Syndicats de la Seine, Comité Général, min. 16–40; *La Bataille*, 2 May 1916; Rosmer, *Le Mouvement ouvrier pendant la première guerre mondiale*, ii. 192–7. Outside Paris, only two conferences hostile to the *majoritaires* were held, by the Unions des Syndicats of the Rhône and Loire. Conferences favourable to the majority were held by the Union des Syndicats of Le Havre (AN F₇ 13619, rep. 27 Apr. 1916, and C. Lepilliez, 'Les Ouvriers et le mouvement ouvrier du Havre', 71); by the Union des Syndicats of the Seine-et-Oise at Versailles (*La Bataille*, 14 May 1916); by the Union des Syndicats of the Aude (Narbonne), Ille-et-Vilaine (Rennes), Oise (Flers), Hérault (Béziers), Tarn (Castres), and Aube (Troyes)—at all of which 'the attitude of the loyalist militants of the CGT was approved' (AN F₇ 13570, rep. 20 May 1916); and of the Bouches-du-Rhône (Aix-en-Provence) (*La Bataille*, 28 May 1916), Morbihan (Lorient) (ibid., 4 July 1916) Pyrénées-Orientales (Perpignan) (ibid., 5 July 1916), and Gironde (*L'Humanité*, 26 July 1916, *La Bataille*, 27 July, and Cavignac (ed.), 'La Classe ouvrière bordelaise face à la guerre', 93–4).

and the Comité Confédéral, it acted in some respects as a subsidiary national forum. At the first session, Rey, of the *terrassiers*, attacked the *majoritaires* for their involvement with government while Bourderon, though not rejecting all the defensive measures undertaken by the CGT, recalled the delegates to the first principles of revolutionary syndicalism. Jouhaux defended the results achieved in the Comité au Secours National, the Commission Mixte pour le Maintien du Travail of the Seine, and elsewhere, retorting:

I am for guaranteeing workers' rights and preparing the struggle which is going to be needed tomorrow . . . The true revolutionary is he who can extract [from the *patronat*] by all means possible (better) wages, laws, and periods of rest . . . [But] if you want to impose your demands on the government you have to be precise. Your demands, Minority, are hollow, empty and imprecise . . .[102]

Bourderon's resolution was defeated by 48 to 24, and the *bloc majoritaire* went on in the subsequent sessions to debate at length the specific issues raised by the war—*la vie chère*, rent control, labour placement, and foreign and female labour.[103]

In effect, the *majoritaires* wrested the initiative from the *minoritaires* in 1916 in a vigorous offensive for their new orientation which forced the opposition on to the defensive. Proof of this comes from the founding of the CDS as a conscious response to *majoritaire* activity. Further confirmation comes from the second syndicalist conference of the war. In sharp contrast to 1915, it was Jouhaux who called for the conference, which was held on 24–5 December 1916. No doubt encouraged by the regional conferences, and confident in the new reformism mapped out in 1915–16 which was consolidated in the programme drafted by the Commission Mixte d'Études Économiques, Jouhaux decided to pre-empt the *minoritaires*. He summoned a secret meeting of the *majoritaires* as early as 11 August, and it was agreed that the big *majoritaire* federations (building workers, railwaymen, and clothing workers) would conduct preparatory 'propaganda tours' to 'enable us to appear at the conference in a very good posture'.[104] In October, in a

---

[102] Union des Syndicats de la Seine, Comité Général, min. 21–2.
[103] Ibid., 23.
[104] AN F₇ 12891, 'Le Mouvement syndicaliste, année 1916', 46–8; AN F₇ 13569, CGT, Comité Confédéral, min. 11 Aug. 1916.

series of acrimonious meetings of the Comité Confédéral, *majoritaire* delegates rejected the criticisms of the CDS and voted a manifesto endorsing the *majoritaire* position by 34 to 6 (6 abstentions).[105] This manifesto was published and circulated with a similarly worded conference convocation.[106] The agenda consisted of the attitude of the Comité Confédéral since August 1914; labour problems; the general conditions for the 'economic reorganization' of France; and war aims. The conference issue of *La Voix du peuple* reported comprehensively on the range of pragmatic reforms advocated since 1914 and on the CGT's international policy. It also reproduced in full the programme of the Commission Mixte d'Études Économiques.[107]

One hundred and thirty-four organizations were represented at the conference.[108] Bourderon, Merrheim, and Péricat simply reiterated their attacks on the previous year, but the *majoritaires* (unlike in August 1915 or at the December 1916 socialist conference) stood on their reformist programme. Jouhaux in particular spoke for two sessions, defending in detail the original 'choice of 1914' and then presenting the new reformism.

The working class must know how to take on its responsibilities and then it will be able, in a more or less distant future, to assume the direction of the economy. That is what I went to say at the industrialists' banquet, with which I am so reproached ... But we must affirm our point of view, which is that economic reforms must no longer be illusory. Other countries are formulating them; we must not lag

---

[105] AN F$_7$ 13569, CGT, Comité Confédéral, min. 7 and 10 Oct. 1916. Personal relations on the committee became extremely strained. Three *majoritaire* delegates (Keufer, of the printers, Thierry, of the Syndicat National des Chemins de Fer, and Boutet, of the municipal workers) presented the manifesto as a deliberate repudiation of the CDS brochure, *L'Action de la majorité confédérale et la conférence de Leeds*. In the imbroglio which followed, Jouhaux had physically to restrain the *majoritaire* postal worker, Descombes, 'built like Hercules', from attacking the *minoritaire* Broutchoux.

[106] AN F$_7$ 13569, CGT, Comité Confédéral, min. 10 Oct. 1916; for the text, see IFHS, 14 AS 213C/18.

[107] *La Bataille*, 24 Dec. 1916; *La Voix du peuple*, Dec. 1916.

[108] For Rosmer, the brief reports in *L'Humanité* and *La Bataille* were the principal sources for the conference, along with a personal account by one delegate in successive issues of *L'Ouvrier chapelier* (*Le Mouvement ouvrier pendant la première guerre mondiale*, ii. 241–2). To these can be added AN F$_7$ 12891, 'Le Mouvement syndicaliste, année 1916', 50–7; an extensive police summary in AN F$_7$ 13583; and F$_7$ 13372, 'La Propagande pacifiste', 'Dans les milieux ouvriers', 29.

behind. It is indispensable that we obtain the coming of industrial democracy.[109]

Although there was no time to debate labour problems and 'economic reorganization' separately, it was clear to all what was at issue between a majority resolution approving the confederal attitude since August 1914 and a minority resolution calling for 'the confederal charter to be respected'. A police report observed that:

In summary, Jouhaux sketched out a programme of syndicalist action which can be defined thus: revolutionary in aim, reformist in action.

His success was very striking ... Merrheim and his friends were literally overwhelmed. They knew that Jouhaux would obtain a majority, but they did not believe he would have such a triumph.[110]

With 99 votes (against 26 for the *minoritaires*, and 8 abstentions), the *majoritaires* improved their position on August 1915—74 per cent as opposed to 68 per cent—and, even more importantly, they gained the support of twenty organizations, where the *minoritaires* lost one.[111] Understandably, Jouhaux was (in the words of another police report) 'very satisfied with the results of the recent conference'. For these vindicated the offensive against the *minoritaires* and confirmed that there was real support within the movement for the *majoritaires*' wartime reformism.[112]

(iv) Jouhaux and Merrheim

The composition of the CGT majority and minority, only fully revealed in 1917–18 when industrial unrest and unionization soared past pre-war levels, will be discussed in the next chapter. But a brief comparison of the two leaders who dominated the conflict down to 1917, Jouhaux and Merrheim, helps to show how the emergence of the *majoritaires*' wartime reformism followed the seismic faults caused by the pre-war crisis of

[109] *La Bataille*, 26 Dec. 1916.

[110] AN F₇ 13583.

[111] *La Bataille*, 26 Dec. 1916 for the figures. The percentages for Aug. 1915 are based on the higher, *majoritaire*, estimate (see n. 85 above).

[112] AN F₇ 13583, CGT, rep. 4 Jan. 1917; Jouhaux, 'Buts d'avenir; paix définitive; travail régénéré', *La Bataille*, 4 Jan. 1917; for a police assessment of the discomfiture of the *minoritaires*, see AN F₇ 13575, CGT, rep. 2 Jan. 1917.

orientation in the CGT, and in revolutionary syndicalism as a doctrine.

Part of the wartime antagonism between the two men—which was frequently intense and made worse by an over-crowded CGT headquarters—sprang from differences of temperament and function. Jouhaux was an administrator and 'politician', adept at manœuvring and popularizing ideas to create a new consensus. At their worst, these qualities resulted in an autocratic or manipulative approach to collective decision-making which deeply offended Merrheim's sense of syndicalist democracy. Not for nothing was Jouhaux known to the *minoritaires* as 'the General'.[113] At their best, they produced an acute sensitivity to shifts in the moods and circumstances of organized labour, which served Jouhaux well in his principal task of maintaining unity in a heterogeneous movement. Merrheim, as most accounts agree, was a born organizer and immensely energetic, possessed of genuine and radical vision. But this was tempered by a strong institutional loyalty which verged on organizational conservatism.[114] The disarray in established

[113] The semi-official biography of Jouhaux remains too close to its subject for a clear perspective (Georges and Tintant, *Léon Jouhaux*, i, *Des origines à 1921*). See also, Maitron (ed.), *Dictionnaire biographique du mouvement ouvrier français* part 3, *1871–1914*, xiii. 122–30; and M. de Lucia, 'The Remaking of French Revolutionary Syndicalism, 1911–1918: The Growth of the Reformist Philosophy' (Ph.D., Brown, 1971).

[114] N. Papayanis provides the first full and balanced biography, *Alphonse Merrheim*, as well as a comparison of Jouhaux and Merrheim during the war, 'Collaboration and Pacifism in France during World War I', *Francia* 5, (1977), pp. 425–51. See also Maitron (ed.), *Dictionnaire biographique du mouvement ouvrier français*, part 3, *1871–1914*, xiv. 14, 70–3; E. Dolléans, *Alphonse Merrheim* (Conférence de l'Institut Supérieur Ouvrier, série histoire syndicale, 1939); Kriegel, *Aux origines du communisme français*, i. 227–30; and C. Gras, 'Merrheim et le capitalisme'. The main sources for Merrheim from 1914 to 1916, in addition to those for the CGT and the Comité d'Action, are Merrheim's speech to the 1919 CGT congress (*20ᵉ Congrès national corporatif . . . (Lyon, 15–21 septembre 1919)* (L'Union Typographique, Villeneuve-Saint-Georges, 1921), 171–89); APP B/a 1605, 'Note sur l'attitude de Merrheim', June 1915; *L'Union des métaux*; the minutes of the Commission Exécutive of the Fédération des Métaux (IFHS 14 AS 219), which down to Oct. 1916, Merrheim wrote himself, almost as a personal diary; Merrheim's correspondence, in the Institute of Marxism-Leninism, Moscow, on microfilm at the Institut de recherches marxistes, Paris, and summarized in V. Daline, 'Alphonse Merrheim et sa "correspondance confidentielle"'; letters to Monatte in Chambelland and Maitron (eds.), *Syndicalisme révolutionnaire et communisme*; and P. Brizon, 'Merrheim', *La Vague*, 12 Jan. 1918.

organizations and procedures during the war favoured Jouhaux's personal initiatives in swiftly adapting the CGT to
changed circumstances, and this in turn fuelled the personal
outrage of Merrheim who, at least until 1917, mounted a
tenacious defence of the ethos of the pre-war movement.

But the significance of the relationship goes deeper. Jouhaux
and Merrheim began as colleagues on the revolutionary wing of
the CGT, and although they seemed to move in stark opposition to each other from the autumn of 1914 to 1917, there was a
strange complementarity in their evolution, stemming from a
shared pre-war concern with the dissolving consensus on revolutionary syndicalism. The most obvious divergence arose over
the relationship between working class and nation. Jouhaux,
under the shock of war, embraced the traditions of republicanism and thus of republican fraternity and self-defence (there
had been hints of this change even before the war).[115] He
constantly invoked the pivotal historical moments when radical
or revolutionary movements forged an ideological unity
between *le peuple* and *la patrie* (the Convention, 1848, 1870–1).
Merrheim remained stamped by the fundamental *ouvriérisme* of
revolutionary syndicalism. He shunned politics and the political values of republicanism, finding his deepest identity in the
syndicalist assertion of the autonomy—economic and cultural—of the working class, and thus in internationalism rather
than nationalism. Faced with the disaster of 1914, Merrheim
could not find within himself either the values or the vocabulary
required for a new synthesis of proletariat and nation. The
alternative was to cling to the hopes of pre-war internationalism, and to seek to renew a popular movement across embattled
frontiers to end the war.

The two conceptions confronted each other especially clearly
at the December 1916 conference. Merrheim, without repudiating national defence, declared it to be incompatible with
any positive developments in the labour movement—'where
national defence begins, socialism and syndicalism disappear'.
Jouhaux retorted that Merrheim ignored the relationship

---

[115] Renauld, 'Documents: mémoires de Léon Jouhaux'; Georges and Tintant,
Léon Jouhaux, i. 124–5; and de Lucia, 'The Remaking of French Revolutionary
Syndicalism', 115–16.

between labour and the nation, and between syndicalist aspirations and 'traditions which we have always affirmed as our own—that of being the sons of the Great Revolution'. Where Merrheim especially condemned symbolic statements of this relationship, such as Jouhaux's role as *délégué à la Nation*, Jouhaux argued that this had been a fumbling attempt to find a new relationship of labour to the nation in the war effort, 'to constitute a public opinion outside military discipline ... What I wanted was to reconstitute the revolutionary organisms of the Convention.' This had failed. But, Jouhaux went on, the subsequent attempt to 'reorganize the economic life of the country' had aimed to 'achieve this end by other means, for it appeared to me to be indispensable, and it still does'.[116]

On the narrower issue of relations between the state and the labour movement, disagreement was more limited. Both Merrheim and Jouhaux had experienced the CGT's inability to influence the state as one of the principal ingredients of the pre-war crisis. The state's economic role in wartime plus the constraints on strike action made it obligatory for labour leaders to establish governmental links, and to act as a labour lobby. In line with his 'pacifism' and aversion to the bourgeois Republic, Merrheim condemned such links if he felt that symbolically or practically they contributed to a new relationship between the proletariat and the nation—a reticence obviously not shared by Jouhaux. But in a limited and instrumental sense, for the protection of labour in trying times, Merrheim contributed a great deal to the labour lobby, as his contact with Albert Thomas and role on the Comité d'Action demonstrate.

This was essentially due to the strong commitment which Merrheim shared with Jouhaux to the need for a powerful trade union movement in France. Both, from different perspectives, had understood the fundamental weakness of a revolutionary syndicalism based on small, militant minorities. Merrheim was determined to preserve the organizational framework of both the metalworkers and the CGT intact in order to continue his pre-war project of creating a powerful, technically well-informed movement. This applied a strong brake to Merrheim's pacifism, for unlike the anarchists (such as Sebastien Faure) or the more

---

[116] AN F₇ 13583, typed report of proceedings.

libertarian *minoritaires* (like Péricat) he was not prepared to jeopardize either the strength or unity of the CGT in pursuing it. This, plus the scepticism which Merrheim had already displayed in 1913–14 towards extreme revolutionary syndicalism, led him to withdraw from the CDS and to oppose thereafter the tendency of the *minoritaires* to separate organization.[117]

On one final, and all-important issue, Jouhaux and Merrheim made different but related judgements. Both men grasped that the deep difficulties of the CGT from 1908 were connected with fundamental mutations in industrial capitalism to which we have referred (a changing labour process, threatening traditional areas of skill, intensified business concentration, the rapid growth of employers' professional and political organizations, etc.). Both Merrheim's pre-war leadership and the explicit philosophy of the *noyau* of *La Vie ouvrière* were founded on the principle that only a labour movement with its own instruments of analysis and capacity for influencing the economy could hope to weather these changes.[118] Jouhaux also came to this view in the two years before the war.[119] The question of whether the new departure envisaged by the *noyau* was revolutionary or reformist is a vexed one, and perhaps wrongly posed. In the context of the edifice of revolutionary syndicalist values still formally intact in the CGT before 1914, the revolutionary ideal remained dominant. But the new emphasis was less on discerning a revolutionary crisis in the new forms of industrial growth than on understanding their dynamic consequences for a currently stagnant labour movement.

The war burst in on these preoccupations. Jouhaux, his revolutionary identity openly altered by the change in relationship between working class and nation implied by the 'choice of 1914', discovered in the war economy and its demonstration of the massive productive potential of capitalism, the core of his

---

[117] APP B/a 1558, rep. 22 Dec. 1916; AN F₇ 12891, 'Le Mouvement syndicaliste, année 1916', 49–50; Papayanis, *Alphonse Merrheim*, 105–10.

[118] N. Papayanis, 'Alphonse Merrheim and Revolutionary Syndicalism' (Ph.D., Wisconsin, Madison, Wis., 1969), 126–89; Chambelland (ed.), *Pierre Monatte: la lutte syndicale*, 61–127; P. Mahony, 'La Vie ouvrière, 1909–1914: History of a Syndicalist Review' (B.A. thesis, Trinity College, Dublin, 1983), 20–39.

[119] L. Jouhaux, 'L'Action directe', *La Bataille syndicaliste*, 9 Jan. 1913; Georges and Tintant, *Léon Jouhaux*, i. 65–101; de Lucia, 'The Remaking of French Revolutionary Syndicalism', 104–18.

new reformism. Labour participation in a planned and reorganized economy seemed to hold out the promise of the moral ascendancy of the working class and the world of labour, which revolutionary syndicalism had sought by other means. Jouhaux of course maintained, in the interests of legitimizing the transition and maximizing unity, that all this conformed with the 'Charter' of Amiens, but there were numerous hints, including references to Proudhon, of the ideological disjuncture which Le Guéry, secretary of the diamond workers, raised explicitly in *La Bataille syndicaliste* as early as June 1915.

Is our charter [of Amiens] still the same; should it remain immutable or be revised? Have the events and the transformations which have occurred in industry and in the political domain made it necessary to trace out a new programme ... ?[120]

Merrheim was initially blocked from following Jouhaux by his perception of the war as entirely negative for labour. In December 1916, *L'Union des métaux* still maintained that:

[The majority] continues to assert that this is a war of 'Right' and 'Civilization' ... To mask the feebleness of their argument, the *jusqu'au boutistes* of the Party and the CGT try to divert the attention, the action of labour organizations towards the economic reorganization of the country.[121]

But Merrheim's extensive co-operation with Jouhaux in the process of lobbying, the pressing nature of many of the issues of post-war reform, and the opportunity which the war seemed to present in 1917–18 for building a mass, disciplined trade unionism, all combined to push him towards the same reformism as the *majoritaires*—especially when the latter reduced some of the friction by accepting the possibility of an international meeting for a negotiated peace.[122]

---

[120] *La Bataille syndicaliste*, 13 June 1915.

[121] *L'Union des métaux*, 65 (Dec. 1916), p. 4.

[122] Additional reasons traditionally cited are Merrheim's disillusionment with the peace movement and its relative lack of working-class support, and the fear of a violent revolution on the Russian model. But to these must be added the positive paths of social evolution apparently opened up by the war, reinforcing the reformism which, as N. Papayanis has shown, Merrheim had already begun to embrace before 1914.

Traditional studies of the wartime CGT have usually portrayed the *majoritaire* leadership as disoriented and lethargic, defending an embarrassed decision to participate in the war effort, taken in the emergency of 1914, against an increasingly strong opposition. The reality was very different, at least down to the end of 1916. The *majoritaires* seized the initiative, especially from the summer of 1915, and explored the implications of the 'choice of 1914' in such a way that by December 1916, they had virtually redefined the basic doctrines and ideological alignment of the syndicalist movement. This was not an abstract effort. It achieved its coherence and its provincial support precisely by providing a programme which encompassed the activities of the CGT since 1914 and which addressed the host of economic and social problems raised by the war. At the same time, it bridged the gulf between the abnormality of war and the more permanent preoccupations of the peacetime labour movement by locating the full reform programme in the realm of post-war reconstruction. In so doing, the CGT *majoritaires* created one of the strongest centres of reflection in wartime France on the economic and social consequences of the mobilization of a 'total' war effort.

This wartime reformism was undoubtedly especially strong in the CGT because it sketched out one resolution to the syndicalist movement's pre-war crisis of orientation. In a Parti Socialiste more deeply involved in the official war effort and not beset by the same pre-war crisis, there was insufficient support for the idea of post-war reform to produce either an internal redefinition of reformist doctrines or durable collaboration with the reformism of the CGT.

5 Consolidating Reformism: The French Labour Movement, 1917–1918

IN 1917–18, the war confronted labour leaders with rapidly and dramatically changing circumstances. War-weariness qualified popular confidence in the national effort. Food shortages and rationing, plus relentless price inflation, heightened the economic difficulties of the working class. Despite Albert Thomas's new regime of industrial relations, which from January 1917 banned all strikes by war workers and provided for regular and compulsory wage rises, a head of industrial discontent built up. Intensified by the manpower crisis, with the continuing inflow of foreign and female labour and in 1918 the 'combing out' of mobilized munitions workers for the front, this pressure ignited in a series of strike movements.

Political perspectives, domestic and international, fractured and diverged. Reaction to faltering military and civilian morale as well as to the political scandals of autumn 1917 brought Clemenceau to power in the sharpest break yet with the consensus of 1914. Conservatives and *jusqu'au boutistes* labelled 'pacifist' all those who failed to share their belief in a purely military outcome or who called for 'democratic' war aims. The majority of the CGT and of the PS rejected such Manichaean divisions and sought to combine a 'Wilsonian' view of the peace with the 'choice of 1914'. They also explored through international labour and socialist contacts the possibility of short-circuiting the military effort by a negotiated peace. Enthusiasm for the February revolution in Russia underwrote such efforts with optimism, until governmental hostility to the international socialist conference at Stockholm and the 'revolutionary defeatism' of the Bolshevik revolution in the autumn reinforced the divisions within the labour and socialist movements. In particular, the conjunction of heightened industrial unrest with more explicitly 'defeatist' currents of pacifism strengthened the threat of the *minoritaires* (especially in the CGT) to the *majoritaire* leaderships and to the government alike.

Yet these apparently adverse developments did not necessarily undermine the reformism established openly in the CGT in 1915–16. If anything, the *majoritaires* consolidated their earlier conviction that reforms both should and could emerge from the war and from organized labour's participation in it.

(i) The Persistent Commitment to Republican Defence

Clemenceau's accession to power was a shock for labour. The old *briseur de grèves* of 1907–8 was supported by a broad coalition of centre-right (and some left) opinion. He also received, and selectively utilized, the vocal endorsement of the nationalist Action Française.[1] The climate of French politics became distinctly more repressive from the autumn of 1917. Although Clemenceau's attitude to organized labour and strikes was carefully nuanced, differentiating between 'reasonable' economic grievances and unacceptable pacifism, the CGT *majoritaires* and many socialists felt that the 'policy of confidence' in labour's support for the war effort had been jeopardized. They also feared that Clemenceau's premiership was engendering a resurgence of the authoritarian right.[2] As early as September 1917, two months before Clemenceau took office, six leading members of the CGT (Jouhaux, Bled, Luquet, Toulouse, Bourderon and Merrheim) drafted a manifesto (*Au*

---

[1] E. Weber, *Action française* (Stanford Univ. Press, Stanford, Calif., 1964), 103–12. For public opinion and politics in 1917–18, see Bibliography, Secondary Works, part 3.

[2] Early in Nov. 1917, a CGT delegation, led by Jouhaux, warned Poincaré that a Clemenceau government would be a 'provocation to the working class' (AN F₇ 13575, CGT, Comité Confédéral, rep. 10 Nov. 1917). Jouhaux also considered Clemenceau's bellicose inaugural speech to be the antithesis of labour's understanding of the war effort (*La Bataille*, 21 Nov. 1917).

prolétariat français) repudiating any attempt to turn the political scandals into a witch-hunt against organized labour and demanding a reaffirmation of the 'policy of confidence'.[3]

Labour fears were symbolized by the fate of Malvy. Forced to resign in August 1917 by the right-wing 'anti-pacifist' campaign, and especially by the attacks of Léon Daudet (the leading Action Française polemicist and parliamentary deputy), Malvy eventually stood trial at his own request before the Sénat acting as High Court, in July and August 1918.[4] Out of office and battling for political survival, he personified for the CGT *majoritaires* the 'policy of confidence' which seemed under such threat. Already on his resignation, the CGT leaders, according to a police report, 'regret the departure of M. Malvy, "faithful interpreter of the feelings of the working class"'.[5] During the trial, the conservative Sénat seemed especially to focus on Malvy's tenderness towards labour and his role in the strikes of May–June 1917 rather than on the more lurid charges of treason favoured by Daudet and the nationalist right.

Jouhaux testified on behalf of Malvy. He praised his co-operation with CGT leaders in 1917, even when their solutions for specific strikes differed, and he saw in Malvy's attitude an augury of the fundamental changes which he hoped would emerge from the war.

The CGT represents a million workers: it demands that expression of [governmental] confidence which it has never ceased meriting. M. Malvy, to whom we render tribute, only brought us a portion of that confidence. In England, in America, in the Central Empires, the working class occupies a more important position than in this country. This position must be given to us after the war, if one wishes to see the economic recovery of France ... [We] have adopted this formula for progress: the maximum production in the minimum time for the maximum wage. But the *patrons* must, on their side, implement the necessary improvements, and the policy of confidence inaugurated by M. Malvy must be enlarged.[6]

---

[3] AN F₇ 13575, CGT, Comité Confédéral, min. 4 Sept. and 13 Sept. (rep. 15 Sept.) 1917, plus copy of the manifesto.
[4] *La Bataille*, 8 and 9 Aug. 1918; Malvy, *Mon crime*, 270–83; Bonnefous, *Histoire politique de la troisième république*, ii. 400–1.
[5] AN F₇ 13575, CGT, Comité Confédéral, rep. 8 Sept. 1917.
[6] *La Bataille*, 31 July 1918.

Malvy saw his own significance in comparable terms when he wrote to the CGT thanking it for its support. He suggested that since the *haute bourgeoisie* had difficulty in accepting the rights and importance of organized labour and the latter's aspirations to social reform, it was up to some new combination of progressive republican forces to ensure these after the war.[7] When the High Court finished by condemning Malvy for dereliction of duty and banished him from France for three years, *La Bataille* ran a petition of protest which by October 1918 had become a campaign 'For justice in victory'. The signatories included the major national federations of the CGT (though not the Métaux), the Comité Confédéral, and the Union des Syndicats de la Seine, as well as three to four hundred local organizations—syndicats, Unions départementales, sections of the PS and of the Ligue des Droits de l'Homme, and local coalitions républicaines.[8]

In fact, Malvy's idea of a new association of left republican forces echoed reality. The concept had surfaced in labour circles shortly after Clemenceau came to power. In January 1918, *La Bataille* conducted an 'enquête républicaine' amongst syndicalist leaders to discover their response to the threat of political reaction. The replies by and large argued that the defence of the Republic remained the concern of organized labour, and that socialists and syndicalists incarnated the republican spirit. Many went further, maintaining that a new alignment of advanced republicans was needed not only to counter reactionary interpretations of the national defence but also to keep alive the possibilities of post-war reform.[9]

Such an alliance took shape in February 1918. The founding meeting of the Ligue, or Coalition, Républicaine, as it became known, was called by two Radical deputies, Dalbiez and Poncet, worried by the alleged incapacity of their party to prevent an anti-republican reaction under Clemenceau.[10] Among those responding were 'numerous militants of all the left-wing parties, of labour organizations, of secular and youth groups, of

[7] Ibid., 5 Oct. 1918. The letter was well received by the Comité Confédéral (AN F$_7$ 13576, CGT, Comité Confédéral, 4 Oct., rep. 5 Oct., 1918).

[8] *La Bataille*, 22 Sept. 1918.

[9] Ibid., 9, 14, and 18 Jan. 1918.

[10] The founding meeting of the Ligue Républicaine was on 28 Feb. 1918 (ibid., 1 Mar. 1918). For Dalbiez's anxieties, see *La Vérité*, 2 Feb. 1918.

students' associations', though the principal support came from the CGT, the PS, the Ligue des Droits de l'Homme, plus various Radical deputies.[11] Jouhaux and Merrheim attended the opening meeting for the CGT. Jouhaux joined the Commission Exécutive, and although Merrheim at first refused, not through hostility but owing the the Coalition's initial lack of clarity on international policy, he later joined it together with Bourderon and leading *majoritaires*—Bled, Bartuel, Luquet, and Bidegaray. Despite doubts as to whether syndicalists should join a political body, the Comité Confédéral agreed that the CGT should support the Coalition while reserving the right to dissociate itself from individual campaigns.[12]

The Coalition Républicaine could never be more than a loose propaganda organization.[13] Its main activities were the production of a manifesto in support of Malvy during his trial and a campaign in the final months of the war against nationalist calls for total military victory and the dismemberment of Germany.[14] But in early March, its aims were broadened to include a Wilsonian peace without annexations, and by the time the manifesto, originally drafted by the socialist intellectual, Raymond Lefebvre, had been published on 6 April, it endorsed the argument that a 'democratic' war effort required greater equality in treatment between social groups and the full inclusion of the labour movement. The government needed to:

Practise a social policy which, abandoning the old methods of brutal authority, would accord confidence to the working class and call on its organizations, instead of treating them with distrust.[15]

Together, the translation of Malvy into a political symbol and the formation of the Coalition Républicaine reformulated, in

---

[11] *La Vérité*, 2 Mar. 1918.

[12] AN F₇ 13576, CGT, Comité Confédéral, 19 Mar. 1918 (rep. 21 Mar.) and *La Bataille*, 6 Apr. 1918. For Merrheim, see *La Vérité*, 2 Mar. 1918.

[13] M. Sembat, 'Pour la ligue', *Le Midi socialiste*, 13 Mar. 1918. Sembat argued that in order to unite disparate voices ranging from very moderate socialists like Groussier to former pacifists like Merrheim, it must concentrate on the lowest common denominator of Republican defence.

[14] *La Vérité*, 12 Aug. 1918, for the Coalition's support for Malvy; *La Clairière*, 15 Nov. 1918, 1578–9, for the anti-annexationist appeal, 'A la nation française', issued by the Coalition together with the CGT, PS, and Ligue des Droits de l'Homme.

[15] *La Bataille*, 6 Apr. 1918; *La Vérité*, 13 Mar. 1918 (Lefebvre's orig. draft); S. Ginsburg, *Raymond Lefebvre et les origines du communisme français* (Éditions Tête de Feuilles, 1975), 53–4.

opposition to Clemenceau and his style of government, the values of left-wing republicans. The latter thus maintained, despite the polarization of French politics, an alternative conception of the war effort which, for the CGT, continued to stress 'confidence' in organized labour and recognition of its demands for both domestic and international reforms in the post-war world.

(ii) Industrial Conflict and Mass Syndicalism

Although national leaders had re-established contact with local syndicalist *cadres* in 1915–16 and had attuned their action and programmes to obvious working-class anxieties, they had met (whether *majoritaires* or *minoritaires*) with a good deal of silence and inertia beyond the organizational hierarchy of the CGT. The strikes of 1917–18 and soaring CGT membership reversed this relationship, resulting in multiple, and often novel, contacts between the CGT and the working class. Virtually without exception, the strikes were initiated locally or at most regionally—so that national organizations were reacting to autonomous waves of grass-roots militancy. This same activism funnelled new members into the CGT at a vertiginous rate. From a skeletal 100,000 in 1916, the confederation's membership rose to 300,000 in 1917 and doubled to 600,000 in 1918.[16]

Central to this ferment in French industrial relations was the munitions work-force—resulting, as we have noted, from a substantial reconstruction of the pre-war working class. It was often only in 1917–18 that this heterogeneous body of women, foreigners, civilian males, and mobilized workers, these last including displaced activists from pre-war centres of syndicalism (notably Paris and the *Nord*), succeeded in establishing effective local *syndicats* and launching strikes to protect living standards in the burgeoning centres of munitions production. But the industrial unrest went beyond armaments workers. Significantly, the trigger of the first main strike wave in spring 1917 was the unprecedented action of low-paid women workers in the textile and clothing industries, a sector which, despite the Comité Intersyndical d'Action contre l'Exploitation de la Femme, had remained largely ignored by, and ignorant of, trade unionism. It

[16] See Append. III.

produced a large number of the strikers of 1917–18. White-collar workers were no more immune than others to the erosion of living standards, and 1917 saw strong pressure on the CGT to organize commercial employees and sections of the civil service. Traditional strongholds of trade unionism such as the miners, railway and local transport workers, and building workers were also forced by inflation into more aggressive postures.[17]

The obvious risk of large-scale and, in the defence industries, illegal strike-waves was that they would provoke equally large-scale repression by the government, a temptation the latter would find even harder to resist if the strikes became politicized and explicitly pacifist. Such developments would severely erode the credibility of the 'choice of 1914' and of the 'policy of confidence' in organized labour. But it does not follow that the CGT *majoritaire* leadership was therefore antipathetic to all strike activity. The despair felt by CGT leaders in late 1916 and early 1917 at persuading the government (and the Sénat) to tackle inflation and shortages more energetically, had already led to predictions of public unrest. The Comité Confédéral feared 'revolts by women, or riots provoked either by the lack of coal or, eventually, by bread shortages' and it threatened to campaign publicly against the government.[18] Since the strikes of 1917–18, whatever other issues and levels of motivation they expressed, focused on prices and wage demands, they seemed to prove the CGT's point and to supply that popular pressure on the government, for which labour leaders had been groping, after the failure of the Comité d'Action and effective syndicalist-socialist co-operation. The lobbying of ministers and civil servants was supplemented from 1917 by the role of CGT leaders as spokesmen for the strikers and as negotiators in the settlement of the conflicts. By attributing the strikes to the

[17] Among the most important archival sources are AN F$_7$ 13353–76 (usines de guerre); F$_7$ 13891 (metallurgical strikes); AN 94 AP 139–40 (Fonds Thomas); F$_{22}$ 170 (Ministry of Labour), strikes 1917–18; SHAT 6N 149 (Fonds Clemenceau). See also Ministry of the Interior, *Statistique des grèves survenues pendant les années 1915–1916–1917–1918* (Imprimerie Nationale, 1921), and the contemporary studies by R. Picard, *Les Grèves et la guerre* (Enquêtes soumises au Comité National d'Études Sociales et Politiques, 1917) and id., *Le Mouvement syndical durant la guerre*. For secondary works, see Bibliography, Secondary Works, part I.

[18] AN F$_7$ 13575, CGT, Comité Confédéral, meeting of the *majoritaires*, 8 Feb. 1917 (rep. 11 Feb.); the *Déclaration* in *La Bataille*, 21 May 1917.

glaring shortcomings of government policy and inadequate 'confidence' in organized labour, *majoritaire* leaders could present their successful resolution as a measure of real achievement to the syndicalist rank-and-file and as evidence of their continuing, critical support of the war effort to the government.

The Paris clothing trade strikes of May–June 1917, the first major strike wave of the war, were a textbook model of the *majoritaire* approach to industrial unrest.[19] The seamstresses struck almost without warning, following the lead of the Maison Jenny on 11 May. They demanded the *semaine anglaise* without loss of pay as well as an overall wage increase. Within days the action involved forty thousand workers, many of them on army contracts.[20] We have seen that women clothing and textile workers were, on the admission of contemporaries, appallingly paid, and had suffered large cuts in 1914 without subsequent increase.[21] The authorities, including the two ministers concerned, Malvy and the minister of Labour, Léon Bourgeois, were under no illusions as to the cause of the strikes. As a report of 28 June by the Préfet de Police concluded:

The strike movement ... had as its legitimate motive the quest for wages bearing some relationship to the cost of living: it never degenerated into a political movement. It should, moreover, be noted that women workers, notoriously at a disadvantage from the point of view of wages, played the principal role.[22]

From the outset, the two ministers, and especially Malvy, took a vital part.[23] They pressured the conservative clothing employers to the negotiating table and more or less coerced them

---

[19] AN F$_{22}$ 170 (Ministry of Labour) for extremely full documentation of the negotiations settling the strikes; Malvy, *Mon crime*, 64–75; Picard, *Les Grèves et la guerre*, 17–18; id., *Le Mouvement syndical durant la guerre*, 107–9; C. Morel, 'Le Mouvement socialiste et syndicaliste en 1917 dans la région parisienne' (DES diss., Paris, 1958).

[20] Reports in F$_{22}$ 170.

[21] See Chap. 3, above.

[22] Malvy, *Mon crime*, 74.

[23] Technically, the minister of Labour was responsible for strikes outside the war industries. But security considerations gave Malvy an important, and probably preponderant, role. Bourgeois had a record of interest in social reform, and both ministers were undoubtedly sympathetic to the labour side, as were the civil servants involved—Arthur Fontaine and Charles Picquenard from the Ministry of Labour and François Simiand from the Ministry of Armaments (AN F$_{22}$ 170, n. of 22 May; Malvy, *Mon crime*, 71).

into accepting the strikers' demands. They also drafted a law in the middle of the negotiations to introduce the *semaine anglaise* into the industry (it was passed in June 1917).[24] The official CGT leadership was fully involved in the strike negotiations and in consultation over the law. The labour delegations were composed equally of members of the strike committees and of the leaders of the Fédération de l'Habillement (Dumas, Millerat, and Vignaud who, since 1915, had animated the Comité Inter-syndical d'Action contre l'Exploitation de la Femme), while Jouhaux exerted a strong, continuous influence on Malvy.[25]

The result was interpreted as a notable syndicalist victory, the more so since it took the form of collective contracts monitored by permanent joint committees of employer and trade union representatives. The very form of the settlement conferred recognition on syndicalism as an institution.[26] *La Bataille* greeted the first gains with the characteristic observation that:

the victory carried off by the seamstresses is not only the work of the trade [*corporation*] but of Parisian syndicalism as a whole, represented by the Syndicat, the Fédération de l'Habillement, the Union des Syndicats de la Seine, and the CGT, on all of which the strike committee called as the natural mouthpiece of the organized working class.[27]

Although perhaps the most dramatic example, many other strikes down to the end of the war were either settled or pre-empted by syndicalist leaders 'taking responsibility' for local movements and negotiating settlements with employers under the more or less well-disposed influence of ministers, senior civil servants (Simiand at the Ministry of Armaments, and Picquenard at the Ministry of Labour), or local military labour controllers, and even magistrates. According to the official figures, ministerial intervention settled conflicts affecting 69 per cent of strikers in 1917, and 25 per cent in 1918, when the emphasis shifted to intervention by local officials (over 50 per cent of strikers).[28] The obvious impact of inflation on wages

---

[24] F$_{22}$ 170, n. of 22 May; Malvy, *Mon crime*, 68.
[25] Malvy, *Mon crime*, 60–1, 78; *Journal officiel, chambre des députés, débats parlementaires*, 1917, p. 1707 (Malvy's self-defence).
[26] AN F$_{22}$ 170, rep. 8 Feb. 1918.
[27] *La Bataille*, 21 May 1917.
[28] Oualid and Picquenard, *Salaires et tarifs*, 393–8.

predisposed officialdom to a certain tolerance of strikes even when technically illegal and involving mobilized workers, provided that they were not marked by pacifism. This was the *manière douce* symbolized by Malvy and whose elimination the CGT *majoritaires* feared with Clemenceau's arrival in power. As early as July 1917, with criticism mounting of Malvy's handling of the strikes, Jouhaux observed that:

Two attitudes which have always proved irreconcilable are in conflict; on one side the *manière forte*, on the other, conciliation.

All that this country contains in the way of backward minds, of unintelligent authoritarianism, of conservative resistance, is waging a campaign to re-establish a restrictive and repressive regime.[29]

As we have noted, both Clemenceau and Loucheur, on the strict question of economic grievances, preferred the *manière douce*, at least until the crisis of spring 1918. In the September 1917 strikes in the Paris aircraft industry, for example, Loucheur convoked both sides, promised to keep the military away from strikers' meetings and to take no reprisals against mobilized workers, offered to back labour demands for an eight-hour day, and, under pressure from Merrheim and the Fédération des Métaux, forced a higher wage-scale on reluctant employers.[30] But the fundamental conflict between politically motivated strikes and a government committed to restoring morale by rooting out all signs of 'pacifism' threatened to destroy the *majoritaire* approach by polarizing French industrial relations into a self-reinforcing cycle of revolt and repression.

This tension was apparent early on. When the Paris strikes of May–June 1917 spread from the clothing workshops to the munitions factories they posed a more obvious threat to the war effort. Malvy estimated that the combined clothing, munitions, and other strikes brought out 100,000 strikers in Paris itself, 80,000 of them women, and the movement was paralleled in many provincial centres. The strikes also showed some signs of anti-war sentiment. Red banners appeared on the marches, while striking *munitionnettes* called for their men to be returned

[29] *La Bataille*, 7 July 1917.

[30] F₇ 13366, reps. on the Sept. strike; L. Loucheur, *Carnet secrets 1908–1932* (Brussels, 1962), 45–6; S. D. Carls, 'Louis Loucheur: A French Technocrat in Government, 1916–1920' (Ph.D., Minnesota, 1982), 180–1; Robert, 'Ouvriers et mouvement ouvrier parisiens', 667–8.

home and the *patrons* to be sent to the front.[31] With government anxiety running high over the failure of Nivelle's 'final push' and extensive mutinies on the western front, it took all of Malvy's 'confidence' in labour and the CGT leadership's powers of persuasion to retain the *manière douce*. At the crucial moment, Jouhaux told Malvy: 'Continue your confidence in us, and we will take responsibility, in the name of the working class, for preventing all disorder in the streets.' Armed with this reassurance and his own police intelligence reports, Malvy was able to fend off calls for the army to break up the strikes and close down the CGT.[32] As movements of industrial protest developed more explicitly anti-war goals, this type of compact between the government and the CGT became harder.

The unreliability of official statistics, swamped by the scale of events, and the shortage of detailed analysis of the wartime strikes (especially for 1918) make it difficult to establish precisely the depth of influence of such pacifist protest. Most studies agree that the strikes of spring and autumn 1917 remained essentially economic in motivation. But in 1918, more explicit demands for an end to the war and even a vaguely revolutionary repudiation of the existing order characterized many strike movements. *Délégués d'atelier* (shop stewards), local metalworkers' *syndicats* which emerged in the state arsenals and private munitions factories, and the Unions des Syndicats of the most radical *départements*, all played a vital role. Together, they constituted local and regional networks of

[31] AN F$_7$ 13366, various reps.; Malvy, *Mon crime*, 73; Morel, 'Le Mouvement socialiste et syndicaliste en 1917 dans la région parisienne', 65–88; Dubesset, Thébaud, and Vincent, 'Les Munitionnettes de la Seine', 213–15; Thébaud, *La Femme au temps de la guerre de 1914*, 258–64; Robert, 'Ouvriers et mouvement ouvrier parisiens', 1489–583.

[32] CGT, *19ᵉ Congrès national corporatif ... Paris, 15–18 juillet 1918*, 229 (Jouhaux's speech); Malvy, *Mon crime*, 79. Malvy came under considerable pressure. The High Command, including Pétain, connected the strikes with the mutinies of May–June, and criticized Malvy for inaction (Poincaré, *Au service de la France*, ix, *L'Année troublée: 1917*, entries for 3 June (p. 154) and 21 June (pp. 171–2)). Laurent, the Préfet de Police, was sufficiently rattled by the strikes and criticisms to oppose his political master's line and call for the imprisonment of Jouhaux and the CGT leadership. He and Malvy were summoned by Ribot, the premier, to argue their positions. Ribot backed Malvy's *manière douce* and Laurent had to resign. But Malvy's victory, with such influential opposition, was clearly tenuous (*Mon crime*, 77–9; H. Maunoury, *Police de guerre, 1914–1919* (Éditions de la Nouvelle Revue Critique, 1937)).

militancy which combined overt pacifism with more aggressive
strike tactics. Nationally, the CDS proved influential in disse-
minating pacifist and revolutionary propaganda.[33]

There were portents of this conjunction of political pacifism
with industrial unrest from the autumn of 1917. In October,
Péricat and others in the CDS began to talk of a possible general
strike against the war in the munitions factories.[34] In
November, a police report warned that 'pacifist propaganda'
was edging into increasingly frequent meetings by munitions
workers in all regions, even if 'corporative' questions remained
predominant.[35] At the end of the month, a triumphant strike in
the Loire (second only to Paris as a munitions centre) rescued
the local metalworkers' leader, Andrieu (a pre-war revolutionary syndicalist mobilized to St-Étienne), from being transferred
for militancy and undisguised pacifism.[36]

But it was only from January 1918 that the movement
heralded by these diffuse signals began to cohere. It had a
number of dimensions. First, there were four epicentres—
Paris, the Loire, Lyons and the Rhône, and the Cher, especially

---

[33] The official strike statistics seriously underestimate numbers, especially for 1918
(Oualid and Picquenard, *Salaires et tarifs*, 368; Robert, 'Ouvriers et mouvement
ouvrier parisiens', 9–52). On the 1918 strikes, see Picard, *Le Mouvement syndical
durant la guerre*, 114–16 (who minimizes the importance of pacifism); Oualid and
Picquenard, op. cit., 368–9 (who, as civil servants with access to archival documentation, do not); Kriegel, *Aux origines du communisme français*, i. 214–19; M. Gallo,
'Quelques aspects de la mentalité et du comportement des ouvriers dans
les usines de guerre, 1914–1918', *Le Mouvement social*, 56 (July–Sept. 1966), pp.
3–33; E. Pelé, 'Le Mouvement ouvrier lyonnais pendant la première guerre mondiale', (Maîtrise diss., Lyon II, 1970); G. Raffaelli, 'Les Mouvements pacifistes dans
les usines d'armement de la région de Saint-Étienne', *Actes du 98ᵉ congrès national des
sociétés savantes* (St-Étienne, 1973), ii. 221–37; Y. Cohen, 'La Naissance du syndicalisme de masse dans le pays de Montbéliard' (Maîtrise diss., Besançon, 1976), 296–
344; G. Hatry, 'Les Délégués d'atelier aux usines de Renault', in Fridenson (ed.),
1914–1918 : l'autre front, 222–35; Brunet, *Saint-Denis: la ville rouge*, 174–83; Becker,
The Great War and the French People, 251–301; J. Bond-Howard, 'The Syndicat des
Métallurgistes de Bourges during the 1914–1918 War: A Study of a Minoritaire
Trade Union' (Ph.D., London, 1984), 187–280; ead., 'Le Syndicalisme minoritaire
dans les usines d'armement de Bourges de 1914 à 1918', *Le Mouvement social*, 148
(July–Sept. 1989), pp. 33–62; K. Amdur, *Syndicalist Legacy: Trade Unions and
Politics in Two French Cities in the Era of World War I* (Univ. of Illinois Press,
Urbana, Ill., 1986), 83–107; Robert 'Ouvriers et mouvement ouvrier parisiens',
1666–721.

[34] AN F₇ 13372, 'La Propagande pacifiste', 'Dans les milieux ouvriers', 40.

[35] Ibid., 43.

[36] Raffaelli, 'Les Mouvements pacifistes dans les usines d'armement de la région
de Saint-Étienne'; Becker, *The Great War and the French People*, 266–76.

Bourges. These were all major munitions—and in the case of the Loire, mining—centres. Here, conditions favoured the effort by *minoritaire*-led syndicats and *délégués d'atelier* to turn rising disaffection over material grievances into explicitly pacifist industrial action designed to end the war, or at least to force the government into exploring a negotiated peace. On 3 January, for example, a meeting of a thousand *délégués d'atelier*, representing up to 180,000 munitions and aircraft workers in the Paris region, affirmed that syndicalism was the only effective form of working-class action and also demanded a negotiated peace.[37] In February, a police report summarized the *minoritaire* message heard with growing insistence at meetings:

> The question of wages is nothing, that of Peace is everything; the working class must therefore organize itself in anticipation of a revolutionary movement which will break out simultaneously in all countries to impose Peace.[38]

Secondly, woven into pacifist militancy was an offensive against the CGT *majoritaires*, formulated in particular by the CDS. This turned on two related questions. The CDS and local *minoritaire* activists wanted to use 1 May to unleash a general strike against the war—though whether this should be token, limited to one day, or open-ended, was not clear. At the same time, they wished to convene a fully fledged congress of the CGT in advance, in order to maximize their support and co-ordinate the action. As both the CGT *majoritaires* and the leadership of Fédération des Métaux opposed any May Day strike (especially after the Germans opened their western offensive on 21 March) and postponed a congress until midsummer, the *minoritaires* bitterly attacked the *majoritaires*, and planned their own May Day action and *minoritaire* congress. This confirmed the breach between the metalworkers' leadership and the CDS, and between Merrheim and Péricat.[39]

---

[37] AN F₇ 13367, rep. n.d.; Hatry, 'Les Délégués d'atelier aux usines de Renault', 228–9.

[38] AN F₇ 13372, 'La Propagande pacifiste', 'Dans les milieux ouvriers', 54.

[39] Ibid., 54–88; AN F₇ 13272 ('Le 1er mai, 1915–1918'); AN F₇ 13576, CGT, Comité Confédéral, min. 4 Apr. 1918 (postponing congress until after the German offensive), and meeting of 18 Apr. (rep. 19 Apr.), rejecting strike action for May Day; IFHS 14 AS 219, Fédération des Métaux, Commission Exécutive, min. 13 and 23 Apr. 1918; P. M. Arum, 'Georges Dumoulin: Biography of a Revolutionary Syndicalist, 1877–1923' (Ph.D., Wisconsin, Madison, Wis., 1971), 340–53.

Thirdly, co-ordination of the movement proved hard. This was partly because communications (in the face of censorship and repression) were difficult, partly because local strikes with their own specific causes kept erupting and jeopardizing a general movement, and partly because military and international circumstances weighed on calculations of the likely success of any such movement. Thus, in February Andrieu (increasingly influential as a spokesman for the provincial movements) urged the end of a strike in St-Étienne while counselling local militants 'to act with their followers so that, at the agreed hour, which will sound soon, they may all rise up at the first signal from Paris'.[40] Impressive links were indeed established, including a Comité Intercorporatif du Centre founded early in 1918 to connect Bourges, Lyons, and the Loire.[41] But the CDS, obvious source of the 'signal from Paris', found it impossible to provide the leadership for which many militants called. The dynamic of the movement was too diffuse for the national body to be much more than a centre for communications and propaganda. In particular, it failed to bridge the gap between the activists of the centre and southeast, declaring themselves ready in April for an anti-war offensive to be launched on 1 May, and Paris militants, fearful that public opinion in the capital, faced with the gravest military crisis since September 1914, would turn against them. The Parisians insisted that the nature of the action on May Day should be left to local decision and that the *minoritaire* congress should be postponed until the middle of that month.[42]

Finally, interposed between the material grievances favouring strike action (wages, prices, provisioning shortages, etc.) and explicit opposition to the war, was an issue which contributed a powerful stimulus to the movement of industrial militancy and which triggered many of the May strikes. This was the 'combing out' of mobilized workers for the front. Faced with a manpower crisis, the Mourier law of August 1917 did not (like the 1915 Dalbiez law) merely seek to restore equity to the

---

[40] AN F₇ 13372, 'La Propagande pacifiste', 'Dans les milieux ouvriers', 56–7.
[41] Kriegel, *Aux origines du communisme français*, i. 209–10; Bond-Howard, 'The Syndicat des Métallurgistes de Bourges', 212–16.
[42] AN F₇ 13372, 'La Propagande pacifiste', 'Dans les milieux ouvriers', 78 (meeting of the CDS, 6 Apr. 1918).

allocation of *mobilisés* between front and factory, and winkle out the flagrant *embusqués*. It also sought to retrieve genuine skilled workers for the front. From the beginning of 1918, this effort centred on twenty-four- to thirty-five-year-olds—that is, on those pulled back from combat in 1914–15 for war work and who had spent most of the war in factories. Many had been seasoned workers before 1914, and it was from their ranks that most of the local level militants were drawn. Although slowed by the German offensive, the move to return these men to the front quickened in the late spring, at the same time as the call-up of the class of 1919 (i.e. nineteen-year-olds), including those in factories. Resistance to 'combing out' or call-up, especially during the German offensive, was tantamount to a refusal of the moral obligation to military service (*impôt du sang*) and a rejection of the 'choice of 1914'. It provided a personal and pragmatic motivation for a core of pacifist strikers.[43]

The strikes of May 1918 took the form of a series of loosely connected but barely overlapping actions (Paris was over before the Loire started) which combined wage-demands and other economic issues with protests at the departure of workers for the front. And everywhere militant pacifists declared that workers had 'gone on strike to protest against the war'. Andrieu informed a police commissioner that

We have had enough of war, we want peace, and for that we have only one means of winning the workers to our cause, to halt all the war factories and thus paralyse the production of the instruments which for four years have been used in mutual slaughter.[44]

On 19 and 20 May, the postponed and rather chaotic *minoritaire* congress was held at St-Étienne. It condemned the *Union sacrée*, called for an immediate, negotiated end to the war, and voted (by 115 to 4, with 60 abstentions) for an immediate general strike.[45] At the peak of the various strikes, sizeable minorities had abandoned work in the munitions factories and other industries of Paris, the Loire, Cher, Rhône, and other

---

[43] Horne, 'L'Impôt du sang: Republican Rhetoric and Industrial Warfare in France', 220–1.

[44] Quoted by Becker, *The Great War and the French People*, 297.

[45] AN F₇ 13372, 'La Propagande pacifiste', 'Dans les milieux ouvriers', 88–90; AN F₇ 13576, rep. May 1918; Brécy, *Le Mouvement syndical en France, 1871–1921*, 101–3; Arum, 'Georges Dumoulin', 351–2.

centres, though the majority remained at work.[46] The government responded with some negotiations and a display of military force. There were widespread but selective arrests (during the strikes and in the subsequent months), plus transfers of *mobilisés* to regimental depots, in order to break up the networks of *minoritaire* militancy.[47] By early October, one member of the CDS reckoned that 35,000 activists had been transferred since May, and the *minoritaires* undoubtedly received a setback from which they did not recover before the end of the war.[48]

The strikes of May 1918 failed for a number of reasons. Their organization was weak and confronted by an exceptionally strong state. Moreover, they did not win the expected depth of support among munitions workers, perhaps due, as suggested by M. Gallo, to the apathy of much of the work-force to unions and politics, more probably because most workers remained unwilling to compromise the national defence, especially at a crucial moment.[49] None the less, with their challenge to the 'choice of 1914', they were the most serious threat faced by the

---

[46] Picard, *Le Mouvement syndical durant la guerre* (p. 115), estimates the total strikers in the metallurgical industry at 180,000. Hatry, utilizing statistics in AN F₇ 13367, broadly corroborates this with a figure of 200,000 ('Les Délégués d'atelier', 232). At under 15%, this was a small minority of the one and a half million labour force in the war factories. But such a figure is of limited significance, since what counted more for the authorities and strikers alike was the degree of disruption to the major centres. In Bourges, only the militant *minoritaires* struck (2,000 out of a national defence workforce of 24,000, 8,000 of whom belonged to broadly *minoritaire* unions (Bond-Howard, 'The Syndicat des Métallurgistes de Bourges', 278–9)). In the Loire, too, a minority of the national defence force of over 100,000 went on strike, though in some localities the strike was almost solid at the beginning (Becker, *The Great War and the French People*, 289; Amdur, *Syndicalist Legacy*, 92–3). In Paris, 100,000 workers out of a total of 300,000 in the defence industries were on strike between 13 and 18 May (Robert, 'Ouvriers et mouvement ouvrier parisiens', 1693). None of this should minimize the significance of the strikes, and to the possible total of 200,000 must be added strikers from other industries, especially textiles, who participated in complex patterns of local solidarity. But the May strikes seem to have gained the active support of only the militant core of dissatisfied or pacifist workers.

[47] Hatry, 'Les Délégués d'atelier aux usines de Renault', 232–5; Bond-Howard, 'The Syndicat des métallurgistes de Bourges', 281–98; Carls, 'Louis Loucheur', 252; Robert, 'Ouvriers et mouvement ouvrier parisiens', 1674–5.

[48] AN F₇ 13372, 'La Propagande pacifiste', 'Dans les milieux ouvriers', 117.

[49] Gallo, 'Quelques aspects de la mentalité et du comportement ouvriers dans les usines de guerre', 29–31; Kriegel, *Aux origines du communisme français*, i. 216; Robert, 'Les Luttes ouvrières pendant la première guerre mondiale', 60–1; Becker, *The Great War and the French People*, 298–301.

majoritaire CGT leadership during the war. The fact that all the strikes involved issues on which the *majoritaires* insisted on remaining the accepted voice of labour, plus the danger of losing control of the mushrooming syndicalism of the big munitions centres, made it perilous to disown the radical movement entirely. This emerged clearly on the Comité Confédéral as early as the end of 1917, in a discussion of the arrest of Hélène Brion, the pacifist teachers' leader, and of the threatened transfer of Andrieu from the Loire. Dumas argued that Clemenceau had decided to repress only pacifism, leaving normal syndicalist activity alone. 'Take care!', he went on. 'If you absolutely insist on protesting, do it in a form that no one can implicate in [the pacifists'] propaganda.' But Jouhaux replied that Malvy's methods, and the solid national morale resulting from them ('to which we have largely contributed'), meant the CGT taking responsibility for strikes and dissuading the authorities from creating martyrs by repression. A protest over the Brion and Andrieu cases was accordingly made.[50]

Majoritaire responses in 1918 were consistent with this approach. While the government was informed that it must take responsibility for the conditions causing unrest, the CGT leadership (and especially Merrheim and the Fédération des Métaux) tried to give the unrest an acceptable shape.[51] Merrheim, in a series of articles in *La Vérité* throughout the spring of 1918, expounded *majoritaire* logic.

The duty [of all metallurgical workers] is to join their respective organizations, to bring to these the force which will create cohesion, not confusion, of action, and which will impose the observation of collective contracts on the *patronat* and on all the workers.

Above all, let them not forget that it is only supported by this force that the workers' organizations will be able to act efficiently . . .[52]

In May, the CGT and the Fédération des Métaux flatly condemned the attempt by the CDS to supply an alternative,

---

[50] AN F$_7$ 13575, CGT, Comité Confédéral, 30 Nov. 1917, rep. 3 Dec; ibid., meeting, 1 Dec. 1917, min. and rep. 5 Dec.; meeting 5 Dec. 1917, rep. 7 Dec.; for the text of the protest, CGT, *Rapports des comités . . . pour l'exercice 1914–1918*.

[51] IFHS 14 AS 219, Fédération des Métaux, Commission Exécutive, min. 26 Jan., 2 Feb., 13 Mar., 13 Apr., 23 Apr., and 11 June 1918; *L'Union des métaux*, 68 (July 1918).

[52] A. Merrheim, 'La Question des salaires', *La Vérité*, 16 Mar. 1918, and articles of 28 Apr., and 4, 8, 9, and 12 May 1918.

pacifist leadership to the syndicalist movement. They preached against the strikes, especially given the military situation, arguing that the *minoritaires* would find themselves totally isolated by public opinion.[53] When the strikes none the less occurred, the national leaders 'took responsibility' for them and, while minimizing their political content, insisted on being consulted over their settlement. On 16 May, the *métaux* leadership assumed direction of the Paris strike and, after negotiations between Clemenceau, Loucheur, Merrheim, and Renaudel (for the Groupe Socialiste), the strike ended two days later.[54] Labe and Blanchard, assistant secretaries of the federation, went to Bourges and St-Étienne respectively to try to end these movements, but found themselves shunned.[55] In these cases, the authorities themselves isolated the movements and forced a return to work.

The attempt by the state systematically to break up the networks of industrial pacifism after the strikes, though probably stopping short of mass repression, was serious enough to heighten *majoritaire* fears of a further polarization of feeling in the war factories.[56] In a specially convened meeting of left-wing deputies on 7 June (subsequently published as a CGT brochure, *La Leçon des faits*), Jouhaux and Merrheim defended the *majoritaire* approach. Merrheim was at pains to emphasize that the Fédération des Métaux accepted the Mourier law and thus, implicitly, the 'choice of 1914' ('we have always declared that the fact of being a metallurgical worker did not constitute a privilege, a right for workers not to go into the trenches'). Ignoring the ambivalence of pacifist militancy, he argued that

[53] AN F₇ 13576, rep. May 1918; IFHS, 14 AS 219, Fédération des Métaux, Commission Exécutive, min. 13 Apr. 1918; *La Vérité*, 13 May (Merrheim's condemnation of the Comité Intercorporatif du Centre). The Fédération des Métaux issued a circular condemning the *minoritaire* St-Étienne congress.

[54] AN F₇ 13576, rep. 21 May 1918; AN F₇ 13367, rep. 16 May 1918; Poincaré, *Au service de la France*, x, *Victoire et armistice*, 178–9; Hatry, 'Les Délégués d'atelier aux usines de Renault', 232.

[55] Bond-Howard, 'The Syndicat des Métallurgistes de Bourges', 273; Becker, *The Great War and the French People*, 271.

[56] IFHS, 14 AS 219, Fédération des Métaux, Commission Exécutive, min. 11 and 29 June 1918; L. Jouhaux, 'Mesure de justice', *La Bataille*, 21 Aug. 1918, and 'Confiance, oui ou non', *La Bataille*, 22 Aug. 1918.

even in the Loire the strikers had not intended to support the enemy but merely to defend their own principles. He blamed the strikes on the way in which the government and industrialists had tried to 'comb out' seasoned workers in their twenties and thirties without due warning or any indication of French war aims, and without assurances that they would not be supplanted on a mass scale by foreign workers (hostility to whom was a theme of the strikes). Above all, he maintained that by ignoring official trade unionism, the government had created a leadership vacuum which the more radical *délégués d'atelier* had exploited to their own advantage.

Jouhaux endorsed this view, stressing that the strikes stemmed from the failure of successive governments to adopt the war aims or domestic reforms proposed by labour leaders.[57] Elsewhere, he warned against further alienating the working class from the war effort by repression:

> The government would be short-sighted and impolitic if it created the false impression that the National Defence is, for the working class, incompatible with its rights, its feelings of dignity, and its duty of [labour] solidarity.[58]

And in the following months, the *majoritaires* redoubled their intercession with the authorities on behalf of imprisoned and transferred militants of the May strikes.

The strikes of 1917–18 thus revealed two opposed attitudes to industrial relations in the CGT. The *majoritaires* and the leadership of the Fédération des Métaux, for all their hostility to the ban on strikes by civilian war workers and to compulsory arbitration, saw in the war the opportunity to develop an essentially contractual relationship with employers, based on collective bargaining and backed up by a disciplined, mass trade unionism. The role of strikes, orderly and led from above, was

---

[57] CGT, *Rapports des comités . . . pour l'exercice 1914–1918*, 44 ff.; *La Leçon des faits: la délégation confédérale devant les parlementaires de gauche* (June 1918); 'La CGT adresse une lettre à la représentation nationale', *La Bataille*, 27 June 1918; M. Laurent, 'La Délégation de la CGT au Palais Bourbon', *La Clairière*, 1 July 1918, pp. 1137–54.

[58] *La CGT devant la situation ouvrière*, published after the May strikes, and putting the same argument as *La Leçon des faits*.

to support the labour leadership in this process.[59] The *minori-taires*, both the CDS and the local networks of militants in the big munitions centres, favoured a quite different approach. The belief in the general strike, the *élan* of local movements using cross-trade and cross-grade solidarity to compensate for meagre financial resources, and the readiness to ascribe non-economic goals to strike movements, recalled classic revolutionary syndi-calism, with which Péricat and others claimed an unbroken connection.[60] The originality of the radical approach in 1917–18 was that it now extended to many semi-skilled workers in munitions work, as well as skilled, and threatened to find a mass following.

This opposition of approach between *majoritaires* and *minoritaires* resumed, in transformed circumstances, the clash of attitude to strikes which had threatened the internal unity of both the metalworkers and the building workers on the eve of the war. But wartime conditions obliged the *majoritaires* to formulate much more consciously and explicitly a contractual and institutionalized view of industrial relations which, until then, had been associated with overtly reformist currents of syndicalism and with certain industries (printing, mining, the railways).[61]

The question of a shopfloor and factory level of worker representation (the *délégués d'atelier*) revealed especially clearly the difference between *majoritaire* and *minoritaire* conceptions of industrial action, and between both and the views of different industrialists and ministers. Indeed, the *délégués d'atelier*, far from being a point of convergence or consensus, resembled a

[59] Ministère du Travail, *Tarifs de salaires et conventions collectives pendant la guerre 1914–18*, 3 vols. (Imprimerie Nationale, 1921); R. Picard, *La Conciliation, l'arbitrage et la prévention des conflits ouvriers* (Comité National d'Études Sociales et Politiques, Sept. 1918); M. Leroy, *Les Techniques nouvelles du syndicalisme* (Garnier, 1920), esp. 53–4; G. Pirou, 'Le Problème du contrat collectif du travail en France', *Revue internationale du travail/International Labour Review*, Jan. 1922, pp. 35–50; Oualid and Picquenard, *Salaires et tarifs, passim*; Dubreuil, *Employeurs et salariés*, 42–54.

[60] See Péricat's pamphlet, *Maîtres et valets*; his presentation of it to the CDS (AN F$_7$ 13372, 'La Propagande pacifiste', 'Dans les milieux ouvriers'); and his speech to the Dec. 1917 CGT conference at Clermont Ferrand (CGT, *Conférence extraordi-naire des fédérations nationales, bourses du travail et unions des syndicats (Clermont-Ferrand, 23–5 déc. 1917)*. *Compte rendu* (Maison des Syndicats, n.d.), 80).

[61] See Chap. 1, above.

revolving mirror in which the different groups reflected their own preoccupations.[62]

The initial demand for their institution came from the skilled metalworkers' organizations in January 1917. The Union des Ouvriers Mécaniciens de la Seine, in concert with the Fédération des Métaux, proposed the idea to Albert Thomas in response to compulsory arbitration. Thomas approved in principle, since the idea accorded with his policy of using the industrial mobilization to strengthen recognition of the labour movement as well as with his overriding need to avoid disruption in production. In a series of circulars, he urged industrialists to establish *délégués d'atelier* in order to foster 'regular relations' with the work-force (employers in Nantes had been experimenting with them in this capacity since late 1916). But the system remained voluntary and, until September 1917, without any clear principle of selection.[63]

The CGT *majoritaires* demanded a factory-wide system (Jouhaux preferred the term *délégués ouvriers*) on a broad franchise so as genuinely to reflect the wartime transformation of the labour force. They also insisted that the *syndicats* be allowed to field official candidates so as to make the delegates an instrument of syndicalist control. *Délégués d'atelier* had emerged before the war in engineering factories faced with technological change.[64] But the scale of wartime developments plus the vulnerability of the mobilized workers seemed to make some form of local control over basic conditions especially important, as we have already

[62] Sources for the *délégués d'atelier* are AN F$_7$ 13366 (dossier on the delegates); AN F$_7$ 13595 (reps., press cuttings, 1917–1918); AN 94 AP 141 (Fonds Thomas), for official circulars, press cuttings, and Thomas's own views; *Bulletin des usines de guerre*, for official circulars; and APP B/a 1375, for the delegates of the Seine.

[63] AN 94 AP 141, letter from the Fédération des Métaux to Albert Thomas, 21 Aug. 1917, stating that the metalworkers originally prepared the idea in Jan. 1917 to facilitate wage-negotiations under the new regime; *L'Union des métaux*, 67 (May–Dec., 1917), pp. 2–5; A. Merrheim, 'Les Réformes de M. Thomas: les délégués ouvriers', *L'Œuvre économique*, 25 Sept. 1917, pp. 553–60; R. Picard, *La Conciliation et l'arbitrage*, 31–2 (with details of the Nantes experiment); Oualid and Picquenard, *Salaires et tarifs*, 420–1.

[64] *La Voix du peuple*, 1 May 1917; L. Jouhaux, 'Les Délégués ouvriers', *La Clairière*, 15 Nov. 1917, pp. 345–53, for the *majoritaire* view of the delegates. For their pre-war history, M. Perrot, 'Lo Sviluppo del movimento sindacale in Francia: forme di contrattazione e di rappresentanza (1900–1920)', in Antonioni, *et al.*, *Sindacato e classe operaia nell'età della seconda internazionale*, 80–1.

noted.[65] The Fédération des Métaux felt that *délégués d'atelier* were the 'only guarantee of security for mobilized workers'.[66] The new system of negotiated regional minimum wages which Thomas introduced for war industries in January 1917 reinforced the argument for a factory tier of syndicalist discipline, if the system were to be turned to labour's advantage.

In fact, the *majoritaires* saw the *délégués d'atelier* as the local counterpart to the growing national recognition of the CGT and, as such, felt that they should be firmly integrated into the syndicalist hierarchy. Jouhaux considered them a powerful symbol of the participation of organized labour in the industrial mobilization and of the democratization of the economic sphere to which he hoped the war experience would lead. He felt that *délégués ouvriers* would allow organized labour to help remodel the production process and social relations in the factory, and that they represented 'a right of management and control' over aspects of the workplace directly concerning labour. He even envisaged permanent councils for each military district, with full syndicalist involvement, to crown the system of delegates.[67] Nor was the munitions industry the sole focus of *majoritaire* demands. The idea of worker delegates was canvassed just as strongly in mining and the railways. Even the Fédération du Bâtiment saw them as the means of ensuring the application of union rates of pay and conditions to the public works projects which it was hoped would cushion the eventual military demobilization.[68]

Not surprisingly, industrialists by and large resisted this conception of the *délégués d'atelier*. According to an official report of the Ministry of Armaments, many employers resented

---

[65] See pp. 69–70, above.

[66] AN F$_7$ 13595, Fédération des Métaux circular, *Aux organisations, aux militants*, 7 July 1917; Comité Fédéral National of the Fédération des Métaux, Sept. 1917, reported in *L'Union des métaux*, 68 (July 1918), p. 11.

[67] L. Jouhaux, 'Pour une bonne marche économique', *La Bataille*, 27 Aug. 1917; 'Les Délégués ouvriers', *La Clairière*, 15 Nov. 1917, pp. 345–53.

[68] For the miners, see C. Bartuel, 'La Féodalité industrielle doit disparaître', *La Clairière*, 15 Oct. 1917, pp. 241–52; id., 'La Réorganisation des mines', ibid., 1 Apr. 1918, 785–98; Bartuel and Rullière, *La Mine et les mineurs*. For the *cheminots*, see *Fédération nationale des travailleurs des chemins de fer. Compte rendu du 1er congrès national, Paris, 28–30 juin 1918* (Imprimerie Nouvelle, 1918), 194–6. For the building-workers, see *La Bataille*, 26 Feb. 1918 (rep. of the federation's Comité National, 24–5 Feb.).

the challenge to established factory discipline and feared lest the delegates 'install the regime of Soviets in France'. Such employers tended either to ignore the whole idea or to hand-pick worker delegates, thus obviating any possibility of syndicalist influence.[69] The Union des Ouvriers Mécaniciens de la Seine discovered that in one of Loucheur's own factories, 'the chief engineer has certain workers called and announces to them that they are the officially recognized delegates'.[70] Other industrialists, like Louis Renault, drafted conditions of candidacy so restrictive as to limit the delegate system to the workshop (rather than factory) level and to exclude as candidates all workers not employed in the establishment before the war.[71] An employers' paper, *La Métallurgie*, considered retrospectively that because of the connection with syndicalism, the *délégués d'atelier* had been 'rarely useful and often harmful', while another business paper, *La Journée industrielle*, summarized the conflict of views thus:

The real difficulty in the functioning [of the delegates] comes from an attempt by the *patrons* to restrict them by reducing the delegates' role to that of a simple intermediary, charged with transmitting individual grievances, and from an attempt at emancipation by the labour side, which considers the delegate to have a veritable syndicalist mandate, qualifying him to intervene in general questions concerning the factory.[72]

Early September 1917 found Thomas rather uncomfortably adjudicating this conflict between industrialists and the CGT on the frontier of 'control' in the munitions factories. His circular of 5 September, based on the accord worked out by Louis Renault and the delegates in Renault's Paris factory late in August, was a compromise. The criteria for candidates and voters made concessions to the CGT, since they embraced those employed during as well as before the war, including women, although immigrants remained excluded. But Thomas, privately accepting that many employers still refused to recognize trade unions,

[69] AN F, 13595, rep. 16 May 1918.
[70] AN 94 AP 141, complaint from the union to Thomas, Dec. 1918.
[71] Oualid and Picquenard, *Salaires et tarifs*, 422–5; Picard, *La Conciliation et l'arbitrage*, 31–4; Hatry, 'Les Délégués d'atelier aux usines de Renault', 222–5.
[72] *La Métallurgie*, Nov.–Dec. 1919, p. 346; J. Hardy, 'Les Délégués d'atelier', *La Journée industrielle*, 27 Mar. 1918.

restricted the functions of the delegates and sharply distinguished them from those of the *syndicat*. The *délégués d'atelier* were to be confined to the workshop, rather than factory, to concern themselves with the more efficient functioning of production and with individual grievances, and to act as mediators and conciliators between management and the work-force.[73] The CGT and metalworkers' leaderships were not slow to condemn what they considered an endorsement of the industrialists' point of view which destroyed the value of the institution.[74]

In practice, these distinctions proved impossible to maintain. *Délégués d'atelier* overlapped with syndicalist activism, operated at the factory level, and raised broader issues. But this in turn produced divergent *majoritaire* and *minoritaire* views, as workshops and factory delegates in the large munitions centres became one of the principal elements of the militant industrial pacifism culminating in the strikes of May 1918.[75] This development, in quite a different way, also opposed the *délégués d'atelier* to the CGT hierarchy. A remarkable record kept in the spring of 1918 by the *délégués d'atelier* of the war factories in Paris's thirteenth *arrondissement* illustrates clearly how radical delegates used Thomas's decree, '[which] would have been really inoffensive if followed to the letter [for] it would merely have made the *délégués d'atelier* auxiliaries of the *patronat*', in order to build an explicitly anti-war movement. Pointing out that they were more representative than the official hierarchy in factories where much of the work-force remained ununionized, the report commented that 'the *délégués d'atelier*,

[73] *Bulletin des usines de guerre*, 10 Sept. 1917, pp. 153–5; Hatry, 'Les Délégués d'atelier aux usines de Renault', 222–5. In a revealing passage of an early draft of the circular (dated 27 Aug.), omitted from the final version, Thomas admitted that 'despite the intimate collaboration (of labour) in the war effort, and owing to the prejudices and memories of yesteryear, and to political apprehensions, many *patrons* refuse to enter into relations with the secretaries of workers' syndicats, with those whom too often they call "agitators" ...' (AN 94 AP 141).

[74] *L'Union des métaux*, 67 (May–Dec. 1917); *La Vérité*, 21 Feb. 1918; AN F₇ 13366 and F₇ 13595, typed report on delegates, with syndicalist reactions; Jouhaux, 'Les Délégués ouvriers', *La Clairière*, 15 Nov. 1917, 351.

[75] Hatry, 'Les Délégués d'atelier aux usines de Renault'; Cohen, 'La Naissance du syndicalisme de masse', 200–2; Bond-Howard, 'The Syndicat des Métallurgistes de Bourges', 190–2.

enjoying the workers' complete confidence, had not all become delegates just to act as *agents de liaison* between the *syndicat* and the factory'. It went on to accuse the Fédération des Métaux of refusing to convoke further meetings of delegates from the whole Paris region once the pacifist campaign was under way.[76]

Some *majoritaires* indeed felt that the delegates undermined the central authority of the CGT, and in Poincaré's account, Merrheim admitted, when negotiating the end of the May strike in Paris, that they had proved one of Albert Thomas's less happy innovations.[77] The *délégués d'atelier* obviously meant many different things in 1917–18, and operated in various ways. The CGT majority continued to support the principle. But squeezed between restrictive official interpretations (in February 1918 Loucheur ruled that delegates who were *mobilisés* could not also be syndicalists) and the challenge from militant pacifist delegates, the *majoritaires'* conception of the delegates as agents of syndicalist 'management and control' failed to find widespread acceptance.[78]

Yet overall there were sufficient positive developments in industrial relations in 1917–18, from the CGT majority's point of view, to confirm its orientation. Trade unionism, nationally and locally, played an unprecedented role in bargaining. If many employers resisted recognition of organized labour, others were increasingly open to it. In early 1917, for example, the Fédération des Industriels et des Commerçants Français approached the CGT suggesting 'a new relationship' between employer and labour organizations based on the collective

---

[76] Musée social (uncatalogued).

[77] Poincaré, *Victoire et armistice*, 178–9. The *métaux* continued to endorse the principle, and protested against the further restriction of the delegates by Loucheur ('Rapport Fédéral, 1914–1918', *L'Union des métaux*, 68 (July 1918), pp. 11–12). But the Commission Exécutive repeatedly discussed the dangers of local militancy based on the *délégués d'atelier* escaping national control in the big munitions centres (IFHS 14 AS 219, Fédération des Métaux, Commission Exécutive, min. 2 Feb., 13 Mar., 13 Apr., and 29 Oct., 1918).

[78] *Bulletin des usines de guerre*, 4 Mar. 1918, p. 355. According to Oualid and Picquenard, 347 establishments instituted *délégués d'atelier* during the war, 315 working for the national defence, and 290 of them engineering companies. Only one-sixth of these establishments still had delegates in 1921–4 (*Salaires et tarifs*, 439–40). Picard confirms that the delegates had become 'widespread' by 1918, despite initial employer resistance (*La Conciliation*, 39–41).

contract.[79] Important figures in the coalowners' and metallurgical industry's professional bodies (the Comité des Houillères
and Comité des Forges) supported this view, as did the influential business paper, *La Journée industrielle*.[80] Moreover, the
state, through the Ministry of Armaments and the Ministry of
Labour, possessed real power to force employers to recognize
trade unions, especially through the regional wage negotiations.
The *syndicats* often appealed to officials to enforce the revised
regional wage-scales on recalcitrant employers, with some
effect, as the reduced gap between prices and wages in 1918
testifies (see Appendix I). The Fédération du Sous-Sol similarly used the state to intervene against the coalowners in
1918.[81] It was above all the power and potential of the wartime
state, along with the growth of syndicalism itself, which
encouraged the CGT leadership to believe, as the war came to
an end, that the role and status of organized labour within
industry might be transformed.

(iii) The Dimensions of Syndicalist Reformism

The proliferation of syndicalism in 1917–18 allows some
measurement of the dimensions attained by wartime reformism
within the CGT. Although it was tempting for *minoritaires* to see

---

[79] AN F_7 13575, CGT, Comité Confédéral, meeting 8 Feb., rep. 11 Feb. 1917.
The federation also approved the widespread introduction of *délégués d'atelier*,
though mainly as a grievance procedure (*Bulletin de la fédération des industriels et
des commerçants français*, May–June 1917, 77–80).

[80] Notably R. Pinot, secretary of the Comité des Forges and key figure behind the
Union des Industries Métallurgiques et Minières, founded in 1900 as an umbrella for
heavy industry. Certainly by early 1919, Pinot and the UIMM accepted collective
bargaining (A. François-Poncet, *La Vie et l'œuvre de Robert Pinot* (Colin 1927), 281–
3). For examples from *La Journée industrielle*, see J. Hardy, 'La Lutte de classe', *La
Journée industrielle*, 14–15 Apr. 1918, p. 3, and B. Précy, 'Il faut s'entendre', ibid., 30
Apr. 1918, p. 1.

[81] To the point of threatening a strike. See the remarkable documentation in F_{22}
286. Three-way negotiations were conducted late in 1917 between de Peyerimhoff,
of the Comité des Houillères, Colliard, minister of Labour, and Bartuel, on
minimum and increased wages, *commissions mixtes*, and eight-hour shifts. The
miners' leaders signed an accord on the first two, but claimed subsequently that the
employers refused to implement it. By mid-1918, thoroughly disillusioned, the
Fédération du Sous-Sol insisted that the government force the employers to comply
(report by Bartuel to the *sous-sol* congress in F_{22} 286).

the majority orientation purely as a personal betrayal by syndicalist functionaries, some attempted a deeper analysis. Both
Hyacinthe Dubreuil,[82] in a CDS publication, *La Vraie Cassure*
(1917), and Georges Dumoulin,[83] assistant secretary of the CGT
who returned from the trenches to the coal-mines of the Loire in
1916–17 and wrote a bitter attack on the majority (*Les Syndicalistes français et la guerre*, June 1918), traced the wartime
divisions to differences between types of worker.[84] For both, the
central distinction was between the harsh environment of the
private sector, which generated a genuine, class-conscious militancy (metallurgy, building, clothing, and textiles), and the
narrowly corporative approach engendered by the cushioned
state or state-regulated sectors. As secretary of the skilled *mécaniciens* of the Paris region, Dubreuil saw the wartime *métallo* as a
man with skill but no security and a revolutionary temperament
honed by constant resistance to the private industrialist.[85] He was

[82] (1883–1971) son of a Norman labourer, Dubreuil became a skilled engineering
worker. Moving to Paris after his military service, he was a keen syndicalist and was
elected secretary of the Union des Mécaniciens de la Seine in 1912. *Minoritaire*
during the war, which he spent as a war worker in Paris, he was close to Merrheim
and active in the CDS. But after the divisive Paris engineering strike of 1919, he
rallied to the CGT majority. An impressive autodidact, he wrote a stream of articles
and books between the wars elaborating the new CGT orientation and examining the
implications of American mass-production techniques for France. From 1931, he
worked for the International Labour Organization. Strongly sympathetic to Vichy,
he none the less remained a prolific writer and lecturer until his death (Maitron (ed.),
Dictionnaire biographique du mouvement ouvrier français, pt. 3, *1871–1914*, vol. xii; M.
Fine, 'Hyacinthe Dubreuil', *Le Mouvement social*, 106 (Jan.–Mar. 1979), pp. 45–63).

[83] (1877–1963) born in the Pas-de-Calais, Dumoulin became a miner at 16. Active
in the Parti Ouvrier Français, he was imprisoned and sacked following a strike at
Courrières in 1901. Involved from 1906 in the revolutionary syndicalist *jeune
syndicat*, he came under the influence of its temporary organizer, Monatte, who
persuaded Dumoulin to move to Paris. He became a journalist and CGT administrator, frequenting anarchist and revolutionary syndicalist circles, and was a key figure
in the *noyau* of *La Vie ouvrière*. Mobilized from 1914 to 1916, and active in the
syndicalism of the Loire, where he returned as a miner, in 1916–18, Dumoulin
strongly supported Monatte's pacifism. But in 1918–19, he rallied to the *majoritaires*
and stuck to the CGT in 1921. He resigned from national office in 1923 but remained
a strong influence in the CGT and SFIO of the *Nord*. Close to the pacifist
syndicalism of Bélin in the 1930s, he took part in the Ministry of Labour at Vichy. At
the Liberation, he was stripped of all syndicalist functions (Maitron, (ed.), *Dictionnaire biographique du mouvement ouvrier français*, pt. 3, *1871–1914*, vol. xii; Dumoulin, *Carnets de route*, 65–97; Arum, 'Georges Dumoulin', and id., 'Du Syndicalisme
révolutionnaire au réformisme; Georges Dumoulin (1903–1923)', *Le Mouvement
social*, 87 (Apr.–June 1974), pp. 35–62).

[84] Copies of both are in the Institut de Recherches Marxistes, Paris.

[85] H. Dubreuil, *J'ai fini ma journée* (Librairie du Compagnonnage, 1971).

thus the archetypal *minoritaire* and inheritor of the moral qualities of the pre-war revolutionary syndicalist. The *majoritaire*, by contrast, was a state or municipal employee or a transport worker 'long ripe for the *Union sacrée*'. For Dumoulin, too, 'all the militants of the [metalworkers'] *syndicats* became *minoritaires*', whereas the traditional material self-interest of the miner lay at the root of the *sous-sol*'s wartime moderation, and a sense of hierarchy and obedience explained the (not uncontested) *majoritaire* allegiance of the *cheminots*.

There is an important kernel to these observations. The voting at the July 1918 CGT congress (as a rough indicator) suggests that at the federal level, the *minoritaires* were well-represented in private-sector federations (i.e. over 30 per cent of the relevant delegation's vote), a number of which were associated with pre-war revolutionary syndicalism.[86] Some of these, outside the war economy, were either numerically weak (laundry workers, brush makers, hatmakers, dyers) or relatively unresponsive to the boom in union membership (building workers). Others had been swollen by defence needs—most obviously, the metalworkers' and vehicle- and aircraft-workers' federations. These last two were clearly *minoritaire* bastions, (with 32 per cent and 60 per cent respectively of their federal delegations' votes), though both encompassed semi-skilled as well as the traditional skilled workers. Equally, the *majoritaire* notion of a 'statute' for the worker, specifying recognition of labour representatives and mechanisms for settling wages and conditions, was historically more characteristic of the outlook of workers in state or state-regulated industries (such as mining or railways) than in the private sector (with the notable exception of printing). The miners, railwaymen, merchant marine, postal workers, match workers (a state concession), and hospital workers all furnished a solid base for the *majoritaires*.

Brief reference to three categories of worker—miners, railwaymen, and the massed ranks of direct state employees in the post office and civil service—suggests how the wartime orientation of the *majoritaires* built on prior reformist traditions. As we have noted, Bartuel and the executive of the Fédération du Sous-Sol condemned the government for failing to reorganize

---

[86] CGT, *19ᵉ Congrès national corporatif ... (Paris, 15–18 juillet 1918)*, 271–300.

the mines in order to make full use of the *capacités profession-nelles* of the miners, recalled *en masse* from the front by 1917. They argued that the state had simply allowed the 'occult powers of the Comité des Houillères' to let real wages slide while abrogating the eight-hours legislation of 1905 and 1913 (by 1916, shifts ran to ten hours).[87]

This threw into sharp relief a series of issues dating back to the 1890s, on which Bartuel himself had focused the campaigns of the federation when, with the almost complete amalgamation of the miners' unions, he had become secretary in 1911.[88] These demands, restoration of the eight-hour shift, minimum regional wages, as well as overall increases, and miners' pensions, formed the essence of the programme defined by the Bureau Fédéral in 1916, approved by the March 1917 and August 1918 congresses, and pursued in the miners' campaign and strike in 1919.[89] The federation also significantly extended the concept of safety and hygiene delegates to the demand for a regional system of *paritaire* commissions to determine wages and conditions, plus a national commission to settle disputes. In short, the miners' leaders reacted against worsening living standards and a more authoritarian regime (since the bulk of the mining workforce was subject to military discipline) by invoking the key *majoritaire* themes— technical modernization (to raise productivity on shorter hours), 'confidence' in the miners' *syndicats*, and a new order in the management of the industry. But this remained essentially a reformulation of long-standing concerns.

The *cheminots* offer a close parallel with the miners. Still decimated, on the outbreak of war, by the strike of 1910, the railway unions achieved amalgamation in January 1917, becoming the largest federation in the CGT. Like the miners, the

[87] See pp. 94–5, above; Bartuel, 'Pourquoi nous manquons de charbon', *La Clairière*, 1 Aug. 1917, pp. 11–22.

[88] Bartuel and Rullière, *La Mine et les mineurs*, 491–525; D. Cooper-Richet, 'La Fédération nationale des mineurs' (3ᵉ cycle thesis, Paris, n.d.), chap. 5.

[89] Arts. by Bartuel in *La Clairière*, 1 Aug. 1917, pp. 11–22; 1 Oct. 1917, pp. 202–19; 15 Oct. 1917, pp. 241–52; 1 Dec. 1917, pp. 406–16; 15 Jan. 1918, pp. 576–80; 1 Apr. 1918, pp. 785–98; 1 Oct. 1918, pp. 1432–40; *La Bataille*, 13 Jan. 1916, for 1916 conference; ibid., 25 Mar. 1917, for 1917 congress, with *Fédération nationale des travailleurs du sous-sol. Compte rendu officiel des travaux du 3ᵉ congrès national extraordinaire, 23–6 mars 1917* (Imprimerie des Travailleurs Réunis, Carmaux, 1917); *La Bataille*, 22–6 Aug. 1918, for 1918 congress (no proceedings were published); ibid., 12 June–12 July 1919, for the strike.

leadership of the new Fédération Nationale des Travailleurs des Chemins de Fer condemned the failure of the companies to halt the decay of the system and protested against worsening wages, hours, and conditions. The authoritarian style of railway management, a bitter issue in 1910, was exacerbated by the militarization of the railways. The companies were under military control and the work-force, much of it on automatic *sursis d'appel*, was subject to military discipline.[90] The government had to intervene to assure minimum trade union rights.

The moderate leadership of the *cheminots* in 1917–18 therefore composed a programme of immediate demands which centred on wage increases and a *statut du personnel*, defining the career grades and union rights of employees. Such a programme was rooted in the special world of the railways, where family allowances, company pensions at an early retirement age, and a secure career structure carefully graded by function and seniority, had long been the main battleground between a restrictive company paternalism and unions seeking a statutory role in securing and administering such work conditions. The programme also reflected a tradition of *cheminot* reformism in which pressure on the state, owner of one network and licensing authority for the private companies, was the favoured form of action. A *statut* had existed in a partially satisfactory form since 1913 on the state network. The *cheminot* programme was approved by the June 1918 congress of the new federation.[91]

In the case of both the miners and *cheminots*, however, the war and the expectation that it would bring significant economic reforms endowed the traditional demand for nationalization—which had resurfaced shortly before the war—with special significance. The Syndicat National of the railwaymen voted the principle of nationalization at their April 1912 congress and, with the encouragement of Albert Thomas, adopted a report two years later (drafted by the executive) which embraced the autonomous and decentralized model of a nationalized industry

---

[90] *La Bataille*, 29 Jan. 1917, for the unity conference.

[91] *La Tribune des cheminots*, 1 Jan. 1918 ('Une Année d'efforts'); Toulouse, 'L'Action syndicale chez les cheminots', *La Clairière*, 15 Apr. 1918, pp. 851–6; and *Fédération nationale des travailleurs des chemins de fer. Compte rendu du 1er congrès national, Paris 28–30 juin 1918* (Imprimerie Nouvelle (Association Ouvrière), 1918), 177–94. For the 'special world of the railways', see Ribeill, *Le Personnel des compagnies de chemins de fer*, i, *Des origines à 1914*, 556–65.

(run by representatives of the consumers and workers).[92] The transport crisis from 1916, and above all the eventually successful demand of the companies for an increase in railway rates (which required parliamentary approval), underlined the critical economic and military role of the railways while evoking differences in the relative wartime sacrifices of companies and *cheminots*. The new federation responded with a strong campaign for railway nationalization which was launched in 1917 by the secretary, Marcel Bidegaray,[93] with the backing of socialist deputies, and approved by the June 1918 congress. It was to become the leitmotiv of *cheminot* action, *majoritaire* and *minoritaire*, in 1919–20.[94]

The Fédération du Sous-Sol, also reacting to the perceived differential in sacrifice, spearheaded its wartime critique of the coal companies with nationalization demands. A bitter debate between reformists and revolutionary syndicalists before the war had been tentatively resolved by the leadership with the adoption of the autonomous model of nationalization.[95] In

---

[92] *Le Mouvement socialiste*, 255 (Sept.–Oct. 1913), pp. 243–4; *Syndicat national des travailleurs des chemins de fer. Compte rendu du 25ᵉ congrès national, avril 1914* (Société Ouvrière d'Imprimerie, Courbevoie, 1914), 115–17, 174.

[93] (1875–1944) born in Bayonne, Bidegaray became a driver with the Chemin de Fer de l'Ouest (state-owned from 1909) after serving as a fireman in the Midi. Elected as the 'neutral' candidate (between the revolutionary syndicalist and reformist) as secretary of the Syndicat National in 1909, he held the same post in the unified Fédération Nationale. A moderate, he favoured arbitration in the 1920 railway strike. An unsuccessful candidate in the 1932 elections, he joined the Neo-Socialists in 1933. Arrested at the Liberation, he died (or was executed) in Dec. 1944.

[94] M. Bidegaray, *Contre les compagnies: pour la nation* (Société Ouvrière d'Imprimerie, Seine, 1917), with prefaces by Cachin and Jouhaux; id., *L'Information ouvrière et sociale*, 17 Mar. 1918; *Fédération nationale des travailleurs des chemins de fer. Compte rendu du 1ᵉʳ congrès national*, 194–6.

[95] A resolution of the Montceau-les-Mines *syndicat* at the 1912 congress condemned the traditional policy of nationalization on the grounds that it would reinforce the *état-patron*. The policy was referred to an executive commission, which in 1913 came out in favour of the *socialization* of mines—implying a different form of collective ownership. But it recommended maintaining the existing policy for the time being. A report to the 1914 congress suggested that the entire question needed to be studied afresh. It was this reconsideration which surfaced in the fuel crisis of 1916 (*Fédération nationale de l'industrie des mines... Compte rendu officiel des travaux du 23ᵉ congrès national des mineurs... février 1912* (Imprimerie des Travailleurs Réunis, Carmaux, 1912), 108–9; *Fédération nationale des travailleurs du sous-sol... Compte rendu officiel des travaux du 25ᵉ congrès national... avril 1913* (Imprimerie des Travailleurs Réunis, Carmaux, 1913), 32; *Fédération nationale des travailleurs du sous-sol... Compte rendu officiel des travaux du 26ᵉ congrès national... janvier 1914* (Imprimerie des Travailleurs Réunis, Carmaux, 1914), 24–5).

1916, also backed by socialist deputies, Bartuel and the Bureau
Fédéral, as we have observed, demanded nationalization in this
form as the ultimate solution to the fuel crisis. The industry was
to be administered regionally and nationally by councils representing the state, consumers, and the producers (in the shape of
representatives of the engineers and of the Fédération du Sous-
Sol).[96] As in the case of the *cheminots*, nationalization was to
play a strategic role in the reconstruction of post-war France.
Bartuel considered that

It will be a consolation ... to see our socialist conceptions ineluctably
imposing themselves on humans who have been battered by the most
frightful trials, and whose future can only be preserved by the
reorganization of their society.[97]

As for direct state employees, the *majoritaire* approach
coincided with, and substantially reinforced, the long-running
attempts by many of these, notably postal workers and
civil servants (*fonctionnaires*), to unionize. Technically, this
remained illegal under the 1884 law on *syndicats*. Organizations
of some of these groups had affiliated to the CGT before 1914,
but the threat of illegality hung over them (the interdiction did
not apply to workers in state manufacturing enterprises). Here,
too, the demand for a *statut* governing career grades, conditions, and representation rights, was central.[98] Wartime
insistence by the *majoritaires* on full recognition of *le droit
syndical* referred to this ban.[99] As economic pressures spurred a
revival of activity among state employees (including strikes and
strike threats by telephonists and telegraphists in 1917), their

---

[96] 'Proposition de loi tendant ... à la nationalisation des mines concédées',
Journal officiel, chambre des députés, documents parlementaires, 1916, no. 2672,
pp. 1631–3; Bureau Fédéral, Fédération du Sous-Sol, 'La Crise du charbon', *La
Bataille*, 24 Nov. 1916; and C. Bartuel, 'La Féodalité industrielle doit disparaître',
La Clairière, 15 Oct. 1917, pp. 241–252.

[97] C. Bartuel, 'La Féodalité industrielle', 252.

[98] L. Harmel, 'Le Syndicalisme des fonctionnaires', *La Clairière*, 15 Dec. 1917,
pp. 441–52, and 1 Jan. 1918, pp. 497–506; C. Laurent, *Le Syndicalisme des fonction-
naires: aperçu historique* (Institut Supérieur Ouvrier, n.d., but 1938), 16–24;
G. Frischmann, *Histoire de la fédération CGT des PTT* (Éditions Sociales, 1967);
J. Wishnia, 'French Fonctionnaires: The Development of Class Consciousness and
Unionization, 1884–1926' (Ph.D., Stony Brook, NY, 1978); J. Siwek-Pouydesseau,
Le Syndicalisme des fonctionnaires jusqu'à la guerre froide (Presses Universitaires de
Lille, Lille, 1989).

[99] e.g. L. Jouhaux, 'Extension du droit syndical', *La Bataille*, 10 Aug. 1917.

membership was actively solicited by the CGT majority leaders. Although the Fédération des Instituteurs was predominantly *minoritaire* (it represented the more radical and illegal minority of primary school teachers, most of whom belonged to the non-syndicalist *Amicales*), the *fonctionnaires* and different grades of postal employee all endorsed the CGT reformism developed in 1915–16.[100]

Yet if Dubreuil and Dumoulin were perceptive about the link between reformism and workers in the large penumbra of the state, they also over-simplified and missed out the real originality of the federal composition of the CGT majority. Within the strongly reformist groups, there was sometimes a vigorous *minoritaire* opposition. This was particularly true of the *cheminots*, who had a long revolutionary syndicalist as well as reformist tradition, and where a group initially centred on Gaston Monmousseau (and the Paris-Rive Droite, or St-Lazare, organization) gained just over 30 per cent of the vote for an anti-*majoritaire* resolution at the 1918 congress.[101] Even more importantly, most of the private sector federations in 1918 remained *majoritaire*. The cases of the Fédération des Métaux and the Fédération du Bâtiment show clearly how, for pre-war revolutionary syndicalists, one resolution of the CGT's crisis of orientation led to wartime reformism.

The convergence of Merrheim and Jouhaux over the need to defend the material interests of war workers by interceding with the government was strongly reinforced in 1917–18 by their accord on an essentially contractual approach to industrial relations. Above all, they shared a revulsion at the pacifist industrial militancy of spring 1918 and condemned the schismatic tendencies of the CDS. Differences remained. Merrheim never forgave Jouhaux his open embrace of republican patriotism. The *majoritaire* endorsement of an international process by which the labour and socialist movements might explore a

[100] Harmel, 'Le Syndicalisme des fonctionnaires'; Bordères, 'Le Droit syndical des agents de l'état', *L'Information ouvrière et sociale*, 14 Apr. 1918; reps. of the conferences of the *agents* and *sous-agents* of the PTT, on 9 May and 13–16 June respectively, in *La Bataille*, 10 May and 14–17 June (1918). For the teachers, see M. Ferré, *Histoire du mouvement syndicaliste révolutionnaire chez les instituteurs: des origines à 1922* (Société Universitaire d'Éditions de la Librairie, 1955), 174–85.
[101] *Fédération nationale des travailleurs des chemins de fer. Compte rendu du 1er congrès national*, 73–7.

negotiated end to the war removed a major source of discord. But Merrheim sounded a more pacifist tone, echoing his earlier 'Zimmerwaldian' stance, right to the end, while opposing disruptive action in support of such goals. Often, in 1918, his attitude must have seemed deeply contradictory to his erstwhile supporters in the CDS.[102] This convergence with the confederal *majoritaires*, not just by Merrheim but also by his principal lieutenants in the metalworkers' leadership (Labe, Blanchard, and Lenoir), led naturally to the Fédération des Métaux adopting the principal themes of *majoritaire* reformist thinking.

Thus, where the *Union des métaux* had condemned the idea of 'economic reorganization' in late 1916 with Merrheim accusing the majority of leading the CGT to 'the *Millerandisme* of the past', a more cautious note was sounded by September 1917, with Merrheim wondering simply whether 'the CGT would be capable of working usefully at the economic reorganization' in the face of the *patronat*'s power.[103] In 1918, Merrheim endorsed various aspects of the *majoritaire* approach. Citing (along with so many other European Socialists) the American munitions industry, he argued that new production processes could, if properly controlled, increase productivity and wages while shortening hours. He thus underwrote the central, productivist tenet of the *majoritaire* programme.[104] The *métaux* leaders were also preoccupied from 1917 by the looming problem of demobilization and the apparent likelihood of a complete disruption of the wartime engineering industry. This made a strong syndicalist influence on the process of transition from war to peace essential, and by 1918, Merrheim was calling for an economic plan—a kind of peacetime economic mobilization—to cushion the military demobilization, in whose elaboration the CGT was to play a key role.[105] At the federation's first wartime congress, in July 1918,

---

[102] AN F₇ 13372, 'La Propagande pacifiste', 'Dans les milieux ouvriers', 58, 70.

[103] *L'Union des métaux*, 65 (Sept.–Dec. 1916), p. 4; ibid. (July 1918), p. 7.

[104] 'Dans les usines de guerre d'Amérique', *La Vérité*, 7 July 1918.

[105] *L'Union des métaux*, 68 (July 1918), rep. of the Comité Fédéral National, Sept. 1917, p. 15; ibid. (Sept. 1918), rep. of congress of Fédération des Métaux, July 1918, p. 7. As the war ended, Merrheim cited the example of British labour's demobilization and reconstruction programmes (AN F₇ 13367, rep. 6 Oct. 1918, of a speech to *métallos* in Rouen; 'Dans les usines de guerre anglaises', *La Vérité*, 27 Nov. 1918). AN F₇ 13576, rep. 16 Nov. 1918, suggested that he was 'disposed to collaborate with the Ministry of Armaments' in order to secure syndicalist participation in 'the demobilization councils and the transformation of production in the factories'.

Merrheim and the leadership were condemned along with the CGT *majoritaires* for class collaboration by the CDS minority. But on the crucial resolution, which carefully distinguished the federation's position from that of the CDS and repudiated the May strike movement, Merrheim received an impressive vote of confidence—157 to 15. He made an explicit connection between the federation's attitude and the 'effort at regeneration' undertaken by the 1913 congress.[106] As the war ended, the *métaux*'s Commission Exécutive approved the CGT's *Programme minimum*, and in a speech of January 1919, subsequently published as a brochure (*La Révolution économique*), Merrheim indicated how the *majoritaire* perspective had finally fused with his pre-war concerns.[107]

If today the CGT counts in this country and enjoys an immense moral credit, ... if [the authorities] are considering according to syndicalists their full rights, the eight-hour day, demands which we have struggled for during twenty, twenty-five years, it is thanks to this reconstituted unity of the working class, forming a bloc, and saying to our rulers, to the bourgeoisie, to the *patronat*: 'we do not forget the general interests of the nation, but we, the working class are ... a power with whom you must reckon' ...[108]

The moderate leaders of the Fédération du Bâtiment who had triumphed at the 1914 congress (notably Chanvin, Charbonnier, and Picart) played a central part in defining the themes of confederal reformism while also applying these to their own wartime situation. By 1917–18, this included the need to fend off a powerful attack by the anarcho-syndicalists of the Paris organizations who had become, with Péricat, Hubert, and others, a central pillar of the CDS.[109]

The building workers' leaders enthusiastically participated in the Comité d'Action and throughout the war maintained their interest in the reconstruction of the devastated north-east. In

---

[106] *L'Union des métaux*, 69 (Sept. 1918), p. 6; A. Dumercq, 'Confrontation indispensable', *La Bataille*, 25 Aug. 1918.

[107] IFHS 14 AS 219, Fédération des Métaux, Commission Exécutive, min. 24 Dec. 1918.

[108] *La Révolution économique*, 27; Papayanis, *Alphonse Merrheim*, 113–20.

[109] AN F₇ 13649, various reps.; Syndicat Général des Ouvriers Terrassiers de la Seine, *A nos adhérents: rapport moral ... du 1er août 1914 au 1er janvier 1918*.

July 1917, Picart proposed a tripartite Office Public de Reconstruction des Régions Envahies, composed of representatives of the state, consumers, and the building workers, which would rebuild the public infrastructure of the north-east and act as a check on profiteering in private-sector building.[110] Like the Comité Confédéral of the CGT, the building workers' executive also stressed the need to prepare general plans for the postwar world from as early as June 1915.[111] In a report to the federation in February 1918, it outlined the value of the *majoritaire* approach to the building workers during the war on a range of issues (apprenticeship, labour placement, foreign labour, control over building sites through *délégués ouvriers*, etc.).[112] It also presented its own general plan, closely modelled on the November 1916 programme of the Commission Mixte d'Études Économiques, for a planned, collectivized, but decentralized economy,

> not on the capitalist path of the unlimited development of capitalist trusts and cartels . . . nor on the *étatiste* path of bureaucratic administration by the state . . . but on the path of economic federalism, with the administration directly under the control of the consumers and producers, grouped in their representative organisms . . .[113]

The first wartime congress of the federation, in July 1918, approved this plan, together with the whole range of reforms proposed by the CGT majority, by the narrow head of 50 votes to 46.

The wartime reformism of the CGT thus marked a fundamental realignment in which pre-war reformists sympathetic

---

[110] IFHS 14 AS 407 (Fonds Picart), doss. 5.

[111] The internal history of the building-workers' leadership can be reconstructed from the collection of circulars in IFHS 14 AS 407, doss. 1; the propaganda material, ibid., doss. 4; and the mins. of the Commission Exécutive, Jan. 1916–Jan. 1917, ibid., doss. 10 (all from the Picart collection). For the origins of post-war planning, see circular, June 1915, and *Le Travailleur du bâtiment*, Oct. 1915.

[112] *La Bataille*, 26 Feb. 1918; P. Chanvin, 'Comment la fédération ouvrière du bâtiment envisage la réorganisation économique', *L'Information ouvrière et sociale*, 7 Mar. 1918.

[113] *Fédération nationale des travailleurs de l'industrie du bâtiment, 6ᵉ congrès national, Versailles, 10 . . . 13 juillet 1918. Compte rendu des séances* (Imprimerie Nouvelle, 1918), 265. The report was circulated to delegates before the congress, with a letter from Chanvin and Charbonnier indicating that it was to be the main business (IFHS 14 AS 407, doss. 4).

to state action (miners, railwaymen) and reformists and revolutionaries from the dominant anti-state tradition coalesced around a new programme and approach. As the hegemony of classic revolutionary syndicalism, established in 1904–8 and still formally predominant, though undermined, down to 1914, openly disintegrated under the impact of the war, the reformist hegemony which replaced it drew support from the entire spectrum of pre-war currents. The composition of the majority on the Comité Confédéral, as well as the policies of individual federations, demonstrates this. If Bartuel and Bidegaray represented the continuity of state-oriented reformism, many of the leading *majoritaires* came from the heartlands of revolutionary syndicalism. Bled (gardeners), Luquet (hairdressers), Dumas (clothing), Vignaud (docks), Savoie (food), Lefevre (jewellers and watchmakers), Picart (building), and Dret (leatherworkers) were, like Jouhaux and Merrheim, former revolutionary syndicalists from private-sector organizations. Ironically, both Dumoulin and Dubreuil succumbed to the pull of this realignment, for they emerged in 1918–19 as two of the leading exponents of the new orientation.[114]

The twin ideological pivots of this realignment were the reformulation of nationalization proposals on the autonomous model and the November 1916 programme for the economic reorganization of post-war France. The former released the idea of nationalization from the traditional objection that it would strengthen the tyranny of the state (the *état-patron*). It thus allowed the state-oriented tradition of reformism to escape from its pre-war isolation in the CGT to become part of

---

[114] Dumoulin took up his pre-war post as a CGT functionary in July 1918. Though bitterly attacking the *majoritaires* at the July Congress, he accepted the connection between war and social change and rallied to Merrheim as the latter backed Jouhaux, ostensibly to preserve syndicalist unity against the CDS (CGT, *19ᵉ Congrès national corporatif ... (Paris, 15–18 juillet 1918)*, 135–48; Dumoulin, *Carnets de route*, 95–7; Arum, 'Georges Dumoulin', 357–65; id., 'Du syndicalisme révolutionnaire au réformisme', 42–4). But since Dumoulin helped draft the *Programme minimum*, he openly embraced *majoritaire* reformist ideas almost immediately (see n. 138, below). Dubreuil, who had acted as a kind of lieutenant of Merrheim in the Fédération des Métaux, sided with him in 1918 and, at the July 1918 *métaux* congress, defended Merrheim's policy of interceding with the authorities (*L'Union des métaux*, 69 (Sept. 1918), p. 4).

broader wartime syndicalist thinking on the need for public control of the economy. By 1917–18, the CGT majority as a whole endorsed the nationalization of the mines, railways, and certain other industries (notably hydro-electricity).[115]

That broader concept of a decentralized, 'democratic' economy with a major institutional role for organized labour—which lay at the heart of the 1916 post-war reform programme—represented in turn a reformist, gradualist version of the 'anti-authoritarian' and anti-political values prevalent in pre-war French syndicalism. It framed a host of other themes—the harnessing of industrial growth to labour's advantage, the collectivization of part of the economy and regulation of the rest, the contractualization of industrial relations—all of which found strong support among private-sector syndicalists and erstwhile revolutionaries, as well as among traditional reformists.

Of course, the craft and industrial federations formed only one dimension of the CGT, since syndicalists enrolled twice, by locality as well as trade. Ever since the independent Fédération des Bourses du Travail in the 1890s, there had been a tendency for the local and regional cross-trade groupings to express a more militant syndicalism than the national federations. The Bourses du Travail and Unions départementales were also more likely to reflect the transformed economic geography of wartime France and its impact on labour militancy. They corresponded more closely to the framework of *minoritaire* syndicalism, which was in part the revolt of the factory and the industrial locality against the national structures of the CGT. Here, the voting in July 1918 is an even rougher indication than in the case of the federations, since the networks of *minoritaire* militancy had been seriously eroded by the repression following the May strikes.

None the less, the votes of the eleven biggest Unions départementales, correlated with each *département*'s order of importance in the industrial war effort (as indicated by the size of its munitions work-force in January 1917), show that *minoritaire* strength was well above average in the largest Unions départementales, though the Seine-Inférieure, Ille-et-Vilaine, and Gironde are exceptions (see Table 3). And there is a broad

---

[115] *La Voix du peuple*, 1 May 1917, pp. 11–12, 16; ibid., Dec. 1917, p. 17; H. Prêté and L. Jouhaux, *La Houille blanche: une solution ouvrière* (Dec. 1917).

TABLE *3*.   Majoritaires *and* Minoritaires *by Union départementale*, *1918*

Unions départementales (ranked by size to the nearest 500) in 1918[1]		*Département* by size of munitions labour force[2]	Min. (% vote)[3]	Maj. (% vote)
Seine	108,500	1	31	72
Seine-Inférieure	24,000	6	8	82
Rhône	18,500	3	35	56
Loire	16,500	2	38	62
Haute-Garonne	16,000	5	26	63
Seine-et-Oise	14,000	9	24	74
Bouches-du-Rhône	12,500	—	49	51
Ille-et-Vilaine	12,000	—	5	95
Gironde	11,500	4	6	91
Loire-Inférieure	11,000	8	4	77
Cher	11,000	10	—	71
Average (90 Unions départementales)			20	72

Sources:
[1] *Rapports des comités confédéraux et des commissions pour l'exercice 1918–1919* (1919), 151–2.
[2] J.-L. Dereymez, 'Les Usines de guerre (1914–1918) et le cas de la Saône-et-Loire', *Cahiers d'Histoire (Lyon-Grenoble)*, 26/2 (1981), pp. 151–81 (161).
[3] M. Labi, *La Grande division des travailleurs* (Éditions ouvrières, 1964), 272–3.

relationship between the most industrially active *départements* in the war effort and *minoritaire* bastions. The importance of the May 1918 strike movements in those *départements* (Seine, Loire, Rhône) underlines the connection, which has been demonstrated by J.-L. Robert. Politicized industrial militancy in 1918 and the strength of the *minoritaires* were connected to the impact of armaments production, both on the composition and distribution of the working class.[116] Adding other *départements* with a high *minoritaire* vote—Bouches-du-Rhône (49 per cent) Ardèche (50 per cent), Drôme (38 per cent), Hérault

---

[116] J.-L. Robert and M. Chavance, 'L'Évolution de la syndicalisation en France de 1914 à 1921: l'emploi de l'analyse factorielle des correspondances', *Annales ESC*, Sept.-Oct. 1974, pp. 1092–107; Robert, *La Scission syndicale de 1921*, 176–9.

(50 per cent), Isère (84 per cent), Lot (33 per cent), Finistère (40 per cent), a map of *minoritaire* sentiment emerges along two axes, one to the centre and south-east (Paris–Lyons–St-Étienne–Marseilles), the other to the west and south-west. These corresponded with areas well sheltered from the western front but strongly marked by the relocation of French industrial production for the war effort.[117]

On the other side, the *majoritaire* orientation within these Unions départementales remained strong. In important munitions *départements* (the Seine-Inférieure, close to the front, and the Gironde in the south-west) the *majoritaires* remained overwhelmingly predominant. Other *départements* near the front (Meurthe-et-Moselle, Saône-et-Loire, Aube, but not the Meuse), and less industrialized *départements* outside the main *minoritaire* areas, were also *majoritaire* strongholds.

More local studies are needed. But it is clear that the distinction between *majoritaires* and *minoritaires* was not simply one between national leaders and a militant rank-and-file. The *majoritaire* conception of syndicalism struck a responsive chord in many localities. In the Seine-Inférieure (Rouen, Le Havre) and Ille-et-Vilaine, for example, its themes were actively pursued by local organizations.[118] But in some of the most intense concentrations of war workers a quite different variant of trade unionism, combining the techniques of revolutionary syndicalism with a potentially mass following, threatened the authority of the new reformism.

(iv) *Consolidating Reformism: The Political Contest in the CGT*

The final year of the war witnessed a realignment of tendencies at the national level of the CGT. Since December 1916, the *majoritaires* had modified their refusal to meet German labour

---

[117] Robert, *La Scission syndicale de 1921*, 98–9; Becker, *The Great War and the French People*, 231.

[118] For the Seine-Inférieure, various reports in AN F, 13619; for the Ille-et-Vilaine, various reps, in AN F, 13603 and Rennes municipal archives, Ix 79 1/2 9, and J. Horne, 'Labour Leaders and the Post-War World, 1914–1919' (Ph.D., Sussex, 1980), 439–41.

leaders before the end of hostilities. In 1917, they participated in the attempt to explore a negotiated peace through an international labour and socialist conference. And when the Painlevé government refused passports for Stockholm, they co-operated with the British labour movement in a new, allied move to secure agreement with the socialists of the Central Powers on how to end the war. At the same time, the CGT *majoritaires* supported the campaign in 1918 to pressure Clemenceau and the French government into committing themselves to 'Wilsonian' peace aims.

In part, this shift of attitude was a response to obvious war-weariness among French workers and to fears that, through Clemenceau, expansionist interests were gaining control of French foreign policy. But there was also an element of political calculation. Jouhaux, in particular, remained sceptical of the readiness of German labour leaders to repudiate their own government's expansionism, and to carry out the democratic revolution which might open the way to German acceptance of a non-annexationist peace. As he told the British TUC in September 1917: 'Unless ... peace can be made by free peoples wars are bound to continue'.[119] A secret meeting of the confederal majority in November 1917 made it clear that espousing the idea of an international conference was partly a tactical move, dramatizing the CGT's rejection of Clemenceau's unspecific and 'undemocratic' war aims, and stealing the *minoritaires'* clothes before the third CGT conference of the war, at Clermont Ferrand in December 1917.[120] Certainly none of this undermined the 'choice of 1914', even though it marked the distance between the CGT and the government on war aims. During the German spring offensive in 1918, the *majoritaires* firmly endorsed the national defence.[121]

For their part, the moderate *minoritaires*, exemplified by Merrheim, rallied to the 'choice of 1914' in two crucial regards. They discovered a shared apprehension with the *majoritaires* at the idea of a Russo-German peace treaty. As early as 4 April

---

[119] *Report of the Trades Union Congress, Blackpool, September 1917* (1917), 279.
[120] AN F₇ 13575, CGT, meeting 23 Nov., rep. 25 Nov. 1917.
[121] Both the Comité Confédéral of the CGT and the Union des Syndicats of the Seine demanded a more active role for organized labour in defending Paris, in a resurgence of the sentiments of autumn 1914 (*La Bataille*, 14, 18, and 22 June 1918).

1917, Merrheim told the Comité Confédéral that 'while he remained a partisan of peace, he formally repudiated any idea of a separate peace between Russia and Germany.'[122] The bulk of French syndicalists and socialists continued to view the revolution in Russia through the lens of French national defence until the Armistice, and considered Bolshevik 'defeatism' and the treaty of Brest-Litovsk in March 1918 as a kind of betrayal, which placed France gravely at risk.[123]

The May 1918 strikes also compelled the moderate *minoritaires* to acknowledge the incompatibility of political strikes with support for the national defence. Merrheim stressed that the working class could use 'legitimate' pressure for its ideas.[124] But the *métaux* leaders showed in May 1918 that this did not extend to the paralysis of war production. Bourderon made his position clear in December 1917 when, in the Comité Confédéral, he distinguished 'pacifist' from 'defeatist' campaigns, and, in opposing the latter, declared that he would rather be a Frenchman than a German. If the duty of the working class was still 'to strip the bourgeoisie of all its advantages, notably the means of production', Bourderon added significantly that 'it must also think about the interests of the country'.[125] Even Dumoulin, in chairing the *minoritaire* congress at St-Étienne in May 1918, considered that it was unwise to jeopardize the national defence at such a moment, and in the summer rallied to Merrheim and Jouhaux.

Consequently, at the Clermont Ferrand conference and at the first full congress of the CGT during the war, in Paris in July 1918, the *majoritaires* and moderate *minoritaires* found substantial grounds for *rapprochement*. They swung their combined weight behind an international policy designed to push the government along the path towards a 'democratic' and possibly negotiated peace, without jeopardizing the war effort. And they both strove to defend syndicalist unity against what were considered the divisive tactics of the CDS.

---

[122] AN F₇ 13575, CGT, Comité Confédéral, min. 4 Apr. 1917. Merrheim made his disapproval of Brest-Litvosk clear to the 1918 CGT congress.

[123] See Chap. 8, below.

[124] 'Les Ouvriers anglais et la guerre', *La Vérité*, 28 Jan. 1918; for Merrheim's uncompromising support for the national defence, see his speech to the July *métaux* congress, in *La Vérité*, 13 July 1918.

[125] AN F₇ 13575, CGT, Comité Confédéral, 5 Dec., rep. 7 Dec. 1917.

The Clermont Ferrand resolution achieved its immediate aim. It was voted with only two abstentions.[126] The common approach was confirmed in the succeeding months. In February 1918, the Comité Confédéral called for prudent syndicalist meetings to force the government to declare its 'democratic' war aims.[127] Bourderon and Merrheim, in contrast to the earlier part of the war, supported the *majoritaires* as they both renewed their wartime moratorium on May Day strikes and reserved the right to step up the peace aims campaign once the military crisis of the German offensive was past.[128] As if to clinch the new alignment, Bourderon and Merrheim were included in a small executive committee (with Luquet, Bidegaray, and Bartuel), established in February 1918, to aid Jouhaux in the event of a major domestic crisis.[129]

This *rapprochement* in turn helped redefine a more radical and obdurate minority, hovering on the brink of defeatism and ready to challenge the consensus on maintaining the military effort. The twenty *minoritaire* delegates who met the day before the Clermont Ferrand conference resolved to 'carry out a general strike or create disturbances throughout the whole country' if the CGT refused to approve an international conference.[130] Temporarily concealed by the façade of unity, the rift broke through again in April–May 1918 as the CDS under Péricat and the pacifist strike movements openly challenged the *majoritaire* realignment. At the July 1918 congress, a motion which both reaffirmed the Clermont Ferrand unity resolution and condemned *minoritaire* separatism was opposed by a strong minority (253 to 908, with 46 abstentions), in a vote whose sociological significance we have already discussed. As the war came to an end, the minority was swelled by a number of disillusioned *syndicats* which had approved the July resolution mainly in the interests of unity and on the mistaken assumption

---

[126] CGT, *Conférence extraordinaire ...* (*Clermont-Ferrand, 23–25 décembre 1917*), 154–5.
[127] AN F₇ 13576, CGT circular.
[128] Ibid., CGT, Comité Confédéral, 18 Apr. 1918, rep. 19 Apr.
[129] Ibid., CGT, Comité Confédéral, min. 10 Feb. and 19 Mar. 1918.
[130] AN F₇ 13583, rep. of the St-Étienne Commissariat Central to the Préfet of the Loire, 22 Dec. 1917.

that the congress marked the end of the wartime orientation of the *majoritaires*.[131]

The last twelve months of the war, therefore, were decisive in deepening, along a modified internal frontier, the antagonism in the CGT between the 'choice of 1914' and a more intractable syndicalist pacifism. Spring 1918 provided a variation on the emergency of autumn 1914, with the original themes amplified. The possibility of pacifist repudiation of the national effort was more real, as was the danger, in syndicalist eyes, of political reaction. The threat of German conquest was every bit as menacing and posed again, in stark terms, the question of the relationship between working class and nation, labour movement and Republic.

Some historians have argued that this process amounted to a *rassemblement centriste*, or realignment on the centre.[132] But the adherence of the *majoritaires* to the 'choice of 1914' was not in essence modified by their qualified and partly tactical agreement to explore a negotiated peace. The moderate *minoritaires*, by contrast, embraced much of the 'choice of 1914' by the primacy which they accorded the military effort and by the clear limits which they placed on any popular movement for peace. It was the CDS which turned the earlier pacifist critique of the implications of the 'choice of 1914' for revolutionary syndicalist values into a total rejection of the practice and principles of wartime labour reformism. In this, it foreshadowed the line of fracture within French trade unionism from the Armistice to the schism of 1921. The *majoritaires* thus found their strength consolidated, at least nationally, by the realignment of 1917–18. Even allowing for the under-representation of *minoritaire* strength at the July 1918 congress, the *majoritaires'* position compared favourably with that at previous wartime meetings (see Table 4).

The reformist policies and programme defined earlier in the war played a vital role in, and were correspondingly strengthened by, the *rapprochement* of *majoritaires* and moderate *minoritaires*. Perhaps inevitably, the programme of post-war 'economic reorganization' and reform placed by the *majoritaires* on the

[131] Ibid., n. of 1 Nov. 1918.
[132] Georges and Tintant, *Léon Jouhaux*, i. 299–302; Kriegel, *Aux origines du communisme français*, i. 204–33.

TABLE 4. Majoritaire *Votes at Wartime Conferences of the CGT*

Conference or Congress	*Majoritaire* Vote (%)
Aug. 1915	68
Dec. 1916	74
Dec. 1917	unity resolution
July 1918	75

agenda of the December 1917 conference was eclipsed by discussion of peace aims and the attempt to patch up syndicalist unity. But it re-emerged into full prominence in 1918. Most of the *majoritaires* who spoke at the July 1918 congress, or who were interviewed beforehand by *La Clairière*, took as their theme (after a vigorous defence of the 'choice of 1914') the need for a 'democratic' peace and a gradualist approach to social change.[133] Although the resolution largely reiterated that of Clermont Ferrand, there was no doubt what the *majoritaires* stood for.

Paradoxically, a specific programme of reforms was not this time presented. It is evident from the agenda that the majority leaders hoped that the congress itself, much the largest and most representative syndicalist gathering of the war, would define one.[134] The fact that the debates were formally preoccupied with the Comité Confédéral's wartime record precluded this, and it was only in the subsequent months that reform plans were finalized for the rapidly approaching peace.

There were two aspects to the process. The first affected the organization of the CGT, the second its policies. The congress had unanimously voted the principle of a major constitutional change to strengthen the central institutions of the CGT. An enlarged Comité Confédéral (Comité Confédéral National) was envisaged which would be more representative of the movement as a whole and which would meet regularly to guide a small executive. Doubtless the vote was unanimous because both factions saw it as a means of consolidating their power.

---

[133] *La Clairière*, ser. of arts., 15 Apr.–1 July 1918, on 'Le Congrès de la CGT et le problème économique'; CGT, *19ᵉ Congrès national corporatif . . . Paris, 15–18 juillet 1918*, 221–36 (Jouhaux); 178–88 (Savoie), and 169–75 (Bidegaray).

[134] The agenda simply listed the international conference and domestic reforms as the elements of the programme to be defined (IFHS 14 AS 213 c/18).

Such centralization did not automatically favour the *majoritaires*. In practice, however, they dominated its implementation, and it certainly accorded with their ideas of a mass, disciplined syndicalism.[135] By the September 1919 congress, Monatte (once more a leading figure in the *minoritaires*) argued that the *majoritaires* had simply used the reform to expel 'troublemakers' from the central organs of the CGT.[136]

The specific programme of post-war reforms sought from the congress was subsequently drafted by the majority leaders themselves. A commission was established composed of five *majoritaires* (Jouhaux, Bled, Dumas, Auguste Savoie,[137] and Lenoir, of the *métaux*), plus Dumoulin. It was this commission which, from August to November 1918, drew up the *Programme minimum*.[138] This was unveiled at a mass meeting of Paris trade unionists on 24 November 1918, at the Cirque d'Hiver, and was endorsed unanimously by the first Comité Confédéral National, on 15 December 1918.[139]

The *Programme minimum* opened by reiterating the CGT's 'democratic' peace aims. It also rejected protectionism and

---

[135] The Bureau Confédéral, enlarged into a commission administrative of 14, replaced the Comité Confédéral in the latter's wartime function of an executive body. It was predominantly *majoritaire*, and consisted of 7 secretaries of federations and 7 secretaries of Unions départementales. The Bureau Confédéral implemented the remaining changes in Oct.–Dec. 1918 (*Rapports des comités . . . pour l'exercice 1918–1919*, 4–7).

[136] CGT, *20ᵉ Congrès national corporatif . . . (Lyon, 15–21 septembre 1919)*, 108.

[137] (*c.* 1876–?) a Parisian bakery worker, Savoie was, from 1908 to 1913, secretary of the Union des Syndicats de la Seine. In 1908 he also became secretary of the Fédération de l'Alimentation. A pre-war revolutionary syndicalist (he was, with Jouhaux, one of the five who in 1912 signed the reaffirmation of the Amiens charter in *La Bataille syndicaliste*), he joined Jouhaux in the wartime majority, with his federation. He remained *majoritaire* in 1921, when the bulk of his members passed to the communist CGTU. During the Vichy years, he was vice-president of the commission which drafted the Charte du Travail.

[138] CGT, *Rapports des comités . . . pour l'exercice 1918–1919*, 14–15; AN F₇ 13576, CGT, Comité Confédéral, 1 Aug., rep. 3 Aug. 1918. The full text of the programme is in *Rapports des comités . . . pour l'exercice 1918–1919*, 28–35. It was published in Dec. 1918, with additional comment by Jouhaux, as a pamphlet entitled *Les Travailleurs devant la paix*. It is reproduced in Robert, 'Les "Programmes minimum" de la CGT de 1918 et 1921'.

[139] AN F₇ 13576, rep. 24 Nov. 1918, and *La Bataille*, 25 Nov. 1918, for the mass meeting; *Rapports des comités . . . pour l'exercice 1918–1919*, 7; and for the Comité Confédéral National, CGT, *Première réunion du comité confédéral national (Paris, 15–16 décembre 1918). Compte rendu sténographique* (L'Union Typographique, Villeneuve-Saint-Georges, 1919); *La Bataille*, 16 Dec. 1918.

economic reprisals after the war, and referred to the international version of economic and social reforms which it hoped labour representatives would inscribe in the peace settlement. It then turned to the issues raised by the strikes of 1917–18, demanding *le droit syndical* for all, including state employees, and widespread recognition of trade unions by employers, through *délégués ouvriers* and collective bargaining. The eight-hour day was claimed as tangible proof of the confederal majority's contention that within a reformed and technically updated capitalism, there was a real margin for improved living standards. On demobilization, it repeated the 1915 Comité d'Action plan for the reconstruction of the devastated regions. It also added the idea of a Conseil National Économique, with state, business, and syndicalist representatives, whose function would be to master-mind the return to the peacetime economy. But the bulk of the programme, as we have seen, was taken verbatim from the November 1916 plan for the reconstruction of post-war France. The *Programme minimum* was a summation of the *majoritaires'* wartime reformism as well as the basis on which they confronted *l'après-guerre*.

Changing circumstances in 1917–18 refined but did not destroy the reformist hegemony established by the majority leaders of the CGT earlier in the war. If anything, this hegemony was consolidated nationally, as the moderate *minoritaires* accepted its basic tenets and as the majority leaders adopted a cautious but credible approach to the industrial unrest. At precisely the point where relations with the state came under greatest strain, the new reformism preserved the essence of the 'choice of 1914'. The surge of syndicalist numbers suggested that support for the reformism of the majority extended far beyond the Comité Confédéral. But it also crystallized a pacifist syndicalism deeply antagonistic to the *majoritaires*, and redrew the frontier of internal opposition. The CGT which in November 1918 faced the return to a peace economy was profoundly divided.

6 The Road to 'Reconstruction': The British Labour Movement and Post-War Reform, 1914–1918

LABOUR reformism in wartime France was a highly differentiated plant. It grew in the space between the more negative and coercive features of the mobilization process, on the one hand, which legally and, early on numerically, weakened syndicalism while turning industrialists into the privileged partners of the state, and the growth of *minoritaire* hostility on the other. Yet this terrain was fairly substantial, even if in some combatant societies, such as Russia, it barely existed at all. It comprised not only continuing support by much of labour opinion for the 'choice of 1914', but also the collaborative aspects of the mobilization process, in which the state accredited syndicalist leaders as the authoritative voices of labour and, under pressure from acute labour shortages and the disruptive potential of labour militancy, imposed constraints on the autonomy of the *patronat*. Through its wartime reformism, the CGT sought to use this terrain to define a more critical participation in the war effort and to demand that the social forces unleashed by the war should be applied to far-reaching domestic reforms, especially once the conflict was over.

We now turn to the question of whether the wartime reformism of the CGT was an isolated plant or part of a wider species. Here the British comparison will help to establish whether we are dealing with a more general feature of industrialized societies experiencing multiple mobilization for a 'total' war, or whether the responses of different labour movements, and societies, remain too varied to permit generalization.[1]

(i) The War Emergency: Workers' National Committee and 'After the War' Questions

In the British case, a variety of factors worked against the emergence of a specific war reformism comparable to that in France in the first eighteen months of the war. The importance of maintaining a voluntary military mobilization focused the attention of most labour leaders on the recruitment drive. At the same time, trade union leaders were more officially involved than in France in an industrial mobilization which remained technically voluntary for a full year, until July 1915. In principle, the bargaining which occurred between Lloyd George and the unions over the Munitions of War Act gave labour leaders an opportunity unparalleled in France to establish their own conditions for participating in the industrial mobilization.[2] The bargaining was not entirely one-sided, but it is hard to disagree with G. D. H. Cole's verdict, late in 1915, that in reality trade union leaders gained little and conceded a lot.[3] They neither obtained an unequivocal guarantee on the post-war restoration of suspended trade union customs, nor did they extend the scope of the bargaining to encompass a broad range of issues which touched the working class closely during the war (price controls, housing, social welfare, etc.). In this, they reflected both the strength of the patriotic mood in 1914–15 and their own fairly narrow conception of trade union concerns.

Additionally, the internal ideological conflict which from December 1914 helped sharpen the *majoritaire* reformism of

[1] Rare exceptions to the lack of comparative economic and social histories of the First World War are M. Ferro, *The Great War 1914–1918*, (1969; English trans., Routledge & Kegan Paul, 1973); G. Hardach, *The First World War, 1914–1918* (1973; English trans., Allen Lane, 1977); A. Marwick, *War and Social Change in the Twentieth Century: A Comparative Study of Britain, France, Germany, Russia and the United States* (Macmillan, 1974); and J. M. Winter, *The Experience of World War I* (Macmillan, 1988).

[2] See pp. 77–9, above.

[3] Cole, *Labour in Wartime*, 198–9.

the CGT had no parallel in most of the British labour movement. This might seem paradoxical, since there was clear, public opposition to the war from the outset in the shape of the ILP and a new organization founded in December 1914, the Union of Democratic Control (UDC), which formed a bridge between ILP socialists and dissident Liberals. But the ILP and UDC concentrated on the immorality of a war caused in their view by undemocratic, secret diplomacy, and on the special immorality of British involvement. By and large (the more revolutionary Scottish ILP apart), the reformist socialists who predominated in the ILP did not condemn labour participation in the national effort as a fundamental betrayal of deeper class principles.[4] This reflected the pragmatic and relatively undoctrinal nature of the pre-war British labour movement, in which ideological debates comparable to those in the CGT and SFIO had, except on the revolutionary fringes, no significant place.[5]

Throughout 1915, both the Labour Party and TUC supported the official war effort without demur and with little reference to the labour movement's more general pre-war (let alone postwar) concerns. The first wartime Trades Union Congress, in September 1915, reaffirmed the commitment to 'prosecute the cause of the Allies to a final and complete victory'. But when F. Bramley proposed a 'new workers' charter', containing the standard TUC demands since the mid-1890s, the nationalization of coal-mines, railways, and land, together with an eight-hour day and minimum wage, plus a vigorous campaign to implement them, he failed completely. The resolution had been on the agenda of the cancelled 1914 congress. But Bramley himself agreed that it would be inopportune to enact the resolution

---

[4] Dowse, *Left in the Centre*, 21–2; H. Hanak, 'The Union of Democratic Control during the First World War', *Bulletin of the Institute of Historical Research*, 36 (Nov. 1963), pp. 168–80; M. Swartz, *The Union of Democratic Control in British Politics during the First World War* (Clarendon Press, Oxford, 1971). For the Clydeside movement, see R. K. Middlemas, *The Clydesiders: A Left-wing Struggle for Parliamentary Power* (Hutchinson, 1965), 58–113; W. Kendall, *The Revolutionary Movement in Britain, 1900–1921* (Weidenfeld and Nicolson, 1969); J. Hinton, 'The Clyde Workers' Committee and the Dilution Struggle', in A. Briggs and J. Saville (eds.), *Essays in Labour History, 1886–1923* (Macmillan, 1971), 152–84; and I. McLean, *The Legend of Red Clydeside* (John Donald, Edinburgh, 1983).

[5] See Chap. 1, above.

during the war, and he simply asked for a vote of principle. The resolution fell for lack of a seconder.[6]

Yet the British case was not totally dissimilar to the French. If the sense of ideological hiatus was much less serious, the economic and social disruption occasioned by the war was felt keenly, and provoked a comparable response of working-class self-defence. A national organization was established which directly paralleled the Comité d'Action—the War Emergency: Workers' National Committee (WEWNC). Founded by a special conference on 5 August 1914, it represented the major national labour committees (the PCTUC, the LPNEC, and the Management Committee of the General Federation of Trade Unions (MCGFTU)), leading trade unions, socialist groups, and various women's and co-operative organizations. Moderate craft and 'new Union' leaders predominated. But they rubbed shoulders with more radical trade unionists (such as Robert Smillie, socialist president of the MFGB, and chairman of the WEWNC from late 1915), with socialists such as J. Ramsay MacDonald and W. C. Anderson of the ILP and H. M. Hyndman, veteran leader of the British Socialist Party, and with a phalanx of influential women labour activists. A significant presence was that of Sidney Webb, for whom the committee proved the first step to institutional participation in the labour movement (he graduated to the LPNEC in 1916), now that Labour had become the chosen vehicle of Fabian reformism.[7]

The new committee's initial task was to ensure adequate food distribution and to 'guard against the exploitation of the people by unnecessarily high prices'.[8] Under its energetic secretary, J. S. Middleton,[9] it broadened its concerns while skirting purely

---

[6] *Trades Union Congress Annual Report, 1915*, 60.

[7] For the founding of the WEWNC, see *Report of the War Emergency: Workers' National Committee (August 1914–March 1916)*, 3; R. Harrison, 'The War Emergency: Workers' National Committee, 1914–1920', in Briggs and Saville (eds.), *Essays in Labour History*, 211–59; J. M. Winter, *Socialism and the Challenge of War: Ideas and Politics in Britain, 1912–1918* (Routledge & Kegan Paul, 1974), 184–233; and McBriar, *Fabian Socialism and English Politics*, 307–45.

[8] *Report of the War Emergency: Workers' National Committee (August 1914–March 1916)*, 3.

[9] (1878–1962) a printer and activist in the local labour movement of Workington (Cumberland), Middleton moved to London as a young man. He came to the attention of Ramsay MacDonald who appointed him assistant secretary (i.e. permanent administrator) to the Labour Representation Committee, a post which he retained in the Labour Party until 1940. He was a member of the ILP from 1897.

trade union questions and general issues of policy belonging to the established national labour committees. Instead it sought out common ground in the urgent problems arising from the war, and acted as a national lobby for labour, interceding with government to propose solutions, and organizing public campaigns to back these up. Like the Comité d'Action, it was in close contact with labour organizations in the provinces, which it encouraged to engage in similar action locally.[10]

The issues which preoccupied the WEWNC closely matched the concerns of the Comité d'Action, allowing for obvious differences of national experience, such as the refugee problem and the physical destruction of northern France. The WEWNC pressed for higher military separation allowances (of a 'pound-a-week') and like the Comité d'Action, successfully urged their extension to common-law wives. It also confronted a sharp bout of unemployment though less protracted and severe than in France (6.2 per cent of insured trades in August 1914, 5.4 per cent in September, falling to 2.6 per cent in January 1915).[11] Here the WEWNC advanced Sidney Webb's ideas on unemployment relief, which were essentially those of the Minority Report of the 1909 Poor Law Commission. These ideas, which were to resurface in other contexts during the war, amounted to a condemnation of the Poor Law system. They advocated prevention (through state expenditure to sustain employment) in preference to relief, and relief was envisaged in the form of constructive projects rather than simple maintenance.[12] The government ignored these proposals, but by early 1915 the problem itself was evaporating.

The defence of the working-class consumer, by contrast, remained urgent and became the most durable of the WEWNC's concerns for the entire war. Again, the approach showed remarkable similarities with that of the Comité d'Action. From the start,

---

[10] *Report of the War Emergency: Workers' National Committee (August 1914–March 1916)*, 4, 21; WEWNC/ADD/22; Clinton, *The Trade Union Rank and File*, 54–62.

[11] Board of Trade figures for insured trades, quoted in Cole, *Labour in Wartime*, 70. The trade union estimates were slightly different. For the range of issues covered by the committee, see *Report of the War Emergency: Workers' National Committee (August 1914–March 1916)*, 10–21.

[12] Cole, *Labour in Wartime*, 101–7; Winter, *Socialism and the Challenge of War*, 191–4.

profiteering was condemned, especially on government contracts, and seen as a major cause of price inflation. This remained a common working-class conviction throughout the war. The WEWNC advocated the compulsory acquisition and sale at controlled prices of the wheat crop (i.e. *réquisition* and *taxation*) and it co-ordinated widespread local campaigns for price controls and rationing. It demanded compulsory cultivation of idle land in 1917 as a step towards securing 'the complete social ownership and control of the land of the country'.[13] And like the Comité d'Action, the WEWNC took on the coal-owners and retailers in an effort to limit the soaring price of domestic coal. It also systematically fought rent increases.[14]

The WEWNC also intervened on a subject which goaded the CGT into action in 1915—female sweated labour in a clothing industry experiencing a boom on army contracts. Like the Comité Intersyndical d'Action contre l'Exploitation de la Femme, the women members of the WEWNC campaigned on government committees for reduced hours and minimum wages. As dilution in munitions production gathered pace in the autumn of 1915, they also urged women workers to unionize and fight for equal wages and conditions.[15]

The WEWNC was not the only organ of labour and working-class self-defence against the immediate social repercussions of the war. The ILP, which actively supported the WEWNC, also campaigned on its own behalf on the same issues. The other national committees overlapped to some extent with the WEWNC. The co-operative movement, as in France, expanded considerably under the impetus of the war (membership

[13] The WEWNC organized various conferences, and lobbied the government, on food supplies and prices throughout the war (WEWNC/35/1/41; WEWNC/ADD/22/17/1; booklet of 21 Apr. 1917, *The National Food Supply*, WEWNC/20/1/2/16; *Report of the War Emergency: Workers' National Committee (August 1914–March 1916)*, 13–15). In 1918, members of the committee participated in the Consumer Council, newly established largely as a concession to Labour criticisms of provisioning policies (Winter, *Socialism and the Challenge of War*, 199–202).

[14] *Report of the War Emergency: Workers' National Committee (August 1914–March 1916)*, 16–17; WEWNC, various docs. in 13/7 and ADD/29/1/64; Winter, *Socialism and the Challenge of War*, 202–5.

[15] *Report of the War Emergency: Workers' National Committee (August 1914–March 1916)*, 7–9; *Women's Appeal to Women*, issued late Sept. 1915, WEWNC/ADD/22/33/1.

increased from three million to well over four million).[16] None the less, the WEWNC occupied the crucial seat in defining national labour attitudes to the war as an economic and social emergency outside the cluster of questions concerning labour relations in the industrial mobilization.

Until the winter of 1915–16, the connection with longer-term labour preoccupations was barely made. The war, for the reasons we have suggested, continued to be seen as a hiatus. But at that point an issue arose which began simultaneously to extend the range of labour criticism of government policies and to evoke the nature of the post-war world—demobilization. The issue had surfaced briefly earlier in 1915, when the government pondered the reintegration of disabled servicemen into civilian life. Concluding that the problem was inseparable from demobilization generally, officials resurrected a pre-war scheme depending largely on local voluntary bodies, including the trade unions, 'to befriend the ex-fighting men on their return to their homes'.[17] This was clearly unacceptable in labour eyes, and the WEWNC set up a subcommittee on the subject, mainly to guard labour against becoming enmeshed in totally inappropriate official schemes.[18]

Little was done by the WEWNC until the end of the year. Only then did rising pressure, in the labour movement and more generally, force the matter to the top of the agenda.[19] This

---

[16] For the ILP, see the *Annual Conference Report*, 1915–1918 and the party's official paper, *Labour Leader*. For the Co-operative movement, see the *Co-operative Congress Annual Report*, 1914–1918; G. D. H. Cole, *A Century of Co-operation* (Co-operative Union, Manchester, 1945), 264–71; Pollard, 'The Foundation of the Co-operative Party'.

[17] Social Welfare Association, *The Civil Employment of Soldiers and Sailors on their Discharge* (1915), 6. The pre-war scheme, though concerned with able-bodied as well as disabled servicemen, contained no measures to deal with mass unemployment or the transition to a peace economy.

[18] J. M. Winter gives the founding date of the subcommittee as June 1915 (*Socialism and the Challenge of War*, 216). But a letter from Middleton to O'Grady of the GFTU, of 23 Nov. 1915, indicates that the committee had made little progress owing to the pressure of other work (WEWNC/14/5/5).

[19] Social Welfare Association, *The Civil Employment of Soldiers*, 6. On 16 Dec. 1915, the Joint Board (representing the three senior executive committees, the PCTUC, LPNEC, and MCGFTU) met to consider the problems of the disabled servicemen.

suggests that perception of the gravity of the issue was directly related to the rhythm and nature of the mobilization process itself. Only as the scale of voluntary recruitment produced a mass army comparable to those of continental powers and as organized labour made major concessions to facilitate the equally spectacular growth of munitions production, did the corresponding seriousness of demobilization strike labour leaders. At the same time, the resolutely civilian approach to the mobilization process (since there was no pre-existing military model for it) suggested that, unlike in continental countries, demobilization might also be the subject of a form of social compact. The CGT only began to discuss demobilization, and to challenge the prevailing assumption that it was a purely military process, in 1917–18.[20]

The WEWNC's approach to demobilization was wide-ranging. Indeed, such was the seamless tissue of questions which demobilization unrolled that the committee's response took the form of a *First Report on Labour after the War*. Issued in February 1916, this report held a deeply pessimistic view of the likely state of the economy on the return to peace.[21] It predicted that the turning tide of demobilization would inundate the labour market and bring massive dislocation. 'Organized labour', it considered, 'has never before been confronted with so great a crisis'. The solutions proposed were twofold. In a development of ideas already outlined during the brief unemployment of autumn 1914, serious social welfare reform was demanded. In particular, the Poor Law 'with its "Stoneyard"

---

[20] The Fédération des Métaux was worried from autumn 1917 by a military demobilization. The cooling of state–labour relations after Sept. 1917 also helped push the CGT into action. In Oct., Jouhaux criticized the government for convoking the Conseil Supérieur du Travail rather than the Commission Nationale de Placement to consider demobilization. The labour delegates on the former (created by Millerand in 1900), unlike the latter, were not chosen by the CGT. In 1918, the Commissions Mixtes Départementales were invited to discuss the question, but the government refrained from involving the CGT nationally. In Nov. 1918, therefore, as the problem became critical, the CGT proposed the Conseil National Économique to oversee demobilization (L. Jouhaux, 'Conseil supérieur du travail', *La Bataille*, 17 Oct. 1917, and 'Incohérence-directives', *La Bataille*, 21 Oct. 1917; *Bulletin du ministère du travail*, Aug.–Oct. 1918, 353–60; L. Jouhaux, 'Le Pays attend', *La Bataille*, 27 Dec. 1918).

[21] WEWNC/8/4/18.

and Workhouse' was to be replaced by an extension of the 1911 Unemployment Insurance Act, currently covering only the sectors most prone to unemployment, to all industries. At the same time, the level of employment was to be maintained through a planned demobilization, starting up key industries first to power a general recovery, and through local authority spending on social programmes, especially housing and schools. In short, wartime economic controls were to be applied to a demobilization and a post-war recovery guided to social ends.

The proposals only applied to a specific transition period. But by identifying the goals of social welfare reform and full employment, the report explicitly raised the question of how these were to be secured more permanently. The final section of the report evoked the idea of a British economy emerging permanently reorganized along vaguely collectivist lines from the experience of the war.

> The occasion calls for far-reaching changes in industrial organisa-
> tion—for a cessation of the present wasteful competition and indivi-
> dual profit-seeking; for the deliberate reorganisation of agriculture . . .
> for a systematic organisation of the whole transport system under
> public control; for the nationalisation of such indispensable services as
> the supply of coal—through which alone the nation can be enabled to
> meet effectively the competition of better educated and more system-
> atically organized communities.[22]

The influence of Sidney Webb on the report was strong. The central proposition that there should be no fall in the 'Standard of Life' through a reduction in the 'Standard [wage] Rate' was Fabian phraseology however general the sentiment.[23] When Middleton had reactivated the subcommittee he suggested to Smillie that Webb, who 'has been studying the whole problem . . . for several months and has got some definite ideas', should present his views.[24] But the subcommittee also contained other influential labour figures, including Smillie himself, Marion Phillips of the Women's Labour League, and Ramsay Mac-Donald. There is no reason to suppose that the critical and

---

[22] *First Report on Labour after the War*, 8.
[23] McBriar, *Fabian Socialism and English Politics*, 329.
[24] WEWNC/14/5/16/ii.

implicitly socialist tone of the report did not also represent their views.[25]

The report marked the apogee of the WEWNC's influence and also provoked a crisis in its existence, which has been described in detail by both Royden Harrison and J. M. Winter.[26] Only the broad significance of this turning-point need concern us here. The PCTUC, the GFTU and the Labour Party had all expressed their own interest in demobilization over the winter of 1915–16. Indeed, one reason why Middleton reactivated the demobilization subcommittee was to ensure that the WEWNC kept its pre-eminence in dealing with war-related issues.[27] The PCTUC was busy with plans for war pensions and the disabled.[28] The GFTU, in Middleton's words, 'has been dabbling in After the War problems for some time', and in 1916 it called on the government to ensure the post-war competitiveness of British industry and hence adequate working-class living-standards through the existing system ('the Labour movement is not out to defend systems but to secure margins').[29] Most seriously, the first Labour Party conference of the

---

[25] When the full committee discussed the report, the extremes were represented by H. M. Hyndman of the BSP and Appleton of the GFTU. Hyndman approved the report as the basis for even more far-reaching changes ('I do not believe that the capitalist competitive wage system can be safely left to cope with such a crisis as we have to face' (WEWNC/14/5/26)). Appleton criticized the extravagance of the report, fearing the burden which extended unemployment insurance would place on non-war workers during the demobilization period (letter to Middleton, 16 Feb. 1916, WEWNC/14/5/29/i). The committee's approval of the report suggests broad support for the wide and fairly radical view which the subcommittee had taken of post-war questions.

[26] Harrison, 'The War Emergency: Workers' National Committee', 242–3; Winter, *Socialism and the Challenge of War*, 215–19.

[27] The Joint Board, representing the three senior committees, met on 16 Dec. to discuss the disabled, agreed that the demobilization of the able-bodied and disabled should be treated together, and established a subcommittee to consider the problem to which the WEWNC was invited to provide delegates (printed min. WEWNC/14/4/10). On 18 Dec., Appleton wrote to Middleton asking for some action from the WEWNC's own subcommittee on the question (WEWNC/14/5/13/i). Middleton then wrote to Smillie, chairman of the WEWNC on 22 Dec., recommending that the subcommittee start work in earnest (WEWNC/14/5/16/ii). Reviewing the Joint Board's initiative on disabled servicemen, in Mar. 1916, Middleton felt that it had poached on the terrain of the WEWNC (WEWNC/15/1/24/i).

[28] The PCTUC, together with the subcommittee of the Joint Board, were concerned above all with pension and re-education schemes.

[29] Middleton to Smillie, 25 Feb. 1916 (WEWNC/14/5/34/i); GFTU, *Annual Report*, 1916, 7–8.

war, in late January 1916, raised 'After the war' questions, and
the LPNEC set up a subcommittee to consider them in February, consisting of Middleton, Webb, Henderson, W. H.
Hutchinson, W. C. Robinson, and J. R. Clynes.[30]

The first meeting of this subcommittee, on 24 February
1916, suggested a conference with the other bodies considering
post-war problems, including the WEWNC. Middleton naturally felt that this undermined the WEWNC's unique position as
the strategic hub of labour's response to the war. But the
conference, representing the PCTUC, MCGFTU, and
LPNEC, as well as the WEWNC, decided otherwise and
established a common 'After the war' committee with representatives of all four national labour bodies.[31] The WEWNC
subsequently tried to reverse this decision. But the other three
national committees confirmed the existence of the Joint Committee on Labour Problems After the War at a further conference on 19 April 1916, which granted it financial support from
the three executives and the right to appoint subcommittees.[32]

This crisis of the WEWNC, which firmly clipped its wings as a
rival of the established national committees, has obvious parallels
with that of the Comité d'Action in 1916. Both committees began
with a primary reaction to the 'war emergency', improvising
measures of labour self-defence to problems as they arose. The
strong parallels between many of the measures stem from the
similarity of the war's impact on the two working classes. Both
committees moved to a more structured and critical response to
these wartime problems which inevitably raised general, endur-
ing preoccupations. In different ways, they found themselves
pondering the social processes of the war and their likely impact

[30] See in particular the presidential address to the conference by W. C. Anderson, also prominent in the ILP and MP for Attercliffe (Sheffield). This was issued
as a pamphlet, *Labour and War Problems*, by the ILP in 1916. For the After the War
subcommittee, see LPNEC, min. 22 Feb. 1916.

[31] Middleton wrote to Smillie after the Labour Party subcommittee had issued
invitations to the joint conference that 'there has been a very quiet but studied
attempt to undermine the work of the Workers' National Committee' (25 Feb.
1916, WEWNC/14/5/34/i). Smillie agreed with Middleton (letter to Middleton, 28
Feb. 1916, WEWNC/14/5/57/1). The joint conference was finally held on 9 Mar.
1916 (WEWNC/14/5/53/i). The WEWNC representatives on the new joint committee, when it had been accepted, were Webb, Bellamy, and Smillie (WEWNC
min. 27 Apr. 1916, WEWNC/ADD/23/3).

[32] LPNEC, min. 1916, vol. 8a, 69.

on post-war society. Though the level of ideological intensity differed markedly, both found themselves trying to locate the abnormality of war in the longer-term perspectives of labour interests and plans. The war itself, by its own complexities, exceeded their original brief, and exposed them to deeper tensions within the labour movement. In the British case, these consisted of the unwillingness of the established committees to let consideration of post-war plans (and the attitude to the official war effort which they implied) out of their hands, plus fears among cautious trade union leaders that the WEWNC might strike out in too radical a direction (it was J. O'Grady, chairman of the GFTU, who tried unsuccessfully to exclude the WEWNC from the new committee).[33] 'After the war' questions were not an accidental by-product of the war but an expression of attitudes to it. As such, they were simply too significant to be left in the hands of the WEWNC.

In 1916 and early 1917, concern with 'After the war' questions became widespread within the labour movement. As the war distorted traditional patterns—and perceptions—of the distribution of wealth, it heightened labour criticism of the economic mobilization. High profits in war-related businesses seemed to stand in sharp contrast to the soaring price inflation and uncertain supplies which confronted working-class consumers. Unilateral sacrifices by industrial labour in 1915 rubbed more sorely in 1916 as the constraints on workers grew. Together with unabated fears of massive post-war unemployment, this more critical spirit found expression not only in proposed remedies for the war effort (economic controls, greater mobility for munitions workers, etc.) but also in the growing projection of the post-war period as the measure and anticipated recompense of labour's participation in the national effort.

Evidence for this broadened appeal of post-war reform comes from several quarters, including both leadership circles and the base of the movement. The Joint Committee on Labour Problems After the War took up where the WEWNC had left off, and in a series of reports on specific problems, mainly issued in 1916, it fleshed out the connection between demobilization and wider post-war reforms.[34] The committee was composed of

[33] Ibid., vol. 8a, 69.
[34] For the new committee's principal reports, see Bibliography, part 1.

representatives of the four national committees (including Webb for the WEWNC), but subcommittees brought in a wide spectrum of labour opinion.[35] The Joint Committee identified the restoration of trade union customs suspended in 1915 as the pivot of trade union attitudes to the post-war period. It also urged that a massive housing programme should provide the core of the government's employment programme through the demobilization period, and that the trade unions should be involved nationally in establishing wages and conditions during the transition to a peace economy. A report on women issued under the aegis of the committee saw the war as a major opportunity to introduce equal pay legislation and to undertake a unionization drive amongst women workers.

The Joint Committee on Labour Problems After the War reflected the views of influential national labour figures. But the Trades Union Congress held in September 1916 at Birmingham and the Labour Party conference at Manchester, in January 1917, indicate that broader trade union and Labour opinion was receptive to the more critical tone of official labour, and to post-war reform as a central theme in the war effort itself. Indeed, in many respects, local feeling set the pace for this change.

The mood of the 1916 Trades Union Congress contrasted sharply with that of a year earlier. Harry Gosling, moderate London rivermen's leader and TUC president, had participated in a British Association enquiry earlier in the year on wartime working-class grievances and possible post-war reforms.[36] In his opening address, he urged the congress to propose changes in the organization of the war effort and of the post-war order, in view of 'After the War' problems 'which will be so tremendous in character'.[37] Although Gosling was not

[35] The committee's membership in Sept. 1916 consisted of PCTUC, H. Gosling, W. Thorne, and C. W. Bowerman; LPNEC, J. R. Clynes, J. R. MacDonald, and G. J. Wardle; GFTU, J. O'Grady, B. Cooper, and B. Tillet; and WEWNC, A. Bellamy, F. Bramley, and S. Webb (from *The Restoration of Trade Union Customs after the War: A Statement and Analysis of the Government Guarantees* (1916)). For Webb's influence, see Winter, *Socialism and the Challenge of War*, 218–19.

[36] Report of the British Association on industrial unrest, 1916, in A. W. Kirkaldy (ed.), *Labour, Finance and the War* (British Association, 1916), 20–55.

[37] *Trades Union Congress, Annual Report, 1916*, 59–61; H. Gosling, *Peace: How to Get it and Keep it* (Cassell, 1917).

advocating wholesale collectivization, but rather greater recognition and status for labour within the system of industrial relations, his reforms extended to the nationalization of mines, railways, and shipping and state control of grain and meat supplies. He also clearly distinguished labour's voice from the official post-war reform (or 'reconstruction') planning initiated by Asquith in March 1916. 'I at least', he declared, 'am not going to pretend that the course indicated by the government is going to satisfy even the most moderate amongst us.'

The congress took up the theme. Even if its breadth of vision remained more limited than that of the WEWNC or the Joint Committee on Labour Problems After the War, the upheaval of the war effort revitalized old shibboleths—such as the nationalization of key, infrastructural industries, which had been TUC policy since 1896. J. Hill of the Boilermakers presented a PCTUC resolution which declared that:

The war has proved beyond all doubt the national weakness and danger of our pre-war industrial system, and the need for immediate reform.

Our vital industries should no longer be left in the hands of capitalists whose object is profit, and workers whose first object is wages. Such industries should be regulated by the State in the national interest.[38]

The resolution specified the nationalization of railways and mines, and urged extensive state control of the food industry and shipping. Carried without division, it testified to a significant shift of trade union opinion in favour of broadly collectivist measures. J. Jones, of the National General Workers' Union observed that the war had demonstrated more effectively than thirty years' propaganda both the exploitation in British society and the need for an independent labour programme and organization to overcome it.

The same view was even more evident at the Labour Party conference four months later. For over a year, Middleton had been bombarded with suggestions on post-war reform by local organizations. The Leicester Labour Party had written as early as December 1915 proposing a conference on 'Labour After the War'.[39] The Manchester, Salford, and District Women's War Interests Committee provided Middleton with resolutions of a

[38] *Trades Union Congress, Annual Report, 1916*, 250–1.
[39] WEWNC/15/1/6.

conference on women war workers and demobilization.[40] The Birmingham Trades and Labour Council circulated other trades councils with demobilization schemes, and by July 1916 had published its own memorandum on the *Problems of Labour and the War*. Middleton requested twenty copies for the WEWNC, declaring that he was 'very glad indeed that local organizations are thinking out these After the War problems. The national bodies are just getting to work.'[41] In October, the secretary of the Newcastle Labour Representation Committee sent a copy of local demobilization proposals to Middleton, 'not that we consider them any value but just to acquaint you with our activities.'[42] On 16 August 1916, J. Bromley, general secretary of the Associated Society of Locomotive Engineers and Firemen, suggested directly to Henderson that Labour should hold a national conference on 'After the war' problems.[43]

It was thus in response to strong local demands for the discussion of demobilization and post-war issues, as well as to the logic of its own growing concern with the peacetime future, that the LPNEC decided to give such questions a central place at the January 1917 party conference.[44] On 3 November 1916 the committee resolved

with a view to securing adequate discussion upon the various aspects of Labour Problems after the War; that a subcommittee be appointed to draft suitable resolutions on the question of Restoration of Trade Union Conditions, Demobilization, Unemployment, and the Position of Women . . .

These resolutions, plus the pamphlets issued by the Joint Committee on After the War Problems, were circulated to the affiliated organizations of the party.[45] They provide the clearest possible indication that the Labour Party was seizing the initiative within the labour movement nationally on the question of post-war reform.

---

[40] Ibid./15/12/i.

[41] Ibid./15/1/23; /15/1/50; and /15/1/51; J. Corbett, *The Birmingham Trades Council 1866–1966* (Lawrence and Wishart, 1966), 104–17.

[42] WEWNC/15/1/54/ii.

[43] Ibid./15/1/52. Henderson's reply two days later assured Bromley that the LPNEC had been considering the question since the Jan. 1916 conference (WEWNC/15/1/53).

[44] Clinton, *The Trade Union Rank and File*, 75.

[45] LPNEC, min. 3 Nov. 1916.

The response was considerable. About a hundred resolutions came in from local organizations. For the conference, the LPNEC reduced these, together with its own original proposals, to ten composite resolutions on post-war reform, all of which were passed (some slightly amended) and issued as a brochure, *Labour Problems after the War*.[46] The resolutions demanded the reform of the labour exchanges and the maintenance of the 'Standard of Life' during the initial economic chaos of peace-time. But they went much further and advocated a permanent minimum wage, the nationalization of mines and railways, the retention of government controls on agriculture and food, better conditions for women workers, educational and child welfare reform, and universal adult suffrage. Fundamental fiscal reform lay at the heart of proposals for meeting the cost of the war.

Overall, the reforms straddled three basic sectors—economic production and regulation, with specific collectivist and inter-ventionist solutions favoured; redistribution of economic and social benefits, through welfare and education proposals; and political reform. In each sector, the reforms can be visualized in two dimensions, reawakening pre-war debates in the Labour Party while responding to specific wartime conditions which were felt to be rapidly approaching the intolerable. The motion on coal nationalization, for example, considered that

this country should no longer be dependent for its coal supply on a small number of capitalist colliery proprietors, coal merchants and dealers, among whom there is an increasing tendency to combinations and price arrangements, by which the consumer is made to pay a quite unnecessary price for coal.[47]

Suffrage reform awoke the long-standing issue of Labour's electoral strategy and alliance with the Liberals. At the same time, it was of immediate and quite specific importance if the Labour Party was to win political support for its own indepen-dent programme of 'After the War' reforms.

Although the conference resolutions remained a list rather than an integrated programme, such as that of the Commission Mixte d'Études Économiques in November 1916, their critical function in relation to the war effort was similar, and their

[46] *Report of the Labour Party Conference, Manchester, January 1917*, 7; 'Labour and its Voice', *New Statesman*, 27 Jan. 1917, pp. 389–91.
[47] *Labour Problems After the War*, 9.

implications for Labour's post-war policy were quite clear. It was not until 1918, with the more overt separation of Labour from the official war effort, that the reform impulse was codified in a programme—*Labour and the New Social Order*. But in all of its essentials, the later programme was anticipated by the resolutions passed at the January 1917 conference.

(ii) Conscription of Men and 'Conscription of Riches'

It is no coincidence that 'After the War' questions began to be seriously discussed in the labour movement at the very point when military conscription was introduced, in the first half of 1916. We have already seen that the switch from voluntary to compulsory military recruitment marked a fundamental up-heaval in the type of national effort which labour leaders saw themselves as participating in. Conscription seemed to introduce into Britain the 'Prussianism' against which the war was suppo-sedly being fought. It also seemed a potential harbinger of the worst 'Prussianism' of all—industrial conscription, or the full subjection of industrial workers to military authority (this was indeed implemented for male German workers by the Patriotic Auxiliary Service Law of 2 December 1916, though, paradoxi-cally, with official labour support and at the price of a certain recognition of trade unions by the military).[48] Both the LPNEC and the PCTUC eventually accepted conscription, persuaded by the government's evidence of a grave crisis in military recruit-ment, or unwilling to let continued antipathy to the measure outweigh overall support for the national effort.[49] The important point, however, is that conscription undoubtedly began to change their attitude to that effort, and the basis on which they participated in it. It was as if, from the perspective of labour leaders, the war effort began again in 1916 on revised terms.

One of the principal instruments of that revision of terms was a campaign which sought the compulsory mobilization (i.e. expropriation) of wealth as a reciprocal measure of social

---

[48] G. Feldman, *Army, Industry, and Labor in Germany, 1914–1918* (Princeton Univ. Press, Princeton, NJ, 1966), 197–249.

[49] See Chap. 2, above.

equality for the conscription of men. Perhaps not surprisingly, the 'Conscription of Riches' movement originated in bodies which had already established a critical distance from the official war effort—the ILP and the WEWNC.

The ILP, displaying a spectrum of pacifism ranging from revolutionary socialists and conscientious objectors, who totally repudiated the war, to those who urged a negotiated end to the conflict and a 'democratic' peace, found unanimity in its hostility to conscription. The 'Conscription of Riches' figured prominently in its reaction when compulsory military service became law. A version of the idea had emerged as early as May 1915. Like Bedouce, Mistral, and Auriol among French socialist deputies, Philip Snowden, the ILP's financial expert, simply applied his pre-war critique of the fiscal system to soaring wartime budgets, funded by loans rather than progressive tax reform. In particular, he feared that all possibility of post-war social reform was being mortgaged to the swelling burden of government indebtedness, turning the war into profit for the rich and impoverishment for the poor.[50]

Refocused through the lens of anti-conscription feeling, these arguments concentrated attention on the moral as well as financial implications of the war effort. A resolution on the 'Conscription of Riches' (proposed by Ben Riley, of the ILP's National Administrative Committee (NAC)) was passed unanimously by the Newcastle upon Tyne conference of the party in April 1916.[51] Riley argued that both as a matter of equity in the mobilization process and also to secure the post-war future as a period of social 'reconstruction', it was necessary to conscript 'the great incomes and resources of wealth owned by the rich'. It was agreed to mount a campaign to this end. Ramsay MacDonald rehearsed the arguments in a pamphlet, *The Conscription of Wealth*, in 1916 ('the treatment of the two essentials to national success in the War—life and wealth—is flagrantly unequal').[52] The ILP pursued the conscription of wealth—

[50] P. Snowden, 'How to Pay for the War', *Labour Leader*, 20 May 1915 (speech to the Commons, 12 May); 'Paying and not Paying for the War', *Labour Leader*, 30 Sept. 1915; *An Autobiography*, (Ivor Nicholson and Watson, 1934), i. 367–76.
[51] *ILP Annual Conference*, 1916, 79.
[52] *The Conscription of Wealth*, MacDonald Papers, PRO/30/69/3A/90.

interpreted essentially as progressive tax reform—until the end of the war.[53]

The WEWNC launched a parallel campaign at the same moment as the ILP, in the spring of 1916.[54] Again, the issue had surfaced earlier. Late in 1915, a WEWNC pamphlet bitterly opposing conscription, *Compulsory Military Service and Industrial Conscription: What they Mean to the Workers*, had concluded by pointing to the social injustices highlighted by the conscription controversy. It was to these that the focus shifted once conscription had been introduced.

> The proposed [conscription] law . . . does not touch 'property' at all. It does not interfere with the power of the idle, absentee owner of land or investments to draw, year after year, an income in rent, interest or dividends from the labours of those who *are* rendering National Service . . .[55]

Although there were differences within the WEWNC on the grounds of opposition to conscription (Middleton and Smillie rejected it as part of a more general trend toward centralized political authority, whereas Webb, normally an apostle of enlightened bureaucratic power, limited his objection to conscription *per se*), these did not impede a common and continuing repudiation of the military service acts or a shared anxiety over the growing cost and social inequality of the war effort.[56] Like Snowden, Webb had been pondering these questions throughout 1915.[57]

In January 1916, with the conscription of unmarried men, W. C. Anderson, an ILP member of parliament who was also prominent in the WEWNC and the Labour Party, introduced an unsuccessful bill into the Commons for the conscription of wealth, which had in fact been drafted by Webb, and which proposed the appropriation of all unearned income during the

---

[53] e.g. *ILP Annual Conference*, 1917 (NAC Report), 21; *Labour Leader*, 11 Apr. 1918.

[54] Harrison, 'The War Emergency: Workers' National Committee, 1914–1920', 238–52; Winter, *Socialism and the Challenge of War*, 208–15.

[55] *Compulsory Military Service and Industrial Conscription: What they Mean to the Workers*, 14–15.

[56] Winter, *Socialism and the Challenge of War*, 208–10.

[57] Cole (ed.), *Beatrice Webb's Diaries, 1912–24*, 47.

war.[58] At the same time, Middleton felt that the TUC's initial opposition to the government's military service bill created favourable circumstances for preparing a 'Conscription of Riches' campaign. This was launched in the late spring, with the extension of conscription to married men. Although the PCTUC was reluctant to participate, having by then, with the LPNEC, accepted both conscription acts, Middleton pressured it into holding a special conference on the issues raised by conscription, by using the continued hostility to compulsory recruitment of several of the larger unions, notably the miners, dock workers, textile unions, railwaymen, and postal unions.[59] The conference was held in London on 30 June, with an agenda corresponding closely to the original WEWNC proposal, and which included the 'conscription of accumulated riches for the service of the nation'. The conference duly passed a resolution to that effect.[60]

In principle, therefore, the 'Conscription of Riches' became an official aim of the trade union movement as early as the summer of 1916. In reality, the ILP and the WEWNC continued to generate much of the energy behind the idea. It was the WEWNC, unrepentant at its defeat over responsibility for 'After the war' questions, which published the June conference resolutions, including the conscription of wealth, and which condemned Asquith's indifference to the deputation which presented them to him.[61] Sidney Webb defined his ideas on the conscription of wealth in a Fabian pamphlet published in July 1916, *How to Pay for the War*, which developed the theme of radical fiscal reform to encompass not only the appropriation by the state of all unearned income during the war, but also much severer income tax and an overall levy on capital. These were the concepts which prevailed in the WEWNC from August to October 1917, when H. M. Hyndman made the far more radical suggestion that the conscription of wealth should be interpreted

---

[58] Ibid., 64; 'The Conscription of Wealth', *New Statesman*, 22 Jan. 1916, p. 367.
[59] Middleton to C. W. Bowerman, secretary of the PCTUC, 26 May 1916 (WEWNC/29/102-3); WEWNC/29/10/6.
[60] PCTUC, min. 30 June 1916.
[61] Harrison, 'The War Emergency: Workers' National Committee, 1914–1920', 247. The WEWNC issued a leaflet, *Labour and Social Conditions Caused by the War: Some Notes on the Speech of the Prime Minister in Replying to the Trade Union Congress Deputation on July 19th 1916*.

to mean the collectivization of 'the entire riches of this Island'.[62]
Webb's views largely coincided with those of Snowden and
MacDonald, in what became a broad labour consensus on the
subject. A WEWNC pamphlet of October 1917 which summarized Webb's views was endorsed by the PCTUC, the LPNEC,
and the MFGB, while Snowden, for the ILP, proposed a
successful resolution along similar lines to the Labour Party
conference in January 1918.[63]

Yet if the ideas on the conscription of wealth continued to
come from the left, they acted from the start as a leaven on the
broad mass of labour opinion. One of the signals of a more
critical attitude to the war effort at the Birmingham Trades
Union Congress in September 1916 was a composite resolution
on the conscription of wealth. Advocating a detailed census of
wealth and its 'conscription' to pay for the war, in the name of
national equality, it was passed unanimously.[64] On 15 February
1917, the PCTUC presented this resolution to Bonar Law,
Conservative Chancellor of the Exchequer, and demanded a
variety of wealth taxes to finance both the war and post-war
'reconstruction' (Bonar Law, diplomatic but unimpressed, told
the delegation that it overlooked 'the enormous contribution
that is being made by the accumulated wealth of the country
during this war', and condemned a capital levy as 'folly').[65] In
June 1917, a conference of the Triple Alliance (the NUR,
MFGB, and National Transport Workers' Federation)
approved the conscription of wealth.[66] The demand also constituted the financial proposals presented to the Labour Party
conference in January 1917:

this Conference demands that an equitable system of conscription of
accumulated wealth should be put into operation forthwith, believing

---

[62] The WEWNC issued a pamphlet summarizing Webb's approach, *The Conscription of Riches*, in direct refutation of Hyndman's more radical proposals. For
this dispute, see WEWNC/5/3/3 to WEWNC/5/3/24, and Winter, *Socialism and the
Challenge of War*, 212–15.

[63] Winter, *Socialism and the Challenge of War*, 215; for Snowden's resolution, see
Report of the Labour Party Conference, Nottingham, January 1918, 133–4.

[64] *Trades Union Congress, Annual Report, 1916*, 378–81.

[65] PCTUC, *Quarterly Reports*, Mar. 1917, 82–4.

[66] *Railway Review*, 15 June 1917; typewritten notes on the wartime history of the
Triple Alliance, TUC Library, HD6664.

that any attempt to tax food or other necessities of life would be unjust and ruinous to the mass of the people.[67]

It has been assumed that the activities of the WEWNC in 1915–16, and especially its interest in 'After the war' problems and the 'Conscription of Riches', led directly to *Labour and the New Social Order* as the first, integrated wartime programme of the Labour Party.[68] Despite the undoubted significance of the committee, such a view ignores not only the role of the ILP but also the crucial process whereby labour leaders, especially in the Labour Party, absorbed growing criticisms of the organization of the war effort, particularly from local Labour and trade union bodies, and turned these into an incipient post-war reform programme which became a comment on the war itself. The anticipated difficulties of demobilizing a massive industrial effort focused attention on the post-war period. But this rapidly became the canvas on which mounting labour criticisms of the war effort were painted in bold colours. At the same time, the shift from voluntary to compulsory military service cast a new and harsher light on the mobilization process. Hostility to profiteering had been endemic in the labour movement from the outset, and excess profits taxation was one of the principal trade union conditions for accepting the Munitions of War Act in mid-1915. But military conscription provided a moral yardstick for the war effort, and the 'Conscription of Riches' represented labour's measurement of the inequalities involved. If the lead on these questions was taken by individuals and bodies on the left of labour opinion, whose critical distance from the war effort was already established, their ideas were soon adopted by the major labour organizations as they were pushed into a more independent understanding of the war, through which they slowly sought to divine the post-war future.

(iii) Labour and the 'New Social Order'

The accelerating momentum of the war in 1917–18 radically altered the circumstances confronting labour leaders in Britain.

---

[67] *Labour Problems after the War*, 11.
[68] Winter, *Socialism and the Challenge of War*, 219; Harrison, 'The War Emergency: Workers' National Committee 1914–1920', 256.

Working-class dissatisfaction grew over numerous issues, especially consumer grievances and the intensifying pressure on munitions workers (with restrictions on their freedom of movement plus the government's successive attempts, following the haemorrhages of the Somme and Passchendaele, to 'comb out' male engineering workers for the front). In May 1917 this discontent erupted in a major wave of engineering strikes, through which the unofficial shop stewards' movement consolidated a national network. Further strikes disrupted a number of industries in July 1918.[69]

Additionally, as in France, changing international circumstances transformed the horizon of the national labour movement. The February revolution in Russia and the 'democratic' peace demands to which it gave rise, plus the entry of the USA into the war on a Wilsonian programme, powerfully reinforced labour and working-class demands in Britain for allied commitments to such war aims and for openness to a negotiated peace. Where the January 1917 conference of the Labour Party reaffirmed by a large majority its commitment to the pursuit of military victory over Germany, the Trades Union Congress in September 1917 decided that the British labour movement should lead an international labour and socialist initiative for a negotiated, 'democratic' peace.

Even more than in the French case, these developments consolidated, and indeed considerably extended, the labour reformism which had emerged in 1916. We have already seen that the conversion of the Labour Party and TUC to 'democratic' peace aims in 1917 remained entirely compatible with the 'choice of 1914' and continued support for the war effort— both confirmed in the military crisis of spring and summer 1918.[70] Equally, Labour's gradual separation from government (despite continued ministerial participation by several right-wing members of the PLP), gave it the independence to intensify its criticisms of government policies, domestic and

---

[69] Orton, *Labour in Transition*, 88–150. For the sources of working-class unrest, see *Commission of Enquiry into Industrial Unrest*, 1917, Cd. 8662–8669, and summary, Cd 8696. For strikes, see Append. II, and for the 'unofficial' movement, see Hinton, *The First Shop Stewards' Movement*, 196–272.

[70] See p 55, above.

international. There was no threat of political reaction comparable to that perceived by French socialists and syndicalists under Clemenceau.[71] Indeed, Lloyd George and the government more generally (especially the radical Liberal supporters of the prime minister) talked the language of post-war reform and scaled up the earlier Reconstruction committees (of Asquith in 1916 and Lloyd George in 1917) into a full Ministry of Reconstruction in August 1917.[72] None the less, national consensus on the significance of the war fragmented in 1917–18, and labour, especially the Labour Party, found itself increasingly playing the role of an unofficial 'loyal opposition', translating protest and criticism into an alternative version of the war effort and an alternative view of the post-war future.

This consolidation of a specific war reformism took several forms. The intensity of working-class discontent over food prices (the official Commission of Enquiry into Industrial Unrest, set up in response to the strikes of May 1917, found these to be the biggest single grievance) pushed the Co-operative movement into the forefront of labour protest.[73] Prior to the war, successive Co-operative congresses had avoided political involvement, whether through direct representation in parliament or formal association with the Labour Party. But in 1917, two Co-operative congresses, in May and October, established a National Co-operative Representation Committee, which in 1919 became the Co-operative Party.[74] In alliance with the Labour Party, it fought a by-election in January 1918, and

---

[71] This is not to say that repression did not occur nor that Labour leaders did not protest against it (see LPNEC, min. 28 Nov. 1917, p. 193, resolution protesting against police raids under the Defence of the Realm Act, and ibid., 13 Dec. 1917, p. 213, for a protest against pamphlet and book censorship; see also A. Henderson's condemnation of the 'policy of repression and regimentation', *The Aims of Labour* (1918), 68). But Lloyd George did not share Clemenceau's pre-war notoriety with labour, nor was there a comparable apparent danger in Britain of anti-parliamentary reactionaries gaining influence in 1917–18.

[72] P. B. Johnson, *Land Fit for Heroes: The Planning of British Reconstruction, 1916–1919* (Chicago Univ. Press, Chicago, Ill., 1968).

[73] *Commission of Enquiry into Industrial Unrest*, summary, 1917, Cd. 8696, 153–4.

[74] *New Statesman*, 27 Oct. 1917, p. 77; Pollard, 'The Foundation of the Co-operative Party'; and for a contrary view, T. Adams, 'The Formation of the Co-operative Party Reconsidered', *International Review of Social History*, 32/1 (1987), pp. 48–68.

saw one of its ten candidates in the December general election returned to parliament.

Part of the explanation for this sharp change of approach lay in the accumulation of grievances since 1914 against governments which ignored Co-operative advice on provisioning and even discriminated against the movement itself. But the political alignment of the Co-operative movement went beyond such specific resentments. It also demonstrated that Co-operative members no less than other elements of organized labour shared in the changing, more critical response to the war and, at the national level, endorsed the basic language of a wartime labour reformism. The Co-operative movement participated in the WEWNC, and lobbied the government over consumer affairs with Labour leaders. At the congress of May 1917, strictly Co-operative questions were linked to wider issues such as nationalization and the conscription of wealth. The emergency congress in October advocated closer collaboration with the trade union movement, amid near unanimous support for the idea that 'both movements have made up their mind that industry in all its forms shall be for public service, and not for the growth and further entrenchment of capital'.[75] It also agreed on a provisional programme of social and political reform, including the principle that 'the processes of production, distribution and exchange . . . shall be organised on co-operative lines in the interests of the whole community'.[76] In short, the Co-operative movement switched to a broadly Labour political commitment in 1917 because it shared with Labour and trade union leaders a growing conviction that the war marked a significant change in forms of social and economic organization, and that the different sections of organized labour needed independent programmes of post-war reform and collaboration if they were to harness that change for the benefit of the working class.

Trade union leaders confirmed in 1917–18 the quickening interest in post-war reform which had surfaced at the September 1916 Trades Union Congress. But for several reasons, their interest remained more restricted than that in the Labour Party. It was, in the first place, in the logic of the structure of

[75] Opening address by the chairman, T. W. Allen, cited in Pollard, 'The Foundation of the Co-operative Party', 201.
[76] Resolution quoted ibid., 203.

the British labour movement that the Labour Party, established as the agent of the trade unions in legislative and broadly political matters, should take the lead in converting an increasingly critical labour participation in the war effort into reform proposals which were premissed on electoral and parliamentary action. Post-war 'reconstruction', in labour eyes, became identified with an independent Labour Party programme for the election which it was assumed would follow (and possibly precede) the end of hostilities. Although the Trades Union Congresses in September 1917 and September 1918 saw considerable discussion of post-war reforms, it was the Labour Party which took responsibility for devising a 'reconstruction' programme in the winter of 1917–18.

The ideological traditions of British labour reinforced this distinction between the roles of party and trade unions in the field of post-war reform. The production-centred socialism characteristic of the CGT (the reformist reformulation of which Jouhaux sought to legitimize by reference to Proudhon) was not matched by any comparable tradition in Britain, where the bulk of trade unionists, after all, did not even consider themselves socialists before 1914. The willingness to accept the liberal parliamentary state when legislative intervention was required (so different from both libertarian syndicalist and marxist currents of socialism in France, with their traditional hostility to the 'bourgeois' state) predisposed most national trade union leaders to adopt a parliamentary and political approach to 'reconstruction' under the leadership of the Labour Party.

The obvious exception to this occurred among the radical leadership of the shop stewards' movement, which generated a syndicalist, producer-centred view of socialism from its industrial defence of the skilled engineering worker. But outside the rank-and-file movement in the engineering industry such views had a limited impact.[77] Among those unions (notably the MFGB and the NUR) which had been influenced more broadly by Syndicalism and Guild Socialism, these ideas usually

---

[77] B. Pribicevic, *The Shop Stewards' Movement and Workers' Control, 1910–1922* (Blackwell, Oxford, 1959), 91; Kendall, *The Revolutionary Movement in Britain*, 142–69; Hinton, *The First Shop Stewards' Movement*, 275–97; A. W. Wright, 'Guild Socialism Revisited', *Journal of Contemporary History*, 9/1 (1974), pp. 165–80; Winter, *Socialism and the Challenge of War*, 121–49.

resulted at the national level in a reformulation of nationalization plans to encompass the right of the producers (in the case
of the miners), or of producers and consumers (in the case of the
railwaymen), to play a major role in running the industry. The
NUR had introduced such ideas at its last pre-war congress, in
1914, and the 1919 proposals of the MFGB gave the union,
along with the state, a crucial role in running a nationalized coal
industry.[78] The vague notion of worker participation in nationalized concerns had, by 1918, made its way on to the Labour
Party's programme.[79] But though important as an indicator of
labour demands for an enhanced status in industry, these ideas
did not challenge nationally the consensus on a parliamentary
approach to post-war 'reconstruction'.

In addition to such vital differences of structure and tradition
between the two labour movements, the central issues which
inspired the syndicalist-centred war reformism of the CGT—
the protection of the skilled worker and the modernization, and
mechanization, of French industry on the skilled workers'
terms—were treated much more defensively in Britain. The
restoration of trade union customs provided the first and most
obvious line of defence against the possibility that employers
might use the war to establish permanent dilution, substitution
by women workers, and Taylorism. Here, as we have argued, a
return to the pre-war status quo, not change, was demanded as
the minimum price of labour's wartime co-operation.[80] The
reports of the Commission of Enquiry into Industrial Unrest
confirmed almost universal scepticism among skilled workers
over the intentions of government and employers to honour the
verbal commitments on restoration given in 1915. Restoration

---

[78] R. Page Arnot and G. D. H. Cole, *Trade Unionism on the Railways: Its History
and Problems* (Trade Union ser. no. 2, 1917), 105; F. Hodges, *Nationalisation of the
Mines* (Leonard Parsons, 1920), Append. II ('Bill of Miners' Federation'), 151–69;
E. Eldon Barry, *Nationalisation in British Politics: The Historical Background*
(Cape, 1965), 102–3, 239–43.

[79] Numbers XIX and XXI of the reconstruction resolutions voted at the June
1918 Labour Party conference, dealing with the nationalization of railways and of
iron- and coal-mines respectively. Both called for increased worker participation in
the management of the collectivized industries (*Report of the Labour Party
Conference, Westminster, June 1918*, 75–6).

[80] See pp. 4–5, 79–80, above.

became a central post-war demand not only of the ASE, but of the TUC as a whole.[81]

In general, therefore, the TUC co-operated with the Labour Party's approach to 'reconstruction' in late 1917 and 1918, while considering on its own account such questions as the restoration of trade union customs or nationalization which specifically affected trade unions. On one issue, however, trade union leaders were forced by outside pressure to respond directly—the system of industrial relations. Unlike in France, this question lay at the heart of the broader debate in Britain on the nature of post-war society. Doubtless, this was a backhanded tribute to the strength of the trade unions and to the scale of the pre-war unrest, as well as an expression of the growing preoccupation with the threat to Britain's industrial position from more dynamic competitors. However else their prognoses differed, politicians, businessmen, and commentators tended to agree that a better climate of industrial relations was vital to Britain's post-war recovery, and a multitude of enquiries and reports suggested schemes by which this might be achieved.[82]

The government's own Reconstruction Committee was responsible for the most influential of these schemes. In 1917, it established a Committee on Relations between Employers and Employed, known (after its chairman, the Speaker of the Commons) as the Whitley Committee, 'to make and consider suggestions for securing a permanent improvement in the

---

[81] *Commission of Enquiry into Industrial Unrest*, summary, 1917, Cd. 8696, 153–4. The Joint Committee publication, *The Restoration of Trade Union Customs after the War*, was drafted with the participation of leading PCTUC members (C. Bowerman, the secretary, and Fred Bramley), and subsequently circulated to the movement, with an incorporated form for registering wartime changes in work practices.

[82] See the report of the British Association on industrial unrest, in Kirkaldy (ed), *Labour, Finance and the War*, 20–55; *Memorandum on the Industrial Situation after the War* (Garton Foundation, 1916), 72–3; Lord Milner, *The Elements of Reconstruction* (Nisbet, 1916), Chap. 3; A. C. Pigou, A. Greenwood, S. Webb, and A. E. Zimmern, *The Reorganisation of Industry* (Ruskin College, 1916); H. Carter (ed.), *Industrial Reconstruction: A Symposium on the Situation after the War and How to Meet It* (T. Fisher Unwin, 1917), including statements by Labour and business representatives; War Cabinet, *Report for 1917*, 1918, Cd. 9005, p. xvii; S. J. Chapman (ed.), *Labour and Capital after the War* (John Murray, 1918), with a variety of labour and business views; and *Liberal Policy in the Task of Political and Social Reconstruction* (Liberal Party, 1918), 71–3. For a discussion of post-war industrial relations planning, see Middlemas, *Politics in Industrial Society*, 94–151.

relations between employers and workmen'.[83] The four Whitley reports outlined a plan for joint labour-business consultation at all levels and in every type of industry, from those already well-organized, with trade unions and employers' associations, to those where such organization was minimal or non-existent. In effect, the government used the initiative provided by its wartime economic intervention in an attempt to universalize the voluntary, consultative procedures which had characterized some pre-war industries (cotton, the iron and steel trades), and which had been established locally in the munitions industry during the war itself.[84]

The first report, published in July 1917, dealt with already well-organized industries, and thus directly with the power of the trade unions. It envisaged a consultative system for each industry extending from individual works committees to an overall industrial council with joint worker and employer representation. This machinery, operating through the trade unions on the labour side, was intended to give labour 'a definite and enlarged share in the discussion and settlement of industrial matters with which employers and employed are jointly concerned'.[85]

Several trade union leaders participated in the Whitley Committee.[86] Within the movement at large, however, the evidence of congress debates plus a series of conferences sponsored in late 1917 by the Fabian Research Department suggests that reactions were muted and diverse.[87] Ultimately, they were determined by the interaction of two considerations—a varying appraisal among trade union leaders of the aim of change in industrial relations, and a strong defensive reflex for the preservation of trade union autonomy.

Support for the Whitley proposals might well signify a relative conservatism of economic perspective, as with J. R.

[83] Committee on Relations between Employers and Employed, *Final Report* (1 July 1918), Cd. 9153, 3. This summarizes the four substantive reports, Cd. 8606, Cd. 9002, Cd. 9085, Cd. 9099.

[84] A. Flanders, 'Collective Bargaining', in A. Flanders and H. A. Clegg, *The System of Industrial Relations in Great Britain* (Blackwell, Oxford, 1967), 272–8; Clegg, *A History of British Trade Unions since 1889*, ii. 204–7.

[85] Whitley Committee, *Final Report*, 3.

[86] J. R. Clynes, R. Smillie, F. S. Button, and J. J. Mallon.

[87] For the Fabian Research Department conferences, see *Fabian News*, Dec. 1917 and Jan. 1918.

Clynes and J. J. Mallon (both participants in the committee), who felt that the new institutions would begin to make labour 'real partners in industry' under the existing economic regime.[88] Yet if the Whitley reports tended to be attacked from the left for their assumption that the interests of labour and capital were identical (Frank Hodges, the Guild Socialist-influenced secretary of the MFGB made precisely this accusation), many felt that joint consultation, by strengthening organized labour, would encourage more fundamental change.[89] A critical acceptance of Whitley, in other words, and hence of the ideal of more harmonious industrial relations based on the recognition of trade unionism, was compatible with a belief (however vague) in the need for deeper change in the organization of industry—and this was indeed a common response. The NUR considered that the Whitley proposals could be incorporated into its own railway nationalization proposals, and that the principle of joint consultation 'opened the door for new and still greater developments ... There is no violent cataclysm, no sudden break, but a gradual remoulding of industry under the co-operative aim and the national idea.'[90]

Even more significantly, the trade union side on the Whitley Committee (predominantly moderate) attached a proviso to the final, summarizing report of 1 July 1918.

[While] recognising that the more amicable relations thus established between capital and labour will afford an atmosphere generally favourable to industrial peace and progress, we desire to express our view that a complete identity of interests between capital and labour cannot be thus affected, and that such machinery cannot be expected to furnish a settlement for the more serious conflicts of interest involved in the working of an economic system primarily governed and directed by motives of private profit.[91]

---

[88] *Trades Union Congress, Annual Report, September 1917*, 230 (Clynes); *Fabian News*, Dec. 1917 (Mallon).

[89] *Trades Union Congress, Annual Report, September 1917*, 232. For a sustained Guild Socialist critique of Whitley, see M. B. Reckitt and C. B. Bechofer, *The Meaning of National Guilds* (Palmer and Hayward, 1918), 244.

[90] *Railway Review*, 13 July 1917. The Executive Committee of the NUR considered Whitley to be in line with existing NUR policy (*Railway Review*, 21 July 1917, p. 5).

[91] Whitley Committee, *Final Report*, 4. The note was signed by J. R. Clynes, J. A. Hobson, Susan Lawrence, J. J. Mallon, and M. Wilson. Smillie had been unable to attend.

Yet it was the anxiety to preserve trade union autonomy which really shaped the response to Whitley. Beatrice Webb wrote a prescient memorandum to the Reconstruction Committee in mid-1917 predicting that the proposals would meet with 'indifference' or outright 'hostility' by most union leaderships.[92] She proved correct. Where trade unionism was weak or divided, Whitley was dangerous. Even in the best-organized industries trade unionism was uneven, and generalized works committees opened up the twin possibilities of dissident local radicalism or employer unionism. The proposals also played on the tensions over skill which had been sharpened by dilution, with craft unions doubly anxious lest their special interests should be outvoted and obliterated in national industrial councils.[93] Where trade unionism was strong, by contrast, as with the powerful industrial or general unions, the Whitley proposals seemed superfluous. Smillie, a member of the committee, considered them useful for small disputes in unionized industries which did not already possess negotiating machinery, but irrelevant to coal-mining with its developed collective bargaining. Ernest Bevin, of the National Transport Workers' Federation, also felt that there was little to be gained by forcing a uniform strait-jacket on diverse industries.[94]

In the end, the Whitley reports were ignored by the major trade unions, and only took permanent root in the civil service, where they met a long-standing need for a national negotiating structure (precisely what the public service unions in France sought unsuccessfully during the war).[95] The PCTUC approved Whitley, partly as an attempt to gain a role for trade unions in the demobilization process, but it took care to avoid a

[92] Passfield Papers, IV/8, 13.

[93] B. C. Roberts, *The Trades Union Congress, 1868–1921* (Allen & Unwin, 1958), 290.

[94] *Trades Union Congress, Annual Report, September 1917*, 227–30.

[95] E. Halévy, *The Era of Tyrannies: Essays on Socialism and War* (1938; English trans., Allen Lane, 1967), 82–122; Roberts, *The Trades Union Congress*, 288–91. The Fabian and Labour Research Departments, late in 1918, observed that 'The great Trade Unions, for the most part, took little notice of the Report, preferring their own methods of negotiation; and the Councils have therefore been set up in trades which only a very elastic interpretation could include under the term "well-organised"' (Fabian Research Department/Labour Research Department, *Monthly Circular*, 1 Dec. 1918, p. 46).

major debate on the subject in congress. It mounted no campaign on their behalf, and the Whitley proposals did not figure in the post-war plans of either the TUC or the Labour Party.[96] Labour reactions to the government's initiative on industrial relations reform provide further evidence that even among moderate trade union leaders, the war had shaken confidence in existing arrangements and produced a mood of change. But they also show that the desire to consolidate trade union strength outweighed any impulse to embark on risky experiments in industrial constitution-building.

The Labour Party acknowledged the primarily political and electoral nature of 'After the war' questions, and hence the pre-eminence of its own role, when the LPNEC established a subcommittee on 16 October 1917 to report on 'reconstruction after the war'. Consisting of Sidney Webb, Ramsay Mac-Donald, and Arthur Henderson, the subcommittee produced a draft of *Labour and the New Social Order*, which the parent committee had accepted by 13 December 1917.[97] The document proclaimed itself to be a 'systematic and comprehensive plan' not simply for 'this or that Government Department, or this or that piece of social machinery, but, so far as Britain is concerned, [for] society itself'.[98] Presented to the January 1918 party conference, *Labour and the New Social Order* was referred to the constituency organizations and, somewhat modified, approved as the Labour Party's official post-war 'reconstruction' programme at a special conference, on 26–8 June 1918.

The significance of *Labour and the New Social Order* varies according to the context which it mirrors. Most often, it is seen

[96] B. C. Roberts argues that the PCTUC was mainly interested in avoiding embarrassing division. It therefore wrongly asserted at the 1918 congress that the Whitley proposals had been approved by the Sept. 1917 congress, whereas they had merely been referred back to the PCTUC. Late in the Sept. 1918 congress, the PCTUC asked for confirmation of approval 'in connection with the rapidly approaching readjustment period' (*Trades Union Congress, Annual Report, September 1918*, 70; B. C. Roberts, *The Trades Union Congress*, 291). The PCTUC itself had approved the first report on 18 Aug. 1917 (*Trades Union Congress, Annual Report, September 1917*, PCTUC report), and approved it again in Dec. Following reports of its rejection by trade unionists, J. Roberts, the Labour Minister for Labour, asked the PCTUC for clarification. It was in response to this that the PCTUC affirmed that the TUC had accepted the plan (PCTUC, min. 11 Dec. 1917).

[97] LPNEC, min. 1917, pp. 152, 213.

[98] *Labour and the New Social Order*, in A. Henderson, *The Aims of Labour* (1918), Append. II, p. 91.

as an expression of the moderate socialism adopted explicitly by the party in February 1918 with its new constitution, committing Labour to the 'common ownership of the means of production'. Yet it can be understood merely as a reformulation in Fabian language of demands which had long featured at party conferences. Its precise nature as a reflection of Labour attitudes to the war has more rarely been examined. Yet this, arguably, provides the key to the programme, and renders it less paradoxical than it might otherwise appear.

For *Labour and the New Social Order* expressed the by now widespread perception that the war's social and domestic impact would prove as significant as its international consequences. It also stated the broad labour sentiment that the war had discredited and somehow destroyed 'the individualist system of capitalist production'.[99] The programme explicitly presented itself as a measure by which the supposedly superficial and fragmentary approach of government 'reconstruction' planning might be criticized. And it thus affirmed its central function as the programme on which Labour would assert its electoral autonomy and base its post-war activity, whether in opposition or 'in due time called upon to form an administration'.[100] Whatever else its significance, *Labour and the New Social Order* was a summation of the process by which the increasingly critical participation of labour leaders in the national effort found expression in a vision of reforms, arising from the war itself, but projected in an idealized, programmatic form on to the post-war world. The report affirmed the continued relevance of Labour's peacetime concerns, but it also transformed these by endowing them with a national vocation. Where the CGT *majoritaires* hoped to create an 'economic democracy' on behalf of society as a whole, *Labour and the New Social Order* cast the Labour Party as the only organization capable of ensuring the full democratization, through economic and social reforms, of the entire nation, in contrast to the sectional 'capitalist' principles supposedly represented by both Liberal and Conservative parties.

The 'Four Pillars' on which the programme was erected each had a specific significance in relation to the war, and all, as we

[99] Ibid. 92.
[100] Ibid.

have noted, had been anticipated by the resolutions passed at the January 1917 Labour Party conference. The 'National Minimum' (the first 'pillar'), which saw public works and social works, plus the extension of wartime minimum wage legislation, as the solution to unemployment, was first and foremost Labour's answer to the dislocation of demobilization. The second 'pillar', the 'Democratic Control of Industry', was a résumé of Labour's wartime insistence on the nationalization of key industries and a measure of economic regulation over all industry. The third 'pillar', the transformation of taxation in order to pay for both the war and social reforms, was in effect the conscription of wealth. The final 'pillar', the 'Surplus Wealth for the Common Good', proclaimed Labour's commitment to broad welfare reforms, many of which had featured in 'After the war' proposals since 1916.

Most of these demands (nationalizations, extended unemployment insurance, tax reform) had pre-war antecedents. But the programme codified them by underpinning them with socialist principles. Central among these were the assertion, first, of collective rights over production ('the Labour Party looks to ... a genuinely scientific reorganization of the nation's industry, no longer deflected by individual profiteering, on the basis of the Common Ownership of the Means of Production'), and secondly, of the responsibility of the collectivity (i.e. the state) for protecting the individual from want ('the Labour Party today stands for the universal application of the Policy of the National Minimum ... of Leisure, Health, Education and Subsistence').[101] It was the war which gave conviction and even a sense of urgency to these principles. By generating a high tension between the 'choice of 1914' and the economic disadvantages suffered by the working class, the war imparted a powerful charge to basic Labour demands and induced their reformulation into a more coherent programme. In fact, the reception of *Labour and the New Social Order* suggests that the war made a moderate, pragmatic socialism relevant to much of organized labour.

Each of the three members of the subcommittee responsible for *Labour and the New Social Order* illustrates an important

---

[101] Ibid., 94, 99.

aspect of the programme's relationship to the Labour Party. Sidney Webb is usually credited with responsibility for the document. But Ramsay MacDonald's involvement suggests more complex roots. Both MacDonald and the ILP officially shared the broad assumptions of the programme. In 1917, MacDonald wrote a short book, *Socialism After the War*, which advocated, in addition to the conscription of wealth, the nationalization of key industries and the implementation through social services of a national minimum living standard.[102] The ILP published a post-war reform programme as early as May 1915 which argued that the war was making converts to socialism with the hostility aroused by profiteering and the example of massive state intervention in the economy.[103] By September 1917, the *Labour Leader* felt that the broad mass of trade union opinion had adopted positions close to those of the ILP on domestic and international matters.[104] *Labour and the New Social Order* thus represented a community of ideas between ILP leaders and pro-war figures like Webb and Henderson— and indeed expressed that broader Labour consensus on 'After the war' questions which had emerged in 1916. Ben Turner, the trade union leader, argued in the *Labour Leader* that:

[the programme's] chief sponsors are no doubt Sidney Webb and J. Ramsay MacDonald. Both men have put their soul into it . . . Men like Henderson, Wake, Anderson, Jowett and other doughty servants of Labour have put their bit into it. The Movement has also played a good part in its shaping, for the result of the constant direct contact of the Executive members with the Movement in the provinces as well as in London, is well expressed in the wideness and yet intensely practical nature of the document.[105]

None the less, the doctrinal hallmark of Webb and the Fabians is clearly stamped on *Labour and the New Social Order*. From early in the war, the Fabians had turned their attention not only to the conscription of wealth but to the demobilization and post-

---

[102] Like Henderson and Webb, MacDonald premised his programme on the Labour Party as an independent opposition party ('The first parliamentary task of Socialists should now be to form an opposition with an imperial, foreign and domestic policy of reconstruction and reform', *Socialism After the War*, 43).
[103] 'The War and Social Conditions', *Labour Leader*, May 1915.
[104] 'Review of the Week', *Labour Leader*, 13 Sept. 1917.
[105] *Labour Leader*, 10 Jan. 1918.

war 'reconstruction' in general.[106] Sidney Webb, in addition to his role on the WEWNC and LPNEC, published a series of works in 1916–17 adapting the pre-war Fabian understanding of social reform to wartime perspectives. In addition to the Fabian pamphlet, *How to Pay for the War*, he dealt in Fabian tract 181, *When Peace Comes: The Way of Industrial Reconstruction*, with the 'Great disbandment problem' and the opportunity it represented for permanent social reform. In the same month, September 1916, Webb and Arnold Freeman published *Great Britain after the War*, which speculated more broadly on the long-term significance of the war for the labour movement and Webb's own views on social progress and collectivism.

How soon will boldly-conceived Reconstruction follow the mere palliation of evils? . . . Will the power of the State be used when Peace comes, in the interests of the few or in those of the many? Are we destined, during the first years of dislocation to witness a period of plutocratic tyranny? . . . Will this be followed by 'Labour Governments' and 'Socialist Legislation'?[107]

The LPNEC's requirement of a more integrated and coherently formulated post-war 'reconstruction' programme presented the occasion for an optimistic reply to these questions, and Fabian reformism provided the language and basic concepts with which to shape the impulse emanating from the party. The 'national minimum', the emphasis on a rational, reforming state acting for the benefit not of the working class

---

[106] The Fabian Society saw the war as its opportunity to win the support of 'the leaders of the industrial and political wings of the Labour movement whose training or temperament fits them for taking part in the work of research or in the discussion of its results' (resolution, annual meeting, 1915, *Fabian News*, May 1915). The Society acknowledged the WEWNC as the 'recognised medium for bringing organised Labour and Socialist pressure upon the Government in connection with all questions affecting the welfare of the masses arising from the war' (ibid.). In the autumn of 1915, the Webbs ran a course of lectures on 'The World after the War' (*Fabian News*, Sept. 1915). The Fabian concern with social reform arising from the war was thus clearly established in 1915, and was developed throughout the war with publications and conferences (see *Fabian News*, the *New Statesman*, Fabian tracts and pamphlets, annual reports, minutes of meetings, and correspondence, all in the Library, Nuffield College, Oxford; for the Webbs, see also the Passfield Papers, Library, the London School of Economics; for discussions of Fabianism and the war, see McBriar, *Fabian Socialism and English Politics*, 340–5, and Winter, *Socialism and the Challenge of War*, 29–66, 184–233).

[107] *Great Britain after the War*, 8.

alone but of all citizens, and the complete absence of reference
to worker participation in the control of industry, all bore the
Fabian imprint. The fundamental ideas were close to the
eclectic socialism of the ILP. And no other tradition of socialist
thought (Guild Socialist, Christian Socialist) was sufficiently
central to Labour or adequately represented in the party during
the war, to provide a rival intellectual framework.[108]

Henderson saw the question of post-war reform, domestic
and international, as the occasion for a basic reorientation of the
Labour Party. In part, the need for a new strategy and organization was imposed from without—by the resolution of the
unfinished business of Edwardian electoral reform in the shape
of the 1918 Representation of the People Act (completing the
enfranchisement of working-class males and extending limited
representation to women). This alone would probably have
produced the overhaul of independent Labour constituency
organizations which occurred between 1917 and 1920. But it
would not automatically have determined the shape of the
party's new constitution nor designated the political goals to
which a fully autonomous party was to be directed. Henderson
felt that the war itself, and the issues it raised, had presented
Labour with an opportunity not just to break with the divided
Liberals but to become the party of social—and socialist—
reform.[109] Webb and MacDonald shared this view. From 1916,
leading ILP figures such as Jowett hoped that the war would
convert the Labour Party to socialism and thus strengthen 'the
Trade Union and Socialist Alliance'.[110] But Henderson's role,
as leader of the Labour Party (especially after his effective
dismissal from the cabinet in 1917), was decisive.

Henderson was certainly deeply impressed by the social
impact of the war and its consequences for Labour. In *The Aims
of Labour*, published in January 1918 with *Labour and the New
Social Order* as an appendix, he condemned the organization of
the war effort, including the repression of Labour dissidents,
while reaffirming the basic 'choice of 1914'. The central assertion

[108] Winter, *Socialism and the Challenge of War*, 270–88.
[109] Ibid., 234–69; Pugh, *Electoral Reform in War and Peace*, chap. 13; Laybourn,
The Rise of Labour, chap. 3.
[110] F. W. Jowett, 'The ILP and the Labour Party', *Socialist Review*, Jan.–Mar.
1916, p. 31.

of the book was the familiar theme that the economic mobilization had demonstrated the power of the state but that only an independent Labour Party could be counted on to use such power to effect a genuine post-war 'reconstruction' of society along socialist lines ('the hard, cruel, competitive system of production must be replaced by a system of co-operation under which the status of the workers will be revolutionised').[111]

In order to achieve this, Henderson and Webb proposed a new party constitution, in which local branches recruiting individuals would parallel the block membership of the trade unions, and replace the affiliation of the individual socialist societies. Such a reorganization opened up the party socially— to the 'producers by hand or by brain', and hence to much of the lower middle class and middle class—and also broadened its political appeal to all 'democratic' forces in the country as well as organized labour. The new constitution met stiff resistance at the January 1918 party conference from two quarters. A significant number of trade unionists feared that a mass individual membership would weaken the party as the political defender of specifically trade union interests. The ILP, under attack from much of trade union opinion for its opposition to the war (it had already been driven off the LPNEC at the January 1917 conference), resisted its permanent exclusion from the executive. The constitution was passed at a special conference late in February 1918, but not before a worried Henderson had toured the hesitant areas, in which a Lib–Lab. tradition remained strong, in order to promote it.[112]

The conflict over the new constitution is instructive. It revealed, firstly, a sharp tension between two conceptions of the Labour Party—as the trade unions' political pressure group or as a national party. Many trade unions hesitated to accept the electoral logic of the movement's growing demand that the Labour Party wage a broad, independent campaign on post-war 'reconstruction'. It is all the more significant, therefore, that in their majority they eventually did so, and that the subsequent attempt by conservative trade unionists to set up a purely Trade Union Labour Party was firmly repudiated by the PCTUC and

[111] *The Aims of Labour*, 74.
[112] Orton, *Labour in Transition*, 133–5; McKibbin, *The Evolution of the Labour Party*, chap. 5.

by the September 1918 Trades Union Congress.[113] The conflict indicated, secondly, the irony for the ILP of the Labour Party's commitment to a moderate socialism. A result which the ILP during the war had undoubtedly helped secure undermined the logic of a distinct socialist body within the Labour Party and thus contributed to the marginalization and eventual demise of the ILP.

There is no doubt that opinion within the Labour Party and the trade union movement in 1918 by and large considered post-war reform, domestic and international, to be the dominant issues, and that it rallied behind the Labour Party's *Memorandum on War Aims* and *Labour and the New Social Order*. Both were circulated by the LPNEC in spring 1918 for discussion as the basis of Labour's election campaign, and by June, the committee reported that *Labour and the New Social Order* had aroused widespread interest not only in the press, but also 'from soldiers and sailors on all fronts, from Flanders to Mesopotamia, from the Irish Sea to the Pacific'.[114] The June Labour Party conference passed, in addition to *Labour and the New Social Order*, a large number of 'reconstruction' resolutions. And from August 1918, the LPNEC (with Webb playing a central role) translated the work of the June conference and of a series of Advisory Committees established in 1918 into an election programme centred on 'reconstruction'.[115]

The Labour Party denies that there is, at this Election, no other issue than the War. Such a pretext is a device for enabling the representatives of capitalistic interests to creep into Parliament without avowing their object ... The Labour Party ... declines to go back to the

---

[113] PCTUC, min. 9 Apr. 1918; *Trades Union Congress, Annual Report, September 1918*, 261.

[114] LPNEC, min. 27 Feb. 1918; *Report of the Labour Party Conference, June 1918*, 13; C. Howard, 'Expectations Born to Death: Local Labour Party Expansion in the 1920s', in J. M. Winter (ed.), *The Working Class in Modern British History* (CUP, Cambridge, 1983), 65–6.

[115] The advisory committees were established in late Mar.–Apr. 1918 (LPNEC., min. 1918, 104). By the end of the year they covered Trade Policy and Finance, Industrial Policy, Machinery of Government, Local Government, Public Health, Education, Rural Problems, Temperance Policy, and International Questions, and produced a variety of pamphlets (LPNEC., min. 1918, 480). Four new standing subcommittees were also created, one of which, the Policy and Programme subcommittee, drafted an electoral statement in Aug., on Webb's inspiration, which summarized much of the work of the subcommittees (MacDonald Papers, diary, 31 July 1918).

conditions of penury and starvation which were all that society used to allow millions of workers. It stands for such a systematic reconstruction of industrial and social relations as will give to the workers by hand or brain the full fruits of their labour.

The Labour Party demands, when peace has been secured, the wide measures of reform that are described in 'Labour and the New Social Order'.[116]

The PCTUC both supported the Labour approach and pursued its own particular 'After the war' issues.[117] And the ILP, in October 1917, launched a 'Great Forward Movement' to influence the Labour Party both on the new constitution and on 'reconstruction'. Though defeated on the former, the ILP campaigned in close co-operation with the Labour Party on post-war reform throughout 1918.[118] Labour was thus remarkably united in contesting the December 1918 election on the issue of post-war reform.[119] The victory atmosphere and the deprivation of three-quarters of the armed forces of the right to vote by the unseemly haste with which the election was held,

[116] LPNEC, min. 1918, 304. For the various drafts, see 303–17.

[117] Henderson proposed a joint campaign to the International Joint Committee of the Labour Party and TUC on 8 Jan. 1918 (LPNEC, min. 8 Jan. 1918). At a joint PCTUC/LPNEC meeting the following day, the PCTUC was averse to the idea until it was clarified that reconstruction referred to post-war social reforms rather than Henderson's plans for the Labour Party's constitution (LPNEC and PCTUC, mins. 9 Jan. 1918). On 20 Feb., the International Joint Committee set up a subcommittee to settle details of the 'War Aims and Reconstruction' campaign. It consisted of Henderson and Webb for the Labour Party and G. H. Stuart Bunning and C. W. Bowerman, chairman and secretary respectively, of the PCTUC (LPNEC, min. 20 Feb. 1918). In the election campaign, the PCTUC issued a manifesto which saw the main issue as 'Reconstruction proposals', and which derived its main demands from the Labour Party programme—nationalizations, the prevention of unemployment, and minimum standard wages (PCTUC *Quarterly Reports*, Dec. 1918, p. 2).

[118] See, for statements on the 'Great Forward Movement', *Labour Leader*, 25 Oct. (P. Snowden, 5), 1 Nov. (F. Jowett, 5), 8 Nov. (Snowden, 2), 15 Nov. (MacDonald, 5), and 29 Nov. and 6 Dec., for local responses. See Snowden's 'Review of the Week' column in *Labour Leader*, 1918, for ILP endorsement of *Labour and the New Social Order*. For the ILP and the 1918 election, see the *Labour Leader*'s 'Striking Points for Propagandists', 12 Dec. 1918. Snowden asserted that his reconstruction proposals drew on ILP programmes since the party's inception (*Labour Leader*, 5 Dec. 1918). Ramsay MacDonald, however, both in his address 'To the Electors of the West Division of Leicester' (MacDonald Papers, PRO/30/69/7/51) and in an interview with *Le Populaire*, 3 Dec. 1918, defined reconstruction in terms of *Labour and the New Social Order*.

[119] For Labour's immediate electoral policy, see *Labour's Call to the People!*.

contributed to a disappointing result. But the Labour Party still increased its seats from 42 in December 1910 to 63, becoming the largest opposition party in the Commons.

Recent years have seen a substantial debate on the significance of the Labour Party's apparent commitment to socialism in 1918. Some confirm the traditional view of the 1918 constitution as a turning-point in the adoption by the bulk of the trade union movement of a moderate 'Labour socialism'. Others reject this interpretation and stress the continuity of evolution across the war years.

In particular, R. McKibbin, in his organizational study of the Labour Party from 1910 to 1924, argues that 1918 saw not the victory but the defeat of socialism.[120] According to this view, moderate, patriotic, non-socialist trade union leaders consolidated their hold on the Labour Party, eliminating the representation of the ILP and defeating, by their dominance of the electoral machinery, Henderson's and Webb's conception of a socially broad-based party. The war confirmed the political autonomy of the party, through the widened franchise of 1918 and the disintegration of the Liberals. It also strengthened trade union commitment to a pragmatic 'collectivism'. But, it is argued, these developments were well in the making before the war and owed nothing essentially original to it. The war simply reinforced the nature of the Labour Party as the expression of a class-conscious but non-socialist trade union leadership, which tended to see socialism as the alien product of middle-class intellectuals, such as those recruited during the war to the ILP. This leadership pursued through electoral independence the pragmatic reforms and defence of trade union interests which it had previously advanced through parliamentary coalition with the Liberals.

The revisionists have rightly focused attention on some of the longer-term factors in the organizational consolidation of Labour and its gradual replacement of the Liberals in major working-

---

[120] McKibbin, *The Evolution of the Labour Party*. Winter, *Socialism and the Challenge of War* reaffirms the more traditional view. For the debate, see, *inter alia*, S. McIntyre, 'Socialism, the Unions and the Labour Party after 1918', *Bulletin of the Society for the Study of Labour History*, 23 (1975), pp. 101–11; and Winter, 'Trade Unions and the Labour Party in Britain'.

class areas. But in so far as they touch on Labour during the war, they appear to misunderstand, if not totally ignore, the disruptive effects of the conflict on the labour movement and the specific reformism which these helped produce. The 'class consciousness' of the trade union leaders was less unchanging than is suggested, nor was socialism confined to middle-class intellectuals. As we have noted, criticisms of the war effort generated a strong feeling that the economic system as such required fundamental change. Combined with the moral charge levied on society by Labour for its support for the war effort, plus apprehensions about the demobilization, and couched in terms of post-war reform, this feeling led much of Labour and trade union opinion to demand a major 'reconstruction' of post-war society. Moderate socialism provided the language and terminology for this demand. 'Reconstruction' thus led to socialism, so that the adoption of the latter never took the form of an abstract intellectual leap—an ideological rupture.[121]

Nothing in this process was incompatible with labour patriotism. On the contrary, the demand for reform stemmed as much from the 'choice of 1914' as from the ILP's opposition to the war. At the same time, the shift in labour opinion greatly facilitated the dissemination of the socialists' ideas—including, ironically, those of the ILP. Nowhere is this shown more clearly than in the eventual acceptance by the Trades Union Congress and the Labour Party of the ILP and WEWNC initiative on the conscription of wealth—perhaps the turning-point in the relationship of labour leaders to the war effort.

---

[121] At the June 1918 Labour Party conference, a first reconstruction resolution called for 'the gradual building up of a new social order' by (*inter alia*) 'deliberately planned cooperation in production and distribution and exchange'. E. C. Fairchild, of the BSP, condemned the vagueness of the formula in contrast with the commitment to collectivization in the Labour Party's new constitution. Webb conducted a skilful defence which, without denying the constitutional commitment, argued the need to mute the terms of labour's mass electoral appeal. Presented as a clash between the electoral programme of post-war reconstruction and socialist principles, the former prevailed, and Fairchild's amendment was defeated (*Report of the Labour Party Conference, June 1918*, 43–4). The second resolution dealt specifically with the transition to peace. It rejected wage reductions and called for increased production as the only basis of 'any genuine reconstruction'. An amendment was proposed by the Northampton Labour Representation Committee declaring the 'socialisation of industry' to be the only means of achieving this. This time, socialism stemmed from reconstruction. The amendment was passed by 1,225,000 to 843,000 (ibid., 44).

The conflict with the ILP had more to do with the latter's opposition to the war (its refusal of the 'choice of 1914') than with its socialism. This is not to deny that trade union leaders and the PCTUC were organizationally cautious, concerned above all to defend the considerable achievements of organized labour. This emerged clearly in their insistence that the restoration of trade union customs was pivotal to post-war reform, and in their reluctance to venture too far into the marshes of 'Whitleyism'. For the same reason, there was a tussle over the precise balance of influence in the new constitution of the Labour Party. But the February and June 1918 party conferences indicate that much of the predominantly trade union membership accepted that an independent Labour campaign on post-war 'reconstruction' required a rather different, socially broadened Labour Party.

In these ways, therefore, a specifically wartime labour reformism emerged in Britain as in France, and imparted a fresh impulse to the development of the labour movement and its ideological orientation. Beneath obvious differences in form and chronology, due to the differing traditions and structures of organized labour in the two countries, and due also to the distinctive forms of war mobilization in the two cases, there were many broad similarities. It is to a more systematic comparison of the causes and function of this wartime labour reformism that we must now turn.

7 Labour Reformism in Wartime: A Comparison

THE labour reformism which emerged between 1914 and 1918 in the French and British labour movements can be analysed in three dimensions. Most obviously it represented the awakening of organized labour to the societal and economic implications of the war itself. But it was also an important moment in the evolution of the two labour movements. Wartime reformism was related to longer-term changes and is only fully explicable by reference to these. Additionally, labour participation was one component in the larger process of societal mobilization for the war effort. To understand how the two societies coped, it is as important to see how wartime reformism structured and sustained labour support as it is to know how labour dissidence and pacifism weakened it.

(i) The Nature and Functions of Wartime Labour Reformism

At the core of labour reformism as a distinctive wartime phenomenon was the tension between the 'choice of 1914' and the attempt by labour leaders to defend working-class interests, politically and industrially, in the upheaval caused by a long, industrial war effort. Labour reformism reinjected complexity into an artificially narrow national consensus on the war and differentiated labour terms of participation from those of the state.

At the same time, it delineated a vital relationship between past and future. The war was experienced as a rupture with the

past, and with normal preoccupations, in both labour movements. Not only did it erupt suddenly and expose the illusion of
the Second International that it could prevent a European war,
but it also confounded all expectations by its scale and duration.
Once the initial emergency was over, both labour movements
confronted a certain ideological disjuncture caused by the
International's collapse and the difficulty of absorbing the war
experience into the longer-term language and concerns of
organized labour. This was especially acute in the CGT, where
it brought to the boil a long-simmering crisis of orientation. But
it is significant that in both cases, the organizations established
to cope with the initial emergency had refocused by 1916 on the
broader implications of the war experience for labour.

These two central aspects of wartime labour reformism
converged on the post-war future. Official programmes of
reconstruction related the upheaval of the present to the shape
of *l'après-guerre*, thus distilling much of labour thinking on the
war as a complex set of economic, social, and political issues.
But criticism of the war effort as such pointed in the same
direction. The idea of post-war reform was above all a by-
product of the process of societal mobilization. It represented,
for moderate labour leaders, an extension and idealized version
of changes demanded in that process, in the name of social
equality.

This explains many of the similarities between reform demands in the two cases. Condemnation of 'profiteering' naturally suggested the need for radical fiscal reform. Regulation
of the supply and pricing of provisions fed the idea of a
rudimentary form of permanent state regulation and planning
of the economy. Wartime control of the labour supply suggested the importance of permanent trade union involvement in
the operation of the labour market, through labour exchanges in
both cases and through the strict regulation of immigrant
labour in that of the CGT. The obviously vital role of coal and
railways in the economic mobilization, and the varying degrees
of control imposed by the state, seemed to prove the labour case
for nationalization. 'Dilution' of the munitions labour force and
changes in engineering production processes reinforced demands for labour 'participation' and 'control' in determining
working conditions and even the way production was organized.

Fears of a massive post-war slump on both sides of the Channel produced demands for a planned economic demobilization.

Perhaps there is no automatic reason why these post-war programmes should have assumed the form of reformist socialism. Reformism, as a term in labour history, covers several phenomena. It can denote a systematic interest in piecemeal reforms within an acceptance of the prevailing economic order. Or it can indicate a variety of evolutionary projects for transforming capitalism and class relations from within by the gradual expansion and penetration of organized labour into prevailing institutions and economic arrangements.[1] The emphasis has frequently been on organization and practice as much as on theory. Reformism was not a common term in the British labour movement where the weakness of overtly revolutionary currents rendered such self-definition nugatory. Nor was it popular in the French labour and socialist movements where, conversely, the rhetoric of revolution prevailed.[2] Moreover, 'socialism' itself was not a welcome appellation in much of the CGT since it implied the state-oriented approach against which the bulk of pre-war syndicalist leaders (reformist as well as revolutionary) defined themselves.

None the less, stepping back from contemporary terminology, it was indeed a moderate socialism, suggesting the possibility of transforming capitalism by a strategy of reforms, which shaped the programme of the CGT *majoritaires* from 1916 and of the Labour Party in 1918. This was rarely a matter of

---

[1] There is a dearth of comparative history or conceptual analysis of reformism. But see T. Judt, introduction to special issue of *Journal of Contemporary History*, 'Conflicts and Compromise: Socialists and Socialism in the Twentieth Century', 11/2–3 (1976), pp. 1–10; G. Quazza (ed.), *Riforme e rivoluzione nella storia contemporanea* (Einaudi, Turin, 1977); D. S. White, 'Reconsidering European Socialism in the 1920s', *Journal of Contemporary History*, 16/2 (1981), pp. 251–72; and F.-G. Dreyfus (ed.), *Réformisme et révisionnisme dans les socialismes allemand, autrichien et français* (Éditions de la Maison des Sciences de l'Homme, 1984), especially the conclusion by L. Hamon (185–94). Among studies which reflect on the moderate nature of the twentieth-century British labour movement are R. Miliband, *Parliamentary Socialism* (Allen & Unwin, 1961), and J. Cronin, *Labour and Society in Britain, 1918–1979* (Batsford, 1984). Studies of French reformism are 'Réformismes et réformistes français', *Le Mouvement social*, 87 (Apr.–June 1974), and D. Blumé, R. Bourderon, *et al.*, *Histoire du réformisme en France depuis 1920* (Éditions sociales, 1976), 2 vols.

[2] Hamon, 'Conclusions générales', in Dreyfus, *Réformisme et révisionnisme*, 191.

abstract definitions. The programmes grew from the conviction that the war had brought major changes to the *laissez-faire* model of capitalism and from labour demands for a change in the principles of economic organization and in the status of the worker. Socialist ideas were culled from the traditions to hand in each case in order to codify post-war ideas. Fabian collectivism and eclectic ILP socialism, in the British case, and the producer-oriented, anti-state collectivism of the Proudhonist tradition in France, provided the fundamental concepts of the two programmes. Neither was a blueprint for a socialist economy or a strategy for achieving it. Rather, both were moral declarations of organized labour's reluctance to remain aboard the existing economic system and an embryonic plan of how it might embark on an alternative, essentially collectivist voyage—along very different routes in the two cases.

The history of this wartime reformism has been overshadowed, especially in France, by the emphasis on labour opposition to the war. Few studies in either country have tried to account for its resilience or the support which it rallied. Yet since it represented the majority response of organized labour, such an assessment is overdue, and to that end it is important to look more closely at the principal features and functions of the phenomenon.

'Pro-war' labour leaders faced two powerful pressures for the absorption of their movements into the existing order—politically, through the 'self-mobilization' of labour behind the national cause, and economically, through their role in the industrial mobilization. The specific characteristics of wartime reformism, as both practice and programme, stemmed from the growing reluctance of labour leaders to accept these assimilationist tendencies.

The fundamental dimension was political, since the war irrupted into the labour movements as an extraneous, unanticipated emergency requiring a swift political response. War reformism started from the premiss of the working class's incorporation into the nation. This was partly determined by the permeability of the labour movement and many of its activists to the mood of national solidarity of 1914. But the 'choice of 1914' was also shaped by specifically labour and socialist traditions in which class and national perspectives combined. Hence the conviction that the war was in essence a conflict between 'democracy' and 'militarism', whose outcome affected the prospects of the labour and socialist movements themselves. Modified in favour of the possibility of a negotiated peace, this 'choice' was not fundamentally repudiated by the British labour or CGT majorities, or by many French socialists, throughout the war. Whether or not pro-war labour leaders were 'right' in their view is scarcely the point. It was a powerful conviction with its own logic. It is curious, therefore, to see it explained away, especially in the French case, as the aberration of an isolated leadership. No such difficulties attend the discussion of labour and socialist participation in the national defence twenty-five years later, under the sign of anti-fascism.[3]

In order to restore a critical brake to the political incorporation of the working class and organized labour into the nation, many pro-war labour leaders turned sooner or later to the notion of working-class sacrifice in the war effort. The mobilization process, though exceptional, was felt by its differential impact on various groups to highlight social inequalities prevalent in peacetime. At the same time, it demonstrated graphically the economic indispensability of the industrial worker. If the political mobilization turned on the claims of the nation over groups and individuals, labour reformism reversed the argument and expressed the claims of labour on the nation. To cite two among many examples, J. H. Thomas declared to the NUR in June 1917:

> We cannot afford to return to pre-war conditions with their low wages and irksome surroundings. The sacrifices which railwaymen have made ought at least to be recognised to the extent of assuring them very much improved conditions in the future. These things I suggest are strong reasons why the Government should never again lose its control of our railways.[4]

At almost the same moment in France, and also in the context of nationalization demands, the executive of the Fédération Nationale des Cheminots maintained: 'The *cheminots* claim to have contributed a large share to the national defence and they

---

[3] A. Kriegel seems to be the only person to have made the comparison for France, in 'Août 1914: nationalisme et internationalisme ouvriers', 219.

[4] *Railway Review*, 22 June 1917.

have the right to claim, for the future, greater liberty, greater well-being . . .'[5]

The language of sacrifice allowed labour leaders to present labour as not merely a sectional interest within the nation but as the legitimate expression of the nation, and thus to claim a pre-eminent role for the labour movement in national affairs. In both cases, the idea that labour had come of age was widely asserted. Business and 'capital', by contrast, were seen as self-interested and sectional. *Labour and the New Social Order* stressed throughout that the reforms proposed were not 'class measures' but in 'the interests of the community as a whole'. The November 1916 programme of the Commission Mixte and the *Programme Minimum*, in outlining the economic reorganization of France, averred that 'the working class must therefore direct the national effort in this direction'.

Such claims rested on the assertion that the labour movement represented, actually or potentially, a numerical as well as moral majority. In industrialized Britain, where on any reckoning a large proportion of society could be thought of as working class, this was easier than in France. Even here, the social coalition behind the Labour Party envisaged by Webb and Henderson extended to the clerical, professional, and intellectual middle and lower middle classes, and white-collar and civil-service trade unionism increased sharply.[6] In partially industrialized France, where the *classes moyennes* and peasantry outnumbered industrial workers, the definition of a social coalition to underpin the national claims of CGT leaders was more problematic—especially since these other classes bore disproportionately the 'sacrifice' of the trenches.

Indeed, workers in munitions, mines, and railways were often seen by other social groups as protected by their privileged status. So insistent was this resentment against war workers that the Comité Confédéral of the CGT attempted to straighten the record (as it saw it) in September 1916 by issuing a circular which accused industrialists and deputies of deliberately caricaturing war workers as protected and overpaid in order to deflect attention from war profits, and it reasserted 'the

[5] *La Voix du peuple*, 1 May 1917, p. 16.
[6] B. Waites, *A Class Society at War: England, 1914–1918* (Berg, Leamington Spa, 1987), 240–64.

measure of sacrifice which [war workers] bring to the general work of national defence'.[7]

These difficulties seriously hampered the effort by the CGT *majoritaires* to project themselves, morally speaking, as the voice of the nation. None the less, the CGT attempted to speak for agricultural workers, consolidated support among public service workers, and made contact with professional organizations of the engineers and technicians who assumed an increasingly prominent role in production.[8] In short, it consciously sought to enlarge on its traditional constituencies in manual industrial labour. In both countries, therefore, broadened social definitions of the labour movement accompanied the latter's claim to speak for the nation.

But this qualification of organized labour's incorporation into the political mobilization of opinion behind the war inevitably remained in the realm of criticism and prescription, since the prior and continuing commitment was to support the national effort, not to hinder it by imposing labour's terms—even supposing that to have been possible. This gave the post-war reform programmes much of their coherence and relevance while the war lasted. Pro-war labour leaders had written, if not a blank, at least an uncrossed cheque to the nation, and through it, to government and business. The conversion to peace was the moment when the cheque was to be repaid and the political credit invested in a reformed post-war order.

Labour leaders were exposed to a more tangible form of incorporation through the industrial mobilization which, as we have seen, generated powerful 'corporatist' tendencies in both societies.[9] At the heart of these tendencies, from the labour

[7] *La Bataille*, 21 Sept. 1916; Horne, 'L'Impôt du Sang: Republican Rhetoric and Industrial Warfare in France, 1914–1918'.

[8] M. Descostes and J.-L. Robert (eds.), *Clefs pour une histoire du syndicalisme cadre* (Éditions ouvrières, 1984), 57–60.

[9] The literature on corporatism is considerable. For useful summaries and conceptual distinctions, see P. Schmitter, 'Still the Century of Corporatism?' *Review of Politics* (Jan. 1974), pp. 85–131; R. Harrison, *Pluralism and Corporatism: The Political Evolution of Modern Democracies* (Allen & Unwin, 1980); and S. Berger (ed.), *Organizing Interests in Western Europe: Pluralism, Corporatism and the Transformation of Politics* (CUP, Cambridge, 1981), especially the opening essay by C. S. Maier, 'Fictitious Bonds of Wealth and Law', 27–61. Specifically historical studies bearing on the period of the First World War are Fine, 'Towards Corporatism'; C. S. Maier, *Recasting Bourgeois Europe: Stabilization in France, Germany and Italy in the Decade after World War I* (Princeton Univ. Press, Princeton, NJ, 1975); Middlemas,

point of view, lay two partly overlapping relationships. The first was that of organized labour with the state, as an agent not only of coercion but also of reform. The pre-war period had witnessed interventionist tendencies by the state in a range of fields, from labour conditions, the labour market, and industrial relations to social welfare. With varying effect in the two countries, reforming civil servants and politicians had sought to define an enlarged social role for the state in mediating economic and class relationships.

The war immeasurably strengthened this tendency, necessitating as it did unprecedented state intervention in the economy. The massive munitions efforts moved labour questions to the centre of the political stage. Both Lloyd George and Albert Thomas recognized that the interests of labour had to be respected and accommodated by state action over working conditions and welfare, and by consultation with labour leaders in the process. The munitions effort was by definition exceptional, but it suggested the potential for substantial post-war reform in the same fields. Equally, the powers exercised by the wartime state inevitably raised the broader issues of the control and ownership of economic wealth. Lloyd George and Albert Thomas hinted constantly that the munitions effort was indirectly working in favour of longer-term labour aspirations.[10]

The second relationship was that between business and labour. National traditions of industrial relations differed, as we have noted. Although in Britain employer recognition of trade unions, let alone collective bargaining, were far from universal, a strong tradition existed of voluntary joint negotiation up to and including the national level between employers' and workers' organizations. The government endorsed this trend before the war, and this essentially voluntary and contractual system was strained but not destroyed by the pre-war industrial strife. Under a much more directive state, it was significantly

---

Politics in Industrial Society; Kuisel, *Capitalism and the State in Modern France*; A Rossiter, 'Experiments with Corporatist Politics in Republican France, 1916–1939' (Ph.D., Oxford, 1986).

[10] Lloyd George, *Through Terror to Triumph*, and speech to the 1915 TUC (*Trades Union Congress, Annual Report, 1915,* 359–60); for Albert Thomas, see speeches reported in the *Bulletin des usines de guerre*, 1916–17.

expanded during the war, incorporating large segments of non-skilled workers.

Many employers faced the reality of increased trade union strength and expanded institutional contact and bargaining by defensively strengthening their own professional organizations, as a counterweight to trade union influence on the government. This was especially the case with the powerful Engineering Employers' Federation. But there was also a distinct current of business, academic, and government opinion, as we have noted, which considered industrial conflict and the entrenched power of skilled workers to be the core of Britain's relative industrial decline—sharply highlighted by the war—and which, in consequence, aimed for more radical reform. This resulted in a plethora of proposals, of which the Whitley scheme was merely the most influential, somehow to enhance the consultative status of labour and the material well-being of workers in return for the renunciation of trade union 'customs' and industrial conflict. The newly formed Federation of British Industries (FBI) and its president, Dudley Docker, beat this particular drum in 1917–18.[11] The National Alliance of Employers and Employees (NAEE), founded in 1917 by a group of trade unionists and businessmen, promoted a comparable compact between the 'enlightened and progressive employer and the constructive, evolutionary trade unionist'.[12]

Trade unionism loomed less large in the preoccupations of French than British employers, as a report in 1919, by the American National Industrial Conference Board, on conditions of production in Europe, commented.[13] Paternalism, employer welfare schemes, and company unions remained widespread. As in Britain, the war shone a spotlight on the inadequacies of

[11] FBI, Report of the Nationalisation Committee, in A. Gleason, *What the Workers Want: A Study of British Labor* (Harcourt, Brace and Howe, NY, 1920), 296; Dudley Docker in Huntly Carter (ed.), *Industrial Reconstruction*, 39–91, and in Chapman, *Labour and Capital after the War*, 129–40; J. Turner, 'The Politics of "Organised Business" in the First World War', in id. (ed.), *Businessmen and Politics: Studies of Business Activity in British Politics, 1900–1945* (Heinemann, 1984), 33–49.

[12] Manifesto of the NAEE, *The Times*, 14 Sept. 1918, p. 3. For the origins of the NAEE, see ibid., 23 May 1917, p. 3, and *Unity*, Oct. 1919, pp. 5–6.

[13] *Problems of Labor and Industry in Great Britain, France and Italy. Report of the European Commission of the National Industrial Conference Board, November 1919* (Washington, DC, 1919), 287–92.

France's industrial economy by comparison with Germany. The barriers were reduced between business and government, and both became acutely concerned with questions of national efficiency and economic competitiveness.[14] As we have seen, French industrialists were compelled to recognize organized labour and engage in compulsory wage bargaining, in 1917–18, in an unprecedented manner. But the fact that skilled labour was much less deeply entrenched in the engineering industry, that employers benefited from a substantial restructuring of the wartime working class (deploying, for example, the foreign labour which the unions forbade in Britain), and that, overall, trade unionism remained weaker, meant that industrial relations with organized labour seemed less crucial to employers than other considerations.

The short-term logic of the war encouraged trade union leaders to accept, and even advocate, labour participation in these interlocking relationships with business and the state. The suspension of 'official' strikes pushed them down the path of closer contact, formal and informal, with both, and of collective bargaining under the sanction of state compulsion. This 'partnership', we have argued, was generally understood by labour leaders to be unequal, given the privileged role of private capital and enterprise in the industrial effort, but none the less one which yielded tangible benefits. It provided a framework for defending individuals and groups of workers and for criticizing aspects of the industrial mobilization. It yielded some influence on the state's direction of the labour supply (the abolition of 'leaving certificates' in Britain, the terms of employment of foreigners in France) and a labour voice on welfare issues in the war factories. The introduction of machinery in both countries in 1917 for regularly revising wages in the war industries made workers somewhat less vulnerable to inflation. Locally, trade unions and the co-operative movement helped organize food and other vital supplies, while the pressure of the labour movement helped bring about national rationing in the last year of the war. These, despite the criticisms of radical rank-and-file minorities, were not insubstantial benefits even if

---

[14] Fine, 'Towards Corporatism', 4–46; Peiter, 'Men of Goodwill'; Kuisel, *Capitalism and the State in Modern France*, 31–58; Godfrey, *Capitalism at War*.

they failed to satisfy many of the grievances and criticisms engendered by the war.

It was precisely to respond to the latter and to try and transcend the limits of labour participation in the industrial effort that many labour leaders developed the criticisms and alternative approaches which lay at the core of their wartime reformism. The corporatist tendency promoted by the war—that is, the changed relationship of state, business, and organized labour—influenced the elaboration of this wartime reformism. But it did so as much through labour leaders' perceptions of its potential as by its wartime substance. Here, when it came to projecting wartime experience into prescriptions for the war itself and the post-war future, the divergence from government and business views was considerable.

Undoubtedly, what impressed labour leaders most in the wartime arrangements was the vitality and adaptability of the wartime state and the relative ease with which ministers and bureaucrats overrode the traditional constraints imposed by the *laissez-faire* model of the economy. This became the central economic lesson of the war. It encouraged labour leaders to ask whether the powers and methods used by the state for the industrial mobilization could not be adapted to the goals of post-war reconstruction.

In Britain, from 1916, governments themselves sought to build a secondary political compact around the issue of post-war reform—partly in response to labour expectations and the potential menace of working-class disaffection. The war cabinet in its 1917 and 1918 reports identified 'reconstruction' as a fundamental consequence, and therefore goal, of the war.[15]

But the pivot of government 'reconstruction', as we have seen, was the reform of relations between employers and workers, through the Whitley scheme. And, ironically, this got a mixed and generally muted reception in the trade union movement and was ignored by the Labour Party. In common with other schemes for creating 'industrial harmony', it threatened the twin strengths of British trade unionism, the entrenched 'customs' of the skilled and the mass organization of many sectors, well beyond the skilled.

---

[15] *Report of the War Cabinet for 1917*, Cd. 9005, esp. introduction and chap. 16; Johnson, *Land Fit for Heroes*.

What was at issue, in fact, was nothing less than the terms on which 'efficiency' should be promoted in industry through wartime and post-war reorganization, and the degree to which labour should remain free, in relations with business, to exert its organized strength on the outcome. Trade union leaders fought a campaign which, in terms of the system of industrial relations, was essentially defensive. Following the 'patriotic bargain' of the Munitions of War Act, they sought doggedly to limit state control of labour (within the constraints of support for the war). The 'restoration' of trade union 'customs' was the pivot on which bargaining turned because it was an acknowledgement that the wartime restrictions on the formal powers of trade unions were temporary and reversible. 'Restoration' was the first step in extending labour 'control' over production in the face of reorganization. And if the epicentre of 'control' remained the defence of skilled grades in the engineering industry, it also had wider connotations. 'Restoration', commented the Commission of Enquiry into Industrial Unrest for the north-east,

is meant to cover not only the protection of existing craft industries but also the improvement of the conditions of labour, and the more adequate realisation of the right of the worker to secure his fair share in the product of his industry.[16]

Although this produced tensions with some general unions (notably the Workers' Union), the rapid expansion of semi-skilled and unskilled unionization confirmed the tendency of union leaders to conserve their autonomy and negotiate from positions of strength. Participation in joint bodies with employers to discuss the post-war world or to improve industrial relations varied, but was usually accepted only as an *adjunct* to growing trade union power and as a means of pressing for 'efficiency' on labour's terms.[17] Significantly, the

[16] Cd. 8662, 7. Reports for other regions corroborated this.

[17] Jack Beard, president of the Workers' Union, participated in the NAEE and favoured collaboration with employers on intensifying production through accords. Perhaps significantly, the union pursued an independent strategy, clashing with the ASE and resisting amalgamation with other general unions (Hyman, *The Workers' Union*, 198–201). But Ernest Bevin, rising star of the National Transport Workers' Federation, though debating Reconstruction with employers in 1917, did so to determine 'what is capital prepared to concede?' (A. Bullock, *The Life and Times of Ernest Bevin* (Heinemann), i, *Trade Union Leader, 1881–1940* (1960), 69–72).

NAEE secured the adhesion of only a small number of conservative unionists (the PCTUC, which discussed membership twice, shelved it on each occasion).[18]

Of course, there was also a radical vein of ideas on labour control of production and industrial self-government—notably in the shop stewards' movement and the Guild Socialists. But their impact on mainstream labour leaders, as we have seen, was subordinated to reform planning which was essentially political and proceeded via the state. This, we have argued, was the predominant characteristic of British Labour's post-war thinking. It is not just that the Labour Party was its principal vehicle and electoral success the designated path, but also that the cluster of reforms concerning social welfare and the ownership and control of economic wealth, which emerged in 1916–17 through the WEWNC, ILP, and Labour Party, was predicated on action by the state. Here, too, government efforts to consolidate the national consensus around the war as a social process were attuned to Labour aspirations. Yet what stands out is the absence of a bargain or compact between government and Labour on economic and social reform—despite the participation by important Labour figures (Beatrice Webb, J. H. Thomas, Marion Phillips) in Lloyd George's Reconstruction Committee of early to mid-1917.[19]

The welfare measures which preoccupied that committee and the subsequent Ministry of Reconstruction under Christopher Addison (health, housing, poor relief), as well as Fisher's reform of primary education, overlapped with Labour concerns and to some extent with Labour Party policies. But the reforming impulse on welfare issues was contested within government. Addison, for example, was bitterly resisted by the Local Government Board in his bid to create a Ministry of Health,

---

[18] PCTUC, min. 13–15 Feb. 1917, and 13 Mar. 1917. Trade union members of the NAEE executive which signed the manifesto were W. A. Appleton, W. B. Cheeseman, J. T. Clatworthy, W. F. Dawtry, H. Dubery, J. Solomon Hill, B. Kenyon, Arthur Pugh, and J. Havelock Wilson. Wilson, the fiercely anti-socialist leader of the Sailors and Firemen, provided the only overlap with the PCTUC. Significantly, J. Hodge, Labour minister and increasingly isolated on the right of the party, took part in meetings (*The Times*, 15 Jan. 1917 and 29 Jan. 1919).

[19] Johnson, *Land Fit for Heroes*, 56; P. Abrams, 'The Failure of Social Reform, 1918–20', *Past and Present*, 24 (1963), p. 61; Middlemas, *Politics in Industrial Society*, 130.

while the Ministry of Labour, established by Lloyd George as part of the price for Labour support of his coalition government, has been described as a 'graveyard of reform' over the next few years.[20] On economic questions, the government rejected the 'conscription of of wealth' via a capital levy, or indeed any radical change in financing the war. Nor did it have a clear view on nationalization, and there was no support for the degree of immediate nationalization envisaged by the Labour Party.[21] Here, ministers were closer to business opinion. Even the FBI, with its keenness on union consultation, rejected nationalization or any form of worker control which infringed 'commercial management', while the mine and railway owners, directly in Labour's firing-line, vehemently opposed nationalization and, as the war ended, urged economic decontrol.[22]

The Liberals were closer to many Labour Party proposals, with the Asquithian wing consciously fighting to retain the mantle of reform. But as Addison recognized, the Liberals were only likely to be able to participate in reconstruction through a Lloyd George coalition and this, especially after the 'coupon' election in December 1918, was dominated by the Conservatives.[23] It was clear to the keenest protagonists of reconstruction

---

[20] R. Lowe, 'The Ministry of Labour, 1916–1924: A Graveyard of Social Reform', *Public Administration*, 52 (1974), pp. 415–38; id., *Adjusting to Democracy*, 87–105. Labour was critical both of the 1918 Education Act and of official hesitation over a Ministry of Health. Even when established in 1919, the latter did not abolish the Poor Law system, as both the 1909 Minority Report of the Poor Law Commission and *Labour and the New Social Order* demanded. The insurance principle, with worker contributions for sickness and unemployment relief, at the core of government policy since 1911, was accepted by *Labour and the New Social Order*, although greater subvention of the unions' own schemes was urged.

[21] The programmes of non-government Liberals and Conservatives differed. Liberals were prepared to accept the nationalization of the railways (and 'national systems' of transport more generally), and of electricity. A strong Liberal current also supported widespread minimum wages (C. S. Addison, *Four and a Half Years* (Hutchinson, 1934), ii. 553–4; *Liberal Policy in the Task of Political and Social Reconstruction*). The coalition election manifesto did not advocate nationalization and was vague in its social welfare proposals (*The Times*, 22 Nov. 1918).

[22] FBI, Report of the Nationalisation Committee, in Gleason, *What the Workers Want*, 284–9. For FBI hostility to retention of the National Factories in public ownership and to railway nationalization, see *The Federation of British Industries: Third Annual Report for the Period ending 30 June 1919*, 10, 17.

[23] Addison, *Four and a Half Years*, ii. 602; Middlemas, *Politics in Industrial Society*, 134–6.

within the government in 1917–18 that Labour was devising an alternative post-war programme in part to cut free of coalitions.[24] Tom Jones, one of Lloyd George's two cabinet secretaries (and like Addison, on the radical wing of the party) dreamt early in 1918 of reconstituting the cabinet to include key Labour leaders (Henderson, J. H. Thomas, and Smillie), in order to facilitate both a 'democratic' peace and a 'period of democratic reconstruction at home'. But after consulting the Webbs, he concluded that Henderson's desire for autonomy plus fundamental policy differences made this impossible.

Henderson has vowed he will not again enter the Government without (a Labour majority). They could only enter on conditions that would not be accepted viz. the abolition of profiteering, conscription of capital—in a word the equalitarian state.[25]

In France, government concern with post-war reform generally, and with organized labour's aspirations in particular, was weaker and more diffuse than in Britain.[26] Significantly, there was no cabinet-level initiative on post-war reconstruction. In the crises of 1917, governments re-emphasized national self-defence as the sole and sufficient justification for the war, with Clemenceau in particular eschewing any secondary compact around reform. Nothing illustrates more clearly the minority, and relatively isolated, position of the working class in French society.

Yet in France, uniquely among the combatant powers, a socialist presided over the creation of the munitions effort. Judgements by CGT leaders about the reforming potential of the state centred on their contacts with ministers and sympathetic civil servants engaged in the industrial effort—that is, the socialist academics drafted in as administrators by Albert Thomas to the Ministry of Armaments and the progressive

---

[24] Addison, *Four and a Half Years*, ii. 459.

[25] T. Jones, *Whitehall Diary*, ed. K. Middlemas (OUP, Oxford), i, *1916–1925* (1969), 46.

[26] H. Carter, 'Reconstruction Literature in France', *The Sociological Review*, 10 (1918), pp. 55–9, 141–3; C. Bloch, 'The Literature of Economic Reconstruction in France', *Manchester Guardian Commercial*, special issue on 'Reconstruction in Europe', 4 Jan. 1923, pp. 744–8; and Kuisel, *Capitalism and the State in Modern France*, 59–62.

bureaucrats of the Ministry of Labour.[27] For, paradoxically perhaps, the *réorganisation économique* envisaged by the CGT as the core of post-war reform depended on the state itself providing the institutional framework through which organized labour could help fashion a decentralized, publicly owned and controlled economy. With the failure of joint reform planning between the CGT and PS nationally, the political strategy of the CGT turned on its capacity to influence the state directly.

A broad set of assumptions characterized the various agencies and *commissions mixtes* in which labour participated, locally and nationally. The imperative of industrial growth and efficiency was recognized, for the war and afterwards. The continued inter-relationship of organized labour, business, and the state in tackling agreed crucial questions—such as the labour market and labour supply, or the demobilization—was generally assumed. Within this consensus, which perhaps harked back to the Saint-Simonian tradition of collaboration between the state and productive forces in technically modernizing the economy, there was a privileged link between syndicalist leaders and progressive civil servants on reforms which particularly concerned labour. It was this, as we have noted, which produced Henri Sellier's labour placement plans for the Paris region, a sympathetic hearing for CGT views on female and foreign labour, and a bias towards labour in the settlement of strikes, at least in 1917.[28]

But despite this, the limitations on Thomas and his advisers in a munitions effort dependent on private enterprise meant that no accord, formal or informal, was possible which might respond to the broader aspirations of the CGT towards the *réorganisation économique* of post-war France. Not only Merrheim but also Jouhaux, on occasions, queried Thomas's ability to control the industrialists on whom he relied. On the central questions of the ownership and organization of production and a 'democratic' system of industrial relations, the gap remained wide.

[27] See p. 76, above.
[28] See Chap. 3, above. For the 'Saint-Simonian' consensus, see Fine, 'Towards Corporatism', 4–46, and id., 'Guerre et réformisme en France, 1914–1918', *Recherches*, 32/33 (Sept. 1978), pp. 305–24.

Thomas' reliance on private enterprise framed by state control led naturally to the *régie intéressée* as the vehicle of the future. Not only did this run foul of the Jacobin intransigence of the Groupe Socialiste until April 1917 (with its demand for outright requisitioning), but it was far removed from the forms of federalist collective ownership and control advocated by the Commission Mixte d'Études Économiques. Thomas's major innovation in state ownership, the sophisticated arsenal at Roanne, was a traditional *étatiste* enterprise. Yet the scandal and conservative opposition which ultimately sank it indicated the limits to business and political acceptance of a permanently enlarged public sector.[29] Thomas undoubtedly saw the wartime recognition and consultation of organized labour as a significant step forward. But compulsory arbitration remained an exceptional measure, repudiated in principle by the CGT, while Thomas was torn over the *délégués d'atelier* between the integral version espoused by CGT leaders and the frequently minimalist and paternalist version of those *patrons* prepared to accept them.[30]

Thomas's central conviction, that the transformation of the engineering and metallurgical industries by the war and the development of mass-production techniques would benefit working class, *patronat*, and nation, overlapped the productivism of the CGT. But where Thomas saw the benefits flowing from the work in hand, CGT leaders kept a critical distance and proposed a more far-reaching reform prospectus than he could match.

Thomas's departure from office none the less removed the key connection between syndicalist leaders and the state. The Ministry of Labour remained an important link, especially in 1918–19. But Loucheur replaced Thomas's advisers at the Ministry of Armaments with his own business associates and, although not rejecting organized labour's association with the

---

[29] Godfrey, *Capitalism at War*, 257–88 (for the Roanne arsenal). For Thomas's conception of the rapport between state and business in the war effort, see Fine, 'Guerre et réformisme en France'; Hennebicque, 'Albert Thomas et le régime des usines de guerre, 1915–1917'; G. Hardach, 'La Mobilisation industrielle en 1914–1918: production, planification et idéologie', in Fridenson (ed.), *1914–1918: L'autre front*, 81–109; and Kuisel, *Capitalism and the State in Modern France*, 34–7.

[30] See Chap. 5, above.

munitions effort, he became, as the war ended, the principal architect of economic decontrol.[31]

Out of office, Thomas was freer critically to develop the insights gained in power. He championed railway nationalization, urged the redeployment of the state arsenals as the pivot of a planned economic demobilization, and endorsed syndicalist efforts to establish a contractual style of industrial relations.[32] The network of contacts between Thomas's experts, civil servants of the Ministry of Labour, and business and labour leaders, assumed new forms. *L'Information ouvrière et sociale* was founded in early 1918 as a vehicle for continued exploration of Thomas's 'practical corporatism'. The Comité National d'Études Sociales et Politiques heard papers on current problems. The Comité Permanent d'Études Relatives à la Prévision des Chômages Industriels (founded in 1911 by administrators in the Ministry of Labour and re-established in 1917–20 under Thomas's presidency) considered the demobilization throughout 1918.[33]

By these means, the basic assumptions applied to the munitions effort were kept alive for the reconversion to peace. Jouhaux, Merrheim, Dumoulin, and other CGT leaders were able to exchange ideas with industrialists like André Citroën and Louis Renault, and with Robert Pinot, secretary of the Comité des Forges, as well as with figures like Arthur Fontaine, François Simiand, Lucien March (head of the national statistical service), and the economist and philanthropist, Max Lazard. This helped sustain the idea, prominent in CGT thinking in 1918–19, that the state might yet provide support for syndicalist reform plans. But it is quite clear that CGT

[31] J.-M. Chevrier, 'Le Rôle de Louis Loucheur dans l'économie de guerre, 1914–1918' (Maîtrise diss., Université de Paris X, 1972); Kuisel, *Capitalism and the State in Modern France*, 48–50; Carls, 'Louis Loucheur'.

[32] The evolution of these ideas can be traced in *L'Information ouvrière et sociale* from early 1918 and in Thomas's parliamentary speeches.

[33] Papers of the Comité National d'Études Sociales et Politiques in AN 94 AP 401; Ministère du Travail, *Comité permanent d'études relatives à la prévision des chômages industriels. Compte rendu des travaux. Années 1917–1920* (Imprimerie Nationale, 1920); and for the same, Fine, 'Towards Corporatism', 35–40, and 'Guerre et réformisme en France, 1914–1918', 318–19. 'Practical corporatism' is Fine's term.

leaders used these contacts to explain their policies, not to negotiate on them.[34]

If this phase of Thomas's career brought him closer to the CGT's post-war plans, it was Jouhaux, as Thomas accepted, who 'gives the direct impression of the new spirit which animates the whole world of labour ... a mixture of worker sentiment, national preoccupations, and ideal aspirations.'[35] Thomas himself became an increasingly isolated figure on the right of the PS, so that at the end of 1919, despite being re-elected, it was logical for him to accept the post of director of the new International Labour Office, and to transfer his 'practical corporatism' to a less troubled plane. It was here, in the post-war international field, that he and his circle of wartime advisers and administrators developed more fully their connection with the reformism of the CGT.

In the absence of sustained action by the state, it was inherently unlikely that enhanced wartime contact between business and labour leaders would produce the economic reforms and changed industrial relations sought by the latter. Certainly, the shift by many employers (under state compulsion) to recognizing and negotiating with syndicalists was an unexpected development. Additionally, a significant current of business opinion (especially in metallurgy and mining) was prepared to contemplate an expanded role for the state in the organizational co-ordination of French industry, its technical modernization, and its commercial expansion—though this did not mean maintaining state controls on the economy longer than strictly necessary

[34] On Fine's evidence, *L'Information ouvrière et sociale* was used by Dulot and Thomas to proselytize their own productivism and facilitate exchanges of ideas between syndicalist leaders and industrialists. In fact, the former contributed much more to the paper than the latter, with well-known CGT and metalworker leaders expounding *majoritaire* policy. The Comité National d'Études Sociales et Politiques—which heard papers from guest speakers, including trade unionists—was used by Jouhaux, Laurent, and Dumoulin, in 1919–20, to present different aspects of CGT policy, national and international. No CGT leaders, apart from Keufer, were actually on the Comité Permanent ... des Chômages Industriels, as it discussed the forthcoming demobilization in 1918. Jouhaux and Merrheim were invited to present the CGT's views in Nov., but business representatives—and Thomas himself—expressed reservations about the extent to which workers' organizations should be involved in broad economic decision-making (*Comité permanent ... des chômages industriels*, 38–9, 64–8).

[35] A. Thomas, 'La Classe ouvrière et l'affaire Malvy', *L'Information ouvrière et sociale*, 11 Aug. 1918; see also 'Le Programme confédéral', ibid., 15 Dec. 1918.

after the war. This approach was powerfully seconded by Étienne Clémentel, minister of Commerce, until beached by the ebb-tide of state disengagement from the economy in 1919.[36] But as we have suggested, industrial relations, by contrast with Britain, were less crucial to business opinion. Reparations, the level of protectionism, the benefits of maximizing output compared to the dangers of overproduction, were the essential calculations of industrialists faced with the transition to peace.

For the CGT, the approach to industrial relations was virtually the opposite to that of British trade unions. The latter, defending their organizational strength and established skilled 'practices', were wary of employer or government schemes to rearrange labour relations in the name of 'industrial harmony'. The CGT faced a more fundamental restructuring of the industrial labour force, socially and geographically, during the war. Yet it lacked, precisely, organizational strength (until the surge of 1917–20) and a tradition of craft 'customs'. So, with the aid of the state, it sought reforms which would compensate for both—in the face of caution, and sometimes outright hostility, from employers.

Thus, the Fédération des Métaux and the CGT accepted the changes which were occurring in the engineering industry, but hoped to control them on their own terms. They did not repudiate mass production, or even 'Taylorism'. But they demanded that such changes—the technical core of syndicalist productivism—should yield dramatically improved conditions for labour, beginning with higher wages and shorter hours. In the absence of 'customs' as a bargaining-counter, or even widespread employer recognition, they sought to use the state to impose *délégués d'atelier*. And they promoted the idea of a *contrôle ouvrier* which meant the right of local syndicalist delegates, subordinated to the national organization, to determine how, and on what terms, the division of labour should be restructured.[37] Similarly, the CGT majority's emphasis on institutionalizing the economic power of labour locally and

---

[36] M. Trachtenberg, '"A New Economic Order": Clémentel and French Diplomacy during the First World War', *French Historical Studies*, 10/2 (1977), pp. 315–41; Kuisel, *Capitalism and the State in Modern France*, 37–48; Godfrey, *Capitalism at War*, 82–105.

[37] See Chap. 5, above; R. Picard, *Le Contrôle ouvrier sur la gestion des entreprises* (Marcel Rivière, 1922), 73–101; Cross, 'Redefining Workers' Control'.

nationally, through collective bargaining and *commissions mixtes*, can be regarded as an attempt to compensate, again via the state, for the most obvious weaknesses of pre-war syndical-ism—the lack of employer recognition and mass support.

The collectively organized economy envisaged by the CGT was therefore to emerge through a reformed capitalism. Poten-tially, as Jouhaux pointed out to the Fédération des Industriels et des Commerçants Français in March 1916, the interests of reforming syndicalist and modernizing industrialist coincided, at least in the shorter term. But in reality, there were fundamen-tal divergences of strategy and interest.

The new receptiveness to collective bargaining and formalized co-operation with organized labour through *commissions mixtes* was a crucial step in the direction envisaged by the CGT. Yet even this was not without *arrière-pensées*. When the heavy industry organization, the Union des Industries Métallurgiques et Minières, was re-formed in 1918–early 1919 specifically to deal with labour and social questions, the continuing importance of non-union labour, alongside union recognition, was underlined, as were the possibilities of building bridges to the work-force by way of employer welfare schemes. New tunes by no means drowned out the old.[38] More seriously still, the basic productivist case put by the CGT—that technical and organizational change must, as a minimum, yield higher wages and shorter hours—was by no means universally accepted by employers.[39] Metallurgical producers and the Comité des Forges were anxious about excess capacity, induced by the war, and sought ways to regulate the market rather than pursue all-out growth.

Big producers and heavy industry also tried, through bodies like the ANEE, to preserve the balance and interests of French manufacturing as a whole, with its plethora of small, often rather

---

[38] UIMM, *Assemblée générale du 18 février 1919* (Imprimerie Chaix, 1919), 4–6.

[39] André Lebon warned against the high wages argument as soon as Jouhaux made it in Mar. 1916 (*Bulletin de la fédération des industriels et des commerçants français* (Feb.–Mar. 1916), p. 186). *La Journée industrielle* also rejected the argument (J. Hardy, 'Le Mirage des hauts salaires', 11 Dec. 1918). The UIMM was equally cautious, accepting that concessions should be made to workers 'to a degree compatible with the productivity of industry', but warned against 'dangerous or premature experiments which might ruin the very basis of economic organization and compromise the prosperity of the country' (UIMM, *Assemblée générale du 18 février 1919*, 4–5).

inefficient companies.[40] Hence the CGT's constant complaints of 'economic malthusianism' and protectionism at the cost of low working-class living-standards. The issue emerged with acute bitterness, as we shall see, when for political reasons, in the face of strong union pressure, the government forced the eight-hour day on largely reluctant employers in the spring of 1919.[41]

When it came to continued regulation of the economy, let alone public ownership, the principal employer organizations—the ANEE, the Fédération des Industriels et des Commerçants Français, the Radicals' Comité Républicain du Commerce, de l'Industrie et de l'Agriculture, as well as the fiercely free enterprise Union des Intérêts Économiques—all spelt out their hostility.[42] This directly countered the CGT's commitment to structural economic reform via different types of public ownership and control, including nationalization.

CGT and employer thinking equally parted company over syndicalist notions of worker control and industrial democracy. André Lebon, shipping magnate and president of the Fédération des Industriels et des Commerçants Français, who had invited Jouhaux to address the organization in March 1916, rejected outright the syndicalist leader's pretension to a labour role in management.[43] Legouëz, the vice-president and a Paris industrialist, considered Jouhaux's views in 1917 on hydroelectricity nationalization to be unworkable and hostile to capital.[44] Unsurprisingly, the mouthpiece of political conservatism, *Le Temps*, scathingly condemned the *Programme minimum* as the

---

[40] François-Poncet, *La Vie et l'œuvre de Robert Pinot*, 232–4; H. D. Peiter, 'Men of Goodwill', 287–8.

[41] See Chap. 9, below.

[42] Fédération des Industriels et des Commerçants Français, *Les Origines et le but de la fédération* (n.d., but during the war), 10–11; 'Pour la liberté industrielle', declaration by the Comité Républicain in *La Journée industrielle*, 25–6 Dec. 1918; joint programme of the Union des Intérêts Économiques and Confédération des Groupes Commerciaux et Industriels de France, 3 Apr. 1919 (in the Bibliothèque Marxiste de Paris); B. Précy, 'Étatistes ou anti-étatistes', *La Journée industrielle*, 17–18 Mar. 1918; H. D. Peiter, 'Men of Goodwill', 267; G. Lefranc, *Les Organisations patronales en France du passé au présent* (Payot, 1976), 55; Kuisel, *Capitalism and the State in Modern France*, 40–1, 53–4.

[43] *Bulletin de la fédération des industriels et des commerçants français* (Jan.–Feb. 1916), pp. 185–6.

[44] R. Legouëz, *Bulletin de la fédération des industriels et des commerçants français* (Jan.–Feb. 1918), pp. 24–6.

first step towards a collectivist revolution.[45] But even the pragmatic and moderate business paper, *La Journée industrielle*, though considering recognition of syndicalism to be the price paid for 'social peace', and counselling the government to negotiate on elements of the CGT programme, drew the line at syndicalist claims to organize production.[46]

Perhaps the fullest debate on *le contrôle ouvrier* outside the CGT took place in the Association Nationale Française pour la Protection Légale des Travailleurs, a body connected with the Ministry of Labour and dating from 1900. In 1919, it adopted a lengthy report in favour of voluntary *commissions mixtes* in each factory (strongly influenced by the Whitley proposals) as a consultative framework for wages, conditions, discipline, and the implementation of collective contracts. But this remained the view of progressive administrators (Keufer, the printing workers' leader, was the only syndicalist participant) and, significantly, a minority current of opinion, including Legouëz, was sceptical, repudiating any infringement of entrepreneurial authority.[47]

As the war ended, employers were forced as never before to organize themselves politically and confront the unprecedented strength of labour and its post-war demands, amid the uncertainties of the demobilization. To many, the need for concessions was evident. These extended to the recognition of syndicalism and certain material gains (over wages and hours). But even here the battles were hard fought, while over the CGT leadership's more far-reaching proposals the rift, as Albert Thomas acknowledged, was profound.[48]

The 'corporatist' tendencies inherent in the economic mobilization were an important component of the behaviour and experience of pro-war labour leaders. They undoubtedly helped incorporate trade union leaderships into a structured system of industrial relations and closer contact with the state.

---

[45] *Le Temps, inter alia*, 'Menaces à retenir', 30 Nov. 1918, and 'Le Programme de la CGT', 1 Dec. 1918.

[46] J. Hardy, 'Le Programme de la CGT', *La Journée industrielle*, 7 Jan. 1919, and 'Incertitudes', ibid., 2–3 Feb. 1919.

[47] R. Fagnot, *La Part du travail dans la gestion des entreprises* (Félix Alcan/Marcel Rivière, 1919); Lavergne, *Les Idées politiques en France de 1900 à nos jours*, 131–2; Rossiter, 'Experiments with Corporatist Politics in Republican France', 57–68.

[48] 'Conversations patronales', *L'Information ouvrière et sociale*, 5 May 1918.

In the French case, a critical extrapolation of wartime organizational arrangements contributed directly to labour's post-war reform plans. But it was precisely this critical response—in both cases the core of labour's post-war thinking—which marked sharp boundaries to the 'corporatist' tendencies of wartime. There was no bargain or compact in either case between labour leaders and government or industrialists over the goals and procedures for the post-war period. The wartime reformism in both labour movements expressed more than organized labour's role as one element in a system of industrial relations or as one political interest group. It aspired to transcend sectional interests and make the labour movement into a counterveiling power, generating its own vision of the national interest through alternative views of the economic system and role of the state.

It was the scope of such claims which aroused the resistance of business organizations and non-labour or non-socialist politicians, even where these had accepted the wartime role of the state as unavoidable and contemplated a different relationship with organized labour over the longer term. But because the reformist programmes also envisaged working through the existing order, via the sectional role of the labour movement within it, their more immediate elements left room, after the Armistice, for bargaining and concessions.[49]

(ii) Continuities and New Departures

Labour reformism was thus distinctly reformulated through the experience of the war. There were, naturally, strong continuities with the pre-war period. But the war itself, in the case of the CGT and Labour Party, crystallized new reformist programmes and rallied national majorities behind them.

Elements of the new CGT reformism were apparent before 1914. Some leading revolutionary syndicalists had begun a critical appraisal of French industrial capitalism. A pragmatic attitude to collective bargaining and social legislation had emerged. Despite the prevalent hostility to the state, miners

[49] Cf. the conclusions of Martin Fine, who stresses the corporatist consensus between industrialists, progressive administrators, Thomas, and the CGT leaders—especially between Thomas and Jouhaux—in 'Towards Corporatism', 21–2, and 'Guerre et réformisme en France'.

and *cheminots* espoused a parliamentary reformism. Jouhaux and Merrheim led a campaign in favour of a new realism and sense of organization. But as police reports and syndicalist commentaries on the anticipated congress in September 1914 indicated, the CGT had found no new synthesis for its orientation.[50]

It was the war and the process of societal mobilization which provoked the realignment. Jaurès, in a prescient passage of *L'Armée nouvelle*, had commented that the revolutionary syndicalists 'forget that the law of evolution, of transaction and of compromise which they apply to the morrow of the Revolution, necessarily applies ... to the inevitably gradual conquest of power by the proletariat.'[51] The war, both by explicitly relating nation to class through the 'choice of 1914' and by disrupting the composition and organization of the industrial work-force to such a degree, made many CGT leaders openly accept 'evolution, transaction, and compromise'. The image conjured up by the industrial mobilization of a potentially powerful and industrialized economy, generating a more 'organized' capitalism with higher living standards, provided a strong impulse in this direction. The various forms of syndicalist participation in the war effort indicated *how* organized labour might extend its control over the economy from within. And from 1917, wartime circumstances seemed to be creating the mass syndicalism which had eluded the CGT in the last years of peace.

In Britain, the war resolved the question of Labour's relations with the Liberals. The imperative in 1917–18 of defining an alternative, and specifically Labour view of the domestic mobilization process and of allied war aims, plus the possibilities of a mass electoral party opened up by the 1918 suffrage reform, pushed the Labour Party into independence from the Liberal Party. Additionally, the theme of reconstruction and the need for a distinctively Labour project for the post-war state effected the bridge between a moderate socialism and much of trade union opinion which pre-war socialists had never managed to build.

Despite similarities in theme and function, the two labour movements adopted doctrines and strategies of post-war reform

[50] Chap. 1 n. 104.
[51] Jaurès, *L'Armée nouvelle*, 305.

which were fundamentally opposite—political in one case, industrial in the other. Here, deeper historical differences were crucial. In Britain, the road to reconstruction and a moderate socialism went via the state and the political role of the Labour Party. This corresponded to the structure of the movement and to most trade unionists' understanding of the specific and circumscribed nature of the industrial sphere. The strength of British labour's organization lay in the availability to trade unionists of a directly political vehicle for their criticisms and post-war proposals.

The corresponding political option in France was foreclosed by the division of the PS between a moderate pacifism and a Jacobin conception of the national defence which absorbed the *majoritaires* to the detriment of post-war reform, as well as by the disjuncture between party and syndicalism. These factors, rooted in the traditions and structure of French labour, determined the crucial failure of the CGT *majoritaires* and sympathetic socialists to turn the Comité d'Action into a genuinely joint agency for planning post-war reform. The undoubted interest of socialists, especially at the municipal level, in the connection between the war and reform, remained diffuse and nationally unfocused. And the CGT *majoritaires* were reinforced in what, for many of them, was a natural inclination to conceive of post-war reform in an essentially industrial mode. This resulted in an original and distinctive variant of reformism—for they proposed nothing less than an economic version of the *démocratie sociale* preached by Jaurès and others before 1914. But it also meant that the realignment of the CGT around this vision perpetuated the fundamental rift between *mouvement ouvrier* and *Parti Socialiste*.

The limitations of the two reformisms, mirroring their predominant characteristics, also stood in sharp contrast to each other. In the French case, the absence of a political instrument for enacting or pursuing syndicalist reform plans remained one of the latter's most glaring weaknesses. It meant that any substantial ebb-tide in syndicalist numbers or marginalization of sympathetic figures in government would jeopardize the scheme of progressive economic reform. By contrast, the dependence of Labour's reconstruction plans on electoral victory resulted in a difficult hiatus following the disappointing outcome of the

general election in December 1918. The question of an industrial, 'direct action' strategy for essentially political reforms
therefore surfaced almost as soon as the war had ended.

It is a commonplace that the redefinitions and realignments
of revolutionary socialism during and after the war thrust
intellectuals into an unusually prominent position. Something
analogous occurred within the reformist currents of labour, as
the rapid economic and political changes which they confronted
stimulated an abnormal degree of theorizing and doctrinal self-
expression. The role of Sidney Webb and the Fabian tradition
is clear in this regard, although, as we have noted, the intellectual origins of *Labour and the New Social Order* also derived
from MacDonald, Snowden, and the ILP, while the modified
Guild Socialism of G. D. H. Cole and others crept into
nationalization proposals. The ideological genesis of French
wartime reformism is more obscure. It drew on at least three
currents within the pre-war labour and socialist movements.

The first was that favouring municipal and national enterprises in the autonomous form of the *régie directe*, administered
by representatives of the employees and consumers on behalf of
the municipality or state. The attempt to devise a form of public
enterprise which would both avoid reinforcing the authoritarian
power of the state and provide a vehicle for the gradual introduction of socialism, emanated from a group of administrative and
intellectual socialists particularly associated with the École Normale Supérieure in Paris. From 1907, a number of the coterie
who were to play such a vital role in organizing the French
munitions effort participated in a Groupe d'Études Socialistes
organized by a young intellectual, Robert Hertz, and loosely
based on the school. They included Albert Thomas himself,
Hubert Bourgin, François Simiand, and Maurice Halbwachs. In
the years before 1914, this group published various studies,
concentrating on municipal socialism in particular. They were
also influenced by the Webbs and by British experiments in
municipal socialism.[52] Albert Thomas and Edgar Milhaud, the
founder of the influential *Annales de la Régie directe*, converted

[52] D. Lindenberg, *Le Marxisme introuvable* (Calmann-Lévy, 1975), 125–73; C.
Prochasson, 'Le Socialisme normalien (1907–1914): recherches et réflexions autour
du groupe d'études socialistes et de l'école socialiste' (Maîtrise diss., Université de
Paris I, 1981), esp. 16, 53; id., 'Place et rôle des intellectuels dans le socialisme
français 1900–1920' (thèse de doctorat, Paris I, 1989).

these ideas, as we have seen, into a political tendency on the right of the PS which challenged the Guesdist view of the class state, established links with reformist socialists in the important Fédération de la Seine, and won both the miners' and *cheminots'* organizations to the autonomous form of nationalization.[53]

'Economic federalism' was the second pre-war current flowing into the new reformism. Perhaps it was less a current than several partly-connected sources whose confluence was only reached in 1916 with the November programme of the Commission Mixte. Growing pre-war emphasis by Jouhaux and other CGT leaders on the gradual extension of syndicalist control over industry, rather than a cataclysmic general strike, raised as many questions as it answered. What form would such control take, and who would exercise it? How could such an economy be co-ordinated without reinforcing the power of the state? When would 'integral emancipation' be deemed to have occurred? Such questions received no answers, nor were they debated by syndicalist congresses before the war. But Jouhaux, in particular, detecting the vacuums created by the shifts in revolutionary syndicalist language, made hesitant attempts to fill them. He drew on Proudhon's vision of an 'economic federalism' of self-administering workshops not just as the final goal of revolutionary syndicalism but as the means of achieving it: 'thus it is work which must be improved, transformed, making out of the workshop-boss the workshop without a master'.[54] In two prescient articles published in 1912 and 1913, he rejected a generalized nationalization, because of the danger of a 'parasitical and irresponsible bureaucracy', and advocated instead that industries should be run by the 'associated delegates of the collectivity in question'.[55] He also urged syndicalists to think in terms of the 'industrial and commercial techniques indispensable for cooperating in an intelligent and rational production'. But this merely hinted at the problems of technical change and economic control, and Jouhaux ignored entirely the question of whether any but the workers should be involved in industrial self-government.

[53] See Chap. 1, above.
[54] 'Syndicalisme et socialisme', *Revue socialiste, syndicaliste et coopérative*, 1913, 1, 214.
[55] 'La Nationalisation', *L'Encyclopédie du mouvement syndicaliste* (Marcel Rivière), 2 (May 1912), pp. 53–5, and 'Syndicalisme et socialisme', 209–16.

Others, outside the CGT, could not afford to. Two important additional, and partly overlapping, centres of pre-war reflection on 'economic federalism' were the socialist co-operative movement (especially in Paris) and elements of Parisian socialism which advocated municipal socialism and reformist perspectives. Susceptible to the influence of the academic socialism of the Groupe d'Études Socialistes and also frequently sympathetic to revolutionary syndicalist ideas, these Parisian *coopérateurs* and socialists feared the dangers of a 'syndicalist corporatism' in any scheme of public ownership which placed economic power solely in the hands of workers as producers.[56] Thus Jean Gaumont, the *coopérateur*, published a book in 1911 which endorsed the Proudhonist ideal of replacing the 'government of men' by the 'administration of things'. But he posed two questions ignored by Jouhaux—the possible variety of new industrial forms (co-operatives, municipal enterprises, public services administered under the authority of the state) and the relationship of producers' to consumers' organizations.[57] Ernest Poisson, as secretary of the newly created FNCC, raised similar points in his *La Coopération nouvelle* (1914).

The Fédération de la Seine, debating the orientation of French socialism prior to the 1913 socialist congress, discussed three resolutions—one marked by orthodox Guesdism, but two which showed clearly the importance of this Parisian milieu, where socialism, co-operatives, and syndicalism intersected, for the formulation of new socialist perspectives. Both of these resolutions favoured the progressive achievement of socialism through municipalizations and nationalizations in the autonomous form, and one, drafted by Poisson, foreshadowed the 1916 programme of the Commission Mixte in its emphasis on the role of co-operatives and *syndicats* in extending working-class management (*gestion*) to the economy as a whole.

---

[56] E. Poisson, 'Municipalisme et syndicalisme', *Le Mouvement socialiste*, 230 (Apr. 1911), pp. 241–4, and *La Coopération nouvelle* (Marcel Rivière, 1914), 36–7; C. Muetschler, 'Coopératives et syndicats', *Le Mouvement socialiste*, 230 and 231 (Apr. and May 1911), pp. 245–61 and 336–47; *Parti socialiste. 8ᵉ congrès national tenu à Saint-Quentin . . . avril 1911*, 230–345, 441–3 (municipalization debate); Dommanget, *Edouard Vaillant*, 138–9; Howorth, *Edouard Vaillant: la création de l'unité socialiste en France*, 183–4.

[57] J. Gaumont, *L'État contre la nation: le fédéralisme professionnel et l'organisation économique de la société* (Giard et Brière, 1911), 137–8.

The replacement of the government of men by the administration of things ... will result from the participation of consumers' organizations in the collective management [of the economy], and from the technical organization of work by the free and responsible collective endeavour of the associated producers.[58]

The significance of the Comité d'Action, especially within the Paris labour and socialist movements, is that it both concerted these different reflections on 'economic federalism' and made the CGT their principal beneficiary at the national level.

A third line of thought contributing to wartime reformism came from certain intellectuals who diagnosed the malaise of revolutionary syndicalism as a doctrine and sought to redefine it accordingly. Hostile to the centralizing power of the state and to the Jacobin tradition, which were felt to blight the creative resources of society, these intellectuals found the antidote in revolutionary syndicalism conceived not as an industrial tactic but above all as an original social morality and set of institutions, capable of progressively democratizing the economy and liberating society from the tutelage of politics. Best-known was Hubert Lagardelle, a former theorist of classic revolutionary syndicalism who, from about 1908, used his prestigious review, *Le Mouvement socialiste*, to rethink his earlier ideas. In Lagardelle's new definition, revolutionary syndicalism became the 'socialism of institutions'.[59] Even more important for the future was a young magistrate and sociologist, Maxime Leroy, who wrote several pre-war studies of the labour movement culminating in a detailed examination of the ethos, practice, and institutional arrangements of syndicalism, *La Coutume ouvrière* (1913).[60]

Lagardelle and Leroy both made the problem of authority in industrial societies the pivot of their analysis. They saw in the associative life of the working class and the ethos of the skilled

---

[58] *La Revue socialiste, syndicaliste et coopérative*, 1 (1913), pp. 222–7.

[59] H. Lagardelle, *Le Socialisme ouvrier* (Giard et Brière, 1911), esp. 'Les Caractères généraux du syndicalisme', 325–45 (an art. of May 1908); 'La Politique syndicaliste', *Le Mouvement socialiste*, Dec. 1910, pp. 345–8; and 'La Critique syndicaliste de la démocratie', ibid., Feb. 1911, pp. 81–6, virtually a manifesto of Lagardelle's new position. For Lagardelle's pre-war biography, see Maitron (ed.), *Dictionnaire biographique du mouvement ouvrier français*, pt. 3, *1871–1914*, xiii. 176.

[60] 'In Memoriam: Maxime Leroy', *Le Contrat social*, 1/5 (1957) (special issue). A certain number of Leroy's personal dossiers and correspondence are in the Institut d'Histoire Sociale (Avenue Raymond Poincaré), Paris.

worker an alternative, co-operative concept to the authoritarianism of the workplace under industrial capitalism and to that of the state, thinly disguised by representative politics. Their views found concrete expression in the widely-publicized pre-war problem of the right of state employees to unionize. The demand by various categories of *fonctionnaires* for unions and a *statut* defining their rights, raised the double authoritarianism of the state as lawmaker and employer. Lagardelle and Leroy (and other sympathetic intellectuals) sought to provide theoretical justification for these demands in the face of conventional wisdom and the overwhelming hostility of government.[61]

Such ideas carried an obvious appeal for revolutionary syndicalists seeking to reformulate their basic orientation in a more gradualist mode and who were themselves concerned to organize state employees.[62] Lagardelle's periodical publicized this doctrinal shift.[63] Leroy frequented CGT circles before the war, was a close confidant of Merrheim, and knew Jouhaux well enough to show him *La Coutume ouvrière* in proofs (Jouhaux was favourably impressed).[64] The emphasis during the war by Jouhaux and the *majoritaire* leaders on the 'new rights of workers' as well as on the participation by the CGT in all levels of the economy, showed the undoubted influence of these pre-war ideas. Although Leroy was possibly in less close contact with syndicalism during the war, his influence was sharply renewed in the *après-guerre*.[65]

---

[61] Leroy's first two books tackled the problem (*Les Transformations de la puissance publique: le syndicat des fonctionnaires* (Giard et Brière, 1907), and *Syndicats et services publics* (Colin, 1909)). For Lagardelle's views, see 'Les Services publics et le syndicalisme', *Le Mouvement socialiste* (Mar. 1911), pp. 161–6.

[62] See Chap. 5, above.

[63] e.g. 'Nouveaux Problèmes', *Le Mouvement socialiste* (Dec. 1911), pp. 321–4.

[64] For Leroy's relations with Merrheim, see the originals of Merrheim's correspondence with him from 1906 to 1914 in the Institut d'Histoire Sociale, and V. Daline, 'Alphonse Merrheim et sa "correspondance confidentielle"', 245. For the connection with Jouhaux, see the letter from Dumoulin to Leroy, 10 Oct. 1913 (Institut d'Histoire Sociale).

[65] Leroy's 'Cahiers noirs', a manuscript diary from June 1916 to July 1917 (Institut d'Histoire Sociale), reveal no contact with labour leaders. But in his 1918 book on political reform, *Pour gouverner*, he approved the *délégués d'atelier*, though considering them too weak, and endorsed Jouhaux's and Prêté's ideas on hydroelectricity nationalization, in *La Houille blanche* (Grasset, 1917).

Symptomatic of the entire doctrinal realignment represented by wartime reformism was the growing reference to the enigmatic figure of Proudhon. The Proudhonist heritage of French labour was continuous and complex. But the immediate prewar period had witnessed a recrudescence of interest in the thinker among revolutionary syndicalist intellectuals, notably Lagardelle, as well as among a group of academics, the Amis de Proudhon, who undertook the republication of his works in a cheap edition.[66] During the war, as before, Jouhaux invoked Proudhon's formulae, notably 'the workshop will replace the government', to define the *majoritaire* approach. As early as autumn 1914, Jouhaux, in correspondence with a syndicalist journalist, Léon Harmel, referred to Proudhon as a figure of inspiration for a CGT confronting the disorientation caused by the war.[67] In 1918–19, Harmel published a series of substantial articles in *La Clairière*, describing Proudhon's life and ideas with the aim of helping the CGT to redefine its doctrine.[68] In contrast to the insistence on the state and violent revolution seen as characteristic of Marxism, Proudhon appeared to legitimate the aspiration of the syndicalist *majoritaires* gradually to create a kind of democratic and co-operative constitution for the economy. And in the post-war period, as the *minoritaires* increasingly defined themselves by reference to the Bolshevik revolution, the *majoritaires* turned 'Proudhonism' into a semi-official reformist ideology.

It might be objected that the war was incidental to the longer-term evolution of labour reformism in the two countries. At one level, this is true. The definition of new relationships between organized labour and the state, the bid for a more central place for the working class in the life of the nation, the attempt by trade unions to extend their power by engaging in new institutional connections with business, constitute a frame on which reformism, as ideas and practice, has been woven over the much longer term. But this would also be an unjustifiably

---

[66] C. Bouglé, *Socialismes français*, chap. 10 (Bouglé was one of the *amis*); A. Kriegel, 'Le syndicalisme révolutionnaire et Proudhon', in *Le Pain et les roses*, 69–104.

[67] Referred to in a reply by Harmel, 3 Jan. 1915, repr. in Georges and Tintant, *Léon Jouhaux*, i. 511–12. Harmel (real name, Louis-Antoine Thomas) remains a shadowy figure about whom hard biographical information seems scarce.

[68] Eleven articles in *La Clairière*, 1 Aug. 1918–1 Mar. 1919.

abstract view. The First World War defined these themes with exceptional clarity, and it is by no means certain that without it, reformism in either France or Britain would have taken the precise forms it did. Wars have been major events in twentieth-century European societies, and the combination of deeper shifts in the direction of development of those societies with the experience of war has resulted in distinctive forms of change. Wartime reformism, as far as organized labour is concerned, was not the least remarkable of these.

(iii) Labour Reformism and the Process of Societal Mobilization

It remains to clarify the relationship of labour reformism with the broader process of societal mobilization behind the war effort. Fundamentally, it provided a language for the self-mobilization of organized labour during the conflict precisely at the point where criticisms of the official mobilization began to multiply—over consumer questions, industrial conditions, manpower policy, and so on. It created, therefore, a plurality of views within the mobilization process.

This contributed to the resilience of both France and Britain during the war. Not only did it maintain the crucial mediating function of labour leaderships between the state and the labour rank-and-file, but labour reformism also represented the attempt to preserve some basic assumptions about political democracy in a situation which lent itself to authoritarian solutions— hence the crucial importance of the 'policy of confidence' in France, and of British labour's attempt to fend off 'industrial conscription'. By this, their condemnation of repressive measures against 'pacifist' minorities, and their assertion of alternative views on the significance of the war, moderate labour leaders acted as a brake on the powerful tendency in both countries, and especially in France during the last eighteen months of the conflict, towards unquestioning patriotic allegiance and subordination to the state.

Both labour leaders and the government, however, were acutely aware of the danger that working-class dissatisfaction and unrest might swamp moderate trade union and socialist leaderships. In France and Britain, ministers were careful not to undermine the authority of the latter by negotiating independently with radical industrial movements—the shop stewards' movement in Britain and the militant *délégués d'atelier* and strike leaders of May 1918 in France. Where such contact did occur it was carefully framed by the involvement of accredited national leaderships.[69]

Furthermore, one of the essential functions of labour reformism was to contest more radical movements by providing ideological ammunition in defence of the 'choice of 1914'. This was perhaps less important in the British labour movement. The failure of the shop stewards' leaders to convert a movement of industrial protest into a repudiation of the war marked the limits of a distinctively trade union pacifism, while the pacifists of the ILP and UDC, in their majority, shared the moderate and reformist approach to domestic change espoused by the Labour Party in 1917–18.

In the CGT, however, the deepening rift between *majoritaires* and *minoritaires*, and the real possibility in May 1918 of a mass industrial pacifism, contributed to the explicit programmatic definition of the *majoritaires'* reformism. The challenge of the *métaux* leadership and of the *noyau* of *La Vie ouvrière*, as they tried to pick up the broken threads of pre-war internationalism, encouraged the *majoritaires* to seize the initiative in 1915–16 in redefining the orientation of the CGT. In the last two years of the war, reformist ideas provided a bulwark against the more revolutionary pacifism of the CDS and the menace of schism.

The connection of labour reformism with broader working-class opinion during the war is not easy to assess in view of the difficulties in measuring the latter. When claiming to speak for the working class, labour leaders and activists, of whatever hue, reduced a complex, multiple reality to the dimensions of their own aims and formulations. The actual connections were necessarily more allusive.

One possibility is that direct working-class patriotism, supporting the war effort as it was organized and endorsing the

[69] As in the case of the May 1918 negotiations in France, or the ASE's official involvement in the resolution of the May 1917 strikes in Britain (Jefferys, *The Story of the Engineers*, 184). On 16 May 1917, the War Cabinet reaffirmed its policy of 'recognising only the constituted authorities of the Trades Unions', unless the latter requested it to treat with shop stewards (PRO, Cab/23/2).

imperative of allied military victory, retained considerable influence throughout. In France, the right-wing socialist, Hubert Bourgin, claimed that the Comité de Propagande Socialiste pour la Défense Nationale achieved real influence, but outside official socialist networks.[70] The *France libre* group of socialist deputies backed the Clemenceau government in 1918, and it is quite likely, as the state's apparatus of surveillance maintained, that substantial working-class opinion approved of the 'Tiger's' conduct of the war.[71]

In Britain, a Socialist National Defence Committee was formed in 1915 on almost identical lines to the similarly named French body, becoming the British Workers' League in May 1916, and the National Democratic and Labour Party in 1918. Linking trade unionists and 'patriotic' socialists (its secretary, Victor Fisher, was a former Fabian and BSP member), the British Workers' League drew lessons of national and imperial 'efficiency' from its socialist pedigree, establishing close links with the Conservative imperialism of Lord Milner. It attacked both the pacifism of the ILP and the Labour Party itself in 1917–18, as the latter realigned on a socialist programme and broadened constitution. The strength of this working-class patriotism is indicated by the return of ten National Democratic and Labour Party MPs in the 1918 election.[72] It is corroborated by the schism which occurred in several local trades councils (notably Birmingham and Sheffield) between patriotic and pacifist trade unionists.[73]

Yet in the British as well as the French case, the organizational significance of this form of working-class patriotism remained limited in 1917–18 compared to the early part of the

---

[70] Bourgin, *Le Parti contre la patrie*, 105.

[71] Chap. 2 n. 53, above; Duroselle, *Clemenceau*, 834.

[72] *Socialists and the War* (manifesto of the Socialist National Defence Committee), PRO 130/69/5/103 (MacDonald papers); *The Times*, 20 July 1916 (founding of British Workers' League), 14 May 1917 (manifesto against the ILP), and 2 Nov. 1917 (post-war ideas); R. Douglas, 'The National Democratic Labour Party and the British Workers' League', *Historical Journal*, 15/3 (1972), pp. 503–32; J. O. Stubbs, 'Lord Milner and Patriotic Labour 1914–1918', *English Historical Review* (1972), pp. 717–54.

[73] Corbett, *The Birmingham Trades Council, 1866–1966*, 104–17; J. Mendelson, W. Owen, *et al.*, *Sheffield Trades and Labour Council 1858–1958* (Sheffield Trades Council, 1958).

war. *La France libre* signally failed to rally the PS to Clemenceau, and the leadership of the British Workers' League
(including G. H. Roberts, as a Labour minister) lost their battle
to retain Labour support for the Lloyd George government.
And unless we are to assume that there was no relationship
between the proportionate strengths of different currents
within organized labour and broader working-class opinion,
this marginalization of strident labour patriotism, by comparison with the consolidation of war reformism in the CGT and
Labour Party, can reasonably be held to have wider meaning.

Crucially, war reformism was not a pact with government or
business, let alone a simple expression of the *Union sacrée*. It
sought to mitigate official patriotism and restore a sense of
autonomy to working-class support for the war. This was
especially important since the war was a period of abnormal
disturbance in social awareness and in the moral perceptions by
different groups of their relationships to each other and to the
nation state. Unqualified labour patriotism found it hard to
articulate class-based criticism of the war effort, while pacifists
of varying kinds faced the thorny issue of defining just where
they stood on national integrity and defence. Wartime labour
reformism held class and nation in a kind of balance which,
arguably, was connected with key aspects of working-class
experience during the war.

The first of these was the military effort itself. Mass conscription and the associated threat of militarized work raised in acute
form the question of the state's authority in relation to the
working class. In France, despite the pre-war anti-militarism of
the labour movement, the legitimacy of universal military
service was accepted, until a militant minority repudiated it in
the May strikes of 1918.[74] In Britain, however, with its different
traditions and historical reliance on a professional navy rather
than a conscript army, the shock of compulsion was a turning-
point. Although the vast bulk of the working class acknowledged its necessity, it produced a sharp sense of differential
sacrifice, between capital and labour, and encouraged a more

---

[74] Horne, 'L'Impôt du Sang: Republican Rhetoric and Industrial Warfare in
France', 219–21.

critical attitude to the war effort.[75] In both countries, moreover, the power conferred on the state by compulsory military service made it vital to distinguish between the militarization of the bulk of adult males in the army, and the retention of a basic civilian status for those engaged in the industrial mobilization. Burgeoning trade union membership was a defensive response not only to inflation but also to the authoritarian tendencies of the wartime state. It was an attempt to moderate the state's grip on mobilized, or mobilizable, men in the war industries.

The essential hierarchy within the working class was shaken during the war by the threat to the status and wage differentials of skilled workers, especially in engineering. In one sense, this was a divisive question, especially in Britain, where the 'trade card' scheme conferred on skilled engineers the effective power of self-exemption from conscription. Bitter resentment by unskilled grades doing comparable work helped decide the cabinet to end the scheme in 1917. In France, there was considerable reserve shown by skilled males to women and immigrant workers, as we have seen. Yet wartime inflation also reduced the spread of wage differentials in the two countries, extended the organization of the unskilled and semi-skilled (often initiating the latter in France), and promoted cross-grade wage-settlements, as through the machinery for regularly revising pay introduced by both munitions industries in 1917. On balance, the sectional barriers within the industrial labour force were reduced, rather than augmented, by the war.[76] This contributed to the enhanced sense of class consciousness and unity which was an evident ingredient of the language of war reformism in both cases.

The war also intensified working-class self-definition and action outside the workplace. Military call-up disrupted the family as an earning unit, and brought vast numbers of working-

---

[75] Criticism of the way the Military Service Acts functioned and, as the cabinet's labour reports in mid-1917 indicated, a waning of the enthusiasm characteristic of the earlier, voluntarist response, were far from amounting to a repudiation of conscription (T. Wilson, *The Myriad Faces of War: Britain and the Great War* (Polity Press, Cambridge, 1986), 526–8).

[76] March, *Le Mouvement des prix et des salaires*, 266–7, 276; Robert, 'Les Luttes ouvrières pendant la première guerre mondiale', 42–3; A. L. Bowley, *Prices and Wages in the United Kingdom, 1914–20* (OUP, Oxford, 1921), 106–107; Waites, *A Class Society at War*, 130–59.

class families into contact with the state as welfare recipients, through military separation allowances. Working-class mutual aid and solidarity with soldiers and their families became a vital adjunct to official measures. Rent and food prices were the focus for working-class action—with rent strikes (as in Glasgow in 1915) and campaigns for moratoriums on rent increases in both countries, and the proliferation of consumer co-operatives. Especially at the municipal level, such issues stimulated the labour and socialist movement to campaign on behalf of working-class interests and to enter local administration.[77] As we have noted, there were numerous local equivalents of the Comité d'Action and the WEWNC. It seems clear that in both countries, the growing burden on the working-class consumer in 1917–18 was the single largest grievance, and one which was judged by the standards of a severe popular 'moral economy'. Official reports stressed that the 'profiteer' or *spéculateur*, meaning anything from the small shopkeeper to the big merchant and, in France, even the hoarding peasant, was a detested figure in working-class opinion. Certainly, food protests occurred in Britain and France and popular feeling demanded national rationing in both countries ahead of its introduction by the government.[78] The sense of moral outrage at the spiralling cost of living, and a sharpened sense of identity on the part of the working-class consumer, were central to the formulation of the reformist critique.

The disruption of war also heightened working-class sensitivity to the relationship of labour with capital and management

---

[77] Cavignac (ed.), 'La Classe ouvrière bordelaise face à la guerre', 28–48; Dogliani, 'Stato, imprenditori e manodopera industriale in Francia durante la prima guerra mondiale', 531–9; Clinton, *The Trade Union Rank and File*, 54–80; J. Bush, *Behind the Lines: East London Labour, 1914–1919* (Merlin Press, 1984), 35–68.

[78] It was stated as the major cause of unrest in all areas by the Commission of Enquiry into Industrial Unrest, in June 1917 (Cd. 8696, 153), and on 1 Jan. 1918, Barnes, as minister for Labour, told the cabinet that the solution to the mounting industrial conflict 'is not by raising wages all round, but by keeping down the cost of living' (Cab/23/5). See also Waites, *A Class Society at War*, 221–31. In France, the summary monthly police reports to the minister of the Interior on public opinion, from Oct. 1917, contained a separate section on the cost of living—seen as the overriding popular urban grievance (Oct.–Dec. 1917, in SHAT 16N 1538; Jan. 1918 on, in BDIC F△ 43 Res. 2). Thus, the report of February 1918 considered that 'in the working class, doubts grow about the equality of sacrifice . . . Overall, the working class demands vehemently requisitioning and the general food [rationing] card' (5).

in the industrial economy. Abnormally high profits in war industries, the physical expansion of many companies, and the ostentatious evidence of war fortunes, contrasted with the relentless pressure on nominal wages. The unfamiliar scramble to keep wages abreast of spiralling inflation, and the disturbance of wage differentials long internalized as 'natural', contributed to the sense of disadvantage among wage-earners, even if, in terms of real income, war workers were not always worse off—and in some cases were clearly better off—than before the war.[79] The legal constraints experienced by most indigenous male workers and the physical fatigue felt by all workers, women and men, by 1917–18, powerfully endorsed the impression of worsening economic inequality resulting from the war. The Commission of Enquiry into Industrial Unrest, in 1917, concluded that a sense of 'inequality of sacrifice' was widespread.[80] In France, the reports on public opinion by the Ministry of the Interior indicated that hostility to 'hoarders' and 'speculators', in late 1917 and 1918, was intense and encompassed both food suppliers and the *patrons* who paid inadequate wages while amassing profits.[81] The 1919 report of the American National Industrial Conference Board on labour and industry in Europe considered that in both countries, the main cause of working-class unrest was 'the challenge being thrown down to the present system of industry'. And as we have seen, it fuelled the preoccupation with ownership and control in industry which lay at the heart of reformist post-war planning.[82]

War reformism in both labour movements, it can be suggested, was not isolated in the antechambers of power, the abstract formulation of remote leaders. It sought to translate various aspects of wartime working-class experience into immediate action and programmes of post-war change. In so doing, it paralleled, and was in touch with, local developments. The Labour Party in east London, for example, was strengthened by its activity on a variety of issues from 1914 to 1918. Throughout 1918, it prepared its election campaign—

---

[79] See Append. I.
[80] Cd. 8696, 154. See also Askwith, *Industrial Problems and Disputes*, 471.
[81] SHAT 16N 1538 and BDIC F△ 43 Res. 2.
[82] *Problems of Labor and Industry in Great Britain, France and Italy*, 3; Cronin, 'Labour Insurgency and Class Formation', 20–48.

independently, but on themes which mirrored those of the party nationally. The concerns and ideas which furnished the CGT with its reform programme in 1915–16 were expressed quite autonomously by local and departmental syndicalist and socialist organizations.[83]

Yet the rejection of pacifism imposed by the 'choice of 1914' and the constraints on protest necessitated by support for the war effort, quite obviously circumscribed the ability of moderate national or local leaders to channel working-class discontent, *especially* if it assumed an explicitly anti-war form. This begs the question of how widespread working-class opposition to the war effort became in 1917–18. Certain areas, described by the summary of the British Commission of Enquiry into Industrial Unrest as lacking 'communal sense', were clearly less integrated into the national effort. This is most obviously the case with South Wales and Clydeside, where a strong sense of regional or national distinctiveness combined with equally strong traditions of revolutionary socialism or Syndicalism to produce a real recalcitrance in the face of the war effort (though even here, patriotic responses should not be overlooked). But other major centres of munitions production—Sheffield, the west Midlands, Paris, the Loire district, Lyons—also generated more militant and even pacifist movements which outbid moderate leaders for the allegiance of organized workers.

The British shop stewards' movement, however, failed to create a mass industrial protest against the war and the French strikes of May 1918 never involved more than an activist minority, even in the major munitions centres. Although undoubtedly biased towards comforting conclusions, the Commission of Enquiry into Industrial Unrest found that the patriotic allegiance of most workers in June 1917 was unshaken, and that 'feelings of a revolutionary character are not entertained by the bulk of men'.[84] In France, the reports of the Ministry of the Interior in 1918 stressed that pacifists were in a minority and that 'the labouring and thinking mass ... understands clearly that a peace without victory would be for France

---

[83] Bush, *Behind the Lines*, 139–62; Cohen, 'La Naissance du syndicalisme de masse', 340–4.
[84] Cd. 8696, 153; Waites, *A Class Society at War*, 231–5.

an irreparable disaster'.[85] In both countries, the military crisis of the spring and summer 1918 undoubtedly helped curb pacifist tendencies.

Differences suggest themselves between the two societies. The British working class, longer formed and more fully integrated into a less conflictual national political culture, and also less directly exposed to the war, may well have remained as a whole more enthusiastically supportive of the war effort. This would certainly accord with the obvious chronological difference in the development of war reformism. Where syndicalist and socialist circles in France formulated a critical response to the mobilization as early as 1915, British labour, by and large wholeheartedly (with the exception of the ILP), endorsed the war effort on more-or-less official terms until the crisis of compulsion in 1916. In France, a less well-established working class which was exposed to greater convulsion during the war in its composition, geography, and physical organization was perhaps more fundamentally altered—resulting in a significantly changed entity which both *majoritaires* and *minoritaires,* in opposing ways, strove to enrol and direct.[86]

But, to return to organized labour, none of this suggests that the relative integration of the working class into the nation and the simultaneous affirmation of class autonomy, which wartime labour reformism represented, was fundamentally out of tune with a good deal of labour opinion. It was not accidental that it should be these leaders who consolidated a national majority in 1918 and furnished the programme for the first months of peace—when the moment of reckoning seemed at last to have arrived.

---

[85] BDIC F△ 43 Res. 2, rep. of Mar. 1918, p. 4.

[86] For a broad, sociological analysis of differences between the two working classes across the twentieth century, see D. Gallie, *Social Inequality and Class Radicalism in France and Britain* (CUP, Cambridge, 1983).

8 The International Dimension

ALTHOUGH wartime reformism was engendered above all by the domestic impact of the conflict, international questions were vital to majority labour leaders throughout. This was so, first, because a belief in the rectitude of allied war aims and their special relevance to organized labour was central to the 'choice of 1914' and, secondly, because the desirability—and feasibility—of a negotiated peace became the most immediate cause of internal dissension in labour circles. Additionally, the war whose outbreak devastated the internationalist assumptions of labour and socialist leaders posed the problem of the form in which international contacts might be resumed, and of whether this was appropriate while the war lasted. International socialism during the war, and its conflicting responses to the question of peace, is the subject of an abundant literature and does not form part of this study. But it is important to establish, from the perspective of majority labour leaders, the relationship between international issues and the theme of the war as an agent of reform.[1]

(i) Labour War Aims and the 'New Diplomacy': Majoritaire Perspectives

Almost from the outset in France, the logic of a defensive struggle influenced socialist and syndicalist war aims. Both Jouhaux, in his funeral oration to Jaurès, and Guesde, on behalf of the Groupe Socialiste, warned the government that the left would not tolerate annexations (apart from the 'return' of Alsace-Lorraine) or the destruction of the German nation.[2] The

---

[1] See Bibliography, Secondary Works, part 2.
[2] Jouhaux, *A Jean Jaurès*, 11; Rouger, *L'Action socialiste au parlement*, 4.

particular revolutionary traditions of French socialism encouraged many socialist and syndicalist leaders to construe the defence of France, Belgium, and Serbia as a crusade liberating Europe, and ultimately the Central Powers themselves, from the 'militarism' exemplified by the Prussian and Austrian élites. It was but a small step to envisage the eventual peace as the triumph of democratic internationalism—that is, of the peaceful association of self-determined and demilitarized nations. A new 'open' diplomacy, international arbitration, disarmament, and some form of supra-national democratic authority had, by 1915–16, become the hallmarks of *majoritaire* conceptions of the post-war settlement in both the PS and CGT.

At the same time, the supposed 'betrayal' by the German and Austrian socialist and trade union movements in supporting their governments' aggression—coming on top of the national tensions within the pre-war ISNTUC and Socialist International—appeared to preclude the revival of working-class internationalism as a means of ending the war and achieving such a peace. At most, *majoritaire* leaders would contemplate only inter-allied discussions to consolidate their war aims. The military defeat of the central powers was seen as the sole road to peace.

Majority British labour leaders were no less adamant in their refusal to meet enemy socialists while the war was in progress. The manifesto issued in October 1914 to dispel 'misconceptions' about Labour's attitude to the war referred briefly to a peace-settlement premissed on arbitration, but primarily endorsed the military effort.[3] Generally, British labour leaders showed less interest than their French counterparts in the shape of the future peace. This reflected the lower level of pre-war concern by British trade unionists with international questions as well as the initial degree of absorption of British labour into the war effort on official terms. The case for a 'democratic' peace and the 'new diplomacy' was, of course, made much more forcefully in Britain than in France during the first fifteen months of the war, by the ILP and UDC.[4] But the fact that it

---

[3] Cole, *Labour in Wartime*, 55–7.
[4] Mayer, *Political Origins of the New Diplomacy*, 46–9; M. Swartz, *The Union of Democratic Control in British Politics during the First World War* (Clarendon Press, Oxford, 1971), 147–8.

was yoked to a campaign for a negotiated peace only reinforced mainstream labour's reluctance to contemplate it. Arthur Henderson was unusual in riding both horses, and belonging to the UDC (until his entry into government in May 1915) while leading the 'pro-war' Labour Party.[5]

These attitudes and constraints emerged with particular clarity at the inter-allied socialist meeting held in London on 14 February 1915. The PS as well as the CGT had rejected the invitation by Dutch and Scandinavian socialists in November 1914 to an international gathering in Copenhagen (held in January 1915).[6] But the neutral socialists' initiative, plus the publicity achieved by the ILP's stance, prompted allied socialists to hold their own meeting in London, at the invitation of Vandervelde, the Belgian socialist leader exiled in France, and the British section of the International. The latter included the ILP along with the Labour Party and the BSP. Foreign delegates represented the PS, the Parti Ouvrier Belge, and Russian socialists, though not the Mensheviks and Bolsheviks.[7] Although technically ineligible, the CGT also engineered an invitation and voted for the inclusion of Merrheim in its delegation, despite his initial hostility to the conference.[8]

The resolutions, voted unanimously, were a compromise between the 'pro-war' majority and the ILP backed by Merrheim. The 'profound general causes' of the war were identified in capitalism and 'aggressive imperialism', but the immediate culpability of 'German imperialism' was highlighted. The need to 'fight until victory is achieved' was proclaimed, but it was made clear on minority insistence that the 'political and economic crushing of Germany' was not intended. The war was seen as one of liberation in favour of oppressed nationalities, not of conquest, and as the prelude to 'the peaceful federation of the

[5] Swartz, *The Union of Democratic Control in British Politics*, p. 148.

[6] APP B/a 1605, 'Note sur l'attitude de Merrheim ... depuis la déclaration de guerre' (June 1915); AN F₇ 13574, rep. 25 Jan. 1915, on the CGT since Nov. 1914.

[7] APP B/a 1470, reps. 29 Mar. and 3 May 1915; APP B/a 1605, 'Note sur l'attitude de Merrheim ... depuis la déclaration de guerre'; *L'Union des métaux*, 61, May 1915; Maitron and Chambelland (eds.), *Syndicalisme révolutionnaire et communisme*, 86–135; and Daline, 'Alphonse Merrheim et sa "correspondance confidentielle"', 316–22.

[8] AN F₇ 13574, rep. 15 May 1915; APP B/a 1605, 'Note sur l'attitude de la CGT et des organisations syndicales du département de la Seine depuis le mois de janvier dernier', Apr. 1915, 6–11.

United States of Europe and the world'. Again on minority insistence, the meeting concluded by condemning Tsarist Russia's repression of socialists and minority nationalities. This issue continued to trouble the *majoritaires'* view of the allied effort as a democratic crusade down to February 1917.[9]

The London meeting, despite Merrheim's view to the contrary, was no simple manifestation of the *Union sacrée* or the product of allied government machinations. It was condemned by much of the French press, and Marcel Sembat faced severe censure from his government colleagues (including Guesde) for having attended.[10] There was a perceptible tension between total support for the national effort and war aims emanating from one point of the political compass. This tension barely affected the CGT in view of its more distant and indirect participation in the official mobilization of political support for the war effort. Already in early February 1915, in response to a separate invitation by the American Federation of Labor (AFL) to ponder the eventual peace-making process, the confederal majority proclaimed its war aims to be the abolition of secret diplomacy, the introduction of compulsory international arbitration, respect for nationalities, and arms limitation.[11] Together with 'the possibility of forming the federation of nations', these constituted the platform which the *majoritaires* defended against Merrheim and Bourderon at the first CGT conference of the war, in August 1915, and further elaborated in 1916.[12]

But the PS was directly exposed to the tension between the *Union sacrée* and its own specific war aims. The Conseil National of mid-July 1915 referred to the programme outlined in London, while endorsing the national and allied efforts.[13] Yet already the far right of the party criticised unnecessary discussion of the peace as a distraction from the national mobilization.[14] From December 1915, the PS demanded a more specific

[9] *L'Humanité*, 16 Feb. 1915, and Cole, *Labour in Wartime*, 57–9.
[10] Poincaré, *Au service de la France*, vi, *Les Tranchées*, 67–70; APP B/a 1605 'Note sur l'attitude de Merrheim . . . depuis la déclaration de la guerre'.
[11] 'A l'Internationale ouvrière: aux organisations centrales nationales' (brochure in IFHS 14 AS 213b/18).
[12] *L'Union des métaux*, 62 (May–Dec. 1915), p. 17.
[13] *Le Parti socialiste, la guerre et la paix*, 123–7; Van Der Slice, *International Labour Diplomacy and Peace*, 68.
[14] Bourgin, *Le Parti contre la patrie*, pp. 57 ff.

declaration of war aims from the government and developed further its views on a 'democratic peace', including the prickly matter of a retrospective plebiscite in Alsace-Lorraine to square the return of the provinces with the principle of self-determination.[15] Broadly, there was a considerable overlap of views between the *majoritaires* of Renaudel and the moderate *minoritaires* associated with Jean Longuet on the shape of the peace, the real conflict crystallizing, as we have noted, over the possibility of a negotiated end to the war and the desirability of an international socialist meeting to promote this.

In Britain, by contrast, the legacy of the London meeting was quietly buried by the bulk of the Labour Party in favour of unconditional endorsement of the political mobilization. In early July 1915, for example, in response to the cautious effort of the International Socialist Bureau (ISB)—moved from Brussels to neutral Holland—to sound out the common ground between belligerent socialists, Ramsay MacDonald proposed that the British Section of the International issue a war aims manifesto. Though initially agreeing, the LPNEC (as one component of the British Section) subsequently vetoed the manifesto.[16] In March 1916, the Labour leadership refused a further ISB invitation—this time to discuss possible peace terms at the Hague with French and Swedish socialists—on the grounds that the party's only concern was the 'prosecution of the War to a victorious termination'.[17] An ILP resolution in favour of a democratic (but not negotiated) peace was resoundingly defeated at the January 1916 conference, and it was not until the conference a year later that the Labour Party accepted the concept of a post-war 'International League', as advocated by President Wilson.[18]

American diplomatic, and then military, involvement in the war combined with the February revolution in Russia to impart a strong leftward realignment to labour and socialist peace

[15] Notably at the congresses of Dec. 1915 and 1916 (*L'Humanité*, 30 Dec. 1915; *Le Parti socialiste, la guerre et la paix*, 152–4).

[16] LPNEC, min. 15 Sept. 1915; *ILP Annual Conference*, 1916 (NAC report), 8–9; Van Der Slice, *International Labour Diplomacy and Peace*, 98; Marquand, *Ramsay MacDonald*, 198.

[17] LPNEC, min. vol. 9, 3; *Report of the Labour Party Conference, Manchester, January 1917*, 44.

[18] Van Der Slice, *International Labour Diplomacy and Peace*, 99–100.

plans. Wilson's interpretation of the United States international role and the gradual predominance in Russia of the forces
supporting non-annexationist peace aims (especially through
the Petrograd Soviet) powerfully reinforced both the idea that
the war might engender a new system of international relations
and the possibility that diplomacy—starting with labour and
socialist diplomacy—might yield an alternative resolution of
the war to the military effort, apparently mired in stalemate.[19]

At the same time, both Wilson and the Russian revolution
turned a critical searchlight on to French and British official
war aims, especially as news leaked out of the secret talks and
accords with Italy and Russia. Once the embarrassment of the
Tsarist alliance had gone, the French and British governments,
with their continued propensity to think in terms of old-style
secret diplomacy and the balance of power, appeared the major
obstacle to an allied declaration of democratic, non-annexationist war aims. As early as April 1917, Jouhaux was censored in
La Bataille when he declared that 'not to recognize that the
time has come to talk loud and clear, about peace aims, is to
declare oneself an adversary of democracy'.[20]

The importance of democratic peace aims was thus accentuated for socialist and syndicalist *majoritaires* in France while
British labour in 1917 was definitely enlisted behind the 'new
diplomacy'. Majority leaders in both countries were pitted
against their own governments over the definition of peace
aims. And the Petrograd Soviet's initiative for an international
socialist gathering, converging with the renewed effort to the
same end by the northern neutral socialists (the Dutch-Scandi-
navian Committee), resulted in the Stockholm conference and a
fundamental challenge to the majority leaders' embargo on
meeting 'enemy' socialists and trade unionists.[21]

[19] Mayer, *Political Origins of the New Diplomacy*, 147–241.
[20] SHAT, 5N 494 (*La Bataille*, 29 Apr. 1917); D. Stevenson, *French War Aims
against Germany, 1914–1919* (Clarendon Press, Oxford, 1982), 61–93; V. H. Rothwell, *British War Aims and Peace Diplomacy 1914–1918* (OUP, Oxford, 1971),
145–53.
[21] On Stockholm, see M. Fainsod, *International Socialism and the World War*
(Harvard Univ. Press, Cambridge, Mass., 1935), 124–46; Mayer, *Political Origins
of the New Diplomacy*, 191–241; H. Meynell, 'The Stockholm Conference of 1917',
International Review of Social History, 5 (1960), pp. 1–25 (pt. 1) and pp. 203–25
(pt. 2); D. Kirby, *War, Peace and Revolution: International Socialism at the
Crossroads, 1914–1918* (Gower, 1986), 152–70.

The resulting adjustment was most dramatic in the case of British Labour. Henderson's role was crucial. His experience as an official emissary of the British government to the progressive forces in Russia in June–July 1917, as he urged the latter to harness revolutionary mobilization to a redoubled war effort of democratic liberation, rekindled his enthusiasm for the international goals associated with the UDC and ILP, and eventually convinced him of the need for British Labour to participate in the planned Stockholm conference.[22] Henderson's conversion undoubtedly played a crucial part in winning the special Labour Party conference on 10 August, called in advance of a new Anglo-French meeting, to support the Stockholm venture.[23]

Yet other forces tended in the same direction. Sidney Webb and the Fabians, accepting the invitation refused by Labour in 1916, drafted a memorandum on *The Terms of Peace* in July–September 1916 for submission to the ISB which stressed the importance of a scheme of 'international government' (based on the ideas of the radical Liberal intellectual, Leonard Woolf) 'that will prevent future war'.[24] Webb wrote the first comprehensive Labour Party statement on international aims, the *Memorandum on War Issues*, for the Labour and Anglo-French

---

[22] Swartz, *The Union of Democratic Control*, 162–6; Winter, *Socialism and the Challenge of War*, 245–53.

[23] *Report of the Labour Party Conference, Nottingham, January 1918* (LPNEC report), 4–6; A. Henderson, *A People's Peace*, 4; M. I. Cole (ed.), *Beatrice Webb's Diaries 1912–24*, 12 and 22 Aug. 1917, 93–4; Winter, *Socialism and the Challenge of War*, 257–8.

[24] Initially, the Fabian Society was split over the causes of the war and international aims. But in 1915, L. S. Woolf, a member of the Research Department also active in the UDC, and later a member of the ILP, published two reports, issued in 1916 as a book, *International Government*. They sketched proposals for a supra-national authority to arbitrate disputes (McBriar, *Fabian Socialism and English Politics*, 135–45). Beatrice and Sidney Webb had expounded the idea in a course of lectures to the 1915 Fabian Summer School on 'The World after the War' (*Fabian News*, Sept. 1915). In 1916, the Fabian Society (like the ILP) took up the challenge rejected by the Labour Party and submitted their own peace plans to the ISB. S. Webb wrote a draft in July, which appeared under the title *The Terms of Peace*, as an executive committee statement in *Fabian News*, Sept. 1916 (draft in Fabian Society papers, Nuffield College, Oxford). He called again for an international authority, but also stressed economic aspects (post-war free trade, the regulation of unemployment in all countries through public works, and reparations). These figured in the *Memorandum*, but the *political* aspects of the post-war order were greatly enhanced in the 1917 documents by comparison with 1916.

conferences. Acknowledging the influence of American intervention and the Petrograd Soviet's peace programme, he advocated a League of Nations and enumerated a series of points
which sought, in practical Fabian style, to implement the
principles of national self-determination and non-annexation—
though Alsace-Lorraine was to be 'restored' to France.[25]

A major shift in rank-and-file sentiment underpinned (and in
some cases outran) these developments. After the government's
interdiction on participation in the Stockholm conference, a
new international policy was unveiled at the Blackpool Trades
Union Congress in September 1917 by which British labour
would take the lead in securing first allied, then international,
labour agreement on 'democratic' peace aims.[26] John Hill,
secretary of the Boilermakers and vice-chairman of the PCTUC
in 1916–17, pointed out the novelty of trade union interest in
international questions, and argued for a 'people's peace',
relying internationally as well as nationally on the control of
capital by labour through some kind of 'world democracy'.
Robert Smillie proposed the new strategy which, in the teeth of
opposition from the conservative and nationalist minority led
by J. H. Wilson of the Sailors' and Firemen's Union, was
overwhelmingly approved by 2,849,000 to 91,000.[27]

The Labour Party and TUC jointly endorsed the new
approach in the form of a special conference on 27 December
1917, which approved a *Memorandum on War Aims*. This, the
definitive statement of Labour's international policy, was
Webb's original document substantially enlarged by an
LPNEC-PCTUC Joint International Committee, of which (as
with *Labour and the New Social Order*) Henderson, Webb, and

[25] *Memorandum on War Issues*, esp. 3; LPNEC, min. 14 Aug. 1917; *Report of the
Labour Party Conference, Nottingham, January, 1918* (LPNEC rep.); M. I. Cole
(ed.), *Beatrice Webb's Diaries, 1912–24*, 12 Aug. 1917, 92–3. The first draft was
prepared for circulation before inter-allied socialist and British Labour conferences
on war aims, planned for the 8, 9, and 10 Aug. respectively in London. The inter-
allied conference was postponed until 28–29 Aug., after a British Labour delegation
had conferred with the PS in Paris on 29–30 July. But the draft was still presented
to the Labour Party meeting on 10 Aug. A revised version was formulated by an
LPNEC subcommittee (consisting of Henderson, F. W. Purdy, and W. C. Robinson, as well as Webb), for the inter-allied meeting at the end of the month (LPNEC,
min. 22 Aug. 1917)).
[26] PRO, CAB/23/3, 10 Aug. 1917; *Report of the Labour Party Conference,
Nottingham, Jan. 1918*, 8; Winter, *Socialism and the Challenge of War*, 257–8.
[27] *Trades Union Congress, Annual Report, September 1917*, 56–8.

MacDonald were the key members.[28] The *Memorandum* began by approving the resolution of the February 1915 London conference. To end all war and begin 'Making the World Safe for Democracy', it repudiated secret diplomacy and imperialism (defined as territorial aggrandisement rather than an economic feature of capitalism). It also extolled the classic precepts of liberal internationalism—national self-determination and arms reduction. Above all, it proposed a comprehensive League of Nations as an international legislature with coercive powers to prevent aggression. Significantly, there was also an important section on 'Economic Problems', which rejected any 'Economic War after Peace has been secured' and urged a co-ordinated, international approach to post-war economic reconstruction and social reform to remove economic rivalry as a source of national conflict.[29]

By a process paralleling the definition of Labour's domestic reform plans, ideas associated originally with the left of the party had become the new orthodoxy in a more sharply critical mainstream view of the war and its international consequences. The ILP was shut out of the inter-allied diplomacy in 1918 as an independent force just as its views were being adopted by the Labour Party.[30] For as Ramsay MacDonald commented:

Since it issued its War Aims, the Labour Party has come more and more to speak in our language and to look at Europe from our point of view . . . As the rains abate it is the Ararat of the Independent Labour Party upon which the ark is finding a resting place.[31]

---

[28] Full membership of the committee was, for the LPNEC, Henderson, Mac-Donald, Webb, Hutchinson, McGurk, Purdy, and Wardle, and for the PCTUC, Bowerman, Bramley, Gosling, Hill, Thomas, and Thorne (LPNEC, min. 1917, 147; PCTUC, min. 27 Sept. 1917). By 17 Oct. Webb had redrafted the memorandum (PCTUC, min. 17 Oct. 1917). Accepted by the Joint International Committee on 24 Oct., it was endorsed after some PCTUC amendments by a meeting of the two executive committees on 12 Dec. and, with virtual unanimity, by the special joint conference on 27 Dec. (PCTUC, min. 24 Oct., 12 Dec., and 27 Dec. 1917).

[29] *Memorandum on War Aims*, reproduced as Append. I in Henderson, *The Aims of Labour*.

[30] The 1918 NAC report of the ILP expressed broad agreement with the *Memorandum on War Aims* but bitterly condemned the exclusion of the ILP from participation in the Feb. 1918 inter-allied Labour and socialist conference (*ILP Annual Conference*, 1918, 16 ff.; LPNEC, min. 13 Feb. 1918).

[31] Manuscript article notes, 1918, PRO 30/69/3A/67, 9.

And by 1918, many of the intellectuals (such as Leonard Woolf) who had pursued their liberal radicalism through the UDC had gravitated to the Labour Party and were busily fleshing out a programme of post-war international reform through its various subcommittees.[32]

The CGT majority, as we have seen, managed to win near unanimity at the Clermont Ferrand conference in December 1917 for a resolution which reiterated the democratic peace programme outlined in 1915–16, but which also invoked Wilson and the Russian revolution against Clemenceau's obdurate refusal to define French war aims, and accepted CGT participation in an international labour conference to discuss peace terms. Yet unanimity was only possible because the *minoritaires* dropped an alternative resolution which had denied any special validity to the French war effort and the CGT's participation in it, and had demanded an all-out international campaign to impose peace. The *majoritaires* saw the 'unity' motion confirmed—but against rising dissension—at the July 1918 congress.[33]

The French socialist majority, like the Labour Party, responded to the Russian revolution, and the conversion of its own emissaries to Russia (Cachin and Moutet) to the case for a renewal of the International, by approving participation in the Stockholm meeting. The decision, taken by the Conseil National in May 1917, was subsequently qualified by the majority's insistence that responsibilities for the outbreak of war (i.e. admission by the SPD of German war guilt) should be established before any international conference met—a stand which deprived the Anglo-French socialist conference, when it was finally held in late August, of a united policy on the international meeting.[34] From June to August 1917, a reply was drafted to a questionnaire on peace aims from the Dutch–Scandinavian

---

[32] Notably the Advisory Committee on International Questions, with S. Webb as chairman and Woolf as secretary (LPNEC, min. 1918, memo dated Apr., 104; L. S. Woolf, *Beginning Again: An Autobiography of the Years 1911 to 1918* (1964; OUP, Oxford, 1980), 134–6; Swartz, *The Union of Democratic Control*, 206–7).

[33] See Chap. 5, above.

[34] *L'Humanité*, 29 May and 3 Sept. 1917; *Report of the Labour Party Conference, Nottingham, January 1918* (LPNEC report), 9.

Committee which, approved by a significant majority at the
October 1917 congress of the PS, became the principal *majoritaire* statement on the international consequences of the war.[35]

The October 1917 programme paralleled and anticipated
Labour's *Memorandum on War Aims*. The war was being
fought to 'escape the hegemony which a powerful industrial and
military organization might give to Germany and her allies', but
also for national self-determination and in order to establish
through 'the Society of Nations the guarantee of a peaceful
equilibrium for the world'. The achievement of a new international order turned not merely on government treaties but on
'the foresight and will of the proletarian masses as well as on the
democratic and socialist institutions which they will need to
perfect or establish'. Less concerned than the *Memorandum on
War Aims* to prescribe solutions for particular international
problems, the October 1917 programme above all sought to
intensify the campaign begun in December 1915 to persuade
the French government to commit itself to democratic war
aims. To end the war on this basis, the programme also sought
to reconcile support for the military effort with an international
socialist diplomacy. In the spirit of this programme, the socialist majority supported British Labour's inter-allied and international peace aims campaign in 1918.[36] It was only at the
October 1918 congress, as German resistance crumbled and
intervention in Russia seemed to presage an anti-revolutionary
offensive by the allies, that the case for supporting the military
effort evaporated and the moderate *minoritaires* triumphed.[37]

For the labour and socialist majorities, 1917–18 defined, in
the British case, and amplified, in the French, a vision which
was implicit in the 'choice of 1914' and which had emerged
explicitly at the London conference in February 1915. If the
war was perceived by labour leaders as a clash of political
systems and ideologies, it involved more, by definition, than
merely resisting territorial aggrandisement. It meant creating
the circumstances which would prevent any recurrence of the

---

[35] *Le Parti socialiste, la guerre et la paix*, 189–99.
[36] With the exception of the far-right of the party, including forty deputies (see
Chap. 2).
[37] *L'Humanité*, 7–11 Oct. 1918.

disaster of 1914 in the future. Eliminating the political regimes of Austria and Germany was crucial but insufficient in this process. The war must also found a new international order which would remove the possibility of war and counteract tendencies within the allied powers toward an expansionist or punitive peace. To fight the war merely for the *status quo ante* (shorn of the German 'menace') increasingly seemed to most 'pro-war' labour leaders as unwarrantable in the international as in the domestic sphere.

There was, therefore, a common assumption in both spheres that the war itself was a dynamic force which made any return to the pre-war world impossible. Moreover, the nature of change in the domestic and international spheres was perceived as being intimately linked. International peace, not to mention an international attempt to regulate the economic problems generated by the war, were the preconditions of plans for domestic reform. Henderson wrote in 1918, in *The League of Nations and Labour*:

The specific programme of reconstruction in which Labour is interested presupposes two essential conditions which must be fulfilled before it can be carried into practical effect: the first condition is the defeat and destruction of Prussian militarism; the second is the establishment of a League of Nations which will make the world safe for democracy.[38]

At the same moment, Jouhaux suggested that the CGT's domestic and international reform plans were two parts of the same programme.

We want ... French workers to be able in the future to continue the task which we have already begun in order to implement, not any longer the bourgeois Republic, but the full social Republic, that which will be able to achieve the union of all peoples and thus create the domain of the international worker.[39]

The two dimensions, domestic and international, were also seen as complementary aspects of a single propaganda campaign. This was so as early as the CGT majority's programme

---

[38] *The League of Nations and Labour*, 5.
[39] *La Clairière*, 1 June 1918, pp. 1016–17 and 1020–1.

at the December 1916 conference, which Jouhaux summarized as 'new rights for labour in the sense of an economic democratization; new rights for humanity, with the aim of avoiding a return of the current massacres, by the constitution of the Society of Nations.'[40] As we have noted, the Labour Party mounted a campaign in 1918 based equally on 'War Aims and Reconstruction'.

But the connections between wartime reformism in the domestic and international spheres went deeper still. Majority socialists and syndicalists envisaged that change would occur, during and after the war, through the institutions of a liberal democracy—internationally (where they had yet to be created) as well as domestically. They assumed that war, though an innate tendency of capitalism and economic 'imperialism', could be contained and prevented in advance of the construction of a full international socialist order. A symbiosis of labour and socialist movements with the programmes of liberal, 'bourgeois' pacifism, would suffice. As the October 1917 programme of the PS reasoned:

The Parti Socialiste does not forget that the capitalist regime of economic competition, colonization, and imperialism can make peace always precarious. But claiming to represent the interests of the peoples, [the PS] intends to achieve the maximum guarantees against the risk of conflict by the installation of this Society of Nations which the thinkers of the bourgeoisie itself have considered to assure a durable and just peace.[41]

Rather than socialism being the precondition for eliminating war, the prevention of war thus became a condition of achieving socialism. This retreat from an exclusively socialist alternative to a system based on international conflict had been anticipated by the Second International, especially the 1910 Copenhagen Congress, which had agreed on little else except the relevance of the 'bourgeois' peace programme—to the strong disapproval of the left. But to the congress's unanswered question of what anti-war strategies socialists should pursue, the 'choice of 1914'—as worked out by the wartime majorities in France and Britain—

---

[40] 'Buts d'avenir: paix définitive, travail régénéré', *La Bataille*, 4 Jan. 1917.
[41] *Le Parti socialiste, la guerre et la paix*, 190.

returned an unambiguous reply: the defence of liberal democratic nation-states and the construction of a new diplomatic
system on that foundation. The labour and socialist movements were, of course, to be the motor force of this process. But
internationally, as domestically, the *majoritaires* were brought
by war *explicitly* to claim the inheritance of liberal democracy as
the foundation of social—and socialist—progress.

Just as the domestic reform programmes of both French and
British labour movements were compatible with continued
support for the war effort, so were the international policies
adopted or consolidated in 1917–1918. The change in attitude
towards contact with 'enemy' socialists and trade unionists was
determined by several considerations. First was the conviction
(down to the October revolution) that an international socialist
conference was the minimum price for keeping Russian socialists in the war. Albert Thomas, like Henderson a government
emissary to the Russian revolutionaries in April–June 1917, was
won to Stockholm on these grounds.[42] Second was the possibility after the Reichstag peace resolution of July 1917 that
German Social Democrats might initiate a reform process
leading to a negotiated, non-annexationist peace.[43] Third was
the need to fend off the minority challenge (especially in
France) by taking the lead in a campaign to achieve internationally agreed labour peace aims and to lever a commitment to
the 'new diplomacy' from the French and British governments.

But the majorities refused to adopt the minority view that
war origins or the relative legitimacy of the two alliances had no
place in a renewal of the International. Rather, they sought to
reconcile the renewal of international labour and socialist
contact to explore peace aims with unflinching commitment to
the allied cause as a democratic crusade. For this reason, the
CGT and PS *majoritaires* and British Labour saw Stockholm
not as an unconditional, open-ended diplomatic process but as a
platform for persuading both Russian and German socialists of

---

[42] I. Sinanoglou (ed.), 'Journal de Russie d'Albert Thomas, 22 avril–19 juin
1917', *Cahiers du monde russe et soviétique*, 14/1–2 (1973), p. 200; Henderson,
Labour's Peace Terms, (early 1918); Mayer, *Political Origins of the New Diplomacy*,
84 ff.; Winter, *Socialism and the Challenge of War*, 247.

[43] Mayer, *Political Origins of the New Diplomacy*, 118–25; Fischer, *Germany's
Aims in the First World War*, 399–404.

the fundamental rectitude of the allied effort.[44] The Labour-led diplomacy of 1918 aimed at the same goal. With minor amendments, the *Memorandum on War Aims* was approved by French socialists and the CGT at an inter-allied conference in London in February 1918, and issued to the socialists of the Central Powers as the basis of an accord on peace aims.[45] But in the absence of a clear conversion by the SPD to this view of a 'democratic', non-annexationist peace or the beginning of a democratic revolution in Germany, majority labour and socialist leaders in France and Britain continued to back the military effort as the only alternative to a *paix allemande*.[46] They were thus unwilling to take any *action* to secure passports for an international meeting or to pressure their governments to adopt democratic war aims, especially when the separate Russo-German peace at Brest-Litovsk placed the allies in greater peril

[44] Hence the crucial issue of whether or not Stockholm was to be considered binding on participating organizations. The PS *majoritaires* and the Labour Party insisted on prior consultation among the allies to reach a common war aims policy and also refused to accept Stockholm as more than consultative, so as to avoid being trapped by 'pacifist' manœuvres. Jouhaux and the CGT *majoritaires* agreed, insisting that a putative CGT delegation should be armed with—and constrained by—a mandatory war aims policy before attending. It is clear that all three currents expected the concessions to come from the labour and socialist movements of the Central Powers, which were to condemn their own governments' aggression and align themselves with their Entente colleagues' conception of the peace (*Report of the Labour Party Conference, Nottingham, January 1918*, 8–9; 'Déclaration de la majorité, 2 septembre 1917', *Le Parti Socialiste, la guerre et la paix*, 183–7; AN F₇ 13575, CGT, Comité Confédéral, 28 Aug. 1917, rep. 30 Aug. 1917; *La Bataille*, 16 Aug. 1917 (art. by Jouhaux on Stockholm)).

[45] The PS and CGT were consulted from the start in the preparation of the inter-allied conference. A British delegation visited both in Paris beforehand, and a basic agreement to accept the *Memorandum on War Aims* as allied labour and socialist policy (with some qualifications) was reached, and ratified by a CGT commission (consisting of Jouhaux, Laurent, Luquet, Merrheim, and Lenoir) and by a meeting of the Conseil National of the PS. The socialist *minoritaires* opposed the British document. Both the CGT and socialist delegations approved the *Memorandum* at the London conference, 20–4 February 1918 (LPNEC, min. 1918, International Joint Committee, 8 Jan. 1918; *L'Humanité*, 16, 18, and 19 Feb. 1918, for the British visit and Conseil National; AN F₇ 13576, CGT, Comité Confédéral, 19 Feb. 1918, rep. 21 Feb., for the CGT commission; *L'Humanité*, 22, 23, 25 and 27 Feb., for the conference; Van Der Slice, *International Labour Diplomacy and Peace*, 40–6).

[46] Considerable importance was attached in the spring and summer to the replies from the Austrian and German movements, neither of which was favourable (Labour Party Archives, LSI/1/29 and LSI/2; *L'Humanité*, 19–23 Sept. 1918; SFIO, *Conférence interalliée de Londres: les résolutions adoptées*; Van Der Slice, *International Labour Diplomacy and Peace*, 46–9).

than at any time since autumn 1914. The rift in assumptions and strategy between the majority and those *minoritaires* who, in the name of the same peace aims, believed that steps to achieve a negotiated peace should pre-empt all else, remained fundamental.

In practice, allied labour diplomacy in 1918 experienced a double defeat. It failed to win the support of either the SPD or the French and British governments. Lloyd George made a vague concession to the 'new diplomacy' in his speech to a trade union audience on 5 January 1918, Clemenceau not at all.[47] Yet despite, or perhaps because of, this stasis, President Wilson reached the pinnacle of his symbolic and practical significance for allied labour opinion. The 'Fourteen Points', published in January 1918 as a counter-manifesto to the Brest-Litovsk negotiations (disguised by the Bolsheviks as a call to a general non-annexationist peace) vindicated all, *majoritaires* or *minoritaires*, who saw the war as a crusade for a new international order. Yet Wilson also endorsed military victory as the only alternative to a domestic revolution in the central powers.[48] With the Armistice signed on the basis of the 'Fourteen Points', Wilson arrived in France on 13 December 1918 to a tumultuous welcome from the labour and socialist movements of both countries, the apparent guarantor that their views, and even their direct presence, would help shape the peace-settlement.[49]

(ii) Trade Union Internationalism and Economic Reforms, 1915–1918

In parallel with their political war aims, moderate 'pro-war' labour leaders in France and Britain developed distinctive international plans for economic reform. These were largely, though not exclusively, the preserve of the trade union movements, with the essential momentum coming from the CGT.

[47] Mayer, *Political Origins of the New Diplomacy*, 322 ff.
[48] Ibid., 160–1, 182–3, and 352. The Sept. 1918 inter-allied labour and socialist conference firmly endorsed the 'Fourteen Points' as 'a summary of the principles which the Interallied Memorandum has set out in detail' (report of the conference's Commission on War Aims, Labour Party Archives, LSI/2/13/18).
[49] LPNEC, min. 6 Nov. 1918; *La Bataille*, 14 Dec. 1918; *L'Humanité*, 14 Dec. 1918; A. J. Mayer, *Politics and Diplomacy of Peacemaking: Containment and Counter-revolution at Versailles, 1918–1919* (Weidenfeld and Nicolson, 1968), 172–3.

The impulse was supplied by various preoccupations. Internationally, as domestically, the spectre of economic chaos haunted labour thinking on the eventual process of demobilization, complicated as it would be by the allied blockade of the Central Powers and the issue of reparations. The first inter-allied economic conference of June 1916, and the rising tide of economic nationalism in conservative circles, suggested that attempts would be made to institutionalize allied economic co-operation against post-war Austria and Germany. Such economic antagonism was seen as the antithesis of the conciliatory peace required as the basis of a new diplomatic system. It also seemed to menace national reform programmes of labour legislation, and especially the eight-hour day, which depended on simultaneous implementation in the major economies to ensure that relative levels of productivity and competitiveness were not disrupted. More generally, the conviction that the war had transformed the status of the working class was easily projected on to an international screen via the anticipated peace-making process. The treaty, in the eyes of moderate labour leaders, was to lay the basis not just of a new political, but also of a reformed economic and social, order.

As in the political sphere, the issue of whether a resumption of contact with 'enemy' labour leaders was appropriate during the war proved crucial. It also proved extremely bitter, since it exacerbated both the pre-war antagonism between French and Germans in the IFTU and the former's sense of betrayal by their German *confrères* in August 1914. The question of international economic reforms was interwoven throughout the war with a struggle between Jouhaux and Legien for the upper hand within the fractured trade union international.

With the expectation of a short war, the idea that the international labour movement should try to influence a new European settlement, widely expected to be on the scale of 1815, surfaced almost at the outset. The AFL, which had affiliated to the ISNTUC in 1910 and, under its indefatigable general secretary, Samuel Gompers, assumed an increasingly active role in international trade union affairs, sought in the early months of the war to play the role of mediator.[50] At its

---

[50] Lorwin, *Labor and Internationalism*, 123–33.

Philadelphia congress in November 1914, the AFL passed a resolution of Gompers proposing that an international labour meeting should be held at the same time and place as the 'general Peace Conference', with the aim of 'protecting the interests of the toilers and thereby assisting in laying foundations of a more lasting peace'.[51]

The Comité Confédéral of the CGT, alone of the major European trade union movements, welcomed this suggestion, and when the confederal majority voted on 7 February 1915 to go to the inter-allied socialist conference in London, it identified the need to consider the economic as well as political dimension of labour war aims.

If international law has to be established for the stability of world peace, syndicalist militants would not wish to forget that there are equally international guarantees for labour which need to be obtained, so that syndicalism can accomplish its work of liberating labour without having to fear henceforth the opposition between nationalities.[52]

Preparing a distinctively syndicalist programme for the post-war period, however, meant re-establishing some form of trade union links while the conflict lasted. Jouhaux used the opportunity presented by the London conference to recontact the main body representing British trade unions internationally, the General Federation of Trade Unions, and its general secretary, William A. Appleton,[53] over the form such links might take.[54]

In some respects, the GFTU was an odd partner for the CGT. Founded in 1899 in an attempt to provide more coherent

[51] J. T. Shotwell, *The Origins of the International Labor Organization* (Columbia Univ. Press, New York, 1934), ii, *Documents*, 3; S. Gompers, *Seventy Years of Life and Labour: An Autobiography* (Hurst and Blackett, 1924), ii. 390.

[52] *Rapports des comités ... pour l'exercice 1914–1918*, 58; AN F₇ 13574, CGT, Comité Confédéral, min. 7 Feb. 1915; AN F₇ 13572, rep. 'La CGT et la paix', 15 May 1915.

[53] (1859–1940) Born in London and brought up in Nottingham, Appleton became a lace worker. General secretary of the Amalgamated Operative Lacemakers in 1896, he became general secretary of the GFTU in 1907, a post he held until 1938. Active in international trade unionism since 1900, he was elected president of the IFTU in Aug. 1919. An advocate of craft unionism and by temperament cautious and pragmatic, he was out of tune with the more radical temper of post-war labour and resigned as president of the IFTU in Nov. 1920.

[54] A Prochaska, *History of the General Federation of Trade Unions, 1899–1980* (Allen & Unwin, 1982), 144–6.

industrial leadership for the labour movement, the GFTU rapidly became an insurance organization (for strikes, sickness, and unemployment), recruiting increasingly among the smaller trade unions. In the face of the TUC's withdrawal from, and subsequent indifference to, the international scene, following early disappointments, the GFTU assumed the habit of speaking for British trade unionism on international affairs and was the British member of the IFTU.[55] By 1914, the GFTU was under pressure. Its membership overlapped with that of the TUC but, at a million, was little more than a third the size. It had failed to provide the impulse towards stronger, industrial unionism hoped for by some radicals during the unrest of 1911 to 1914. Yet it also clashed with an increasingly active PCTUC and the leaderships of some of the larger unions over industrial tactics and the place of unions in the National Insurance Scheme.[56]

Although, when the war came, the GFTU lobbied the government on a number of specific issues, it resisted (as we have noted) the attempt by the WEWNC to broaden the emergency committee's function into one of articulating an alternative and critical Labour vision of the mobilization—and demobilization—process.[57] The relative conservatism and anti-socialism of the GFTU leadership, in addition to its declining representativity of British trade unionism as a whole, rendered it ill-suited to express the left-ward shift of British labour under the impact of the war and of post-war plans. None the less, its international role remained uncontested until 1918, and the GFTU was the obvious counter-poise for the CGT leadership to the continued preponderance of the German free trade unions in the international movement.

The CGT and GFTU delegates who met in London agreed that there should be no direct contact with German and Austrian trade unionists while hostilities lasted, and that the bitterness engendered by the conflict made the removal of the international secretariat from Berlin to neutral Berne essential.

[55] GFTU, *Annual Report*, 1914–18; GFTU, *Jubilee Souvenir: Fifty Years' History of the General Federation of Trade Unions, 1899–1949* (1949); Prochaska, *History of the General Federation of Trade Unions*, 142–68; M. Nicholson, *The TUC Overseas: The Roots of Policy* (Allen & Unwin, 1986), 9–11.
[56] Prochaska, *History of the General Federation of Trade Unions*, 101–23.
[57] Ibid., 126–8.

Legien had already anticipated the issue by setting up a corresponding bureau under Oudegeest, secretary of the neutral Dutch trade unions (though seen by the French and British as a *protégé* of the German movement), in Amsterdam. But Legien systematically blocked the proposal of Jouhaux and Appleton (transmitted by Gompers in spring 1915) by insisting that only the full international congress foresworn by Appleton had the authority to remove the secretariat to another country.[58] The CGT had little option but to parallel Legien's earlier move and propose a corresponding bureau sympathetic to the Entente movements in Paris.[59] By late 1915, therefore, it was clear that the immediate framework for discussing a syndicalist peace programme, plus the AFL's original suggestion of a labour meeting coincident with a peace conference, would be the allied trade union movements themselves.

Just what such a strategy might entail was considered by the CGT in the months following the February 1915 conference in London. The leadership of the Fédération du Bâtiment, which had taken a major part in defining *majoritaire* attitudes to the war since November 1914, presented a resolution to the Comité Confédéral on 13 May 1915 which reiterated the basic right of the working class ('which has payed its large tribute to the defence of the country') to shape the outcome of the peace by holding an international conference at the end of the war and presenting its demands.[60] The latter, the motion went on, should consist of 'economic labour clauses' (*clauses économiques ouvrières*) to be included in the peace treaty. These were to prescribe international standards on questions such as working hours, the three-shift system of continuous production, protection of women and children, social insurance, and trade union rights.

The Fédération du Bâtiment proposal provided the kernel of a longer report on the *clauses ouvrières*, which was drafted

[58] AN F₇ 13572, rep. 27 Sept. 1915; GFTU, *Annual Report 1915*, 19–33; Sassenbach, *Twenty-Five Years of International Trade Unionism*, 46–9; Lorwin, *Labor and Internationalism*, 178–9; Gompers, *Seventy Years of Life and Labour*, ii. 389; Georges and Tintant, *Léon Jouhaux*, i. 222–4.

[59] AN F₇ 13572, CGT brochure, 'Aux centrales nationales des organisations syndicales' (13 Nov. 1915).

[60] IFHS, 14 AS 407 (Fonds Picart), doss. I, circulars of the Fédération du Bâtiment. The motion was signed by Chanvin, and almost certainly drafted by him and/or Picart.

between autumn 1915 and spring 1916 (and signed by Jouhaux) as part of the *majoritaire* offensive to seize the ideological and political initiative within the CGT. Indeed, published in the May Day issue of *La Voix du peuple*, the report was nothing less than an international extension of the domestic reformism which served to reorientate the CGT in 1916, and it was underpinned by many of the same assumptions.[61]

The report on the *clauses ouvrières* started from the proposition that working-class sacrifices in the war entitled organized labour to claim substantial economic and social reforms, and that it should begin to do so immediately if it really wished to influence the post-war settlement. The cost of not doing so was evoked by the sombre prediction that, left to its own devices, the *patronat* would pass on the burden of war debts and physical reconstruction to the working class, pleading international competition in order to justify continued long hours and low wages. Here the argument fused with that on domestic economic reform. The introduction of international standards on labour conditions and social welfare, plus international regulation of the labour market, were the indispensable corollary of the CGT's domestic productivism, based on high wages, shorter hours, and technical transformations.

The range of issues specified for international legislation was similar to that of the original Fédération du Bâtiment proposal. But migration occupied a central place, reflecting the CGT's growing concern with the 'vacancies caused by the hecatombs of the battlefield' and the inevitable post-war labour famine in many industrial areas of Europe. More broadly, the CGT report acknowledged the importance of a long *bourgeois* tradition of thinking on international labour legislation by philanthropists, politicians, and reforming industrialists and civil servants. This tradition was embodied in the International Association for the Legal Protection of Labour, founded in 1900 as a voluntary body but accorded semi-official status by several governments—including the British and the French.

---

[61] Despite the mistaken claim by the report to the 1918 congress that the *clauses ouvrières* were drawn up in the first half of 1915 (*Rapport des comités . . . pour l'exercice 1914–1918*, 60), they were drafted in late 1915 to early 1916, as part of the *majoritaire* response to the minority challenge at the Aug. 1915 conference, and circulated to syndicalist organizations in Feb. 1916 (F, 12891, 'Le Mouvement syndicaliste, année 1916', 13–14).

The Association had pioneered international conventions on labour conditions (notably in 1906, restricting women's night work), encouraged inter-governmental labour treaties (such as that between France and Italy in 1904, focused on migration), and established a rudimentary international labour office to monitor the application of agreements.[62] The CGT explicitly annexed this tradition as the special preserve of international trade unionism.

Migration was also an urgent matter for other trade union movements. We have already seen that the British (GFTU) and Italian (CGL) delegations visiting Paris for 1 May 1916 approved the CGT's report on regulating migrant labour and agreed that, together with the *clauses ouvrières*, migration should be placed on the agenda of an inter-allied trade union conference to be held in London, in tandem with the annual conference of the GFTU.[63] The CGT was asked to submit a report on both issues, and its existing document, plus a set of summarizing *clauses ouvrières* for inclusion in the peace treaty, were duly circulated to the participating movements.

In fact, when the conference finally took place in Leeds on 5–6 July, it revealed the disarray of even the moderate trade union leaderships of the Entente, faced with the question of appropriate international responses to the war. Russian labour leaders, though invited, could not attend.[64] Rigola and the CGL were keen to participate but were vetoed by Serrati and the socialist leadership—intent on preserving Italian labour's neutrality towards the war. Only an *ad hoc* and unofficial delegation of Italian syndicalists went to Leeds. Apart from two Belgian trade union leaders, the GFTU provided the only substantial national delegation apart from the CGT.[65]

Jouhaux and the CGT delegation (with the *minoritaires* excluded) undoubtedly had the greatest ambitions for the

---

[62] Shotwell, *The Origins of the International Labor Organization*, i. 29–47; J. W. Follows, *Antecedents of the International Labour Organization* (Clarendon Press, Oxford, 1951), 157–76.

[63] See p. 109, above; and *L'Avenir*, July 1916, p. 260.

[64] AN F$_7$ 12891, 'Le Mouvement syndicaliste, année 1916', 35.

[65] Ibid., 34–5; *La Constitution du comité syndical italien pour l'émigration et les intérêts ouvriers internationaux: conférence inter-prolétaire de Leeds, 5–6 juillet 1916*, brochure in IFHS.

conference.[66] They wished to achieve four ends—allied agreement on the transfer of the IFTU secretariat to a neutral country; approval for the original AFL proposal for an international labour conference coincident with the peace negotiations; agreement on the political basis of a democratic international order; and the endorsement of the *clauses ouvrières*.[67]

There was broad agreement on the first goal. Hostility to Legien's pre-war domination of the IFTU was widespread and, despite the rebuff to Jouhaux and Appleton's manœuvrings in 1915, it was hoped that the international secretariat might yet be transferred to Switzerland. Meanwhile, the Paris corresponding bureau was approved.

But the GFTU objected on patriotic grounds to any meeting with German or Austrian labour leaders before the conclusion of peace. The French printers' leader, Keufer, managed to rescue a commitment in principle to the original AFL idea, provided no political questions were envisaged for such a conference. The British delegates also rejected Jouhaux's elaborate resolution on the political foundations of a new international order (previously approved by the majority of the Comité Confédéral).[68] In effect, Jouhaux sought to profit by the temporary eclipse of Legien's influence to resolve the CGT's long-standing quarrel with the Germans in the IFTU, by expanding the body's scope beyond purely economic questions. The GFTU had always stood closer to the Germans on this issue, and it ruled Jouhaux's initiative firmly out of order. The *clauses ouvrières*, passed unanimously but without discussion at the end of the conference, were thus the one unequivocal victory for the CGT.

Yet if Leeds was a partial set-back for the international tactics of the CGT *majoritaires*, the French movement's originality in defining a distinctive economic programme for international trade unionism had major repercussions, at home and abroad,

---

[66] AN F₇ 13569, CGT, Comité Confédéral, min. 8 and 22 June 1916; *L'Union des métaux*, 64 (Aug. 1916), p. 4; AN F₇ 12891, 'Le Mouvement syndicaliste, année 1916', 32–3.

[67] *Rapports des comités ... pour l'exercice, 1914–1918*, 72–6; AN F₇ 12891, 'Le Mouvement syndicaliste, année 1916', 33–9; AN F₇ 13569, min. of Leeds conference; *La Bataille*, 5–7 July 1916; *L'Union des métaux*, 64 (Aug. 1916), pp. 4–5.

[68] AN F₇ 13569, CGT, Comité Confédéral, min. 22 June 1916; AN F₇ 12891, 'Le Mouvement syndicaliste, année 1916', 33; *L'Union des métaux*, 64 (Aug. 1916), p. 4.

over the following year. Both the CGT and GFTU lobbied their respective governments on behalf of the *clauses ouvrières*, and endorsed them at end of year conferences.[69] The French syndicalist *minoritaires* bitterly ridiculed them, while the *majoritaires'* unapologetic defence of the Leeds programme further inflamed the polemic within the CGT in the run-up to the December conference.[70]

Externally, Jouhaux took the lead in trying to build a wider consensus around the programme. Shortly after Leeds, he circulated the *clauses ouvrières* to the trade union organizations affiliated to the IFTU.[71] The ground was well-chosen. The prewar congresses of the IFTU had discussed how the international trade union movement might campaign for government recognition of the conventions on night work, domestic work, and industrial poisons drafted by the International Association for the Legal Protection of Labour.[72] The IFTU had also been acutely concerned before the war with worker migration between states.[73] The CGT, in suggesting that the peacemaking process should have a social and economic dimension, also pointed to a new programme and strategy for the IFTU.

With German leadership so clearly under attack, Legien was swift to respond. On 4 October 1916, he issued an invitation, in conjunction with the Swiss trade union movement, to an international syndicalist conference in Berne in December—thus contesting the legitimacy of Leeds, which he dismissed as an attempt to foster wartime divisions in the trade union international.[74] Although acceding to a request from the Scandinavian trade unions that the conference be postponed, so that fuller consideration could be given to the kind of proposals urged by the British and French movements, Legien drove home his riposte in early 1917 by circulating IFTU members

---

[69] GFTU, *Jubilee Souvenir, 1899–1949*, 33–4; AN F₇ 13575, CGT, Comité Confédéral, rep. 4 Oct. 1916; *La Bataille*, 17 Dec. 1916.

[70] See Chap. 4, above.

[71] Via the brochure, *Questions ouvrières*.

[72] Shotwell, *The Origins of the International Labor Organization*, i. 35–47.

[73] Lorwin, *Labor and Internationalism*, 123, 130; J. A. Moses, *Trade Unionism in Germany from Bismarck to Hitler, 1869–1933*, i, *1869–1918* (Barnes and Noble, Towota, NJ, 1982), 174.

[74] AN F₇ 13572, report by the Bureau de Presse Français, 20 Sept. 1917; Lorwin, *Labor and Internationalism*, 182–3; Shotwell, *The Origins of the International Labor Organization*, i. 65–8.

with a detailed critique of the Leeds resolution and his own counter-proposals. He intended these to form the basis of discussion at the deferred international conference, now being organized by the Swiss for autumn 1917, in Berne.[75]

Legien, echoing pre-war German and American fears, was slightly more restrictive on migration than the *clauses ouvrières*, agreeing that it should be rationally co-ordinated between supplying and receiving states, but reserving the right of a nation to halt immigration during an economic slump. He was sceptical of the idea, emanating from the CGT, that *paritaire* organizations including employer representatives could regulate immigration in the interests of workers. And he was especially anxious at the incorporation of 'coloured labour' in the Leeds provisions on immigration—a point clearly determined by the post-war needs of the French economy. Legien also implied that other countries were less developed than Germany in their provision of social welfare and labour relations, and expressed fears that minimum standards required by the Leeds clauses might undermine the achievements of the socially most advanced states. Legien endorsed the Leeds programme's demand for the *semaine anglaise* and a reduction of working hours, although he went further by substituting an eight-hour for a ten-hour day as the general maximum (as had the CGT conference of December 1916).[76] Finally, where the CGT had proposed that the International Association for the Legal Protection of Labour become an international labour office which, with the support of the IFTU, would foster international labour legislation and arbitrate in disputes, Legien wanted such a body to have mandatory powers to impose new conventions on contracting states through periodic conferences.

Yet for all the nuances of difference, the essential thrust of the German proposals was similar to that of the *clauses ouvrières* adopted at Leeds. Nor is this surprising, since Legien and the General Commission of Free Trade Unions had consolidated

---

[75] Shotwell, *The Origins of the International Labor Organization*, ii. 30–43; AN F₇ 13572, CGT, Comité Confédéral, min. 19 Oct. 1916; rep. by the Bureau de Presse Français, 20 Sept. 1917.

[76] The resolution at the CGT conference of Dec. 1916 approving the *clauses ouvrières* had also reduced the maximum working day from ten (endorsed at Leeds) to eight.

their own variant of labour reformism in relation to the wartime mobilization of German society.[77] As elsewhere, the notion of international reform was an extension of this. But the pre-war tensions of the IFTU, exacerbated by wartime divisions, frustrated any convergence of these programmes while the war lasted.

The Scandinavian trade unionists, together with Oudegeest and the Dutch movement, attempted to produce just such a convergence by convoking an international conference in Stockholm, in June 1917, to discuss the issues raised at Leeds. But Gompers and the AFL executive rejected the initiative, while the GFTU and CGT ignored it.[78] Although the conference cabled its agreement with the *clauses ouvrières* to Jouhaux, it proved a dead end—flawed, in the view of Entente trade union leaders, by being little more than the German 'bloc' of the IFTU (i.e. Germany, Austria, Hungary, Holland, Bulgaria, and the Scandinavian states).[79]

The principal intermediary in 1917 seeking to arrange an international trade union gathering continued to be the Swiss trade union movement, working in association with Legien and the international secretariat in Berlin, but also enjoying close contacts with the French and Italian movements. On 29 March 1917, the Swiss movement, having confirmed with Legien that the German 'bloc' would attend a conference in Berne, sounded out the AFL, CGT, GFTU, CGL, the Spanish UGT, and the exiled Belgian movement.[80]

The CGT leadership had already indicated to the Swiss fraternal delegates at its December 1916 conference that it would reverse its policy and meet German labour leaders, provided the transfer of the international secretariat to neutral territory was on the agenda.[81] The CGT response in May 1917

---

[77] Moses, *Trade Unionism in Germany*, i. 197–212.

[78] AN F$_7$ 13572, rep. by the Bureau de Presse Français, 20 Sept. 1917; Gompers, *Seventy Years of Life and Labour*, ii. 395–6.

[79] AN F$_7$ 13572, rep. by the Bureau de Presse Français, 20 Sept. 1917; Sassenbach, *Twenty-Five Years of International Trade Unionism*, 55–7; Lorwin, *Labor and Internationalism*, 183.

[80] AN F$_7$ 13572, rep. by the Bureau de Presse Français, 20 Sept. 1917.

[81] AN F$_7$ 13572, rep. by the Bureau de Presse Français; 'A propos de la conférence de Berne', *La Clairière*, 15 Aug. 1917, 90–3; Sassenbach, *Twenty-Five Years of International Trade Unionism*, 55.

to the Swiss sounding confirmed this shift, though it insisted on the need for a prior allied conference. The CGL also accepted in principle. But the GFTU maintained its patriotic refusal to meet 'enemy' trade unionists, simply calling for a further allied meeting. And the AFL, now deeply committed to the patriotic mobilization of America behind the war, rejected the conference as untimely.[82]

The formal convocation by the Swiss unions of the Berne conference in October placed the fate of the international secretariat, plus the *clauses ouvrières*, firmly on the agenda.[83] But the continuing divisions within the Entente labour movements emerged painfully at the prior allied conference in London, on 10–11 September.[84] Where the CGT argued for attendance at Berne to secure the transfer of the secretariat, the GFTU and AFL refused—urging the Swiss unions instead to conduct a plebiscite on the issue. Even had the French and Italian delegations gone to Berne, they would have been outvoted by the German 'bloc'. But their governments forbade them to attend. The conference in Berne was thus dominated by Legien, who refused to contemplate the transfer of the secretariat, considering this a question of confidence in his leadership. It was essentially Legien's programme of international economic reforms which the conference voted.[85]

This stalemate lasted until the Armistice. None the less, in relation to international economic and social reforms, the final

---

[82] AN F$_7$ 13575, CGT, secret meeting of confederal majority, 25 May 1917, rep. 26 May; Comité Confédéral, 2 June 1917, rep. 4 June; AN F$_7$ 13572, rep. of the Préfet of the Gironde, 3 July 1917, with attached CGT brochure *Aux organisations syndicales*, setting out reasons for going to Berne; L. Jouhaux, 'L'Action des trade unions et l'internationale', *La Clairière*, 1 Aug. 1917, p. 8; L. Marchetti, *La Confederazione generale del lavoro negli atti, nei documenti, nei congressi, 1906–1926* (Edizioni Avanti, Milan, 1962), 235; Prochaska, *History of the General Federation of Trade Unions*, 146–7.

[83] AN F$_7$ 13572, rep. by the Bureau de Presse Français; Lorwin, *Labor and Internationalism*, 183.

[84] AN 94 AP 249 (Fonds Thomas), press cuttings; *La Voix du peuple*, Dec. 1917; *La Bataille*, 14 and 15 Sept. 1917; GFTU, *Annual Report*, 1918; CGT, *Rapports des comités ... pour l'exercice 1914–1918*, 78–9.

[85] AN F$_7$ 13575, series of reps., Oct. 1917; *La Bataille*, 10 Oct. 1917; CGT, *Rapports des comités ... pour l'exercice 1914–1918*, 80; Sassenbach, *Twenty-Five Years of International Trade Unionism*, 57–60; Shotwell, *The Origins of the International Labor Organization*, ii. 44–9 (Berne resolutions); Lorwin, *Labor and Internationalism*, 184.

year of the war strengthened the hand of the allied labour movements in three ways, even before military victory dealt them organizational supremacy. First, the connection between economic reforms and the political framework of the 'new diplomacy' was accepted, along with the right of international trade unionism to concern itself with both spheres. At the September 1917 conference in London, the GFTU dropped its hostility of the previous year to 'political' questions and supported a French resolution summarizing the CGT's attitude to democratic diplomacy and the Society of Nations as it had developed during the war.[86]

Secondly, the allied Labour and socialist parties displayed a reciprocal interest in international economic reforms and labour legislation. This, as we have noted, had marked Sidney Webb's interest in the post-war settlement from the outset. The theme was taken up by the *Memorandum on War Aims* in its section on 'Economic Relations' and in 1918 the Labour Party repudiated economic nationalism and argued for a co-ordinated reconstruction of the international economy.[87] In February 1918, Henderson insisted on inviting the CGT as well as the PS to the inter-allied labour and socialist conference in London.[88] The CGT presented a lengthy policy document which included the idea of the *clauses ouvrières*. A comparable but more general statement of principle, drafted by the AFL, was included in the resolutions voted by the subsequent conference in London in September (attended by the AFL as well as the CGT).[89]

Thirdly, and most importantly, 1918 tilted the geographical balance of influence within the IFTU to the west, as English-speaking labour movements (British, American, and dominion) became involved to an unprecedented degree. With the initiative taken by the September 1917 Trades Union Congress in calling for a specifically labour diplomacy, following the fiasco of Stockholm, it was inevitable that the PCTUC would contest the right of the GFTU to represent British trade unionism in the IFTU. The PCTUC had turned down the invitation to the

[86] *La Bataille*, 15 Sept. 1917.

[87] e.g. *Labour and an After War Economic Policy* (Labour Party pamphlet, no. 35, Nov. 1917), and *Economic War after the War* (Oct. 1918), produced by the Labour Party Advisory Committee on International Questions.

[88] See n. 45, above.

[89] *La Voix du peuple*, 1 May 1918.

September 1917 inter-allied trade union conference in London.[90] But on 9 July 1918, stimulated both by the ideas of the CGT and by a visit from an AFL delegation, the PCTUC proposed co-ordinated action between the 'Trade Unions representing the Allied and Neutral countries working in consultation with the colonial organisations', in order to challenge German leadership in a reconstituted trade union international.[91] The conflict with the GFTU erupted at the September 1918 Trades Union Congress. Although a compromise solution of joint representation was agreed, the TUC and its leading figures dominated British participation in international trade unionism during the last months of war and the post-war period.[92]

This TUC initiative was a belated step in the direction taken by the CGT three years earlier. The AFL's interest in international trade union contacts also revived in late 1917 and 1918, but in a rather different sense. In 1916 and early 1917, polarizing American sentiments on the war induced a keen anti-German hostility in the AFL which, on American entry, turned into unqualified commitment to military victory. Additionally, the AFL formulated a broadly Wilsonian peace programme and sketched out a list of international labour reforms loosely akin to those of Leeds and Berne.[93] But the adamant refusal to make any contact with 'enemy' labour leaders before the signature of peace—reminiscent of French and British official trade union attitudes earlier in the war—potentially conflicted with the latter's subsequently more qualified views on labour diplomacy

[90] PCTUC, min. 6 Sept. 1917.

[91] Labour Party Archives, LSI/5/1/3, PCTUC memo, *Proposed International Bureau*; PCTUC, min. 10 July 1918; LPNEC, min. 1918, 256.

[92] PCTUC, min. 4 Sept. 1918; GFTU, *Annual Report*, 1919; Prochaska, *History of the General Federation of Trade Unions*, 135–6, 148–51; Nicholson, *The TUC Overseas*, 22–3. The decisive shift in the locus of British trade union internationalism was marked by the Sept. 1918 inter-allied conference in London, to which the CGT and TUC went as industrial bodies alongside political parties, and from which the GFTU was excluded.

[93] Van Der Slice, *International Labour Diplomacy and Peace*, 141–62; M. Fine, 'French and American Labor: Reformism and the Crucial Years, 1918–1921' (M.A., Wisconsin Madison, Wis., 1967), 2–25; id., 'Syndicalisme et réformisme: Samuel Gompers et le mouvement ouvrier français (1918–1919)', *Le Mouvement social*, 68 (July–Sept. 1969), pp. 3–33.

for a possible negotiated end to the conflict.[94] The AFL condemned the central thrust of the British-led allied labour diplomacy during the final year of the war. Gompers in particular felt that it rendered moderate leaders vulnerable to the 'pro-German' *minoritaires* of the PS and CGT and to the ILP in Britain. Behind these he saw the looming influence of Bolshevism—epitome of the AFL's traditional antipathy to socialism and revolution.[95]

Two AFL delegations, the second led by Gompers himself, visited western Europe in May and September 1918 (with the official blessing of the American government) in order to strengthen the commitment of the French, British, and Italian working classes and labour leaderships to the military effort.[96] Gompers failed to get the September 1918 inter-allied labour and socialist conference in London to repudiate the possibility of an international meeting with the labour leaderships of the Central Powers. But he utilized the obvious desire of the British and French delegates to incorporate the powerful American trade union movement into the councils of inter-allied labour, in order to secure recognition of the AFL's unflinching view of the war as a contest between 'Autocracy and Democracy', in which the continued prosecution of the military effort was central.[97]

The American delegations revealed divergences on strategy from mainstream views in the French and British labour and socialist leaderships, having more in common with the *jusqu'au boutiste* labour right in the two countries. None the less,

[94] Gompers, *Seventy Years of Life and Labour*, ii. 396; AN F₇ 13569, CGT, rep. 15 Feb. 1917 (CGT regret that the AFL had abandoned its earlier commitment to an international labour conference co-terminous with the peace conference). The GFTU shared the AFL's refusal to meet with 'enemy' trade unionists, but was marginalized in 1918 by the Labour Party's and TUC's role in an allied labour diplomacy premissed on just such contact.

[95] Gompers, *Seventy Years of Life and Labour*, ii. 400–7; Fine, 'Syndicalisme et réformisme', 7.

[96] M. Laurent, 'La Conférence des travaillistes franco-américains', *La Clairière*, 1 June 1918, pp. 1015 ff.; P. Dumas, 'Samuel Gompers en Europe', *La Clairière*, 15 Sept. 1918, pp. 1369 ff.; P. Dumas, 'La Délégation américaine à Paris', *La Clairière*, 1 Nov. 1918, pp. 1473 ff.; CGT, *Réceptions de Gompers à la Confédération Générale du Travail, 24 et 26 septembre 1918*; CGT, *Rapports des comités . . . pour l'exercice, 1914–1918*, 87–8; Gompers, *Seventy Years of Life and Labour*, ii. 408–72.

[97] Labour Party Archives, LSI/2/13/18, 'Commission sur "buts de guerre"' (resolutions of Sept. conference); Gompers, *Seventy Years of Life and Labour*, ii. 432–3; Lorwin, *Labor and Internationalism*, 186–7.

American organized labour was recognized through the AFL as a vital element in the plans by moderate allied leaders to influence the peace settlement. And the contacts of 1918 fostered awareness of the nature of organized labour on both sides of the Atlantic and of some of the parallels in domestic post-war planning. Jouhaux, for example, wrote in September 1918 that even though

> our American comrades do not entirely share our view of things [and] are not, like us, imbued with the spirit of class struggle, ... they are perfectly well aware of the shocking inequality of the wage-earning class and, like us, wish to see it abolished.

And he approved of the protective concessions extracted by the AFL from the American government in return for its participation in the economic mobilization.[98]

A certain ideological convergence was even clearer between the CGT and British Labour on post-war reform. As early as September 1916, Jouhaux had expounded his views on the subject to the Trades Union Congress.[99] And in 1918, CGT *majoritaires* were impressed by the reconstruction plans of the Labour Party and TUC.[100] Symptomatic of this common concern with war as the generator of reform was the virtually synonymous publication of Kropotkin's 'Open Letter to the Western Workingmen' in *La Bataille* and in the NUR's *Railway Review* (see p. vii, above). In designating the combined labour movements of the 'west' (in conjunction with those released by the February revolution in Russia) as the agents of post-war economic and social transformation, the celebrated anarchist turned champion of the Entente struck a resonant chord in 'western' labour opinion.

As the war came to an end, the political programme of the allied labour and socialist movements for constructing a 'democratic' peace was matched by a complementary view of economic and labour reforms, summarized by the *clauses ouvrières*

---

[98] *L'Heure*, 28 Sept. 1918; Fine, 'Syndicalisme et réformisme', 24–5.

[99] *Trades Union Congress, Annual Report, 1916*, 289–94.

[100] Jouhaux welcomed Labour's reconstruction programme, and evoked the consensus between the two movements on the possibility of a gradual, peaceful reorganization of capitalism, entrenching the power of organized labour, as a consequence of the war ('La Voix du travail', *La Bataille*, 29 June 1918). See also, M. Laurent, 'Le Mouvement ouvrier britannique dans la guerre', *La Clairière*, 1 May 1918, pp. 926–34.

and by the parallel German programme approved at Berne in October 1917. To the extent that these programmes were intimately connected to domestic post-war reconstruction plans, it is perhaps not surprising that the Labour Party had proved the decisive influence on the one and the CGT on the other. By 1918, the major allied labour organizations had also accepted the idea that labour should both be represented in the official peace negotiations (as part of the national delegations) and seek to influence these by holding a simultaneous international labour conference. With the Armistice signed, French and British labour leaders lobbied their governments for the former. Meanwhile, the international commission appointed at the September 1918 conference in London, to reconvene the Second International when the fighting ended, began its task. Jouhaux, on Henderson's initiative, had been asked on to that committee.[101] But in early January 1919, he invoked the authority of the Paris corresponding bureau approved by the Leeds conference in 1916 to summon a separate but simultaneous trade union congress.[102] The hostility of the French government ruled out Paris as a venue. But as the representatives of the victorious governments negotiated in the French capital in February 1919, the wartime leaders of the international socialist and trade union movements assembled in Berne.

(iii) Between Reaction and Revolution: International Labour Reformism, 1919–1920

The Berne conferences, along with subsequent efforts to re-establish the internationals in 1919–20, were traversed by two sets of tension. The first derived from the wartime hostilities

[101] Labour Party Archives, LSI/3/1; Van Der Slice, *International Labour Diplomacy and Peace*, 309–14.

[102] Jouhaux endorsed the socialist conference but also wished to confirm the autonomy of trade union internationalism with a distinct conference. Oudegeest, on 26 Oct. 1918, sent an exploratory telegramme to IFTU members on a congress at the same time and place as the peace negotiations. But it was Jouhaux who seized the opportunity and formally convoked this meeting (Labour Party Archives, LSI/3/205/1; AN F₇ 13576, CGT, Commission Administrative, 13–14 Jan. 1919, rep. 15 Jan.; Sassenbach, *Twenty-Five Years of International Trade Unionism*, 61–5; Lorwin, *Labor and Internationalism*, 187–8; Van Der Slice, *International Labour Diplomacy and Peace*, 326–7).

between nations. The second came from the divisions engendered or exacerbated by the war within nations and within national labour movements. Though not unimportant, the former was rapidly eclipsed by the latter as the fundamental determinant of the fate of international labour reformism.

War guilt was a predictably bitter issue for labour leaders who, to the end, had accepted the logic of an armed conflict between nations. At Berne, Albert Thomas presented a resolution on behalf of the ex-*majoritaire* French socialists accusing the SPD of complicity in German aggression. The Germans evaded the issue by relocating their own legitimacy in the revolution of November 1918 '[by which] the German proletariat has overthrown and destroyed the old system which was responsible for the war.'[103] This was the minimum shift in the German socialists' position which allied labour diplomacy had unsuccessfully demanded in 1918. The conference agreed that it was sufficient to settle the war guilt issue temporarily and permit the SPD to collaborate in drafting an international socialist peace programme. But when a founding congress for a new Labour and Socialist International was held in Geneva, in July–August 1920, it was still felt necessary, citing the resolutions of Berne and the London inter-allied conference of February 1915, to underline the particular war guilt of Germany and Austria.[104]

Hostility between the former enemies was even more bitter at the Berne trade union conference. The AFL (despite originating the idea in 1914), the GFTU, and the Belgians boycotted the gathering. The CGT delegation considered the minimum price for participation to be the realization of its long-standing desire to remove the international secretariat from Berlin.[105] In

---

[103] *International Labour and Peace. Berne International Labour and Socialist Conference, i. Conference Resolutions; ii. British Delegation, Declaration; iii. Permanent Commission: Amsterdam Resolution, Preliminary Peace Proposals; iv. International Committee of Action: Manifesto; v. British Labour Party: Manifesto* (Labour Party, n.d. but 1919), 3; Van Der Slice, *International Labour Diplomacy and Peace*, 317; Mayer, *Politics and Diplomacy of Peacemaking*, 389.

[104] 'The International Labour and Socialist Congress, Geneva, 1920: The Resolutions', *The Labour Party Local Government, Parliamentary and International Bulletin*, 1/10 (1920), p. 117 (Labour Party Archive, LSI/10/12/1).

[105] *La Bataille*, 5, 6, and 10 Feb. 1919; Sassenbach, *Twenty-Five Years of International Trade Unionism*, 64–5; Van Der Slice, *International Labour Diplomacy and Peace*, 327–31.

fact, the conference decided that the two wartime corresponding bureaux (Paris and Amsterdam) should jointly convene a constituent congress to refound the IFTU and settle the
location of its headquarters.

When that congress was held in Amsterdam, in late July–
early August 1919, the CGT—with the combined weight of the
AFL, GFTU, TUC, and Belgian delegations behind it—
succeeded in permanently relocating the IFTU in the Dutch
city. The occasion was marked by bitter exchanges between the
Belgians and Germans, and also between Jouhaux and Legien,
confronting each other for the first time since Brussels in late
July 1914. Although Legien refused to accept German labour's
complicity in the outbreak of war or in the occupation of
Belgium and deportation of Belgian civilians, a statement
'regretting' the latter was extracted from the Germans, paper-
ing over the issues if not the passions they aroused.[106]

Yet the process of reconciliation was made easier for French
and British labour leaders by their unprecedented prestige and
influence within the post-war internationals. The Labour Party
moved from the periphery of the pre-1914 Second International to the core of the post-war Labour and Socialist International (LSI), whose secretariat in 1920 was moved to London
for several years. The divisions of French and Italian socialism
made the Labour Party the natural partner of the SPD in
reconstructing a socialist international on reformist foundations. The CGT, supported by the TUC, resolved the long-
running battle over the proper scope of a trade union international in favour of its own views when, at the Berne syndicalist
conference, it committed the projected new organization to
shaping the political as well as economic future of post-war
Europe.[107] Possibly helped by the death of Legien in 1920, the
way was open for the British, French, and German movements
to collaborate on a broader and more independent trade union

[106] IFTU, *Compte rendu du congrès syndical international tenu à Amsterdam . . . du
28 juillet au 2 août 1919, précédé par le rapport sur la conférence préliminaire tenue les
25, 26 et 27 juillet 1919, Le Mouvement syndical international,* supplement II, July
1921; Sassenbach, *Twenty-Five years of International Trade Unionism,* 68–70.
[107] *La Bataille,* 6 Feb. 1919; P. Dumas, 'La Conférence syndicale internationale
de Berne', *La Clairière,* 1 Mar. 1919, pp. 1882–3.

internationalism than before the war.[108] And in both bodies, political and trade union, the imperative of demonstrating that labour could achieve within its own ranks the peace of reconciliation which it preached more generally obliged labour leaders to minimize wartime rancour and recrimination.

Hopes that organized labour might make a real impact on the peace settlement were undoubtedly high at Berne, and the two conferences drew on labour's wartime international programmes as the basis for their post-war claims.[109] A League of Nations, composed not of government but parliamentary delegates, according to party strength ('a league of peoples and not a league of governments'), was confirmed as the indispensable means—for socialists and non-socialists alike—of securing the world against war.[110] National self-determination (the product of democracy not nationalism), international arbitration, and disarmament were the chief ingredients of this recipe for international harmony. Although the socialist conference proclaimed that 'the true liberation of the nations will be their liberation from the yoke of capitalism', the goal of a pacific world democracy became the working definition of socialist internationalism.[111]

---

[108] The role of trade unionism in pressing for the reform of the League of Nations as the precondition for safeguarding peace became a central and unquestioned feature of IFTU activity, where before the war anti-militarist questions had been shunned as 'political' (despite CGT objections) (*Premier rapport sur l'activité de la fédération syndicale internationale (juillet 1919–décembre 1921) présenté au congrès ordinaire de Rome, avril 1922, Le Mouvement syndical international*, supplement V, Apr. 1922, 59–62; Sassenbach, *Twenty-Five Years of International Trade Unionism*, 131–4).

[109] Thus Jouhaux was reported as optimistic in late Feb. that a 'supranational labour parliament' might emerge from Versailles (AN F₇ 13576, CGT, Comité Confédéral, min. 24 Feb. 1919), while Luquet believed that 'it is . . . a new world which the international labour office of the Society of Nations will have to organize' ('Pour une législation internationale du travail', *L'Humanité*, 26 Feb. 1919). For accounts of the two Berne conferences, see P. Renaudel, *L'Internationale à Berne: faits et documents* (Grasset, 1919); *Les Résolutions de la conférence internationale ouvrière et socialiste de Berne, 3–10 février 1919* (SFIO, Imprimerie Nouvelle, 1919); *International Labour and Peace. Berne International Labour and Socialist Conference*; CGT, *Rapports des comités . . . pour l'exercice 1918–1919*, 90–148; *Report of the Labour Party Conference, Southport, June 1919*, 3–20 (LPNEC rep.); reps. in *La Bataille* and *L'Humanité*; Van Der Slice, *International Labour Diplomacy and Peace*, 309–42; Mayer, *Politics and Diplomacy of Peacemaking*, 373–409.

[110] *Les Résolutions de la conférence internationale ouvrière et socialiste de Berne*, 3.

[111] *International Labour and Peace. Berne International Labour and Socialist Conference*, 5.

The economic dimension to the peace settlement was stressed both through the attribution of economic functions to the League of Nations in regulating the international economy and through the idea of a Labour Charter. Labour Party advisory committees furnished the British delegation with memoranda on the urgent need to convert the wartime allied partnership into a 'wider system of international economic co-operation'. Such co-operation was to overcome the immediate economic chaos of central Europe and subsequently, as a World Economic Council attached to the League of Nations, to substitute co-operation for competition and to compensate for the inadequacies of the world market by a kind of international state intervention, of which labour legislation would form a part.[112] The CGT took a comparable view, considering that 'the Society of Nations will include the rational and scientific organization of work in all countries, the international allocation of raw materials, and the internationalization of the means of transport and exchange'.[113]

Paralleling the argument on international democracy, the trade union conference's resolution considered that 'the emancipation of the workers cannot be completely realized except by the abolition of the capitalist system itself'. But it proposed economic regulation and 'an international system for fixing labour conditions' as an interim structure for 'lessening the evil' of capitalism, and enabling the industrial worker to 'fulfil his duties as a citizen under modern democracy'. The trade union conference went on to outline a Labour Charter for insertion into the peace treaty—including the eight-hour day, spearhead of national labour reform campaigns in the spring of 1919—which was based on the twin wartime programmes of Leeds and Berne.[114]

The divergence between the Berne conferences and the Big Four allied powers (Three following Italy's defection) over the political settlement rapidly became apparent. The principles

---

[112] Memorandum of Advisory Committee on Trade Policy and Finance (Labour Party Archives, LSI/5/3/1), and *Memorandum on International Labour Legislation and the Economic Structure of the League of Nations*, prepared by various advisory committees (LSI/5/3/2).
[113] *La Bataille*, 10 Feb. 1919.
[114] CGT, *Rapports des comités ... pour l'exercice 1918–1919*, 44–8.

enunciated at the socialist conference were sent to Clemenceau.[115] They were also translated into specific proposals by a meeting in late April, in Amsterdam, of the Permanent Commission set up by the socialist conference.

This meeting demanded self-determination for 'German-Austria', objected to the removal from Germany of German-settled areas in east Prussia and suggested plebiscites in all the disputed segments of the new German-Polish frontier. It repudiated French efforts to separate the Saar or Rhineland from Germany, and proposed that *all* colonies, not just Germany's, should be placed under League of Nations mandate. The principle of reparations was endorsed. But the meeting stressed that these should be economic, finite, and administered by the League of Nations. The League itself was to begin disarmament, engage in compulsory arbitration of international disputes, and have the power to sanction its decisions with international forces.[116]

The Big Three had no interest in hearing such a critique of the actual peace terms which they were drafting on very different criteria, and which they issued as a virtual ultimatum to the German government. They refused in May to receive a socialist delegation, and the Permanent Commission's executive retaliated with a public denunciation of the published peace terms ('this peace is not our peace').[117] Both British Labour (in a manifesto of 1 June, condemning the League as merely 'a restricted instrument of a victorious coalition'), the CGT majority, and the PS condemned the Treaty of Versailles as an extension, not a resolution, of the war.[118]

The divergence between the allied governments and international trade unionism over the economic dimension to the peace settlement was no less severe. Without any prompting from organized labour, the French and British governments agreed to include the kind of international labour questions

[115] Van Der Slice, *International Labour Diplomacy and Peace*, 353–4.

[116] *International Labour and Peace. Berne International Labour and Socialist Conference*, 12–18; *Bulletin de la deuxième internationale*, (May 1919), pp. 1–5; Labour Party Archives, LSI/3/252.

[117] Labour Party Archives, LSI/3/265; *International Labour and Peace. Berne International and Socialist Conference*, 19–20.

[118] Ibid., 21, for Labour Party memorandum on the peace terms; *La Bataille*, 28 May 1919, for the CGT; *L'Humanité*, 9–12 May 1919, for the PS.

considered before the war by the International Association for the Legal Protection of Labour in the peace treaty. Arthur Fontaine, as permanent head of the Ministry of Labour and a prime mover in the pre-war International Association and its French branch, had been preparing the official French position on this since 1917, and he was strongly supported by the British government from the Armistice.[119] Although both governments turned down organized labour's request for direct representation in the plenary peace negotiations, they conceded labour participation in the official delegations to the labour commission—one of a host of subordinate committees beavering away in the late winter and spring of 1919 in obscure corners of Paris (in this case at the Ministry of Labour). Thus Gompers (who, boycotting Berne, set great store by the Paris deliberations), Jouhaux, G. N. Barnes, and Vandervelde, now a minister in the Belgian coalition government, all took part. The defeated powers, as in the main forum of negotiations, were absent.[120]

Within the labour commission, Jouhaux served as the dissonant voice of the Berne trade union conference. Where the conference had planned an 'international ... parliament of labour' with mandatory authority to regulate labour conditions, the International Labour Organization (ILO) envisaged by the commission was far more restricted in its legislative powers. Although the labour view that the defeated states must immediately be included in the ILO, ahead of their entry into the League, was accepted, there was further division over the scope and status of a Labour Charter. Where Jouhaux insisted on the full inclusion of the Berne programme in the peace treaty, a much more limited set of principles was adopted, essentially to guide the first plenary conference of the ILO in drafting international conventions.[121]

---

[119] G. N. Barnes, *History of the International Labour Office* (Williams and Northgate, 1926), 38–48; Shotwell, *The Origins of the International Labor Organization*, i. 83–97, 105–26.

[120] Barnes, however, was not recognized by the Labour Party or TUC as a Labour representative.

[121] Barnes, *History of the International Labour Office*, 42–5; Shotwell, *The Origins of the International Labor Organization*, i. 127–220; Lorwin, *Labor and Internationalism*, 190–1; E. Vandervelde, *Souvenirs d'un militant socialiste* (Éditions Denoël, 1939), 287–9; Gompers, *Seventy Years of Life and Labour*, ii. 490–9.

Part XIII of the Treaty of Versailles, which covered labour issues, thus by no means contained the 'guarantees' sought by trade union leaders at Berne that labour conditions would improve internationally as a result of the war. The CGT executive accepted that the labour commission had endorsed vital issues such as the eight-hour day, but condemned it for entering too timorously on the novel path of international social reform.[122] And at the beginning of August, the bulk of the delegates attending the constituent IFTU congress in Amsterdam (except the AFL and the British representatives) castigated the inadequacy of Versailles by the light of the aspirations of Berne.[123]

By the early summer of 1919, therefore, the brief mood of optimism among moderate labour leaders in the possibility of a reforming Wilsonian peace had evaporated. The Treaty of Versailles had turned out to be largely an exercise in traditional big power diplomacy. Allied military intervention in Russia maintained the spectre of war over a Europe nominally at peace. In conjunction with sharpening domestic industrial conflict, it confirmed fears of a growing mood of political reaction in the French and British governments. At the same time, the founding of the rival Communist International in March 1919 and the revolutionary upheavals in central Europe had placed revolution, not the peace settlement, firmly on the agenda of more radical currents of labour and socialism. Yet this by no means spelt the end of moderate labour's wartime aspirations. Rather, former 'pro-war' leaders elaborated new variants of programme and strategy with the explicit aim of keeping open a middle path, economically and diplomatically, between reaction and revolution, and thus of realizing the reform potential which they considered inherent in the war years.

Before the Armistice, the attitudes of French and British majority labour leaders to the Bolshevik revolution primarily reflected their own preoccupation with the military predicament of the western allies. Reservations were expressed—in the

---

[122] At the Comité Confédéral National in late Mar. (*La Bataille*, 26 Mar. 1919), and late May (*La Bataille*, 28 May 1919).

[123] IFTU, *Compte rendu du congrès syndical international tenu à Amsterdam . . . du 28 juillet au 2 août 1919*, 44–5.

ILP and CGT, for example—on the methods and representativity of the Bolsheviks.[124] Kerensky was welcomed by the Comité Confédéral of the CGT in July 1918 as the real embodiment of the Russian revolution.[125] But the question of allied military intervention in Russia turned principally on the needs of the allied effort against the Germans—especially in the face of Russian withdrawal from the war at Brest-Litovsk.

The Armistice and revolutionary developments in central Europe transformed the significance both of rapidly escalating military intervention by the western allies in Russia and of the Bolshevik revolution itself. The obvious danger that instead of a non-annexationist peace, respecting national self-determination, Europe might experience a prolonged civil war made moderate western labour leaders critical of allied intervention— even if the fiercest opponents were naturally those identifying most closely with Bolshevism as a symbol of their own revolutionary desires. With increasing insistence in 1919–20, the IFTU and the moderate socialists seeking to revive the Second International condemned military intervention as a manifestation of allied 'imperialism' and as a violation of Russian self-determination.[126]

But a Bolshevik Russia whose legitimacy and sovereignty were perforce accepted, even defended, also represented a fundamental threat to moderate labour and socialist leaders—

---

[124] S. R. Graubard, *British Labour and the Russian Revolution, 1917–1924*, (Harvard Univ. Press, Cambridge, Mass., 1956) 44–63; R. Page Arnot, *The Impact of the Russian Revolution in Britain* (Lawrence and Wishart, 1967), 117–20; A. Kriegel, 'L'Opinion publique française et la révolution russe', in V. Fay, *et al.*, *La Révolution d'octobre et le mouvement ouvrier européen* (Études et Documentation Internationale, 1967), 75–104; I. Sinanoglou, 'Frenchmen, their Revolutionary Heritage and the Russian Revolution', *International History Review*, 2/4 (Oct. 1980), pp. 566–84; J.-P. Ménage, 'Les Majoritaires de la CGT et la révolution russe, *1917–1923*' (Maîtrise diss., Paris I, 1981); G. Frischmann, 'La Révolution d'octobre 1917 et les syndicats français', *Cahiers de l'institut CGT d'histoire sociale*, 3 (Dec. 1982), pp. 11–30.

[125] AN F₇ 13576, CGT, Comité Confédéral, 9 July 1918, rep. 11 July.

[126] The CGT condemned allied intervention in Russia at its July 1918 congress (CGT, *19ᵉ Congrès national corporatif . . . (Paris, 15–18 juillet 1918). Compte rendu des travaux*, 261–2). The LPNEC followed suit in September (LPNEC, min. 18 Sept. 1918). The new majority of former *minoritaires* in the Conseil National of the PS condemned allied intervention on 28 July 1918, though the former *majoritaires* were prepared to accept it as part of the military effort against Germany (*L'Humanité*, 30 July 1918). The Sept. 1918 inter-allied labour and socialist conference came out against intervention (Labour Party Archives, LSI/1/29).

especially when it spawned a rival international with a new, schismatic approach to revolution. The issue of 'Democracy and Dictatorship' had already figured on the agenda of the socialist conference at Berne in February 1919. The ex-*majoritaire* French socialists (Renaudel and Thomas) took the lead in attacking the Bolshevik 'dictatorship of the proletariat' and warned of the the danger for the west of any attempt to carry out a violent revolution in conditions of economic disruption. Others wished to suspend judgement (accurate information on Russia was scarce). A compromise majority resolution, drafted by the Swedish leader, Branting, and supported *inter alia* by the French ex-*majoritaires*, Labour, the SPD, and half of the Austrian socialists, rejected the Bolshevik conception of revolution (while also deploring the use made of 'Bolshevism as a bogey' by 'counter-revolutionary forces'), and counter-posed a gradual, reformist approach within a liberal democratic framework.

True socialisation implies methodical development in the different branches of economic activity under the control of democracy. The arbitrary taking over a few concerns by small groups of workers is not Socialism . . .[127]

A minority resolution supported above all by the new French majority and the more radical Austrian socialists (it was drafted by Longuet and Adler) repudiated the majority's condemnation of Bolshevism, and the whole issue was referred to the Permanent Commission.[128] A potential fracture was clear at the very moment of the attempted reunification of the Second International, and although the majority at both Berne conferences undoubtedly still hoped that Bolshevism might be marginalized internationally, the need for an ideological counter-offensive became increasingly urgent.

The IFTU congress in Amsterdam, early in August 1919, and the meeting of the Permanent Commission of the Berne socialist conference, held at the same period in Lucerne, were thus equally preoccupied with defining attitudes to the peace settlement and to Bolshevism. A minority at the socialist

[127] *International Labour and Peace. Berne International Labour and Socialist Conference*, 6; Mayer, *Politics and Diplomacy of Peacemaking*, 400–5.
[128] *International Labour and Peace. Berne International Labour and Socialist Conference*, 7.

meeting was openly pessimistic at the possibility of revising the peace treaty. Rejecting all compromise with 'bourgeois parties', it defined the international's duty as being to use the 'revolutionary situations created by the war in order to gain and exercise political power everywhere for the realisation of socialism and the abolition of classes'.[129]

But the clear majority at both gatherings agreed to accept Versailles as a starting-point for peace and to work for its comprehensive revision. This meant turning the League of Nations into a 'league of peoples' and, for the socialists, redrafting the territorial provisions of Versailles. The IFTU congress emphasized the inadequacy of the 'Labour Charter', demanding the integral application of the Berne programme of February 1919. But it agreed to work through the ILO and to participate in the latter's founding conference in Washington, scheduled for September and finally held in October–November 1919.[130]

At the same time, both conferences affirmed their belief in the moral and political bankruptcy of the existing economic order and proposed, as a more-or-less explicit alternative to violent revolution and the 'dictatorship of the proletariat', the progressive socialization of the means of production. The IFTU congress stressed that socialization, for its success, required 'normal production, scientifically and progressively developed', and instructed the IFTU executive to effect an extensive enquiry into past and current socialization experiments (a delegation was sent to Russia to that end). The socialist meeting equally envisaged that the opening congress of the new socialist international (scheduled for Geneva in February 1920) would prepare 'plans for socialisation in view of the struggle upon which the world has now definitely entered between proletariat and capitalist power'. Additionally, that congress was to consider 'the forms of democracy and representative institutions'

[129] *The International at Lucerne, 1919: The Resolutions. The Provisional Constitution* (Labour Party, 1919), 5–7; 'The International', *New Statesman*, 9 Aug. 1919, pp. 461–2.

[130] *The International at Lucerne*, 3–5; IFTU, *Compte rendu du congrès syndical international tenu à Amsterdam ... du 28 juillet au 2 août 1919*, 44–52; IFTU, *Premier rapport sur l'activité de la fédération syndicale internationale (juillet 1919–décembre 1921)*, 27–33.

and the 'place of revolutions in the transformation of Society'.[131]

It would be too easy to see this merely as a rhetorical response to Bolshevism and to the surge of revolutionary sentiment and activity in central, and even western, Europe in the spring and summer of 1919. The spectre of political breakdown and economic chaos which Bolshevism symbolized was ideologically and temperamentally abhorrent to moderate labour and socialist leaders. It was precisely what their entire approach to post-war planning had sought to avoid. The transition which they envisaged was to be achieved by peaceful, continuous reconstruction. Antagonism to Bolshevism simply emphasized an approach rooted in the 'choice of 1914' as this had been variously experienced in the different combatant societies. There is no reason to suppose that Huysmans, for example, was posturing when, in a private circular sent to socialist leaders by the ISB in November 1919 to prepare the Geneva congress, he stated:

> There exists no difference of opinion within the international Socialist and Labour movement as to the fact that the war has sealed the fate of the capitalist system as we knew it before the war ...[132]

But internationally as domestically, socialism was to proceed via new forms of 'organized capitalism' and encroaching working class influence.

This double-edged programme—political and economic revision of the June 1919 peace-settlement and socialization of the means of production—thus had the dual function from the summer of 1919 of reformulating the claims of international labour on governments while furnishing an ideological counter-project to violent revolution broadly inspired—or symbolized—by Bolshevism.[133] In both respects, this international dimension served as a paradigm of the assumptions which had

[131] IFTU, *Compte rendu du congrès syndical international tenu à Amsterdam ... du 28 juillet au 2 août 1919*, 53; *The International at Lucerne, 1919*, 3; *Rapport du secrétariat international au congrès international de Genève, le 31 juillet 1920* (Internationale Ouvrière et Socialiste, Imprimerie Coopérative Lucifer, Brussels, 1920), 1; J. Wrynn, *The Socialist International and the Politics of European Reconstruction, 1919–1930* (Graduate Press, Uithoorn, 1976), 30–1.

[132] Labour Party Archives, LSI/19/2/5, circular of 21 Nov. 1919.

[133] See Bibliography, Secondary Works, part 2.

underlain labour reformism in the French and British labour movements during the war. The two internationals were seen as pressure groups, seeking to perfect the nascent institutions of democracy, political and economic, on a world scale. Politically, the revision of the peace depended on the strengthening of the League of Nations itself, which in turn could only be achieved by the democratic accession of socialism to power nationally. The domestic preoccupation with the electoral path was thus translated on to the international plane. As the founding congress of the Labour and Socialist International resolved when it finally met in Geneva, in July–August 1920:

The International Socialist Congress ... calls upon the national Labour and Socialist Parties to secure the entry of their delegates to the League as organised at present ... so as to change the constitution from within and extend its powers, in order that the League may guarantee the security and harmony of all nations ...[134]

Economically, both the LSI and the IFTU envisaged the League operating as an international interventionist state to effect the physical and economic reconstruction of Europe, and to resolve the gathering reparations crisis in 1920–2, both of which were seen as preconditions for basic changes in the organization of national economies. 'The new system of economy', declared Jouhaux in opening the second IFTU congress in London, in November 1920, 'must be based on the abolition of armaments, the international distribution of raw materials, and the socialisation of the means of production'.[135] The ILO was seen specifically as the instrument of international social reform. The CGT *majoritaires*, in particular, considered it a vast international *commission paritaire* on the tripartite model, through which reforms could be secured and defended. Jouhaux, along with Arthur Fontaine and the young Jean Monnet, French socialist and assistant secretary of the League of Nations, was instrumental in getting Albert Thomas made first

---

[134] 'The International Labour and Socialist Congress, Geneva, 1920', 118.

[135] IFTU, *Report of the Special International Trades Union Congress held in the Throne Room, Holborn Restaurant, November 22nd to 27th 1920*, (IFTU, London, 1921), 7; L. Jouhaux, *La Fédération syndicale internationale et la réorganisation économique* (IFTU, Amsterdam, 1922); B. Georges, D. Tintant, and M.-A. Renauld, *Léon Jouhaux dans le mouvement syndical français* (Presses Universitaires de France, 1979), 44–71.

director of the permanent International Labour Office in
Geneva.[136] The general decline in industrial productivity during and after the war—the optimistic productivism of the CGT
notwithstanding—meant that any shift of political and economic circumstances in favour of employers was likely to
produce a counter-attack on labour reforms conceded for
mainly political reasons. As this occurred in 1920, the IFTU
mounted a campaign for the international defence of the
accords signed at the first ILO conference in November 1919—
and especially the eight-hour day—which it conducted in part
through the ILO itself.[137]

The issue of socialization of the means of production elevated
to the international plane a fundamental dimension of
reformism which, during the war, had remained confined to
national movements and their thinking on domestic post-war
change. In December 1919, the ISB set up commissions on
'Socialization' and the 'political form of socialism' in preparation for the founding congress of the LSI.[138] The congress, in
July–August 1920, was dominated by the British, the Germans,
and the Dutch Social Democrats.[139]

The Dutch particularly influenced the resolution on socialization (with a carefully prepared report, itself influenced by
Otto Bauer and Austrian socialist thinking on socialization in
1919), though the resolution also incorporated statements from
Labour (drafted by the Webbs) and the SPD.[140] The resolution

[136] IFTU, *Premier rapport sur l'activité de la fédération syndicale internationale
(juillet 1919–décembre 1921)*, 27–36; *The International Trade Union Review*, I/I
(Jan. 1921), pp. 7–8; L. Jouhaux, *L'Organisation internationale du travail* (La
Sirène, 1921); Fine, 'French and American Labor', 63–5.

[137] ILO, *Enquiry into Production, Introductory Memorandum*, (Bastable, 1920), 5–
10; IFTU, *Enquiry on the Eight Hours Day* (1922); G. Lefranc, *Les Expériences
syndicales internationales: des origines à nos jours* (Aubier, 1952), 29–30.

[138] *Rapport du secrétariat international au congrès international de Genève, le 31
juillet 1920*, 3–5, 24–5; Horne, 'L'Idée de nationalisation dans les mouvements
ouvriers européens jusqu'à la deuxième guerre mondiale', 16–27.

[139] 'The International Labour and Socialist Congress Geneva, 1920. The Resolutions'; *X^e congrès international socialiste et ouvrier, Genève, 1920. Compte rendu*
(ISB, Brussels, 1921); ILO, *The Congress of the Labour and Socialist International
(Geneva, July 31st–August 6th 1920)* (1920); Labour Party Archives, LSI/10/1/8,
typescript notes on Geneva proceedings (51 pp.); Wrynn, *The Socialist International and the Politics of European Reconstruction*, 32–3.

[140] ILO, *The Congress of the Labour and Socialist International*, 10; Labour Party
Archives, LSI/9/14, file with various socialization reports presented to the congress.

on the 'political system of socialism' was abstracted by the Webbs from their *Constitution for the Socialist Commonwealth of Great Britain*, which had been written as a preparatory document for the congress and circulated (in synopsis) to all the delegations.[141] Together, the two resolutions formed a manifesto of gradualist socialism in contradistinction to Bolshevism. They declared the bankruptcy of capitalism, but emphasized the progressive nature of its replacement by a collectively owned economy, in order to preserve living standards. Socialization of the most monopolistic industries in a tripartite form, maintaining a role for managers alongside workers, together with state and consumers' representatives, and with compensation for shareholders, was to be the instrument for superseding capitalism. The essential framework was to be parliamentary democracy with a socialist majority. The defensive use of 'direct action' was allowed, doubtless in recognition of the defeat by a general strike of the Kapp Putsch in Germany. But 'terrorism' (Bolshevism) was condemned, along with 'any tendency to convert an industrial strike automatically into political revolution' (i.e. revolutionary syndicalism).[142]

Socialization was no less important for the IFTU, especially at its second, London, congress in November 1920. Gompers and the AFL had withdrawn from the federation, in part over the commitment to socialization made in August 1919, thus marking the difference (despite overlapping concerns and strategies) between the narrower perspectives of Gompers's business unionism and variants of European trade union reformism.[143] There was broad support at the London congress for a resolution which demanded the progressive socialization 'of all branches of production which in the estimation of the proletariat of every country is realisable', starting with the

---

[141] Labour Party Archives, LSI/9/14/11, 'Socialisation and the Political System of Socialism'; B. and S. Webb, *A Constitution for the Socialist Commonwealth of Great Britain* (1920; repr. CUP, Cambridge, 1975), esp. introd. by S. Beer, pp. ix–xxxiii.

[142] 'The International Labour and Socialist Congress, Geneva, 1920. The Resolutions', 'The Political System of Socialism', 121.

[143] IFTU, *Premier rapport sur l'activité de la fédération syndicale internationale (juillet 1919–décembre 1921)*, 17–18; Lorwin, *Labor and Internationalism*, 263–70; cf. Fine, 'Syndicalisme et réformisme', 31–2, who emphasizes the similarity of Gompers's and Jouhaux's orientations.

mines, and in a manner entailing the 'active participation of the whole population in industrial and national control, exercised in conjunction with the appropriate Trade Unions.' Again, the Dutch labour movement played a key role in formulating the proposal. But its tenor was in complete harmony with the wartime thinking of the CGT.[144]

Despite the euphoria of rising numbers in 1919–20—especially apparent in the IFTU, peaking at over three times its pre-war maximum with twenty-three million in 1919—the unity on which the hopes of moderate labour and socialist leaders were premissed was the first casualty of the political polarization following the birth of the Comintern and the signing of the peace.[145] The schism, moreover, was not two, but threefold, as substantial numbers of socialists broke with reformism in the name of a revolutionary ideal but remained cautious (and sometimes hostile) towards Bolshevism and the Third International. This was especially the case with some of the new French socialist majority, the German Independent Social Democrats, and the Austrian socialists—for whom revolutionary events in Vienna and Germany were as significant as those in Moscow. Herein lay the roots of the Vienna International, as well as of adherence to Moscow, following the withdrawal of the above elements from the Berne organization in the winter of 1919–20.[146]

Trade union unity was more resilient—partly because the primary communist emphasis was on political rather than industrial schism. For this reason, the IFTU saw itself as the custodian of moderate reformism in 1920, and took over the organization of May Day from the fractured socialist international with the twin slogan of 'socialization' and the 'Washington (ILO) accords'.[147] But by mid-1921, the first congress of

[144] *Report of the Special International Trades Union Congress . . . November 22nd to 27th 1920*, 55–6; 'Le Congrès syndical international, Londres, 22–28 novembre', *L'Information ouvrière et sociale*, 9 Dec. 1920, 7; Lorwin, *Labor and Internationalism*, 208–9.

[145] Sassenbach, *Twenty-Five Years of International Trade Unionism*, 79.

[146] Union des Partis Socialistes pour l'Action Internationale, *Textes des résolutions prises à la conférence socialiste de Vienne (22–27 février 1921)* (n.p., n.d.); Lindemann, *The 'Red Years'*, 249–86.

[147] *The International Trade Union Review*, I/I (Jan. 1921), pp. 13–14; Lorwin, *Labor and Internationalism*, 233–4.

the Moscow Red International of Labour Unions had confirmed the schism of international trade unionism as well.

Yet, ironically perhaps, it was the very fact of division and schism, along with the frustration of moderate labour's immediate post-war hopes, which produced the fullest international expressions of the distinctive labour reformism which the war itself had generated.

9 The Reckoning: L'Après-guerre and the Longer-Term Legacy

THE significance of the post-war future for French and British labour reformism during the war made demobilization the moment of reckoning. It was the test both of the power acquired by organized labour and of the relevance of the reformist orientation to working-class aspirations.

Demobilization, in the broadest sense, was nearly as complex a process as the wartime mobilization had been. The disbanding of vast armies, with the risk of unemployment and disaffection among returned servicemen, was central. But as labour leaders had long emphasized, demobilization was also an industrial process. The question here was whether wartime state intervention would be jettisoned, retained for an interim period, or permanently adapted to the purposes of peace. This raised the even more fundamental issue of whether the state would act to modify relations between economic interests and social groups as a consequence of the war. Government economic policy and the balance of political forces which determined it were thus of critical concern to labour leaders.

At the same time, inflation continued and even accelerated in both countries, while the needs of peacetime economic conversion, plus physical reconstruction in France, absorbed the demobilized with un-anticipated ease, sustaining a buoyant labour market down to the second half of 1920.[1] Peacetime industrial relations were thus resumed in the context of substantially the same economic pressures which had fuelled

---

[1] Créhange, *Chômage et placement*, 82; D. Aldcroft, *The Inter-War Economy: Britain 1919–1939* (Batsford, 1970), 31–5.

industrial unrest in 1917–18. The years 1915–20, as we have noted, marked a peak of labour militancy in both countries.[2]

Just as there was also a political mobilization (and self-mobilization) of opinion behind the war, so there was a corresponding dimension to the demobilization process. The peace-settlement with Germany antagonized labour in part because it defined deeper differences over the purpose and significance of the war itself. But other questions, such as the burden of war debts, measures for returned servicemen, social and labour reforms, and women's suffrage, translated the wartime service by various groups, and their sense of reciprocal national obligation, into post-war claims for recompense.

Understood in this sense, the conversion from war to peace was many-sided and its duration varied between sector and society.[3] The fate of labour's reform plans during this *après-guerre* period represented the culmination of war reformism as a phenomenon and was retrospectively revealing about some of its characteristics and limitations.

(i) From Hope to Disillusion: Organized Labour and the Demobilization Process

The most fundamental constraint on moderate labour in France and Britain during the post-war period was its exclusion from government. Whereas in defeated Germany and Austria, the process of political transformation furnished socialist leaders in power with certain opportunities for reform, political developments in victorious France and Britain consolidated the forces of conservatism. Although the elections of December 1918 in Britain and November 1919 in France increased the absolute and proportionate size of the Labour and socialist votes, the number of deputies remained small. It actually fell from 103 to 64 in the case of the PS, due to a change in the electoral system.

---

[2] See pp. 8–10, above.
[3] J. A. Dowie, '1919–20 is in Need of Attention', *Economic History Review*, 27/3 (1975), pp. 429–50; *Geschichte und Gesellschaft*, 9 (1983), special no. on demobilization in Europe after the First World War.

And although the number of Labour MPs rose, the principal socialist leaders (including Henderson and MacDonald) lost their seats. But in any case, both parties shunned participation in a coalition government, even had this been possible.[4] They were thus inevitably excluded from office during the critical transition from war to peace.

It therefore appeared virtually from the outset in both countries that labour influence on the demobilization process depended essentially on the same approach as wartime reformism—lobbying, dialogue with the more progressive, reforming elements of government, campaigns to influence public opinion, and the unshackled potential of industrial organization and action, as wartime constraints on the labour force were gradually dismantled. Both the emergency Labour Party conference in November 1918 and the PCTUC made it clear that Labour was to use its role in parliamentary opposition, if it failed to win the election, to push demobilization in the direction of its larger reform plans.[5] The subsequent string of Labour Party successes in by-elections down to 1921, especially that of Henderson at Widnes in August 1919, confirmed the Labour leadership in this approach.[6]

Although limited co-operation between the CGT and PS continued, both in the Commission Mixte d'Études Économiques and through socialist legislative proposals in the Chambre des Députés, the crucial failure in 1916 to construct durable organizational links or joint post-war programmes meant that the CGT confronted the demobilization on the basis of syndicalist autonomy, without any parliamentary strategy (significantly, the *Programme minimum* made no reference to the nature of the state).[7] This approach was confirmed by worsening relations with the PS after the moderate socialist *minoritaires* triumphed in October 1918.

---

[4] G. Ziebura, *Léon Blum et le parti socialiste, 1872–1934* (Presses de la Fondation Nationale des Sciences Politiques, 1967), 152.

[5] *Report of the Labour Party Conference, Southport, June 1919*, Append. V, 184; PCTUC, *Quarterly Reports*, Dec. 1918, p. 2; *L'Humanité*, 16 Jan. 1919 (interview with Henderson).

[6] LPNEC, min. 1919, 268–70 (for Widnes); M. Cowling, *The Impact of Labour, 1920–1924* (CUP, Cambridge, 1971), 25; C. Howard, 'Expectations Born to Death', 65–6.

[7] Robert, 'Les "Programmes minimum" de la CGT de 1918 et 1921', 61.

Despite these political constraints, initial optimism about labour's capacity to shape the demobilization process was as high domestically as internationally. In both countries, labour leaderships sought through the winter of 1918–19 to relate specific (and comparable) demobilization demands to more permanent reconstruction perspectives. The CGT campaigned on a set of points derived from the *Programme minimum*. Central were the eight-hour day (recompense for working-class 'sacrifice' and pivot of syndicalist productivism) and the Conseil National Économique.[8] The latter translated the wartime experience of participation in economic regulation through *commissions paritaires* into a potential instrument for planning and controlling the national economy—'both for the demobilisation and for the rapid readjustment of war production to peace production'. Composed of labour and business representatives, technical advisers (such as engineers), and government delegates, it was to co-ordinate five basic aspects of the economy (transport, production, raw materials, retooling, and the labour supply), and thus to supplant a *laissez-faire* capitalism deemed incapable of avoiding post-war chaos.[9]

Additionally, the CGT demanded protection of real wages against inflation, social welfare measures, and a political amnesty for the strikers arrested in 1918.[10] Little emphasis was placed at this point on nationalization—it had figured in the *Programme minimum* in the vague form of 'the return to the Nation of national riches'—since a measure of general control over the economy seemed more urgent in view of demobilization. But individual federations, notably the *cheminots*, pursued the issue.[11]

CGT leaders gained wide press publicity for these ideas, and after intense lobbying of ministers and parliament, appeared to win some acceptance for them in government circles. Clemenceau assured Jouhaux immediately after the Armistice that he

---

[8] See p. 217, above.

[9] CGT, *Rapports des comités ... pour l'exercice 1918–1919*, 31, 49–51; L. Jouhaux, 'Organisation', *L'Information ouvrière et sociale*, 21 Nov. 1918.

[10] CGT, *Rapports des comités ... pour l'exercice 1918–1919*, 51; AN F₇ 13576, rep 13 Jan.; *La Bataille*, 1 and 13 Jan. 1919.

[11] *La Tribune des cheminots*, 1 Jan. 1919; *La Bataille*, 1 Feb. 1919, for the delegate conference which adopted the executive resolution calling for nationalization.

favoured the eight-hour day and adequate protection for
workers during demobilization, and in late December he lis-
tened sympathetically to syndicalist ideas on the Conseil National Économique.[12] A police report in January 1919 commented on the optimism of the CGT leaders that the wartime
role of the working class would be recognized by the eight-hour
day and union rights for civil servants, while the Conseil
National Économique was felt to have 'the assent of parliament
and the government'.[13]

In Britain, the differences in perspective between the Labour
Party, the PCTUC, and individual trade unions meant that
there was no single lobbying programme comparable to that of
the CGT. None the less, there was an underlying unity of
approach.[14] Restoration of pre-war 'customs', and hence the
defence of established positions, was of course strategically
pivotal for the bulk of trade unionists, and endorsed by the
Labour Party. After prolonged government equivocation and
employer opposition, the promise of restoration was honoured
by parliament in August 1919, and pre-war practices were
generally reinstated.[15] Continued state regulation of industrial
production in order to sustain employment was equally central.
This meant not only the conversion of the 'national' factories to
peace production and public works programmes (notably
house-building on a massive scale) but also the retention of
broad state planning of industry.[16] Railway and coal nationalization were generally considered by the Labour Party to be
crucial to the orderly conversion to a peace economy. But it was
the MFGB which set the pace on coal nationalization, successfully balloting its members on, and threatening the new Lloyd

---

[12] AN F$_7$ 13576, CGT, Comité Confédéral, 14 Nov. 1918 (rep. 16 Nov.); *Le
Radical*, 3 Jan. 1919 (rep. of meeting of 31 Dec.); CGT, *Rapports des comités . . .
pour l'exercice 1918–1919*, 51.

[13] AN F$_7$ 13576, rep. 23 Jan. 1919.

[14] Gleason, *What the Workers Want*, 18–24, for a perceptive view of these
divisions. For Labour views on demobilization, see *The Labour Year Book* (1919);
LPNEC, min. 1919; PCTUC, min. 1919; *Report of the Labour Party Conference,
Southport, June 1919* (rep. of the LPNEC); *Trades Union Congress, Annual Report,
September 1919* (rep. of the PCTUC).

[15] LPNEC, min. 1919, 185.

[16] Ibid., 63; *The Labour Year Book* (1919), 158–97; *Report of the Labour Party
Conference, Southport, June 1919* (LPNEC rep.), 51.

George government with, a strike to secure it.[17] Continued state regulation was demanded to protect wages and to secure food supplies at controlled prices, through the Ministry of Food. And although less prominent than in the CGT as an official demand, reduction in work-time became the focus of a multi-form, often unofficial, strike-movement in early 1919, spear-headed by engineering and shipbuilding workers and by certain key localities, notably Glasgow and Belfast.[18]

The British government, pressured by industrial unrest, also apparently yielded some ground to labour demands in late February 1919. Under the ultimatum of a miners' strike, it conceded the Sankey Royal Commission on the organization of the coal industry (in which the MFGB was persuaded to participate), and the cabinet seemed to commit itself in advance to the commission's pronouncement, even if this ran to nationalization.[19] Sidney Webb optimistically declared in late March, on the basis of Sankey and a government bill to reorganize the railways, that '[in] all probability the mines, railways and canals would be publicly owned before the end of another year'.[20]

Additionally, the government instituted an experimental National Industrial Conference on 27 February, with some 900 trade unionists and industrialists. The idea had originated towards the end of the war in the NAEE and in the Ministry of Labour under G. H. Roberts. More limited than the CGT's idea of a Conseil National Économique, in that it was less concerned with overall planning than with industrial relations and fostering 'co-operation between capital and labour', it was intended by Lloyd George and Robert's successor, Sir Robert Horne, to pursue the Whitley idea by creating a constitution for industrial self-regulation. To this end, the conference established a Provisional Joint Committee. Although the ASE and

[17] Orton, *Labour in Transition*, 217–21; Page Arnot, *The Miners: Years of Struggle*, 220–5.

[18] Askwith, *Industrial Problems and Disputes*, 465, 468–70; Clegg, *A History of British Trade Unions since 1889*, ii. 270–4.

[19] Orton, *Labour in Transition*, 218–19; S. M. H. Armitage, *The Politics of Decontrol in Industry: Britain and the United States* (Weidenfeld and Nicolson, 1969), 116–28. B. Webb deduced from a conversation with Tom Jones that the Commission was designed by the government to find against nationalization (M. I. Cole (ed.), *Beatrice Webb's Diaries, 1912–24*, 147).

[20] *Fabian News*, May 1919.

Triple Alliance unions were conspicuously absent, leaders of both the Labour Party and the PCTUC (including Henderson) cautiously participated.[21]

Yet this apparent susceptibility of both governments to labour leaders' views on the broad demobilization process turned out, by and large, to be an optical illusion. It is true that the spectre of discontented returned servicemen and unemployed munitions workers was a sobering one. The stirrings of mutiny among soldiers and sailors angry at the slow pace of demobilization, plus the strikes of the beginning of 1919 in Britain, pushed the two governments into a pragmatic, relatively generous response.[22] In both cases, a temporary 'dole' was instituted and prolonged for most of 1919. For British demobilized servicemen it was extended to March 1921, while their French counterparts received a substantial lump sum based on length and type of service.[23] These measures, plus massive pressure on women and, in France, immigrants, to quit their wartime jobs, along with the upturn of industrial production from mid-1919, moderated the impact of unemployment.[24] Within a year of the Armistice, over four million men had been

[21] *The Times*, 28 Feb. and 5 Mar. 1919; *Unity* (organ of the NAEE), Mar., Apr., and Nov. 1919; *Report of the National Industrial Conference . . . 4 April 1919*, Cmd. 139; Gleason, *What the Workers Want*, 70–8, 371–90; Orton, *Labour in Transition*, 171–2; Johnson, *Land Fit for Heroes*, 376–84, 473–7; R. Lowe, 'The Failure of Consensus in Britain: The National Industrial Conference, 1919–1921', *Historical Journal*, 21/3 (1978), pp. 649–75; Middlemas, *Politics in Industrial Society*, 139–40.

[22] The French government, from the start, had liberated soldiers on the strictly egalitarian basis of their original call-up year by order of seniority, despite the CGT's demand for an 'economic' demobilization, with key categories of workers being released first. Significantly, the socialists approved the 'Jacobin' justice of the government's approach. The British government, by contrast, attempted just such an 'economic' approach before serious unrest forced it to switch to the French solution (AN F_7 13576, rep. 18 Jan. 1919; A. Prost, 'Die Demobilmachung, der Staat und die Kriegsteilnehmer in Frankreich', in *Geschichte und Gesellschaft*, 9 (1983), pp. 178–94; C. L. Mowat, *Britain between the Wars, 1918–1940* (Univ. of Chicago Press, Chicago, Ill., 1955), 22–3).

[23] Ministère du Travail, *Mesures tendant à maintenir l'activité nationale pendant la démobilisation* (Imprimerie Nationale, 1919); Créhange, *Chômage et placement*, 82; Prost, 'Die Demobilmachung'; Orton, *Labour in Transition*, 186–7; Wolfe, *Labour Supply and Regulation*, 301–2; Montgomery, *British and Continental Labour Policy*, chap. 24; Clegg, *A History of British Trade Unions since 1889*, ii. 239–42.

[24] Nogaro and Weil, *La Main-d'œuvre étrangère et coloniale*, 27–8, 57; McMillan, *Housewife or Harlot*, 159–60; Thébaud, *La Femme au temps de la guerre de 1914*, 287–91; G. Braybon, *Women Workers in the First World War* (Croom Helm, 1981), 173–215.

demobilized in each country without unemployment rising significantly above pre-war levels.[25] Both governments also continued some controls on the supply and prices of key foodstuffs. But such measures had no significance beyond the demobilization itself. When it came to the critical issue of how to reactivate the peacetime economy, the divergence between government and reformist labour leaders gradually became apparent.

Initially Loucheur, in his capacity as minister of Industrial Reconstruction (as the armaments ministry now became), together with certain leaders of heavy industry, had shown some sympathy for the use of state arsenals and factories for economic reconstruction. This was partly to retain a munitions capacity until the formal signature of the peace.[26] The Sénat, the conservative press, and the bulk of business opinion, however, were overwhelmingly hostile to the idea, as they were to any delay in decontrolling the economy. By early 1919, Loucheur, though envisaging a limited co-ordinating role for the state, was re-emphasizing his underlying belief in private enterprise, and this dominated subsequent official policy. In mid-February, in a speech to the Chambre des Députés, he declared a 'hymn to production' based on private enterprise and decontrolling the economy as quickly as feasible. A month later, he told the Sénat 'that it would constitute an economic mistake to transform the state establishments into veritable competitors of private industry'.[27] The only alternative voice in government—Clémentel at the Ministry of Commerce, who favoured a continuing, interventionist role for the state in regulating foreign trade and reorganizing production—was rapidly marginalized.[28]

---

[25] M. Huber, *La Population de la France pendant la guerre* (Presses Universitaires de France, 1931), 471; S. R. Graubard, 'Military Demobilization in Great Britain following the First World War', *Journal of Modern History*, 19/4 (1947), p. 309; ILO, *Enquête sur la production* (Berger-Lavrault, 1923–5), vol. iv, pt. 2, 320, 413–20.

[26] Notably Pinot and De Peyerimhoff. Ministère du Travail, *Comité permanent d'études relatives à la prévision des chômages industriels*, 64–7; Carls, 'Louis Loucheur', 311–13.

[27] *Journal officiel, chambre des députés, débats parlementaires*, 14 Feb. 1919, 636–46; *L'Information ouvrière et sociale*, 20 Feb. 1919; AN 94 AP 367 (typescript of Albert Thomas on reconstruction developments, for the quote to the Sénat). In Feb., Loucheur set up, and then ignored, a committee on the future of state factories (Carls, 'Louis Loucheur', 328).

[28] Kuisel, *Capitalism and the State in Modern France*, 51–7.

In Britain, the Ministry of Munitions also eliminated state contracts in the munitions and engineering industry as rapidly as possible rather than using them, along with 'national' factories and shipyards, to guide the transition to peace production.[29] Sir Robert Horne paralleled Loucheur in stating to the National Industrial Conference on 27 February that the only means of reactivating the economy 'was to restore confidence in private enterprise'.[30] The cabinet generally, despite certain differences over timing, favoured the return to full private enterprise, with the possibility of an element of permanent state regulation lingering only over a few sectors, such as coal, shipping and railways.

Inevitably, in these circumstances, any government interest in a major role for trade unions in running a controlled economy evaporated. The CGT's Comité Confédéral National of late March condemned the government's failure to create new bodies with syndicalist representation to reconstruct the devastated regions (these were still being demanded in 1921).[31] Already in late February, the Chambre des Députés had rejected a socialist resolution in favour of the CGT's conception of the Conseil National Économique by 396 to 51, approving instead a proposal that any Conseil National Économique should merely help the government to 'hasten the return to normal life'.[32] When, under pressure from a threatened strike in mid-July, the government produced its own plan for a Conseil National Économique, it followed suit by proposing an extremely limited and purely advisory body, attached to the ministries concerned with economic policy.[33]

---

[29] R. H. Tawney, 'The Abolition of Economic Controls, 1918–21', *Economic History Review*, 13/1–2 (1943), pp. 1–30; Armitage, *The Politics of Decontrol in Industry*, 14–15.

[30] *The Times*, 28 Feb., 1919.

[31] *Rapports des comités ... pour l'exercice 1918–1919*, 62–3; Conseil Économique du Travail, *Rapport de la commission d'enquête du Conseil Économique du Travail dans les régions dévastées* (Jan. 1921), 39; L. Jouhaux, 'The French Trade Union Movement and the Reconstruction of the Devastated Areas', *International Trade Union Movement*, 2/5 (Sept.–Oct. 1922), pp. 249–56.

[32] AN F₇ 13576, rep. 2 Mar. 1919; *Journal officiel, chambre des députés, débats parlementaires*, 28 Feb. 1919, p. 939.

[33] *La Bataille*, 18 July 1919; *Rapports des comités ... pour l'exercice 1918–1919*, 123.

In Britain, the conflict with Labour views reached its peak in the Sankey Commission. Labour's cross-examination of the coal owners was conducted almost as a microcosm of the new alignments in the party by Smillie, Frank Hodges, the Syndicalist-influenced secretary of the MFGB, and Herbert Smith, president of the Yorkshire Federation, for the miners, and Webb, R. H. Tawney, and the radical Liberal convert, Sir Leo Chiozza Money, as their economic experts. Wartime service and sacrifice were frequently cited in making both a moral and a 'business' case for nationalization. But the ambiguity created in June by the commission's four reports, with a bare majority approving nationalization through two different reports (Sankey endorsing state ownership, the miners' report advocating a form of worker participation), allowed the government to withdraw from its initial undertaking, and reject nationalization outright in August.[34] The passage of the Ministry of Ways and Communication Act equally dashed all hope of railway nationalization.[35]

The rejection in both countries of anything remotely resembling labour views on the economic demobilization left social questions and industrial relations as the principal fields in which the labour movements might exert sufficient pressure to extract long-term reform. Here the reduction in work-time was a central issue. The eight-hour day, a traditional labour demand, had been the object of renewed interest by the CGT and TUC before the war, and of active campaigning by several trade unions in each country.[36] The war itself accentuated the significance of reduced hours because of widespread work fatigue and because of the emphasis placed by both munitions

[34] Coal Industry Commission (1919), Cmd. 210 (reps.) and Cmd. 359–61 (mins., evidence, and appends.); Gleason, *What the Workers Want*, 33–55, for an eyewitness account; G. D. H. Cole, *Chaos and Order in Industry* (Methuen, 1920), 62–85; Page Arnot, *The Miners: Years of Struggle*, 203–23; Armitage, *The Politics of Decontrol in Industry*, 125–8.

[35] Armitage, *The Politics of Decontrol in Industry*, 68–73.

[36] Clegg, *A History of British Trade Unions since 1889*, ii. 112; G. Cross, 'The Quest for Leisure: Reassessing the Eight Hour Day in France', *Journal of Social History*, 18 (Winter 1984), pp. 195–216; id., 'Les Trois Huit; Labor Movements, International Reform and the Origins of the Eight Hour Day, 1919–1924', *French Historical Studies*, 14/2 (1985), pp. 240–68; id., *A Quest for Time*, chaps. 6 and 7. I am grateful to Prof. Cross for showing me the relevant sections of the last-mentioned work before its publication.

ministries on the possibility of reducing the working day via modernized production. Simiand made the point in 1917 that the spring strikes in Paris were almost unprecedented in recent years in making hours, as opposed to wages, the principal goal.[37] The eight-hour issue also symbolized more general working-class aspirations to a changed status in post-war society since it was related to leisure and the role of the family.

The manner in which the goal was pursued reflected differences in the two industrial relations systems already outlined.[38] Although in Britain the state had legislated the eight-hour day for miners before the war (reduced to seven in 1919), and used its wartime powers to satisfy the railwaymen's insistence on the same measure in December 1918, the bulk of the accords on a forty-eight-hour week or less in late 1918–19 were reached bilaterally between unions and employers, though sometimes with the aid of wartime joint machinery.[39] In March, under pressure from proliferating action on hours, the employers' delegates to the Joint Provisional Committee agreed with the trade union side to make legislation on a forty-eight-hour week the first of its recommendations to government. The law never materialized, but 6,305,000 workers experienced a reduction in work hours in 1919 of an average of six and a half hours a week (with over half before the end of March).[40]

In France, by contrast, the CGT pressured the state to impose the eight-hour day by legislation on a largely recalcitrant *patronat*.[41] By March, Jouhaux was increasingly impatient with the government's failure to translate promise into reality, and, warning that 'France is currently sitting on a volcano', issued veiled threats of the consequences if the eight-hour day

[37] AN 94 AP 141, rep. 9 Aug. 1917.
[38] See Chap. 7, above.
[39] Askwith, *Industrial Problems and Disputes*, 465; Clegg, *A History of British Trade Unions since 1889* ii. 253–5, 267–8; Dowie, '1919–20 is in Need of Attention'; R. Lowe, 'Hours of Labour: Negotiating Industrial Legislation in Britain, 1919–1939', *Economic History Review*, 35 (1982), pp. 245–68.
[40] Dowie, '1919–20 is in Need of Attention', 439.
[41] Ministère du Travail, *Travaux préparatoires de la loi du 23 avril 1919* (Imprimerie Nationale, 1919); *Bulletin du ministère du travail*, 1919, append., 26–7 (for the text of the act); J. Cavaillé, *La Journée de huit heures: la loi du 23 avril 1919* (Marcel Rivière, 1919); Cross, 'The Quest for Leisure'; id., 'Les Trois Huit'; I. Lespinet, 'La Journée de huit heures' (Maîtrise diss., Paris X, 1985).

were not introduced by 1 May.[42] The CGT leadership preferred to organize May Day demonstrations on the issue rather than a general strike, partly not to hinder the Versailles labour commission from enshrining the eight-hour day in the peace treaty, and partly to avoid repeating the failed general strike for the same issue following May Day 1906. Instead, a more sophisticated industrial strategy was prepared whereby union demands on the eight-hour day and other matters to each company and sector were backed up by the sanction of a 'cartel' of unions—miners, railwaymen, seamen, dockers, and transport workers—which was inspired by the Triple Alliance and established at the end of March.[43]

Meanwhile, the government had adapted a bureaucratic committee at the Ministry of Labour into an emergency *commission paritaire* on the eight-hour issue by adding ten delegates each from the CGT and industrialists, as well as Loucheur.[44] It was clear from its deliberations as well as from an enquiry run in the spring of 1919 by the business paper, *La Journée industrielle*, that the bulk of business opinion viewed the eight-hour day either as a total disaster in view of France's weakened state and low industrial productivity or as feasible provided it was introduced slowly and related to productivity increases.[45] But the insistence of Clemenceau, Loucheur, and a small minority of business leaders (generally those most open to bargaining with the CGT) on the inescapable *political* necessity of the measure to placate industrial workers, as well as the

[42] AN F₇ 13576, n., 12 Mar. 1919. He similarly warned a meeting of the Comité National d'Études Sociales et Politiques, in early Apr. 1919, that 'today the working class is demonstrating in the street; if a cataclysm is to be avoided, one must give in (to the working class)' (AN 94 AP 401, min. 7 Apr. 1919).

[43] AN F₇ 13576, reps. 26–7 Mar.; *La Bataille*, 24–6 Mar. 1919; and *La Voix du peuple*, 1919, pp. 147–74, on the Comité Confédéral National of 23–5 Mar., which turned the eight-hour issue into the central, immediate demand of the CGT; AN F₇ 13576, n. of 1 Apr., on first meeting of 'Cartel' (30 Mar.); AN F₇ 13576, CGT, Commission Administrative, min. 7 Apr. 1919; AN F₇ 13576, rep. 22 Apr. 1919; L. Jouhaux, 'Force et volonté', *La Bataille*, 27 Mar. 1919; three articles by Jouhaux on the eight-hour campaign, 'Les huit heures: où en sommes-nous?', *La Bataille*, 3 Apr., 'Transformations nécessaires', ibid., 5 Apr., and 'La Conséquence', ibid., 10 Apr. 1919; and *La Bataille*, 16 Apr. 1919 on the 'Cartel'.

[44] Ministère du Travail, *Travaux préparatoires de la loi du 23 avril 1919*; 'Commission des traités internationaux du travail', *Bulletin du ministère du travail*, 1919, append., 1–27.

[45] *La Journée industrielle*, 16 Feb.–18 Apr. 1919.

conviction of the progressive functionaries at the Ministry of Labour, resulted in the eight-hour law being rushed through parliament in late April 1919.[46] The modalities of its implementation were left to collective contracts for each sector, facilitated by a law of March 1919.[47] Most of the strikes occasioned by the reduction in work-time in France concerned the detailed application of the eight-hour law (an unprecedented 557 collective contracts were signed in 1919, 331 of them involving reduced hours).[48]

The cost to national economic recovery in both countries of the eight-hour day is a matter of debate.[49] But it was a relatively easy reform for governments to allow or enact since it involved no direct charge on the exchequer. It was quite otherwise with reforms requiring immediate state expenditure, especially from 1920, as governments began to switch from their easy continuation of inflationary wartime policies to budgetary retrenchment.[50] This was of more consequence in Britain, where government promises of post-war social 'reconstruction' had been far more important since 1916. The surviving radical Liberals in government, and notably Addison, were severely handicapped, though not totally incapacitated. Unemployment insurance was extended in 1920 and a Ministry of Health established in 1919 (with Addison in charge) which pursued a limited public housing programme.[51] In France, where a Ministry of Hygiene and Social Assistance and Protection was created (in 1920), a full decade elapsed before the foundations were laid of national social insurance and public

[46] J.-J. Mordacq, *Le Ministère Clemenceau: journal d'un témoin* (Plon), iii, *novembre 1918–juin 1919* (1931), 251–3; François-Poncet, *Robert Pinot*, 277–80; for the role of Picquenard, Fontaine and the Ministry of Labour, see 'Commission des traités internationaux du travail', session of 27 Mar. 1919.

[47] G. Pirou, 'The Theory of the Collective Labour Contract in France', *International Labour Review*, Jan. 1922, p. 37.

[48] *Bulletin du ministère du travail*, June–Aug. 1919, pp. 301–5, and Nov.–Dec. 1920, pp. 506–7; Oualid and Picquenard, *Salaires et tarifs*, 493–7.

[49] Dowie, '1919–20 is in Need of Attention'.

[50] F. Goguel, *La Politique des partis sous la IIIᵉ république* (1946; new edn., 1958), 193–6; Aldcroft, *The Inter-War Economy: Britain, 1919–1939*, 303.

[51] Abrams, 'The Failure of Social Reform', 43–64; Johnson, *Land Fit for Heroes*, 288, 410; B. S. Gilbert, *British Social Policy, 1914–1939* (Batsford, 1970), 98–161; L. Orbach, *Homes for Heroes: A Study of the Evolution of British Public Housing, 1915–1921* (Seeley, Aldershot, 1977), 68–88.

housing policies.[52] In the short term, high wartime hopes of social reform in both countries evaporated to leave a disappointing residue of achievement.

Reformist labour leaders were not simply the victims of astute manipulation. Tactical manœuvring certainly took place by political élites concerned at the vulnerability of the state to workers' and soldiers' unrest, framed by militant and even revolutionary movements, in the aftermath of the war—a concern which fed exaggerated images of Bolshevik subversion.[53] It made sense in such circumstances to engage moderate leaders—who were not merely demanding reforms but also proposing to collaborate, on their own terms, in the all-important battle for production and economic recovery—in some kind of political process, either to defuse or to settle at the minimum price working-class pressure for change. But such manœuvring worked both ways. If the Sankey Commission successfully bought time for the government and defused a miners' strike in February 1919, Clemenceau and Loucheur conceded the eight-hour day to avoid an industrial collision in April–May.

In fact, there was a good deal of genuine confusion in government policy in both countries. Neither Clemenceau nor Lloyd George were necessarily side-tracking labour leaders by discussing the Conseil National Économique or establishing the National Industrial Conference.[54] And the interventionist and reforming thrust of labour policies overlapped with 'statist' and

[52] G. Weil, *Histoire du mouvement social en France, 1852–1924* (Alcan, 1924), 447–9; A. Hirsch, 'Le Logement', in A. Sauvy, *Histoire économique de la France entre les deux guerres*, iii (Fayard, 1972), 79–88; A. Barjot, 'La Sécurité sociale', ibid., 370–4; H. Hatzfeld, *Du paupérisme à la sécurité sociale, 1850–1940* (1971; new edn., Presses Universitaires de Nancy, Nancy, 1989), 142–54.

[53] For British examples, see T. Jones, *Whitehall Diary*, i. 73, 99–102; Kendall, *The Revolutionary Movement in Britain*, 187–95; C. Wrigley (ed.), *A History of British Industrial Relations*, ii. 75–82. For France, see Mordacq, *Le Ministère Clemenceau*, iii. 183–4; J. Prévost, *Histoire de la France depuis la guerre* (Éditions Rieder, 1932), 102–18.

[54] Halévy, *The Era of Tyrannies*, 152 (for the most influential statement of the 'manipulation' thesis). Armitage, *The Politics of Decontrol in Industry*, 70, 124, and Lowe, *Adjusting to Democracy*, 22–3, emphasize the confusion of government policy. CGT leaders were well aware of the competing approaches to, and incoherence of, government economic policies in the first months of peace. Jouhaux told the Comité Confédéral on 22 Nov. 1918, 'we are traversing an exceptionally difficult period and we feel that the government, like the *patronat*, is disoriented . . .' (AN F$_7$ 13576, rep. 23 Nov.).

reforming elements of government (the Ministry of Reconstruction in Britain, the Ministry of Commerce in France, and
the Ministries of Labour in both countries). Only gradually did
it become apparent that business and parliamentary opinion, as
well as the political conservatism which became predominant in
both governments in 1919, intended to jettison, rather than
convert, the economic apparatus of the wartime state. And the
ministerial and bureaucratic advocates of social reform were
only decisively marginalized when the two governments declined to frame economic and fiscal policies capable of tackling a
social and redistributive national 'reconstruction' as well as the
burden of war debts.

The growth of labour leaders' protest in both countries
reflected the crystallization of these political realities. The
meetings of the CGT's Comité Confédéral National in late
March and late May remonstrated with increasing vehemence
against the government's approach to demobilization as well as
peace-making, while that of 21–2 July condemned 'an economic
and financial policy which is leading the country to ruin'.[55] The
socialist deputies kept up a running critique of the official
failure to maintain adequate controls on supplies and prices of
food, and Albert Thomas criticized his erstwhile deputy, Loucheur, for dismantling the state sector as a potentially modernizing force for French industrial production.[56]

Although the British government acted on a number of the
minor recommendations adopted by the second National
Industrial Conference in April, it failed to deliver laws on the
two key labour demands—the forty-eight-hour week and minimum wages.[57] Yet the trade union delegates of the Joint
Provisional Committee had submitted a memorandum (drafted
by G. D. H. Cole) to the April conference announcing the
'breakdown of the existing capitalist system of industrial organization', condemning government and business for failing

[55] *Rapports des comités . . . pour l'exercice 1918–1919*, 62–3, 77–8; L. Jouhaux,
'Force et volonté', *La Bataille*, 27 Mar. 1919; id., 'Notre comité national', *La
Bataille*, 29 May 1919.
[56] Rouger, *L'Action socialiste au parlement*, 43–57; A. Thomas, 'Reconstruction',
L'Information ouvrière et sociale, 17 July 1919.
[57] R. Lowe, 'The Failure of Consensus in Britain'.

even to understand working-class desires for a radical alternative such as that proposed by labour, and calling for 'the widest possible extension of public ownership and democratic control of industry'.[58] The rhetoric was Cole's, but the sentiment suggested how even fairly staid (let alone more radical) union leaders accepted the moderate socialism embodied in Labour's post-war programme. The Parliamentary Labour Party, largely composed of such men, sharply condemned the government's disposal of 'national' factories and failure to nationalize coal, and put forward its own bill on full unemployment maintenance and the right to work. Both the Labour Party conference in June and the Trades Union Congress in September underlined labour's repudiation of the government's conversion to peace.[59]

The defeat of moderate labour hopes for the immediate post-war period dismantled the specifically wartime reformism characteristic of both countries. It dispelled the central optimism that the powers assumed by the state in order to co-ordinate the war effort might be turned to the very different end of fundamental economic and social reforms, merely by labour claims that these were in the national interest and owed to the working class for its role in the war. But as internationally this disillusionment served to reformulate, rather than simply discredit, reformist options and invited a reassessment of the strategies of organized labour.

(ii) Revising Reformism, 1919–1920

The Parti Socialiste by no means turned its back on the issue of post-war reform in 1919. As the Armistice removed the Jacobin imperative of national defence, and socialist membership (declining throughout the war) soared in 1919, a more polarized political dynamic began to remodel internal socialist divisions.[60]

---

[58] Cole, *Chaos and Order in Industry*, 247–72; Gleason, *What the Workers Want*, 371–90.

[59] *Report of the Labour Party Conference, Southport, June 1919* (rep. of the PLP), 57 ff.

[60] Membership rose from 30,000 at the end of 1918 (90,000 in July 1914) to 132,000 a year later, and 180,000 by the time of the Tours congress in Dec. 1920 (J. Charles, *et al.*, (eds.), *Le Congrès de Tours. 18ᵉ congrès national du parti socialiste. Texte intégral* (Éditions sociales, 1980), 41).

The extreme right of the party (the 'quarante' deputies who had established *La France libre* in support of the military effort in July 1918) and the former *majoritaires* displaced in October 1918 sought, as the war ended, to constitute a 'Groupe d'action de reconstitution économique de la France'. Albert Thomas, Dubreuilh, Renaudel, and Gaston Lévy were key figures behind this attempt to parallel the orientation of the CGT and combine retrospective justification of participation in the national defence with support for the *Société des Nations*, and a socialist programme for the transition to peace.[61] But the initiative proved fragile. The extreme right had few rank-and-file supporters and separated from the party in autumn 1919–early 1920, while the ex-*majoritaires* were progressively marginalized within the party.[62] In the first months of 1919, public opinion took the CGT, not the PS, to be the voice of labour on demobilization while *L'Humanité* itself tended to defer to the CGT's views on the economic aspects of the conversion to peace.[63]

The only possibility of a post-war reform campaign rallying the support of a socialist majority was one from the centre, which revived the pre-war Jauressian 'synthesis' and incorporated—or at least restrained in a dynamic equilibrium—the divisions stemming from the war and the Russian revolution. It was precisely this that Léon Blum attempted, consciously taking up the doctrinal mantle of Jaurès and grasping the opportunity presented by the elections anticipated for 1919.[64]

Blum proved the dominant figure in a commission formed in December 1918 to draft an electoral programme for submission to the first post-war socialist congress, eventually held in April 1919. In this document, in his speech to the congress, and in a

[61] *L'Humanité*, 11 Nov. 1918, for the manifesto adopted by ex-*majoritaires* on 25 Oct. following their congress defeat (presented by Thomas, Bracke, Louis Dubreuilh, and Renaudel); APP B/a 1470, rep. 27 Nov. 1918, on the meeting which discussed fusing the *Quarante* and the former *majoritaires* into the new group.

[62] M. Prélot, *L'Évolution politique du socialisme français, 1789–1934* (Éditions Spes, 1934), 218–19.

[63] e.g., 'Démobilisation pour renaître!' special no. of *L'Humanité*, 5 Jan. 1919.

[64] Blum came from the right of the PS and had been Sembat's assistant at the Ministry of Public Works down to Dec. 1916. But thereafter he sought a conciliatory position in the centre in association with some of those who tried to reconcile *majoritaires* and moderate *minoritaires* in Oct. 1917 (Ziebura, *Léon Blum et le parti socialiste*, 141–5; J. Lacouture, *Léon Blum* (Seuil, 1977), 144–54).

subsequent brochure, *Pour être socialiste*, he tackled a multiple agenda—seeking to re-synthesize the doctrines of French socialism while adressing immediate and longer-term post-war perspectives and, above all, preserving unity.[65]

Blum endorsed socialist participation in the national defence, but the significance which he attributed to the war was essentially dialectical. The war economy, which generated organizational forms anticipating socialism, had also intensified the class conflicts which only socialism could resolve.

The war proved that socialism was not a Utopia because universal labour and capital, mobilized for four years for destruction could be mobilized just as well in order to create.

The war proved that class antagonism really is the law of contemporary society because ... it accentuated fortune and misery, [and] concentrated capitalism as well as the international proletariat.[66]

Blum reasserted 'social revolution'—that is, the substitution of a collectivized economy for the current order founded on 'private capitalist property'—as the goal of the PS. But obliquely addressing the October revolution, he affirmed that although in western Europe the political acquisition of power by the working class *might* be a violent process, it might also be legal and peaceful. The latter, in view of the connection which Blum drew between socialism and liberal democracy, seemed infinitely preferable. In either case, the *economic* revolution would be a long, cumulative process of reform. Having blurred the sharp distinction between revolution and reform characteristic of both the far left gravitating to Bolshevism and traditional Guesdism, Blum proposed parallel programmes of political and economic reforms which would engender the ultimate socialist society from the contradictions of the current system: '[this new] order is sketched out and defined within bourgeois society itself through a profound renovation of the latter's

[65] Electoral programme of the PS, *L'Humanité*, 11 Apr. 1919 (also a brochure); L. Blum, *Commentaires sur le programme d'action du parti socialiste (discours prononcé le 21 avril 1919 au congrès national extraordinaire)* (Librairie Populaire, 1919); id., *Pour être socialiste* (Librairie de l'Humanité, 1919); Kriegel, *Aux origines du communisme français*, i. 327–9; Wohl, *French Communism in the Making*, 127–31; Ziebura, *Léon Blum et le parti socialiste*, 99–100 and 147–9.
[66] *L'Humanité*, 11 Apr. 1919.

framework and institutions.'[67] The revolution was the point at which this process gained critical mass politically and decisively remodelled social organization, and the 'dictatorship of the proletariat' was merely the label applied to the transition.

The core of Blum's project was to line up by this compass of ultimate revolution the more immediate reforms which would ensure that 'after the war, the social and political worlds do not turn out identical to the eve of the war'. Politically, the socialist programme involved sweeping constitutional changes to the parliamentary system, including women's suffrage and abolition of the Sénat, and the expansion of the wartime Commissions Mixtes Départementales into a parallel industrial constitution for restructuring the economy. Direct economic reforms included the retrospective taxation of war profits, extensive nationalizations (railways, canals, mines, the merchant fleet, banks, and war factories), including participation by consumers, and some kind of state 'plan' for retooling the industrial economy and reorganizing manpower. The programme ended with a series of immediate measures on working conditions and social welfare.

Clearly influenced in its economic and social aspects by the CGT's *Programme minimum*, the socialist programme was a new departure, far exceeding pre-war programmes in the scale of reforms considered possible and especially in its advocacy of nationalization. But although it was opposed at the congress only by the relatively small 'kienthalian' left which identified with Bolshevism, the consensus achieved and the enthusiasm generated by Blum's self-assured speech were deceptive and short-lived. Through other issues discussed—including a separate motion on the 'general orientation' of the party—and through a further congress in September to concert the party's electoral campaign, it became evident that the impulses which converged on Blum and secured his sudden pre-eminence were those not of reform, but unity. On the contrary, the significance attached to post-war reforms was divergent and potentially conflictual.

Thomas, Renaudel, and the ex-*majoritaires* envisaged a continuous process of economic and political reform as the sole alternative to Bolshevism and saw the PS as building on the

[67] Ibid.

post-war strategy of the CGT. Renaudel wrote in late August that

for us, what was once called in our discussions 'the socialism of institutions' is the *raison d'être* and the goal of syndicalism and the co-operative movement. It is the prelude, the means and the aim of political socialism itself.[68]

Much of the centre, however, including many Guesdists, saw reforms essentially as a question of tactics in building a united revolutionary party. They denied the possibility of achieving socialism by cumulative reforms, stressing instead what they took to be the increasingly revolutionary situation in France and the seizure of power by the working class. Thus, the stalwart Guesdist, Paul Faure, presented the long motion on 'general orientation' to the April 1919 congress. It repudiated the war as imperialist, condemned the *droits des peuples* as an illusory foundation for the peace, and—without mentioning reforms—rejected in advance any participation in coalition governments. It also called for the party to reassert its commitment to revolutionary class struggle against the 'bourgeois dictatorship'. With the right (789 votes) abstaining, the resolution received 962 votes, against 232 for the 'kienthalian' alternative.[69] Just before the September congress, Paul-Faure unambiguously affirmed that:

In asking capitalist society, even 'democratized', to carry out real reforms of a socialist inspiration ... [the reformists] are trying to rekindle a dead hearth where there are no longer any cinders.[70]

At the September congress, another Guesdist, Alexandre Bracke, won a majority (again excluding the 'kienthalians') for the April document as the basis of the socialist electoral programme, but on condition that the party shunned alliances. Renaudel and Blum, in the interests of unity, supported this condition.[71] On this catch-all platform, widely differing and often contradictory campaigns were fought.[72] With the

---

[68] 'Pour l'unité', *L'Humanité*, 31 Aug. 1919.
[69] *L'Humanité*, 23 Apr. 1919.
[70] 'De la réforme à la révolution', *L'Humanité*, 6 Sept. 1919.
[71] *L'Humanité*, 13 Sept. 1919; Ziebura, *Léon Blum et le parti socialiste*, 151–2.
[72] Kriegel, *Aux origines du communisme français*, i. 328–40; Wohl, *French Communism in the Making*, 151–2.

November election result, in practical terms, a clear reversal for the party, the purely circumstantial association of right and centre evaporated, and the notion of a socialist post-war reconstruction programme faded (although mentioned at the Strasburg congress in February 1920, it was no longer the focus of attention).[73]

Instead, the balance within the party continued to swing to the left as the advocates of close organizational links with Moscow contested the traditional revolutionary positions of the party. In December 1920, at the fateful congress of Tours, the upholders of the latter divided between those who accepted that the path of revolutionary unity proceeded via adherence to the Comintern, and who therefore joined with the pro-Bolsheviks, and those who refused to accept Moscow affiliation at the price of schism. Blum defended the Jauressian heritage against all the advocates of the Comintern. But his case for reforms as part of the revolutionary process was now largely theoretical—a defence against Lenin—rather than a matter of immediate practicality. And the tenor of the delegates' speeches made it clear that for many of the party's new militants, not just the right-wing reformism of Renaudel but the Jauressian heritage itself were anathema—along with the wartime participation in the national defence which Blum also retrospectively defended.[74]

The reformist initiative in France thus remained with the CGT *majoritaires*. In the crucial twenty months from May 1919, the confederation's war time orientation was revised not only in response to stiffening government opposition to any reform beyond the eight-hour day but also to counter a reviving, revolutionary minority whose potential strength was considerably amplified by popular militancy and industrial unrest.

The threat from the latter quarter became apparent with 1 May. Pierre Monatte relaunched *La Vie ouvrière* the day

---

[73] *Parti Socialiste, 17ᵉ congrès national tenu à Strasbourg les 25, 26, 27, 28 et 29 février 1920. Compte rendu sténographique* (1920), 562–4; Ziebura, *Léon Blum et le parti socialiste*, 153–5; Wohl, *French Communism in the Making*, 154–7.

[74] Charles, *et al.* (eds.), *Le Congrès de Tours*, 410–35; M. Sembat, *La Victoire en déroute* (Éditions du Progrès Civique, 1925; English trans., *Defeated Victory* (The Labour Publishing Co., 1925)), chap. 5; T. Judt, *La Reconstruction du parti socialiste, 1921–1926* (Presses de la Fondation Nationale des Sciences Politiques, 1976), 8–13.

before, preceded by a circular drawing attention to the revolutionary aspects of the post-war situation, condemning the *majoritaires* for persisting with the *Union sacrée*, and declaring an unshaken faith in pre-war revolutionary syndicalism—of which events in Russia seemed the apotheosis ('What then is the Russian revolution, if not a revolution of a syndicalist nature?').[75] This was to be the *minoritaire* leitmotiv for the next year. Massive demonstrations took place on May Day, and bloody clashes with the police in Paris were privately attributed by the *majoritaire* leaders as much to the *minoritaires* and 'shady elements' as to governmental repressiveness.[76] Meanwhile, talk circulated among Parisian *minoritaire* railway leaders (Sirolle, Monmousseau) of a general railway strike as a prelude to revolution, and two prominent *minoritaires* among the Paris building workers declared the imminence of a dictatorship of the proletariat.[77]

But the full danger of insurrectionary and revolutionary ideas in a soaring trade union membership was only manifested with the wave of strikes in May–June 1919, which accounted for nearly half the strikes and 62 per cent of the strikers for the whole year. Metallurgy, with 28 per cent of strikers, and Paris, with nearly a third, played a central role in the 1919 unrest, and the Paris metalworkers' strike in June produced the most flagrant clash between *majoritaires* and *minoritaires*.[78]

For the *métaux* and CGT leaderships, the strike was one which should never have occurred, and its scale and militancy took them by surprise.[79] A national collective contract between the Fédération des Métaux and the Union des Industries

[75] Chambelland (ed.), *Pierre Monatte: la lutte syndicale*, quot. 159.

[76] AN F$_7$ 13576, CGT, Commission Administrative, min. 3 May 1919; ibid., rep. 6 May 1919.

[77] Hubert, of the *terrassiers*, and Vallet, of the *charpentiers*; see AN F$_7$ 13576, rep. 5 May 1919.

[78] Ministère du Travail, *Statistique des grèves survenues pendant l'année 1919* (Imprimerie Nationale, 1922), 330–3.

[79] *L'Union des métaux*, 72 (Apr.–May 1919), and 73 (June–July 1919); APP B/a 1386, ser. of general reports on the strike, 2 June–early July; CGT, *Rapports des comités . . . pour l'exercice 1918–1919*, 94 ff.; N. Papayanis, 'Masses révolutionnaires et directions réformistes: les tensions au cours des grèves des métallurgistes français en 1919', *Le Mouvement social*, 93 (Oct.–Dec. 1975), pp. 51–73; B. Abhervé, 'Les Origines de la grève des métallurgistes parisiens, juin 1919', ibid., 75–85; Brunet, *Saint Denis: la ville rouge, 1890–1939*, 210–32: Papayanis, *Alphonse Merrheim*, 131–4; Robert, 'Ouvriers et mouvement ouvrier parisiens', 1910–25.

Métallurgiques et Minières had been signed on 17 April agreeing to the eight-hour day.[80] The *majoritaires* hailed it as a triumph for their approach to industrial relations. The detailed implementation of the accord, however, depended on local negotiations, and in the case of Paris, sharp tensions emerged between the national and local *métaux* leaderships over central features of the national accord. In particular, the Paris *syndicats* criticized the productivist core of the agreement which envisaged that real wages would be maintained for the shorter working day by the workers 'sympathetically adapting themselves to mechanization and to rational working methods', rather than by increased rates of pay, especially for piecework.[81] The Paris *syndicats* also demanded the forty-four-rather than forty-eight-hour week. The industrialists were determined to resist these modifications. They dragged their feet in replying to the local demands, thus precipitating a strike of 165,000 workers which they immediately converted into a lock-out and used to switch their factories from war to peace production.[82]

To these discords between the national and Parisian levels of the Fédération des Métaux was added a political dimension. The more radical leaders of the Paris *syndicats* saw the strike in a revolutionary light, although the co-ordinating Comité d'Entente eventually co-operated with the Fédération des Métaux in trying to resolve the conflict on a strictly economic basis. This further division allowed the strike to gravitate to the overtly political and revolutionary leadership of a Comité d'Action de Grève, whose support came essentially from the industrial suburbs swollen by the war (Saint-Denis, Boulogne-Billancourt, Puteaux, Courbevoie, Nanterre, etc.). The temper of popular opinion in these districts was undoubtedly radical, and local militants sought to convert the strike not merely into a political campaign against the government (notably its intervention in Russia and apparent refusal of an amnesty for

[80] *La Journée industrielle*, 19 Apr. 1919; *L'Union des métaux*, 72 (Apr.–May 1919), p. 2.

[81] Abhervé, 'Les Origines de la grève des métallurgistes parisiens', 79–83.

[82] From 85,000 on 2 June, the strikers reached a peak of 165,000 on 7 June, and were still 135,000 on 26 June when the movement began to crumble (reps. APP B/a 1386).

imprisoned wartime activists), but also into a 'revolutionary general strike'.[83]

By no means all the strikes in the May–June wave fitted this pattern. From mid-June to mid-July, a disciplined miners' strike achieved the eight-hour day in conjunction with parliamentary legislation and mediation by the Ministry of Labour.[84] Other strikes, in the Paris métro and in the capital's clothing industry, were also seen as exemplifying the *majoritaire* approach.[85] But when the metalworkers' conflict ended, after nearly a month, in compromise and recrimination, it confirmed the *majoritaires'* rejection of the tactics of pre-war revolutionary syndicalism and the revolutionary use of the strike weapon. Yet if this correspondingly reinforced their determination that strikes for specific 'corporative' aims should not be diverted from their purpose, the June strike clarified the need for appropriate tactics to press for the CGT's broader programme.

This tactical reassessment became entwined with a planned twenty-four hour strike in July against the international policy of the Allied powers, especially their intervention in Russia and indirect backing for the suppression of the Hungarian revolution. The suggestion of internationally co-ordinated protests and strike action had emerged from more militant elements in the Berne Socialist International (notably Italian socialists and syndicalists) in the face of the allied governments' indifference to labour criticisms of the peace terms.[86] The CGT's Comité Confédéral National of late May endorsed the idea, adding the amnesty issue and slow demobilization to the list of grievances, and it instructed the 'Cartel' of unions, established in late March, to co-ordinate action with the British Triple Alliance.[87]

[83] APP B/a 1386, rep. 23 June 1919; AN F, 13576, rep. 26 June 1919; *L'Union des métaux*, 73 (June–July 1919), pp. 7–11.

[84] CGT, *Rapports des comités . . . pour l'exercice 1918–1919; La Bataille*, arts. by Bartuel, 14 June (history of dispute) and 12 July (outcome).

[85] CGT, *Rapports des comités . . . pour l'exercice 1918–1919*; *Fédération Nationale des Moyens de Transport, Congrès extraordinaires; juillet 1918, avril 1919, et septembre 1919* (1920), 'Rapport moral', Apr.–Sept. 1919, 157–8.

[86] CGT, *Rapports des comités . . . pour l'exercice 1918–1919*; AN F, 13576, various reps. June–July 1919; AN F, 13310, doss. on 21 July; *La Bataille*, July 1919; Georges and Tintant, *Léon Jouhaux*, i. 367–71; and, for the international context, Mayer, *Politics and Diplomacy of Peacemaking*, 853–73.

[87] *La Bataille*, 28 May 1919; *Rapports des comités . . . pour l'exercice 1918–1919*, 77–8.

Significantly, the meetings of both the leadership of the *métaux* and the 'Cartel' in late June, which refused to declare a general strike in support of the Paris metalworkers, confirmed the commitment to a symbolic international political strike in conjunction with the Italian and British trade unions.[88] Despite combined socialist and syndicalist delegations from France and Italy to the Labour Party conference at the end of June, the PCTUC refused to summon the special Trades Union Congress necessary to decide on British participation in the strike. By itself, the LPNEC claimed that it had no authority to do more than suggest demonstrations to local Labour organizations, on Sunday 20 July, while the Triple Alliance was dogged by cumbersome decision-making machinery and also preferred to work for common action by the whole trade union movement.[89]

Although CGT leaders bitterly condemned what they saw as a British defection, they committed themselves in early July to the one-day strike, scheduled for the twenty-first, though they now added more domestic issues to the protest—notably the soaring cost of living and the entire CGT programme of economic reconstruction.[90] By 18 July, Clemenceau was sufficiently anxious to summon the CGT leadership to an interview. He offered various concessions—accelerated demobilization, a political amnesty, and a purely consultative Conseil National Économique—though he refused to negotiate on foreign policy questions.[91] After a long, intense meeting of the Commission Administrative on the night of 18–19 July, the CGT leadership called off the strike. Though they rejected Clemenceau's version of the Conseil National Économique, they seized as an excuse on the defeat of the government in the Chamber on 18 July over food prices, and the resignation of the minister concerned. But the real reason was the double fear that radical elements might take over the protest locally and, even more critically in view of the reports coming in, that the strike might

[88] AN F₇ 13576, rep. 26 June 1919.

[89] *Report of the Labour Party Conference, Southport, June 1919*, 155–6; Bagwell, 'The Triple Industrial Alliance', 107–8.

[90] AN F₇ 13576, CGT, Commission Administrative, 1 July 1919, rep. 2 July; Commission Administrative, 3 July, min.; rep. 5 July; *La Bataille*, 4 July 1919.

[91] AN F₇ 13576, CGT, rep. 19 July 1919; *La Bataille*, 19 and 20 July 1919; Watson, *Georges Clemenceau*, 382–3; Duroselle, *Clemenceau*, 837–9.

win only lukewarm support from organized labour, leaving the CGT isolated in the face of a hostile public opinion.[92]

The fiasco of the cancelled strike (technically only post-poned)—which left the Italian syndicalists to go it alone—illustrated, without resolving them, the difficulties of using the disciplined strength of a volatile and divided trade union movement as a means of applying political pressure on the government. It also precipitated a further programmatic reor-ientation of the CGT majority. At the Conseil Confédéral National convoked on 21–2 July to consider the crisis, Jouhaux, apparently spontaneously, delivered a powerful speech which began to shift the emphasis of post-war reform—and which rallied the majority with a vote of 91 to 16 (with 8 abstentions) in favour of the leadership's handling of recent events.[93] Jou-haux, like Merrheim in *La Révolution économique*, stressed that revolution was not, for syndicalists, a violent political catas-trophe but 'the long precursor of evolution which, little by little, penetrates the system, the action which saps a regime and constitutes the new organism which will succeed it'. But, admitting that he might have believed too readily in the possibility of major reforms immediately following the war, he now invoked Proudhon to hint that the CGT should prepare by itself the instruments for creating a collective, co-operative system in the shell of the old. The need to be less dependent on the good will of the state in providing leadership for the mass influx of inexperienced syndicalists underlined the need for a new departure.

The exact nature of this programmatic revision (prepared in advance by the *majoritaires*) was revealed by Jouhaux at the CGT congress at Lyons, in mid-September, and developed over the following year.[94] It turned on three pivots. The first was the reconception of the Conseil National Économique as a purely labour body, the Conseil Économique du Travail, whose function was to map out a new approach to fundamental economic reorganization and the immediate problems of

[92] AN F$_7$ 13576, n., 11 July 1919; ibid., Commission Administrative, min. 16 July; *La Vie ouvrière*, 23 July 1919.

[93] CGT, *Rapports des comités ... pour l'exercice 1918–1919; La Voix du peuple*, 1919, pp. 410–19; *La Bataille*, 25 July 1919 (Jouhaux's speech).

[94] CGT, *20ᵉ Congrès national corporatif ... (Lyon 15–21 septembre 1919)*, 246–51.

post-war reconstruction. The second was the proclamation of
'industrial nationalizations' as the principal instrument for
embarking on the transformation of the economy. The third
pivot was a renewed attempt, especially by the Fédération des
Métaux, to achieve a measure of 'worker control' over production.
Majoritaire leaders pointed constantly to the parallels
between their renewed programme and radical developments
elsewhere. Merrheim cited Lenin's use of technical experts in
war communism as justification for the inclusion of this category
in the Conseil Économique du Travail. Jouhaux, at
Lyons, claimed similarities between the CGT's view of nationalization
and Otto Bauer's concept of socialization (recently
publicized through a translation of *The Way of Socialism* in
L'Humanité). But, as Jouhaux insisted, the revision of the CGT
programme came essentially from within and descended directly
from the original post-war plan of the Commission Mixte
d'Études Économiques in November 1916.[95]

The Conseil Économique du Travail, inaugurated in January
1920, appealed to that expanded social constituency which the
CGT had sought to address during the war.[96] Represented on
its committee, in addition to the confederation, were consumers
through the FNCC, civil servants through the newly

[95] Ibid., 182, 246–50.
[96] Jouhaux insisted at Lyons (against Monatte's accusations) that the idea for the
Conseil Économique du Travail came from the Bureau Confédéral of the CGT (ibid.,
247). Its germ (and name), along with the emphasis on nationalizations, is already
contained in an art. by Jouhaux in *L'Information ouvrière et sociale* of 20 July 1919.
Albert Thomas, in Jan. 1920, saw Jouhaux as the principal spokesman for the idea
(AN 94 AP 266 (Fonds Thomas), typescript 'Idées à mettre en lumière après le
Conseil Économique du Travail'). It almost certainly owed something to Roger
Francq, an engineer who in Apr. 1919 dreamed of a Congrès National du Travail to
run the economy (AN 94 AP 266, typescript 'Project de dictature du prolétariat'), and
who became secretary of the Union Syndicale des Techniciens de l'Industrie, du
Commerce et de l'Agriculture, a future component of the Conseil Économique du
Travail. His ideas on economic reorganization were very close to those of the CGT
majoritaires ('Armes de la production', *La Bataille*, 6 July, and 'Des remèdes? En
Voilà!', ibid., 15 Aug. 1919). The CGT issued a preliminary declaration on the
Conseil Économique du Travail (ibid., 4 Nov. 1919) and it was inaugurated on 8 Jan.
1920. For its form and work, see Leroy, *Les Techniques nouvelles du syndicalisme*, 107–
65; Picard, *Le Mouvement syndical en France durant la guerre*, 173–203; G. Gemelli,
'Un'Istituzione ambivalente: le origini del conseil national économique', *Rivista di
storia contemporanea* (1984), pp. 539–77; Fine, 'Towards Corporatism', 87–91; Rossiter,
'Experiments with Corporatist Politics in Republican France', 99–107.

formed Fédération Nationale des Fonctionnaires, and technicians and engineers through the most radical of their professional organizations—the Union Syndicale des Techniciens de l'Industrie, du Commerce et de l'Agriculture (USTICA), founded in June 1919.[97] The USTICA reflected the profound mutations in the division of labour in manufacturing which potentially aligned some technical experts with organized labour, and made them crucial to the *majoritaire* conception of a working association of all genuinely productive forces. The *fonctionnaires* likewise represented an intellectual and administrative capital for economic reorganization—being those 'who have, or rather should have, as their professional role the coordination of collective activities'—as well as a group provoked by inflation into a sharp sense of collective grievance.[98]

The Conseil Économique du Travail's main purpose, apart from embodying 'a new Society in gestation' as a kind of shadow, alternative economy, was research, and like the wartime Comité d'Action it consisted of subcommittees on different aspects of the economy—national retooling, economic reorganization, industrial production, agricultural production, 'social life' (urbanization, education, and social welfare), the devastated regions, and so on. During 1920, its most urgent task was to develop proposals for the second fulcrum of the CGT's doctrinal revision—nationalization.

Nationalization, in general, and of coal, railways, hydroelectricity and banking in particular, stemmed directly from the CGT's wartime preoccupations. But in November 1918 it had been subordinated to *majoritaire* ambitions to use national recognition of the CGT's wartime role to gain a controlled economy with substantial syndicalist participation. With disillusionment, specific nationalizations became the potential spearhead of a political campaign by syndicalism to impose its brand of post-war reconstruction on the state. They also dovetailed with the importance accorded to nationalization by the IFTU from August 1919.

---

[97] Descostes and Robert (eds.), *Clefs pour une histoire du syndicalisme cadre*, 57–65; A. Thépot (ed.), *L'Ingénieur dans la société française* (Éditions ouvrières, 1985), 284.
[98] CGT declaration on the Conseil Économique du Travail, *La Bataille*, 4 Nov. 1919.

The CGT's conception of nationalization was clarified in the process. The autonomy of nationalized concerns from the state and the management function of workers' and consumers' delegates had sharply marked syndicalist thinking from *étatiste* conceptions of national ownership. But the role envisaged for central and local representatives of the state within this decentralized schema had been vague. Both Jouhaux's speech at Lyons and the outline scheme of nationalization (which was drafted by a young academic *coopérateur* on the Conseil Économique du Travail, Bernard Lavergne) specified that nationalization would be tripartite in form, administered by delegates of the state, producers (technicians as well as workers), and consumers.[99] Here the Austrian model of socialization may have influenced Jouhaux, although the plan also reflected the syndicalist conception of the Conseil National Économique in 1918 and the tripartite shape both of the wartime proposal for coal nationalization and of the Fédération des Cheminots' renewed demand for railway nationalization in the spring of 1919, which Albert Thomas had sponsored in parliament. But by virtue of their financial and administrative independence, nationalized industries continued to be seen as reflecting above all the interests of consumers and producers. With possible indemnification of shareholders, they were peacefully to supplant competitive with co-operative enterprises and prepare the way for further 'works of transformation'.[100]

Enthusiastically endorsed by various intellectual *amis de Proudhon*, especially Maxime Leroy who devoted a major work, *Les Techniques nouvelles du syndicalisme* (1921), to the CGT's post-war orientation, the revised or 'revolutionary reformism' (as Dumoulin described it) of the confederation undoubtedly

[99] CGT, *20ᵉ Congrès national corporatif ... (Lyon, 15–21 septembre 1919)*, 248; CGT, *La Nationalisation industrialisée. (Les raisons, la nécessité de sa réalisation)* (mid-1920), 15–22; B. Lavergne, 'Principes directeurs de nationalisation ...' (typescript proposal on behalf of the FNCC to the first meeting of the Conseil Économique du Travail, in the Musée Social; id., *Les Idées politiques en France*, 150–4.

[100] M. Bidegaray, *L'Exploitation d'aujourd'hui par les compagnies: l'exploitation de demain par la nationalisation des chemins de fer* (Imprimerie Ouvrière, Courbevoie, 1919); 'Proposition tendant à la nationalisation de tous les réseaux de chemins de fer', *Journal officiel, chambre des députés, documents parlementaires*, 1919, no. 6046, pp. 1280–8; G. Lefranc, 'L'Origine de l'idée de nationalisation industrialisée en France, 1919–1920', *Essais sur les problèmes socialistes et syndicaux* (Payot, 1970), pp. 115–16.

expressed an impulse for fundamental transformation.[101] There were nuances between the explicitly revolutionary goals of erstwhile revolutionary syndicalists like Jouhaux, Merrheim, and Dumoulin, who proclaimed their fidelity to the 'integral emancipation' of the working class enunciated by the 'charter' of Amiens, and the more narrowly focused concerns of pre-war reformists like Bidegaray.[102] But the ubiquitous references to Proudhon expressed the goal of a radical break with *laissez-faire* capitalism. The same references also marked the gulf between *majoritaire* gradualism and the political revolution, whether by party or by general strike, symbolized by events in Russia since October 1917, and which the CGT majority leaders, no less than Blum or the socialist right, repudiated.[103]

But the means of implementing this revised reformism remained unclear. Shunning the open-ended general strike, the *majoritaires* seemed to waver between legislative action by sympathetic deputies, educational campaigns to convince public opinion, and limited industrial action in favour of specific reforms—what Leroy termed the 'constitutional strike'. Events did not allow the luxury of hesitation. The revised programme consisting of the Conseil Économique du Travail and 'industrial nationalizations' won a large majority at Lyons—larger than that for the majority leadership's performance since 1918, suggesting a tactical aspect to Jouhaux's leftward move.[104] But gathering industrial unrest and the revolutionary militancy of local syndicalist cadres in certain industries and regions precipitated the two railway strikes of February and May 1920—the second of which the *majoritaire* leaders sought to control by

[101] G. Dumoulin, *La Vie ou la mort du syndicalisme: le programme de la CGT* (Maison des Syndicats, 1921), 13; Kriegel, *Aux origines du communisme français*, i. 541–2; M. Augé-Laribé, *et al.*, *Proudhon et notre temps* (Étienne Chiron, 1920).

[102] Jouhaux, Merrheim, and Dumoulin all wrote pamphlets or books in 1920–1 to stress the revolutionary goals of CGT action and the historical continuity with the Amiens 'charter' (Jouhaux, *Le Syndicalisme et la CGT* (Éditions de la Sirène, 1920); Merrheim, *Amsterdam ou Moscou? Le syndicalisme en danger* (Éditions du Cercle d'Études, n.d.); Dumoulin, *La Vie ou la mort du syndicalisme*, 1921). Bidegaray, in talking of railway nationalization, tended to stress its immediate significance for workers and community alike rather than its linkage to further changes.

[103] e.g. Jouhaux at the congress of Lyons, CGT, *20ᵉ Congrès national corporatif*, 249–52; D. J. Saposs, *The Labor Movement in Post-War France* (Columbia Univ. Press, NY, 1931), 73–6.

[104] One thousand six hundred and thirty-three for, 324 against, as opposed to 1393 for, 588 against.

converting it into a general strike for an ill-prepared scheme of railway nationalization.[105]

When this strike ended disastrously in defeat and repression, it marked the turning-point of the *après-guerre*, sending CGT membership plummeting in advance of the autumn economic recession, and confirming an employer counter-offensive against the syndicalist gains, in hours and wages, of the previous year. It was in this unpropitious atmosphere, in 1921, that the Fédération des Métaux tried to implement the third element of the CGT's readjusted reformism—a scheme for syndicalist-dominated 'commissions of worker control' in each engineering factory, to watch over collective contracts, hiring and dismissals, and the implementation of labour legislation.[106] This built directly on the *majoritaire* experience of the *délégués d'atelier* in 1917–18 and the Lyons congress's approval of collective contracts. It was essentially defensive in inspiration, seeking to counteract growing unemployment in engineering and the erosion of the eight-hour day. But it was summarily rejected by the UIMM, which claimed that the *métaux*'s involvement in the May 1920 general strike vitiated the April 1919 collective contract.[107] Significantly, Robert Pinot wrote a series of articles in 1920–1 which repudiated the Proudhonist orientation of the *majoritaires*, and their plans for economic controls and nationalization, counterposing, as the principle of industrial organization, the renewed authority of the *patron*.[108]

From the point of view of the *majoritaires*, the Orléans congress of the CGT in September–October 1920 (and the modified programme which the leadership drew up in February 1921) simply consolidated the revision of the CGT's post-war reconstruction policy initiated in July–September 1919. This

[105] CGT, *L'Action confédérale et la grève des cheminots* (Éditions de la CGT, 1920); Kriegel, *Aux origines du communisme français*, i. 476–94; A. Jones, 'The French Railway Strikes of January–May 1920: New Syndicalist Ideas and Emergent Communism', *French Historical Studies*, 12/4 (1982), pp. 508–40.

[106] ILO, *Une demande de contrôle ouvrier en France* (ILO, Études et documents, ser. B, no. 8, 1921); A. François-Poncet, *Une Formule nouvelle: le contrôle syndical* (Société d'Études et d'Informations Économiques, 1921); Picard, *Le Contrôle ouvrier*, 73–101; Cross, 'Redefining Workers' Control'.

[107] ILO, *Une demande de contrôle ouvrier*, 9–12.

[108] R. Pinot, 'La Confédération générale du travail et les idées proudhoniennes', *La Revue hebdomadaire*, 1 May 1920, pp. 3–34; 'Le Chef dans la grande industrie', *Revue de France*, 15 Mar. 1921, pp. 109–22; 'L'Organisation permanente du travail', *Revue de Paris*, 1 May 1921, pp. 165–99.

seemed to have been successful since the *minoritaires* had barely increased their hold over the intervening year. The *majoritaires*, with 67 per cent support at Lyons (75 per cent at Paris in July 1918), still won 66 per cent of the vote at Orléans.[109] But the *minoritaires*, confirmed in their rejection of *majoritaire* moderation by the events of spring 1920, and experiencing an analogous polarization to that in the PS with the Comintern's decision in mid-1920 to establish the RILU, began to develop their own parallel organizations. By the next congress, at Lille in July 1921, *majoritaire* support had sunk to 53 per cent, the decline being mirrored to varying degrees in the Fédérations and Unions départementales. When formal schism occurred after intensive feuding in December 1921, the reformists retained a bare majority.[110]

In Britain, frustrated Labour reconstruction hopes refocused on nationalization, especially of coal and railways, though as in France, the labour movement also formulated the immediate goal of ending intervention in Russia and dismantling the coercive powers of the wartime state, including conscription and censorship. The clash of views between Labour and the government over nationalization had been dramatized by the fate of the Sankey Commission. The Labour Party conference in June 1919 endorsed the majority recommendation of Sankey, while the September Trades Union Congress overwhelmingly supported a motion by Smillie in favour of unspecified action to force the government to nationalize coal.[111] Both Henderson and Webb felt that a fresh general election might be precipitated by a political crisis, and saw nationalization as the key to a Labour electoral breakthrough.[112]

Nationalization also straddled some of the principal doctrinal currents in the post-war labour movement. As we have noted

---

[109] CGT, *21ᵉ Congrès national corporatif ... (Orléans, 27 septembre–2 octobre 1920). Compte rendu des travaux* (L'Union Typographique, Villeneuve-Saint-Georges, 1921); Labi, *La Grande Division des travailleurs*, 265–81; Robert, 'Les "Programmes minimum" de la CGT'.

[110] Saposs, *The Labor Movement in Post-War France*, 49–73; Georges and Tintant, *Léon Jouhaux*, i. 393–440; Kriegel, *Aux origines du communisme français*, ii. 731–54; L. Batsch and M. Bouvet, *CGT, autour de la scission de 1921* (Éditions de la Brèche, 1983).

[111] *Report of the Labour Party Conference, Southport, June 1919*, 51; *Trades Union Congress, Annual Report, September 1919*.

[112] Gleason, *What the Workers Want*, 96.

different kinds of 'joint control' involving producers and consumers, which derived from pre-war Syndicalism and Guild
Socialism, crept into mainstream Labour thinking via the
MFGB and NUR nationalization proposals. The influence of
R. H. Tawney's 'ethical' socialism and of Guild Socialists such
as G. D. H. Cole, who increasingly qualified his Guild Socialism with a Labour pragmatism, tempered the *étatiste*, administrative conception of nationalization favoured by the Webbs.
The last-mentioned made limited concessions to ideas of
worker participation in running industry in their 1920 *Constitution for the Socialist Commonwealth of Great Britain*.[113]

As in France, however, the revision of wartime labour
reformism was linked to basic issues of method and tactics,
whose particular colouring in Britain came from the discrepancy between labour's industrial strength and its political
weakness in relation to a 'reconstruction' programme premissed
on parliamentary action. In particular, the potential industrial
might of the Triple Alliance and the overt socialism of some of
its leaders (Smillie and Frank Hodges of the MFGB, C. T.
Cramp, president of the NUR, and Robert Williams, secretary
of the National Transport Workers' Federation), conjured up
the possibility of industrial 'direct action' for political ends.

The issue had already emerged in February 1919 when
nationalization was designated one of the goals of the miners'
threatened strike. It resurfaced in the spring and summer as the
PCTUC resisted Triple Alliance attempts to drag the TUC into
what the committee's moderate majority considered the unconstitutional waters of political direct action against the government's intervention in Russia and extension of conscription in
April 1919 for a further year.[114] In the process, 'direct action' was
thoroughly debated by both the Labour Party conference in June
and the Trades Union Congress in September.

At the former, more moderate trade unionists (often of the
older generation in leadership positions well before the war),

---

[113] R. H. Tawney, *The Nationalization of the Coal Industry*, (1919), 30; Winter,
Socialism and the Challenge of War, 277–85; B. and S. Webb, *A Constitution for the
Socialist Commonwealth of Great Britain*, 168–202.

[114] *Trades Union Congress, Annual Report, September 1919* (PCTUC report),
74–5, 98–9; Clegg, *A History of British Trade Unionism since 1889*, ii. 284–8.

such as Sexton, Clynes, and the outgoing LPNEC chairman, McGurk, repudiated any industrial action which might jeopardize Labour's legitimacy as a parliamentary party and deepen the challenge of radical rank-and-file militancy. 'Supposing they destroyed the Government by a national strike', demanded Sexton, 'what were they going to put in its place?'[115] Smillie and Hodges, however, denied the charge that political strikes were unconstitutional and argued the need to compensate for labour's political weakness by its industrial strength. With all due safeguards for the consultation of individual unions, they called for the TUC to discuss co-ordinating a 'direct action' campaign against intervention in Russia, and a resolution to that effect, notwithstanding the LPNEC's caution over the international strike on 21 July, was voted by 1,893,000 to 935,000.[116]

At the Trades Union Congress in September, the continued inaction of the PCTUC (in July it decided on a split vote not to hold a conference on 'direct action') caused bitter discord and was condemned by a narrow majority.[117] The same arguments appeared as in June.[118] The mood in favour of at least the possibility of 'direct action' was confirmed by the vote for Smillie's resolution on coal nationalization, while a motion by Shaw (of the Textile Workers) banning all political strikes (Shaw painted Smillie and Williams as Bolsheviks) was in effect defeated.[119]

By autumn 1919, therefore, a narrow majority existed in favour of possible industrial action for political ends in both the Labour Party and TUC. But the question was fraught with ambiguity, and it is important to understand, especially in contrast with France, what it represented for the bulk of labour. None of the leaders who identified nationally with the call for 'direct action' against intervention in Russia considered strikes to be a weapon of revolution. Here the difference in labour traditions and in the social disturbance caused by the war was crucial. Only on the fringes of British labour and in the rapidly

---

[115] *Report of the Labour Party Conference, Southport, June 1919*, 119.
[116] Ibid., 161.
[117] PCTUC, min. 22 July 1919.
[118] *Trades Union Congress, Annual Report, September 1919*, 216–31; Gleason, *What the Workers Want*, 112–35.
[119] *Trades Union Congress, Annual Report, September 1919*, 288–300.

waning shop stewards' movement was there any equivalent of the CGT *minoritaires'* tendency, in 1919–20, to consider 'direct action' the path to a soviet-inspired revolution.[120]

Instead, the national advocates of 'direct action' were scrupulously careful to observe the constitutional proprieties of individual unions and the TUC, and hence the formal hierarchy of trade union power, in seeking concerted industrial action on specific political issues. They considered this an additional, and for the moment superior, instrument to parliament and public opinion—paralleling the CGT's hesitant definition of the idea of a *grève constitutionnelle*. The obvious difference is that British labour was by its structure and traditions committed primarily to political action through elections, and thus to socialism through the continuity of the parliamentary process. Both sides appealed to this reality. Where the antagonists of 'direct action' accused its proponents of destroying the legitimacy of a future Labour government in advance, Hodges argued that judicious use of labour's real industrial power was vital to satisfy the demands for post-war change and thus *preserve* Britain from breakdown and violent revolution.

'This country', he maintained at the Labour Party conference, 'can move through to the social revolution differently from any other country, but if you deny it the right to move through constitutional channels provided by the Labour Party and the trade union movement, you bring into being those elements of social chaos and disaster which may not be the best for the country in the long run.'[121]

In fact, to many the appeal of 'direct action' was less as an open-ended instrument for political change than as a vent for political frustration. It was thus most likely to be invoked where the moral rights of organized labour were apparently denied by government deception or arbitrariness (the protagonists of 'direct action' were wont to accuse the *government* of 'unconstitutional' behaviour).[122] Intervention in Russia and the maintenance of conscription provoked the broadest support for political

[120] Miliband, *Parliamentary Socialism*, 70; Kendall, *The Revolutionary Movement in Britain*, 261–3; Hinton, *The First Shop Stewards' Movement*, 318–23; R. Challinor, *The Origins of British Bolshevism* (Croom Helm, 1977), 270–1.

[121] Gleason, *What the Workers Want*, 101–2.

[122] e.g. Smillie and Robert Williams at the Labour Party 1919 conference (*Report of the Labour Party Conference, Southport, June 1919*, 87, 89).

strikes since they were tantamount to a refusal by the government to complete the process of military demobilization, and
finally end the war. Significantly, the only real 'direct action'
campaign flared suddenly in August 1920 over the renewed
possibility of British military action against Russia in the
Russo-Polish war.[123]

'Direct action' for nationalization, especially coal (in view of
the government's 'broken pledge'), also commanded support,
and a majority in the MFGB, although the Trades Union
Congress in September 1919 had merely approved the possibility of taking this path. In the event, the reluctance of the
Labour Party leadership and PCTUC prevailed. A special
Trades Union Congress in December 1919 settled on a 'Mines
for the Nation' publicity campaign rather than a general strike.
And although a miners' conference in March 1920 confirmed
the appeal for general 'direct action' in favour of nationalization, this was decisively rejected by a further special Trades
Union Congress the same month, which voted overwhelmingly
instead for 'intensive political propaganda in preparation for a
General Election'. The unwieldiness and internal divisions
which hampered the Triple Alliance as an instrument of
industrial action were sharply revealed in April 1921 ('Black
Friday'), with the abandonment of sympathetic action on behalf
of the miners, as they faced decontrol and severe wage cuts.[124]

Thus there was no political general strike in Britain, unlike in
France, although the strength of the trade union movement
made it an infinitely more serious prospect for the state. The
circumscribed approach of much of organized labour to industrial action as appropriate only to economic, and indeed professional, questions, predominated. Its corollary was the decisive
confirmation of the electoral primacy of Labour politics. The
Appeal to the British Nation by the Labour Party, issued by the
LPNEC in late 1920, was an ironic and comprehensive indictment of the 'first great Peace and Reconstruction Government',

---

[123] Miliband, *Parliamentary Socialism*, 76–82; Clegg, *A History of British Trade
Unions since 1889*, ii 292–4.

[124] *Report of the Labour Party Conference, Scarborough, June 1920*, (LPNEC
report), 7–9; Page Arnot, *The Miners: Years of Struggle*, 216–19; Bagwell, 'The
Triple Industrial Alliance', 111–17; Clegg, *A History of British Trade Unions since
1889*, ii. 287–92.

and indirectly a statement of Labour's post-war disillusion-ment. But in making nationalization and the 'democratization of industry' the pivot of Labour's domestic policy, there was no hint of 'direct action'. The sole alternative for what was held to be a profoundly unrepresentative House of Commons was electoral victory by Labour.

(iii) L'Après-guerre *and the Longer-Term Legacy of Wartime Labour Reformism*

Deep working-class discontent in 1919–20 placed enormous strains on the established structures of both labour movements. This was especially so in France, where syndicalist and socialist organizations, decimated in the early war years, struggled to cope with the influx of new members. Reformist leaders of all hues placed a premium on organizational discipline as they engaged in processes of reciprocal recognition and bargaining with other elements of society. Translating a national legiti-macy acquired during the war into post-war gains meant continuing to represent the 'national' interest as well as the working class. Inevitably, reformist approaches were threat-ened by movements which spoke the language of class violence or open-ended industrial conflict.

But it does not follow from this that reformism was the affair only of organizational 'oligarchies' and national leaderships, any more than it had been during the war.[125] Broader, more complex dynamics were at work. To take the more obvious British case first, overtly revolutionary opinion remained weak despite the scale of industrial unrest in 1919–21. The shop stewards' movement faded with the wartime conditions which had given rise to it, and its principal leaders gravitated to communism.[126] The ILP, which increased to 37,000 members by 1920 (80 per cent more than in 1914) mirrored in more radical form the debate in the Labour Party over 'direct action'.

---

[125] Cf. Roberto Michels's classic analysis, using the SPD as a case study, *Political Parties: A Sociological Study of the Oligarchical Tendencies of Modern Democracy* (1911; English trans., 1915; Dover, NY, 1959).

[126] Kendall, *The Revolutionary Movement in Britain*, 169; Hinton, *The First Shop Stewards' Movement*, 319–20.

But although the ILP diverged from Labour by joining the Vienna International in 1921 and adopting a Guild Socialist programme in 1922 (over the opposition of 'constitutionalist' leaders like MacDonald and Snowden), the party continued in its majority to reject violent revolution and to envisage working through the Labour Party and (increasingly) the trade unions.[127] When the Communist Party of Great Britain was founded in 1920–1, it was a fusion of marginal revolutionary organizations and numbered no more than three to five thousand adherents.[128]

By contrast, the Parti Communiste Français emerged from the schism of the PS in December 1920 with 110,000 members, as opposed to 40,000 who remained socialists.[129] There was no direct link between the new majority of late 1918, product of wartime pacifism, and that approving affiliation to Moscow at Tours. But the failure of the right-wing 'Groupe d'action de reconstitution économique de la France', or of Albert Thomas as an individual, to define a reformist programme comparable with that of the CGT, and the deep contradictions within the majority which Léon Blum rallied behind his 1919 electoral programme, indicate the opposition of the bulk of party activists to a reformist socialism culled from the war.

Yet the experience of the CGT, directly in touch with the wave of post-war industrial unrest, was different. Worker attitudes to syndicalism were above all volatile, as well as varied. This presented considerable problems for CGT leaders wishing to secure support for national and local collective contracts or to orchestrate an impressive display of disciplined industrial strength to bring pressure to bear on government. The June strikes of 1919 caught syndicalist leaders unawares. Yet the 21 July action was aborted as much through feared lack of support, and it was the combination of these which made the May 1920 general strike such a devastating defeat for the *majoritaires*. What is significant, given this reality, is the strength of the majority position until the winter of 1920–1.

[127] Dowse, *Left in the Centre*, 54–5, 65–8; Kendall, *The Revolutionary Movement in Britain*, 276; Marquand, *Ramsay MacDonald*, 256–7.

[128] H. Pelling, *The British Communist Party: A Historical Profile* (A. & C. Black, 1958), 1–14.

[129] A. Kriegel, *Le Congrès de Tours (1920): naissance d'un parti communiste français* (Julliard, 1964), p. xxix.

The erosion of *majoritaire* support occurred *after* a decisive industrial defeat, and in the context of rapidly falling syndicalist numbers and the redefinition of revolutionary options, through the launching of the RILU and the birth of French communism.

Conversely, this suggests that in the first eighteen months of peace the reformist programme of the CGT leaders and their contractual approach to industrial relations were congruent with some fundamental aspects of the labour unrest. The *majoritaires* were deeply apprehensive about the flood-tide of inexperienced syndicalists unfamiliar with the traditions of the CGT.[130] But probably a good deal of worker sentiment and strike motivation in 1919 was ambiguous, and not easily categorized as 'economic', 'reformist', or 'revolutionary'. Where the *minoritaire* leaders possessed little in the way of immediate goals, the *majoritaires* offered a pragmatic industrial leadership tested during the war, as well as a rhetoric of moral claims derived from the war, which provided one formulation of working-class demands. Only as the conditions underpinning both of these collapsed, in the summer of 1920, did the majority's hold on the apparatus of syndicalism seriously weaken. By the same token, syndicalist reformism (as it had done during the war) provided a moderate focus for working-class dissaffection when the state was most vulnerable, during the military demobilization. By the time the decisive confrontation occurred, both government and employers were well-prepared.[131]

Overall, the post-war period pointed up sharply the excessive optimism of pro-war labour leaders over their potential influence on government and continued bargaining strength in industry. As we have seen, the enlargement of trade union power across the decade of 1910–20 assumed multiple forms, moderate and radical. In 1920–1, the ebb-tide set in. Determined resistance by employers and much of the state, aided by an economic slump, undermined the institutionalized power and collective bargaining favoured by moderate trade union

---

[130] E.g. the lament of an anonymous CGT leader, reported in *La Journée industrielle*, 6 June 1919, that among the newcomers, 'strikes are declared with scorn for all discipline. The authority of the CGT is belittled'.

[131] Kriegel, *Aux origines du communisme français*, i. 431–75.

leaders as well as the 'direct action' or revolutionary syndicalist ambitions of the radicals. In neither country did the Ministries of Labour, weakened and isolated in the climate of post-war politics, manage to preserve the wartime approach to industrial relations based on the recognition of trade unions and their active incorporation into bargaining arrangements. As trade union numbers dropped in the 1920s, with employers in many sectors attacking or bypassing trade unions, the authority of the latter waned and their contacts with the state (by comparison with wartime) languished.

In Britain, the overall strength of trade unions and the tradition of collective bargaining tempered this erosion of trade union power. French trade unions were much more severely affected. The number of collective contracts, 557 in 1919 and still 345 in 1920, sank well below 200 in each of the next five years before dwindling to a handful.[132] The May 1920 strike permitted employers to ignore collective contracts in operation (as in the case of the UIMM) and the state to attack the CGT— to the point of obtaining its legal, though purely nominal, dissolution.[133] The *commissions paritaires* through which the CGT had sought to influence different aspects of the economy—although not entirely abandoned—were stripped of real significance.

The caesura of 1920–1 was not absolute, even in France. A minority of *patrons* continued to bargain with unions. Corporatist connections between the CGT and the state persisted in a minor key, notably when the Cartel des Gauches introduced a more satisfactory, though still diluted, version of the Conseil National Économique in 1925.[134] The wartime approach of the CGT to industrial relations became most relevant to the fairly

---

[132] G. Lefranc (pseud. J. Montreuil), *Histoire du mouvement ouvrier en France des origines à nos jours* (Aubier, 1946), 43; T. Rodgers, 'Employer Organizations: Unemployment and Social Politics in Britain during the Inter-War Period', *Social History*, 13/3 (Oct. 1988), 313–41.

[133] Saposs, *The Labor Movement in Post-War France*, 339–40; Dubreuil, *Employeurs et salariés en France*, 60–1; Lefranc, *Les Organisations patronales en France*, 74–5, 94–5.

[134] Saposs, *The Labor Movement in Post-War France*, 91, 201–10; Fine, 'Towards Corporatism', 129–56; Gemelli, 'Un'istituzione ambivalente: le origini del conseil national économique', 566–77; Rossiter, 'Experiments with Corporatist Politics in Republican France', 107–23 (who argues that the scaffolding of corporatist politics was extended in the early 1920s).

stable environment of public sector employees, from which the organization drew a substantial portion of its members by the late 1920s. But the state and employer counter-offensive undermined the role and credibility of the CGT leadership and marginalized its influence among private-sector workers.[135]

The *après-guerre* period both underlined and confirmed the difference in attitude to the state between British and French variants of war reformism. The tensions resulting from frustrated post-war expectations in the British case produced pressure for 'direct action' in the political vacuum following the December 1918 election. Fabian views on a parliamentary and administrative path to socialism had to contend with alternative currents emphasizing notions of industrial democracy. None the less, the essentially parliamentary road to socialism formulated through wartime 'reconstruction' thinking was confirmed by the way these post-war tensions were resolved in the Labour Party—at the cost, perhaps, of tethering socialist aspirations to the electoral progress of the party and reducing the question of the state to that of a parliamentary majority.[136]

The crucial role of the state in French definitions of socialism and syndicalism, as well as the actual experience of 1919–20, produced connections between wartime and longer-term reformism of a different and more problematic order. The difficulty experienced by Blum, in 1919, in devising a feasible programme of reforms for French conditions while adhering to a marxist view of the class state, formed one of the parameters of inter-war socialism.[137] The coalition government which a reform programme realistically required ran counter to the socialist control of the state obligatory for the achievement of socialism. Younger socialists like Marcel Déat (significantly, one of the 'front' generation) who sought to escape these 'old quarrels' by elaborating a flexible socialist reformism, were forced in the crisis of the Depression to quit the party.[138]

[135] Saposs, *The Labor Movement in Post-War France*, 136–9.
[136] Miliband, *Parliamentary Socialism*, 96–8; D. Coates, *The Labour Party and the Struggle for Socialism* (CUP, Cambridge, 1975), 17–18; Winter, *Socialism and the Challenge of War*, 276–7.
[137] L. Blum, *Bolchévisme et socialisme* (Librairie Populaire, 1927); Ziebura, *Léon Blum et le parti socialiste*, 283–90; Judt, *La Reconstruction du parti socialiste*, 71–97.
[138] M. Déat, *Perspectives socialistes* (Librairie Valois, 1930), 10; A. Bergounioux, 'Le Néo-socialisme: Marcel Déat: réformisme traditionnel ou esprit des années trente?' *Revue historique*, 528 (Oct.–Dec. 1978), pp. 389–414.

This helps to explain the continued separation, yet functional interdependence, of the PS and CGT. As during the war, the syndicalist movement was better placed to take up certain ideas of reform with fundamental political implications by virtue of its assertion of syndicalist autonomy and of the primacy of the economic sphere. French social democracy, in the post-1914 sense of the term, wore a syndicalist as much as a socialist visage. Yet the corresponding absence of any analysis of the state, or means of exerting political leverage on it, remained a fatal weakness, especially in view of significantly reduced numbers and a refusal to revive the experiment of the *grève constitutionnelle*. As during the war, the CGT leadership sought contact with progressive administrators and potentially reforming political parties—the Radicals during the Cartel des Gauches and the socialists during the Front Populaire. The price was especially clear in the 1930s, when the CGT's distinctive 'Plan' for dealing with the Depression (which echoed some of Déat's concerns) was subordinated to the different and more limited preoccupations of the Blum government.[139]

It is an ironic comment on the continued isolation of the CGT in the Third Republic after the Front Populaire that several leading syndicalists, disaffected with a regime to which their ideological roots little disposed them, and lured by the Proudhonist vision of an economy freed from 'politics', plus a deep pacifism, should have ended up in Vichy's Ministry of Labour. Among them were Auguste Savoie and Georges Dumoulin.

The industrial and political constraints on French syndicalist reformism in the *après-guerre* were reinforced by a third, fundamental limitation—its social composition in the wake of the wartime upheaval of the French working class. We have seen that the strength of the *minoritaires* was rooted in the sectors and localities dominated by war production. The correlation holds for the subsequent evolution of the minority down

---

[139] CGT, *Contre la crise, pour l'économie dirigée, exposé sur le plan de rénovation économique* (1934); G. Lefranc, 'Le Courant planiste dans le mouvement ouvrier français de 1933 à 1936', *Le Mouvement social* (Jan.–Mar. 1966), pp. 69–89; J. Amoyal, 'Les Origines socialistes et syndicalistes de la planification en France', *Le Mouvement social*, 87 (Apr.–June 1974), pp. 137–69; Kuisel, *Capitalism and the State in Modern France*, 114–25.

to, and beyond, the 1921 schism. The touchstone of *minoritaire* militancy remained the newly assorted working class of the major munitions centres, to which was added the large railway workforce much of it newly recruited.[140] This revolutionary orientation prevented or limited the enrolment of the most dynamic elements of the working class by the *majoritaires*.

The latter, better represented in the more traditional segments of the working class as well as in the public sector, proved more resistant to the decline in working-class organization, political as well as industrial, in the 1920s. The CGT was consistently, and sometimes substantially, more numerous than its communist counterpart (the PS also outnumbered the rapidly declining Communist Party membership). But in the bastions of post-war *minoritaire* support, such as metallurgy and railways, the communist federations remained larger than those of the CGT.[141] And the resurgence of working-class organization through the Front Populaire decisively favoured the communists, party and unions, over the PS and reformist CGT.[142]

Social discontinuity in the working class during and after the war thus combined with a rapidly deteriorating climate of industrial relations, the internal tensions of French syndicalist and socialist traditions, and the external pull of the October revolution, to fracture the labour movement. The *majoritaire* leaders failed in their aim of converting the heritage of skilled 'trade socialism' into a reformist syndicalism encompassing and permanently organizing the mass, non-skilled membership temporarily brought in by the war. In Britain, greater continuity in the social composition of the working class, more deeply entrenched trade unions, and a less conflictual labour culture, sustained the unity of the labour movement and its reformist orientation.

---

[140] Robert, *La Scission syndicale de 1921*, 173–87; Ribeill, *Le Personnel des compagnies de chemins de fer*, ii. *Les Cheminots en guerre*, 53–89.

[141] Saposs, *The Labor Movement in Post-War France*, 136–9.

[142] A. Prost, *La CGT à l'époque du front populaire, 1934–1939* (Colin, 1964); J. Girault (ed.), *Sur l'implantation du parti communiste français dans l'entre deux guerres* (Éditions sociales, 1977); Noiriel, *Les Ouvriers dans la société française, xixᵉ– xxᵉ siècles*, 157–70.

Yet, for all these differences, there are certain affinities between the longer-term ideological legacies of both variants of wartime labour reformism. At the core of the Comité d'Action's November 1916 programme, as of *Labour and the New Social Order*, was a tension between the aspiration to replace a morally condemned capitalism with a collectivist alternative and the proposal to work toward that goal via economic and social measures to reform capitalism from within. Rejection of capitalism coexisted with the aim of making it more efficient and tolerable. Since the war created the impression that the days of capitalism were numbered (reflecting the economism of much pre-war socialist thought), and since resentment at specific wartime grievances was expressed through jeremiads on the evils of capitalism, this side of the post-war programmes was inevitably stressed.

In reality, of course, the war had initiated new forms of capitalist organization, breaking with the *laissez-faire* past. Even this lesson was obscured by post-war decontrol and the drive for a return to pre-war 'normality'. The latter was impossible to achieve, but in France and Britain, at least, the strategies adopted by governments and industrialists in the 1920s to stabilize the post-war order, along with organized labour's own circumstances, rendered the terrain less favourable than during the war to reformist projects. The Labour Party, in its first government of 1924, had a distinctly more restricted agenda than in 1918. The CGT reduced its wartime concern with productivism and 'worker control' to a defensive, syndicalist version of employer 'rationalization' of industrial processes.

But the Depression and a second world war, followed in both countries by left-wing governments, reactivated the wider relevance of the earlier reformist perspectives. They also triggered a similar duality. The tension between reforming and transforming capitalism, the ambiguity over reforms as the goal of the former or the instrument of the latter, defined the principal dilemmas and internal divisions of the labour and socialist movements in both countries.

Although altered circumstances changed the emphasis, the reformist ideas of the First World War retained much of their relevance. The CGT 'Plan' owed a great deal (including its stress on nationalizations and the rudimentary concept of economic planning) to *majoritaire* thinking during the First World War. The form of nationalization espoused by the French left in 1945 was that defined by the CGT during and after the earlier conflict. The British labour movement during the Second World War was sharply aware of the fate of its 'reconstruction' plans following the First. Historians have rightly stressed the complexity of the relationship between popular participation in 'total' wars and subsequent social change. In the case of the First World War, it may well be that the more substantial, if indirect, legacy of French and British labour reformism should be sought not in the first but in the second *après-guerre*.

Appendix I. The Cost of Living, 1914–1920

1. Rise in Prices (Food and other Items)

		1914	1915	1916	1917	1918	1919	1920
Britain	Jan.	100	110/15	135	165	185/90	220	225
	Oct.	110	130	150/5	175/80	215/20	220	264
Paris	1st qu.	100	120	135	135	190	240	295
	4th qu.	100	120	135	180	235	280	370
Provincial France	1st qu.	100	110	130	150	210	280	320
	4th qu.	100	120	145	190	260	300	390

Sources: *Labour Gazette*, Aug. 1919, p. 318; Apr. 1921, p. 184;
L. March, *Le Mouvement des prix et des salaires pendant la guerre*
(1925), 244.

2. Rise in Wages, 1914–1919

	1914	1915	1916	1917	1918	1919	1920
Britain	100	105/10	115/20	135/40	175/80	210/15	260
France	100	110	125	130	175	250	360

Note: The British figures average 12 major industries; the French
figures average ten sectors, and are for male workers.
Sources: A. L. Bowley, *Prices and Wages in the United Kingdom
1914–20* (1921), 106; L. March, *Le Mouvement des prix et des
salaires pendant la guerre* (1925), 297.

Appendix II. Workers Involved in Strikes, 1914–1921

	France	Britain
1914	161,000	326,000
1915	9,000	401,000
1916	41,000	235,000
1917	436,000	575,000
1918	386,000	923,000
1919	1,173,000	2,401,000
1920	1,317,000	1,779,000
1921	402,000	1,770,000

Note: see Chap. 1, n. 17, above.

Sources: *Annuaire statistique de la France, 1966, Résumé rétrospectif,* pp. 120–1; J.-L. Robert, 'Ouvriers et mouvement ouvrier parisiens pendant la grande guerre èt l'immédiat après-guerre' (Thèse d'état, Paris, I, 1989), 49; *British Labour Statistics. Historical Abstract, 1886–1968* (1971), 396.

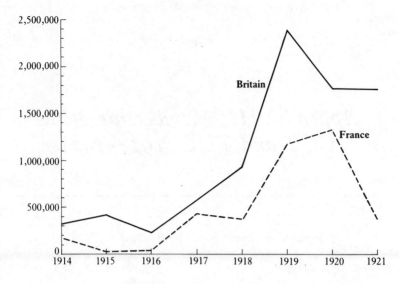

Appendix III. Membership of the CGT and TUC, 1914–1921

	CGT		TUC
	Unions départementales	Fédérations	
1913	238,477	355,466	2,232,446
1914	237,145	256,761	—
1915	32,068	49,549	2,682,357
1916	82,958	100,549	2,850,547
1917	263,678	295,862	3,082,352
1918	576,828	598,528	4,532,085
1919	1,204,829	1,229,532	5,283,676
1920	1,322,741	1,333,103	6,505,482
1921	663,125	699,248	6,417,910

Sources: J.-L. Robert, *La Scission syndicale de 1921: essai de reconnaissance de formes* (1980), 159–60; B. C. Roberts, *The Trades Union Congress, 1868–1921* (1958), 380.

Appendix IV. The Industrial Work-force during the War

1. Munitions work-force (controlled establishments), Britain, October 1916–January 1918

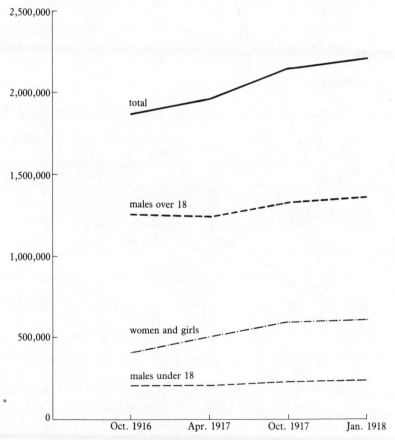

Source: *History of the Ministry of Munitions*, vol. vi, pt. 1, p. 57 (table XX)

2. *Munitions and aircraft work-force, France, 1916–1918*

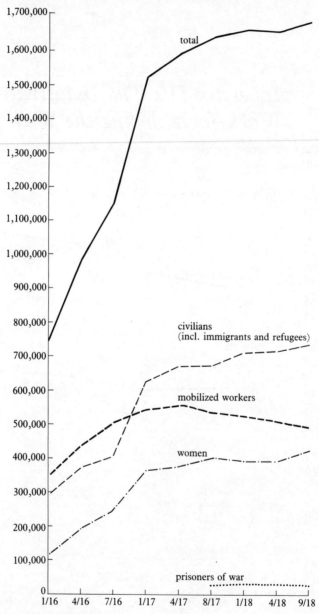

Source: SHAT 6N 58

3. *Women as a percentage of the industrial work-force, 1914–1920*
i. *France*

	% of ind. work-force	% of work-force in metal trades
Pre-Aug. 1914	29.8	6.5
Jan. 1915	38.2	14.2
Jan. 1916	38.0	18.3
Jan. 1917	37.2	21.2
Jan. 1918	37.1	22.3
Oct. 1920	32.0	12.9

Source: *Bulletin du ministère du travail*, Nov.–Dec. 1920, p. 485.

ii. *Britain*

	% of ind. work-force	% of work-force in metal trades
July 1914	26.1	9.4
July 1915	29.8	11.4
July 1916	32.8	17.8
July 1917	35.1	22.8
July 1918	36.1	24.6
July 1920	27.0	13.0

Source: *History of the Ministry of Munitions*, vol vi, pt. 1, p. 31 (table VIII); A. W. Kirkaldy (ed.), *British Labour: Replacement and Conciliation, 1914–1921* (1921), 3

Bibliography

The place of publication, unless otherwise indicated, is Paris for books in French and London for books in English.

I. SOURCES

MANUSCRIPT SOURCES

A. FRANCE

1. Archives Nationales

F_7 (Ministry of the Interior, Sûreté Générale)
F_7 12891 'Le Mouvement syndicaliste, année 1916'
F_7 13073–4 Parti Socialiste and Comité d'Action
F_7 13272 1 May 1915–18
F_7 13273 1 May 1919
F_7 13310 planned strike, 21 July 1919
F_7 13357–69 war factories
F_7 13371–76 pacifism (esp. the cumulative reports in F_7 13372)
F_7 13569–76 CGT and Comité d'Action during the war
F_7 13595 report on *délégués ouvriers*
F_{14} (Ministry of Public Works)
F_{14} 11333–4 Commission inter-ministérielle de la main-d'œuvre
F_{22} (Ministry of Labour)
F_{22} 170 strikes (outside munitions), 1917–18
F_{22} 286–99 mines
F_{22} 401 preparation of eight-hour law, 1919
94 AP (papers of Albert Thomas), esp.:
94 AP 135 foreign and female labour
94 AP 137–40 industrial disputes and strikes
94 AP 141 industrial questions, délégués ouvriers
94 AP 362 post-war reform, 1919 election
94 AP 367 war factories after the war

94 AP 373–5 labour demands
94 AP 401 Comité National d'Études Sociales et Politiques
94 AP 406 Commission Mixte d'Études Economiques

2. Archives de la Préfecture de Police de Paris

B/a 1375 *délégués ouvriers* (Seine)
B/a 1386 Paris metalworkers' strike, 1919
B/a 1470 Parti Socialiste, 1910–18
B/a 1492 Parti Socialiste, sections
B/a 1494 CGT tracts
B/a 1605 reports on the CGT, 1913–15

3. Institut Français d'Histoire Sociale

14 AS 213 Picart papers
14 AS 219 minutes of the Commission Exécutive of the Fédération des Métaux
14 AS 407 minutes and circulars of the Commission Exécutive of the Fédération du Bâtiment, 1916–17

4. Musée Social

Minutes of the Comité Général de l'Union des Syndicats de la Seine, Aug. 1915–Dec. 1917 (uncatalogued)
minutes of the Commission Exécutive of the *délégués d'atelier* of the 13ᵉ arrdt, 1918 (uncatalogued)
B. Lavergne, *Principes directeurs de nationalisation ...*, typescript prepared on behalf of the FNCC for the Conseil Économique du Travail

5. Service Historique de l'Armée de Terre (Vincennes)

6N Clemenceau papers
16N 1538 Monthly police reports to the Ministère de l'Intérieur on public opinion (from Oct. 1917). This series continues in the Bibliothèque de Documentation Internationale Contemporaine (Nanterre), F △ Res. 2.

B. BRITAIN

1. Labour Party Archives

Henderson papers
International Advisory Committee

Labour Party National Executive Committee, minutes, 1914–19
Labour and Socialist International (for international affairs, 1918–20)
Middleton papers
War Emergency: Workers' National Committee papers

2. *London School of Economics, Library*

Passfield papers (for the Webbs)

3. *Nuffield College, Oxford*

Annual reports, minutes and correspondence of the Fabian Society,
plus Fabian tracts, 1910–22, and *Fabian News*, 1914–20

4. *Public Record Office*

Cab 23/1 Cabinet minutes from 1916
Cab 25 Cabinet memoranda and papers from 1916
Cab 26 and 27 Cabinet committees
Ramsay MacDonald papers

5. *Trades Union Congress Library*

Parliamentary Committee of the TUC, minutes 1914–19
PCTUC, *Quarterly Reports*

PRINTED SOURCES

A. FRANCE

1. *Labour and Socialist Movements*

(a) CGT—confederal level
*18ᵉ Congrès national corporatif . . . tenu au Havre du 16 au 23 septembre
1912. Compte rendu des travaux* (Imprimerie de l'Union, Le Havre,
1912).
*Compte rendu de la conférence ordinaire des fédérations nationales et des
bourses du travail . . . tenu les 13, 14 et 15 juillet 1913 . . . Paris*
(Maison des Fédérations, 1914).
*Rapports des comités et des commissions pour l'exercice 1912–191 4
présentés au 19ᵉ congrès corporatif . . . tenu à Grenoble du 14 au 19
septembre 1914* (Maison des Syndicats, 1914).
*Conférence extraordinaire des fédérations nationales, bourses du travail et
unions des syndicats (Clermont-Ferrand, 23–5 déc. 1917). Compte
rendu* (Maison des Syndicats, n.d.).

Rapports des comités et des commissions pour l'exercice 1914–1918 présentés au 19ᵉ congrès corporatif ... tenu à Versailles du 15 au 18 juillet 1918 (Imprimerie Nouvelle, 1918).

19ᵉ Congrès national corporatif ... (Paris, 15–18 juillet 1918). Compte rendu des travaux (Imprimerie Nouvelle, 1919).

Première réunion du comité confédéral national (Paris, 15–16 décembre 1918). Compte rendu sténographique (L'Union Typographique, Villeneuve-Saint-Georges, 1919).

Rapports des comités confédéraux et des commissions pour l'exercice 1918–1919 (1919).

20ᵉ Congrès national corporatif ... (Lyon, 15–21 septembre 1919). Compte rendu des travaux (L'Union Typographique, Villeneuve-Saint-Georges, 1920).

21ᵉ Congrès national corporatif ... (Orléans, 27 septembre–2 octobre, 1920). Compte rendu des travaux (L'Union Typographique, Villeneuve-Saint-Georges, 1921).

22ᵉ Congrès national corporatif ... (Lille, 25–30 juillet 1921). Compte rendu des travaux (L'Union Typographique, Villeneuve-Saint-Georges, 1921).

La CGT et le mouvement syndical (Éditions de la CGT, 1925).

(b) CGT—'majoritaire' programmes and brochures

The Comité Confédéral issued many circulars and *ordres du jour* during the war. Those referred to in the text can be found in *Rapport des comités ... pour l'exercice 1914–1918; Rapport des comités ... pour l'exercice 1919–1920; La Bataille; La Voix du peuple;* APP B/a 1494; and Institut Français d'Histoire Sociale, Picart papers (esp. 14 AS 213 c/18). The most important are:

A l'Internationale ouvrière: aux organisations centrales nationales (Feb. 1915).

Une attitude, un programme (Mar. 1916). Jouhaux's speech to the Fédération des Industriels et des Commerçants Français on 4 Mar. 1916.

La Majorité confédérale et la guerre (1916).

Questions ouvrières (1916). Leeds and the *clauses ouvrières*.

'Ordre du jour' of 10 Oct. 1916, condemning minority hostility to *majoritaire* domestic and international reformism.

Au Prolétariat français! (Oct.–Dec. 1917). Opposition to Clemenceau.

La CGT devant la situation ouvrière (spring 1918). The May strikes.

La Leçon des faits: la délégation confédérale devant les parlementaires de gauche (June 1918). The speeches by Jouhaux and Merrheim to the deputies of the left on 7 June.

Réceptions de Gompers à la Confédération Générale du Travail, 24 et 26 septembre 1918.

Les Travailleurs devant la paix (Dec. 1918). Jouhaux's view on post-war reform, with the *Programme minimum* as an appendix.

Modifications aux statuts proposées au comité national confédéral par la commission désignée par le congrès confédéral de juillet 1918 (1918).

La Nationalisation industrialisée. (Les Raisons, la nécessité de sa réalisation) (mid-1920).

L'Action confédérale et la grève des cheminots (1920).

(c) Comité d'Action

Rapport sur l'action générale du comité présenté le 20 novembre 1915 (1915).

Reconstruction des cités détruites et dommages de guerre (1915).

La vie chère (five reports, 1915).

Rapport du comité d'action, 2ᵉ année, octobre 1915 à octobre 1916.

Rapport de la commission mixte d'études économiques (Nov. 1916). First draft in AN F$_7$ 13571. Final, published copy in AN 94 AP 406 and Institut Français d'Histoire Sociale, Picart papers.

(d) CGT—'minoritaire' brochures

Published collections of these are A. Rosmer, *Le Mouvement ouvrier pendant la première guerre mondiale*, vol. i, *De l'union sacrée à Zimmerwald* (Librairie du Travail, 1936), vol. ii, *De Zimmerwald à la révolution russe* (Mouton, 1959), who cites documents extensively, and A. Sowerwine and C. Sowerwine (eds.), *Le Mouvement ouvrier français contre la guerre, 1914–1918* (Éditions d'Histoire Sociale, 1985), vol. iii, *L'Opposition syndicale.* Among the most important syndicalist *minoritaire* declarations are the *Lettres aux abonnés de la Vie ouvrière*, issued in 1915 (after Zimmerwald) and 1916 by Alfred Rosmer, in effect as propaganda for the Comité pour la Reprise des Relations Internationales, and the following brochures published by the Comité de Défense Syndicaliste:

L'Action de la majorité confédérale et la conférence de Leeds (Aug.–Sept. 1916).

Aux organisations syndicales! A leurs militants! (Nov.–Dec. 1916).

Maîtres et valets (1917).

La Vraie Cassure (Sept. 1917).

The relaunching of *La Vie ouvrière* marked the regrouping of the *minoritaires* post-war (see *La 'Vie ouvrière' réapparaîtra!* (30 Apr. 1919)).

(e) CGT—federations

(i) Fédération de l'Alimentation

Fédération nationale des travailleurs de l'alimentation. Compte rendu des travaux et résolutions du 8ᵉ congrès national, 12–13 juillet, Paris 1918 (1918).

(ii) Fédération du Bâtiment

Fédération nationale des travailleurs de l'industrie du bâtiment. Rapport du comité. Questions à l'ordre du jour du congrès national, Bordeaux ... 7 ... 11 avril 1912 (La Cotypographie, Courbevoie, 1912).

Fédération nationale ... Compte rendu des travaux du 4ᵉ congrès national, tenu à Bordeaux, les 7, 8, 9, 10 et 11 avril 1912 (Imprimerie du 'Travailleur du Bâtiment', 1912).

Fédération nationale ... 5e congrès national ... du lundi 13 au vendredi 17 avril 1914. Rapports sur les questions à l'ordre du jour (Maison des Fédérations, n.d., but 1914).

Fédération nationale ... 5ᵉ congrès national, Paris ... 13 au 17 avril 1914. Compte rendu des séances (L'Union Typographique, Ville-neuve-Saint-Georges, 1914).

Fédération nationale ... 6ᵉ congrès national, Versailles, 10 ... 13 juillet 1918. Compte rendu des séances (Imprimerie Nouvelle, 1918).

Syndicat Général des Ouvriers Terrassiers ... du département de la Seine, *A nos adhérents. Rapport moral et financier. Du 1ᵉʳ août 1914 au 1ᵉʳ janvier 1918* (Société Ouvrière d'Imprimerie, Courbevoie, 1918).

(iii) Fédération des Cheminots

Syndicat national des travailleurs des chemins de fer. Compte rendu du 25ᵉ congrès national, avril 1914 (Société Ouvrière d'Imprimerie, Courbevoie, 1914).

Fédération nationale des travailleurs des chemins de fer. Compte rendu du 1ᵉʳ congrès national, Paris, 28–30 juin 1918 (Imprimerie Nouvelle, 1918).

BIDEGARAY, M., *Contre les compagnies: pour la nation* (Société Ouvrière d'Imprimerie, Seine, 1917).

—— *L'Exploitation d'aujourd'hui par les compagnies: l'exploitation de demain par la nationalisation des chemins de fer* (Imprimerie Ouvrière, Courbevoie, 1919).

(iv) Fédération des Métaux

Fédération des Ouvriers des Métaux, Compte rendu des 1ᵉʳ et 2ᵉᵐᵉ congrès nationaux tenus à Paris ... août 1911 et ... septembre 1913 (Maison des Fédérations, n.d.).

Fédération des Ouvriers des Métaux, 4ᵉ congrès national. Rapport moral et compte rendu du congrès extraordinaire tenu ... à Lyon ... septembre 1919 (Maison des Syndicats, n.d.).

(v) Fédération du Sous-Sol

Fédération nationale de l'industrie des mines ... Compte rendu officiel des travaux du 23ᵉ congrès national des mineurs ... février 1912 (Impri-merie des Travailleurs Réunis, Carmaux, 1912).

Fédération nationale des travailleurs du sous-sol ... Compte rendu officiel des travaux du 25ᵉ congrès national ... avril 1913 (Imprimerie des Travailleurs Réunis, Carmaux, 1913).

Fédération nationale des travailleurs du sous-sol ... Compte rendu officiel des travaux du 26ᵉ congrès national ... janvier 1914 ... (Imprimerie des Travailleurs Réunis, Carmaux, 1914).

Fédération nationale des travailleurs du sous-sol. Compte rendu officiel des travaux du 3ᵉ congrès national extraordinaire, 23–6 mars 1917 (Imprimerie des Travailleurs Réunis, Carmaux, 1917).

(vi) Other

Fédération nationale des cuirs et peaux. Compte rendu des 8ᵉ et 9ᵉ congrès nationaux (Paris, 15–18 septembre 1913; 19–20 mai 1918) (1918).

Fédération nationale des moyens de transport. Congrès extraordinaires; juillet 1918, avril 1919 et septembre 1920 (1920).

Comité Intersyndical d'Action contre l'Exploitation de la Femme, *Le Travail de la femme pendant la guerre* (L'Union Typographique, 1917).

(f) Conseil Économique du Travail

Rapport de la commission d'enquête du Conseil Économique du Travail dans les régions dévastées (Jan. 1921).

(g) Parti Socialiste

Parti socialiste. 8ᵉ congrès national tenu à Saint-Quentin ... avril 1911. Compte rendu sténographique (n.d.).

Parti socialiste. 9ᵉ congrès national tenu à Lyon ... février 1912 (1912).

Parti socialiste. 10ᵉ congrès national tenu à Brest les 23, 24 et 25 mars 1913. Compte rendu sténographique (n.d.).

Parti socialiste. 11ᵉ congrès national tenu à Amiens ... janvier 1914. Compte rendu sténographique (1914).

Parti socialiste. 16ᵉ congrès national tenu à Bordeaux, octobre 1918. Compte rendu sténographique (1919).

Parti socialiste. 17ᵉ congrès national tenu à Strasbourg les 25, 26, 27, 28 et 29 février 1920. Compte rendu sténographique (1920).

CHARLES, J., et al., *Le Congrès de Tours. 18ᵉ congrès national du parti socialiste. Texte intégral* (Éditions Sociales, 1980).

Le Parti socialiste, la guerre et la paix: toutes les résolutions et tous les documents du parti socialiste de juillet 1914 à fin 1917 (Librairie de l'Humanité, 1918).

ROUGER, H., *L'Action socialiste au parlement (1914–1919)* (Librairie du Parti Socialiste et de l'Humanité, 1919).

LUQUET, A., *La Législation sur les loyers de guerre: ce que tout le monde doit savoir* (Librairie de l'Humanité, 1919).

BLUM, L., *Commentaires sur le programme d'action du parti socialiste (discours prononcé le 21 avril 1919 au congrès national extraordinaire)* (Librairie Populaire, 1919).

(h) Co-operative Movement

FNCC, *3ᵉ Congrès national et conférence coopérative interalliée tenu à Paris les 22, 23, 24 et 25 septembre 1916* (Bureau de la Fédération Nationale, 1917).

FNCC, *4ᵉ Congrès national tenu à Paris les 30 septembre, 1ᵉʳ et 2 octobre 1917. Compte rendu* (L'Émancipatrice, 1917).

FNCC, *5ᵉ Congrès national tenu à Paris les 22, 23 et 24 septembre 1918. Compte rendu* (FNCC, 1918).

THOMAS, A., *La Coopération et les usines de guerre* (Bibliothèque de l'École Coopérative, 1919).

2. *The State*

(a) Ministère de l'Armement

Protection et utilisation de la main-d'œuvre féminine dans les usines de guerre (1917).

Réglement des différends du travail dans les usines de guerre (1917).

Protection et utilisation de la main-d'œuvre féminine pendant la guerre (Ministère de la Reconstitution Industrielle, 1919). Work of the Comité du Travail Féminin.

(b) Ministère du Travail

Comité permanent d'études relatives à la prévision des chômages industriels. Compte rendu des travaux. Années 1917–1920 (Imprimerie Nationale, 1920).

'Commission des traités internationaux du travail', *Bulletin du ministère du travail*, 1919, appendix, pp. 1–27.

Mesures tendant à maintenir l'activité nationale pendant la démobilisation (Imprimerie Nationale, 1919).

Statistique des grèves survenues pendant les années 1915, 1916, 1917, 1918 (Imprimerie Nationale, 1921).

Statistique des grèves survenues pendant l'année 1919 (Imprimerie Nationale, 1922).

Tarifs de salaires et conventions collectives pendant la guerre, 1914–1918, 3 vols. (Imprimerie Nationale, 1921).

Travaux des commissions mixtes départementales pour le maintien du travail national (1915–18), 4 vols. (Imprimerie Nationale, 1918).

Travaux préparatoires de la loi du 23 avril 1919 (Imprimerie Nationale, 1919).

(c) Parliament

Journal officiel, 1914–1920. *Chambre des députés, Débats parlementaires* and *Documents parlementaires*.

(d) Other

SELLIER, H., and DESLANDRES, E., *La Constitution de l'office départemental du placement et de la statistique du travail de la Seine. Son action et ses travaux, du 1ᵉʳ novembre 1915 au 30 octobre 1918* (Conseil Général de la Seine, 1918).

3. Employers

(a) Association Nationale d'Expansion Économique

Enquête sur la production française et la concurrence étrangère, 6 vols. (1917).

(b) Le Comité des Forges

Comité des forges de France. Assemblée générale ordinaire. Rapport de la commission de direction (1915–1920).
PINOT, R., *La Métallurgie et l'après-guerre* (1917).
—— *Le Comité des forges de France au service de la nation* (Colin, 1919).

(c) Fédération des Industriels et des Commerçants Français

Les Origines et le but de la Fédération (n.d., but during the war).
LEBON, A., *Les Problèmes économiques nés de la guerre*, 2 vols. (Payot, 1918).

(d) Union des Industries Métallurgiques et Minières

Assemblée générale du 18 février 1919 (Imprimerie Chaix, 1919).
Assemblée générale du 17 février 1920 (Imprimerie Chaix, 1920).

B. BRITAIN

1. The Labour Movement

(a) Trades Union Congress

Report of the Trades Union Congress, Bristol, September 1915 (1915).
Report of the Trades Union Congress, Birmingham, September 1916 (1916).
Report of the Trades Union Congress, Blackpool, September 1917 (1917).
Report of the Trades Union Congress, Derby, September 1918 (1918).
Report of the Trades Union Congress, Glasgow, September 1919 (1919).

There were relatively few PCTUC publications independently of the

Labour Party or joint committees. Manifestos and declarations are contained in the committees' minutes and in the *Quarterly Reports*.

(b) General Federation of Trade Unions
GFTU, *Annual Report*, 1914–19.
Jubilee Souvenir: Fifty Years' History of the General Federation of Trade Unions 1899–1949 (GFTU, 1949).

(c) Labour Party Conferences
Report of the Labour Party Conference, Bristol, January 1916 (1916).
Report of the Labour Party Conference, Manchester, January 1917 (1917).
Report of the Labour Party Conference, Nottingham, January 1918 (1918).
Report of the Labour Party Conference, Westminster, June 1918 (1918).
Report of the Labour Party Conference, Southport, June 1919 (1919).
Report of the Labour Party Conference, Scarborough, June 1920 (1920).

(d) Labour Party Publications
The list is far from exhaustive. It includes only manifestos, pamphlets, and books directly relevant to this study.

1915
Opinions on the Munitions of War Act.
The British Labour Movement and the War.

1916
The Labour Year Book (1916).

1917
A People's Peace (Henderson, Sept. 1917).
Labour and an After War Economic Policy (Henderson, Nov. 1917).
Labour Problems after the War (LPNEC resolutions passed at the Jan. 1917 conference).
Memorandum on War Issues Presented by the Labour Party to the International Socialist Conference (28–9 Aug. 1917).
Memorandum on War Aims (Dec. 1917–Feb. 1918).
Why a Labour Party?

1918
The Aims of Labour (Henderson, Jan. 1918).
The Outlook for Labour (Henderson, Feb. 1918).
Labour and the New Social Order.
The New Constitution for the Labour Party.
The League of Nations and Labour (Henderson).
A League of Nations (Oct. 1918, Advisory Committee on International Relations).
Labour's Call to the People (election manifesto).

1919
The Labour Year Book (1919).
International Labour and Peace.
The Peace Terms (Henderson, mid-1919).
The Principles of the Labour Party (B. Webb and S. Webb).
1920
An Appeal to the British Nation by the Labour Party.

(e) The War Emergency: Workers' National Committee

Compulsory Military Service and Industrial Conscription. What they Mean to the Workers (late 1915).
Report of the War Emergency: Workers' National Committee (August 1914–March 1916) (1916).
First Report on Labour After the War (Feb. 1916).
Labour and Social Conditions Caused by the War: Some Notes on the Speech of the Prime Minister in Replying to the Trade Union Congress Deputation on July 19th 1916.
The National Food Supply (1917).
The Conscription of Riches (1917).

(f) Joint Committee on Labour Problems After the War

Restoration of Trade Union Customs after the War. A Statement and Analysis of the Government's Guarantees (1916).
The Munitions Acts and the Restoration of Trade Union Customs (1916).
The Problem of Demobilisation (1916).
The Problem of Unemployment after the War (1916).
The Position of Women after the War (1916).
The Restoration of Trade Union Conditions in Cases not Covered by Munitions Acts (1917).
A Million New Houses After the War (1917).

(g) The Independent Labour Party

ILP Annual Conference Report, Norwich, April 1915 (1915).
ILP Annual Conference Report, Newcastle upon Tyne, April 1916 (1916).
ILP Annual Conference Report, Leeds, April 1917 (1917).
ILP Annual Conference Report, Leicester, April 1918 (1918).
ILP Annual Conference Report, Huddersfield, April 1919 (1919).
ANDERSON, W. C., *Labour and War Problems* (1916) (Presidential address to the January 1916 Labour Party conference, issued as an ILP pamphlet).

ILP manifestos and programmes have been taken from the *Labour Leader.*

(h) Fabian Society and the Webbs

Fabian Tracts, 1910–22

COLE, M. I., (ed.), *Beatrice Webb's Diaries, 1912–24* (Longman, 1952).

The principal writings by the Webbs consulted for this study are:

WEBB, B., and WEBB, S., *The Principles of the Labour Party* (1919).

—— *A Constitution for the Socialist Commonwealth of Great Britain* (1920; repr. CUP, Cambridge, 1975).

WEBB, S., *How to Pay for the War* (July 1916, Fabian pamphlet).

—— *When Peace Comes: The Way of Industrial Reconstruction* (Fabian tract 181).

—— *The Restoration of Trade Union Conditions* (1917).

—— *The Industrial Situation* (1919).

—— and FREEMAN, A., *Great Britain After the War* (Sept. 1916).

For a full list, see *Publications of Sidney and Beatrice Webb: An Interim Check List* (British Library of Political and Economic Science, London School of Economics, 1973).

2. *The State*

(a) Ministry of Labour

Labour and the Peace Treaty (1919).

(b) Ministry of Munitions

Health of Munitions Workers Committee, *Health of the Munitions Worker* (1917).

Official History of the Ministry of Munitions, multi-volume (HMSO, 1920–4).

(c) Parliament (sessional papers)

Commission of Enquiry into Industrial Unrest (1917), Cd. 8662–9, 8696 (summary).

Report of the War Cabinet for 1917 (1917), Cd. 9005.

Committee on Relations between Employers and Employed (1917–18). *First Report* (on Joint Industrial Councils), Cd. 8606; *Second Report* (on Joint Industrial Councils), Cd. 9002; *Third Report* (on works committees), Cd. 9085; *Fourth Report* (on conciliation and arbitration), Cd. 9099; *Final Report* (summary), Cd. 915.

Report of the Committee on Women's Employment (1918), Cd. 9239.

Report of the War Cabinet Committee on Women in Industry (1919), Cmd. 135.

Report of the Provisional Joint Committee Presented to the Meeting of the Industrial Conference, Central Hall, 4 April 1919 (1919), Cmd. 139.

Coal Industry Commission (1919), Cmd. 210 (reports) and Cmd. 359–61 (minutes, evidence and appendices).

3. Employers

Federation of British Industries, *Annual Report* (1917–20).
—— *The Control of Industry*, (1919).

C. INTERNATIONAL

1. International Socialism

Conférence interalliée de Londres. Les Résolutions adoptées (SFIO, 1918). September 1918 inter-allied Labour and socialist conference in London.

RENAUDEL, P., *L'Internationale à Berne: faits et documents* (Grasset, 1919).

Les Résolutions de la conférence internationale ouvrière et socialiste de Berne, 3–10 février 1919 (SFIO, Imprimerie Nouvelle, 1919).

International Labour and Peace. Berne International Labour and Socialist Conference, i. Conference Resolutions; ii. British Delegation Declaration; iii. Permanent Commission: Amsterdam Resolution, Preliminary Peace Proposals; iv. International Committee of Action: Manifesto; v. British Labour Party: Manifesto (Labour Party, n.d., but 1919).

The International at Lucerne, 1919. The Resolutions. The Provisional Constitution (Labour Party, 1919).

Rapport du secrétariat international au congrès international de Genève, le 31 juillet 1920 (Internationale Ouvrière et Socialiste, Brussels, 1920).

Xᵉ congrès international socialiste et ouvrier, Genève, 1920. Compte rendu (ISB, Brussels, 1921).

'The International Labour and Socialist Congress, Geneva, 1920. The Resolutions', [*Labour Party. Local Government, Parliamentary and International Bulletin*, 1/10, 1920].

Union des Partis Socialistes pour l'Action Internationale, *Textes des résolutions prises à la conférence socialiste de Vienne (22–27 février 1921)* (n.d.).

2. International Trade Unionism

IFTU, *Compte rendu du congrès syndical international tenu à Amsterdam ... du 28 juillet au 2 août 1919, précédé par le rapport sur la conférence préliminaire tenue les 25, 26 et 27 juillet 1919, Le Mouvement syndical international*, supplement II, July 1921.

—— *Premier rapport sur l'activité de la fédération syndicale internation-*

ale *(juillet 1919–décembre 1921)* présenté au congrès ordinaire de Rome, avril 1922, *Le Mouvement syndical international,* supplement V, Apr. 1922.

—— *Report of the Special International Trades Union Congress held in the Throne Room, Holborn Restaurant, November 22nd to 27th 1920* (IFTU, London, 1921).

JOUHAUX, L., *La Fédération syndicale internationale et la réorganisation économique* (IFTU, Amsterdam, 1922).

SASSENBACH, J., *Twenty-Five Years of International Trade Unionism* (IFTU, London, 1926).

Le Premier Congrès international des syndicats révolutionnaires. Compte rendu sténographique (Éditions du Bureau de Presse du Congrès, Moscow, 1921).

3. International Labour Office

Le Congrès des trades unions britanniques de 1920 (1920).

XVᵉ congrès de la Confédération Générale du Travail tenu à Orléans du 27 septembre au 2 octobre (1920).

The Congress of the Labour and Socialist International (Geneva, July 31st–August 6th, 1920) (1920).

Le Programme minimum de la Confédération Générale du Travail de France (18 novembre 1921) (1921).

Une demande de contrôle ouvrier en France (1921).

Enquiry into Production, Introductory Memorandum (Bastable, 1920).

Enquête sur la production, 5 vols. (Berger-Lavrault, 1923–5).

SHOTWELL, J., *The Origins of the International Labor Organization* (Columbia Univ. Press, NY, 1934), vol. ii, *Documents.*

4. Other

Problems of Labor and Industry in Great Britain, France and Italy. Report of the European Commission of the National Industrial Conference Board, November 1919 (Washington, DC, 1919).

THE PRESS

A. FRANCE

1. Syndicalist

L'Atelier (from 1920).
La Bataille (syndicaliste).
La Clairière (from 1 Aug. 1917).
L'Encyclopédie du mouvement syndicaliste (1911–12).
Le Journal de la Fédération de l'Habillement.

Le Travailleur du bâtiment.
La Tribune des cheminots.
L'Union des métaux.
La Vie ouvrière (1909–14, and from May 1919).
La Voix du peuple.

2. *Socialist*

La France libre.
L'Humanité.
Le Midi socialiste.
Le Populaire.
La Vague (pacifist paper of Pierre Brizon, from Jan. 1918).

3. *General Left*

Les Annales de la régie directe.
L'Avenir (from Apr. 1916).
L'Information ouvrière et sociale (from 1918).
Le Mouvement socialiste.
La Revue socialiste, syndicaliste et coopérative.
La Vérité.

4. *Co-operative movement*

L'Action coopérative (FNCC).
L'Émancipation (until 1912, organ of the 'neutral' current).

5. *State*

Bulletin de l'association internationale pour la lutte contre le chômage.
Bulletin du ministère du travail.
Bulletin des usines de guerre.

6. *Employers*

L'Expansion économique, from June 1917 (bulletin of the Association
   Nationale d'Expansion Économique).
Bulletin mensuel du commerce et de l'industrie (bulletin of the Comité
   Républicain du Commerce, de l'Industrie et de l'Agriculture).
*Bulletin mensuel de la fédération des industriels et des commerçants
   français.*
La Journée industrielle (from 1918).
Revue mensuelle des questions sociales, ouvrières et fiscales (UIMM, from
   Mar.–Apr. 1920).
Le Réveil économique, 1910–14, and from Feb. 1917 (organ of the
   Union des Intérêts Économiques).

7. General

L'Économiste français.
L'Œuvre économique.
Le Temps.

B. BRITAIN

1. Labour and Trade Union

Amalgamated Engineers' Monthly Journal and Report.
Fabian News.
Forward (Glasgow).
Labour Leader.
Monthly Circular (Fabian Research Department, 1 July 1917–1 Nov. 1918; thereafter published by the Labour Research Department).
New Statesman.
Railway Review (NUR).
Socialist Review.

2. State

The Board of Trade Labour Gazette (down to June 1917; thereafter the *Labour Gazette*).

3. Employer

Federation of British Industry, *Bulletin* (from 1917).
Unity (from 1919) (organ of the National Alliance of Employers and Employees).

4. General

The Economist.
Manchester Guardian.
Sociological Review.
The Times.

C. INTERNATIONAL

1. Labour

Bulletin de la deuxième internationale (1919).
The International Trade Union Review, from Jan. 1921 (in English, French, and German; organ of the IFTU).

2. International Labour Office

International Labour Review, from 1921 (in English and French).

MEMOIRS AND CONTEMPORARY PUBLICATIONS

A. FRANCE

1. Labour, Socialist and Co-operative Movements

BLUM, L., *Commentaires sur le programme d'action du parti socialiste* (Librairie Populaire, 1919).
—— *Pour être socialiste* (Librairie de l'Humanité, 1919).
BOURGIN, H., *La Guerre pour la paix* (Rivière, 1915).
—— *Le Parti contre la patrie: histoire d'une sécession politique* (Plon, 1924).
BOUVIER, J., *Mes mémoires* (Maspero, 1983).
DAUDÉ-BANCEL, A., *Le Mouvement ouvrier français pendant la guerre* (Librairie des Sciences Politiques et Sociales, 1915).
—— *La Coopération pendant et après la guerre* (FNCC, 1916).
—— *Le Protectionnisme et l'avenir économique de la France* (Giard et Brière, 1916).
—— *La Reconstruction des cités détruites* (La Presse Sociale, 1917).
DUBREUIL, H., *Employeurs et salariés en France* (Félix Alcan, 1934).
—— *J'ai fini ma journée* (Librairie du Compagnonnage, 1971).
DUMOULIN, G., *Les Syndicalistes français et la guerre* (Imprimerie de la Société Mutuelle d'Éditions de la Bibliothèque du Travail, 1918).
—— *La Vie ou la mort du syndicalisme* (Maison des Syndicats, 1921).
—— *Carnets de route* (Éditions de l'Avenir, Lille, 1938).
FRACHON, B., *Pour la CGT: mémoires de lutte* (Éditions Sociales, 1981).
FROSSARD, L.-O., *De Jaurès à Léon Blum: souvenirs d'un militant* (Flammarion, 1943).
GRIFFUELHES, V., *Voyage révolutionnaire: impressions d'un propagandiste* (Rivière, 1910).
HAMP, P., *La France: pays ouvrier* (Éditions de la Nouvelle Revue Française, 1916).
JAURÈS, J., *L'Armée nouvelle* (1910; Éditions de l'Humanité, 1915).
JOUHAUX, L., *Notre syndicalisme* (La Publication Sociale, 1912).
—— *Le Syndicalisme français contre la guerre* (Rivière, 1913).
—— *A Jean Jaurès: discours prononcé aux obsèques de Jean Jaurès par Léon Jouhaux, secrétaire de la Confédération Générale du Travail* (La Publication Sociale, P.-M. Delesalle, 1915).
—— *L'Action syndicale* (Éditions de la Bataille, 1918). Jouhaux's speech to the 1918 congress.
—— *Les Travailleurs devant la paix* (Éditions de la Bataille, 1918).
—— *Le Syndicalisme et la CGT* (Éditions de la Sirène, 1920).
—— *L'Organisation internationale du travail* (Éditions de la Sirène, 1921).

—— and PRÊTÉ, H., *La Houille blanche: une solution ouvrière* (Grasset, 1917).

LAGARDELLE, H., *Le Socialisme ouvrier* (Giard et Brière, 1911).

LEBAS, J., *La Guerre et la politique du parti socialiste français* (L'Avenir, 1916).

LEROY, M., *Les Transformations de la puissance publique: le syndicat des fonctionnaires* (Giard et Brière, 1907).

—— *Syndicats et services publics* (Colin, 1909).

—— *La Coutume ouvrière*, 2 vols. (Giard et Brière, 1913).

—— *Pour gouverner* (Grasset, 1918).

—— *Les Techniques nouvelles du syndicalisme* (Garnier, 1921).

LONGUET, J., *La Politique internationale du marxisme* (Alcan, 1918).

MERRHEIM, A., *La Révolution économique* (Éditions de l'Information ouvrière et sociale, 1919).

—— *Amsterdam ou Moscou? le syndicalisme en danger* (Éditions du Cercle d'Études et d'Action Syndicale, n.d., but 1921).

—— 'Alphonse Merrheim et sa "correspondance confidentielle"', in V. Daline, *Hommes et idées* (Éditions du Progrès, Moscow, 1983), 232–342.

—— and DÉLAISI, F., *La Métallurgie: son origine, ses développements* (Éditions de la Fédération des Métaux, 1913).

MONATTE, P., *Syndicalisme révolutionnaire et communisme: les archives de P. Monatte (1914–1924)*, ed. C. Chambelland and J. Maitron (Maspero, 1968).

—— *Pierre Monatte: la lutte syndicale*, ed. C. Chambelland (Maspero, 1976).

POISSON, E., *La Coopération nouvelle* (Rivière, 1914).

—— *La République coopérative* (Grasset, 1920; English trans., *The Cooperative Republic* (Watkins, Manchester, 1925)).

POUGET, E., *L'Organisation du surmenage (le système taylor)* (Rivière, 1914).

ROSMER, A., *Moscou sous Lénine* (P. Horay, 1953).

SEMBAT, M., *La Victoire en déroute* (Éditions du Progrès Civique, 1925; English trans., *Defeated Victory* (Labour Publishing Company, 1925)).

—— *Les Cahiers noirs*, in *Revue de l'OURS*, 142, 145, 153, 156, 160, and 162 (1983–5).

THOMAS, A., *La Politique socialiste* (Rivière, 1913).

—— *Le Parti socialiste et la politique nationale* (1917).

—— *Journal de Russie d'Albert Thomas, 22 avril–19 juin 1917*, ed. I. Sinanoglou, *Cahiers du monde russe et soviétique*, 14 1–2 (1973).

—— *Bolchévisme et socialisme* (Berger-Lavrault, 1919).

2. *Other*

CAMBON, V., *Notre avenir* (Payot, 1916).

CLEMENCEAU, G., *Discours de guerre* (Presses Universitaires de France, 1968).

FERRY, A., *Les Carnets secrets d'Abel Ferry 1914–1918* (Grasset, 1957).

GALLIENI, Général, *Mémoires du général Gallieni: défense de Paris* (Payot, 1920).

HOURST, Commandant, *Le Problème de la main-d'œuvre: la taylorisation et son application aux conditions industrielles de l'après-guerre* (Librairie de l'école spéciale des travaux publics, 1916).

LOUCHEUR, L., *Carnets secrets, 1908–1932* (Brépol, Brussels, 1962).

MALVY, L.-J., *Mon crime*, (Flammarion, 1921).

MESSIMY, General, *Mes souvenirs* (Plon, 1937).

MORDACQ, J.-J., *Le Ministère Clemenceau: journal d'un témoin*, 4 vols. (Plon, 1930–1).

PAUL-BONCOUR, J. *Entre deux guerres: souvenirs sur la IIIe république*, vol. i, *Les Luttes républicaines, 1877–1918* (Plon, 1945).

PINOT, R., 'Les Industries métallurgiques et la guerre', *Le Parlement et l'opinion* (Oct. 1916), pp. 990–1015.

—— *Le Comité des forges au service de la nation* (Colin, 1919).

—— 'La Confédération générale du travail et les idées proudhoniennes', *La Revue hebdomadaire*, 1 May 1920, pp. 3–34.

—— 'Le Chef dans la grande industrie', *Revue de France*, 15 Mar. 1921, pp. 109–22.

POINCARÉ, R., *Au service de la France*, 10 vols. (Presses Universitaires de France, 1926–33), and vol. xi, *A la Recherche de la paix* (Plon, 1974).

B. BRITAIN

1. *The Labour Movement*

BARNES, G. N., *From Workshop to War Cabinet* (Herbert Jenkins, 1923).

BECHOFER, C. B., and RECKITT, M. B., *The Meaning of National Guilds* (Palmer and Hayward, 1918).

COLE, G. D. H., *The World of Labour* (Bell, 1913).

—— *Labour in Wartime* (Bell, 1915).

—— *Self-Government in Industry* (Bell, 1918).

—— *Chaos and Order in Industry* (Methuen, 1920).

GALLAGHER, W., *Revolt on the Clyde: An Autobiography* (Lawrence and Wishart, 1936).

GOSLING, H., *Peace: How to Get it and Keep it* (Cassell, 1917).

—— *Up and Down River* (Methuen, 1927).

HENDERSON, A., *The Aims of Labour* (Headley, 1918).
HOBSON, S. G., *Guild Principles in War and Peace* (Bell, 1917).
HODGES, F., *Nationalisation of the Mines* (Leonard Parsons, 1920).
—— *My Adventures as a Labour Leader* (G. Newnes, 1923).
KIRKWOOD, D., *My Life of Revolt* (Harrap, 1935).
MacDONALD, R., *Syndicalism: A Critical Examination* (Constable, 1912).
—— *War and the Workers: A Plea for Democratic Control* (Union of Democratic Control, 1915).
—— *Socialism After the War* (National Labour Press, 1917).
—— *National Defence: A Study in Militarism* (Allen & Unwin, 1917).
—— *Parliament and Revolution* (National Labour Press, 1919).
—— *A Policy for the Labour Party* (Leonard Parsons, 1920).
SMILLIE, R., *My Life for Labour* (Mills and Boon, 1924).
SNOWDEN, P., *Socialism and Syndicalism* (Collins, 1913).
—— *An Autobiography*, 2 vols. (Ivor Nicholson and Watson, 1934).
THOMAS, J. H., *My Story* (Hutchinson, 1937).
WOOLF, L., *Beginning Again: An Autobiography of the Years 1911 to 1918 (OUP, Oxford, 1964)*.

2. *Other*

ADDISON, C., *Politics From Within, 1911–18*, 2 vols. (Jenkins, 1924).
—— *Four and a Half Years*, 2 vols. (Hutchinson, 1934).
CARTER, H., *Industrial Reconstruction: A Symposium on the Situation after the War and How to Meet it* (T. Fisher Unwin, 1917).
CHAPMAN, S. J. (ed.), *Labour and Capital after the War* (John Murray, 1918).
JONES, T., *Whitehall Diary*, ed. K. Middlemas, vol. i, *1916–1925* (OUP, Oxford, 1969).
KIRKALDY, A. W. (ed.), *Labour, Finance and the War* (British Association, 1916).
Liberal Policy in the Task of Political and Social Reconstruction (1918).
LLOYD GEORGE, D., *Through Terror to Triumph* (Hodder and Stoughton, 1915).
—— *War Memoirs of David Lloyd George* (1933–6; rev. edn., 2 vols., Odhams Press, 1938).
MILNER, Lord, *The Elements of Reconstruction* (Nisbet, 1916).
PIGOU, A. C., *et al.*, *The Reorganisation of Industry* (Ruskin College, 1916).

C. INTERNATIONAL

GOMPERS, S., *Seventy Years of Life and Labour: An Autobiography*, 2 vols. (Hurst and Blackett, 1924).
TROTSKY, L., *My Life* (Thornton Butterworth, 1930).

VANDERVELDE, E., *Souvenirs d'un militant socialiste* (Éditions Denoël, 1939).

II. SECONDARY WORKS

I. LABOUR HISTORY
France

ABHERVÉ, B., 'Les Origines de la grève des métallurgistes parisiens, Juin 1919', *Le Mouvement social*, 93 (Oct.–Dec. 1975), pp. 75–85.

AMDUR, K., *Syndicalist Legacy: Trade Unions and Politics in Two French Cities in the Era of World War I* (Univ. of Illinois Press, Urbana, Ill., 1986).

AMOYAL, J., 'Les Origines socialistes et syndicalistes de la planification en France', *Le Mouvement social*, 87 (Apr.–June 1974), pp. 137–69.

ARUM, P., 'Du syndicalisme révolutionnaire au réformisme: Georges Dumoulin (1903–1923)', *Le Mouvement social*, 87 (Apr.–June 1974), pp. 35–62.

BARTUEL, C., and RULLIÈRE, H., *La Mine et les mineurs* (Librairie Octave Doin, 1923).

BATSCH, L., and BOUVET, M., *CGT, autour de la scission de 1921* (Éditions de la Brèche, 1983).

BECKER, J.-J., *Le Carnet B: les pouvoirs publics et l'antimilitarisme avant la guerre de 1914* (Klincksieck, 1973).

BERGOUNIOUX, A., 'Le Néo-socialisme: Marcel Déat: réformisme traditionnel ou esprit des années trente?' *Revue historique*, 528 (Oct.–Dec. 1978), pp. 389–414.

BLUMÉ, D., *et al.*, *Histoire du réformisme en France depuis 1920*, 2 vols. (Éditions Sociales, 1976).

BOND-HOWARD, J., 'Le Syndicalisme minoritaire dans les usines d'armement de Bourges de 1914 à 1918', *Le Mouvement social*, 148 (July–Sept. 1989), pp. 33–62.

BOUGLÉ, C., *Socialismes français* (Colin 1932).

—— *Le Mouvement syndical en France, 1871–1921: essai bibliographique* (Mouton, 1963).

BRÉCY, R., *La Grève générale en France* (Études et Documentation Internationale, 1969).

BRUHAT, J., and PIOLOT, M., *Esquisse pour une histoire de la CGT* (Éditions de la CGT, 1965).

BRUNET, J.-P., *Saint-Denis, la ville rouge: socialisme et communisme dans la banlieue ouvrière, 1890–1930* (Hachette, 1980).

CARCENAGUES, P., *Le Mouvement syndicaliste réformiste en France* (Schleicher, 1912).

CAVAILLÉ, J., *La Journée de huit heures: la loi du 23 avril 1919* (Marcel Rivière, 1919).

CAVIGNAC, J. (ed.), 'La Classe ouvrière bordelaise face à la guerre, 1914–1918', *Cahiers de l'Institut Aquitain d'Études Sociales* (Bordeaux), 4 (1976).

CAZALIS, E., *Syndicalisme ouvrier et évolution sociale* (Marcel Rivière, 1925).

CAZALS, R., *Avec les ouvriers de Mazamet dans la grève et l'action quotidienne, 1909–1914* (Maspero, 1978).

CHALLAYE, F., *Syndicalisme révolutionnaire et syndicalisme réformiste* (Alcan, 1909).

CHAUMEL, G., *Histoire des cheminots et de leurs syndicats* (Marcel Rivière, 1948).

COHEN, Y., 'Quand les masses viennent aux syndicats', *Les Révoltes logiques*, 10 (1979), pp. 28–51.

—— 'Ernest Mattern chez Peugeot (1906–1918) ou comment peut-on être taylorien?' in M. de Montmollin and O. Pastré (eds.), *Le Taylorisme* (Maspero, 1984).

COLLINET, M., *Esprit du syndicalisme* (Éditions ouvrières, 1951).

CROSS, G., *Immigrant Workers in Industrial France: The Making of a New Laboring Class* (Temple Univ. Press, Philadelphia, Penn., 1983).

—— 'Redefining Workers' Control: Rationalization, Labor Time and Union Politics in France, 1900–1928', in J. Cronin and C. Sirianni (eds.), *Work, Community and Power: The Experience of Labor in Europe and America, 1900–1925* (Temple Univ. Press, Philadelphia, Penn., 1983), 143–72.

—— 'The Quest for Leisure: Reassessing the Eight Hour Day in France', *Journal of Social History*, 18 (Winter 1984), pp. 195–216.

DÉZÈS, M.-G., 'Participation et démocratie sociale: l'expérience Briand de 1909', *Le Mouvement social*, 87 (Apr.–June 1974), pp. 109–36.

DOGLIANI, P., 'Edgar Milhaud e la rivista internazionale "Annales de la régie directe" (1908–1924)', *Annali della fondazione Luigi Einaudi*, 19 (1985), pp. 195–249.

DOLLÉANS, E., *Alphonse Merrheim* (Conférence de l'Institut Supérieur Ouvrier, série histoire syndicale, 1939).

—— *Histoire du mouvement ouvrier*, ii, *1871–1936* (Colin, 1946).

DOMMANGET, M., *Edouard Vaillant: un grand socialiste, 1840–1915* (La Table Ronde, 1956).

DUBESSET, M., THÉBAUD, F., and VINCENT, C., 'Les Munitionnettes de la Seine', in P. Fridenson (ed.), *1914–1918: L'autre front* (Cahiers du mouvement social, 2, Éditions ouvrières, 1977), 189–219.

DUBIEF, H., *Le Syndicalisme révolutionnaire* (Colin, 1969).

FAGNOT, R., *La Part du travail dans la gestion des entreprises* (Félix Alcan/Marcel Rivière, 1919).

FERRÉ, M., *Histoire du mouvement syndicaliste révolutionnaire chez les instituteurs: des origines à 1922* (Société Universitaire d'Éditions de la Librairie, 1955).

FINE, M., 'Albert Thomas: A Reformer's Vision of Modernization, 1914–1932', *Journal of Contemporary History*, 12 (1977), pp. 545–64.

—— 'Guerre et réformisme en France, 1914–1918', in L. Murard and P. Zylberman (eds)., 'Le Soldat du travail', *Recherches*, 32/33 (Sept. 1978), pp. 305–24.

—— 'Hyacinthe Dubreuil', *Le Mouvement social*, 106 (Jan.–Mar. 1979), pp. 45–63.

FRANÇOIS-PONCET, A., *Une Formule nouvelle: le contrôle syndical* (Société d'Études et d'Informations Économiques, 1921).

FRIDENSON, P., 'Les Ouvriers français de l'automobile jusqu' en 1914', *Sociologie du Travail* (July–Sept. 1979), pp. 297–321.

—— 'Un Tournant taylorien de la société française (1904–1918)', *Annales ESC* (Sept.–Oct. 1987), pp. 1031–60.

—— 'The Impact of the War on French Workers', in R. Wall and J. Winter (eds.), *The Upheaval of War: Family, Work and Welfare in Europe, 1914–1918* (CUP, Cambridge, 1988), 235–48.

FRISCHMANN, G., *Histoire de la fédération CGT des PTT* (Éditions sociales, 1969).

FRUIT, E., *Les Cheminots dans l'histoire sociale de la France* (Éditions ouvrières, 1976).

GALLO, M., 'Quelques aspects de la mentalité et du comportement ouvriers dans les usines de guerre, 1914–1918', *Le Mouvement social*, 56 (July–Sept. 1966), pp. 3–33.

GAUMONT, J., *Histoire générale de la coopération en France* (FNCC, 1924).

GEORGES, B., and TINTANT, D., *Léon Jouhaux*, i, *Des origines à 1921* (Presses Universitaires de France, 1962); ii (with M.-A. Renauld), *Léon Jouhaux dans le mouvement syndical français* (1979).

GINSBURG, S., *Raymond Lefebvre et les origines du communisme français* (Éditions Tête de Feuilles, 1975).

GIRAULT, J. (ed.), *Sur l'implantation du parti communiste français dans l'entre deux guerres* (Éditions sociales, 1977).

GOLDBERG, H., *The Life of Jean Jaurès* (Univ. of Wisconsin Press, Madison, Wis., 1962).

GRAS, C., 'Merrheim et le capitalisme', *Le Mouvement social*, 63 (Apr.–June 1968), pp. 143–63.

—— 'La Fédération des métaux en 1913–1914 et l'évolution du syndicalisme révolutionnaire français', *Le Mouvement social*, 77 (Oct.–Dec. 1971), pp. 85–111.

GUILBERT, M., *Les Femmes et l'organisation syndicale avant 1914* (Éditions du CNRS, 1966).

HANAGAN, M., *The Logic of Solidarity: Artisans and Industrial Workers in Three French Towns, 1871–1914* (Univ. of Illinois Press, Urbana, 1980).

HATRY, G., 'Les Délégués d'atelier aux usines de Renault', in P. Fridenson (ed.), *1914–1918. L'autre front* (Cahiers du mouvement social, 2, Éditions ouvrières, 1977), 222–35.

HORNE, J., 'Le Comité d'Action (CGT-PS) et l'origine du réformisme syndical du temps de guerre (1914–1916)', *Le Mouvement social*, 122 (Jan.–Mar. 1983), pp. 33–60.

HOWORTH, J., *Edouard Vaillant: la création de l'unité socialiste en France* (Editions et Documentation Internationale/Syros, 1982).

HUARD, R., 'Aspects du mouvement ouvrier gardois pendant la guerre de 1914–1918: les grèves de 1917', *Annales du Midi*, 80 (1968), pp. 305–18.

—— 'Les Mineurs du Gard pendant la guerre de 1914–1918: guerre, syndicalisme et mentalités', in *Économie et société en Languedoc-Roussillon de 1789 à nos jours* (Univ. de Montpellier, 1976), 275–94.

HUMPHREYS, G. C., *Taylorism in France, 1904–1920: The Impact of Scientific Management on Factory Relations and Society* (Garland, 1986).

JACQUET, J., *Les Cheminots dans l'histoire sociale de la France* (Éditions sociales, 1967).

JONES, A., 'The French Railway Strikes of January–May 1920: New Syndicalist Ideas and Emergent Communism', *French Historical Studies*, 12/4 (1982), pp. 508–40.

—— *La Reconstruction du parti socialiste, 1921–1926* (Presses de la Fondation Nationale des Sciences Politiques, 1976).

JUDT, T., *Marxism and the French Left: Studies in Labour and Politics in France, 1830–1981* (Clarendon Press, Oxford, 1986).

JULLIARD, J., *Clemenceau, briseur de grèves* (Éditions Julliard, 1965).

—— *Fernand Pelloutier et les origines du syndicalisme d'action directe* (Seuil, 1971).

—— 'I Rapporti sindacati–partiti: la pluralità dei modelli storici e il caso francese', in M. Antonioni, I. Barbadori, *et al.*, *Sindacato e classe operaia nell'età della seconda internazionale* (Sansoni editori, Florence, 1983), 358–81.

JULLIARD, J., *Autonomie ouvrière: études sur le syndicalisme d'action directe* (Gallimard/Le Seuil, 1988).

—— 'La C.G.T. devant la guerre (1900–14)', in id., *Autonomie ouvrière* (Gallimard/Le Seuil, 1988), 92–111.

—— 'Modérés et radicaux: jeune et vieux syndicat chez les mineurs du Pas-de-Calais', in id., *Autonomie ouvrière* (Gallimard/Le Seuil, 1988), 69–93.

—— 'Théorie syndicaliste révolutionnaire et pratique gréviste', in id., *Autonomie ouvrière* (Gallimard/Le Seuil, 1988), 43–68.

KRIEGEL, A., *Le Congrès de Tours (1920): naissance d'un parti communiste français* (Julliard, 1964).

—— *Aux origines du communisme français*, 2 vols. (Mouton, 1964).

—— *La Croissance de la CGT* (Mouton, 1966).

—— *Le Pain et les roses* (Presses Universitaires de France, 1968).

—— and BECKER, J.-J., *1914: la guerre et le mouvement ouvrier français* (Colin, 1964).

—— and PERROT, M., *Le Socialisme français et le pouvoir* (Études et Documentation Internationale, 1966).

LABI, M., *La Grande Division des travailleurs: première scission de la CGT, 1914–1921* (Éditions ouvrières, 1964).

LACOUTURE, J., *Léon Blum* (Seuil, 1977).

LAURENT, C., *Le Syndicalisme des fonctionnaires: aperçu historique* (Institut Supérieur Ouvrier, n.d., but 1938).

LEFRANC, G., *Histoire du mouvement syndical français* (Librairie syndicale, 1937).

—— (pseud. J. Montreuil), *Histoire du mouvement ouvrier en France des origines à nos jours* (Aubier, 1946).

—— *Le Mouvement socialiste sous la troisième république* (Payot, 1963).

—— 'Le Courant planiste dans le mouvement ouvrier français de 1933 à 1936', *Le Mouvement social* (Jan.–Mar. 1966), pp. 69–89.

—— *Le Mouvement syndical sous la troisième république* (Payot, 1967).

—— *Essais sur les problèmes socialistes et syndicaux* (Payot, 1970).

LEQUIN, Y., *Les Ouvriers de la région lyonnaise (1848–1914)*, ii, *Les Intérêts de classe et la république* (Presses Universitaires de Lyon, Lyons, 1977).

LEQUIN, Y. C., 'Le Taylorisme avant 1914: réponse technique et idéologique aux exigences du monopolisme', *Cahiers d'histoire de l'Institut Maurice Thorez*, 16 (1976), pp. 14–36.

LEVINE, L., *The Labor Movement in France* (Columbia Univ. Press, NY, 1912).

L'HOMME, J., 'Le Pouvoir d'achat de l'ouvrier français au cours d'un siècle: 1840–1940', *Le Mouvement social*, 63 (Apr.–June 1968), pp. 41–69.

LIGOU, D., *Histoire du socialisme en France, 1871–1961* (Presses Universitaires de France, 1962).

LINDENBERG, D., *Le Marxisme introuvable* (Calmann-Lévy, 1975).

LORWIN, V. R., *The French Labor Movement* (Harvard Univ. Press, Cambridge, Mass., 1954).

LOUIS, P., *Histoire du socialisme en France de la révolution à nos jours* (Marcel Rivière, 1936).

MAITRON, J., *Le Mouvement anarchiste en France*, i, *Des origines à 1914* (1951; Maspero, 1975); ii, *De 1914 à nos jours* (Maspero, 1975).

—— *Paul Delesalle: un anarchiste de la belle époque* (Fayard, 1985).

—— and PENNETIER, C. (eds.), *Dictionnaire biographique du mouvement ouvrier français*, pt. 3, *1871–1914*; pt. 4, *1914–1939* (Éditions ouvrières, 1973–?).

MONTMOLLIN, M. DE, and PASTRÉ, O. (eds.), *Le Taylorisme* (Maspero, 1984).

MOSS, B. H., *The Origins of the French Labor Movement, 1830–1914* (Univ. of California Press, Berkeley, Calif., 1976).

MOUTET, A., 'Les Origines du système taylor en France: le point de vue patronal (1907–1914)', *Le Mouvement social*, 93 (Oct.–Dec. 1975), pp. 15–49.

—— 'Patrons du progrès ou patrons de combat? La politique de rationalisation de l'industrie française au lendemain de la première guerre mondiale', in 'Le Soldat du travail', special no. of *Recherches*, 32/33 (Sept. 1978), pp. 449–89.

—— 'La Première Guerre mondiale et le taylorisme', in M. De Montmollin and O. Pastré (eds.), *Le Taylorisme* (Maspero, 1984), 67–81.

—— 'Ingénieurs et rationalisation en France de la guerre à la crise (1914–1929)' in A. Thépot (ed.), *L'Ingénieur dans la société française* (Éditions ouvrières, 1985), 71–108.

NOIRIEL, G., *Longwy: immigrés et prolétaires, 1880–1980* (Presses Universitaires de France, 1984).

—— *Les Ouvriers dans la société française, XIXᵉ-XXᵉ siècles* (Seuil, 1986).

—— *Le Creuset français: histoire de l'immigration XIXᵉ-XXᵉ siècles* (Seuil, 1988).

PAPAYANIS, N., 'Masses révolutionnaires et directions réformistes: les tensions au cours des grèves des métallurgistes français en 1919', *Le Mouvement social*, 93 (Oct.–Dec. 1975), 51–73.

—— 'Collaboration and Pacifism in France during World War I', *Francia*, 5 (1977), pp. 425–51.

—— *Alphonse Merrheim: The Emergence of Reformism in Revolutionary Syndicalism, 1871–1925* (Martinus Nijhoff, The Hague, 1985).

PELÉ, E., 'Le Mouvement ouvrier lyonnais pendant la première guerre mondiale', *Bulletin du centre d'histoire économique et sociale de la région lyonnaise* (1972), i, 38–46.

PENNETIER, C., *Le Socialisme dans le Cher, 1851–1921* (Éditions de la Maison des Sciences de l'Homme, 1982).

PERROT, M., 'Les Socialistes français et les problèmes du pouvoir (1871–1914)', in A. Kriegel and M. Perrot, *Le Socialisme français et le pouvoir*. (Études et Documentation Internationale, 1966).

—— 'Le Regard de l'autre: les patrons français vus par les ouvriers (1880–1914)', in M. Lévy-Leboyer (ed.), *Le Patronat de la seconde industrialisation* (Éditions ouvrières, 1979), 293–306.

—— 'La Classe ouvrière française au temps de Jaurès', in M. Rebérioux (ed.), *Jaurès et la classe ouvrière* (Editions ouvrières, 1981), 67–81.

—— 'Lo Sviluppo del movimento sindacale in Francia: Forme di contrattazione e di rappresentanza (1900–1920)', in M. Antonioni and I. Barbadori *et al.*, *Sindacato e classe operaia nell'età della seconda internazionale* (Sansoni editori, Florence, 1983), 75–92.

—— (ed.), 'L'Espace de l'usine', special no. of *Le Mouvement social*, 125 (Oct.–Dec. 1983).

PICARD, R., *Les Grèves et la guerre* (Enquêtes soumises au Comité National d'Études Sociales et Politiques, 1917).

—— *La Conciliation, l'arbitrage et la prévention des conflits ouvriers: expérience du temps de guerre* (Lang, 1918).

—— *Le Contrôle ouvrier sur la gestion des entreprises* (Marcel Rivière, 1922).

—— *Le Mouvement syndical durant la guerre* (Presses Universitaires de France, 1927).

PIROU, G., 'Le Problème du contrat collectif du travail en France', *Revue internationale du travail/International Labour Review* (Jan. 1922), pp. 35–50.

PRÉLOT, M., *L'Évolution politique du socialisme français, 1789–1934* (Éditions Spes, 1934).

PROST, A., *La CGT à l'époque du front populaire, 1934–1939* (Colin, 1964).

RAFFAELLI, G., 'Les Mouvements pacifistes dans les usines d'armement de la région de Saint-Etienne', *Actes du 98ᵉ congrès national des sociétés savantes* (Saint-Étienne, 1973), ii, 221–37.

REBÉRIOUX, M., 'Les Tendances hostiles à l'état dans la SFIO (1905–1914)', *Le Mouvement social*, 65 (Oct.–Dec. 1968), 21–36.

—— (ed.), *Jaurès et la classe ouvrière* (Éditions ouvrières, 1981).

—— *Les Ouvriers du livre et leur fédération: un centenaire, 1881–1981* (Temps Actuels, 1981).

—— and FRIDENSON, P., 'Albert Thomas, pivot du réformisme français', *Le Mouvement social*, 87 (Apr.–June 1974), pp. 85–97.

REID, D., 'Guillaume Verdier et le syndicalisme révolutionnaire aux usines de Decazeville (1917–1920)', *Annales du Midi*, 96 (1984), pp. 171–98.

RENAULD, M.-A., 'Documents: mémoires de Léon Jouhaux', *Le Mouvement social*, 47 (Apr.–June 1964), pp. 81–109.

RIBEILL, G., *Le Personnel de compagnies de chemins de fer*, i, *Des origines à 1914* (Développement et Aménagement, 1980), ii, *Les Cheminots en guerre, 1914–1920* (CERTES-ENPC, 1988).

RIDLEY, F. F., *Revolutionary Syndicalism in France* (CUP, Cambridge, 1970).

ROBERT, J.-L., 'Les Luttes ouvrières en France pendant la première guerre mondiale', *Cahiers d'histoire de l'institut Maurice Thorez*, 23 (1977), pp. 28–65.

—— *La Scission syndicale de 1921: essai de reconnaissance de formes* (Publications de la Sorbonne, 1980).

—— 'La CGT et la famille ouvrière 1914–1918: première approche', *Le Mouvement social*, 116 (July–Sept. 1981), pp. 47–66.

—— 'Les "Programmes minimum" de la CGT de 1918 et 1921', *Cahiers d'histoire de l'institut de recherches marxistes*, 16/2 (1984), pp. 58–78.

—— 'Women and Work in France during the First World War', in R. Wall and J. Winter (eds.), *The Upheaval of War: Family, Work and Welfare in Europe, 1914–1918* (CUP, Cambridge, 1988), 251–66.

—— and CHAVANCE, M., 'L'Evolution de la syndicalisation en France de 1914 à 1921: l'emploi de l'analyse des correspondances factorielles', *Annales ESC* (Sept.–Oct., 1974), pp. 1092–107.

—— and DESCOSTES, M. (eds.), *Clefs pour une histoire du syndicalisme cadre* (Éditions ouvrières, 1984).

ROSMER, A., *Le Mouvement ouvrier pendant la première guerre mondiale*, i, *De l'Union sacrée à Zimmerwald* (Librairie du Travail, 1936), ii, *De Zimmerwald à la révolution russe* (Mouton, 1959).

SAGNES, J., *Le Mouvement ouvrier en Languedoc: syndicalistes et socialistes de l'Hérault de la fondation des bourses du travail à la naissance du parti communiste* (Privat, Toulouse, 1980).

SAPOSS, D. J., *The Labor Movement in Post-War France* (Columbia Univ. Press, NY, 1931).

SCHAPER, B. W., *Albert Thomas: trente ans de réformisme social* (Assen, Van Gorcum, 1959).

SCHÖTTLER, P., *Naissance des bourses du travail: un appareil idéologique de l'état à la fin du XIXe siècle* (1982; French trans., Presses Universitaires de France, 1985).

SCHWEITZER, S., *Des Engrenages à la chaine: les usines Citroën, 1915–1935* (Presses Universitaires de Lyon, Lyons, 1982).

SEMARD, P., *Histoire de la fédération des cheminots* (Fédération des Cheminots, 1934).

SÉVERAC, J.-B., *Le Mouvement syndical* (Quillet, 1913).

SHORTER, E. and TILLY, C., *Strikes in France 1830–1968* (CUP, Cambridge, 1974).

SIWEK-POUYDESSEAU, J., *Le Syndicalisme des fonctionnaires jusqu'à la guerre froide* (Presses Universitaires de Lille, Lille, 1989).

STEARNS, P. N., 'Against the Strike Threat: Employer Policy towards Labour Agitation in France, 1900–1914', *Journal of Modern History*, 40/4 (1968), pp. 474–500.

—— *Revolutionary Syndicalism and French Labour: A Cause without Rebels* (Rutgers Univ. Press, New Brunswick, 1971).

TREMPÉ, R., 'Le Réformisme des mineurs français à la fin du XIXe siècle', *Le Mouvement social*, 65 (Oct.–Dec. 1968), pp. 93–107.

VIDALENC, J., 'La Main-d'œuvre étrangère en France et la première guerre mondiale (1901–1926)', *Francia*, 2 (1974), pp. 524–50.

WILLARD, C., *Les Guesdistes: le mouvement socialiste en France (1893–1905)* (Éditions sociales, 1965).

—— *Socialisme et communisme français* (Colin, 1967).

WOHL, R., *French Communism in the Making, 1914–1924* (Stanford Univ. Press, Stanford, 1966).

ZIEBURA, G., *Léon Blum et le parti socialiste, 1872–1934* (Presses de la Fondation Nationale des Sciences Politiques, 1967).

Britain

ADAMS, T., 'The Formation of the Co-operative Party Reconsidered', *International Review of Social History*, 32/1 (1987), pp. 48–68.

ASKWITH, G. R., *Industrial Problems and Disputes* (John Murray, 1920).

BAGWELL, P. S., *The Railwaymen: The History of the National Union of Railwaymen* (Allen & Unwin), (1963).

—— 'The Triple Industrial Alliance, 1913–1922', in A. Briggs and J. Saville (eds.), *Essays in Labour History 1886–1923* (Macmillan, 1971), 96–128.

BÉDARIDA, F., 'Le Socialisme en Grande Bretagne de 1875 à 1914', in J. Droz (ed.), *Histoire générale du socialisme*, ii, *De 1875 à 1918* (Presses Universitaires de France, 1974), 347–99.

BEER, M., *A History of British Socialism* (Bell, 1919).

BELLAMY, J., and SAVILLE, J., *Dictionary of Labour Biography* (Macmillan, 1972–).

BRIGGS, A., and SAVILLE, J., (eds.), *Essays in Labour History, 1886–1923* (Macmillan, 1971).

BROWN, K. D., *Labour and Unemployment, 1900–1914* (David and Charles, Newton Abbot, 1971).

—— (ed.), *Essays in Anti-Labour History* (Macmillan, 1974).

—— *The English Labour Movement* (Gill and Macmillan, Dublin, 1982).

—— (ed.) *The First Labour Party, 1906–1914* (Croom Helm, 1985).

BULLOCK, A., *The Life and Times of Ernest Bevin* (Heinemann), i, *Trade Union Leader, 1881–1940* (1960).

BURGESS, K., *The Challenge of Labour: Shaping British Society, 1850–1930* (Croom Helm, 1980).

BUSH, J., *Behind the Lines: East London Labour 1914–1919* (Merlin Press, 1984).

CHALLINOR, R., *The Origins of British Bolshevism* (Croom Helm, 1977).

CLEGG, H. A., *A History of British Trade Unions since 1889*, ii, *1911–1933* (OUP, Oxford, 1985).

—— FOX, A., and THOMPSON, A. F., *A History of British Trade Unions since 1889*, i, *1889–1910* (OUP, Oxford, 1964).

CLINE, C. A., *Recruits to Labour: The British Labour Party, 1914–1931* (Syracuse Univ. Press, Syracuse, NY, 1963).

CLINTON, A., *The Trade Union Rank and File: Trades Councils in Britain, 1900–1940* (Manchester Univ. Press, Manchester, 1977).

COATES, D., *The Labour Party and the Struggle for Socialism* (CUP, Cambridge, 1975).

COLE, G. D. H., *Labour in the Coal-Mining Industry, 1914–1921* (Clarendon Press, Oxford, 1923).

—— *Trade Unionism and Munitions* (Clarendon Press, Oxford, 1923).

—— *Workshop Organization*, (Clarendon Press, Oxford, 1923).

—— *A Century of Co-operation* (Co-operative Union, Manchester, 1945).

—— *A History of the Labour Party from 1914* (Routledge and Kegan Paul, 1948).

—— and PAGE ARNOT, R., *Trade Unionism on the Railways: Its History and Problems* (Trade Union Ser., no. 2, 1917).

CORBETT, J., *The Birmingham Trades Council, 1866–1966* (Lawrence and Wishart, 1966).

COWLING, M., *The Impact of Labour, 1920–1924* (CUP, Cambridge, 1971).

CRONIN, J., *Industrial Conflict in Modern Britain* (Croom Helm, 1979).

—— *Labour and Society in Britain, 1918–1979* (Batsford, 1984).

CRONIN, J., 'Strikes and Power in Britain, 1870–1920', *International Review of Social History*, 32/2 (1987), 144–67.

DOUGLAS, R., 'The National Democratic Labour Party and the British Workers' League', *Historical Journal*, 15/3 (1972), 533–52.

DOWSE, R. E., *Left in the Centre: The Independent Labour Party, 1893–1940* (Longman, 1966).

DRAKE, B., *Women in Trade Unions* (1920; new edn., Virago, 1984).

ELDON BARRY, E., *Nationalisation in British Politics: The Historical Background* (Cape, 1965).

FLANDERS, A. and CLEGG, H. A., *The System of Industrial Relations in Great Britain* (Blackwell, Oxford, 1967).

FOX, A., *History and Heritage: The Social Origins of the British Industrial Relations System* (Allen & Unwin, 1985).

GLEASON, A., *What the Workers Want: A Study of British Labor* (Harcourt, Brace and Howe, NY, 1920).

GLEASON, A., and KELLOG P. U., *British Labor and the War: Reconstructors for a New World* (Boni and Liveright, NY, 1919).

GOODRICH, C., *The Frontier of Control: A Study of British Workshop Politics* (Bell, 1920).

GREGORY, R., *The Miners and British Politics, 1906–1914* (OUP, Oxford, 1968).

HALÉVY, E., *The Era of Tyrannies: Essays on Socialism and War* (1938; English trans., Allen Lane, 1967).

HAMILTON, M. A., *Arthur Henderson: A Biography* (Heinemann, 1938).

HAMMOND, M. B., *British Labour Conditions and Legislation during the War* (OUP, NY, 1919).

HARRISON, R., 'The War Emergency: Workers' National Committee, 1914–1920', in A. Briggs and J. Saville (eds.), *Essays in Labour History 1886–1923* (Macmillan, 1971), 211–59.

HARRISON, R., and ZEITLIN, J., (eds.) *Divisions of Labour: Skilled Workers and Technological Change in Nineteenth Century England* (Harvester Press, Brighton, 1985).

HINTON, J., 'The Clyde Workers' Committee and the Dilution Struggle', in A. Briggs and J. Saville (eds.), *Essays in Labour History 1886–1923* (Macmillan, 1971), 152–84.

—— *The First Shop Stewards' Movement* (Allen & Unwin, 1973).

—— *Labour and Socialism: A History of the British Labour Movement, 1867–1974* (Wheatsheaf Books, Brighton, 1983).

HOBSBAWM, E. J., *Labouring Men: Studies in the History of Labour* (Weidenfeld and Nicolson, 1964).

—— 'Artisan or Labour Aristocrat?' *Economic History Review*, 38/3 (1985), pp. 355–72.

—— 'The "New Unionism" Reconsidered', in W. J. Mommsen and H. J. Husung (eds.), *The Development of Trade Unionism in Great Britain and Germany, 1880–1914,* (German Historical Institute/ Methuen, 1985) 15–31.

HOLFORD, J., *Reshaping Labour: Organisation, Work and Politics: Edinburgh in the Great War and After* (Croom Helm, 1988).

HOLTON, B., *British Syndicalism, 1900–1914: Myths and Realities* (Pluto, 1976).

HOWARD, C., 'MacDonald, Henderson and the Outbreak of War, 1914', *Historical Journal,* 20 (1977), pp. 871–91.

—— 'Expectations Born to Death: Local Labour Party Expansion in the 1920s', in J. M. Winter (ed.), *The Working Class in Modern British History* (CUP, Cambridge, 1983), 65–81.

HYMAN, R., *The Workers' Union* (Clarendon Press, Oxford, 1971).

JEFFERYS, J. B., *The Story of the Engineers, 1800–1945* (Amalgamated Engineering Union, Lawrence and Wishart, n.d., but 1946).

KENDALL, W., *The Revolutionary Movement in Britain, 1900–1921* (Weidenfeld and Nicolson, 1969).

KIRKALDY, A., (ed.), *British Labour: Replacement and Conciliation, 1914–1921* (Pitman, for the British Association for the Advancement of Science, 1921).

KNOWLES, K. G., *Strikes: A Study in Industrial Conflict* (OUP, Oxford, 1952).

LAYBOURN, K., *The Rise of Labour: The British Labour Party, 1890–1979* (Edward Arnold, 1988).

MCBRIAR, A. M., *Fabian Socialism and English Politics, 1884–1918* (CUP, Cambridge, 1962).

MCINTYRE, S., 'Socialism, the Unions and the Labour Party after 1918', *Bulletin of the Society for the Study of Labour History,* 23 (1975), 100–11.

MCKIBBIN, R., 'James Ramsay MacDonald and the Problem of the Independence of the Labour Party', *Journal of Modern History,* 42/2 (June 1970), 216–35.

—— *The Evolution of the Labour Party, 1910–1924* (OUP, Oxford, 1974).

—— 'Arthur Henderson as Labour Leader', *International Review of Social History,* 23/1 (1978), pp. 79–101.

MCLEAN, I., *The Legend of Red Clydeside* (John Donald, Edinburgh, 1983).

MARQUAND, D., *Ramsay MacDonald* (Cape, 1977).

MARTIN, D., 'Ideology and Composition', in K. D. Brown (ed.), *The First Labour Party, 1906–1914* (Croom Helm, 1985), 17–37.

MARTIN, R., *TUC: The Growth of a Pressure Group, 1868–1976,* (Clarendon Press, Oxford, 1980).

MARWICK, A., 'The Labour Party and the Welfare State in Britain 1900–48', *American Historical Review*, 73 (1967), pp. 380–403.

MEACHAM, S., *A Life Apart: The English Working Class, 1890–1914* (Thames and Hudson, 1977).

MENDELSON, J., OWEN, W., *et al. Sheffield Trades and Labour Council, 1858–1958* (Sheffield Trades Council, 1958).

MIDDLEMAS, R., *The Clydesiders: A Left-Wing Struggle for Parliamentary Power* (Hutchinson, 1965).

MILIBAND, R., *Parliamentary Socialism* (Merlin Press, 1961).

ORTON, W. A., *Labour in Transition: A Survey of British Industrial History since 1914* (Philip Allan, 1921).

PAGE ARNOT, R., *The Miners*, i, *A History of the Miners' Federation of Great Britain, 1889–1910* (Allen & Unwin, 1949); ii, *Years of Struggle: A History of the Miners' Federation of Great Britain from 1910 Onwards* (Allen & Unwin 1953).

PELLING, H., *The Origins of the Labour Party, 1880–1900* (OUP, Oxford, 1952; 2nd edn., 1965).

—— *The British Communist Party: A Historical Profile* (A. & C. Black, 1958).

—— 'La Classe ouvrière anglaise et les origines de la législation sociale', *Le Mouvement social*, 65 (Oct.–Dec. 1968), pp. 39–53.

—— *A History of British Trade Unionism* (Macmillan, 1963; 2nd edn., 1972).

—— *Popular Politics and Society in Late Victorian Britain: Essays* (Macmillan, 1968).

PHELPS-BROWN, E., *The Growth of British Industrial Relations: A Study from the Standpoint of 1900–1914* (Macmillan, 1959).

PHILLIPS, G. A., 'The Triple Industrial Alliance in 1914', *Economic History Review*, 24/1 (1971), pp. 55–67.

POLLARD, S., *A History of Labour in Sheffield* (Liverpool Univ. Press, Liverpool, 1959).

—— 'The Foundation of the Co-operative Party', in A. Briggs and J. Saville (eds.), *Essays in Labour History, 1886–1923* (Macmillan, 1971), 185–210.

POWELL, D., 'The New Liberalism and the Rise of Labour, 1886–1906', *Historical Journal*, 29/2 (1986), pp. 369–93.

PRIBICEVIC, B., *The Shop Stewards' Movement and Workers' Control, 1910–1922* (Blackwell, Oxford, 1959).

PRICE, R., *Labour in British Society: An Interpretative History* (Croom Helm, 1986).

REID, A., 'The Impact of the First World War on British Workers', in R. Wall and J. Winter (eds.), *The Upheaval of War: Family, Work and Welfare in Europe, 1914–1918* (CUP, Cambridge, 1988), 221–33.

ROBERTS, B. C., *The Trades Union Congress, 1868–1921* (Allen & Unwin, 1958).

SAVAGE, M., *The Dynamics of Working Class Politics: The Labour Movement in Preston, 1880–1940* (CUP, Cambridge, 1988).

STUBBS, J. O., 'Lord Milner and Patriotic Labour, 1914–1918', *English Historical Review* (Oct. 1972), pp. 717–54.

TSUZUKI, C., *H. M. Hyndman and British Socialism* (OUP, Oxford, 1961).

WEBB, B., and WEBB, S., *The History of Trade Unionism* (Longman, 1894; new edn., 1920).

—— *Industrial Democracy* (Longman, 1897; new edn., 1920).

WHITESIDE, N., 'Welfare Legislation and the Unions during World War I', *Historical Journal*, 23/4 (1968), pp. 857–74.

WINTER, J. M., *Socialism and the Challenge of War: Ideas and Politics in Britain, 1912–1918* (Routledge & Kegan Paul, 1974).

—— (ed.), *The Working Class in Modern British History* (CUP, Cambridge, 1983).

—— 'Trade Unions and the Labour Party in Britain', in W. J. Mommsen and H. G. Husung (eds.), *The Development of Trade Unions in Great Britain and Germany, 1880–1914* (German Historical Institute/Methuen, 1985), 359–70.

WRIGHT, A. W., 'Guild Socialism Revisited', *Journal of Contemporary History*, 9/1 (1974), pp. 165–80.

—— *G. D. H. Cole and Socialist Democracy* (OUP, Oxford, 1979).

Comparative and Conceptual

ANTONIONI, M., BARBADORI, I., *et al.*, *Sindacato e classe operaia nell'età della seconda internazionale* (Sansoni editori, Florence, 1983).

ARFÉ, G., *Storia del socialismo italiano, 1892–1926* (Einaudi, 1965).

BRIGGS, A., and MAITRON, J. (eds.), 'Avec ou sans l'état? Le mouvement ouvrier français et anglais au tournant du siècle', *Le Mouvement social*, special no. (65) (Oct.–Dec., 1968).

CAHM, E., and FISCERA, V. (eds.), *Socialism and Nationalism in Contemporary Europe, 1848–1945*, 3 vols. (Spokesman Books, Nottingham, 1978–80).

'Conflicts and Compromise: Socialists and Socialism in the Twentieth Century', *Journal of Contemporary History*, special no. (11/2–3) (July 1976).

CRONIN, J., and SIRIANNI, C. (eds.), *Work, Community and Power: The Experience of Labor in Europe and America, 1900–1925* (Temple Univ. Press, Philadelphia, Penn., 1983).

CROSS, G., *A Quest for Time: The Reduction of Work in Britain and France, 1840–1940* (Univ. of California Press, Berkeley, Calif., 1989).

DREYFUSS, F. G., (ed.), *Réformisme et révisionnisme dans les socialismes allemand, autrichien et français* (Éditions de la Maison des Sciences de l'Homme, 1984).

DROZ, J. (ed.), *Histoire générale du socialisme* (Presses Universitaires de France), ii, *De 1875 à 1918* (1974).

FELDMAN, G., *Arms, Industry and Labor in Germany 1914–1918* (Princeton Univ. Press, Princeton, NJ, 1968).

GALLIE, D., *Social Inequality and Class Radicalism in France and Britain* (CUP, Cambridge, 1983).

GEARY, D., *European Labour Protest, 1848–1939* (Croom Helm, 1981).

HAUPT, G., 'Why the History of the Working Class Movement?' *New German Critique* (New York), 14 (1978), pp. 3–24.

—— *L'Historien et le mouvement social* (Maspero, 1980).

HORNE, J., 'L'Idée de nationalisation dans les mouvements ouvriers européens jusqu'à la deuxième guerre mondiale', *Le Mouvement social*, 134 (Jan.–Mar. 1986), pp. 9–36.

MCCARTHY, W. (ed.), *Trade Unions* (Penguin, Harmondsworth, 1972).

MOMMSEN, W. J., and HUSUNG, H. G., (eds.), *The Development of Trade Unionism in Great Britain and Germany, 1880–1914* (German Historical Institute/Methuen, 1985).

MONTGOMERY, B. G. DE, *British and Continental Labour Policy* (Paul, Trench, and Trubner, 1922).

MOSES, J., *Trade Unionism in Germany from Bismarck to Hitler, 1869–1933*, 2 vols. (Barnes and Noble, Towota, NJ, 1982).

MURARD, L., and ZYLBERMAN, P. (eds.), 'Le Soldat du travail: guerre, fascisme et taylorisme', special no., *Recherches*, 32/33 (Sept. 1978).

PROCACCI, G., (ed.), *Stato e classe operaia in Italia durante la prima guerra mondiale* (Franco Angeli, Milan, 1983).

QUAZZA, G. (ed.), *Riforme e rivoluzione nella storia contemporanea* (Einaudi, Turin, 1977).

STEARNS, P. N., *Lives of Labour: Work in a Maturing Industrial Society* (Croom Helm, 1975).

WHITE, D. S., 'Reconsidering European Socialism in the 1920s', *Journal of Contemporary History*, 16/2 (1981), pp. 251–72.

2. THE INTERNATIONAL DIMENSION

'1914: la guerre et la classe ouvrière européenne', *Le Mouvement social*, special no., 49 (Oct.–Dec. 1964).

BARNES, G., *History of the International Labour Office* (Williams and Northgate, 1926).

BRAUNTHAL, J., *History of the International*, i, *1864–1914* (1961; English trans., Nelson, 1966).

CARR, E. H., *The Bolshevik Revolution, 1917–1923* (Macmillan), iii, *Soviet Russia and the World* (1953).

CLAUDIN, F., *The Communist Movement from Comintern to Cominform* (1970; English trans., Penguin, 1975).

COLE, G. D. H., *A History of Socialist Thought* (Macmillan), iii, *The Second International, 1889–1914* (1956); iv, *Communism and Social Democracy* (1958).

CROSS, G., 'Les Trois Huits: Labor Movements, International Reform, and the Origins of the Eight Hour Day, 1919–1924', *French Historical Studies*, 14/2 (1985), pp. 240–68.

DEGRAS, J. (ed.), *The Communist International, 1919–1943: Documents* (OUP, Oxford, 1956).

DRACHKOVITCH, M., *Les Socialismes français et allemands et le problème de la guerre, 1870–1914* (Imprimerie H. Studer, Geneva, 1953).

FAINSOD, M., *International Socialism and the Great War* (Harvard Univ. Press, Cambridge, Mass., 1935).

FAY, V., *et al.*, *La Révolution d'octobre et le mouvement ouvrier européen* (Études et Documentation Internationale, 1968).

FINE, M., 'Syndicalisme et réformisme: Samuel Gompers et le mouvement ouvrier français (1918–1919)', *Le Mouvement social*, 68 (July–Sept. 1969), pp. 3–33.

FISCHER, F., *Germany's Aims in the First World War* (1961; English trans., Chatto & Windus, 1967).

—— *The War of Illusions* (1969; English trans., Chatto & Windus, 1975).

FOLLOWS, J. W., *Antecedents of the International Labour Organization* (Clarendon Press, Oxford, 1951).

FRISCHMANN, G., 'La Révolution d'octobre 1917 et les syndicats français', *Cahiers de l'institut CGT d'histoire sociale*, 3 (Dec. 1982), pp. 11–30.

GALLISSOT, R., 'La Patrie des prolétaires', *Le Mouvement social*, 147 (Apr.–June 1989), pp. 13–25.

—— PARIS, R., and WEILL, C. (eds.), 'La Désunion des prolétaires', special number of *Le Mouvement social*, 147 (Apr.–June 1989).

GRAS, C., *Alfred Rosmer et le mouvement révolutionnaire international* (Maspero, 1971).

GRAUBARD, S., *British Labour and the Russian Revolution, 1917–1924* (Harvard Univ. Press, Cambridge, Mass., 1956).

HAUPT, G., *Le Congrès manqué: l'Internationale à la veille de la première guerre mondiale* (Maspero, 1965).

—— *Socialism and the Great War: The Collapse of the Second International* (Clarendon Press, Oxford, 1972).

—— 'Guerre ou révolution? L'Internationale et l'union sacrée en août

1914', in id., *L'Historien et le mouvement social* (Maspero, 1980), 199–235.

HAUPT, G., 'Socialisme et syndicalisme: les rapports entre partis et syndicats au plan international: une mutation?' in M. Rebérioux (ed.), *Jaurès et la classe ouvrière* (Éditions ouvrières, 1981), 29–66.

—— *Aspects of International Socialism 1871–1914: Essays by George Haupt* (CUP, Cambridge, 1986).

HOWORTH, J., 'The Left in France and Germany, Internationalism, and War: A Dialogue of the Deaf, 1900–1914', in E. Cahm and V. Fiscera, *Socialism and Nationalism in Contemporary Europe, 1848–1945, 3 vols. (Spokesman Books, Nottingham, 1978–80), i, 7–19.

—— 'French Workers and German Workers: The Impossibility of Internationalism, 1900–1914', *European History Quarterly*, 15/1 (1985), pp. 71–97.

JOLL, J., *The Second International, 1889–1914* (1955; rev. edn., Routledge and Kegan Paul, 1974).

—— *The Origins of the First World War* (Longman, 1984).

KIRBY, D., *War, Peace and Revolution: International Socialism at the Crossroads, 1914–1918* (Gower, 1986).

KRIEGEL, A., *Les Internationales ouvrières* (Presses Universitaires de France, 1964).

—— 'Août 1914: nationalisme et internationalisme ouvriers', in ead., *Le Pain et les roses* (Presses Universitaires de France, 1968), 207–43.

—— 'Jaurès en juillet 1914', in ead., *Le Pain et les roses* (Presses Universitaires de France, 1968), 171–205.

LEFRANC, G., *Les Expériences syndicales internationales: des origines à nos jours* (Aubier, 1952).

LINDEMANN, A. S., *The 'Red Years': European Socialism versus Bolshevism, 1919–1921* (Stanford Univ. Press, Stanford, Calif., 1974).

LORWIN, L., *Labor and Internationalism* (Macmillan, 1929).

LYONS, F. S. L., *Internationalism in Europe, 1815–1914* (Sythoff, Leiden, 1963).

MARCHETTI, L., *La Confederazione generale del lavoro negli atti, nei documenti, nei congressi, 1906–1926* (Edizioni Avanti, Milan, 1962).

MAYER, A. J., *Political Origins of the New Diplomacy, 1917–1918* (Yale Univ. Press, New Haven, Conn., 1959).

—— *Politics and Diplomacy of Peacemaking: Containment and Counter-revolution at Versailles, 1918–1919* (Weidenfeld and Nicolson, 1968).

MERTENS, C., *Le Mouvement syndical international* (Imprimerie 'Lucifer', Brussels, 1923).

MEYNELL, H., 'The Stockholm Conference of 1917', *International Review of Social History*, 5 (1960), pp. 1–25 (pt. 1) and pp. 203–25 (pt. 2).

MILNER, S., 'The International Secretariat of National Trade Union Centres 1901–1913', *International Review of Social History*, 33/1 (1988), pp. 1–24.

MIQUEL, P., *La Paix de Versailles et l'opinion publique française* (Flammarion, 1971).

MULLER, I., *De la guerre: le discours de la deuxième internationale 1889–1914* (Droz, Geneva, 1980).

NEWTON, D. J., *British Labour, European Socialism and the Struggle for Peace, 1889–1914* (OUP, Oxford, 1985).

NICHOLSON, M., *The TUC Overseas: The Roots of Policy* (Allen & Unwin, 1986).

PAGE ARNOT, R., *The Impact of the Russian Revolution in Britain* (Lawrence and Wishart, 1967).

PEDRONCINI, G., *Les Négociations secrètes pendant la grande guerre* (Flammarion, 1969).

PRICE, S., 'A "French Revolution" in Britain before the First World War?' *Modern and Contemporary France*, 22 (July 1985), pp. 3–13.

PROCHASKA, A., *History of the General Federation of Trade Unions, 1899–1980* (Allen & Unwin, 1982).

REBÉRIOUX, M., 'Le Socialisme et la première guerre mondiale (1914–1918)', in J. Droz (ed.), *Histoire générale du socialisme* (Presses Universitaires de France), ii, *De 1875 à 1918* (1974) 585–641.

ROTHWELL, V. H., *British War Aims and Peace Diplomacy, 1914–1918* (OUP, Oxford, 1971).

SASSENBACH, J., *Twenty-Five Years of International Trade Unionism* (IFTU, Amsterdam, 1926).

SHOTWELL, J. T., *The Origins of the International Labor Organization*, 2 vols. (Columbia Univ. Press, NY, 1934).

SINANOGLOU, I., 'Frenchmen, their Revolutionary Heritage and the Russian Revolution', *International History Review*, 2/4 (Oct. 1980), 566–84.

STANSKY, P. (ed.), *The Left and War: The British Labour Party and World War I* (OUP, NY, 1969).

STEINER, Z., *Britain and the Origins of the First World War* (Macmillan, 1977).

STEVENSON, D., *French War Aims against Germany, 1914–1919* (OUP, Oxford, 1982).

SWARTZ, M., *The Union of Democratic Control in British Politics during the First World War* (Clarendon Press, Oxford, 1971).

TAYLOR, A. J. P., *The Trouble-Makers: Dissent over Foreign Policy* (Hamish Hamilton, 1957).

VAN DER LINDEN, M., 'The National Integration of European Working Classes (1871–1914)', *International Review of Social History*, 33/3 (1988), pp. 285–311.

VAN DER SLICE, A., *International Labour, Diplomacy and Peace, 1914–1919* (OUP, Oxford, 1941).

WILLARD, C., 'La Connaissance de la révolution russe et l'expérience soviétique par le mouvement ouvrier français en 1918–1919', *Cahiers de l'institut Maurice Thorez*, 12–13 (1975), pp. 318–30.

WRYNN, J., *The Socialist International and the Politics of European Reconstruction, 1919–1930* (Graduate Press, Uithoorn, 1976).

3. FRENCH SOCIETY AND THE FIRST WORLD WAR

AFTALION, A., *L'Industrie textile en France pendant la guerre* (Presses Universitaires de France, 1925).

ALBERT, F., *Le Procès Malvy: examen critique* (Ligue des Droits de l'Homme, 1919).

BARJOT, L., 'La Sécurité sociale', in A. Sauvy, *Histoire économique de la France entre les deux guerres*, iii (Fayard, 1972), 365–93.

BECKER, J.-J., *1914: comment les français sont entrés dans la guerre* (Presses de la FNSP, 1977).

—— 'Union sacrée et idéologie bourgeoise', *Revue historique*, 538 (July–Sept. 1980), 65–74.

—— *The Great War and the French People* (1980; English trans., Berg, Leamington Spa, 1985).

BLOCH, C., 'The Literature of Economic Reconstruction in France', *Manchester Guardian Special*, 4 Jan. 1923, special no. on 'Reconstruction in Europe', pp. 744–8.

BOCK, F., 'L'Exubérance de l'état en France de 1914 à 1918', *Vingtième siècle*, 3 (1984), pp. 41–51.

BONNEFOUS, G., and BONNEFOUS, E., *Histoire politique de la troisième république* ii, *La Grande Guerre, 1914–18* (Presses Universitaires de France, 1957); iii, *L'Après-guerre, 1919–24* (Presses Universitaires de France, 1959).

BRUGGEMAN, H., POËTE, M., and SELLIER, H. *Paris pendant la guerre* (Presses Universitaires de France, 1925).

CARTER, H., 'Reconstruction Literature in France', *The Sociological Review*, 10 (1918), pp. 55–9, 141–3.

CRÉHANGE, R., *Chômage et placement* (Presses Universitaires de France, 1927).

CROSS, G., 'Towards Social Peace and Prosperity: The Politics of Immigration in France during the Era of World War I', *French Historical Studies*, 11/4 (1980), pp. 610–32.

DELATOUR, Y., 'Le Travail des femmes pendant la première guerre mondiale et ses conséquences sur l'évolution de leur rôle dans la société', *Francia*, 2 (1974), pp. 482–501.

DEREYMEZ, J.-W., 'Les Usines de guerre (1914–1918) et le cas de la

Saône-et-Loire', *Cahiers d'histoire (Lyon, Grenoble)*, 26/2 (1981), pp. 151–81.

DOGLIANI, P., 'Stato, imprenditori, e manodopera industriale in Francia durante la prima guerra mondiale', *Rivista di storia contemporanea*, 4 (1982), pp. 523–59.

DUCASSE, A., MEYER, J. and PERREUX, G., *Vie et mort des français, 1914–1918* (Hachette, 1959).

DUROSELLE, J.-B., *Clemenceau* (Fayard, 1988).

'Etrangers, immigrés, français', special no. of *Vingtième siècle*, July–Sept. 1985.

FONTAINE, A., *L'Industrie française pendant la guerre* (Presses Universitaires de France, 1925).

FOURCAUT, A., *Femmes à l'usine en France dans l'entre deux guerres* (Maspero, 1982).

FRANÇOIS-PONCET, A., *La Vie et l'œuvre de Robert Pinot* (Colin, 1927).

FRIDENSON, P., *Histoire des usines Renault*, i, *Naissance de la grande entreprise (1898–1939)* (Seuil, 1972).

—— (ed.), *1914–1918: l'autre front* (Cahiers du mouvement social, 2; Éditions ouvrières, 1977).

—— 'France, États-Unis: genèse de l'usine nouvelle', in 'Le Soldat du travail', special no. of *Recherches*, 32/33 (Sept. 1978), pp. 375–88.

FROIS, M., *La Santé et le travail des femmes pendant la guerre* (Presses Universitaires de France, 1926).

GAILLARD, O., *Histoire économique et financière pendant la grande guerre* (Presses Universitaires de France, 1923).

GEMELLI, G., 'Un'istituzione ambivalente: le origini del conseil national économique', *Rivista di storia contemporanea* (1984), pp. 539–77.

GIDE, C., and OUALID, W., *Le Bilan de la guerre pour la France* (Presses Universitaires de France, 1931).

GODFREY, J., *Capitalism at War: Industrial Policy and Bureaucracy in France, 1914–1918* (Berg, Leamington Spa, 1987).

HARDACH, G., 'La Mobilisation industrielle en 1914–1918: production, planification et idéologie', in P. Fridenson (ed.), *1914–1918: l'autre front* (Cahiers du mouvement social, 2; Éditions ouvrières, 1977), 80–109.

HATRY, G., *Renault usine de guerre, 1914–1918* (Éditions Lafourcade, 1978).

—— *Louis Renault: patron absolu* (Éditions Lafourcade, 1982).

HATZFELD, H., *Du Paupérisme à la sécurité sociale, 1850–1940* (1971; new edn., Presses Universitaires de Nancy, Nancy, 1989).

HENNEBICQUE, A., 'Albert Thomas et le régime des usines de guerre, 1915–1917', in P. Fridenson (ed.), *1914–1918: l'autre front* (Cahiers du mouvement social, 2; Éditions ouvrières), 1977), 111–44.

HORNE, J., 'A Parliamentary State at War: France 1914–1918', in A. Cosgrove and J. I. McGuire (eds.), *Parliament and Community* (Appletree Press, Belfast, 1983), 211–35.

—— 'Immigrant Workers in France during World War I', *French Historical Studies*, 14/1 (1985), pp. 57–88.

—— 'L'Impôt du Sang: Republican Rhetoric and Industrial Warfare in France, 1914–18', *Social History*, 14/2 (May 1989), pp. 201–23.

HUBER, M., *La Population de la France pendant la guerre* (Presses Universitaires de France, 1931).

IZARD, P., *Le Chômage et le placement en France pendant la guerre* (Sagot, 1920).

JEANNENEY, J.-N., *François de Wendel en république: l'argent et le pouvoir, 1914–1940* (Seuil, 1976).

KING, J. C., *Generals and Politicians: Conflict between France's High Command, Parliament and Government, 1915–18* (Univ. of California Press, Berkeley, Calif., 1951).

KUISEL, R. F., *Capitalism and the State in Modern France: Renovation and Economic Management in the Twentieth Century* (CUP, Cambridge, 1981).

LAVERGNE, B., *Les Idées politiques en France de 1900 à nos jours: souvenirs personnels* (Librairie Fischbacher, 1965).

LAZARD, M., *François Simiand, 1873–1935: l'homme, l'œuvre* (Association pour le progrès social, 1935).

LEFRANC, G., *Les Organisations patronales en France du passé au présent* (Payot, 1976).

LÉVY-LEBOYER, M. (ed.), *Le Patronat de la seconde industrialisation* (Éditions ouvrières, 1979).

—— and BOURGUIGNON, F., *L'Économie française au XIXᵉ siècle* (Économica, 1985).

MACDONALD, W., *Reconstruction in France* (Macmillan, 1922).

MCMILLAN, J., *Housewife or Harlot: The Place of Women in French Society, 1870–1940* (Harvester Press, Brighton, 1981).

MARCH, L., *Le Mouvement des prix et des salaires pendant la guerre* (Presses Universitaires de France, 1925).

MAUNOURY, H., *Police de guerre, 1914–1919* (Éditions de la Nouvelle Revue Critique, 1937).

MEILHAC, C., *L'Effort du ravitaillement français pendant la guerre et pour la paix, 1914–1920* (Alcan, n.d.).

NOGARO, B., and WEIL, L., *La Main-d'œuvre étrangère et coloniale pendant la guerre* (Presses Universitaires de France, 1926).

NOIRIEL, G., *Longwy: immigrés et prolétaires, 1880–1980* (Presses Universitaires de France, 1984).

OUALID, W., 'The Effects of the War upon Labour in France', in C. Gide (ed.), *Effects of the War upon French Economic Life* (Clarendon Press, Oxford, 1923), 139–91.

—— and PICQUENARD, C., *Salaires et tarifs: conventions collectives et grèves (la politique du ministère de l'armement et du ministère du travail)* (Presses Universitaires de France, 1928).

PEDRONCINI, G. *Les Mutineries de 1917* (Presses Universitaires de France, 1967).

—— *Pétain: le soldat et la gloire, 1856–1919* (Perrin, 1989).

PEITER, H. D., 'Institutions and Attitudes: The Consolidation of the Business Community in Bourgeois France, 1880–1914', *Journal of Social History*, 9/4 (June 1976), pp. 510–25.

PINOT, P., *Le Contrôle du ravitaillement de la population* (Presses Universitaires de France, 1925).

PRÉVOST, J., *Histoire de la France depuis la guerre* (Éditions Rieder, 1932).

PROST, A., 'Die Demobilmachung, der Staat und die Kriegsteilnehmer in Frankreich', in *Geschichte und Gesellschaft*, 9 (1983), pp. 178–94.

REBOUL, C., *Mobilisation industrielle*, i, *Les Fabrications de guerre en France de 1914 à 1918* (Berger-Lavrault, Nancy, 1925).

RENOUVIN, P., *Les Formes du gouvernement de guerre* (Presses Universitaires de France, 1925).

—— (ed.), 'L'Année 1917', special no. of *Revue d'histoire moderne et contemporaine*, 15 (Jan.–Mar. 1968).

SARDIER, G., *Le Ravitaillement en charbon pendant la guerre* (Larose, 1920).

STONE, J., *The Search for Social Peace: Reform Legislation in France, 1890–1914* (State Univ. of New York Press, Albany, NY, 1985).

THÉBAUD, F., *La Femme au temps de la guerre de 1914* (Stock, 1986).

THÉPOT, A. (ed.), *L'Ingénieur dans la société française* (Éditions ouvrières, 1985).

TOURNERIE, J.-A., *Le Ministère du travail: origines et premiers développements* (Cujas, 1971).

TRACHTENBERG, M., '"A New Economic Order": Clémentel and French Diplomacy during the First World War', *French Historical Studies*, 10/2 (1977), pp. 315–41.

WATSON, D. R., *Georges Clemenceau: A Political Biography* (Methuen, 1974).

WEIL, G., *Histoire du mouvement social en France, 1852–1924* (Alcan, 1924).

WORMSER, G., *Le Septennat de Poincaré* (Payot, 1979).

4. BRITISH SOCIETY AND THE FIRST WORLD WAR

ABRAMS, P., 'The Failure of Social Reform 1918–20', *Past and Present*, 24 (1963), pp. 43–64.

ADAMS, R. J. Q., *Arms and the Wizard: Lloyd George and the Ministry of Munitions* (Cassell, 1978).

—— and POIRIER, P., *The Conscription Controversy in Great Britain, 1900–1918* (Macmillan, 1987).

ALDCROFT, D., *The Inter-War Economy: Britain, 1919–1939* (Batsford, 1970).

ARMITAGE, S., *The Politics of Decontrol in Industry: Britain and the United States* (Weidenfeld and Nicolson, 1969).

BOWLEY, A. L., *Prices and Wages in the United Kingdom, 1914–20* (OUP, Oxford, 1921).

BRAYBON, G., *Women Workers in the First World War* (Croom Helm, 1981).

BURK, K. (ed.), *War and the State: The Transformation of British Government, 1914–1919* (Allen & Unwin, 1982).

CEADEL, M., *Pacifism in Britain, 1914–1945: The Definition of a Faith* (OUP, Oxford, 1980).

DANGERFIELD, G., *The Strange Death of Liberal England* (Constable, 1936).

DEWEY, P. E., 'Military Recruitment and the British Labour Force during the First World War', *Historical Journal*, 27/1 (1984), pp. 199–223.

DOWIE, J. A., '1919–20 is in Need of Attention', *Economic History Review*, 27/3 (1975), pp. 429–50.

GILBERT, B. S., *British Social Policy, 1914–1939* (Batsford, 1970).

GRAUBARD, S. R., 'Military Demobilisation in Great Britain following the First World War', *Journal of Modern History*, 19/4 (1947), 297–311.

HALÉVY, E., *The Rule of Democracy (1905–1914)* (1932; English trans., Ernest Benn, 1934).

HANAK, H., 'The Union of Democratic Control during the First World War', *Bulletin of the Institute of Historical Research*, 36 (Nov. 1963), pp. 168–80.

HURWITZ, S. J., *State Intervention in Great Britain: A Study of Economic Control and Social Response, 1914–1919* (Columbia Univ. Press, NY, 1949).

JOHNSON, P. B., *Land Fit for Heroes: The Planning of British Reconstruction, 1916–1919* (Univ. of Chicago Press, Chicago, Ill., 1968).

LIDDLE, P. H. (ed.), *Home Fires and Foreign Fields: British Social and Military Experience in the First World War* (Brassey's Defence Publishers, 1985).

LLOYD, E. M. H., *Experiments in State Control at the War Office and the Ministry of Food* (Clarendon Press, Oxford, 1924).

LOWE, R., 'The Ministry of Labour, 1916–1924: A Graveyard of Social Reform', *Public Administration*, 52 (1974), pp. 415–38.

—— 'The Failure of Consensus in Britain: The National Industrial Conference', *Historical Journal*, 21/3 (1978), pp. 649–75.

—— 'Hours of Labour: Negotiating Industrial Legislation in Britain, 1919–1939', *Economic History Review*, 35 (1982), pp. 245–68.

—— *Adjusting to Democracy: The Role of the Ministry of Labour in British Politics, 1916–1939* (Clarendon Press, Oxford, 1986).

MARWICK, A., *The Deluge: British Society and the First World War* (Macmillan, 1965).

—— *Britain in the Century of Total War* (Bodley Head, 1968).

—— *Women at War, 1914–1918* (Fontana, 1977).

MIDDLEMAS, K., *Politics in Industrial Society: The Experience of the British System since 1911* (André Deutsch, 1979).

MOWAT, C. L., *Britain between the Wars, 1918–1940* (Univ. of Chicago Press, Chicago, Ill., 1955).

ORBACH, L., *Homes for Heroes: A Study of the Evolution of British Public Housing, 1915–1921* (Seeley, Aldershot, 1977).

POLLARD, S., *The Development of the British Economy, 1914–1967* (Edward Arnold, 1969).

PUGH, M., *Electoral Reform in War and Peace, 1906–1918* (Routledge & Kegan Paul, 1978).

RODGERS, T., 'Employer Organizations, Unemployment and Social Politics in Britain during the Inter-War Period', *Social History*, 13/3 (Oct. 1988), pp. 313–41.

RUBIN, G. R., *War, Law and Labour. The Munitions Act, State Regulation, and the Unions, 1915–1921* (Clarendon Press, Oxford, 1987).

—— 'Explanations for Law Reform: The Case of Wartime Labour Legislation in Britain 1915–1916', *International Review of Social History*, 32/3 (1987), pp. 250–70.

SANDERS, M., and TAYLOR, P., *British Propaganda during the First World War* (Macmillan, 1982).

TAWNEY, R. H., 'The Abolition of Economic Controls, 1918–21', *Economic History Review*, 13/1–2 (1943), pp. 1–30.

TAYLOR, A. J. P., *English History 1914–45* (OUP, Oxford, 1965).

TITMUSS, R. M., *Essays on the Welfare State* (Allen & Unwin, 1958).

TURNER, J., 'The Politics of "Organized Business" in the First World War', in id. (ed.), *Businessmen and Politics: Studies of Business Activity in British Politics, 1900–1945* (Heinemann, 1984), 33–49.

WAITES, B., 'The Effect of the First World War on Class and Status in

England, 1910–1920', *Journal of Contemporary History*, 11 (1976), 27–48.

—— 'The Government of the Home Front and the "Moral Economy" of the Working Class', in P. H. Liddle (ed.), *Home Fires and Foreign Fields: British Social and Military Experience in the First World War* (Brassey's Defence Publishers, 1985), 175–93.

—— *A Class Society at War: England, 1914–1918* (Berg, Leamington Spa, 1987).

WIGHAM, E., *The Power to Manage: A History of the Engineering Employers' Federation* (Macmillan, 1973).

WILSON, T., *The Downfall of the Liberal Party* (Collins, 1966).

—— *The Myriad Faces of War: Britain and the Great War* (Polity Press, Cambridge, 1986).

WINTER, J. M., *The Great War and the British People* (Macmillan, 1985).

WOLFE, H., *Labour Supply and Regulation* (Clarendon Press, Oxford, 1923).

WOODWARD, E. L., *Great Britain and the War of 1914–1918* (Methuen, 1967).

WRIGLEY, C., *David Lloyd George and the British Labour Movement* (Harvester Press, Brighton, 1976).

—— (ed.), *A History of British Industrial Relations*, i, *1875–1914* (Harvester Press, Brighton, 1982); ii, *1914–1939* (Harvester Press, 1987).

5. GENERAL

ANDRZEJEWSKI, S., *Military Organisation and Society* (Routledge & Kegan Paul, 1954).

BADIE, B., and BIRNBAUM, P., *Sociologie de l'état* (Grasset, 1979).

BERGER, S. (ed.), *Organizing Interests in Western Europe: Pluralism, Corporatism and the Transformation of Politics* (CUP, Cambridge, 1981).

BOND, B., *War and Society in Europe, 1870–1970* (Fontana, 1984).

DEMARTIAL, G., *La Mobilisation des consciences* (Éditions Rieder, 1927).

FERRO, M., *The Great War, 1914–1918* (1969; English trans., Routledge & Kegan Paul, 1973).

HARDACH, G., *The First World War, 1914–1918* (1973; English trans., Allen Lane, 1977).

HARRISON, R., *Pluralism and Corporatism: The Political Evolution of Modern Democracies* (Allen & Unwin, 1980).

HOWARD, M., 'Total War in the Twentieth Century: Participation and Consensus in the Second World War', in B. Bond and I. Roy (eds.),

War and Society: A Yearbook of Military History (Croom Helm, 1975), 216–26.

KAZANCIGIL, A., *L'État au pluriel: perspectives de sociologie historique* (UNESCO, 1985).

LANDES, D., *The Unbound Prometheus: Technological Change and Industrial Development in Western Europe from 1750 to the Present* (CUP, Cambridge, 1969).

LASSWELL, H. D., *Propaganda Technique in the World War* (1927; new edn., MIT Press, Boston, Mass., 1971).

LOUIS, P., *Le Bouleversement mondial* (Alcan, 1920).

MAIER, C. S., *Recasting Bourgeois Europe: Stabilization in France, Germany and Italy in the Decade after World War I* (Princeton Univ. Press, Princeton, NJ, 1975).

MARWICK, A., *War and Social Change in the Twentieth Century: A Comparative Study of Britain, France, Germany, Russia and the United States* (Macmillan, 1974).

MICHELS, R., *Political Parties: A Sociological Study of the Oligarchical Tendencies of Modern Democracy* (1911; English trans., 1915; Dover, NY, 1959).

MILWARD, A., *The Economic Effects of the Two World Wars on Britain* (2nd edn., Macmillan, 1984).

NETTL, P., *Political Mobilization* (Faber, 1967).

SCHMITTER, P., 'Still the Century of Corporatism?' *Review of Politics* (Jan. 1974), 85–131.

SORLIN, P., *La Société française*, ii, *1914–1968* (Arthaud, 1971).

WALL, R. and WINTER, J. M. (eds.), *The Upheaval of War: Family, Work and Welfare in Europe, 1914–1918* (CUP, Cambridge, 1988).

WINTER, J. M. (ed.), *War and Economic Development* (CUP, Cambridge, 1975).

—— *The Experience of World War I* (Macmillan, 1988)

6. UNPUBLISHED DISSERTATIONS AND THESES

ARUM, P. M., 'Georges Dumoulin: Biography of a Revolutionary Syndicalist, 1877–1923' (Ph.D., Wisconsin, Madison, Wis., 1971).

BOND-HOWARD, J., 'The Syndicat des Métallurgistes de Bourges during the 1914–1918 War: A Study of a Minoritaire Trade Union' (Ph.D., London, 1984).

CARLS, S. D., 'Louis Loucheur: A French Technocrat in Government 1916–1920' (Ph.D., Minnesota, 1982).

CHEVRIER, J.-M., 'Le Rôle de Louis Loucheur dans l'économie de guerre, 1914–1918' (Maîtrise, Paris X, 1972).

COHEN, Y., 'La Naissance du syndicalisme de masse dans le pays de Montbéliard' (Maîtrise, Besançon, 1976).

COOPER-RICHET, D., 'La Fédération nationale des mineurs' (3ᵉ cycle, Paris, n.d.).

DELAUNAY, Y., 'La C.G.T. durant la première guerre mondiale' (DES, Paris, 1950).

DOWNS, L. L., 'Women in the Engineering Industry, 1914–1939: The Employers' Perspective: A Comparative Study of the French and British Metals Industry' (Ph.D., Columbia, NY, 1987).

DUBESSET, M., THÉBAUD, F., and VINCENT, C., 'Quand les femmes entrent à l'usine: les ouvrières des usines de guerre de la Seine 1914–1918' (Maîtrise, Paris VII, 1974).

DUFOUR, J.-C., 'Les Nationalisations dans l'histoire du mouvement ouvrier français (jusqu'à la deuxième guerre mondiale)' (DES, Paris, 1969).

FINE, M., 'French and American Labor: Reformism and the Crucial Years, 1918–1921' (M.A., Wisconsin, Madison, Wis., 1967).

—— 'Towards Corporatism: The Movement for Capital–Labor Collaboration in France, 1914–1936' (Ph.D., Wisconsin, Madison, Wis., 1971).

GROPPO, B., 'Les Origines de la politique syndicale de la troisième internationale, 1919–1921' (Doctorat d'état, Institut d'Études Politiques, Paris, 1980).

JENNAWI-LE YAOUANC, N., 'La Conception de l'état chez les idéologues du socialisme anglais et français avant 1914' (DEA, Paris II, 1980).

LEPILLIEZ, C., 'Les Ouvriers et le mouvement ouvrier du Havre de 1914 à 1927' (Maîtrise, Rouen, 1972).

LESPINET, I., 'La Journée de huit heures' (Maîtrise, Paris X, 1985).

LUCIA, M., DE, 'The Remaking of French Revolutionary Syndicalism, 1911–1918: The Growth of the Reformist Philosophy' (Ph.D., Brown, 1971).

MÉNAGE, J.-P., 'Les Majoritaires de la CGT et la révolution russe, 1917–1923' (Maîtrise, Paris I, 1981).

MILNER, S., 'The French Confédération Générale du Travail and the International Secretariat of National Trade Union Centres (1900–1914): French Syndicalist Attitudes towards Internationalism and the International Labour Movement' (Ph.D., Aston, 1987).

MOREL, C., 'Le Mouvement socialiste et syndicaliste en 1917 dans la région parisienne' (DES, Paris, 1958).

PEITER, H. D., 'Men of Goodwill: French Businessmen and the First World War' (Ph.D., Michigan, 1973).

PELÉ, E., 'Le Mouvement ouvrier lyonnais pendant la première guerre mondiale' (Maîtrise, Lyon II, 1970).

PROCHASSON, C., 'Le Socialisme normalien (1907–1914): recherches et réflexions autour du groupe d'études socialistes et de l'école socialiste' (Maîtrise, Paris I, 1981).

—— 'Place et rôle des intellectuels dans le socialisme français, 1900–1920' (Thèse de doctorat, Paris I, 1989).

RAFFAELLI, G. and RAFFAELLI, M., 'Le Mouvement ouvrier contre la guerre: introduction bibliographique, méthodologique, et biographique à l'étude de l'évolution économique et sociale de la région stéphanoise, 1914–1920' (Maîtrise, Paris X, 1969).

ROBERT, J.-L., 'Ouvriers et mouvement ouvrier parisiens pendant la grande guerre et l'immédiat après-guerre' (Thèse d'état, Paris I, 1989).

ROSSITER, A., 'Experiments with Corporatist Politics in Republican France 1916–1939' (Ph.D., Oxford, 1986).

TRONQUAY, J., 'Le Combat pacifiste des instituteurs syndicalistes pendant la guerre de 1914–1918; ses étapes, ses limites' (Maîtrise, Paris I, n.d.).

VOLOVITCH, M. C., 'Essai sur l'évolution et la composition de la main-d'œuvre industrielle pendant la guerre de 1914–1918' (Maîtrise, Paris, 1968).

WISHNIA, J., 'French Fonctionnaires: The Development of Class Consciousness and Unionization, 1884–1926' (Ph.D., Stony Brook, NY, 1978).

Index